THE FIRST TO BE DESTROYED
The Jewish Community of Kleczew and the
Beginning of the Final Solution

Judaism and Jewish Life

SERIES EDITOR:
Simcha Fishbane (Touro College, New York)

EDITORIAL BOARD:
Geoffrey Alderman (University of Buckingham, Great Britain)
Herbert Basser (Queens University, Canada)
Donatella Ester Di Cesare (Università "La Sapienza," Italy)
Meir Bar Ilan (Bar Ilan University, Israel)
Andreas Nachama (Touro College, Berlin)
Ira Robinson (Concordia University, Montreal)
Nissan Rubin (Bar Ilan University, Israel)
Susan Starr Sered (Suffolk University, Boston)
Reeva Spector Simon (Yeshiva University, New York)

THE FIRST TO BE DESTROYED
The Jewish Community of Kleczew and the Beginning of the Final Solution

ANETTA GŁOWACKA-PENCZYŃSKA
TOMASZ KAWSKI
WITOLD MĘDYKOWSKI

Edited by
Tuvia Horev

Boston 2015

A catalog record for this book as available from the Library of Congress.
Copyright © 2015 Academic Studies Press
All rights reserved

ISBN 978-1-61811-284-2 (hardback)
ISBN 978-1-61811-285-9 (electronic)

Book design by Ivan Grave

Published by Academic Studies Press in 2015
28 Montfern Avenue
Brighton, MA 02135, USA
press@academicstudiespress.com
www.academicstudiespress.com

This research was initiated by
Dr. Tuvia Horev in memory of his grand-
parents, Tobiasz and Sura Rachwalski of
Kleczew, and in commemoration of the
Jewish community of Kleczew, Poland.

Contents

List of Photographs	xii
List of Tables	xvi
List of Maps	xviii
Acknowledgments	xix
Preface	xxiii
Introduction	1

PART *One*
THE DEVELOPMENT OF THE JEWISH COMMUNITY OF KLECZEW

Chapter 1. The Old Polish Period (Fifteenth–Eighteenth Centuries)	9
Introduction	10
1. Demographic Structure	13
The Jews in Poland	13
The Jews of Kleczew	15
2. Economic Activity	23
3. Organization and Functioning of the Jewish Community (Kehilla)	28
Chapter 2. The Partition and Foreign Occupation Period in Poland (Late Eighteenth–Early Twentieth Centuries)	37
Introduction	39
1. Demographic Structure	42
2. Economic Activity	45
3. Organization and Functioning of the Jewish Community	51
Chapter 3. Interwar Kleczew (1918–1939)	73
Introduction	74
1. Demographic Structure	78
2. Economic Activity	88

3. Social and Political Life 92
4. Organization and Functioning of the Jewish Community 104

PART *Two*
"IN THE EYE OF THE STORM": JEWS IN OCCUPIED KLECZEW AND REICHSGAU WARTHELAND

Chapter 4. The First Occupation Years: "Resettlement" and Deportation 133
  1. The Situation in Kleczew before September 1939 133
  2. The September 1939 Campaign in the Kleczew Vicinity 135
      The Occupation of Kleczew 141
      Abuse of Jews in Kleczew 141
  3. The First Few Months: Consolidating the German Infrastructure and Administration 143
      A "Model District" 143
      Arthur Greiser, Reich Governor (Reichsstatthalter) of the Warthegau 144
      Policy of deportations from the Warthegau 148
        Expulsion of Jews and Poles 148
        Reich Commissioner for the Consolidation of German Nationhood (RKFDV) 149
        The November 8, 1939, Conference 150
      Building Capacity and Infrastructure for Successful Implementation of the Deportation Policy 156
        Organizing the Warthegau Administration 160
      Police organization in the Warthegau 161
      Nazi Legislation Concerning Jews in the Warthegau 163
  4. Expulsions of Jews and Poles from Reichsgau Wartheland 164
      First Displacements, September 1939 164
      Displacements in Lublin 165
      The January 4, 1940, Conference 169
      The First Short-Term Plan (*Der erste Nahplan*): Discussion in January 1940 170
      Difficulties and Challenges in Implementing the Deportation 172
      Mulling Madagascar, July 1940 175
      Challenges and Arguments Presented by Governor General Dr. Hans Frank 178
  5. Attitude toward Jews during the Deportation Period 180

The Beginning of Nazi Policy toward the Jews in Poland	180
Persecution of Jews in Towns and Settlements of Inowrocław Regierungsbezirk	186
The Eviction Method	192
Economic Exploitation of the Jews	196
"Contributions" and Head Tax	196
6. The Jewish Community in Kleczew in 1939–1940	197
The Establishment of Ghettoes in Reichsgau Wartheland	199
Deportation to Zagórów	200
Zagórów (Hinterberg) Ghetto, 1940–1941	203
The Jewish Relief Committee from Lehmstädt (Kleczew) in Zagórów	206
Operation Barbarossa Disrupts the Deportation Process	210
Chapter 5. Forced Labor	224
1. Jewish Forced Labor in the Warthegau	224
Labor Camps	228
Mobilization for Service in Labor Camps	230
Deportation of Young Men to Labor Camps: The Case of Zagórów	231
Siting and Organization of the Camps	234
Living Conditions in the Camps	235
Examples of Forced Labor Camps in the Warthegau	237
Forced Labor in Kleczew	238
The Labor Camp in Inowrocław	238
The Żegotki labor camp	240
2. The Fate of the Forced Labor	242
The Forced Labor Camp in Czarków and its Liquidation	243
3. Estimates of the Number of Poles and Jews Deported	249

PART *Three*
FIRST TO BE DESTROYED: THE BEGINNING OF ORGANIZED MASS EXTERMINATION

Chapter 6. "Piloting" the Organized Mass Extermination of Jews	257
1. Decision-Making in the Extermination of Jews in the Warthegau	257
Inowrocław Regierungsbezirk	257
The Decision to Exterminate the Jews in the Warthegau	258

  Sonderkommando Lange   259
  Rolf Heinz Höppner's Role and his Ideas on Extermination   266
 2. Executions in Kazimierz Biskupi   273
  Transports to the Place of Execution   275
  The Execution Site   276
  The German Detachment   277
  The Polish Detail   279
  Preparations for the Crime   282
  When Did the Executions in Kazimierz Biskupi Forest Take Place?   284
  Method of Execution: Ready-Made Graves and Lime Pits   286
  Burial of Victims   291
  Escape from Execution Sites   294
  Reports about the Mass Murder in the Kazimierz Biskupi Forests   295
  The Sole Surviving Family   299
 3. Executions in Długa Łąka   301
  Methods of Execution   304
  Number of Victims   311
  Mass Graves after the Execution   312
  Masking the Mass Graves   314

Chapter 7. Establishment and Operation of the
  First Extermination Camp   321
 1. The Mass Extermination Camp in Chełmno on the Nerem   321
  The Camp at Chełmno on the Nerem—General Characteristics   322
  'Aktionen' and Transports   324
  Reception at the Rzuchowski Forest Camp   326
  The Extermination Method   329
  Sonderkommando Kulmhof   334
  The Jewish Detail   338
  Information and Disinformation about the Deportation and Mass Murder   341
  Who were the Victims of Chełmno?   346
  First Liquidation of the Chełmno Death Camp   351
  The Second Wave of Extermination in Chełmno on the Nerem and Rzuchów Forest   352

The Second Liquidation of Chełmno: The Jewish Detail Rebels	354
Number of Victims in Chełmno	357
2. Activities of Kommando 1005	358
3. The Tally of Extermination in Inowrocław Regierungsbezirk	366
4. What about the Perpetrators?	368

PART *Four*
EPILOGUE: THE POSTWAR PERIOD

Chapter 8. Kleczew after the War	379
1. Postwar Kleczew	383
2. Survivors and Descendants of Kleczew's Jews	385
3. A Final Remark	397

ANNEXES

Annex 1: Documents, Letters, and Testimonies	403
Annex 2: Stories of Descendants and Survivors of the Jewish Community of Kleczew	462
Annex 3: Tables	498
List of Abbreviations	562
Archival Sources	564
Bibliography	567
Index	599

List of Photographs

1. Tobiasz Rachwalski from Kleczew and his son — 79
2. The Bagno family in Kleczew — 84
3. A family in front of their store in Kleczew — 90
4. Young women with two girls in front of a footwear shop — 90
5. Members of Mizrachi youth movement in Kleczew (1) — 93
6. Tze'irei Mizrachi in Kleczew — 93
7. Members of Hashomer Hadati in Kleczew at the beginning of their organization — 94
8. Members of Hashomer Hadati at training commune in Kalisz, 1932-1933 (1) — 95
9. Members of Hashomer Hadati at training commune in Kalisz, 1932-1933 (2) — 95
10. Hashomer Hadati conference in Bartów, 1933-34 — 96
11. Hashomer Hadati—the Dvora group, November 25, 1934 — 96
12. Hashomer Hadati, Dvora group—names' list — 97
13. Hashomer Hadati, Hashmonaim group, summer 1934 — 97
14. Shlomo Rachwalski in Hashomer Hadati uniform, Kleczew, 1934 — 97
15. Hashomer Hadati summer camp, Golina and Kleczew branches — 98
16. Torah va-Avoda Movement in Kleczew — 98
17. Krzywanowski family, Kleczew — 100

18.	Izaak Traube and his family, during the trip from Kleczew to Palestine, June 1939	101
19.	IzaakTraube as a soldier in the Polish army	101
20.	Exterior view of elementary school building in Kleczew, March 1933	122
21.	Student ID card, Kleczew public school, 1937/1938	122
22.	Report and evaluation card, Kleczew public elementary school, 1938	123
23.	Jewish girls with their teacher, Beit Yaakov school in interwar Kleczew, 1938	124
24.	Polish troops on the battlefield in defensive war, September 1939	137
25.	Arthur Greiser (1897-1946)	145
26.	Arthur Greiser, Governor of the Wartheland and Friedrich Übelhör	146
27.	Arthur Greiser and higher officials welcoming the millionth German settler in the Warthegau	147
28.	Poznań. German troops march with banners on the occasion of second anniversary of the Wartheland, Oct. 1941.	147
29.	Poles being led to trains under German army escort as part of the Nazi German ethnic cleansing of western Poland (the Wartheland), annexed to the Reich, after the 1939 invasion	153
30.	Expulsion of Poles from territories annexed to the Reich (1939–1943)	154
31.	Jewish property in the street after the deportation (1)	154
32.	Jewish property in the street after the deportation (2)	154
33.	Deportation of Jews from Kutno	155
34.	Resettlement of Baltic Germans, column of trucks with displaced belongings, November 1939	159
35.	Płaszów, Kraków: resettlement of ethnic Germans (1939–1940)	159
36.	Resettlement of Volksdeutsche (ethnic Germans), 1940, column of carts of the displaced with their belongings	160
37.	Resettlement of Volksdeutsche (ethnic Germans), January 1940, displaced trucks loaded on railway wagons	160
38.	Jewish property in the street after deportation	195
39.	Members of the Jedwab family in Zagórów ghetto, 1940	203
40.	Jewish forced laborers deported from Sompolno and other localities to Blechhammer in 1941	227
41.	Jewish forced laborers on the way to work	228
42.	A Selbstschutz unit on parade	281
43.	The church in Chełmno, near the palace building whence gas vans drove to the woods	322

44. Herbert Lange, commander of Sonderkommando Lange — 323
45. Deportation of Jews to Chełmno by means of narrow-gauge railway — 326
46. Gas van from Chełmno being examined by a member of the Polish Commission of Inquiry — 333
47. Gas van from Chełmno—wooden construction of mobile gas chamber, originally covered with metal plates — 334
48. Canteen of the Sonderkommando and guards at the camp in Chełmno — 335
49. Hans Bothmann, second commander of Chełmno death center — 336
50. Two-storey building near the no-longer-existent palace at Chełmno, where Jewish prisoners lived and worked — 356
51. Death camp in Chełmno on the Nerem: collection of tombstones from Turek, 2009 — 358
52. Death camp in Chełmno on the Nerem. One of the monuments based on ruins of the crematorium, 2009 — 358
53. Death camp in Chełmno on the Nerem. One of the monuments overlooking the site where victims' mass graves are located, 2009 — 364
54. Witnesses at the Chełmno trial in Bonn, Germany, in 1963 — 369
55. Arthur Greiser, Governor of the Wartheland (middle, with bandaged head), during his extradition to Poland — 370
56. Thresa (Trane) Glucker (*née* Rachwalski). Born in Kleczew, died in US, 1933 — 380
57. Three sons of Tobiasz Rachwalski from Kleczew, who emigrated to the U.S.A. in the early 20th century — 380
58. Farewell party at Tobiasz Rachwalski's house, July 1939 — 381
59. Fojgel Traube *née* Rachwalski with her daughters, January 23, 1939, Kleczew — 381
60. Two sisters of the Traube family with their uncle, Shlomo Rachwalski who perished in the Holocaust — 381
61. Two sisters: Fruma (Frymet) Horev *née* Traube (right) and Hanna Grienfield (*née* Traube), Israel 2012 — 382
62. Jakub Itzkovich Kroner. Soviet certificate of award for good work during the "Great Fatherland War," 1941–1945 — 382
63. Jakub Kroner: membership card in the Professional Association of Miners, Wałbrzych branch, 1946 — 383
64. Jakub Kroner: membership card in Po'alei Tsiyyon-Ha-Shomer ha-Tza'ir in Poland — 383

65. Old monument at one of the mass graves in the forest between Kleczew and Kazimierz Biskupi	392
66. Kleczew, Poland, after the war: group photograph at the site where Jews were murdered	393
67. Krężel forest, near Kleczew: three Monuments commemorating the victims, 2009 (1)	394
68. Krężel forest, near Kleczew: three Monuments commemorating the victims, 2009 (2)	394
69. Krężel forest, near Kleczew: three Monuments commemorating the victims, 2009 (3)	394
70. Jewish headstones, found in Krężel forest near Kleczew, 2009 (1)	394
71. Jewish headstones, found in Krężel forest near Kleczew, 2009 (2)	394
72. Site of the former Jewish cemetery in Kleczew, currently a football stadium: main entrance, 2009	395
73. Site of the former Jewish cemetery in Kleczew, currently a football stadium, 2009	395
74. Former synagogue in Kleczew (main entrance), currently a cinema, 2009	396

List of Tables

1. Number of soldiers for Malbork expedition, 1458, by chosen towns in Greater Poland — 12
2. Jews in towns of Kalisz Province who paid poll tax, 1674 and 1676 — 17
3. Kleczew residents liable to poll tax and hearth tax, 1703 — 18
4. Jewish population of selected towns in Greater Poland, 1765, by per-capita tariff — 19
5. Census of Jewish heads in Kleczew, 1778 (six months) — 20
6. Number of craftsmen, taxes, and property taxes paid by towns of Konin County, 1579/1580 and 1618/1619 — 24
7. Occupational structure of residents of Kleczew, 1807–1809 — 27
8. Population of Kleczew, 1793–1909 — 43
9. Demographic structure of the population of Kleczew, 1807/1808 and 1808/1809 — 44
10. Demographic structure of Kleczew Jewish population, 1807/1808 and 1808/1809 — 44
11. Natural movement of Kleczew Jewish population, 1809–1864 — 45
12. Social and occupational structure of occupationally active Jews in Kleczew, 1836–1867 — 48
13. Structure of Jewish crafts in Kleczew, 1836 and 1867 — 49
14. Social and occupational structure of inhabitants of Kleczew Municipality, 1895 — 50

15.	Workshops and employment in Kleczew, 1895	51
16.	Kleczew kehilla budget, 1845–1850	54
17.	Kleczew synagogue administration, selected years	56
18.	People who pledged donations for construction of synagogue in Kleczew, December 31, 1862–January 12, 1863	61
19.	Information about work of "shysters" in Kleczew, 1840s	68
20.	Population of Kleczew, 1909–1939, selected years	78
21.	Occupational structure of economically active Jews in Kleczew, 1919–1935	82
22.	Distribution of Jewish trade companies, based on data for 1919	83
23.	Structure of municipal and school tax in Kleczew, 1919. Category: real-estate owners	86
24.	Structure of municipal and school tax in Kleczew, 1919. Category: tenants	87
25.	Jews and Jewish organizations registered as "chimney owners" in Kleczew	91
26.	Members of Jewish communities in Eastern Greater Poland, 1921–1939	108
27.	Structure of political influences in Kleczew kehilla managing board, 1924–1939	114
28.	Structure of political influences in managing boards of Jewish communities in Słupca (Konin) County, 1924–1939 (data collected before terms of office elapsed)	115
29.	Structure of political influence in managing boards of Jewish communities in Słupca County, 1924–1939	116
30.	Results of 20th Zionist Congress elections, July 10, 1937, in selected localities of Eastern Greater Poland	117
31.	Structure of Kleczew kehilla budget, 1919–33 (income)	118
32.	Structure of Kleczew kehilla budget, 1919–33 (expenses)	119

List of Maps

1. Greater Poland in the Sixteenth to Eighteenth Century — 11
2. Location of Jewish Communities in the Lodz Province in 1923 — 37
3. Interwar Poland 1919-1939 — 75
4. Administrative Division of the Reichsgau Wartheland — 144
5. Reichsgau Wartheland, General Government and District of Galicia in 1941 — 166
6. General Government (GG) — 169
7. Location of Collective Ghettos, Extermination sites, and Labor Camps in the Neighborhood of Kleczew — 371

Acknowledgements

This study was carried out with the assistance and cooperation of many individuals and institutions. It was initiated, funded, and coordinated by Dr. Tuvia Horev, a descendant of the Rachwalski family of Kleczew. Drs. Tomasz Kawski and Anetta Głowacka-Penczyńska performed extensive research on archival material, mainly in Polish archives, and wrote the first version of this study. Their knowledge of and experience in medieval and early modern history enabled them to research the history of the Jewish community in Kleczew and its surroundings from the time it was founded until 1939. Dr. Witold Mędykowski conducted extensive research mainly in Israeli archives, primarily the Yad Vashem Archive collections, diaries, testimonies, memoirs, and rich research literature, as well as archives and sources aboard; on this foundation he composed the section of this volume relating to the Holocaust period and completed the section on the postwar period. Dr. Mędykowski collaborated with Dr. Tuvia Horev in the second stage of the research; Dr. Horev edited and finalized the work.

The late Ezra Mendelsohn who was Professor Emeritus of Contemporary Jewry at the Hebrew University of Jerusalem assisted in various stages of this project. His advice and critical comments led to many significant improvements in the manuscript. We also thank Dr. David Silberklang of Yad Vashem for his very important advice in the final stages of the project. We are grateful to Ms. Nechama Golan for the initial copyediting of the English version of the manuscript, to Mr. Naftali Greenwood who contributed tremendously in copy-editing a later draft of this manuscript, to Mr. Yochanan Amichai for translating letters from Kleczew and Zagórów written in German, and to Mr. Jarosław Suproniuk for preparing the map graphics.

It is our pleasant duty to thank the Polish Cultural Attaché and Polish Ambassador in Israel at the time, who supported us in the search for researchers in Poland and connected us with the Museum of the History of Polish Jews in Warsaw. The Museum assisted in establishing the research team and created a professional and administrative framework that allowed this work to be produced. We owe special thanks to Mr. Albert Stankowski and Mr. Grzegorz Kołacz, of the Museum, for their strenuous efforts to promote the research in Poland.

Much of this project was based on personal collections of documents and photographs. Among the contributors, we wish to thank the Horev and Traube families in Israel as well as Mr. Merton E. Marks, Dr. Richard Marks, and Ms. Diane Plotkin of the U.S.A., all of them descendants of the Rachwalskis of Kleczew, for making their personal collections available. Ms. Sarah (Sarit) Kav and the Bagno family of Israel contributed a priceless collection of prewar photographs that illustrated our understandings of schoolchildren, youth movement activities, and many other aspects of life in Kleczew. Mr. Yitzhak Kroner of Israel contributed many personal documents that made it possible to reconstruct the fate of the Kroner family of Kleczew during the war and postwar years in Poland and the Soviet Union. Ms. Ada Holtzman and Ms. Edna Dan of Israel, descendants of Lea (Lotka) Holzmann (*née* Krzywanoska) of Kleczew, contributed several important photographs that supplement the other collections.

Our research in Poland benefited from the assistance of many archivists in institutions as diverse as the State Archives in Poznań and the branch in Konin, the State Archives in Łódź, the Jewish Historical Institute Archives, and the Main Archive of Old Records in Warsaw (AGAD).

The research was greatly facilitated by consulting the rich materials available in the libraries of the University of Bydgoszcz.

We owe much gratitude to Ms. Anna Dybała, who assisted in the researching important archival material from the State Archive in Poznań, Konin Branch, regarding the postwar period. Dr. Rafał Leśkiewicz of the Institute of National Remembrance in Poland (IPN) helped us obtain documents relating to the postwar period. Dr. Anna Ziółkowska and her colleagues at the Martyrs' Museum in Żabikowo, near Poznań, contributed priceless photographs concerning the "euthanasia" program in the Reichsgau Wartheland and the concentration camp in Poznań. Dr. Nikodem Bończa-Tomaszewski and Ms. Renata Jankowska of the National Digital Archive in Warsaw assisted us in obtaining photographs illustrating the war period in the Reichsgau Wartheland. We thank the staff of the Federal Archives in Germany with whose assistance we illustrated our account of the population transfer. We also thank Ms. Naama Shilo of the Yad Vashem Photo Archives, who was instrumental in helping us research deportations and the Chełmno extermination center.

The Holocaust period was researched using the archival collections at Yad Vashem Archives. Especially important were collections of testimonies that articulated several survivors' personal views and resolved some as-yet-unanswered questions. Priceless information was obtained from the collection of the Spielberg Foundation Video Testimonies via copies available at the Yad Vashem Archives. This project would not have been possible without access to the rich research literature in the Yad Vashem Library, the National Library of Israel in Jerusalem, and the Bloomfield Library for the Humanities and Social Sciences at the Hebrew University.

We are very grateful to Ms. Madeleine Okladek of the U.S.A., who performed extensive genealogical research on the Rachwalski family of Kleczew. Some of her findings are presented in Annex 2. We would also like to thank the following people who responded to our call for personal information and materials for this book: Shirley Ann Mendelson (U.S.A.), Elizabeth Grainger (UK), Annie Elizabeth Lindo (UK), Linda Geffon, Jim Bennett (Israel), David Conway (UK), Kenneth L. Rattner (U.S.A.), and

Jay Norwalk (U.S.A.). Some of the information they supplied is included in Annex 2. We also express our gratitude to other descendants of Jews from Kleczew, in the United States, UK and Australia, with who we were in contact as this book was being written, for the interest and encouragement they expressed and the information they provided. We apologize for being unable to include all materials we received due to size constraints or the specialized nature of this volume. Last but not least, we wish to express our gratitude to the excellent staff of Academic Studies Press, with special thanks to Ms. Sharona Vedol and, Ms. Kira Nemirovsky for their highly professional assistance which made the publishing of this book such an enjoyable experience.

> The authors and the editor express their special gratitude to the Museum of the History of Polish Jews in Warsaw for its assistance in establishing the professional and administrative framework of the project and the research team in Poland, without which this work could not have been produced.

Preface

As the son of a woman born in Kleczew to a family that had lived there for generations, I could not help but imbibe the reality of Kleczew with my mother's milk. My family had never been nostalgic for Kleczew, and certainly I had never heard any stories about how things had been back there. My grandparents had immigrated to pre-state Israel with their two daughters in July 1939, less than sixty days before the Germans invaded Poland. In doing so, they had left much of their family behind. Nearly all of these relatives perished very shortly afterward, in the Holocaust.

Born in Israel as a member of a new generation that had never smelled the stench of exile and experienced its horrors, I understood nothing about the immensity of the trauma that nestled deep in my grandparents' hearts. I never even felt the need—I admit this in shame—to ask them what they felt or to ask them to share their memories with me, confide in me, or just tell me who those relatives back there had been.

A few years ago, however, I came across an excerpt of the testimony of a Polish veterinarian, Dr. Mieczysław Sękiewicz. Sękiewicz had testified to a Polish judicial committee on October 27, 1945, and again in 1968, to researchers from a regional committee in Poznań for the investigation of

Nazi crimes, about a ghastly crime that had taken place in the Wygoda forest: the massacre of thousands of Jews who had been taken there from several communities in Konin sub-district and the Warthegau (the section of Poland that Nazi Germany had annexed) including Kleczew. As I read Sękiewicz's account, I realized that this events occurred very close to Kleczew. From that moment on, I felt it my duty to ensure that the memory of the Kleczew's community, to which I trace my ancestry (I was named after Tobiasz Rachwalski, born in Kleczew), would not end with that horror. To honor this pledge, I decided to facilitate a historical study that would explore the development of the Jewish community of Kleczew in order to seek lessons that might help to prevent such atrocities in the future.

Before beginning the study, I approached the cultural attaché at the Polish Embassy in Israel for assistance in locating appropriate and skillful researchers in Poland. The attaché and his staff responded in a most useful way, by putting me in touch with the Museum of the History of Polish Jews in Warsaw, which in turn was very helpful in finding Polish researchers and liaising with them. An agreement with two researchers in Poland (Anetta Głowacka-Pęnczyńska and Tomasz Kawski) was signed first. Dr. Witold Mędykowski of Israel joined the team later. Dr. Mędykowski contributed much to the development of the research, chiefly in matters relating to the Holocaust era and the final shaping of the manuscript. I fervently thank these researchers for their professionalism and the enormous investment they made in gathering the material, analyzing it, and placing it in writing. I am also very grateful to the Polish Embassy in Israel and the Museum of the History of Polish Jews in Warsaw for their assistance.

The research team systematically collected findings from many archives in various countries, retraced the history of the Kleczew community from its inception to its extinction, and analyzed the findings thoroughly in view of historical events that unfolded concurrently in Poland and in Europe at large.

At the time I began the project, I could not have guessed one of its revelations: that was evidently in Kleczew district and, more generally, in the Warthegau that the model later applied in the mass murder of Polish and European Jewry evolved.

Given the background of the research initiative, it was decided that in addition to the historic research, which lies at the core of the study, the book would also contribute to the commemoration of the Jewish communities that had existed in this district by presenting, in specific appendices, relevant documentation; tables listing the names of Jewish families that had lived in Kleczew at various times; and events from Kleczew community life, including information that would reveal in detail the histories of several Jewish families from Kleczew. Examples are the survival story of a person who survived the extermination campaign through a last-minute escape from Kleczew to the East (Kroner); and a detailed history of at least one family (the Rachwalskis) as a representative of Jewish families from Kleczew and their fates. The Rachwalskis' travails included the last-minute escape of Pessia Rachwalski and her children from Poland via Gdynia, by ship, on August 24, 1939, seven days before the German invasion of Poland, to join the head of the family, Majer, who had emigrated earlier from Kleczew to the United States.

It is impossible, of course, to pack all the information gathered about life in Kleczew into one book. As the manuscript was being edited, we had to make difficult decisions regarding what would give readers the broadest possible picture without inundating them with material irrelevant to the main topics of concern. We hope these decisions will be accepted with understanding.

I conclude by praising my father, Ze'ev Horev (Horzewski), who died as the book was being edited, and my mother Fruma—may she be graced with long life—who was born in Kleczew, daughter of the late Foigel (*née* Rachwalski from Kleczew) and Yitzhak Abba Traube (born in Kalisz) for their encouragement and warmth. Fruma is probably the last Jew alive who was born in Kleczew.

Last but not least, I offer loving gratitude to my dear ones—my wife, Mazal, and my children, Boaz, Ehud, and Einav—for their love, support, and encouragement.

Tuvia Horev
Karmei Yosef, Israel

A birth certificate, Kleczew, June 20th, 1864 (Tobiasz Rachwalski's)

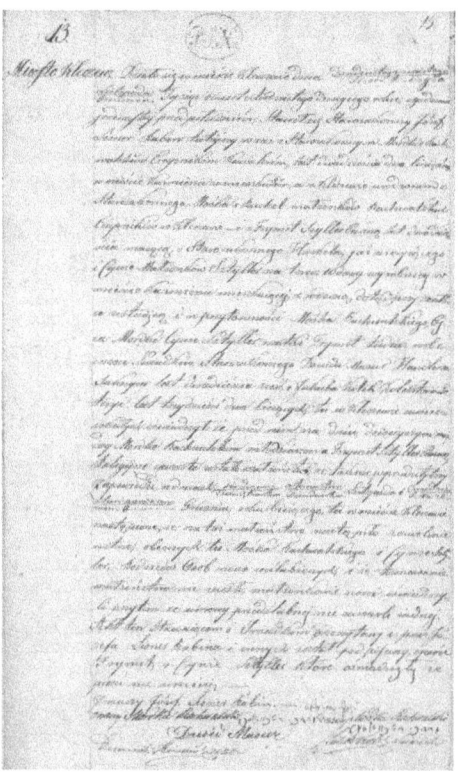

A marriage certificate of Mordke Rachwalski from Kleczew and Frymet Sztyler daughter of Heskel and Cywie from Kazimierz (Tobiasz Rachwalski's parents), 24 Nov 1842

Introduction

Kleczew is a small locality in Eastern Greater Poland, in Greater Poland Province (Wielkopolska), Konin County. At present, it is known as the headquarters of Konin Lignite Mine S.A., the biggest industrial enterprise in the province. Kleczew's industrial history, however, is quite recent. For centuries, the town was a local administrative, trade, and service center for the surrounding agricultural region. Until World War II, it remained multi-religious and multi-ethnic. The Jewish community was one of the groups that considerably influenced Kleczew's development. The present current study elaborates on their role.

The literature on the Jews of Kleczew is relatively scanty, especially in regard to the old Polish period and the partitions era. The information that can be found about its earliest history is provided by Zenon Guldon[1] and Jacek Wijaczka.[2] Information on the later period, often inexact, comes mainly from publications of an encyclopedic nature.[3] Tomasz Kawski[4] and Monika Opioła[5] provide works based on twentieth-century sources.

Literature on Jewish communities elsewhere in Eastern Greater Poland is also relatively scarce in comparison with that on other regions. Separate monographs, in addition to community records and memorial books, were published about several Jewish communities such as those in Kalisz[6] and Błaszki.[7] Some localities, such as Izbica Kujawska, are described in several worthy but exiguous works.[8] The authors of these works, much like those who wrote about Kleczew, concentrate mainly on the twentieth century. *Dzieje Kleczewa*[9] proved to be a valuable source of information about Kleczew itself.

The information gaps were filled in by archival research. For the sixteenth to eighteenth centuries, we examined: the Kleczew town books; the Konin county books; the Kalisz county books; and the records of the Royal Treasury, found in the Central Archive of Historical Records and the State Archive of Poznań. (An example of a draft register page from cities and towns in Greater Poland in 1579 is presented as Document 1 in Annex 1.) Information about the nineteenth and twentieth centuries was harvested mainly from the Kleczew town books for 1807–1950, which are kept in the Konin Division of the State Archive in Poznań. The following archival sources were also consulted, although with fewer results: the Central Denomination Authorities of the Kingdom of Poland (Main Archive of Old Records in Warsaw); Records of the Emperor's Civil Administration in Konin 1915–1918; and Registry Records of the Synagogue District in Kleczew 1808–1905. For the interwar period (1918–1939), the most significant were documents produced by the county and town or state administration authorities and local administration authorities (Kleczew town records 1807–1950, County Local Administration Office in Słupca 1918–1933, County Local Administration Office in Konin 1918–1939, County Police Station in Słupca 1918-1932), found in the Konin Archive. The province administration records were also of some help. Chief among them were the documentations from the Provincial Office in Łódź 1918-1939 and the Provincial Office in Poznań 1919-1939, deposited with the Łódź and Poznań branches of the State Archives. As for the World War II era, the main sources of information were found in the archive of the Jewish Historical Institute in Warsaw, especially the archival sources: the American [Jewish] Joint Distribution Committee; the so-called Ringelblum Archive and Reports; and the Yad Vashem Archives. The Main Archive of Old Records in Warsaw (AGAD) was a valuable source as well. For the post-1945 period, the Central Committee of Polish Jews submitted some interesting information.

The Martyrs' Museum in Żabikowo, the National Digital Archive in Warsaw, the Federal Archives in Germany, and the Yad Vashem Archives in Jerusalem provided valuable photographs. The last-mentioned was a particularly useful source in many aspects of the research, including as it does written testimonies of survivors and the video collection of the Spielberg Foundation.

The structure of this study is chronological and topical. The first section acquaints the reader with the development of the Jewish community in Kleczew from the old Polish period (fifteenth to the late eighteenth centuries), through the partition and foreign occupation period in Poland (late eighteenth to early twentieth centuries) and the interwar period (1918–1939). The second describes the situation of Jews in occupied Kleczew and the Reichsgau Wartheland, often referred to as the Warthegau, during the first period of the occupation. Part three describes the beginning of organized mass extermination. It depicts a process that might be considered the "pilot program" for the organized mass extermination of Jews which took place in several sites in the Reichsgau Wartheland, including in the surroundings of Kleczew. It follows this depiction with a description of the establishment and operation of the first extermination camp in Chełmno on the Ner. This section of the book illustrates the tragic fate of Jewish Kleczew specifically, as well as the Jewish communities of other localities of the Warthegau in general, during World War II. Part four concludes the study, focusing on the postwar period. It includes, among other things, rare information about the few Jews who showed up in Kleczew and its vicinity after World War II and the traces of the material culture that the original Jewish inhabitants left behind.

All of the chapters of this book set the data within a wider context than that of Kleczew itself, the context of Greater Poland in the prepartition period and Eastern Greater Poland after 1815. The shaping of the latter region was influenced by the partitioning of Greater Poland between Prussia (Germany) and Russia in 1815, with the eastern part of the region falling under the sway of the Russian Empire. The results of this division remain visible.

Although the Holocaust period was very short in world history, its tragic consequences brought about the annihilation of the Jewish community of Kleczew and most of its counterparts in the Poznań area, Poland at large, and all of central Eastern Europe. Therefore, the chapter dealing with the Holocaust is the largest in this book, copious enough to present many personal stories and an inside view of what happened to the Jews of Kleczew and its vicinity.

Although this book is the outcome of extensive historical research, it also gives special attention to the commemoration of the Jewish community of Kleczew. It includes copious data and extensive tables in the annexes in which names, occupations, and other details illustrate the everyday lives of the Jews of Kleczew and honor their memory. The names are spelled as they appear in each source. To be true to the sources, we did not try to correct or standardize spellings even when we knew that different sources were making varied references to the same person.

The destruction of Jewish Kleczew and other communities in the area (Golina, Słupca, Wilczyn, etc.) marked the beginning of the systematic mass murder of Jews on Polish soil, only a few months after it commenced in Soviet-annexed territory at the hands of special death squads (*Einsatzgruppen*). The executions of Jews deported from Kleczew to a collective village ghetto in Zagórów in the Kazimierz Biskupi forests in autumn 1941 also marked the beginning of a pilot mass-murder operation performed by Kommando Lange, the unit that had established and activated the death center in Chełmno only a few weeks later. Chełmno, as we know, served as an experimental center and a place where some death-camp commanders came to learn how to better and faster kill thousands of Jews every day. Thus, in a very early stage after the German invasion, the small and distant Jewish community of Kleczew found itself in the eye of the storm of hatred and destruction that would annihilate most of European Jewry. The tragic story of this community, as well as other communities in the area, may be considered the first milestone in what would evolve into the mass murder of Jews in the occupied Polish lands by Nazi Germany: a central part of the Final Solution.

NOTES

1 Z. Guldon, *Skupiska żydowskie w miastach polskich w XV-XVI wieku*, in *Żydzi i judaizm we współczesnych badaniach*, vol. 2, ed. K. Pilarczyk and S. Gąsiorowski (Kraków, 2000).
2 Z. Guldon and J. Wijaczka, "Osadnictwo żydowskie w województwach poznańskim i kaliskim w XVI-XVII wieku," *Biuletyn Żydowskiego Instytutu Historycznego*, nos. 2-3 (1992); Z. Guldon and J. Wijaczka, "Ludność żydowska w Wielkopolsce w drugiej połowie XVII wieku," in *Żydzi w Wielkopolsce na przestrzeni dziejów*, ed. J. Topolski, K. Modelski (Poznań, 1999).
3 Examples are J. Zineman, ed., *Almanach gmin Żydowskich w Polsce*, vol. 1 (Warsaw, 1939); *Jewrejska Enciklopedija*, vol. 1-14 (Petersburg, 1910-1913); *Pinkas ha-Kehilot, Encyclopaedia of Jewish Communities*, vol. 1 (Jerusalem, 1976); and ibid., vol. 4 (Jerusalem, 1989).
4 T. Kawski, "Inwentarze gmin żydowskich z Pomorza i Wielkopolski wschodniej w latach 1918/20-1939," *Kwartalnik Historii Kultury Materialnej*, no. 3-4 (2006): 73-96; T. Kawski, *Społeczność żydowska na pograniczu kujawsko-wielkopolskim w XX wieku*, in *Z dziejów pogranicza kujawsko-wielkopolskiego*, ed. D. Karczewski (Strzelno, 2007), 161-187.
5 T. Kawski, M. Opioła, *Gminy żydowskie pogranicza Wielkopolski, Mazowsza, Małopolski i Śląska w latach 1918-1942* (Toruń, 2008).
6 A. Pakentreger, *Żydzi w Kaliszu w latach 1918-1939. Problemy polityczne i społeczne* (Warsaw, 1988); A. Pakentreger, *Losy Żydów m. Kalisza i powiatu kaliskiego w okresie okupacji hitlerowskiej (od 1940 do 9 VII 1942 r.). Martyrologia i Zagłada* (Warsaw, 1980).
7 H. Marcinkowska, *Miasteczko w kolorze niebieskim. Żydzi z Błaszek* (Błaszki, 2001).
8 Such as P. Nowicki, *Ludność żydowska w Izbicy Kujawskiej w okresie międzywojennym (1918-1939)*, vol. 5 (Włocławek, 2004), 129-150; P. Nowicki, "Zanim 'przybył z zaświatów,' nazywł się Winer. Krąg rodzinny i konspiracyjny Szlamka, uciekiniera z ośrodka zagłady w Chełmnie nad Nerem," *Zagłada Żydów. Studia i materiały*, no. 5 (2009): 163-192.
9 J. Stępień, *Dzieje Kleczewa* (Poznań-Konin, 1995).

PART One

THE DEVELOPMENT OF THE JEWISH COMMUNITY OF KLECZEW

1 The Old Polish Period (Fifteenth–Eighteenth Centuries)

BACKGROUND[1]

Beginning at the end of the fourteenth century onward, the throne of Poland was occupied by monarchs of the Lithuanian Jagiellonian dynasty. The strengthening of relations between Poland and Lithuania led to the Union of Lublin in 1569, which created the Polish Lithuanian Commonwealth, the largest country in sixteenth-century Europe. This vast territory was inhabited not only by Poles and Lithuanians but also by members of numerous other nationalities: Russians, Germans, Armenians, Tatars, and Jews: the commonwealth was multi-religious as well. The very high ratio of nobility to the general population (10%) gave the nobility a degree of influence that diminished the power of the king. For Polish Jews, however, the sixteenth century was a golden age. The Jewish population and the number of Jewish communities were on the rise during this time. By the end of the 16th century, there were 70,000–80,000 Jews in the Polish-Lithuanian Commonwealth, and 300 registered Jewish communities. In several large cities, Jews accounted for about 20% of the population. Poznań was a good example of such a town.

> This increase can be traced in large part to the arrival of Jewish tradesmen, craftsmen, and financiers who had been driven out of Czech lands and German cities and came to Poland in search of better working conditions.
>
> In the seventeenth century, the Polish-Lithuanian Commonwealth engaged in a series of devastating wars with its neighbors that led to political and economic destabilization. One of the worst sufferings inflicted on Jews in that century occurred during the Cossack uprising on the southeastern border of Poland. The insurrection, led by Bohdan Chmielnicki in 1648, was particularly brutal, claiming the lives of 50,000–100,000 Jews. However, the Jewish communities managed to rise from the devastations of the mid-seventeenth century thanks to the privileges granted to them by the rulers. By the end of the eighteenth century, the number of Jewish communities reached 800, and their combined Jewish population totaled 750,000–1,000,000, or 8–10% of the inhabitants of Poland. This percentage remained unchanged until 1939.

INTRODUCTION

The sixteenth and seventeenth centuries saw the advent of dense urban settlement in Poland, the continuation of medieval urbanization based on German law that resulted in the continual establishment of towns in the Kingdom of Poland—300 between the sixteenth century and the first half of the seventeenth.[2] By the end of the eighteenth century, many of these urban centers had grown to several thousand residents. Most, however, were small, often agricultural, with 2,000 inhabitants at the most. By the end of the sixteenth century, such places—known as agricultural towns—constituted almost 90% of all towns in Greater Poland, Lesser Poland, and Ukraine. In Red Ruthenia, almost 95% of the population dwelled in agricultural towns.[3] The most urbanized region of the kingdom was Greater Poland. This can be explained by the rich urban network that it had developed in the Middle Ages. Because it was already heavily settled, settlement activity there was less intense in the new era. Whereas the number

of chartered towns grew by 14.6% in the sixteenth century, it advanced by only 5.3% in the seventeenth.[4]

Kleczew was established under Magdeburg law in 1366, by Janek of Kleczew. Until the eighteenth century, it belonged to Konin County. Like 90% of towns in Greater Poland, Kleczew fell into the class of small centers. Under the demographic criteria proposed by M. Bogucka and H. Samsonowicz for small-center classification, Kleczew can be placed in the third category—that of towns with fewer than 2,000 inhabitants. However, no source materials allow us to determine exactly how large and populous Kleczew was until the late seventeenth century. Using a list of military levies exacted from towns in Greater Poland in 1458 as a guide, one may consider Kleczew middle-sized relative to other towns in Greater Poland at that time. For example, Kleczew had to furnish ten soldiers for the Malbork expedition in 1458, compared with the twenty required of Kłodawa and Słupca, fifteen of Koło and Konin, six of Turek, Brudzew, and Rychwał, and three of Golina and Zagórów (Table 1).

Table 1 Number of soldiers for Malbork expedition, 1458, by chosen towns in Greater Poland

Name of town	Number of soldiers
Kłodawa, Słupca	20
Koło, Konin	15
Uniejów	13
Kleczew	10
Turek, Brudzew, Rychwał	6
Tuliszków	5
Golina, Zagórów	3
Przedecz, Ląd, Ślesin	2
Kwiatkowo, Licheń	NA

Source: *Codex diplomaticum Maioris Poloniae*, Poznań 1840, Quoted from J. Łojko, *Kleczew w XVI-XVIII stuleciu*, [source:] dzieje Kleczewa, p. 16.

On the basis of property tax remittances in 1579, one may deduce that Kleczew was slightly smaller than Koło at that time. According to the Kalisz Province tax register for 1618–1620, the town paid property taxes on twenty-six "street houses"—dwellings built on town streets and around the market square—and on fifteen houses on the outskirts.[5] The population of craftsmen diminished from 112 in 1579 to eighteen in 1618, due to epidemics that claimed many casualties in greater Kleczew in the early seventeenth century.[6] The town's development was also hindered by fires and looting armies. In 1615, the court records of the *wójt* (the governor, sometimes of several settlements) mention the destruction of much of the town by fire.[7] The size of Kleczew in 1672 may be estimated on the basis of poll-tax remittances to the town administration. Kleczew was one of the settlements that paid the highest poll taxes that year (95.25 złoty), surpassed only by Koło and Konin.[8]

The first more exact demographic information appeared in 1673, when the Kleczew tax register counted 103 citizens. By the second half of the eighteenth century, this population had increased almost thirteen-fold. When Kleczew was taken over by the Prussians, a census was carried out and found 1,348 inhabitants.[9]

Who held title to the assets of Kleczew is difficult to determine. The first wójts were Mikolaj Baunvater and a person referred to only as Menclin. Among the settlement privileges granted, they received five lans[10] and the right to use the baths. The Kleczew parish priest was paid for his services with the "coin" of two lans of arable land.

Up to the end of the fifteenth century, there is information about only two owners of the town's property: Jan of Kleczew (d. 1411) and a person referred to as Mikołaj. In the sixteenth century, the Kleczew estate was divided into several parts. It remained so until the late eighteenth century. For example, in the early seventeenth century, Jadwiga Rusocka of the Spławski family—Maksymilian's widow—owned part of Kleczew,[11] and the Rusocki and Borzewicki families owned other parts.[12] At the end of the seventeenth century, Franciszek Kretowski held title to part of the town; at the beginning of the eighteenth century, so did Krzysztof Przyjemski, Władysław Łącki, and Melchior Gurowski.

1. DEMOGRAPHIC STRUCTURE

The Jews of Poland

Jews appeared in Poland in the country's formative years. They required a permit to settle there; the first such permit appeared in a statute issued in Kalisz by Duke Bolesław the Pious in 1264.[13] The statute determined the basis of further legislation related to the Jews and was approved as the law in force by Casimir III the Great (1334) and subsequently by Casimir IV Jagiellon (1453). The Jewish population became the country's urban financial elite and, by the sixteenth century, enjoyed general provincial privileges. Even so, Jews were excluded from the official social structure, their activity largely confined to dealing with money. Evidence of Jewish coin-makers or leaseholders in the duchy's mints in the twelfth and thirteenth centuries confirms the significant role played by Jews in the Polish treasury, occasioned by their knowledge of laws regulating the money market and credit. At this time, the ruler granted Jews special protection and treated transgressions against them as offenses against the treasury.[14]

Casimir III the Great guaranteed Jews the right to move freely from place to place within Poland's borders, the right of residence in Poland, freedom of trade including freedom to grant loans, the right to personal safety, and permission to carry out religious practices. Exempted from town jurisdiction, Jews, like nobles, were subject only to provincial and royal courts.[15] Casimir IV Jagiellon expanded these privileges, adding, among others, the right to issue promissory notes on real estate and for debt obligations. In 1505, the text of the privilege granted by Bolesław the Pious was inserted into the Polish legal code in what became known as Statute of Kalisz.[16] By the fourteenth and fifteenth centuries, these privileges allowed Jews to become owners of real estate in both villages and towns.

In the Middle Ages, the largest concentrations of Jews in Poland were in Silesia. By the mid-fourteenth century, Jewish communities could be found in at least thirty-three towns there. In the course of the German colonization that took place at this time, groups of Jews also appeared in other districts, such as Greater Poland (Poznań, Pyzdry, Kopaszewo, Kościan, Sieradz, and Łęczyca), Kuyavia (Brześć and Inowrocław), Lesser Poland (Kraków, Kazimierz, and Sandomierz), and Masovia (Warsaw). Fifty-four Jewish settlements appear on a list of crown taxpayers in 1507.[17] The Jewish population of Poland increased primarily due to the persecution of Jews in Western and Central Europe and the welcoming policies of the Polish kings and dukes. Jews settled mostly in royal and private towns, where the decree of *de non tolerandis Iudaeis* was observed in the breach. Town owners usually encouraged financiers, merchants, and craftsmen to reside in their towns—not necessarily to alleviate their towns' misery but to improve the value of the owners' property. In the fifteenth century, Mosze Ben Izaak Minc, one of the most eminent rabbis of the day, stated that Poland "… has long been a shelter for the expelled children of Israel."[18]

Jewish migration to Greater Poland accelerated considerably in the sixteenth and seventeenth centuries. A survey in 1565 found fifty-four Jewish-owned buildings and a synagogue in the city of Poznań. At the time, there were approximately 1600 buildings exclusive of those owned by nobility, religious orders, and Jews. By the early seventeenth century, 10% of the city's populace was Jewish. In the mid-sixteenth century, the city of Gniezno boasted twenty-two Jewish-owned buildings, five rented ones, a *shkolnik*'s (synagogue sexton's) residence, and a synagogue; in the first half of the seventeenth century, twenty-six Jewish-owned houses were identified, and Jews made up 10%–15% of the city's population. Other relatively large concentrations of Jews in Greater Poland formed in the towns of Łęczyca and Inowrocław. In the sixteenth century, there were sixteen Jewish-owned houses, two rented ones, and a *shkolnik*'s residence in the former, and twenty-seven Jewish-owned houses and four vacant lots, a *shkolnik*'s house, and a synagogue in the latter. In the first half of the seventeenth century, there were as many as fifty Jewish-owned buildings in Łęczyca.[19] In the period of 1564–1579, Jews in eighteen towns remitted poll taxes in Kalisz Province, which boasted the largest congregation of Jews in its captial, Kalisz. In the early sixteenth century, Jews were allowed to own only seven houses there; for every additional house the community had to remit one *grzywna* (a medieval monetary unit) to the town's treasury.[20] By 1565, there were eighteen Jewish-owned houses, a *shkolnik*'s abode, and a synagogue;[21] by 1629, there were twenty-three Jewish-owned houses in town.[22] In Pyzdry, in 1565, Jews owned four houses and a *shkolnik*'s dwelling.[23] In 1579, they paid 30 złoty in poll tax,[24] and in 1628 there were seven houses with eight Jewish tenants. Despite the small number of Jewish-owned residences, the citizens of Pyzdry complained: "… There are a lot of Jewish houses in town—more than allowed by law or than are essential (*modo obligatorio*)—and Jews do not want to pay the property taxes to the town for the surplus houses, causing losses for the city (*in summum civitatis detrimentum*). [The Jews] use the excuse that they are in constant compliance with the law (*modo perpetua resignationis*) and were not allowed to build more than seven houses."[25]

The Jews of Kleczew

Kleczew is one of the towns where Jews probably first appeared in the sixteenth century. Unfortunately, the sources yield little information about their advent. The first mention of the existence of a Jewish community in Kleczew is found in a register of Jewish settlements of 1507,[26] in which the information is based on a coronation tax imposed on the Jews of Kleczew.[27] Regrettably, until 1695, when Piotr Cieśla with his wife Regina sold their house to the "infidel Jews" Jachim and Jick for 120 złoty, there is no information from any available source regarding the presence of Jews in Kleczew.[28] Why did this void occur? It may have been the result of the Swedish wars that took place in the seventeenth century. The "Swedish deluge" of the time took a grave toll on the area's Jewish population; pogroms by Czarniecki's army in 1656 did the same in Greater Poland in locations such as Kalisz Province, Gniezno, Kalisz, Kcynia, Krotoszyn, Łabiszyn, Łobzenica, Nakło, Września, and Złotów, to name only a few. Many Jews died of starvation and plague.[29] For these reasons, not a single Jewish household survived in some towns, including Nakło and Pyzdry.[30] After the wars, townsmen tried to expel Jews from their homes. At the behest of residents of Nakło, the town auditors made a decision:

> (*In quantum*) In so far as those successful ... [Jews] in that town are willing to settle down, we order them not to settle on the street where they previously owned their houses and residences before the town fire, but for the most just and reverent reasons [...] to relocate to another area of town in accordance with their previous situations.[31]

Something similar may have happened in Kleczew, although there is no explicit source confirming this.

Despite these attempts by the bourgeoisie to eradicate Jewish communities or limit their populations, the estate owners confirmed and expanded the existing Jewish privileges to accelerate the reconstruction of Jewish districts. This occurred in Grodzisk Wielkopolski, and Rawicz, among other places.[32] Thus, in 1674–1676, 4,183 Jewish taxpayers paid poll tax in the towns of Kalisz Province (Table 2) and 5,128 did so in Poznań Province.[33] The registers from 1674 and 1676 mention thirty-three locations in Kalisz Province where Jews paid the tax; unfortunately, Kleczew and several other municipalities are not cited among them.[34]

Of the thirty-three residents of Kleczew who were liable to poll tax and hearth tax (a form of property tax) in 1703, two were Jewish. They are referred to as Zabelik and Łazarek, and they paid 25 tynfs (the popular name of the złoty) each (Table 3). These men were moderately wealthy by the town's standards. (Paweł Lukas paid the highest tax, at 50 timpfs;

Table 2 Jews in towns of Kalisz Province who paid poll tax, 1674 and 1676

Town	1674			1676
	Christians	Jews	Percent of Jews	Jews
Borek	210	21	9.1	14
Chodzież	407	29	6.7	20
Gniezno	220	24	9.8	16
Jarocin	297	37	11.1	-
Jutrosin	285	19	6.2	6
Kalisz	1,293	751	36.7	353
Kazimierz	80	26	24.5	21
Kcynia	224	49	18.0	46
Kiszkowo	98	6	5.8	-
Kobylin	456	17	3.4	12
Koło	180	24	11.8	18
Koźmin	535	37	6.5	25
Koźminek	284	27	8.7	14
Kórnik	220	16	6.8	9
Krajenka	530	37	6.5	18
Krotoszyn	865	213	19.8	82
Łabiszyn	140	32	18.6	16
Łękno	86	8	8.5	9
Łobżenica	958	127	11.7	97
Margonin	135	13	8.8	10
Miłosław	273	5	1.8	4
Nakło	146	4	2.7	2
Nowe Miasto	122	18	12.9	13
Pobiedziska	145	9	5.8	-
Pyzdry	337	63	15.7	56
Raszków	143	30	17.3	16
Sępólno Krajeńskie	152	45	22.9	27
Skoki	261	8	3.0	9
Więcbork	111	5	4.3	-
Września	499	76	13.2	36
Złotów	468	107	18.6	48
Żerków	177	6	3.3	6
Żerniki	128	6	4.5	6

Source: Z.Guldon, J.Wijaczka, *Ludność żydowska*, pp. 30-31.

Table 3 Kleczew residents liable to poll tax and hearth tax, 1703

No.	Taxpayer's first name and surname	Value of tax paid (in timpfs)
1.	Stanisław Mycka	40
2.	Tomasz Olszakiewicz (after Bednarka)	12
3.	Wojciech Narożny	30
4.	Mathias Sztuczny	18
5.	Paweł Wieczorkiewicz	12
6.	Aleksander Rosiński	12
7.	Błażej Kotlarz	4
8.	Walenty Lewandowski	18
9.	Jakub Mielcarz	12
10.	Wojciech Manska	18
11.	Bartłomiej Jaworski	35
12.	Łukasz Borucki	35
13.	Walenty Figas	43
14.	Żyd Zabelik	25
15.	Stanisław Lukas	30
16.	Szymon Sojkiewicz	24
17.	Walenty Roszkiewicz	12
18.	Andrzej Sobczak	12
19.	Walenty Pojatecki	35
20.	Bartłomiej Piemigłowski	35
21.	Palacz Staśkowski	6
22.	Jan Piotrowski	12
23.	Walenty Banasik	15
24.	Paweł Lukas	50
25.	Żyd Łazarek	25
26.	Bartłomiej Spychała	30
27.	Jan Ordziński	35
28.	Andrzej Kowalik	12
29.	Jan Dorywała	12
30.	Organista	12
31.	Jan Bednarz	12
32.	Tomasz Moryson	33
33.	Wojciech Habierski	40

Source: APP, Kleczew town records, classification number I/6, cards 70-71.

only 9 citizens paid over 35 timpfs; and 18–33 inhabitants paid merely 10 timpfs).[35] It must be remembered that there is no comprehensive list of other denizens of Kleczew at that time, and therefore we do not have a full demographic picture of the town.

The first detailed information about the number of Jews in Kleczew dates to 1765. Table 4, comparing seven municipalities in which the number of Jews is known because their taxation was based on a per-capita tariff, finds 262 Jews in Kleczew in 1765.[36] By 1776, this number had grown to 305.[37] The Kleczew *kehilla* (meaning organized Jewish community, pl. *kehillot*) was one of the largest in Konin County, sharing this honor with Koło. Other towns in this county that had *kehillot* or subordinated *kehillot* are not mentioned. The main synagogue congregations in Greater Poland were in Krotoszyn, Złotów, Kalisz, Leszno, Swarzędz, and Poznań. Konin County had the smallest number of Jewish residents,[38] as demonstrated in Table 4.

The first documentation of Jewish names and the size of Jewish families in Kleczew (Table 5) is based on a census taken in 1778 that enumerated people who had lived in the town for at least six months. The list includes names of heads of Jewish households and the number of children and servants in each home. At this time, 257 Jews were living in Kleczew. As for the structure of their households, most taxpaying households (58.7%) that year had children: nineteen had one, fourteen had two,

Table 4 Jewish population of selected towns in Greater Poland, 1765, by per-capita tariff

Location	Jewish population
Golin	142
Kleczew	262
Koło	256
Konin	133
Rachwał	102
Rusocice	57
Wilczyn	39

Source: *Liczba głów żydowskich w Koronie z taryfy 1765*, ed. J.Kleczyński, F. Kulczyński, Kraków 1898, p. 7.

Table 5 Census of Jewish heads in Kleczew, 1778 (six months)

No.	First name and surname	Number			Persons in total
		Parents	Children	Servants	
1.	Salamon Leszczyński	2	3	1	6
2.	Marek Aranowicz	2	3	1	6
3.	Lewek Leszczyński	2	-	-	2
4.	Litman Leszczyński	2	1	-	3
5.	Samuel Hersz	2	-	-	2
6.	Mosiek Leszczyński	2	-	-	2
7.	Izrael Kotlarz	2	1	-	3
8.	Abram Krawiec	2	-	-	2
9.	Abram Szkolny	2	-	-	2
10.	Dawid Padraba	2	2	-	4
11.	Heyzak Pukacz	2	-	-	2
12.	Marek z Pyzdr	2	2	-	4
13.	Mosiek Krawiec	2	1	-	3
14.	Litman Lewek Kuśnierz	2	-	-	2
15.	Salomon Lewek Kuśnierz	2	-	-	2
16.	Jakub Krawiec	2	-	-	2
17.	Jakub Piszczek	2	-	-	2
18.	Jakub Gemblik	2	-	-	2
19.	Joachim Krawiec	2	-	-	2
20.	Marek Leszczyński	2	2	-	4
21.	Icyk Marek	2	-	-	2
22.	Jakub Jelenkiewicz	2	1	-	3
23.	Jakub Olejnik	2	2	1	5
24.	Izrael Jakub	2	-	-	2
25.	Józef Beniamin	2	2	-	4
26.	Abram Rzeźnik	2	5	-	7
27.	Mosiek Smaklerz	2	3	3	8
28.	Jakub Piątkowski	2	-	-	2
29.	Lewek Krawiec	2	1	-	3
30.	Lewek Intrologator	2	2	-	4
31.	Bazyli Krawiec	2	2	-	4
32.	Hersz Kuśnierz	2	1	1	
33.	Katme Rzeźnik	2	1	1	4
34.	Marek Krawiec	2	-	-	2
35.	Samuel Rzeźnik	2	1	-	3
36.	Jakub Komornik	2	-	1	3
37.	Lewek Leimus	2	4	-	6
38.	Józef Dawid	2	1	-	3
39.	Hersz Bakałarz	2	-	-	2
40.	Salomon Lachman	2	2	1	5
41.	Mazur Rzeźnik	2	-	-	2

Table 5 cont.

No.	First name and surname	Number			Persons in total
		Parents	Children	Servants	
42.	Lewek Szmuklerczyk	2	-	-	2
43.	Marek Cyrulik	2	1	-	3
44.	Samuel Lachman	2	2	1	5
45.	Lewek Wdowiec	1	-	-	1
46.	Icek Leymus	2	1	1	4
47.	Lewek Krawiec	2	1	-	3
48.	Icek Malarek	2	4	-	6
49.	Hersz Jelinkiewicz	2	3	1	6
50.	Samson Złotnik	2	1	1	4
51.	Trejma Jelenkiewicz	2	2	1	5
52.	Salomon Jelenkiewicz	2	-	-	2
53.	Hersz Layzerowicz	2	2	1	5
54.	Michał Layzerowicz	2	3	1	6
55.	Layzer Daniel	2	-	-	2
56.	Jakub Bakałarz	2	1	-	3
57.	Joachim Goliński	2	2	-	4
58.	Lewek z Gębic	2	-	-	2
59.	Salomon Kuśnierz z Koła	2	-	-	2
60.	Jakub Kotlarz	2	1	-	3
61.	Joachim Salamończyk	2	1	-	3
62.	Joachim Symso	2	4	-	6
63.	Eliasz Krawiec	2	1	-	3
64.	Józef Krawiec	2	6	-	8
65.	Bram Goliński	2	1	-	3
66.	Aleksander	2	-	-	2
67.	Mosiek Markiewicz	2	-	-	2
68.	Jakub Witkowski	2	2	-	4
69.	Rafał	2	-	-	2
70.	Joachim Kuśnierz	2	7	-	9
71.	Boruch Mośkiewicz	2	-	-	2
72.	Aleks Krawiec	2	-	1	3
73.	Jakub Herszowicz	2	2	1	5
	Sub-Total				257
Families belonging to Kleczew synagogue					
1.	Smerka of Różanna	2	-	1	3
2.	Icek of Radwaneczew	2	1	-	3
3.	Other people				21
	Subtotal:				27
	Grand total:				284

Source: APP, Court Ledger, Kalisz 432, cards 213-214.

and eleven had three or more. As many as eighteen households (24%) employed servants. Mosiek Smaklerz was the only Jew in Kleczew who employed three servants; the other households had only one each.

A statistical estimation of Kleczew's composition was completed in 1793, when Prussia occupied the town. According to the data assembled, the population of Kleczew was 1,348 at that time. Nearly half of this population was Jewish (616 individuals, 45.7%); only one person was Lutheran.[39]

Townsmen's obligations included paying taxes. The size of this liability depended on the craft or service performed by the individual, income, property owned, and household size. The most accurate data about taxes remitted by residents of Kleczew pertain to 1770–1772 and include rents from Catholics, Jews, and those of other confessions as well as information about taxes on production of oil (*tłoczkowe*), taxes paid by the community administration (the *kahal* or *kachalskie*), and taxes on trading in the market (*jarmarczne*). Catholic residents remitted 802 złoty, 919 złoty, and 1,334.26 złoty in the respective years; Jews paid an estimated 278 złoty, 258 złoty, and 290.10 złoty. The amount of further taxes paid by the *kahal* depended on the number of synagogue members. The tax called *tłoczkowy* yielded 230 złoty and 215 złoty in that period; *kachalski* generated 1,200 złoty in revenue; and *jarmarczny*, the trade tax, steadily increased from 50 złoty to 51.14 złoty and then to 109.04 złoty.[40]

The Jewish population was not isolated from the rest of society. Jews lived next to Catholics on almost every street. Despite attempts in some towns in Greater Poland to remove Jews, the general population of Kleczew seems to have adopted a friendly attitude toward their Jewish neighbors and relations were basically sound. This is substantiated by records of property sales between non-Jews and Jews in Kleczew. Another example of the peaceful coexistence between Catholics and Jews is the use of the services of Jewish barber-surgeons by local inhabitants. In January 1772, the Jewish barber-surgeon Maśkowicz, together with town officials Grzegorz Molendski and Bartłomiej Pomianowski, performed an autopsy on Walenty Dobosiewicz.[41] In September of that year, two Jewish barber-surgeons, Chersz Aleksandrowicz and Boruch, examined the severely beaten steward of Kleczew estate owner Great Crown Writer.[42]

Statements by owners of houses and plots in Kleczew in 1783 which were used to calculate *szarwarki* (public works) assessments have been preserved. According to these records, seventy-five of the 203 houses in Kleczew (34%) belonged to Jews. Most often, citizens, including Jews, had to contribute three days of labor per year and pay a five-złoty tax. There were two exceptions: the townsmen Psiupsin and Piszczyk had to work four days a year and pay 6.20 złoty, presumably due to their wealth.

Also preserved is a list of Jewish townspeople. It includes residents at the market square: Fraiem Jelenkiewicz, Salomon the goldsmith, Icek, Chersz Zielenkiewicz, Icek Malarek, Lewek Jelenkiewicz, Bok, Izrael Wolf, Alexanderka, Mosiek Leszczyński, Salomon Leszczyński, Marek Aranowicz, Litman Leszczyński, Boruch Cerulik, and Usier Dawidziak; and residents of houses along the streets: Chersz Layzerowicz, Michał Layzerowicz, Jakub Bakalarz, Jachym Gośliński, Gębicki (a tailor), Salma Kuśnierz, Jachym Lachmańczyk, Eliasz Krawiec, Malarkowski, Jeżowa (a dressmaker), Abraham Gośliński, Aleksander Bałecki, Mosiek Markiewicz, Leymusiak (a furrier), Kuśnierka (a widow), Mosiek Fraiemowicz, Marek Cerulik, Mazur Stary, Salomon Lachman, Lewek Leymusiak, Światowa (a merchant's wife), young Mazur, Marek Koźmiński, Kałme the butcher, Chersz (a furrier), Jóźwiak (a tailor), Szkolnik (a tailor), Bakalarz, (a tailor in Dorynatów, a taxpayer from Wolf's house, Musiek Szmuchlerz, Abram the butcher, Iung Oleynik, Jakub Zielenkiewicz, Maskowa Leszczyńska, Izrael Kotlarz, Jakub Cerulik, and Holibaba.[43]

2. ECONOMIC ACTIVITY

The main occupations of townspeople in Greater Poland were trade and craftwork. Craftsmen constituted 25% of all occupationally active people in Greater Poland in the first half of the seventeenth century.[44] This included various craftsmen, such as those involved with textiles (clothiers, cloth-cutters, linen-drapers, tailors, cap-makers, rope-makers, and others), food (millers, bakers, butchers, brewers, and others), leather products (shoe-makers, furriers, harness-makers, and saddlers), timber (coach-builders, wheelwrights, coopers, carpenters, and woodworkers), metal (locksmiths, blacksmiths, sword-makers, goldsmiths, needle-makers, and knife-makers), pottery and construction (potters and masons) and others (apothecaries, barber-surgeons, bath attendants, etc.). A tax register from 1578 for the town of Borek listed eleven separate occupations and the number of individuals who practiced each: there were twelve shoemakers, five innkeepers, four butchers, four bakers, and four tailors, three linen-drapers, two blacksmiths, two furriers, and two salt merchants, one blacksmith, and one potter. By 1618, the crafts population had diminished to thirty-one (including four bakers and four butchers).[45] In Gostyn in 1577–1583, there were seventy-eight craftsmen (including stall-keepers and innkeepers).[46] In Kłecko in 1580, there were forty-seven craftsmen (including peddlers).[47] Sixteenth-century tax registers from Poniec mention approximately sixty craftsmen.[48]

In the late sixteenth century, Kleczew was one of the economically best-developed towns per capita in Konin County. In the share of craftsmen among its townspeople, it was third countywide, trailing only Koło and Konin (Table 6). Unfortunately, in the second decade of the

Table 6 Number of craftsmen, taxes, and property taxes paid by towns of Konin County, 1579/1580 and 1618/1619

Town	1579/1580					1618/1620				
	Property tax		Taxes		Number of craftsmen	Property tax		Taxes		Number of craftsmen
	Fl*	Gr*	Fl	Gr		Fl	Gr	Fl	Gr	
Brdów	2	-	27	14	30	4	-	27	15	8
Kazimierz B.	12	16	40	26	37	10	6	24	9	12
Kleczew	14	7	73	24	112	14	7	15	11	17
Koło	64	-	238	9	160	56	-	132	2	9
Konin	32	-	181	24	158	21	6	83	8	44
Lądek	3	6	23	27.5	28	3	6	12	17	9
Rychwał	4	4	14	4	24	3	14	8	29	7
Tuliszków	4	24	23	4.5	26	4	24	12	1	9
Zagórów	3	6	34	11	42	3	6	25	26	20
Zduny	-	-	-	-	-	-	-	3	2	17

Source: *Źródła dziejowe*, vol. XII, Warsaw 1883, pp. 242-243; *Rejestry poborowe województwa kaliskiego z lat 1618-1620*, ed. A.J.Parczewski, Warsaw 1879, pp. 139-144.

*fl – florin   gr - grosch

seventeenth century, its economy started to deteriorate. The number of craftsmen plunged from 81 to only seventeen. The economic crisis affected not only Kleczew but all towns in Konin County. In Koło, the population of craftsmen plummeted from 160 in 1579–1580 to nine in 1618 and 1619; in Konin, during the same period, the numbers decreased from 158 craftsmen to only forty-four.[49]

The records from 1579 show twelve potters, twelve brewers, seven bakers, seven salt merchants, four peddlers, two oil-makers, and thirty-seven practitioners of other occupations in Kleczew. The tax register from 1618 mentions only seven shoemakers, four furriers, one clothier, one blacksmith, and four potters.[50]

The Kleczew craftsmen united into guilds. Although no guild documents have survived, these guilds are mentioned in the Kleczew town books and the Konin court records. There is an entry dated 1638 about Wojciech Bednarz, an elder of the blacksmiths' guild,[51] and a note from 1641 mentioning Lukasz Koszyczek, a member of the shoemakers' guild.[52] By 1656, the tailors' guild was up and running.[53] In 1667, the town owners ratified the statutes of a guild that embraced sundry crafts: coopers, cap-makers, coppersmiths, blacksmiths, sword-makers, knife-makers, harness-makers, coach-builders, locksmiths, and carpenters.[54] A receipt issued by the Kleczew estate owner Lukasz Golemowski in 1720 mentions a brotherhood of furriers.[55]

Craft structure was usually influenced by the local market, but trade contacts with larger towns such as Poznań, Gniezno, and Konin were also significant. Very often the development of trade and crafts was determined by a town's location on a trade route. Products manufactured in the towns of Greater Poland were sent to external markets; for example, linen and woolen fabrics from the "cloth" towns of southwestern Greater Poland were sold elsewhere. Several important trade routes crossed Greater Poland. For instance, the great route from Warsaw to the Grand Duchy of Lithuania and to Russia ran through Kleczew, Słupca, Ślesin, and Kłodawa.[56] Fairs and markets in Kleczew were popular among the residents of Koło, Pyzdry, Konin, Trzemeszno, Ślesin, Kazimierz Biskupi, and other towns. Kleczew supplied its residents with basic consumer items and craft products. To satisfy the needs of the bourgeoisie, local merchants imported salt, herring, spices, groceries, and metal products.[57] Trade usually took place at weekly markets or the annual fair. Goods were sold from stalls, booths, and butcher shops; craftsmen sold their wares directly from their rooms or homes.[58] Inns or taverns were also popular trading venues. The range of products sold is known thanks to inventory lists. For example, an inventory of merchandise taken after Mateusz Kramarz's death in 1645 shows ribbons, horn combs, leather belts, Cracow knives, black, orange, green, and red haberdashery, white Poznań hooks and eyes, pepper, caraway seeds, and onion seeds.[59]

By the late eighteenth century, residents of Kleczew practiced a variety of occupations. Table 7 shows the distribution of occupations a short time afterward (1807–1809).

The Jews of Kleczew played a crucial role in the town's economy and figured importantly in local trade, especially trade centering on the market. Thanks to Jewish population censuses in 1778 and 1783, we know that Jewish craftsmen dealt in profitable fields such as the furriers' trade, tailoring, and crafting with copper. Others worked as butchers and glaziers.[60] Apart from popular trades, Jews practiced "exclusive" occupations such as barber-surgeon, goldsmith, bookbinder, and teacher.[61]

Jewish craftsmen did not belong to the local guilds. Instead, they engaged in crafts under a license issued by Władysław Gurowski, high up in the Polish-Lithuanian Commonwealth and for some time the wójt of Kleczew.[62] (See Document 2 in Annex 1.)

In the first half of the eighteenth century, there was a brewery in Kleczew belonging to the town's owner. Other townsmen were allowed to brew beer and distill alcohol, but only for their personal use. To sell these products, they had to remit a fee to the royal treasury plus the levies of the Polish Republic. At that time, brewery and distillery rights were granted exclusively to Catholic residents. Jews in Kleczew acquired these rights only in the second half of the eighteenth century, upon receiving special dispensation from Gurowski.

One of our best sources of information on the development of Jews in trade is the collection of town ledgers and court records from the eighteenth century. As mentioned, from the second half of that century onward Jews were licensed to sell liquor in taverns and inns. In 1782,

Table 7 Occupational structure of residents of Kleczew, 1807–1809

Occupation	1807/1808	1808/1809
Coopers	2	1
Carpenters	2	2
Journeymen	13	13
Stainer	1	-
Tanners	1	-
Hat-makers	2	1
Chimney sweep	1	1
Coppersmiths	1	1
Blacksmiths	2	2
Tailors	42	10
Merchants and all types of traders, peddlers excluded	33	6
Furriers	6	-
Doctors, surgeons	1	1
Millers	2	2
Masons	1	-
Musicians	2	1
City clerks	4	4
Treasury clerks	2	2
Bakers	14	6
Beer brewers and wine-makers	1	1
Peddlers	9	-
Farmers	22	22
Harness makers and saddlers	1	1
Butchers	10	4
Coach-builders and wheelwrights	3	3
Carpenters	4	3
Shoe-makers	36	20
Haberdasher	1	-
Mill owners	2	-

Source: APK, AmK, classification no. 148, cards 12-23.

the "nonbeliever" Efram Lewek was granted the right to run inns in Sławoszewo, Dunajec, and Roztoka; he leased them from Gurowski.[63] Aron Aleksandrowicz also held a pub lease.[64] A person named Lachman sold liquor as well.[65] In 1787, Efraim Lewkowicz, a resident and citizen of Swarzędz, was authorized to sell beer in Kleczew.[66]

Kleczew Jews also traded in herring, salt, and iron after the town owner granted them this privilege.[67] Trading in sheep was a common occupation among the townsmen of Greater Poland in the seventeenth and eighteenth centuries. This line of work was connected with the development of the clothing trade in the district: in the first half of the seventeenth century, at least 20%–30% of craftsmen in Greater Poland dealt in textile manufacturing.[68] At least three Jews in Kleczew—Lewek Leymusiewicz, Litman Leszczyński, and Layzer Salomonowicz—took part in the sheep trade.[69] A Jew named Haym and his sixteen-year-old brother are also listed as dealing in trade.[70] Additional indirect information about Jewish trade is provided by documentation on disputes in court records. For example, a trial was held in Kleczew in 1778 to settle a dispute between the merchant Jakub Jelenkiewicz and a Jew named Samuel.[71] In 1779, there was a Jewish tailors' guild. However, no detailed information about it is available.[72]

Jews were active participants in the town's financial life and real-estate market. The earliest confirmed financial transactions performed by Jews in Kleczew date to the eighteenth century and relate to debts owed to Jews by other townspeople.

Given the character and structure of towns in Poland, Jews in Greater Poland were familiar with farming. Until the end of the eighteenth century, towns included pastureland and gardens, and inhabitants raised crops and livestock as a matter of course. Agrarian reforms in the towns accelerated as a result of the seventeenth-century wars and gradual urban decline. Kleczew, like most towns in Greater Poland, had an agricultural history that can be confirmed by records of ploughed land that belonged to the town in 1768 which document the sizes of the plots owned by Kleczew inhabitants. While no Jewish names appear in these records, entries in town records concerning the sale and purchase of real estate show that Jews owned gardens, meadows, and fields, just like other townspeople.

3. ORGANIZATION AND FUNCTIONING OF THE JEWISH COMMUNITY (KEHILLA)

As noted, the exact date of the initial Jewish settlement in Kleczew is not known. The first mention of Jews dates to 1507 and concerns the imposition of a coronation tax on them. The next mention of Jews in Kleczew appears only in 1695. Nothing is known about the kehilla—the organized Jewish community—or how many members it had. It may be assumed that the kehilla in Kleczew resembled its counterparts in other towns of Greater Poland.

The kehilla had a central administrative body called the *kahal*, a Hebrew word for "assembly" or "collective" that Jewish local governmental bodies in Poland, Lithuania, and Russia used. In medium-sized communities, the kahal had twenty-two to thirty-five members; in small communities it had no fewer than eight. These administrative officers were divided into four classes. At the head were four elders (*rashim*, sing. *rosh*), and directly below them were three to five "honorary" members (*tuvim*). These two classes formed the nucleus of the kahal, the official council that adjudicated all community affairs. The remaining classes were the judgmental authority, consisting of the rabbi and dayanim, and the operational authority, consisting of gabbaim, the *shammes*, the *shochet*, and the *melamed*. The elders took turns of one month each as treasurers (*parnasim,* sing. *parnas*) and, in general, as executive officers. The rabbi confined his activity to teaching and rendering decisions on religious questions.

Above the local institution of the kahal stood the Council of Lands, the central administrative organization of Jewish autonomy in Poland for nearly two centuries—from the mid-sixteenth to the mid-eighteenth.[73]

As mentioned above, the kehilla changed leaders every month; the parnas in authority was referred to as the "monthly parnas." His principal duties included, *inter alia*, representing the kehilla vis-à-vis the community at large, summoning kehilla members to local and other meetings, acting on the kehilla's behalf, collecting revenue and dealing with expenses, inspecting bills, and ensuring proper tax collection. The parnas was authorized to grant couples permission to get engaged and to announce important events such as sales and purchase transactions and *cherem* (excommunication) pronouncements. Parnasim were also responsible for repaying debts of the kehilla; it was they who signed promissory notes. Another group active in the kehilla was the *gabbaim* (sing. *gabbai*), known in Polish as *szpitalnicy*. These officials distributed honors in synagogues and collected donations for the construction of new synagogues and the like. They also supervised, together with the shkolnik (synagogue sexton), the synagogue and the *mikve* (ritual bath).

The kehilla was characterized by its strong commitment to weak individuals and by the deep sense of solidarity among members. Its officials looked after orphans and widows, tried to aid poor unmarried women by providing them with dowries, offered scholarships to schoolchildren and older students who could not afford tuition, and so on. A significant role in the kehilla was played by *dayanim* (rabbinical judges), who performed various social functions apart from their court duties: visiting women who gave birth on the Sabbath, announcing the names of newborn girls, filing marriage contracts, etc. Other kehilla appointees were lay judges, tax collectors, scribes, *memunim* (supervisors) for various trades, and market clerks. Most of these officials served without remuneration. Exceptions were dayanim, the rabbi, the cantor, the shkolnik (also known as the *shammes*), the scribe, the *melamed* (elementary school teacher), and the *shochet* (ritual slaughterer); these were contracted for one to three years. Sometimes they also received an apartment, wood for fuel, or the tools of their trade. It was common practice to entrust several functions to one person.[74]

The records show that in 1769 Salomon Leszczyński, Michał Layzerowicz, and Jakub Alexandrowicz were the elders of the Kleczew synagogue.[75] In 1771, the aforementioned Michał Layzerowicz, along with Chersz Layzerowicz and Lachman Łachmanowicz,[76] were the parnasim. Also noteworthy is the fact that in 1714 the Jews of Kleczew had their own school.[77] Like Catholics, kehilla members were obliged to pay taxes to the state treasury, the town's owner, or the town itself.

One encounters records of occasional disputes between the town authorities and the kehilla. They were not, however, of a religious nature. There is no record of persecution of Jews as such in Kleczew. Rather, such conflicts as may have occurred were personal or economic. A memorandum dated June 2, 1769, in the court register concerns Jewish unrest in town, preceded by a dispute between the brothers Chersz and Jakub Jelenkiewicz, Masiek Cyrulik, and Boruch the barber-surgeon. The synagogue elders—Jakub Aleksandrowicz, Fraym Zelenkiewicz, and Chersz Layzerowicz—turned to the mayor, Mateusz Liszkowski, for help, but the latter was loathe to interfere, as the matter was within the jurisdiction of the kehilla. The disturbances, however, continued. To keep the problem from escalating, Liszkowski sent town guards and several other officials, including the town clerk, to the kehilla. The event earned the witness Maciej Fuga, president of the sundry crafts guild, a beating by one of the Jelenkiewicz brothers. The clash involved the guild masters, Balcer Poradziński, Walenty Dobosiewicz, Antoni Woźnicki, Walenty Gruchalski, Michał Kopczyński, Kazimierz Ściński, Jakub Dzikowski, Maciej Fuga, and Andrzej Oyrzyński,[78] who collectively constituted one of the parties to the dispute.

Confrontations between Jews and non-Jewish townspeople were quite frequent. Cases against Jews were settled in the wójt or county courts. Jews sued their neighbors, both Catholic and Jewish, in the same manner. The town owner was the highest court of appeal, superseding the mayor, the wójt, and the synagogue. Leaseholders also held adjudication rights.[79]

In 1781, a case was brought to the county court in Konin. The parties were the kehilla members (represented by the elder Salomon Lechman), the merchant Jakub Pupiek (a.k.a. Chaskiel), and the town owner, Władysław Gurowski. The suit concerned an incident in which Gurowski arrested fellow Kleczew countrymen, shackling them and placing them in stocks.[80]

In 1786, a Jew named Jek Effaimowicz was accused of stealing liturgical objects. The wójt court in Kleczew received a complaint from the parish priest of Budzisław and from a person named Ulatowski, a captain in the Crown Army. Effaimowicz was accused of possessing two chalices, two paintings, and a monstrance, all stolen from the church in Budzisław. In the course of the trial, it turned out that Effaimowicz had bought these items from two other Jews, residents of Praga near Warsaw, for 25 red guldens.[81]

Criminal cases concerning the assassinations of Jews were noted in the county records numerous times. In 1728, when unidentified perpetrators murdered a Jew named Jakub Cerulik, the synagogue elders turned to the wójt court to "… display the head of the assassinated man on the four corners of the market."[82] In a similar case taken to the wójt court in 1763, the Kleczew synagogue elders asked the town authorities to publicly acknowledge, on the four corners of the market, the assassination of two Jewish residents of Kleczew who had been found slaughtered in Bór Świnogacki (Świnogacki forest).[83] In 1769, after unknown assailants murdered two Jews—Salamon Rachwalczyk and Wolf Gierszczen—the synagogue elders demanded that the town authorities accept the findings of their autopsy. Salamon Rachwalczyk, the elders ruled, "… had been struck on his head with an axe through his brain down to the chin." His legs had been bound with rope. Wolf Gierszczen had "his left cheek beaten and his eyes hemorrhaged, one of them knocked out of its socket." Both victims had been thrown into the water and left to drown.[84] On October 1, 1778, Tadeusz Lubiszewsk of Giewartów and a slagger[85] named Pawel Minicki went on trial for killing the merchant Jachman of Kleczew. The two were accused of assaulting and murdering Jachman, then burying his body in the forest. They were also suspected of having robbed Jachman and then throwing the stolen goods into the lake.[86] Unfortunately, the outcome of the trial is unknown because the case was transferred to a higher court.

In 1779, the eight-year-old son of the locksmith Maciej Zielenkiewicz was killed in a tragic accident caused by Haym Kacper, a sixteen-year-old Jew. Entering the locksmith's house, Haym had noticed four double-barreled firearms. As he picked up one of the weapons, the bolt moved and the gun accidentally discharged in the direction of Zielenkiewicz's son. The boy was struck in the back of the head, causing grievous and ultimately fatal brain damage.[87]

Jews also were victims of battery. In 1772, Michal Metlewski's wife went on trial for having beaten Jakub Jelenkiewicz.[88] The wójt courts very often settled disputes regarding family assets and passed sentence in trials concerning debts. For such cases, they were the competent authority not only for Catholics but also for Jews. For example, on January 15, 1771, one of the trials pending was that of a Jew, Salomon Leszczynski, for 700 złoty in debts.[89]

NOTES

1. Background materials presented in the text boxes are based mainly on: A.Wolska, ed., *One Thousand Years of Jews in Poland* (Warsaw, 2006), and Encyclopedia Britannica.
2. M. Bogucka and H. Samsonowicz, *Dzieje miast i mieszczaństwa w Polsce przedrozbiorowej* (Wrocław, 1986), 332.
3. The smallest centers, with fewer than 600 residents, constituted about 10% of towns in Greater Poland and Royal Prussia, 40% in Lesser Poland, Masovia, and Red Ruthenia, and 75% in Ukraine. M. Bogucka and H. Samsonowicz, *Dzieje miast*, 371-376.
4. M. Bogucka and H. Samsonowicz, *Dzieje miast*, 337.
5. A. J. Parczewski, ed., *Rejestr poborowy województwa kaliskiego z lat 1618-1620* (Warsaw, 1879), 139-144.
6. J. Łojko, "Kleczew w XVI-XVIII stuleciu," in *Dzieje Kleczewa. Collected works*, ed. J. Stępnień, (Poznań-Konin, 1995), 50.
7. Archiwum Państwowe w Poznaniu (State Archive in Poznań; hereafter: APP), Akta miasta Kleczew (Kleczew Town Records, hereinafter: AmK), I/2, card 1.
8. APP, Księga Grodzka Konin (Konin Court Ledger; hereafter: KGK), 67, cards 237-240; J. Łojko, *Kleczew*, 41-42.
9. J. Wąsicki, *Opis miast polskich*, vol. 1 (Poznań, 1962), 137.
10. The term *łan* denotes a "field." It was measured variously—anywhere from several hectares to fifty—in different times and places.
11. APP, KGK, 34, cards 405v-406.
12. APP, KGK, 43, cards 487-491; APP, KGK, 60, card 763.
13. R. Grodecki, "Dzieje Żydów w Polsce do końca XIV w.," in *Polska piastowska*, ed. R. Grodecki, (Warsaw, 1969), 652; S. Ettinger, "Sejm Czterech Ziem," in *Żydzi w dawnej Rzeczypospolitej* (Wrocław, 1991), 35.
14. M. Bogucka, H. Samsonowicz, *Dzieje miast i mieszczaństwa w Polsce przedrozbiorowej* (Wrocław, 1986), 157.
15. M. Bogucka and H. Samsonowicz, *Dzieje miast i mieszczaństwa*, 159. According to J. Łojek, the provincial court in Kleczew was not given competence to adjudicate Jewish cases until the eighteenth century; J. Łojko, "Kleczew w XVI-XVIII stuleciu," in *Dzieje Kleczewa*, 27.
16. S. Kutrzeba, *Przywileje Kazimierza Wielkiego dla Żydów*, "Sprawozdania PAU" 27, no. 10 (1922): 4-5; J. Wyrozumski, "Żydzi w Polsce średniowiecznej," in *Żydzi w dawnej Rzeczypospolitej*, 134-135; H. Zaremska, "Przywileje Kazimierza Wielkiego dla Żydów i ich średniowieczne konfirmacje," in *Małżeństwo z rozsądku? Żydzi w społeczeństwie dawnej Rzeczypospolitej*, ed. M. Wodziński and A. Michałowska-Mycielska (Wrocław, 2007), 13. Laski's statute (1505) is considered the first codification of law published in the Kingdom of Poland.
17. M. Horn, "Najstarszy rejestr osiedli żydowskich w Polsce z 1507 r.," *Biuletyn Żydowskiego Instytutu Historycznego w Warszawie*, no. 3 (1974): p. 11.
18. G.D. Hundert, *Żydzi w Rzeczypospolitej Obojga Narodów w XVIII wieku.Genealogia nowoczesności* (Warsaw, 2007), 23.

19 A. Tomczak, ed., *Lustracja województw wielkopolskich i kujawskich 1564-65* (hereafter: *Lustracja 1564-65*), part II (Bydgoszcz, 1963), 271-275; M. Bogucka and H. Samsonowicz, *Dzieje miast*, 473.
20 K. Stefański, *Mieszczaństwo kaliskie w XVI wieku* (Kalisz, 1933), 30-31; Z. Guldon and J. Wijaczka, *Ludność żydowska w Wielkopolsce w drugiej połowie XVII wieku*, in *Żydzi w Wielkopolsce na przestrzeni dziejów*, ed. J. Topolski and K. Modelski (Poznań, 1999), 23.
21 *Lustracja 1565*, 272.
22 W. Rusiński, ed., *Dzieje Kalisza* (Poznań, 1977), 118.
23 *Lustracja 1565*, 272.
24 Archiwum Główne Akt Dawnych w Warszawie (Central Archives of Historical Records in Warsaw, hereafter: AGAD), Archiwum Skarbu Koronnego I (Crown Treasury Archives I, hereafter: ASK I), 13, card 765v.
25 Z. Guldon, ed., *Lustracja województw wielkopolskich i kujawskich 1628-1632*, part 3 (Bydgoszcz, 1967), 161.
26 The original title of the document is "Taxa Judeorum in civitatibus et opidis Regni existentibus." According to Roman Rybarski, it was issued in 1507–1510; Maurycy Horn dates it to early February 1507. After a detailed analysis, Horn stated that the list was drawn up concurrently with the income and expenditure register associated with the coronation of Sigismund I. M. Horn, *Najstarszy rejestr*, 11.
27 AGAD, ASK I, Royal bills, no. 38, card 131v.
28 APP, AmK, I/5card 152.
29 Z. Guldon and J. Wijaczka, *Ludność żydowska*, 26.
30 Cz. Ohryzko-Włodarska, ed., *Lustracja województw wielkopolskich i kujawskich 1659-1665*, part I (Wrocław, 1978), 115 and 187.
31 *Lustracja województw wielkopolskich i kujawskich 1659-1665*, 187.
32 Z. Guldon and J. Wijaczka, *Ludność żydowska*, 28.
33 Ibid., 28-29.
34 Ibid., 30-31.
35 APP, AmK, I/6, cards 70-71; J.Łojko, *Kleczew w XVI-XVIII stuleciu*, 42-43.
36 APP, AmK, I/7, card 119; J. Kleczyński and F. Kulczyński, eds., *Liczba głów żydowskich w Koronie z taryfy 1765* (Kraków, 1898), 7.
37 APP, KGK, 151, cards 492-495.
38 J. Łojek, *Kleczew w XVI-XVIII stuleciu*, 87.
39 J. Wąsicki, *Opis miast polskich*, vol. 1 (Poznań, 1962), 137.
40 J. Łojek, *Kleczew w XVI-XVIII stuleciu*, 96-97.
41 APP, AmK, I/11, cards 21-23, 32-34.
42 APP, AmK, I/10, card 27.
43 J. Łojek, *Kleczew w XVI-XVIII stuleciu*, 97.
44 *Dzieje Wielkopolski*, 469.
45 *Źródła dziejowe*, vol. XII, *Polska XVI wieku pod względem geograficzno–statystycznym opisana przez Adolfa Pawińskiego*, vol. 1, *Wielkopolska* (hereinafter: *Źródła dziejowe*), (Warsaw, 1883), 220; S. Sierpowski, ed., *Dzieje ziemi gostyńskiej* (Poznań, 1979), 118-119.
46 *Źródła dziejowe*, vol. 1, 95.
47 Ten peddlers, sixteen shoemakers, five butchers, one locksmith, six tailors, five blacksmiths, two coopers, two wheelwrights. *Źródła dziejowe*, vol. 1, 164.

48 In the sixteenth century, guild statutes were awarded to the following trades: linen-drapers (weavers), potters, blacksmiths, carpenters, and wheelwrights. These guilds were recognized later on: bakers, brewers, butchers, shoemakers, tailors, and a combined guild gathering together wheelwrights, blacksmiths, and carpenters, as well as carriage-builders, coopers, binders, locksmiths, sword-makers, goldsmiths, needle-makers, basket-weavers, turners, and practitioners of similar crafts. APP, Cechy miasta Poniec 1, 2, 6, 9, 26, 32, 35, 42, 43, 45; A. Bitner–Nowak, Z. Wojciechowska, and G. Wojciechowski, *Dzieje Ponieca* (Poniec, 2000), 81-82; T. Jurek, "Mikrokosmos prowincjonalny. Nad najstarszą księgą Ponieca z przełomu XVI i XVI wieku," in *Aetas media aetas moderna. Studia ofiarowane profesorowi Henrykowi Samsonowiczowi w siedemdziesiątą rocznicę urodzin* (Warsaw, 2000), 44.
49 *Źródła dziejowe*, vol. XII (Warsaw, 1883), 242-243; *Rejestry poborowe województwa kaliskiego z lat 1618-1620*, 139-144.
50 *Źródła dziejowe*, 242-243.
51 APP, AmK, I/4, card 10.
52 APP, AmK, I/4, card 47.
53 Its wardrobe was placed in the parish church; the guild was still operating in 1775; APP, AmK, I/3, card 215; APP, AmK, I/11, card 165.
54 APP, AmK, I/2, card 118.
55 The guild was represented by the elders Bartłomiej Prusak and one Jan. APP, AmK, I/2, card 118.
56 *Dzieje Wielkopolski*, 476-477.
57 J. Łojko, *Kleczew w XVI-XVIII stuleciu*, 59.
58 The mayor, Franciszek Martynowicz, sold beer in his own house, located on the market square, APP, AmK, I/12, card 104.
59 APP, AmK, I/4, cards 40-41 and 82-83. In the inventory of belongings of Szot Dawid /Christa/ (1641), we also find a list of stall-keeper items: pepper, caraway seeds, anise, Hungarian knives, Gdansk knives, Kraków knives, paper, white hooks and eyes, women's combs, needles, ribbons, dyed threads, and a rope, among other things.
60 The 1783 census mentions a goldsmith, Boruch the barber-surgeon, Eliasz the tailor, Józefowa the dress maker, Leymusiak the furrier, Mark the barber-surgeon, Chudy the tailor, Kałme the butcher, Chersz the furrier, Jóźwiak the tailor, Szkolniak the tailor, Bakalasz the tailor, Abram the butcher, Izrael the coppersmith, Jakub the barber-surgeon, a glazier, and the furrier Izrael. Biblioteka Kórnicka (Kórnik Library), Manuscript 7799, card 37.
61 In the vetting of Jewish heads of household in 1776, a goldsmith named Samson and a barber-surgeon named Hersz are mentioned. APP, AmK, I/7, card 119; and in 1778: Lewek Introlator, Hersz Bakałarz, Marek Cyrulik, Jakub Bakałarz. APP, Księga Grodzka Kalisza (Kalisz Count Leger), 432, cards 213-214.
62 J. Łojko, *Kleczew w XVI-XVIII stuleciu*, 55.
63 APP, AmK, I/12, card 24v.
64 APP, KGK, 118, card 517.
65 In her 1763 will, Józefowa Szeygowska mentioned a debt of 13 złoty for liquor to Lachmanek, a Jew. APP, AmK, I/9, card. 88.
66 APP, AmK, I/9, cards 276-277.
67 APP, KGK, 118, card 27; J. Łojko, *Kleczew w XVI-XVIII stuleciu*, 61.

68 *Dzieje Wielkopolski*, 473.
69 We discover the Jewish sheep merchants from files concerning disputes. In 1777, Lewek Leymusiewicz, Litman Leszczyński, and Józef Dawidziak took the mayor, Kazimierz Ściński, to court over a debt of 1,000 złoty that he owed them for the purchase of 580 wethers. APP, AmK, I/10, cards 89-90, and similar cases: APP, AmK, I/11, cards 137-138, 139, 140-141.
70 APP, AmK, I/11, card 168.
71 Jelenkiewicz had a dispute with Bartłomiej, a sheep-keeper from Lisewo, who did not want to sell him sheep: APP, AmK, I/11, card 199; Jan Szaydziński had a dispute about 300 wethers and 90 sows that Samuel, a Jew, was supposed to sell: APP, Records of the Town of Kleczew, cards 200, 206; Kazimierz Ściński and Franciszek Woźnicki had a dispute with Kacper Szayda about the impeding purchase of 200 pigs for the price of 24 złoty: APP, AmK, I/11, card 221.
72 M. Horn, "Chronologia i zasięg terytorialny żydowskich cechów rzemieślniczych w dawnej Polsce (1613-1795)," in *Żydzi w dawnej Rzeczypospolitej*, 211.
73 More details may be found at http://www.jewishencyclopedia.com/articles/4705-council-of-four-lands.
74 A. Michałowska, *Między demokracją a oligarchią. Władze gmin żydowskich w Poznaniu i Swarzędzu (od połowy XVII do końca XVIII wieku)* (Warsaw, 2000), 31-65.
75 APP, AmK, I/10, card 60.
76 APP, AmK, I/11, cards 22-23.
77 That year, Jews purchased a house in Obłąki for the sum of 28 złoty: APP, AmK, I/6, card 149.
78 APP, AmK, I/10, card 63 and subsequent.
79 J. Łojko, *Kleczew w XVI-XVIII stuleciu*, 70.
80 APP, KGK, 150, cards 435-436, 437-437v, 439-439v.
81 APP, AmK, I/12, cards 37 and next.
82 APP, Aktamiasta Konarzewo (Konarzewo Town Records), 2340, card 4.
83 APP, AmK, I/9, card 45.
84 APP, AmK, I/10, card 60.
85 A person who deals with ashes for commercial use.
86 Tadeusz Lubiszewski, 27, was from Ruthenia; Paweł Minicki was born c. 1754 in Duszniki, Poznań County. Only 16 red złoty were found on the victim. APP, AmK, I/11, cards 153-156.
87 APP, AmK, I/11, cards 169-170.
88 APP, AmK, I/11, card. 46.
89 APP, AmK, I/11, card 18.

2 The Partition and Foreign Occupation Period in Poland (Late Eighteenth–Early Twentieth Centuries)

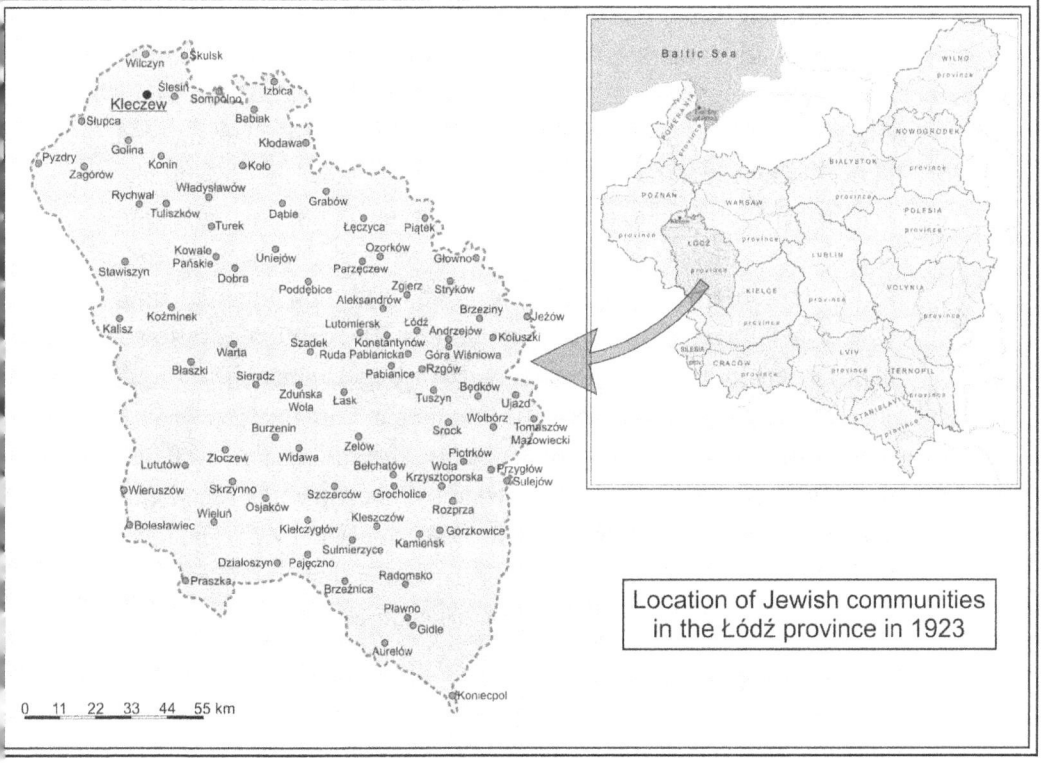

Location of Jewish communities in the Łódź province in 1923

BACKGROUND

In the seventeenth century, the Polish-Lithuanian Commonwealth engaged in a series of devastating wars with its neighbors Russia, Sweden, and Turkey, ushering in a period of decline in the country's ability to govern itself. Although significant internal reforms were introduced in the late eighteenth century, the reform process was not allowed to run its course as the Russian Empire, the Kingdom of Prussia, and the Austrian Habsburg monarchy terminated the Commonwealth's independence in 1795 in a series of invasions and three successive territorial partitions.

After the partition, different parts of Poland became subject to diverse political, economic, social, and cultural influences. The partitioning divided the Polish Jews as well, most (500,000) falling under Russian rule and the rest divided among Prussian (65,000) and Austrian (215,000) governance.

Following Napoleon's defeat of the Prussian army in 1807, an independent Polish authority called the Duchy of Warsaw was established under French protection. After the defeat of Napoleon in 1815, a separate authority called the Kingdom of Poland ("Congress Poland") was created in the Duchy territories. It was controlled by the Russian Tsar and had a parliament and public administration of its own. Not wishing Jews to spread all over Russia, the Tsar introduced laws restricting their residence to the territories of the Kingdom of Poland and those annexed from Poland and Turkey in the eighteenth century. The creation of this Pale of Settlement led to a concentration of Jewish population in these areas.

Until 1864, the Poles engaged intermittently in armed resistance against the Russians as well as the Austrians. After the last uprising failed, the nation preserved its identity by educational uplift and an economic and social modernization program. In 1918, after World War I and revolution brought on the defeat of the partitioning imperial powers, the Second Polish Republic was established; it endured until 1939.

The era described in the following chapter was characterized by frequent changes of governments, influencing the life and culture of Poland in general and the Jews of Poland in particular.

INTRODUCTION

For a brief time in 1772, Kleczew found itself within the boundaries of the Prussian monarchy. Under a Polish–Prussian border agreement signed in 1776, it was returned to Poland along with other towns. After the second partition of Poland, in 1793, the town reverted to Prussia once more and became part of the province of South Prussia. In 1807, it was reassigned to the Duchy of Warsaw; from 1815 to 1918, it belonged to the Russian Empire—initially in Kalisz Province and subsequently in the Kalisz Governorate. During World War I, German forces occupied Kleczew and central Polish territories in 1914 and remained there until 1918, when the independent Polish Republic was born.

As for the socioeconomic situation of the residents of Kleczew, 1793 found the town in dire condition. The town had 152 houses, eight belonging to the owner of the town's property (Anna Gurowska of the Radomicki family), and one elementary school that employed a single teacher. It was mainly a farming town, with stock comprising fifty horses, eighteen sheep, sixty-two head of cattle, 131 pigs, and four goats. Very few residents dealt in crafts. There is evidence of one fisherman, two butchers, one coppersmith, one glazier, one locksmith, three tailors, two wheelwrights, one harness-maker, and various other craftspeople. In addition, there was a small factory managed by Jan Klug as well as five windmills. Several residents brewed beer. In 1800, 170 houses and thirty shops and stalls were counted.[1] A section of town comprising 149 houses and several vacant lots belonged to Mikołaj Gurowski.

In subsequent years, housing stock decreased swiftly: to 151 in 1807–1808, and to only fifty-three the following year, 1808–1809, according to reports of the town council.[2] The most probable reason for the abrupt decrease was a fire in 1808. To gauge the economic significance of the great fire, we need only note that on August 4, 1808, the magistrate of Kleczew was asked to name all people who were able to extend voluntary loans and found none, because

> [...] Almost the whole town inhabited by wealthier residents was destroyed by fire, so every house owner is in need, as all of them

want to rebuild their properties and their own fortunes are too
small and will not get bigger if they cannot run any business.³

In 1812, the livestock resident in Kleczew was enumerated again: twelve pigs, twelve goats, fifty sheep, ninety-five head of horned cattle (twenty heifers, sixty-five cows, and ten oxen), two foals, twenty horses, and ten active beehives.⁴

Throughout the nineteenth century, Kleczew gradually developed economically and enjoyed some population growth. By 1817, it accommodated a city hall, a hospital, a synagogue, an impromptu Jewish house of prayer, and two drugstores. By 1821, the city had added a municipal school, a presbytery, a fever hospital (a hospital for infectious diseases), and two government buildings. The number of buildings in town was 33% higher than it had been in 1800. An assessment in 1846 mentions 157 dwellings that were "built on top of the roof," presumably meaning two-story residences.⁵ In following years, the town's infrastructure improved considerably. Some streets were paved, a sewage system was put in place, and drain ditches were dug. The first streetlights were installed before 1846. The development of small businesses such as cotton gins and weaving mills, a chicory processing plant, tanneries, dye works, and two blacksmith's shops, furthered the town's progress. By 1860, seventeen granaries had shot up among the town's fields.⁶

From 1808, the year of the great fire, to 1860, the number of houses in the town ballooned from only fifty-two to over 160.⁷ The first apartment-houses were erected on Poznańska Street and Niepodległości Square; they came with "annexes," i.e., attics that served as living quarters and balconies. In addition, the buildings on Słupecka, Goranińska Streets and Rynek Streets were thoroughly renovated.⁸

After the January Uprising (1863–1864), the Russian Government deprived many towns of their rights with an 1886 decree.⁹ By 1870, thirty-two towns in the Kalisz Governorate—75% of the total—had met this fate. Kleczew was among them: its magistrate was dissolved and replaced with a municipality. It would not regain its town status until June 1917. Even so, Kleczew gradually developed, as can be seen from the count of brick houses, which may be considered a proxy for economic

> In January 1863, an uprising against the Russian Empire started in the Polish-Lithuanian Commonwealth. Known as the January Insurrection, it began as a spontaneous protest by young Poles against conscription into the Imperial Russian Army, which was considered to be part of a plan to induct all radical Polish youths into the Russian army. The protest escalated into a Polish rebellion against Russian rule in Poland. The rebels gained support among the artisans, workers, lower gentry, and official classes in the cities and triggered peasant revolts against the large landlords in rural areas. Establishing an underground government in Warsaw, the rebels waged a guerrilla war, pitting small units of badly trained troops against Russian regulars. After severe reprisals against the insurgents, including public executions and deportations to Siberia, the insurrection collapsed, resulting in the tightening of Russian control over Poland.

development. In 1871, the town had seventy-nine houses of this type, as well as 446 wooden houses, a great increase over previous years.[10] There were several crafts workshops including two weaving mills, two tanneries, a candle production plant, a soap factory, a brickyard, and a peat dig. Still, farming remained the principal occupation for most people. Residents kept 3,600 sheep, 1,470 head of cattle, 830 pigs, 404 horses, and three goats.[11] In 1899, local animal husbandry included ninety-nine horses, 224 pigs, 102 cows, six heifers, and fourteen calves.[12] By then, however, agriculture had ground to a standstill and the number of animals bred diminished steadily. Within a thirty-year period, the number of livestock raised decreased considerably. This may have been caused in part by price competition or the importation of better meat and grain from other regions. The main reason, however, was growing urbanization and industrialization. These phenomena influenced Kleczew to a limited degree, explaining why many residents still cultivated grain, potatoes, vetch, and peas. Some residents basically became landless farmers,[13] a plight that automatically marginalized them in economic life and forced them to seek alternative sources of income in other sectors of the economy. Kleczew was near the Prussian border and close to where Prussian citizens in Eastern Greater Poland, Eastern Kuyavia, or Masovia settled. This fact fostered economic cooperation. Some goods produced by local industry or crafts—the products of the weaving mills, for example—were exported to Prussia (Germany).

By the end of the nineteenth century, however, Kleczew remained a township of minor significance. The town's sanitary conditions left much to be desired. Over the years, many elements of municipal infrastructure had been destroyed repeatedly in fires, especially those of 1808 and 1862. Even so, Kleczew was still the economic, administrative, and religious hub of its agricultural hinterland. It had a Roman Catholic parish, a synagogue administration, an elementary school, a municipal council, and a post office.[14] In addition, in 1846 a doctor named Neumann was reported as a "permanent resident."[15]

As in previous centuries, Kleczew remained a multi-religious and multi-ethnic place. In 1895, its population structure was 75.6% Catholic, 3.2% Protestant, 19.1% Jewish, and 2.1% other—mainly Christians of different denominations.[16]

1. DEMOGRAPHIC STRUCTURE

Throughout the nineteenth century, despite unfavorable political and economic circumstances, Kleczew gradually developed economically and demographically. Details about its population growth are shown in Table 8.

The town had a population of 1,348 (of whom 616 were Jews) in 1793, 1,140 (496 Jews) in 1808, and 1,570 (802 Jews) in 1827. From then on, there was a steady increase—to 2,480 (1,239 Jews) in 1886 and 3,347 (1,719 Jews) in 1909. The share of Jews in the population was steady at approximately half for most of this time.

Such demographic retreats as occurred were temporary outcomes of catastrophes. Those in 1808 and 1828 resulted from fires that destroyed the town. Although the number of Jewish residents decreased dramatically from 616 in 1793 to 496 after the 1808 blaze, it increased again in the later years considered (Table 8). For instance, we know that there were 628–651 Jews living in the town proper in 1822,[17] 769 (381 men and 388

Table 8 Population of Kleczew, 1793–1909

Year	Total population	Jewish population	Jews as percent of total population
1793	1,348	616	45.7
1808	1,140	496	43.5
1822	NA	628	-
1826	NA	769	-
1827	1,570	802	51.1
1828	NA	628	-
1836	NA	810	-
1857	1,760	985	56.0
1865	1,947	1,051	54.0
1886	2,480	1,239	50.0
1895	NA	1,302	-
1897	2,366	710	30.0
1909	3,347	1,719	51.4

Source: State Archive in Łódź (hereinafter: APŁ), Łódź Kehilla (hereinafter: ŁGWŻ), classification no. 210, card 81; APK, AmK, classification no. 148, cards 12-23; B. Wasiutyński, *Ludność żydowska w Polsce w wiekach XIX i XX. Studium statystyczne*, Warsaw 1930, p. 26; Kołodziejczyk R., *Miasta i mieszczaństwo w Królestwie Polskim w 1965 r. w świetle statystyki*, [source:] *Dzieje burżuazji w Polsce. Studia i materiały*, vol. 2, ed. R. Kołodziejczyk, Wrocław-Warsaw-Kraków-Gdańsk 1980, Table 2, pp. 19-28; *Dzieje Kleczewa*, passim; E. Bergman, J. Jagielski, *Zachowane synagogi i domy modlitw w Polsce. Katalog*, Warsaw 1996, p. 57; J. Wąsicki, *Opis*, p. 137.

women) in 1826,[18] and 802 in 1827. The fire of 1828 depressed the population temporarily; growth resumed afterward.

The records from 1807–1809 shed more light on the destructive effects of the fires. A census in 1807–1808 found approximately 500 Jewish individuals and 139 householders in Kleczew. The first year after the fire (1808–1809), the number of householders plunged to only seventeen. The number of households also decreased, from 248 before the fire to 145 after. The decline was true not only of the Jewish community but also of the population at large. Since the rate of decrease was higher among adults than among children, the impact appears to have been greater among the elderly (Tables 9 and 10).

Intensive construction efforts began after the fire. Many houses were reconstructed by the end of 1810. According to a town register, twenty of seventy-seven houses in town were newly built and nine were temporary;

Table 9 Demographic structure of the population of Kleczew, 1807/1808 and 1808/1809 (before and after fire)

	1807/1808			1808/1809		
	Female	Male	Total	Female	Male	Total
Number of families	-	-	248	-	-	145
Married couples	-	-	NA	-	-	135
Adults	150	141	291	42	38	80
Children under 15 years	75	86	161	55	66	121
Under 20 years	96	98	194	66	68	134
Servants	23	49	72	28	53	81

Source: APK, AmK, classification no. 148, cards 12-23.

Table 10 Demographic structure of Kleczew Jewish population, 1807/1808 and 1808/1809

Status	1807/1808			1808/1809		
	Female	Male	Total	Female	Male	Total
Householders	70	69	139	9	8	17
Household members and relatives	76	80	156	72	63	135
Children*	77	86	163	53	57	110
Servants	22	16	38	7	3	10
Total	245	251	496	141	131	272

Source: see table 8.

* The age limit for "children" is not defined.

thirty-nine had brick chimneys and the others did not. Several brickyards were established in Kleczew to expedite the work.[19] Fifteen homeowners (20.3%) were Jewish. (For details, see Table A in Annex 3).

The number of Jewish households in Kleczew grew from 164 (with a total of 628 people) in 1828[20] to 215 (810 people) in 1836. Unmarried people, even if living alone (44 people), and childless widows/widowers (12) were counted among them.[21] Simple arithmetic informs us that the average household size in 1836 was 3.77. Subtracting the unmarried (56), we arrive at 159 households (754 individuals)—4.74 persons per household. During the Russian occupation, the growth rate of the Jewish

Table 11 Natural movement of Kleczew Jewish population, 1809–1864

Year	Births			Deaths			Marriages
	Male	Female	Total	Male	Female	Total	
1809	5	5	10	-	3	3	-
1810	9	12	21	3	5	8	-
1811	7	5	12	6	11	17	4
1812	10	5	15	4	3	7	5
1820	5	15	20	6	6	12	1
1834	17	22	39	7	6	13	6
1835	13	6	19	7	9	16	2
1837	15	16	31	15	11	26	6
1839	23	13	36	3	12	15	10
1846	15	19	34	9	11	20	12
1864	17	22	39	17	16	33	4

Source: APK, AmK, classification no. 28; APK, Acts of the Registry Office, Kleczew kehilla, call nos. 1, 2, 3, 5.

population in Kleczew accelerated. Births outnumbered deaths, and the number of marriages increased as well (Table 11).[22]

World War I halted the demographic momentum in Kleczew, reducing the Jewish population from 1,719 in 1909 to approximately 1,500 in 1915[23] and around 1,000 in 1917–1918.[24]

2. ECONOMIC ACTIVITY

The residents of Kleczew specialized in trade and several crafts. According to the 1808–1809 census, 18.91% of occupationally active people there were tailors; 16.21% were cobblers; 14.86% were merchants; and 6.3% were bakers (Table 7). The others dealt in farming. Official records list only twenty-two farmers (9.9% of the population); most probably, they were people who owned large tracts of land. The proximity to the Prussian (German) frontier fostered the development of business despite formal obstacles. Some merchants engaged in legal trade; others smuggled various wares across the border. Smugglers' routes passed through Kleczew to Strzałków on to Września, and finally to Powidz and Gniezno.[25]

The case of Szuml Boas illustrates the handling of a debt in a legal business transaction. Boas had not been able to repay his debt to the merchant Julian Sokołowski of Września. In July 1871, the debt was taken over by another merchant from Września, Hersz Jarecki. The contract between the parties is revealing in several ways:

> [...] Szmul Boas testifies that he owed 100 rubles in silver to the merchant Julian Sokołowski from Września; due to inability to pay the debt, he asked Hersz Jarecki to assume responsibility for the outstanding debt and to pay Sokołowski in his name. Hersz Jarecki stated that he had assumed the debt from Boas and would pay the 100 rubles in silver to Sokołowski. He [Jarecki] had already issued a receipt to Sokołowski that also stated that he [Sokołowski] bore no grudge against Boas. Szmul Boas is obliged to repay the 100 rubles to Hersz Jarecki according to the following schedule: 30 rubles in silver by August 2, 1871[26] and the remaining 70 rubles in installments—10 rubles on the 9th of every month for seven months. In case of failure to make timely payments, Szmul Boas will be brought before the municipal court under the debt enforcement procedure.[27]

After 1815, the authorities of the Kingdom of Poland—autonomous though still part of the Russian Empire—made it their goal to develop trade and crafts. Regulations in 1821 promoted industry by allowing craftsmen to settle freely in towns irrespective of their nationality or religion. Reduced taxes and guarantees of government support also encouraged urbanization. Jews benefited from these regulations, settling en masse in the towns of Eastern Greater Poland. In many locations, they were forerunners of industrialization. Elsewhere, they quickly became competitive and began to crowd out local and newly arrived businesspeople alike.

Such was the case in Kleczew. The number of textile manufacturers there surged in 1818, evidenced by the list of people dealing in the field: Michał Woian, Samuel Bartel, Karol Konrad, Fryderyk Szkolny, Michał Gleiman, Samuel Wojner, and Karol Hartung. By 1824, many craftsmen had workshops in town—there were two locksmiths, two blacksmiths, three carpenters, two coopers, two wheelwrights, thirty-seven cobblers, and forty-eight tailors. Most of the shops, especially those that did needlework, belonged to Jews. More important, the largest crafts workshops (if they had automated equipment, one could call them factories) were run by members of the local kehilla. Wolf Szlama Szkolnik and Szmul Krotoszyński owned the town's two main chicory processing mills and employed four and three workers, respectively; Szkolnik owned smaller facilities as well. Tanneries were run by Abram Kalina, Szmul Garbarz, Abram Kluczkowski, Mosiek Ryczywolski, and Lewek Kluczkowski; they employed two to four workers each. There were two factories for woolen and cotton products as well as a tablecloth factory. In 1829, Szmul Garbarz, Abram Salmanowicz, and Abram Kluczewski were listed as tanners.

The textile industry developed apace. In 1834, Lipman Jelonkiewicz produced 1,000 bolts of linen and 600 bolts of hemp cloth. His competitors, Gotfryd Braun and Jakub Bile, produced 960 and 530 bolts and 40 and 650 bolts of material, respectively. Another workshop belonged to Maciej Jelenkowicz, August Berger, and Bogumił Kempel. No records about its doings at the time have survived, but in subsequent years its staff increased steadily. On average, Berger and Kempel employed three workers and Lipman Jelonkiewicz employed six.

Additional textile factories came on the scene swiftly. The one owned by Lewin Krotoszyński was active until 1845. A plant belonging to Pejsach Kryger began to operate in January 1845, and from May 1845 one belonging to Efraim Salomonowicz was active, the owner often working there along with one journeyman (skilled worker) and one to three apprentices. These enterprises were not big on output, producing only 15–270 bolts of plain or striped batiste per year.[28] In 1846, Lewek Jelenkiewicz, Lewek Chaim Krotoszyński, and Peisach Krygier ran cotton workshops that used no automation. In 1851, Szlama Greinfeld, Lewek Jozef Krotoszyński, Abram Jakub Jelonkowicz, Efraim Szlama Jelonkowicz, and Hanno Fogiel all owned textile businesses, together turning out 200–300 pounds of various fabrics.[29]

All told, industrial development in Kleczew was of limited significance. In the second half of the nineteenth century, most of the weavers' workshops went bankrupt due to inability to compete with nearby Kalisz,

Łódź, and Zduńska Wola. Consequently, increasingly specialized services, important crafts, and stratified industry began to grow. Some people combined two professions. Employment increased. The importance of Kleczew Jews in the three aforementioned sectors of the economy was considerable and continued to grow until the outbreak of World War I. Kleczew records dated December 2, 1815, show twenty people registered as dealing in trade and commerce, seventeen of them Jewish (Abram Masiek, Jozef Boile, Jelenkiewicz, the widow Rogozińska, Majer Szlama, Jakub Gembicki, Salomon Mansard, Mosiek Jelenkiewicz, Szlama Wolf, Jozef Lisner, Hersz Lachman, Icyk Jakub Jelonkiewicz, Salomon Boile, Layzer Bauman, Szmul Garbarz, Szymon Szafarz, and Mosiek Izrael).[30]

The distribution of occupations among the occupationally active Jewish population changed over the years. In 1836, 35.7% dealt in trade and services and another 35.7% in crafts; 20.2% were blue-collar workers and 8.4% were active in other ways. In 1851, trade and services were practiced by 27.6% of occupationally active Jews, crafts by 35%, blue-collar occupations by 22.2%, and other activities by 15.2%. In 1867, the proportions among Jews were 55.2% in all kinds of trade and services, 41.6% in crafts only, and 3.2% in all other fields (Table 12).

Table 12 Social and occupational structure of occupationally active Jews in Kleczew, 1836–1867

Sector	1836		1851		1867	
	Number	%	Number	%	Number	%
Trade and services	76	35.7	67	27.6	69	55.2
Crafts	76	35.7	85	35.0	52	41.6
Laborers	43	20.2	54	22.2	-	-
Industrialists	2	0.9	5	2.0	1	0.8
Transportation	-	-	-	-	1	0.8
Community clerks	3	1.4	3	1.2	1	0.8
Real-estate owners	2	0.9	21	8.6	-	-
Others	11	5.2	7	2.9	1	0.8
No data	-	-	1	0.5	-	-
Total	213	100.0	243	100.0	125	100.0

Source: APK, AmK, classification no. 22, 220, comparison by authors.

Among the subgroup of craftsmen, the largest occupational groups were tailors, tanners, bakers, butchers, and glaziers. The remaining occupations (saddlers, hatters, cap-makers, goldsmiths, soap-makers, etc.) were represented by individual people. Many crafts that existed in 1836 disappeared by 1867 (Table 13).

A census of the Kleczew Jewish population in 1836 yields very detailed and valuable information, including each individual's name, age, status in his or her family, and occupation, and notes the people who earned their living as "servants" or "domestic servants." (Table B, Annex 3.) It mentions thirty servants (14.6% of all occupationally active people: twenty females

Table 13 Structure of Jewish crafts in Kleczew, 1836 and 1867

Sort of craft	1836		1867	
	Number of craftsmen	%	Number of craftsmen	%
Tailors	40	52.65	28	53.85
Tanners	8	10.54	8	15.38
Bakers	6	7.9	3	5.77
Butchers	4	5.27	3	5.77
Glaziers	3	3.95	4	7.7
Fishermen	2	2.64	1	1.92
Haberdashers	2	2.64	-	-
Cap-maker	1	1.31	3	5.77
Hat-maker	1	1.31	-	-
Linen-draper	1	1.31	-	-
Saddler	1	1.31	-	-
Gingerbread maker	1	1.31	-	-
Shoemaker	1	1.31	-	-
Goldsmith	1	1.31	-	-
Leather-dresser	1	1.31	-	-
Soap-maker	1	1.31	-	-
Publican	1	1.31	-	-
Optician	1	1.31	1	1.92
Tinsmith	-	-	1	1.92
Total	76	100.0	52	100.0

Source: APK, AmK, classification no. 220.

aged 11–31 and four men aged 20 to 24, all unmarried. The census also gives information on other occupations. Entrepreneurs were a specific occupational group, depending on the margin of trade. The census reports the following people as traders: Anszel Hersz Eliasz, Boruch Czernicki, Layzer Iwańczyk, Szmul Jelenkiewicz, Lewin Krotoszyński, Michał Krotowski, Hersz Kalmanowicz, and Joel Nayfeld. Jews were homeowners as well: at the end of 1885, eight merchants, one factory owner, sixty craftsmen, and twenty-two small businessmen held titles to homes.[31]

Social and political changes in the nineteenth century slowly influenced the evolution of the town's social occupational structures (Table 14). In 1895, 6,801 people lived within Kleczew's municipal limits. Farmers constituted the highest percentage (68.3%), followed by town dwellers (22.6%).

Kleczew remained a production center for local needs. In 1895, it had 129 craft workshops that employed 157 people. Fifty cobblers (shoemakers) provided work for fifty-seven people, making this the largest crafts workshop category, followed by tailors with forty-seven employees (Table 15).

On the social scale, the Jewish population was positioned between farmers and nobles. It was dominant in local trade and, to a certain extent, crafts. These factors led to the emergence of a rather affluent group. Even so, the majority of Jews remained poor.

Table 14 Social and occupational structure of inhabitants of Kleczew Municipality, 1895

Group	Number			Percent
	Women	Men	Total	
Landowners	38	34	72	1.1
Clergy*	-	3	3	0.04
Town dwellers	754	783	1,537	22.6
Farmers	2,294	2,348	4,642	68.3
Others	224	323	547	8.0
Total	3,310	3,491	6,801	100.0

Source: calculations based on J. Stępień, *Kleczew w okresie 1870–1918*, Table 3, p. 131.

* Clergy = leaders of religious services.

Table 15 Workshops and employment in Kleczew, 1895

Type of workshop	Number of workshops	Number of workers	Percent
Shoemakers	50	57	36.3
Tailors	36	47	29.9
Carpenters	9	11	7.0
Bakers	7	7	4.5
Pork butchers	7	7	4.5
Carpenters	7	13	8.3
Blacksmiths	5	6	3.8
Stoneworkers	3	3	1.9
Locksmiths	2	2	1.3
Wash houses	2	2	1.3
Tanneries	1	2	1.3
Total	**129**	**157**	**100.0**

Source: J. Stępień, *Kleczew w okresie 1870–1918,* Table 9, p. 134.

3. ORGANIZATION AND FUNCTIONING OF THE JEWISH COMMUNITY

In the first half of the nineteenth century, the Jewish community of Kleczew branched into several additional localities: Lądek, Ląd, Golina, Ślesin, Wilczyn, and Skulsk. These growing communities eventually separated. In the early nineteenth century, Jews from Lądek and Golina were the first to show dissatisfaction with their subordination to the Kleczew kehilla. In 1822, religious, financial, and personal disagreements became so serious that the provincial authorities decided to solve them by separating the territories. Initially, the kehilla in Golina wished to join the five Jewish families (twenty people) in Lądek; ultimately, however, that area was annexed to Słupca.[32] Disputes among the community administrations in Golina, Słupca, and Zagórów over the governance of the Jews in Ląd and Lądek lasted into the 1930s. This area was especially attractive because it was home to the affluent Nelken family, which owned large estates. The status of Jews in the Rzgów and Ciążeń communities was also disputed.[33]

From 1822 on, the Kleczew kehilla included Kazimierz (known today as Kazimierz Biskupi), Izdebno, Dobrocałowo, Koszewo, Spławie, Wilczyn, Sławoszew, and Kleczew. The supervising authorities, armed with a decree issued on March 29, 1828, regulated the affiliation of different localities with the Kleczew kehilla by incorporating 202 of them into its boundaries. Only a few of these localities actually had Jewish residents; chief among them were Kleczew (164 households, 628 people), Izdebno (one household, five people), Kazimierz (three households, fifteen people), Koszewo (one household, ten people), Mostki (one household, six people), Racięcice (two households, seven people), Skulsk (twenty-eight households, 109 people), Słudzkie Budy (one household, four people), Ślesin (forty households, 198 people), Wilczyn (thirty-one households, 153 people), and Spławce (one household, three people).[34] This territorial division continued in subsequent decades. Other changes occurred in the second half of the nineteenth century, when the Jewish communities of Skulsk, Ślesin, Wilczyn, Słupca, Tuliszków, and Rychwał gained independence.[35]

The kehilla was the basic organizational unit in Jewish community life. All male Jews aged thirteen (the age of majority) and older belonged to it. During the Polish monarchy era, the kehilla enjoyed autonomy[36] (for further details, see Chapter 1). In 1819, a government commission prepared a draft of changes to be introduced in Jewish communities. According to this document, each community would be supervised by a synagogue administration that would control its budget and the distribution of fixed religious costs.[37] On March 21, 1821, under the auspices of General Józef Zajączek, governor of the Kingdom of Poland, the kehilla organization as it had existed until then was abolished and replaced with a "synagogue administration." This entity, under regulations laid down by the Government Commission on Religious Denominations and Public Enlightenment, was to supervise synagogues, houses of study, cemeteries, ritual baths, ritual slaughterhouses, and *chadarim* (elementary schools, sing. *cheder*), deal with religious adjudication and social welfare, take care of the poor, handle administrative and financial matters, manage community assets, represent the Jewish population vis-à-vis the outside world, issue certificates of solvency or insolvency, and collect taxes. The synagogue administration had the right to charge for circumcisions, engagements, and weddings, excuse individuals from having to enter into levirate marriages (the practice of marrying the widow of one's childless brother to maintain his line, as required by ancient Hebrew law), collect funeral fees, receive payment for the use of ritual baths, lease synagogue benches, charge money for *'aliyot* (the honor of being called to the Torah in synagogue), sell wax from candles burnt on Yom Kippur, and collect membership fees.[38] To make the payment of dues just, the community was divided into five classes based on wealth. The first group, the propertied class, paid the highest dues; class 4 paid the lowest. Class 5 was populated by Jews who lived on charity; they were exempt from dues. The synagogue administration was managed by a board (Council of Elders) that supported the rabbi in managing the community. Duespayers in Group 1 sat on the board and had the right to vote. Most often, the board elected three administrators to a three-year term.[39]

Preparing the budget (collecting revenue and planning expenses) was an important element in community life. Budget expenses included the salaries of the rabbi, an accountant, a *shul-klapper* (a person who called community members to prayers), a *melamed* (cheder teacher), and other officials, the costs of lighting and heating the synagogue and house of study, stationery, a newspaper subscription, taxes on community buildings, and charity funds. The budget was based mainly on compulsory fees collected for the synagogue administration and income from leasing ritual baths, ritual slaughterhouses, benches in the synagogue, and 'aliyot. Part of the rabbi's revenue for performing religious ceremonies such as circumcisions, weddings, and funerals also flowed to the community chest.

Data on contributions to the synagogue fund in Kleczew in 1844–1845 yield very detailed and valuable information,[40] including lists of the donations of each member of the community. In 1844, the Kleczew kehilla collected approximately 254 rubles from 114 people in contributions to the synagogue fund. Leases brought in 34.53 rubles that year. In 1845, contributions added up to 236 rubles (exclusive of other sources of income) and were remitted by 125 people (Table C, Annex 3). Table 16 illustrates the structure of budget income and expenses of the Kleczew kehilla in 1845–1850. According to the table, an income of 266.25 rubles

Table 16 Kleczew kehilla budget, 1845–1850

	1845–1847 (yearly)	1848–1850 (yearly)
Income (rubles)		
From fees	213	NA
Rent from lease and religious fees	53.25	27.55
Total:	266.25	NA
Expenses		
Rabbi's salary	135	180
Cashier's salary	13.31	15.56
Shulklapper's salary	-	25
Salary of government official	2.48	
Baker's salary	25	
Stationery	22.50	3
Heating and light for cashier		
Synagogue lighting	30	30
Subscription to *Journal of Rights* and *Government Journal*	2.25	2.25
Taxes from synagogue	15.84	15.84
Amount available for county administrator	19.87	39.60
Total	266.25	311.25

Source: AGAD, CWW, cards 37-39, 43-48.

* No income specification was provided.

in fees and contributions, plus 53.24 rubles from leases, was projected annually in 1845–1847.[41]

The community at large was directed by the kehilla or synagogue administration. This body usually drew its members from a local oligarchy comprising several families, although changes were brought about by generational differences, migrations, social and occupational advancement, or declines of families. In the nineteenth century, the sorting of the population into rich and poor residents created new divisions. Members of the Hasidic movement started to compete with followers of the traditional rabbinic trend. Although contretemps between these schools of Judaism persisted throughout the nineteenth century, they lost their importance in the second half of the century as both populations faced a growing number of followers of the *Haskala* (the Jewish Enlightenment, an eighteenth-century intellectual movement in Western Europe that emphasized reason and science in philosophy and the study of human culture and the natural world) and assimilation. At the end of the nineteenth century, another new rival emerged: Zionism. The Zionists' role gradually grew, especially after the German occupation of Kleczew in 1915.

No sources exist that can trace all representatives of the kehilla administration in Kleczew; we can only refer to random examples (Table 17). As seen in the table in 1815–1823, the synagogue administration was composed of Wolf Szlama Szkolnik, Mosiek Malarek, and Abraham Bauman. In 1825, it was headed by Abram Jelonkiewicz (a grain and spice merchant), Icyk Jakub Jelonkiewicz (a linen and wool merchant), Lipman Jelonkiewicz (a woolen cloth and wool merchant), Berendt Mazur (another woolen cloth and wool merchant), and Wolf Wrenson (an artist and innkeeper).[42] In 1826, they were replaced by Boruch Witkowski, Mejer Szlama Szkolnik, and Szmul Garbarz.[43] In 1848–1849, Hajm Grynfeld, Moszek Rączkowski, and Majer Pietrkowski[44] took over the administration. In 1871, the administrators were M. Hersz, B. Goldbaum, and L. Krotoszyński;[45] followed by Maks Bossak, Izaak Gierszberg, and Szmul Nelkien[46] in 1899–1902. During World War I (1916–1917), H. Wollmann-Goranin, Chil Prost, C. Berendt, S. Lipszyc, and M. Krzyżanowski were in charge, along with deputies M. Krzyżanowski, M. Brisch, Dawid Segał, and S. M. Weingart.[47] After elections in the autumn of 1917, the following joined the Kleczew kehilla administration: H. Woltmann (assimilator [activist in the Haskala] and landowner)—president, S. Lipszytz (Orthodox)—deputy, Chiel Prost (Orthodox), C. Berendt (Zionist), and Rabbi P. Kaufmann. The election results resembled the average among all Jewish community administrations in the Konin and Słupca districts. Of forty-eight seats available, the Orthodox won twenty-four, the assimilators seven, and the Zionists seventeen.[48] In 1918, the Kleczew kehilla was administered by H. Wollmann-Goranin, Chil Prost, S. Lipszyc, M. Krzyżanowski, and Rabbi P. Kaufmann.[49]

The rabbi was the most important community official. Elected by dues-paying members of the community, he served under a contract with the synagogue administration. After elections, the decisive vote

Table 17 Kleczew synagogue administration, selected years

Year	Names
1825	Abram Jelonkiewicz Icyk Jakub Jelonkiewicz Lipman Jelonkiewicz Berendt Mazur Wolf Wrenson
1826	Boruch Witkowski Mejer Szlama Szkolnik Szmul Garbarz
1848–1849	Hajm Grynfeld Moszek Rączkowski Majer Pietrkowski
1871	M. Hersz B. Goldbaum L. Krotoszyński
1899–1902	Maks Bossak Izaak Gierszberg Szmul Nelkien
1916—1917	H. Wollmann-Goranin Chil Prost C. Berendt, S. Lipszyc M. Krzyżanowski the deputies were: M. Krzyżanowski Brisch Dawid Segał, S. M. Weingart
fall of 1917	H. Woltmann (assimilator [activist in the Enlightenment Movement], land owner) – president, S. Lipszytz (Orthodox Jew) Deputies: Chiel Prost (Orthodox Jew), C, Berendt (Zionist), and Rabbi P. Kaufmann.

Sources: 1825—APK, AmK, 21. 1826—AGAD, CWW, 1546, cards 7-9. 1848–9—APK, AmK, 21. 1871—J. Stępień, *Kleczew w okresie 1870–1918*, p. 127. 1899–1902—ibid., p. 137. 1916–1917—APK, KZK, 16.

Notes: In 1825 the following occupations were related to the candidates: Abram Jelonkiewicz, grain and spice merchant; Icyk Jakub Jelonkiewicz, linen and wool merchant; Lipman Jelonkiewicz, local woolen cloth and wool merchant; Berendt Mazur, local woolen cloth and wool merchant; Wolf Wrenson, artist and innkeeper.

belonged to province commissions and, from 1837 on, to governors. Once chosen, the rabbi was directly accountable to the governors and had to pledge allegiance to the Tsarist authorities. His responsibilities included ensuring compliance with religious conventions, disseminating religious knowledge, supervising worshippers' moral conduct, preaching the spirit of the faith, settling religious disagreements, and monitoring community members' loyalty to the secular authorities. The rabbi also performed religious ceremonies such as circumcisions, naming newborns, weddings, and funerals; from 1826 on, he performed the functions of a registry official as well. His salary was paid from the community's membership dues.

It is not known when the first rabbi showed up in Kleczew. Rabbis probably performed their duties in the old Polish period (sixteenth to seventeenth centuries). The first documented rabbi in Kleczew dates to 1822; he eventually left Kleczew and moved to Konin but was not appointed rabbi there. From 1810 to 1849, the post of rabbi in Konin was held by Cwi Hirsz Amsterdam[50] and the vacant position of rabbi of Kleczew was temporarily given to Josef Litnera. By March 1826, Litnera, 49, had held this position for three years. Lacking formal recognition, he was initially treated as an acting rabbi. In time, however, the authorities considered him an unofficial rabbi, and in 1845 he was registered as the rabbi at a salary of 135 rubles. This remuneration was increased to 180 rubles in 1848 (Table 16) and to 200 rubles in 1860–1865.[51] Litnera's lack of proficiency in any language apart from Yiddish and Hebrew was a hindrance to his being appointed an "official" (government) rabbi. In 1848–1849, the synagogue administrators strove to obtain official consent for him to perform the rabbi's duties in Kleczew; after all, they noted, he had been holding the rabbi's office in Kleczew with the utmost care for nearly thirty years. (Gedalie Horowitz[52] was the *shammes/shkolnik*—synagogue sexton—during that time). However, some time between January 6 and January18, 1860, Fałek Auerbach was granted the post of rabbi of the Kleczew synagogue district. Auerbach received his salary retroactively from January 1, 1859. In 1865, Auerbach, aged 47, still held the post.[53] Upon his death in 1878, the position of rabbi was held briefly by Abraham Tzvi Perlmuter and then by Fałek Auerbach's son Shlomo Auerbach, who served until his own death in 1902. Documentation indicates that in 1917–1918, the rabbi of Kleczew was a man by the name of Pinkus Kauffman.[54]

Apart from the rabbi, Kleczew had a cast of additional important officials: rabbis' aides, assistants, cantors, *mohalim* (circumcisers, sing. *mohel*), *shkolniks/shammosim*, and *shul-klappers*. These posts had considerable turnover in the nineteenth century. In 1848, for example, Haskiel Parzyński was a shul-klapper and the aforementioned Gedalie Horowitz who spoke Yiddish, Hebrew, German, and Polish was an unpaid *shammes*. He was preceded by Incze (Lencze) Sam, who had been assisted by Haskiel Parzyński,[55] as shammes; Parzyński himself became *shammes* in 1865 at age sixty-four. Parzyński, who had performed various duties for the kehilla since 1830, received a salary of 25 rubles.[56]

The community had an infrastructure composed of several buildings. One was the mikve (ritual bath), which was customarily community property in the nineteenth and early twentieth centuries. In 1900, for unknown reasons—probably because it was in poor repair—Lejb Bamberg, on behalf of the Kleczew synagogue administration, rented the city baths for use as Jewish ritual baths. The contract was signed by Lejb Bamberg and Izaak Gierszberg on behalf of the kehilla and by Marceli Derengowski, chief official of the municipal office. The annual rent was 51 rubles until 1902.[57]

The school was another indispensable element of the community. Until the late nineteenth century, Kleczew's Jewish children attended traditional chadarim or public elementary schools. In 1899–1902, a Jewish school financed by the synagogue district was established. Adjacent to it was a public elementary school. In 1900, 850 children in total attended school in Kleczew, some of them from the surrounding area. Maurycy Malarek bought the elementary school building for 953 rubles in 1910; the government authorities protested the transaction and blocked it until the end of 1912.[58] In 1915, 300 school-age Jewish children attended school in Kleczew, some of them the two Polish public schools in town. In January 1916, there were 515 children aged 7–14 resident in Kleczew, of whom 155 (30%) were Jewish. Jews paid 543.05 rubles for public school tuition. It was the Jewish residents' goal to establish a separate Jewish school.

Their efforts were successful: in April 1917, a Jewish school was established with Józef Schumper teacher.[59]

The synagogue remained the most important element of the community infrastructure. There had been synagogues in Kleczew since the sixteenth and seventeenth centuries; another was erected in the second half of the eighteenth century. The town had only one synagogue at a time. A description of the Kleczew community on March 30, 1822, reported the synagogue as being in poor physical condition and in need of extensive repair. It was a half-timbered edifice with brickwork underpinnings, most likely one storey tall. The truss between the timberframe (*fachwerk*) was made of poles that were braced by diagonal beams filled with clay or woven fabric. Various sources that provide information about the wooden construction seem to confirm that the wooden frame was reinforced with boards. Before 1822, the community financed the construction of a new foundation; one assumes that the old one was decayed and had to be replaced.[60] Little is known about the synagogue itself, other than that it was considered insufficient for the needs and expectations of the growing community. Therefore, many members of the community did not use it, conducting services in private prayer houses instead.

Efforts to collect donations for the construction of a new brick synagogue began in 1810. Construction began the very next year. However, because of the political chaos that accompanied the fall of the Duchy of Warsaw and the establishment of the Kingdom of Poland under the dominion of the Russian Empire, along with property changes in Kleczew itself, construction ground to a halt with the walls built to only half their intended height.[61] In the meantime, the old synagogue continued to crumble; by 1853, it was in total ruin and beyond any attempt at repair. Several years earlier, members of the synagogue administration had set aside a plot on the corner of Gorańska and Konińska Streets for the construction of a new synagogue.[62] Despite a lack of proper funds, the synagogue administration commissioned the master builder of Konin County to prepare a new cost estimate for a brick synagogue. The designer was probably S. Kozłowski, although it is possible that the county builder, who was also the architect of the project and the designer of each subsequent version, provided this service. The relevant documents were presented to the town authorities and the synagogue administration on January 25, 1853.[63] The construction cost was estimated at 3,524.75 rubles.[64] By 1855, the original plan was embellished with new elements and motifs reminiscent of Middle Eastern architecture. As a result, between the initial sketches for a Neoclassical structure and the fifth version, the intended building acquired Neo-Moorish architectural features.[65] From December 31, 1852, to January 12, 1853, representatives of the kehilla held meetings with town authorities. The rabbi and members of the synagogue administration reported to the magistrate and announced that construction had already begun. The mayor admitted that the old wooden synagogue was so badly ruined as to be unusable, dangerous to approach, let alone to enter. He also acknowledged that services held in private homes were bad for the community and contrary to regulations. Municipal funds (330 rubles had been earmarked for the synagogue construction) and voluntary donations were supposed to cover the building costs of the new synagogue. The money was deposited with the bank of the Kingdom of Poland and a construction committee was appointed, comprising Rabbi Józef Litner, Assistant Rabbi Tobiasz Lipski, Hajman Grinfeld, Hersz Jarecki, Szmul Garbarz, Mosiek Malarek, Jakub Kotek, Josef Goldman, and Hajm Ber. Dozens of community members signed written confirmations of voluntary donations of 25 rubles or more. Hersz Lipszyc pledged 270 rubles and immediately made a first payment of 77 rubles, leaving the remainder to remit in one or two installments. Other donors made similar commitments and paid in installments. Table 18 lists the community members who pledged contributions for the synagogue between December 31, 1862, and January 12, 1863.

Construction soon began. Gotlib Lamprecht was the master builder and executor of the woodwork, mason-work, tin-work, metal-work, painting, paving, and nearly everything else. Construction was finished after 1855[66] at a total cost of 5,864 rubles. For more documents and details regarding the synagogue, including certification of the construction and architectural plans from 1851–1854, see Document 3-6, Annex 1. Members of the kehilla provided the synagogue interior with valuable necessities. Efraim Josef Gruenfeld bought two candelabra from Fraget's workshop, fifteen hanging brass chandeliers with rope riggings, and one

Table 18 People who pledged contributions for construction of synagogue in Kleczew, December 31, 1862–January 12, 1863

Name	Contribution (numbers in parentheses denote first installment given)
Lewin Danzig	180 rubles (45 rubles)
Hajm Grinfeld	180 rubles and 50 kopeks (45 rubles)
Mosiek Rączkowski	112 rubles and 50 kopeks (28 rubles)
Hersz Jarecki	95 rubles and 50 kopeks (7 rubles)
Ber Hajm Saddler	90 rubles (22 rubles and 50 kopeks)
Josef Wilczyński	90 rubles (7 rubles and 22 kopeks)
Szabsia Grinfeld	27 rubles (7 rubles and 67 kopeks)
Szlama Witkowski	150 rubles (37 rubles and 50 kopeks)
widow of Kobie Boes	120 rubles (30 rubles)
Jakub Bosak	120 rubles (30 rubles)
Berendt Mazur	72 rubles (18 rubles)
Josef Gollman	120 rubles (30 rubles)
Dawid Mazur	94 rubles (23 rubles)
Lewek Wilczyński	90 rubles (22 rubles and 50 kopeks)
Mendel Rączka	61 rubles and 50 kopeks (15 rubles and 30 kopeks)
Wołek Gloger	50 rubles and 20 kopeks (14 rubles and 80 kopeks)
Hajm Piekarski	60 rubles (15 rubles)
Szlama Lisner	51 rubles and 75 kopeks (20 rubles and 90 kopeks)
Hersz Kalmanowicz	47 rubles and 25 kopeks (11 rubles and 80 kopeks)
Szymche Iwańczyk	60 rubles (15 rubles)
Hersz Malarek	60 rubles (15 rubles)
Uryn Boes	60 rubles (15 rubles)
Jakub, Teacher	55 rubles and 50 kopeks (13 rubles and 80 kopeks)
Małka, Teacher	52 rubles and 50 kopeks (13 rubles)
Efraim Jeleńkiewicz	45 rubles (25 rubles and 11 kopeks)
Jakub Kohn	42 rubles and 75 kopeks (9 rubles and 90 kopeks)
Josek Rączka	45 rubles (11 rubles and 25 kopeks)
Eliasz Glazer	45 rubles (11 rubles and 25 kopeks)
Zelig Iwańczyk	45 rubles and 75 kopeks (11 rubles and 4 kopeks)
Abram Josef Glazer	38 rubles (7 rubles and 95 kopeks)
Hersz Rączkowski	37 rubles and 70 kopeks (9 rubles and 37.5 kopeks)
Beniamin Roterman	24 rubles and 37 kopeks (6 rubles and 9.5 kopeks)
Mosiek Izrael Piekarski	24 rubles and 37 kopeks (7 rubles and 9.5 kopeks)
Szmul Garbarz	24 rubles (6 rubles)
Aron Zyskind Szmulowicz	24 rubles (6 rubles)
Lajb Baum Orzechowski	25 rubles and 50 kopeks (6 rubles and 37 kopeks)
Szmul Krotoszyński	31 rubles and 50 kopeks (7 rubles and 87 kopeks)
Ichiel Josef Krotoszyński	31 rubles and 50 kopeks (7 rubles and 87 kopeks)

Table 18 cont.

Name	Contribution (numbers in parentheses denote first installment given)
Szymek Grinfeld	31 rubles and 50 kopeks (7 rubles and 87 kopeks)
Lajb Wilczyński	30 rubles (7 rubles and 50 kopeks)
Mordka Rachfalski(Rachwalski)	24 rubles (6 rubles)
Marek Eliaszyk	18 rubles (4 rubles and 50 kopeks)
Ber Kalmiński	18 rubles (4 rubles and 50 kopeks)
Lejb Psipsia	18 rubles (4 rubles and 50 kopeks)
Hajm Krawczyk	17 rubles and 25 kopeks (4 rubles and 31 kopeks)
Mordka Roszer	17 rubles and 25 kopeks (4 rubles and 31.5 kopeks)
Lemel Jelenkiewicz	18 rubles (4 rubles and 50 kopeks)
Jude Lejb Kuczyński	21 rubles (5 rubles and 25 kopeks)
Lejb Jelenkiewicz	18 rubles and75 kopeks (4 ruble and 69 kopeks)
Hajm Psipsia	18 rubles and 75 kopeks (4 rubles and69 kopeks)
Hersz Lejb Apel	18 rubles (4 rubles and 50 kopeks)
Szlama Blitz	25 rubles and 50 kopeks (6 rubles and 37 kopeks)

Source: APK, AmK, classification number 22.

large brass chandelier to be suspended in the middle of the synagogue with rope rigging, paying 157.50 rubles in all.

The master builder of Konin County, W. Taraszuwski, was paid 19.85 rubles for designing the structure and certifying delivery and acceptance. The delivery and acceptance protocol has been preserved; it mentions all expenses and costs incurred during construction.[67] However, the quality of the work done must have been poor, since a collection for synagogue repair was announced only a few years later, in 1867. To this collection, 125 people gave donations that added up to 555.3 rubles. Table D in Annex 3 lists each contributor by name, occupation, and sum donated.[68]

Apart from the synagogue, private houses of prayer played a significant role in Jewish life. Jews who gathered in these facilities often were opposed to the kehilla's official supremacy. Their divergence had various origins. To begin with, there were social divisions—for example, manual workers such as tailors and porters vs. skilled workers and professionals such as mohalim—in addition to disagreements over financial and religious ceremonial customs. The latter issue became acute in the nineteenth century when Hasidic Judaism spread in Kleczew. The strength of the Hasidic influence on Jews in Kleczew is hard to determine with precision, although it is known that Gerrer Hasidim—those of the court centered in Góra Kalwaria—were dominant. The example of nearby Konin allows us to reach some conclusions. There, Hasidic families constituted 10% of the Jewish population. Individual families were numbered as followers of the *tzadikim* (Hasidic pietists/leaders) from Aleksandrów, Sochaczew, and Breslav (Pol. Bracław)—this last being known also as the "*toit* [dead] Hasidim."[69] The situation in Kleczew was probably similar, although due to its small-town character the Hasidic influence there could have been 10% or 30% stronger. Either way, Hasidim and followers of traditional Judaism constituted the majority of the Jewish community.

Several examples of disagreements on social, occupational, and perhaps ritual grounds follow. In the early nineteenth century, the Kleczew kehilla board complained to its governmental superintendents that many Jews were gathering in the private house of the tailor Józef Łabiszynski, among other homes, for prayers. On December 13, 1820, the synagogue elders asked the town leaders to remove two Torah scrolls from Łabiszynski's home because the tailors who congregated in his house were committing "various indecencies"; the scrolls were to be given to the rabbi. On April 10, 1822, the elders of the kehilla (Wolf Szlama Szkolnik, Mosiek Malarek, and Abraham Bauman) presented this grievance to the mayor in the following letter:

> Even though there is a comfortable and spacious synagogue equipped with benches and Torah scrolls, some Jews are holding their services in private homes. There are trade guilds that also perform services in private homes, but we do not know who approved and established them. Such divisions diminish the income of the synagogue treasury under our administration, as only a small number of worshippers, from lower classes, attend the public synagogue; all the others meet in private places. Nor is that all: Jakób Kryger purchased a house that he presumably

wanted to turn into a *cheder* for the community. The walls of the house were pulled down and Kryger had new benches made. Now Jews are holding services there instead of establishing a school. Apart from Jakub Kryger, Elkowi Jarocki is dealing with the newly established school rather than the synagogue [...].

The elders urged the magistrate to demand an explanation from these people about their prayer houses and to force Kryger and Jarocki to document their activities.[70]

The kehilla infrastructure took on its final form in the second half of the nineteenth century. By 1862, the community owned one synagogue, houses of study, and a mikve. There were a rabbi, an assistant, a synagogue custodian, a school, five teachers, and twenty-five students.[71] However, there was no hospital, as only the most affluent communities could afford to maintain one. Therefore, Jews from Kleczew had to go to Jewish hospitals in Kalisz or Warsaw when in need of treatment. In 1820, the Jewish hospital in Warsaw complained to the Government Commission on Internal Affairs and Police that Jewish communities from other provinces were sending poor individuals and beggars to its facility, saddling it with onerous expenses and crowding out local patients. In response, the Commission addressed a decree to the Jewish communities in Kalisz Province on March 19, 1820, warning them not to impetuously send beggars and the poor to the hospitals of Warsaw and Kalisz or, if they were to continue the practice, to cover all costs of their stay.[72] The dictate was delivered to the synagogue elders in Kleczew on October 1, 1820.[73] There is surviving documentation of one David Smulewicz of Kleczew, who was hospitalized in Warsaw at a cost of 21 złoty.[74] On March 17, 1852,[75] the administrator of Konin County advised the mayor of Kleczew by letter that the Jewish hospital in Warsaw was owed 5.55 rubles for having treated a Jewish woman named Ryfka Moszkowa Wołkowicz. Her husband paid the bill.[76] In 1853, Szmul Radziejewski, Ryfka Nejman, and Hajm Birnbaum received care in the Kalisz hospital.[77] Hospitals were repeatedly unable to collect from patients from Kleczew. To set matters right, the Administrative Board of the Jewish Hospital in Warsaw wrote the following to the Kleczew magistrate on or around May 1, 1868[78]:

"Every patient checking into the hospital for treatment must have at least 6 rubles on his person to cover the costs of treatment during the first month. Patients with no money will not be admitted to the hospital."[79] In addition to having difficulties in collecting payments, hospitals found that some families left poor, sick, old, or handicapped relatives on their premises. Around December 31, 1853, a letter was sent to the Kleczew magistrate[80] concerning the stay of Szainya Liba Graydycz in the Jewish Hospital in Warsaw, setting the costs of her treatment at 49.20 rubles. When the mayor of Kleczew tried to trace the patient's family to secure payment, it turned out that Szainya's parents, Józef and Margie Graydycz, had fled the country and "There was no other family [to dun] or assets to foreclose for reimbursement." The kehilla refused to pay because "Szainya Liba Graydycz from our town was not […] approved for treatment in the Jewish hospital in Warsaw, as she was incurably stupid from birth and she cannot be cured." Józef Graydycz and his wife had "fled the country [in 1851], taking their assets with them and remaining aliens in the town of Grzywc near Leszno in Prussia […]. The kehilla administration urges the patient's parents to return to the country, pay for the treatment, and take care of their child."[81]

When the *kehillot* were abolished after 1822, it was assumed that Jewish funeral societies and like associations would be dissolved as well. The funeral societies' functions were transferred to the synagogue administrations.[82] In Kleczew, the Guild of the Assembly of the Jewish Funeral Fraternity, presided over by Dawid Lipman Grynfeld, performed these duties. Beginning on June 10, 1843,[83] it was explicitly forbidden to offer private burial services or charge any fees for doing so, these prerogatives belonging to the synagogue administration. In practice, however, funeral homes continued to operate along with the synagogue administrations, leading to tension. A document issued between December 1 and December 13, 1843,[84] by the Kalisz Government Department of Administration stated that only synagogue administrations were to deal with funerals; services should not be solicited from individual Jews and separate burial entities should not be established. Funeral fees should be collected by the town clerk. Income from funerals—"grave fee" and "burial fee"—should be estimated by the synagogue administrators and the rabbi and remitted to the synagogue treasury immediately after a funeral, with financial supervision provided.[85] According to information from the Kleczew magistrate on December 28, 1850,[86] however, a funeral guild was still operating in town at that time, and the following elders were its members: Hersz Lipszyc, Jakub Kotek, Wowa Mazur, the rabbi, and others. In 1866, senior master Jarecki presided over the guild.[87]

Jews in Kleczew were involved in many disputes with town authorities, their Catholic neighbors, and Jews in other localities. Conflicts between the synagogue elders and the "Jewish street" also arose. The province commissioner advised against such disagreements because "Arguments and quarrels of this type can lead only to punishment. The delegated commissioner has advised Jews that the culprits will be reported to criminal court and, in the matter of hair torn from beards and other injuries, may look forward to justice in court."[88] Unsurprisingly, clashes occurred despite these admonishments. On September 16, 1842,[89] a fight between Wołek Szlama Szkolnik and Szmul Garbarz Dozorca Szumiczny escalated into a brawl. In the middle of the fracas, Szmul Garbarz found refuge in a school administration office. Wołek Szkolnik and his family mounted an attack on the office and "actively insulted Szmul Garbarz." Onlookers sought to rescue Garbarz, setting the skirmish into even higher gear.[90] In 1842, Hemic Byk was punished for hiding meat and resisting the police. Over the course of this incident, the Byks brought a crowd of Jews with them, and Byk's wife Sara, with their son and daughter, insulted a policeman and the mayor. Hemic Byk was sentenced to four hours in prison, a fine of 2.25 rubles, and court and stamp costs; his wife was ordered to spend one hour in prison for disobeying the authorities.[91]

Jews were hauled into court for fighting, arguing, disturbing the peace, embezzlement, fraud, and harmful action against the state. In 1846, Jakub Sure Szkolnik was authorized by the internal revenue service, by decree of the Treasury Commission, to execute "the expulsion [of perpetrators] from the township to a border town because of numerous embezzlements and fraud that were harmful to the state treasury."[92]

On February 2, 1846,[93] the Konin District Magistrate's Court summoned the magistrate of Kleczew to testify about police files and police knowledge in order to obtain:

a) a list of all shysters [unscrupulous lawyers] living in town, dealing with clients, if they formally write complaints and other legal documents;
b) and a list of shysters from nearby localities who write applications to local authorities.

This may have been a request for information about the working methods of unlicensed or inappropriately educated offerers of legal counsel. The idea was to drive "shysters" out of business. To that end, towns were supposed to collect the following information:

1. the shyster's house number;
2. his conduct and the possible harmful influence of his behavior on cases;
3. what he did for a living apart from being a shyster;
4. whether he had been a defendant in criminal court; if so, what he was accused of and whether he was under police supervision;
5. whether he was registered in the book of permanent residents of the town where he had his shyster practice.[94]

The Kleczew town authorities issued a report that answered these inquiries. The main allegations (Table 19) concerned the activities of Jakub Sure Szkolnik, Wolf Szlama Szkolnik, Moszek Szkolnik, and Lewek Jelenkiewicz.

In April 1846, the Kleczew Magistrate's Office provided information about Jews who were often in conflict with the law. The report mentioned Berend Mazur, the owner of House no. 76, married and the father of seven children (known as "a difficult character"); Wolf Szlama Szkulnik, owner of House no. 23, father of four children (known for his impertinence, reprehensible way of thinking, and inciting residents to riot); the butcher Hemie Włydelski, owner of House no. 60 and Włydelski's wife Sarne, parents of four children (known for impertinence and disobeying the authorities); Jakub Boes, owner of House no. 28, married and father of four children (known for inciting residents to riot); and Moszek Szkolnik, who made his living by trade and embezzlement, married and father of

Table 19 Information about work of "shysters" in Kleczew, 1840s

No.	First name and surname	Shyster's conduct and possibility of harmful influence of his behavior on cases	Source of livelihood apart from being a shyster	Is the shyster a defendant in criminal court and, if so, what is he accused of and is he under police supervision?	Registration in book of permanent residents
1.	Jakub Sure Szkulnik	Deserving rebuke under all circumstances because he makes complaints about the authorities, collects fees, and incites others to make complaints	Stall trade, which cannot be continued due to his many frauds		Registered
2.	Wolf Szlama Szkulnik	Wrongdoing: apart from malicious complaints, he collects fees and gives inciteful advice to collectors	Trade in wool and fraud	Several arguments and assaults on mayor's office	Registered
3.	Moszek Szkulnik	As above	Stall trade	As above; accused of fraud in court, under police supervision	Registered
4.	Lewek Jelenkiewicz	Malicious bad advice	Malicious manufacturer	As above	Registered

Souce: APK, AmK, classification no. 227, cards 101-102.

one child (known for all the kinds of deeds that "an evil and ignominious man can have").[95]

After 1864, many Jews tried to escape compulsory conscription into the Tsar's army. Some got away with it. On May 27, 1895, the *Kaliskie Wiadomości Gubernialne* (Kalisz Government News) reported that eight draftees from the Kleczew community, Efraim Cukier among them, had failed to report for enlistment. Others tried to buy their way out. For example, Arnold Gustaw Fibich of Kleczew agreed to replace a Jew, Rafał Rachwalski from Golina, in the army in exchange for a certain sum of money. Local authorities permitted this.[96] The majority of inductees, however, had no choice but to report.

There were also cases of religious conversion. In July 1829, according to Kelczew's town documents, Szmul Grembart declared—apparently before the local priest—his determination to change religions. He was asked questions about his birthplace, parents, age, and occupation. He was also asked why he had decided to change his religion and whether he had his parents' consent. He said that he had been born in Kleczew and was seventeen years old, the son of the tailors Jakub and Eiki Grembart, and an unskilled worker. As for why he had made such a decision, he replied:

> Of my own will. I observed the wonderful Catholic rituals and came to realize that Jews mostly try to live on cheating, which I did not experience among Catholics. So I figured that that religion leads to a goal. Living an honest life will at the same time bring about the redemption of the soul.

Grembart also testified that he could read Yiddish and German but not Polish.[97]

In May 1844, Maryanna Koszerowa of Kleczew went to Warsaw to convert to Roman Catholicism. She was accepted into the Nuns of the Visitation order, where she was to receive the catechism. While there, however, she refused to be baptized and launched a broadside of blasphemies against religion that demoralized others who were taking pre-baptism instruction in the order's monastery. She was expelled from the monastery and returned to Kleczew.[98]

NOTES

1. Archiwum Państwowe w Poznaniu. Oddział w Koninie (State Archive in Poznań, Konin branch; hereinafter: APK), AmK, 92, card 86, 116; J. Łojko, *Miasto w latach 1793-1870*, in *Dzieje Kleczewa*, 111-114.
2. APK, AmK, 148, card 25.
3. APK, AmK, 148, card 40-41.
4. APK, AmK, 148, card 95.
5. APK, AmK, 93, card 8-22.
6. APK, AmK, 91, card 32-34.
7. APK, AmK, 91, card 97.
8. J. Łojko, *Miasto w latach 1793-1870*, 114-115.
9. The records then showed 338 towns in the entire former Kingdom of Poland.
10. APK, AmK, 30, card 11v.
11. APK, AmK,30, card 15.
12. J.Stępień, *Kleczew w okresie 1870–1918*, in *Dzieje Kleczewa*, 126 and table 12, p. 136-137.
13. J.Stępień, *Kleczew w okresie 1870*, 131-132.
14. *Słownik Geograficzny Królestwa Polskiego i innych krajów słowiańskich*, vol. 4 (Warsaw, 1883), 125.
15. AGAD, Centralne Władze Wyznaniowe Królestwa Polskiego (Central Religious Authority of the Kingdom of Poland; hereafter: CWW), 1546, card 53.
16. Estimation based on J. Stępień, *Kleczew w okresie 1870*, Table 4, p. 131.
17. APK, AmK, 20. According to some sources, 150 "souls" inhabited the community (this term probably denoted heads of household, i.e., men having families or men legally responsible according to Jewish law). According to other data, 173 "souls" lived there (56 families), or 164 "souls" and 628 people.
18. APK, AmK, 20.
19. APK, AmK, 148, cards 68-74.
20. APK, AmK, 20.
21. APK, AmK, 220.
22. J. Łojko, *Kleczew w XVI-XVIII stuleciu*, 96, states that there were 135 Jewish weddings in 1835, 146 in 1837, 154 in 1837, 171 in 1839, and 183 in 1840.
23. APK, Kaiserliche Zivilververwaltung Konin 1915–1918 (Imperial Civil Administration Konin; hereafter: KZK), 29.
24. APK, KZK, 16, 20.
25. J. Stępień, *Kleczew w okresie 1870–1918*, 138.
26. August 14, 1871, according to the Julian calendar.
27. Quoted from J. Stępień, *Kleczew w okresie 1870–1918*, 128.
28. In 1844, Samuel Jelenkiewicz produced 800 pieces of batiste and 160 pieces of striped fabric; Lewin Heim Krotoszyński manufactured 410 and 70, and Peisach Kryger 330 and 150.
29. J. Łojko, *Miasto w latach 1793-1870*, 116-118.
30. Ibid., 118.
31. J. Stępień, *Kleczew w okresie 1870–1918*, 128.
32. APK, AmK, 20.

33 For more, see T. Kawski and M. Opioła, *Gminy żydowskie pogranicza Wielkopolski, Mazowsza, Małopolski i Śląska w latach 1918-1942* (Toruń, 2008), passim; T. Kawski, *Funkcjonowanie struktur biurokratycznych gmin żydowskich centralnej i zachodniej Polski w latach 1918-1939*, in *Dzieje biurokracji na ziemiach polskich*, vol. 1, ed. Artur Górak, Ireneusz Łuć, and Dariusz Magier, 495-504 (Lublin, 2008).
34 APK, AmK, 20.
35 APK, Starostwo Powiatowe w Koninie 1918-1939 (County Office in Konin 1918-1939; hereafter SPK), call no. 378, 380; APK, Starostwo Powiatowe w Słupcy 1918-1932 (County Office in Słupca 1918-1932; hereafter: SPS), 216; T. Kawski and M. Opioła, *Gminy*, passim.
36 A. Eisenbach, *Z dziejów ludności żydowskiej w Polsce w XVIII i XIX w.* (Warsaw, 1983), 219.
37 J. Janicka, *Żydzi Zamojszczyzny 1864-1915* (Lublin, 2007), 66.
38 A. Eisenbach, *Z dziejów ludności*, 66-67.
39 A. Eisenbach, *Z dziejów ludności*, 67ff.
40 APK, Am K, classification number 19.
41 APK, AmK, 19; AGAD, CWW, cards 37-39.
42 APK, AmK, 21.
43 AGAD, CWW, 1546, cards 7-9.
44 APK, AmK, 21.
45 J. Stępień, *Kleczew w okresie 1870–1918*, 127.
46 Ibid., 137.
47 APK, KZK, 16.
48 APK, KZK, 16.
49 APK, KZK, 16, 20.
50 T. Richmond, *Uporczywe echo. Sztetl Konin. Poszukiwanie* (Poznań, 2001), 238.
51 AGAD, CWW, 1546, 37-39, 43-48, 138-143.
52 APK, AmK, 21, 220.
53 APK, AmK, 21.
54 APK, KZK,16, 18, 20.
55 APK, AmK, 21.
56 APK, AmK, 21.
57 J. Stępień, *Kleczew w okresie 1870–1918*, 137.
58 Ibid., 137-138.
59 APK, KZK, 29.
60 APK, AmK, 20.
61 APK, AmK, 22.
62 Official property registry, Entry 90.
63 February 6, 1853 (according to the Julian calendar).
64 APK, AmK, 22.
65 E. Bergman, *Nurt mauretański w architekturze synagog Europy Środkowo–Wschodniej w XIX i na początku XX wieku* (Warsaw, 2004), 61-62, and drawing 31 and 32, p. 255.
66 E. Bergman and J. Jagielski, *Zachowane synagogi i domy modlitw w Polsce. Katalog* (Warsaw, 1996), 57.
67 AGAD, CWW, 1546, card 148-176.
68 APK, AmK, 22.

69 Yiddish for disciples of R. Nachman of Humań, who died without a successor. T. Richmond, *Uporczywe echo*, 234.
70 APK, AmK, 23.
71 APK, AmK, 20.
72 APK, AmK, 228, cards 1-2.
73 APK, AmK, 228, cards 1-2.
74 APK, AmK, 228, card 24.
75 March 29, 1852 (according to the Julian calendar).
76 APK, AmK, 228, cards 28-29.
77 APK, AmK, 228, card 41.
78 May 13, 1868 (according to the Julian calendar).
79 APK, AmK, 228, cards 43-45, 234.
80 January 12, 1854 (according to the Julian calendar).
81 APK, AmK, 228, cards 56-58.
82 APK, AmK, 25.
83 June 22, 1843 (according to the Julian calendar).
84 December 13, 1843 (according to the Julian calendar).
85 APK, AmK, 25.
86 February 9, 1851 (according to the Julian calendar).
87 APK, AmK, 25.
88 APK, AmK, 227, card 6.
89 September 28, 1842 (according to the Julian calendar).
90 APK, AmK, 227, card 53-55.
91 APK, AmK, 227, cards 79-83.
92 APK, AmK, 227, cards 97-98.
93 February 14, 1846 (according to the Julian calendar).
94 APK, AmK, 227, cards 99-100, 123.
95 APK, AmK, 227, cards 133-134 and 145-147. By 1847, Moszek Szkolnik had two children. In addition to perpetrating frauds, he was a salt trader. By the early date of 1842, he was accused of attacking the magistrate's office.
96 J. Stępień, *Kleczew w okresie 1870–1918*, 125-126.
97 APK, AmK, 24, cards 23-25.
98 APK, AmK, 24, cards 29-30.

3 Interwar Kleczew (1918–1939)

BACKGROUND

From 1795, when Poland ceased to exist as an independent state, to the beginning of World War I, several unsuccessful uprisings in the cause of independence took place.

When World War I broke out in 1914, Russian and Prussian troops battled in the vicinity of Kleczew, not far from Konin; the clashes ended with a swift Prussian takeover.

In 1918, Poles in the Greater Poland region launched a military insurrection against Germany in the Posen area. This initiative, known as the Greater Poland Uprising, would have a significant effect on the Treaty of Versailles. This pact, which terminated the state of war between Germany and the Allied powers at the end of World War I, also created a reconstituted Poland in the area won by the Polish insurgents plus some additional territory that, although taken from Germany, had been Polish before the three partitions of Poland.

The end of World War I marked the collapse of the powers that had partitioned Poland, resulting in a new European order that allowed for the reconstruction of the Polish state in November 1918.

> The borders of this Second Polish Republic, however, were not recognized by four of its neighbors: Germany, the USSR, Czechoslovakia, and Lithuania.
>
> The Second Republic was a multinational state, comprised of Poles (64%) and other ethnic minorities (36%), including Jews (10%). Within its borders, there were 950 registered Jewish communities, most in the central and eastern regions—the quondam Russian Pale of Settlement—and in old Galicia. The first international Minorities Treaty, ratified by Poland in 1919, guaranteed Jews freedom of religion and allowed them to use their native language in public life, establish associations and schools, and receive government funding for education. The constitution of 1921 ostensibly went farther, guaranteeing equal rights for all citizens. Neither legal acts nor political assurances, however, could prevent discriminatory practices. In 1923, an attempt was made to introduce the *numerus clausus,* a restrictive quota against Jews in access to university education; in 1938, a *numerus nullus*—a total ban on university education for Jews—was proposed.
>
> The 1929–1935 economic crisis and the triumph of nationalistic ideologies in some European countries intensified antisemitic strife in Poland. Nationalist factions called for boycotts of Jewish shops and businesses; brutal assaults took place in several towns.
>
> On September 1st 1939, Nazi Germany invaded Poland. Soon after, on September 17th, the Soviet Union attacked Poland as well, in line with the agreement signed on August 23rd by the German and Soviet foreign ministers, Ribbentrop and Molotov. After the capitulation in October 1939, Poland's territory was divided between Germany and the Soviet Union.

INTRODUCTION

The end of World War I augured a new era in Polish history. In the newly independent country, numerous factors brought new influences to bear on different aspects of civic life. The introduction of republican government rapidly democratized social and political life. It was all novel, especially

for residents of the previously Russian-ruled territories, where all citizen initiatives had been throttled. Under the new political order, citizens were encouraged to be socially and economically active to an extent that they had not expected.

Routines that had developed in the early twentieth century proved useful in following years. A *coup d'état* in 1926 brought the Sanation to power in Poland and anti-democratic tendencies began to ascend. Finally, the Great Depression (1929/30–1935) and Józef Piłsudski's death (1935) put social and political attitudes and behaviors to exploitive use.

To understand the aspects that degraded the quality of life in interwar Poland, one also has to appreciate an additional cluster of micro- and macro-economic factors, all influenced by the policies of all subsequent governments and the state of the market. Historical traditions from the First Rzeczpospolita (Republic) and the post-partition occupation appear to have been dominant in weighing on the economy of all regions in Poland. Despite some modernization processes in the nineteenth and early twentieth centuries, the underdeveloped civilization inherited by the newly-formed Polish Republic could not be brought forward. The third characteristic to keep in mind was the indigenous multi-ethnic and multi-religious nature and its corollary, the multicultural society, of interwar Poland.

As for Kleczew during this period, the town was included in Słupca County until 1932, when Słupca County was dissolved; then it was incorporated into Konin County. Until 1938, Słupca County belonged to Łódź Province and included Koło, Turek, and Kalisz Counties; afterward it was part of Poznań Province. In 1921, Kleczew had a population of 2,744, making it the smallest town in Słupca County. For comparison, Słupca township had 5,534 residents at this time, Pyzdry 4,614, and Zagórów 3,715.[1] The demographic and economic development of Kleczew was stunted by a fire on August 6, 1921, that destroyed part of the town and rendered sixty-eight families homeless. The population grew rather slowly in subsequent years as economic stagnation induced out-migration and local authorities wrestled with constant financial difficulties that were very often caused by personal issues. Matters went so far that the prospect of delisting the town was taken into consideration, even though its population reached 3,000 by the late 1930s.

As it had been before, Kleczew was a local trade and crafts center that supplied goods and services to its agricultural hinterland. Its population of merchants and traders, as well as craftsmen who provided industrial commodities, was not large. Several businesses were established: a candy factory, a groats mill, a dairy, an electric power station, an oil refinery, and windmills. In 1925, the town boasted 112 production mills and workshops. Cooperative enterprises came into vogue; the People's Cooperative Bank, a dairy cooperative, and two savings and loan funds were founded. In the late 1920s, trade guilds for bakers, shoemakers, butchers, millers, carpenters, blacksmiths, locksmiths, and wheelwrights sprouted. Economic life revolved around markets and fairs, the latter taking place on the first Tuesday of each month.

Kleczew remained a seat of local self-government and special administration. The municipality (mayor and magistrate) and county government, the Roman Catholic parish authorities, and the kehilla (organized Jewish community) were located there. The town had a Magistrate's Court, a fire station, and a public school. Its urban character was recognizable not only in its street names[2] but also in its public baths, hotel, beer hall, restaurant, bookshop, photography shop, and wide range of organizations. Residents' needs were met by two or three doctors, a surgeon's assistant, a dentist, a midwife, a notary, a bailiff, and

---

BACKGROUND

The rebirth of sovereign Poland in 1918 was followed by a period of pogroms against the Jews, especially in Eastern Polish borderlands. During the interwar period at large, the situation of Polish Jews was mixed Jews were recognized as a nationality and their legal rights were ostensibly protected under the Treaty of Versailles. De facto, however, Poland observed their legal rights in the breach. The kehilla, the Jewish community governing body, was not allowed to operate autonomously. The government meddled in its elections and controlled its budget. On the other hand, Jews received funding from the state for their schools.

Economic conditions declined for Polish Jews during the interwar years. Jews were barred from the civil service, state-controlled banks, and state-run monopolies (e.g., the tobacco industry), few taught in public schools, and almost none worked for the railroads. Legislation forcing citizens to rest on Sunday was passed, ruining Jewish commerce, which was closed on Saturday. The Jews' economic downfall was accompanied by a rise in antisemitism. In the late 1930s, a new wave of pogroms befell the Jewish population and anti-Jewish boycotts spread.

two lawyers.[3] Situated at the intersections of rail and motor routes from Kutno to Września and from Inowrocław to Konin, Kleczew was a local transportation hub.

Another typical feature of Kleczew was its multi-ethnic and multi-religious character. Ethnic Poles, almost all of whom were Roman Catholic, were the largest sector. Jews were the second-largest religious group. Additionally, a small group of Protestants, descendants of nineteenth-century German settlers, lived in town.[4]

1. DEMOGRAPHIC STRUCTURE

The Jewish population of interwar Kleczew (1918–1939) was much smaller than that preceding World War I. In 1909, the Jewish community numbered 1,719, 51.4% of the total population; by 1921, it had diminished to 894 and 32.6%. Further demographic regression followed, stopping only after 1935. The Jews population of Kleczew during those years was 740–750 (Table 20).

Jewish demographic depletion occurred in all small Jewish communities in the counties of Eastern Greater Poland, neighboring Kuyavia, and larger towns such as Koło, Konin, Słupca, and Zagórów (Table E, Annex 3). The main reason was migration. Many families and young singles left

Table 20 Population of Kleczew, 1909 and 1939, selected years

Year	Total population	Jewish population	Percent of Jews
1909	3,347	1,719	51.3
1921	2,744	894	32.6
1936*	3,512	740	21.0
1938	2,946	Ca. 750	Ca. 25
Sept. 30, 1939	2,996	746	24.9

Source: APŁ, ŁGWŻ, classification number 210, card 81; *Rocznik Statystyczny Królestwa Polskiego. Rok 1913*, prepared by Biuro Pracy Społecznej under the supervision of W. Grabski, Warsaw 1914, Section I, Table III, p. 20; B. Wasiutyński *Ludność*, p. 26.

Note: The data for 1936 in *Dzieje Kleczewa* (p. 234), reporting the number of Jews at about 1,000, should be considered significantly overstated.

unindustrialized provincial towns in favor of more industrialized centers in Eastern Greater Poland and Masovia, such as Kalisz and Łódź, which also had large and well-organized Jewish communities that afforded better opportunities for personal growth. Others left the country altogether. A detailed example of this tendency in several waves and generations may be seen in the story of the Rachwalski family (Annex 2).[5] As expected, the departure of young people affected the average age of the townspeople by lowering the birth rate.[6]

Another factor of influence on the town's demographics was the great fire of August 6, 1921. It claimed the following Jewish victims: Lejzor Kutnowski, Nuchem Gluba, Lejbuś Glauba, Eliasz Grünblat, Leopold Herman, Icek Dyndol, and Szymon Dyner.[7]

Most Jews in Słupca and, consequently, Konin County were town dwellers who accounted for much of the localities' total population (Table E, Annex 3); few Jews lived outside towns.[8] The largest Jewish communities were in villages and settlements that had been deprived of town rights in the nineteenth century (Skulsk, Wilczyn, Władysławów, Tuliszków) and were unable to regain these rights in subsequent years. The Grodziec and Kramsk municipalities suffered similarly,[9] as did the other counties

1. Tobiasz Rachwalski and his son, Abraham Moses (Alfred), who was sent to the U.S. in 1890. The photo was taken during Alfred's visit to Poland in 1924.
(Marks private collection)

of Eastern Greater Poland.[10] Moreover, the migration of Jewish residents from villages continued over the years, further depleting the village population. In Słupca County, the main Jewish communities in 1909 were in Kleczew and Słupca. Sizable groups, however, also existed in Wilcza Góra (381 Jews, 373 of them in Wilczyn), Skulska Wieś (599 Jews, 480 of them in Skulsk), and Pyzdry (390). The Jewish population in the remaining municipalities was smaller: Kazimierz (240; 31 of them in Kazimierz Biskupi), Grodziec (109), Ciążeń (93), Szymanowice (31), Ostrowite (27), Trąbczyn (13), Oleśnica (16), Dłusk (6), and Młodojewo (2).[11] In 1921, the Jewish population of settled localities in Słupca County (town inhabitants excluded) was 439 (10.9% of the total population); 333 Jews lived in villages (0.5%).[12]

Jewish settlement in small Polish towns was peculiar in that nearly all Jews clustered in small urban areas. Kleczew was no exception. Virtually all of its Jews lived on several streets in the town center. The list of voters for the kehilla administrative board (Table F, Annex 3) and those entitled to vote for the Sejm (the lower house of the Polish parliament), the Senate (the upper house), or the municipal council in 1924–1935 shows evidence of this. For a list of Jewish voters for the Sejm in Kleczew (Voting District No. 55, Electoral Constituency No. 19) in 1935, parsed by profession, place of residence in Kleczew, and date of birth, see Table G, Annex 3. The detailed table offers a clear view of the Jewish community, the districts and streets where they lived, their ages, occupations, and other characteristics.

According to the sources, in 1924, twenty-four voters (17.4%) lived on Rynek Street, seventeen (12.4%) on Warszawska Street, sixty-eight (51.8%) on Słupecka Street, seven (5.1%) on Kościelna Street, and eleven (8%) in Konińska Street. Outside Kleczew, two (1.4%) Jewish families lived in the village of Chrzanowo and five (3.6%) in Górne Piaski. No data are available regarding two families (0.3%).[13] More detailed information is supplied by the list of voters—370 Jews among them—for the 1935 parliamentary elections. By the time this list was formed, many of the streets of the town had been renamed. Of the Jews listed, ninety-six (26.7%) lived on Hejmana-Jareckiego Street; sixty-eight (18.9%) on Rynek Street, forty-six (12.8%) on Pierackiego Street;

thirty-nine (10.8%) on Konińska Street; thirty-two (8.9%) on Chrzanowskiego Street; twenty-four (6.7%) at 11 Listopada Square; eighteen (5%) on Kościelna Street, nine (2.5%) on Piaski, nine (2.5%) on Toruńska Street, eight (2.2%) on Słupecka Street, five (1.5%) on Wodna Street, two (0.5%) on Ogrodowa Street, two (0.5%) on Rutki, and two (0.5%) on Stodolna Street.[14] To reconstruct the occupational structure of the Jews of Kleczew, we may cross-reference these data with the list of those who paid sales taxes, those who held trade and industrial certificates, the record of municipal taxpayers in 1919, and the list of paid-up members of the Kleczew kehilla in 1933. On this basis, Table 21 shows the occupational distribution of Jews from Kleczew who were economically active in selected years between 1919 and 1935.

A plurality of Jewish residents earned their income from trade. This tendency crested in 1919, when 100 (78.1% of all Jewish taxpayers) dealt in trade; the proportion declined in subsequent years—112 (53.8%) in 1924, 60 (48%) in 1933, and 72 (42.9%) in 1935. Many were in the food business, especially selling grain, dairy, and fish, in addition to ironware and lumber. Others were horse traders. The largest group, however, sold and traded in groceries, haberdashery, tobacco, clothing, and ready-made shoes. Table 22 presents a snapshot of the distribution of trade companies according to 1919 data.

Craftsmen constituted the second-largest group: twenty-one people (16.4%) in 1919, sixty-three (30.2%) in 1924, forty-two (33.6%) in 1933, and 56 (33.3%) in 1935. Within this category, tailors were the most numerous—twenty-nine in 1924 and thirty-three in 1935. The second-largest group in this category was fishermen: eight in 1924 and seven in 1935. The existence of these two occupational groups corroborates information about the local specializations of Kleczew Jews in the previous century. Another characteristic feature of the Kleczew Jews was that very few dealt in leather crafts such as shoemaking, leather-stitching, or shoe-top making, even though Jewish craftsmen dominated these vocations in other parts of Poland. Furthermore, there were almost no Jewish barbers, goldsmiths, glaziers, harness-makers, cap-makers, hatters, butchers, bakers, tinsmiths, etc. The remaining occupationally skilled Jews were one photographer (Chaim L. Bagno), four teachers

Table 21 Occupational structure of economically active Jews in Kleczew, 1919–1935

Occupation	1919 Number	1919 %	1924 Number	1924 %	1933 Number	1933 %	1935 Number	1935 %
Tinsmith	-	-	4	1.9	1	0.8	3	1.8
Confectioner	-	-	-	-	1	0.8	-	-
Cap-maker, hat-maker	2	1.6	3	1.4	2	1.6	1	0.6
Lodging house	-	-	2	1.0	-	-	-	-
Photographer	-	-	1	0.5	-	-	-	-
Barber	-	-	2	1.0	3	2.4	2	1.2
Carter	-	-	1	0.5	-	-	-	-
Housewife	-	-	1	0.5	-	-	1	0,6
Leather-stitcher	-	-	-	-	2	1.6	-	-
Tailor	8	6.2	36	17.2	26	20.8	33	19.6
Merchant, trader	100	78.1	109	52.4	60	48.0	67	39.8
Furrier	-	-	-	-	1	0.8	-	-
Doctor, dentist	-	-	-	-	2	1.6	2	1.2
Milkman	-	-	1	0.5	-	-	-	-
Teacher	-	-	4	1.9	-	-	2	1.2
Baker	5	3,9	2	1.0	3	2,4	3	1.8
Business	2	1.6	-	-	2	1.6	2	1.2
Rabbi	-	-	1	0.5	-	-	1	0.6
Restaurant keeper	1	0.8	-	-	-	-	-	-
Laborer	-	-	9	4.3	1	0.8	13	7.7
Farmer	-	-	2	1.0	1	0.8	1	0.6
Fisherman	-	-	3	1.4	2	1.6	7	4.2
Harness-maker	-	-	1	0.5	1	0.8	1	0.6
Mohel	-	-	2	1.0	-	-	-	-
Shochet	6	4.7	4	1.9	-	-	5	3.0
Shoemaker	-	-	1	0.5	-	-	-	-
Locksmith	-	-	-	-	-	-	1	0.6
Weaver	-	-	1	-	-	-	-	-
Bookshop owner	-	-	-	-	-	-	1	0.6
Real-estate owner	-	-	4	1.9	13	10.4	17	10.1
Taxi owner	-	-	-	-	-	-	1	0.6
Watchmaker	-	-	4	1.9	-	-	3	1.8
Landowner	-	-	-	-	2	1.6	-	-
No occupation	-	-	1	0.5	-	-	1	0.6
No data available	4	3.1	9	4.3	2	1.6	-	-
Total	**128**	**100.0**	**208**	**100.0**	**125**	**100.0**	**168**	**100.0**

Source: APK, SPS, classification nos. 217, 233; APK, AmK, classification nos. 448, 450, 451.

Table 22 Distribution of Jewish trade companies, based on data for 1919

Type of business	Number of companies
Trade in seeds	3
Trade in eggs and butter	4
Trade in soda water	1
Trade in women's and men's clothing and scraps	1
Trade in used wares	1
Trade in ready-made clothing	2
Trade in haberdashery	16
Trade in china	1
Trade in shoes	2
Trade in fabric	2
Trade in fabric and haberdashery	1
Trade in groceries	34
Trade in restricted merchandise	5
Trade in tobacco	12
Trade in wood	2
Trade in miscellaneous wares	1
Trade in iron	2
Trade in glass	1
Trade in soap	1
Trade in coal	1
Trade in skins	2
Trade in ladies' garments	1
Indefinite type of trade	4
Total	100

Source: APK, AmK, classification no. 451.

(Abram Widawski, Gedalie Szaehsznajder, Szalma Martynbaum, Mojsie Friedenson), one rabbi (Szlama Kaufman/Szlama Hersz Kupferman), seven farmers and landowners (Szmaja Figiel, Icek Figiel, Efraim Kaźmierczak, Adam Iwanczyk, Moryc Malarek, and Jakub Wolman), one restaurateur (Szyja Widawski), and doctors and dentists (Chaskiel Kroner,[15] Rywen Horensztajn, and Emanuel and Eugenia Goldenberg). Detailed information on the Jews of Kleczew emerges from Table F in

Annex 3, which lists those entitled to vote for the Kleczew kehilla on May 27, 1924, by name, occupation, age, and address.[16]

Conspicuous is the fact that as the number of Jews engaging in trade, services, and industry diminished, the number of craftsmen, laborers, and practitioners of "other occupations" grew. The growing share of property owners was especially evident—from only 2.4% of all economically active Jews in 1924 to 10.4% in 1933 and somewhat less, 10.1%, in 1935. This was characteristic of most small Jewish communities.[17] In the 1930s, a bookshop owner named Chaim Bagno and a taxi owner and parcel delivery service provider named Kaufman Światowicz set up businesses in Kleczew.[18] Notably, there were several branches of the Bagno family in Kleczew. Photograph 2 presents the branch of Chaim Bagno's brother, Nachum Israel Bagno.

2. The Bagno family in Kleczew
Seated (right to left): the father, Nachum Israel Ha'Levi; the mother, Mate (née Grinblat), the sister Rivka and her three children: Ester, Ptachya, and Frymet
Standing (right to left): Abraham, Efrayim, Ester, Moshe, and Shmuel Yosef
(Bagno private collection)

The Jews of Kleczew were distinguished for their affluence—a predictable generalization about Jews, but one that the sources in this case confirm. Lists of Kleczew inhabitants who in 1919 declared the value of their assets for the revenue office have been preserved. They were divided into two categories. The first comprised the more affluent, those who had assets worth 30,000–75,000 mp (*markapolska,* Polish marks, the currency of the Polish Republic). Twenty-seven names appear on this list, including thirteen Jews (48%): Rywka Berendt, Nuchem Bagno, Abram Gębicki, Izaak Hirszberg, Mojsie Krzywanowski, D. Wasserman, Sender Lipszyc, Izydor Malarek, Moryc Malarek, Zyskind Pregler, Reich's sons and heirs, Sucher Wajngot, and Sender Rubin. Those in the second category had 10,000–30,000 mp in assets. Forty-seven of the ninety-six people in this category (49%) were Jews. Jews were 32% of the town's population at this time. Detailed but unfortunately incomplete data concerning the value of the second group's asset appear in Table H, Annex 3 and are supplemented by the list of people who were obligated to pay municipal taxes in Kleczew in 1919. Taxpayers were divided into two categories: property owners and tenants. There were 286 people in the first group (Table 23), including eighty-four Jews (29.4%). The taxes remitted by Jews were estimated at 16,790 mp (46.5%) of the 36,145 mp total.

Even though there were only sixty Jews among the 118 people in the second group (Table 24), they paid 2,985 mp (59%) of the 5,060.05 mp in taxes (see also Table H, Annex 3). This information reflects the active and important role that the Jews played in Kleczew's economy. For more data on Jews' contribution to the economic and social development of the town, see Tables 23 and 24.

Table 23 Structure of municipal and school tax in Kleczew, 1919. Category: real-estate owners

Surname and first name	Sum (Polish marka)	Surname and first name	Sum (Polish marka)
Bagno Nuchem	250	Malarek Izydor	600
Bajnisz Michał	10	Malarek Moritz	700
Berendt-sons	200	Nos	50
Berendt Rywka	200	Nüssenbaum	10
Błaszkowska Małka	85	Olejnik Jakub	30
Bock Salomon	60	Patałowski	50
Brysz	300	Pietruszka Zyskind	50
Chaim Fogel	80	Pietrykowski Lejzor	70
Dyner Szymon	15	Piotrowski Jakub	40
Dzieci Idel	500	Pregler Zyskind	400
Ettinger Małka	1,500	Prost Ichiel	250
Ettinger Zygmunt	350	Przedecki Benjamin	25
Fogel Icek	200	Przedecki Jonasz	100
Fogel Szmaja	200	Przedecki Josek	150
Gembicki (Gebicki) Abram-sons	500	Psipsie Chaja	50
Grünblatt Eljasz	100	Psipsie Chaje	80
Grünfeld Dawid	150	Rachwalski	125
Haba Josek	60	Rachwalski Tobjasz	200
Hirszberg Izaak	100	Raczkowski Hersz	50
Huberman Izrael	60	Radziejewski	25
Izydor Malarek	600	Rajchert Mojżesz	60
Justrzyński Wolf	30	Rakowski Majer	320
Kiwała Majer	200	Reich Dorota	1,000
Klamrowski Baer	65	Rogoziński Izrael	20
Klepcz Jukew	200	Rygel Salomon	300
Knopf Szmul	150	Sender Rubin	500
Koner Icek	100	Stachelberg	300
Kottowa Helena	400	Szapszewicz	30
Kroner Icek	150	Szklarek-sons	30
Krotowski Dawid	20	Ślesiński Leiser	500
Krotowski-sons	600	Śliwicki Icek	20
Krzyżanowski Mojżesz	200	Urbach Josek	150
Kuczyński Abram	200	Wajngart Sucher	250
Leonowicz Lejb	20	Wajsman Abram	400
Leszczyński Lewek	150	Warmbrum Szymon	200
Leszczyński Rafał	20	Weinberg Icek	10
Lewkowicz Mojżesz	200	Widawski Szyja	150
Lipszyc Sender	350	Wilczyński Abram	200
Łabuszyński Josek	300	Wilczyński Zelig	50
Łatta Jakub	50	Witkowski Abram	30
Łatta Salomon	50	Witkowski Binem	50
Łatta-sons	50	Witkowski Hejnoch	50
Łepek Sucher	550	Wolf Lejb	130
Izydor Malarek	600		

Source: APK, AmK, classification no. 456.

Table 24 Structure of municipal and school tax in Kleczew, 1919. Category: tenants

Surname and first name	Sum (Polish marka)
Adler Eljasz	60
Bagno Chaim	25
Bajnisz Gerszon	30
Bamber Szajche	10
Berendt Gedalje	40
Berendt Hersz	60
Biederka Izrael	10
Błaszkowski Samuel	5
Boas Josek	30
Brysz Chaja	20
Brysz Henoch	10
Brysz Leizor	40
Brzeziński Dawid	5
Czerwonka Izrael	50
Dawidowicz Chaskiel	10
Dyndol Etta	5
Grünblat Icek	50
Grünblat Rywka	10
Grünfeld-widow	10
Hajnocka Estera	35
Heber Szaje	40
Jakubowski Kas	30
Jastrząb Berek	175
Kauffman Szlama	50
Kazimierski Chemie	15
Klamrowski Hersz	100
Korn Fiszer	80
Kosiarek Lejb	30
Koszer Mojżesz	5
Kott Markus	100

Surname and first name	Sum (Polish marka)
Koza Simce	10
Krause Lejb	80
Krause Salomon	80
Krone Szyfra	20
Kroner Lejb	80
Kutnowski Lejzor	50
Leimer Abram	200
Lewi Itta	300
Lewin Abram	30
Liman Herman	10
Lipszyc Szlama	150
Łódzka Łaje	5
Neimann Mojżesz	50
Pinkus Jakub	15
Prost Lemel	25
Psipsie Anszel	15
Rajchmann Mojżesz	10
Rakowski Izydor	30
Russ Gerszon	100
Samson Lejbuś	60
Segał Dawid	100
Segał Ichiel	25
Sochaczewska Łaja	10
Urbach Icek	50
Wartska Hinda	5
Wasermann Perec	200
Weingart Mejer	30
Weingart Mordka	100
Wolman Herman	10
Wolstein Rafał	5

Source: APK, AmK, classification no. 456.

2. ECONOMIC ACTIVITY

The significant role of Jews in Kleczew's economic life is also reflected in the many business and industrial enterprises that Jews owned in the vicinity of the town, including Słupca (30 kilometers from Kleczew), Ląd (35 kilometers away), and Zagórów (43 kilometers away). The recollections of a Holocaust survivor who gave testimony demonstrate the Jews' important role in the industrialization of these areas:

> The largest plant [...] was a brewery in Słupca founded in 1878, owned by F. Gerszen, who employed seven workers. The second brewery belonged to M.H. Fogiel in Zagórów. In addition, in Słupca there was a motorized mill belonging to Sucher Weisweller and Julian Neuman. They had Jewish-sounding names. In 1900, a steam mill was established in Ląd. Szraga Skowron had a motorized mill in Zagórów. I knew this family. I also do not know if anyone survived. In Ciążeń, there were distilleries. There was also the Nelken fortune in Koponin and Ląd. In Łukom, Ajzyk Nelken owned a sawmill.[19]

Indeed, a register of major trade and industrial companies from 1919 in Kleczew itself reveals that twenty of the town's thirty-four companies (58.8%) were Jewish-owned.[20] This proportion prevailed until the outbreak of World War II. The percentage of Jewish craftsmen was smaller: data from September 12, 1919, show that twenty of the sixty craftsmen working in Kleczew (33%) were Jewish. A year later, thirteen of forty (32.5%) fit this description.[21] Apart from connections in Kleczew itself, local Jews had connections with places nearby. Some did more business outside Kleczew, e.g., in Łęczyca, Gniezno, Powidz, Łódź, or Warsaw, than they did locally.[22]

Table I in Annex 3 lists Jewish inhabitants of Kleczew who paid local taxes and fees for industrial and trade certificates as of January 21, 1919. The table, including names, types of business, and amounts of taxes remitted, gives further evidence of the Jewish community's important economic role both as a partner in local economic activity and as a source of municipal revenue.

The social and occupational structure of the Jews of Kleczew illustrates the spheres of economic activity in which they circulated. Most Jews dealt in petty trade, e.g., in groceries, haberdashery, tobacco, and food (Table F, Annex 3). Larger-scale merchants and traders did business in horses (Eliasz Adler, Mojsie Gębicki, Chaim Gębicki, Abram Krotowski, Fałek Krotowski, Mojsie Nejman, and Jojne Urbach) and lumber (Hersz Berendt, Szaja Heber, and Szlama Lipszyc). In the food sector, the following distributed products manufactured by companies that they owned: Szmaja Fogel (dairy products), Hersz Klamrowski (who owned a butter warehouse), Josek Łabuszyński (who had an oil press), and Mordka Wajngart (who also had an oil press). Apart from the businessmen mentioned in 1919, Szmaja Fogel ran a large fabric warehouse; Dawid Segał a tobacco store; Ichiel Segał a delicatessen; Szyje Widawski a restaurant; and Perec Waserman a general store.[23] Trade on a smaller scale was carried out by the following shopkeepers: groceries—Rywka Berendtowa; haberdashery—Mojsie Brysz, Luzer Brysz, Salomon Rygiel, and Majer Ichel Wajngart; technical and applied glass—Majer Joachimkiewicz and Dawid Druenfeld; and iron and ironware—Fiszel Korn and Szmaja Fogel. One of the two bookshops in Kleczew was run by Chaim Bagno.

Apart from trade, some members of the Kleczew kehilla owned productive enterprises. Several people had small businesses, mostly in food processing. As mentioned above, Josek Łabuszyński and Hersz Klamrowski owned an oil press; Szmaja Fogel ran a dairy. In 1922, Hersz Klamrowski sold the oil press to Moszek Weingarten.[24] Josek Chaba (Haba), Mojsze Lewkowicz, and Mojsie Krzywanowski owned a bakery.[25] After World War I, Icek Dyndol continued to produce hides in his local tannery. His competitor, Majer Jakubowski, did not rebuild his company in the interwar period.[26] Abram Ettinger and Majer Rakowski[27] produced and sold electricity. Twenty-four small businesses in Kleczew in 1925 were associated with the mining of lignite; two of them belonged to Ruchla Psipsie and Zyskind Pregler.[28] Craftsmen also belonged to the group that engaged in production. They specialized mainly in tailoring. Workshops for this craft were run by Mendel Berendt, Hersz Jakubowicz, Majer Kiwała, Ber Klamrowski, Dawid Noss, Chaim Psipsie, Majer Rygiel, Icek Lejb Witkowski, Abram Jakub Gębicki, Lajbuś Koniarek, Simche Koza, Icek Leszczyński, Izrael Rogoziński, Łaja Sochaczewska, and Jojne Witkowski. Other crafts were represented by the tinsmiths Lejb Kroner and Icek Kroner, the clockmaker Izydor Rakowski, the carpenter Jakub Piotrowski, the photographer Chaim Bagno, the butchers Abram Wilczyński, Jukew Klepacz, and Chemje Kazimierski, the bakers Eliasz Grünblatt, Mojsze Lewkowicz, Chaja Patałowska, and

3. Tobiasz and Sura Rachwalski (on right) with two daughters (Fojgel in the center, Frymet on the left) in front of their store in Kleczew
(Horev private collection)

4. Tobiasz Rachwalski's two daughters in front of the family's footwear shop (Fojgel and Frymet), and two granddaughters: Frymet (left) and Hanna (right)
(Horev private collection)

Dawid Segał, the fishermen Azriel Huberman and Zołkind Witkowski, and the cobbler Majer Rachwalski, son of Tobjasz Rachwalski—a Kleczew-born Orthodox Jew. Majer Rachwalski later emigrated later to the U.S.A. (see Annex 2).

The remaining professional groups were represented by the doctor Chaskiel Kroner, the surgeon's assistant Szymon Warbrum, and the dentist Aleksander Horenztejn. In the 1930s, Kaufman Światowicz established a bus company. Technically, Jewish landowners and farmers from neighboring areas also belonged to the Kleczew kehilla. Adam Iwańczyk owned the Siernicze land estate; Jakub Wolman owned the Goranin estate.[29] Both, along with several traders and businessmen, belonged to the local financial elite. The dues they remitted to the kehilla reflect their role in its operation. In 1930, Leopold Piekarski paid 400 złoty into the kehilla's coffers; Dora Reich 100 złoty; Sura Sender 120 złoty; Jakub Wolman 400 złoty; Idel Dzieci 100 złoty; Adam Iwańczyk 1,000 złoty; Dr. H. Kroner 100 złoty; and Itta Lewi 100 złoty—2,320 złoty in all, more than 38% of all dues collected.[30] Jews in Kleczew also owned several properties; the register of "chimney owners" in Kleczew lists sixty-five Jews, 27.5% of the 236 people recorded (Table 25).[31]

Table 25 Jews and Jewish organizations registered as "chimney owners" in Kleczew

First name and surname	First name and surname
Abram Ettinger	Jakub Łatta
Józef Chaba	Icek Śliwicki
Hersz Berendt	Saomon Bok
Idel Dzieci	Majer Kiwała
Józef Łabuszyński	Michał Bajnisz
Chaim Psipsie	Sender Lipszyc
Małka Błaszkowska	Hersz Nisenbaum
Jakub Wajnberg	Abram Witkowski
Szklarek – sons	Zelek Wilczyński
Wołek Jutrzyński	Rafał Leszczyński
Icek Kroner	Salomon Łatta
Josek Przedecki	Bajnisz Giersz
Szyje Widawski	Mojsze Rajchert
Zyskind Pregler	Helena Kott
Majer Rakowski	Izrael Hirszberg
Krotowska-widow	Mendel Wolf
Jakub Klepacz	Szlama Lipszyc
Bine Witkowski	Icek Knopff
Izrael Huberman	Zyskind Pietruszka
Izrael Rogoziński	Abram Wajsman
Jakub Piotrowski	Nuchem Bagno
Chale Brenerowa	Jakub Presberg
Abram Gembicki	Tobiasz Rachwalski
Abram Wilczyński	Szymon Warmbrum
Anszel Psipsie	Dorota Raich
Marje Malarek	Sucher Wajngart
Izydor Malarek	Lewek Leszczyński
Jakub Olejnik	Rywka Berendt
Salomon Rygiel	Icek Kroner
Benjamin Przedecki	Rubin Sender
Jewish kehilla	Hinda Pachciarska
Dawid Krotowski	Marja Hofman
Mojsie Krzywanowski	Hiel Prost
Lajzer Ślesiński	Majer Rygiel
Lajzer Litman	Henoch Bysz
Ekjasz Grynblat	Pieterkowski
Chaim Litman	

Source: APK, AmK, 456.

3. SOCIAL AND POLITICAL LIFE

The beginnings of political activity among Kleczew Jews date to the early 1900s. Followers of leftist ideologies and Zionism were the first to create informal political structures, initially small in membership. The organizations were most often founded by Jewish workers or representatives of the intelligentsia who had settled in Kleczew and spread novel ideas in their new realm. Although members of the young generation were extremely susceptible to innovation, the propagators of these notions encountered many obstacles, both external and internal. The suppression of Jews and any social group disseminating revolutionary ideas, or of those whom the authorities believed to be doing so, began with Russian legislation. As for internal obstacles to these new organizations, the most serious was the attitude of Jewish traditionalists who eschewed any deviation from Orthodox dogma. It was impossible, however, to stop the impending changes; emancipation gradually spread despite the adverse circumstances. The foundations for the absorption of alternative conceptions to those propagated by Orthodox traditionalists had been prepared before the outbreak of World War I. Under the newly favorable political conditions coupled with events that demanded decisions, Jews in Kleczew established a welter of organizations. During World War I, after the German army dissolved the Kingdom of Poland in 1915, the new occupier started to legalize all economic, educational, and cultural organizations that had functioned clandestinely until then and encouraged the institutionalization of political organizations that pursued conservative programs. This policy strengthened the positions of conservative pro-Zionist and anti-Zionist groups alike—the former including members of the Religious Zionist Mizrachi association, the latter comprising those of Agudas Yisroel.

The statutes of Mizrachi were officially approved on April 30, 1921, but the movement's followers there had gotten started several years earlier.[32] Its official local founders were Hersz Wolman, the organization's local leader for a few years; Alje Adler; Nuchem Bagno; Abram Kuczyński; and Chaim Bagno. Headquartered on 1 Rynek Street[33] and using the existing organizational structure, local activists established a

Interwar Kleczew (1918–1939) | 93

5. Tze'irei Mizrachi (Mizrachi youth movement) in Kleczew (1)
Seated (first left in second row): Moshe Bagno
Standing: First left (in the row): Chaim Rachwalski
(Bagno private collection)

6. Tze'irei Mizrachi in Kleczew (2)
Standing (third from left): Moshe Bagno
Seated: first on right—Frymet Rachwalski's fiancé (name unknown)
(Bagno private collection)

branch of Mizrachi in Kleczew in May 1930. Sztachelberg, president of the Kleczew kehilla and director of the administrative board, became its leader.[34] The growing influence and executive abilities of the adherents of Religious Zionism led to the establishment of an illegal house of prayer at the beginning of 1932 in the very building that housed Mizrachi headquarters.[35] Religious Zionists were also very active leaders of the local Mizrachi association and established a community center on Słupecka Street. It was used mainly by youth affiliated with an organization that was not mentioned by name in the records, even though thirty boys and twenty-eight girls were card-carrying members.[36] Photographs and testimonies of family members from Kleczew indicate that the movement in question was probably Hashomer Hadati,[37] a religious version of the Hashomer Hatzair youth movement.[38] Photographs 7-15 present events and people involved in Hashomer Hadati in and near Kleczew. Photograph 16 presents member of another religious Zionist organization in Kleczew—the Torah ve-Avoda movement.

Apart from the Religious Zionists who aligned with Mizrachi, other factions of Zionists formed loose associations. The ideologically centrist General Zionists were bracketed by Revisionist Zionists on the right[39]

7. Members of Hashomer Hadati in Kleczew at the beginning of their organization
(Bagno private collection)

8. Members of HashomerHadati at training commune in Kalisz, 1932-1933
Standing on upper left: Moshe Bagno
(Bagno private collection)

9. Members of Hashomer Hadati at training commune in Kalisz, 1932-1933.
(Bagno private collection)

10. Hashomer Hadati conference in Bartów, 1933-34
(Bagno private collection)

11. Hashomer Hadati—the Dvora group, November 25, 1934
Seated (center): the counselor, Moshe Bagno
Members of the group: Yehudit Yakobowitz, Sarah Reichman, Sarah Lebovitcz,
Lea Berendt, Yehudit Litmann, Shoshanna Livushinska, Frymet Rachwalski, Tova
Sakashawska, Pnina Leibovitcz (Bagno private collection)

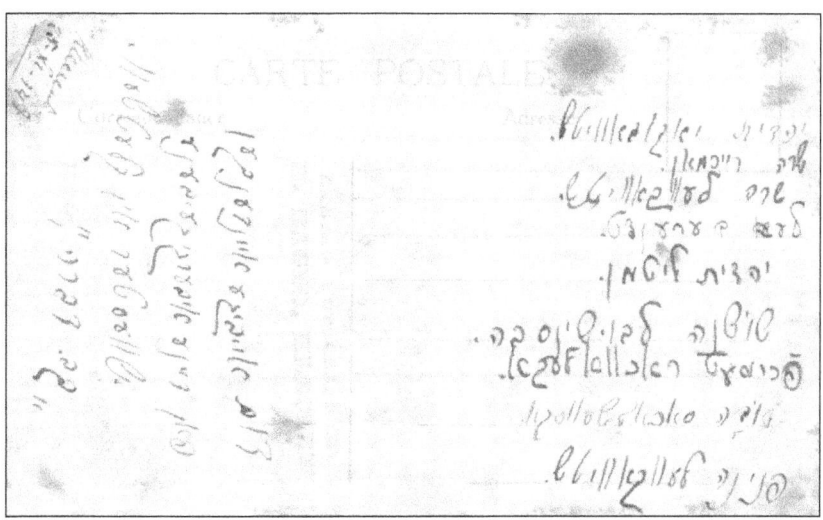

12. Hashomer Hadati, Dvora group, November 25, 1934
Handwritten names (in Yiddish) on back of previous photo
(Bagno private collection)

13. Hashomer Hadati, Hashmonaim group,
summer 1934
Seated (in second row): center—Moshe Bagno, the
group's counselor. First on left (same row): Shlomo
Rachwalski
(Bagno private collection)

14. Shlomo Rachwalski in
Hashomer Hadati uniform,
Kleczew, 1934
(Horev private collection)

15. Hashomer Hadati summer camp, Golina and Kleczew branches.
(Bagno private collection)

16. Torah va-Avoda Movement in Kleczew
(Bagno private collection)

and representatives of leftist Zionism, most likely associated with Po'alei Tsiyyon,[40] on the other side. Members of these groups congregated mainly in various trade or cultural organizations. Zionists inspired the formation of a branch of the Clothing Industry Workers trade union that had among its members thirty less-affluent craftsmen and workers who were employed in the relevant industry.[41] Apart from satisfying the social and occupational needs of union members, the activists concentrated on cultural work, e.g., organizing a performance at the local fire station on January 25, 1930.[42]

In the 1930s, younger-generation Zionists who held radical social and political views became more and more active. On December 15, 1930, Dr. Chaskiel Kroner, Lejzor Ettinger, and Lejb Lewi initiated and founded a branch of 'Hashomer Hatzair' in Kleczew. This organization, its statutes certified by the authorities on May 7, 1931, focused on organizing field trips once or twice a week that offered a combination of education about Palestine, scouting techniques, and ideology. The fourteen boys and twenty girls who belonged to the organization met at the community center on 20 Edwarda Heimana Street.[43] Although Hashomer Hatzair was a secular movement, several of its members came from Orthodox families, fomenting conflicts at home. Lea (Lotka) Krzywanowski was one such person; for more about her, see Annex 2.

Dr. Chaskiel Kroner was the patron and protector of the Jewish Scouts and remained so until the outbreak of World War II.[44] Lay groups subscribing to Zionist and leftist ideologies gathered in the Jewish library that had been established in 1922.[45] From July 1925, activities were supervised by the newly-founded Jewish Association of the Social Library and Reading Room.[46] Zionist affiliates and fellow travelers congregated at the office of the Gemilus Chesed (Free Loan Fund), which they ran.[47]

The existence of the Agudas Yisroel organization in Kleczew (also known locally as "the Orthodox") dated to the beginning of the Second Polish Republic.[48] Its activity was backed by Hasidim after their rebbe[49] in Góra Kalwaria (Gur) so authorized. Some elements in Hasidic society turned their political activity in the specific direction of managing the kehilla. They were perceived as independent religious Jews, a.k.a. independent Orthodox Jews or independent supporters of Orthodox

17. Krzywanowski family, Kleczew. The photograph was taken at a family wedding c. 1936 (Ada Holtzman and Edna Dan private collection) (http://www.zchor.org/kleczew/kleczew.htm).

Lotka (Lea) Holtzman (née Krzywanowski) (standing, second to left) is the only survivor among all these family members. Lotke was a member of the Hashomer Hatzair movement in Kleczew and emigrated to Palestine (pre-state Israel) several months before the beginning of the war.

Seated: Fourth from right—Hana Krzywanowski (née Herszlik), Lotka's mother. Seated in the front—Lotka's two brothers, Jakob (6 years old) and Machel (8 years old). Standing: Franja (14 years old) and Rosa (Ruzka) (12 years old).
Also in the photograph: Towa Watman née Krzywanowski (Lotka's sister), her husband Szmuel (a watchmaker from Wilczyn), and Berta (Lotka's sister), a tailor.
Other persons in the photograph are not identified. Lotka's father, being ultra-Orthodox, refused to participate in this photograph on religious grounds.

Jews. Hasidim in Kleczew leaned in two main directions, the majority preferring the court of the rebbe in Góra Kalwaria and the minority favoring the rebbe of Aleksandrów. One organization was supported by Orthodox Jews irrespective of their internal differences: Agudas Szomrej Umachzikej Szabbos[50] (Association of Sabbath Observers and Guardians). The president of the Łódź Province branch of this organization registered the Kleczew branch, headed by Dawid Segał, on September 11, 1925.[51]

In the 1920s, representatives of professional groups of sundry political inclination stepped onto the stage. At the initiative of Nuchem Bagno, Jakub Sztachelberg, Abram Kuczyński, J. Fogel, and Luzerz Brysz, the Jewish Small Business Association was founded on August 18, 1924.[52] An Association of Jewish Craftsmen also came into being under Izaak Traube (see photographs below),[53] Załme Leszczyński, and Chaskiel Szyke.[54] Operations of the Cooperative Fund of Jewish Merchants, amalgamating 120 members, were supervised by Gerszon Russ.[55]

The aforementioned credit cooperative, People's Cooperative Bank Ltd., was established in the mid-1930s. Located at 11 Listopada Street, it offered small traders and farmers loans at 10% annual interest. Wigdor Warmbrum, Majer Łepek, Hersz Segał, Lajb Jude Samson, and Icek Klepacz sat on its executive board.[56] The Jewish Free Loan Fund granted small loans to merchants and craftsmen in Kleczew. It had 107 members. For many years, Chaim Markowski was its president. In the first half of

18. Izaak Traube (seated, center). To his right: his daughter Frymet; to his left: his daughter Hanna. Behind him (center): his wife Fojgel (*née* Rachwalski); to her left: her sister Frymet; to her right: her sister-in-law Pessa (Mayer Rachwalski's wife). Photographed in Warsaw in Mayer and Pessa's home during the Traubes' trip to Palestine. (Horev private collection)

19. Izaak Traube as a soldier in the Polish army (after WWI) (Horev private collection)

the 1920s, it was led by Jakub Wolman, Zelig Gembicki, Szyje Leszczyński, Hersz Segał, and Rafał Strzeliński.[57] Appointed to its executive board on February 8, 1930, were Chaim Markowski, Abram Kuczyński, Perec Waserman, Lejb Gerszon, Ichel Prost, Josek Habe, and Szmul Łatte.[58]

The evolution of an attitude remains a moot issue that is difficult to measure. Using other communities in the Kleczew vicinity as models, we may infer that many activists switched political positions and organizations even if the new organization embraced a completely different platform. However, this happened only occasionally. More often, an individual's personal or political alliances or interpersonal connections were at stake.[59] Kleczew offers several cases in point. From the early 1920s into the 1930s, the political preferences of leaders of the kehilla changed perceptibly. Josef Boas, initially a follower of Mizrachi, switched his allegiance to Agudas Yisroel. Jakub Sztachelberg walked away from Agudas Yisroel in favor of Zionism. Jechel Rakowski's views evolved from Religious Zionism to a more radical branch of Zionism.[60]

Apart from being active in their own milieu, Jews in Kleczew were visible players in town life. Józef Lipszyc and Hersz Bernd sat on the town council in 1918. Majer Rakowski, elected in December 1918, was a member of the Food Committee. In 1934, Chaskiel Kroner and Gerszon Russ were town councilors. (Russ resigned in 1935.) Moryc Reich was member of the town executive board. In 1939, after town council elections, two out of twelve councilors were Jewish.[61] Before the parliamentary elections in 1927, Jakub Sztachelberg was named to the election committee, together with five non-Jewish Poles.[62] Most other representatives of the community continued to support the pro-government approach. National holidays as well as Marshal Piłsudski's birthday and the anniversary of his death were celebrated in earnest. Rabbi Hersz Zawłodawer and Dr. Chaskiel Kroner (leader of the Jewish Scouts) participated in celebrating the tenth anniversary of the Air and Anti-Gas Defense League (*Ligi Obrony Powietrznej i Przeciwgazowej*) on May 11, 1938. In 1935, patriotic and religious meetings were sponsored by Hersz Wolman.[63] These examples not only demonstrate the active role that Jews played in Kleczew's political life but also suggest that relations between the Jewish and non-Jewish communities were correct at the very least. The accuracy of this assumption, however, is difficult to determine due to the scarcity of source texts from that period. Reports from local police or authorities to higher administrative echelons do not mention hostile behavior toward Jews. The political situation in the village of Skulsk was much the same;[64] relations between the Jewish and non-Jewish populations appear to have been sound there.

Nevertheless, external factors that may have had indirect effects on the residents of Kleczew should be taken into account. Peaceful coexistence prevailed at certain times and places; antagonism abounded elsewhere. For example, throughout the interwar period, especially in the second half of the 1930s, Jews were consistently loathed in most constituencies of Eastern Greater Poland. Organized propaganda and intimidation against Jewish companies began in the early twentieth century.[65] A visceral wave of tension swept the country in the formative stages of Polish nationhood and during the Polish-Bolshevik war (1918–1921). The local authorities in Słupca (30 kilometers from Kleczew) frowned on Jews ever since Poland regained its independence. The *starosta* (chief administration officer) of Konin noticed that Jews had greeted Poland's independence without enthusiasm. The Jews did not try to assimilate and did not support the new authorities. It was emphasized that the Jews, unlike the Polish population, had been favorably disposed toward the German occupation authorities in 1914–1918. In November 1918, several Polish-Jewish clashes took place. Members of the Polish Military Organization initiated antisemitic incidents. To quell them, a ten-member commission was established on November 16, 1918, to contact the authorities and thereby eliminate misunderstandings and offenses against Jews.[66]

In the years that followed, especially during the Great Depression and the evolution of the Polish political system after Piłsudski's death in 1935, economic boycotting of Jewish-owned shops and stalls became a common occurrence. Anti-Jewish posters and leaflets were distributed in many neighboring towns. In Słupca, for example, posters loudly advising "Jews to the ghettos" were hung on fences and walls in February 1938.[67]

Jews were also not spared from physical assault. In Pyzdry (50 kilometers from Kleczew), on February 5, 1936, Jews were thrown out of a fair in Zagórów (43 kilometers from Kleczew) by National Party combat squads from the two localities. Afterwards, the squads started to demolish

Jewish-owned shops.[68] In December 1937, Konin County police reported an escalation in the boycotting of Jewish enterprises. Incidents such as the slashing of goods with razor blades in Jewish-owned shops took place. The most popular form of boycott was the picketing of shops and stalls, mainly on fair days. The picketers were financed by Polish merchants affiliated with the National Party and the National Union Camp. Leaflets with anti-Jewish slogans and endorsements of Polish trade were distributed in large quantities. Customers buying in Jewish-owned shops were persecuted. In the mid- and late 1930s, attempts to forcibly divide the market between Jews and Christians were made. In Władysławowo, under pressure from Polish national groups, these efforts succeeded.[69] Several cases of antisemitic vandalism were reported.[70] On February 16, 1936, local members of the National Party, supported by activists from Sompolno (25 kilometers from Kleczew), planned a pogrom against Jews who had come to the fair in Ślesin (11 kilometers from Kleczew). Thanks to police intervention, it ended as a small demonstration resulting only in the shattering of four windows of Jewish-owned houses.[71] On January 12, 1938, a Jew was beaten in Ślesin.[72] In the town of Golina (23 kilometers from Kleczew), Polish merchants affiliated with the National Party and the National Union Camp paid picketers to harass customers in Jewish-owned shops. Several life- and health-threatening acts of anti-Jewish misconduct were reported in Golina, e.g., the spilling of foul-smelling toxic liquids in Jewish-owned shops.[73] In December 1938, an attempt was made to force Jewish merchants to pay a 100-złoty protection fee to a racketeer in order to end the boycott. The man behind this initiative was arrested.[74]

These examples of events that reflected a change in the attitude toward Jews in the near neighborhood must have influenced relations between Poles and Jews in Kleczew. Since no source texts document hostilities in this town, we can go no farther than to assume that Polish–Jewish tension in Kleczew escalated during the 1930s.

4. ORGANIZATION AND FUNCTIONING OF THE JEWISH COMMUNITY

The status of Jewish communities in newly independent Poland was determined on February 7, 1919, by a decree from the Chief of State titled "Changes in the Organization of Jewish Communities in the Territory of the Former Congress of Poland." The new edict slightly modified the regulations that the German occupation authorities had laid down on November 1, 1916. The confessional character of the Jewish religious communities was preserved. Membership in religious communities remained compulsory. A new five-point electoral law was introduced, limiting suffrage to male citizens over age twenty-five (active suffrage) or over thirty (passive suffrage) who resided within municipal limits for at least one year. The state authorities' ambit concerning Jewish representations was broadened. The Ministry of Religious Denominations and Public Enlightenment (*Ministerstwo Wyznań Religijnych i Oświecenia Publicznego*—MWRiOP) approved elected rabbis and the appointments to religious councils, which would be the main authorities of the Jewish Religious Association. However, since this Association had not been constituted, MWRiOP was effectively the highest decision-making authority when it came to approving the budget and validating resolutions of the kehilla administrative board. MWRiOP made decisions on the imposition of mandatory contributions from Jewish community members and how large the contributions should be. The minister was represented by the starost and the *voivode* (province governor) of the region.[75]

A decree from MWRiOP on April 5, 1928, concerning "announcement of a uniform text of the decree of the President of the Polish Republic on October 14, 1927, systematizing the legal status for the organization of Jewish religious communities in the Polish Republic, with the exception of the province of Silesia,"[76] stated that a Jewish religious community might be formed by residents of a single political municipality if they could afford to finance it or (Article 2) by those of several municipalities if they could not. The legislator divided Jewish communities into small (Article 4) and large ones, the latter having more than 5,000 members (Article 14). Smaller communities would be ruled by executive boards initially comprising four—and after the 1931 elections, eight—elected members, including the kehilla's rabbi in every case (Article 4). The work of the kehilla would be led by the president of the administrative board, to be elected from its members (Article 9). Large communities would be administered by an administrative board composed of an executive body and a community council. The administrative board would have legislative powers. Separate regulations from MWRiOP determined the number of hired officials.[77] The elections were prepared by election commissions that were staffed by three members of the administrative board, seven members of the kehilla, and three deputies in smaller communities; and five administrative board members, eleven kehilla members, and five deputies in larger ones (Article 14).[78]

The administrative board was the only organ that supervised the administration of the kehilla, except for powers vested in the community council by the legislative body. Its functions included approval and revision of the budget, setting and collecting dues and contributions, contracting loans, establishing and managing foundations and enterprises, and electing the rabbi and assistant rabbis (Article 21). Regardless of their size, all kehillot were to meet their members' religious needs, including organizing and maintaining the rabbinate, synagogues, houses of prayer, *mikvaot* (plural of mikve, ritual baths), and cemeteries, arranging religious education for the young, procuring kosher meat, and managing community assets. Kehillot were empowered to engage in charity and to establish institutions in order to fund it (Article 3).

The rabbi was the principal figure in the kehilla. His attitudes, views, and actions strongly influenced the community. The posts of rabbi and assistant rabbi could easily be told apart: assistant rabbis were uncommon in the region whereas rabbis were appointed for life (Article 44). Rabbis supervised religious appurtenances, teachers in Jewish religious schools, and mohalim (circumcisers). Within their municipal limits, they and they alone were allowed to officiate at weddings and grant divorces. They issued certificates permitting religious education, presided over the rabbinical court, and adjudicated religious matters. They were required to deliver sermons on Sabbaths (Saturdays) and other religious and national holidays (Article 47). In smaller communities, the rabbi was elected by kehilla members who had active voting rights (Article 8); in large communities he was chosen by members of the council (Article 21). Applicants for rabbinical posts had to know spoken and written Polish and Hebrew. In the 1930s, a state exam was introduced for rabbis: they had to demonstrate their fluency in Polish before a state commission if they had not graduated from a Polish elementary school, a Jewish school of the same level, or a high school. A regulation from MWRiOP dated October 24, 1930, concerning election rules for the organization of Jewish religious communities in the Polish Republic except for Silesia, set the minimum age of a rabbinical candidate at twenty-three.[79] The rabbi's salary was regulated by a contract between him and the kehilla authorities. Three factors were taken into account in determining the rabbi's pay: the community's financial strength, the number of its members, and the candidate's level of general and religious education. If a rabbi died, his widow received half of her deceased husband's salary. The combined benefits for a rabbi's widow and her children, however, could not exceed the rabbi's original pay.[80] Several officials (rabbis, cantors, and synagogue sextons), apart from receiving the salary defined in the budget, indirectly benefited from the community's additional income, e.g., when they were paid for officiating at weddings.

Another MWRiOP directive, handed down on September 9, 1931, and effective January 1, 1933 (Article 20), regulated the Jewish communities' finances.[81]. All adult members of the kehilla were obliged to contribute directly to the kehilla budget. This included every male and female residing within the municipal boundaries for at least one year on the day the dues were set; anyone who profited from trade, a craft, or an industry; and all owners of real estate (Article 14). The amounts were calculated on the basis of the revenue from industrial, land, and/or property tax paid by the individual in the year preceding the year of kehilla dues collection, to a maximum of 10% of taxes paid and a minimum of 5 złoty (Articles 16 and 17).[82] The poor and those receiving charity from the public or the rabbi were exempt from this direct charge (Article 18). Until the regulation came into effect, the fee was estimated.[83] The estimation committee, operated by the kehilla, took into consideration each taxpayer's income, assets, family status, and previous generosity toward the kehilla (Article 21). In case of delinquent payments, an enforcement procedure was applied (Articles 31–32). The direct taxes paid by community members included fees for ritual slaughter, a cemetery plot, and erecting a gravestone.[84]

The Kleczew kehilla was one of 900 kehillot in Poland and one of twenty-five in Eastern Greater Poland (Table 26).[85] Like most communities in the region, it was classified as a small one.

Table 26 Members of Jewish communities in Eastern Greater Poland, 1921–1939

Seat of kehilla	1921	1925	1928	1932	1934	1937	1939
Babiak, Koło County	270*						250*
Dąbie, Koło County	1,500*			1,200*	1,200*	1,200*	1,200*
Dobra, Turek County	1,300-1,400*	1,800-1,900*					2,000-2,200*
Golina, Konin County	873	800		643	650	725	750*
Izbica Kujawska Koło County	1,405					1,550*	1,600*
Kleczew, Słupca County (Konin County)	950-1,000*	800*	800*	768	750*		700*
Kłodawa, Koło County	1,200*						1,350-1,400*
Koło, Koło County	5,200-5,500*			5,000-5,200*			4,700*
Konin, Konin County	3,000*	2600-2,700		3,150		2,386	2,500*
Koźminek, Kalisz County	800*		800*		850*		850-900*
Pyzdry, Słupca County (Konin)	450*	250	250		240	232	230-240
Skulsk, Słupca County (Konin County)	270	235-242	255	230	200*	190*	180*
Słupca, Słupca County (Konin County)	1,600*		1,550*	1,523	1,132	1,200*	1,150*
Sompolno, Koło County	1,200*			1,150*			1,150*
Stawiszyn, Kalisz County	800-850*			750*		ca. 650	600-660*
Ślesin, Konin County	410		308	323		304	300*
Tuliszków, Konin County	282	205	225	218	220	227	230*
Turek, Turek County	3,000*	3300					3,000*
Uniejów, Turek County	1,200*						1,000*
Wilczyn, Słupca County (Konin County)	200*	141		148	162	176**	174
Władysławów, Konin County	293			250	227		280
Zagórów, Słupca County (Konin County)	1,300	1,000*	850	860	720		730-740*

Source: APK, SPK, classification nos. 342, 375, 377, 378, 381, 382, 383, 393; T. Kawski, *Społeczność żydowska na pograniczu*, Table 1, pp. 162-163; T. Kawski, M. Opioła, *Gminy*, passim.

*= ca.

** data from 1938.

Table J in Annex 3 lists those who paid dues to the Kleczew kehilla in 1919 by name and size of contribution. Dues payers were divided into three categories by economic status and earnings. Those in Category 1 remitted the largest contributions (100 mp and above); only nineteen names (16% of taxpayers) appear in it. The largest contribution, 800 mp, was made by Eli Iwańczyk. Sixty-two people fell into Category 3 (52% of dues payers). The other thirty-eight (32%) belonged to Category 2, each paying 50–80 mp. Further details can be found in Table J.

The Kleczew kehilla numbered 950–1,000 people in 1921, around 800 in 1925, 790 in 1930, 800 in 1931, 768 in 1932, 823 in 1933, 750 in 1934–1936, and approximately 700 in 1939.[86] It encompassed the greater municipal district of Kleczew as well as three nearby municipalities: Sławoszewek (Konin County), Ostrowite, and Kazimierz Biskupi (the latter two in Słupca County and, later, in Konin County).[87] A few member households lived outside Kleczew. In 1921, five individuals lived on the Goranin farm in Sławoszewek; three others lived on the Siernicze farm in Ostrowite.[88]

Table K in Annex 3 lists payers of "supplemental dues" to the Kleczew kehilla in 1921. The largest contribution, 3,000 mp, was remitted by Iwańczyk Adam. The total sum collected was 44,050 mp.

Table L in Annex 3 lists those who paid dues to the Kleczew kehilla in 1933, including each individual's name, occupation, and annual contribution. It also sheds light on many families in the community and their occupations.

In 1935, the kehilla's assets were estimated at 43,150 złoty: 31,500 złoty in buildings, 6,000 złoty in cemetery land, and 5,650 złoty in mobiliers. The synagogue on Górańska Street was the community's most valuable property and its central building; it accommodated the house of prayer, the *cheder* (young boys' religious elementary school), the Talmud Torah (older boys' religious school), and, next door, the mikve.[89]

The examples of political preferences that appear in the foregoing subchapter on social and political life, as revised by representatives of the local elite, were reflected in the evolution of awareness of and changes in political preferences on a larger scale. In the years to follow, the Kleczew Jews' political views became more polarized, as confirmed by the results of elections to the kehilla administrative board. Initially, until the 1924 elections, the kehilla was run by the Orthodox and independent officers who had been elected during World War I. In 1919, the administrative board consisted of Rabbi S.H. Kaufman, Sucher Mendel Waingot (Weingot) as president, Szlama Josek Lipszyc, and Ch. J. Prost.[90]

The next year, Szlama Josek Lipszyc took over the presidency for some time. Two board members (names unknown) left town or resigned; they were replaced by Hersz Wolman and Berendt or, according to some sources, Krzyżanowski. Documents from 1921 list Rabbi S. H. Kaufman, Hersz Wolman, Ch. Prost, and M. Krzywanowski as members of the administrative board. In a letter dated August 21, 1924, Rabbi Kaufman informed the starost of Słupca County that two members of the synagogue administration, Wolman and Berendt, had died and that Szlama Josek Lipszyc had moved away. Rabbi Kaufman proposed to introduce new members into the kehilla organs before a new administrative board could be formed;[91] he had the backing of one board member, Sucher Mendel Weingot. In a letter to the starost on July 24, 1924, Weingot seemed to indicate that the rabbi and several administration members were embroiled in a conflict with the president, Szlama Josek Lipszyc. Specifically, Lipszyc was accused of moving from Kleczew to Łódź for business purposes and had been dismissed from the city council by the Kleczew authorities for this reason. The president of the administrative board considered these accusations false.[92] The real motives of Szlama Lipszyc's opponents became evident in the argumentation they used in their communication with the starost. The opponents wished to strengthen their positions by brushing other members aside or filling supposedly vacant positions with substitutes whose views resembled theirs. The situation was interesting because as of July 1, 1924, the new administrative board had already been elected but had not yet begun to serve; therefore, the efforts that were being made to replace board members concerned the old, lame-duck board. The nature of these contentions had become clear back on October 27, 1922, when Kleczew Magistrate's Court had decided to fine the board members for "fostering social unrest."[93] There was also a festering dispute, years long, between the kehilla authorities and members of a private house of prayer on the premises of S.J. Latte. The Orthodox liturgy has different versions of wording and style; this may have been the background of the establishment of the new house of prayer. Be this as it may, the administrative board of the Kleczew kehilla demanded that the Ministry of Religious Denominations and Public Enlightenment order the prayer house to close its doors. On August 6, 1919, the ministry dismissed the demand as groundless, stating that even though the kehilla had a synagogue, a private prayer house could function as well.[94] The motives of the kehilla authorities in this matter remain murky; they probably trace to economic factors since the alternative place of worship, by reducing attendance at the kehilla's synagogue, presumably took a toll on public contributions.

The new administrative board, elected on July 1, 1924, comprised Nuchem Bagno (president—Mizrachi, a merchant, age 45), Sender Rubin (Agudas Yisroel, a merchant, age 40; he died in the late 1920s), Abram Icek Ettinger (Independent, unemployed, age 63), and Jakub Sztachenberg (Mizrachi, a merchant, age 32). The following were alternates: Josef Boas (Mizrachi, a cap maker, age 62), Luzer Brysz (Agudas Yisroel, a merchant, age 35), Jechel Rakowski (Mizrachi, a clock-maker, age 36), and Icek Lejzor (Izydor) Malarek (Mizrachi, retired, age 72).[95] Before the elections in 1931, one of the board members representing Mizrachi changed his political preferences and declared his views as "Zionist."[96] Although representing three different groups (Mizrachi, Agudas Yisroel, and Independent), all candidates embodied a similar mentality rooted in Jewish tradition and identified with the Orthodox value system. As if to prove it, they formed one electoral bloc before the elections, causing the voting to be cancelled.[97] The same thing happened ahead of the next elections, for the community board, on May 20, 1931. This cancellation was preceded by an agreement signed on May 5, 1931, among the three political parties—the Zionists (represented by Chaskiel Kroner, Lemel Prost, and Lejzer Etyngiel), Agudas Yisroel (Gerszon Russ, Dawid Segał, Luzer Brysz, and Tobjasz Rachwalski), and the Independents (Jakub Wolman and Jojne Witkowski)—to form a joint list of agreed-upon contenders. The board consisted of two seats assigned to the Orthodox (Agudas Yisroel), one to a leftist Zionist (probably a follower of Po'alei Tsiyyon), two seats to Mizrachi, and three to Independent candidates. The following were elected to the administrative board: Chaim Markowski (Mizrachi, a merchant, age 36), Abram Kuczyński (Mizrachi, a merchant, age 39), Dawid Segał (Orthodox, a merchant, age 60), Luzer Brysz (Orthodox, a merchant, age 41), Idel Dzieci (Independent, a merchant, age 64), Majer Jakubowicz (Independent, a furrier, age 60), Ber Pacanowski (Independent, a merchant, age 38, son in law of Tobisz Rachwalski), and Lemel Prost (Zionist, connected to the Communist Youth, a merchant, age 37). All the alternates were Independent: Symcha Koza (a merchant, age 48), Jakub Szmul Łatta (a merchant, age 59), Mojsze Lewkowicz (a baker, age 48), Chune Chojnacki (a tailor, age 40), Luzer Kutnowski (a merchant, age 45,), Załme Leszczyński (a tailor, age 39), Lejb Kroner (a tinsmith, age 69), and Icek Chaba (a baker, age 46). Initially Lemel Prost, a communist Zionist, was chosen as president, but after the Orthodox objected, the factions negotiated and settled on Chaim Markowski of Mizrachi.[98]

The worst of the Great Depression coincided with the escalation of preexisting conflicts among kehilla potentates, prompting the resignations of all members of the administrative board in May–November 1932.[99] The growing anarchy in the kehilla forced the starost to call new elections for July 26, 1933. Again an agreed-upon list was composed and the voting was canceled. The new administrative board, taking office on September 10, 1933, was comprised of Rafał Strzeliński (Mizrachi, age 32), Berek Jastrząb (Mizrachi, age 58), Pinkus Kleczewski (Orthodox, age 55), Mojsze Brysz (Orthodox, age 50), Icek Jojne Urbach (Mizrachi, age 42), Hersz Lejb Jakubowicz (Mizrachi, age 42), Icek Kroncer (Zionist, age 60), and Abram Wolstein (Orthodox, age 60). The alternates were Lejb Kiwała (Mizrachi, age 38), Szmul Jakub Łatte (Orthodox, age 62), Icek Klepacz (Independent, age 38), Majer Joachimkiewicz (Orthodox, age 36), Mojsie Witkowski (Mizrachi, age 37), Salomon Rygiel (Mizrachi, age 65), Chaim (Chune) Chojnacki (Mizrachi, age 38), and Josef Eljasz Chaba (Mizrachi, age 42). Berk Jastrząb was elected president of the administrative board on August 13, 1933.[100] On February 20, 1934, Icek Kroner replaced him.[101]

This administrative board, however, was prematurely dissolved before the official announcement of the next elections on August 30, 1936, and no new list of candidates was revealed before the deadline.[102] Under such circumstances, no voting took place. After several weeks of administrative pressure, a consensus was hammered out; again a unanimous ballot was proposed. The new administrative board consisted of

Jankel lter Jakubowicz (president), Abram Patałowski, Majer M. Bruksztajn, Symche J. Psipsie, Josef Eliasz Chaba, Chaim Fogel, Fajwisz Jojne Urbach, and Icek Dyndol. The alternates were Icek Lewkowicz, Mojsie Fajeńczyski, Mordka Przedecki, Nachman Huberman, Jakub Pinkus, Majer Aron Gembrocki (probably W.M. Gembicki), Jakub Spale, and Icek Korzew.[103] Curiously, from 1934 onward, the members of the administrative board gave only two options for party membership or political affiliations: Orthodox or Independent (apolitical). A parallel formal structure remained in effect after the elections of 1936, although it may be supposed that real political preferences were suppressed. The composition of the kehilla's administrative board shows that the elite in authority changed from what it had been in earlier years: those who had led the community in the 1920s and first half of the 1930s were removed.

In the 1930s, the board complained about Rabbi Zawładower, alleging that he had antagonized local society, tried to prevent the board of directors from appropriating funds from ritual slaughter, and violated regulations. The rabbi was supported by some community members who opposed the board and made its work difficult. A rabbinic council composed of the rabbis of Konin, Słupca, and Golina was asked to settle the argument. When Rabbi Zawłodawer questioned their competence even before they began to discuss the matter, these dignitaries left Kleczew in a huff and, to protest their treatment, refrained from handing down a decision. The resulting chaos paralyzed the work of the administrative board but probably strengthened Rabbi Zawłodawer's position; therefore, he strove to delay the dissolution of the board, which would have entailed a call for new elections.[104] The attitude of the local elite is noteworthy. They managed, despite all their animosities and conflicts, to reach an agreement and issue a joint list of candidates. This indicates that they were harmonious enough to do so and dominated by traditionalists who were unwilling to allow the state to supervise the community's work and meddle in their internal affairs.

The decision in 1938 to incorporate Kalisz, Konin, Koło, and Turek counties into Poznań Province, with its seat in Poznań, was greeted with a frown by the Jewish inhabitants. On April 19, 1938, in Kalisz, twenty-three representatives of the kehillot in these counties convened. At the session, presided over by Mojsze Heber, they concluded that the administrative changes put the kehillot into a difficult position. They were now farther from the provincial authorities, which in any case were prejudiced against Jews, especially Orthodox Jews. The representatives were afraid of trouble in Poznań because people there were unaccustomed to men in traditional Hasidic dress. Their resolution noted that the Poznań kehilla now had to tend the affairs of the kehillot in the four counties that were newly incorporated into Poznań Province; what is more, these kehillot were supposed to cover all the expenses that arose.[105] The resolutions flowing from the meeting, however, were reviewed by neither the county nor the state authorities.

Throughout the interwar period, the Orthodox and the Religious Zionists grouped under the Mizrachi banner, creating a majority in Kleczew (tables 27–29). In the 1930s, however, the Religious Zionists gradually lost influence to secular Zionism. Interestingly, the latter in Kleczew were not General Zionists, as they were in neighboring communities. Neither did the Revisionist Zionists, the Folkspartei (Jewish People's Party), and the Bund socialists wield organized political power in the town. Everyone who identified with a national Jewish ideology, irrespective of differences, favored the establishment of a Jewish state in Palestine. Consequently, all supported the amalgamated Working Palestine Support League. The changes of thinking among the Jews of Kleczew seem to have been more unhurried than those of Jews from larger neighboring towns. The two dominant political currents in Kleczew were

Table 27 Political influences in Kleczew kehilla managing board, 1924–1939

Political party	1924-1931		1931-1933		1933-1936		1936-1939	
	Members	Alternates	Members	Alternates	Members	Alternates	Members	Alternates
Agudas Isroel	1	1	2	-	3	2	2	2
Independent Orthodox	1	-	3	8	-	1	6	6
Mizrachi	2	3	2	-	4	5	-	-
Zionists	-	-	1	-	1	-	-	-
Total	4	4	8	8	8	8	8	8

Source: APK, SPS, classification nos. 199, 200, 217, 233; APK, SPK, classification no. 383, 385.

Table 28 Political influences in managing boards of Jewish communities in Słupca (Konin) County, 1924-1939 (data collected before terms of office elapsed)

Political party	Term of office 1924-1931	%	Term of office 1931-1936**	%	Term of office 1936-1939**	%
Szlojmej Emunej Isroel (Agudas Isroel)	5	20.8	14	29.1	15	31.2
Independent Religious Jews	4	16.7	8	16.7	8	16.7
Mizrachi	3	12.5	7		5	10.4
Zionists	8	33.3	11		16	33.3
Merchant environments	3	12.5	2	4.2	-	-
Independent craftsmen environment	1	4.2	4	8.3	-	-
Folkist Party	-	-	-	-	3	6.3
Bund	-	-	-	-	1	2.1
Revisionist Zionism	-	-	2		-	
Total	24	100.0	48	100.0	48	100.0

Source: APK, SPS, classification nos. 199, 200, 217, 225, 233; APP, SPK, classification nos. 379, 382, 383, 385, 391; see: T. Kawski, Społeczność żydowska na pograniczu, Table 5, p. 176.The results presented by the author for 1931-1936 are different because data collected at the beginning of each term of office were taken into consideration.

Notes:
* Słupca county was dissolved in 1932 and its territory was incorporated into Konin County. Consequently, the number of Jewish communities in Konin County (Golina, Konin, Rychwał, Ślesin, Tuliszków, Władysławów) increased by six (Kleczew, Pyzdry, Skulsk, Słupca, Wilczyn, Zagórów). To preserve the data, six municipalities that had belonged to Słupca County were included after 1932.
** In Kleczew, the managing board was dissolved in 1931. A subsequent election was held on August 26, 1933.

evidently strong enough to thwart the formation of improvised electoral blocs before elections, allowing followers to mask their political views. Much the same happened in the smaller Jewish collectives in Skulsk, Wilczyn, and Pyzdry. The practical impact of individual Zionist parties in Konin County may be judged on the basis of Table 30. It allows us to generalize somewhat about whether the Kleczew Jews' political preferences were exceptional.

The kehilla's financial condition was an important source of influence on its work, and it was bad—like that of the entire town. The fire of 1921 only made the difficulties worse. Consequently, more and more people went on the dole. The kehilla had two main sources of income for

Table 29 Political influences in managing boards of Jewish communities in Słupca County, 1924–1939

Political party	Kleczew 1924	Kleczew 1931	Kleczew 1936	Pyzdry 1924	Pyzdry 1931	Pyzdry 1936*	Słupca 1924	Słupca 1931	Słupca 1936	Zagórów 1924	Zagórów 1931	Zagórów 1936	Wilczyn 1924	Wilczyn 1931	Wilczyn 1936	Skulsk 1924	Skulsk 1931	Skulsk 1936
Agudas Isroel	1	2	2	2	2	2	1	2	2	-	3	2	-	2	8	1	3	-
Independent Orthodox Jews	1	3	6	-	2	2	1	2	-	-	-	-	-	-	-	2	1	8
Mizrachi	1	2	-	1	2	2	-	1	1	-	1	-	1	-	-	-	1	-
Zionists	1	1	-	1	2	2	1	1	2**	1	-	2	3	6	-	1	1	-
Merchant environments	-	-	-	-	-	-	1	-	-	2	2	-	-	-	-	-	-	-
Craftsmen environments	-	-	-	-	-	-	-	2	-	1	2	-	-	-	-	-	-	-
Folkist Party	-	-	-	-	-	-	-	-	3	-	-	-	-	-	-	-	-	-
Bund	-	-	-	-	-	-	-	-	1	-	-	-	-	-	-	-	-	-
Revisionist Zionism	-	-	-	-	-	-	-	-	-	-	-	4	-	-	-	-	2	-
Total	**4**	**8**	**8**	**4**	**8**	**8**	**4**	**8**	**8**	**4**	**8**	**8**	**4**	**8**	**8**	**4**	**8**	**8**

Source: APK, SPS, classification nos. 199, 200, 217, 225, 233; APK, SPK, classification nos. 379, 382, 383, 385, 391; cf. T. Kawski, *Społeczność żydowska na pograniczu*, Table 5, p. 176. The author presents slightly different results for 1931–1939 because he considered data from the beginning of each term of office

Notes:
* No data available; estimated data for 1931 were taken into consideration.
** Bloc of General Zionists and Po'alei Tsiyyon Right.

Table 30 Results of 20th Zionist Congress elections, July 10, 1937, in selected localities of Eastern Greater Poland

Location	Zionist organization	Mizrachi	Labor Palestine Support League
Konin	54	92	336
Słupca	83	5	22
Zagórów	17	2	15
Kleczew	1	48	-
Golina	26	62	20
Skulsk	2	6	14
Razem	-	-	-

Source: APK, SPK, classification no. 139.

this and other uses (Table 31): membership dues and revenue from ritual slaughter, with emphasis on the latter. Between 1919 and 1936, customer payments for kosher slaughter brought in 48%–64% of the kehilla's total income; in most years, depending on the season, the two sources together accounted for 80%–100% of revenue. As for expenses, most of the money was spent on the salaries of the kehilla's officials—mainly the rabbi and ritual slaughterers—and on synagogue maintenance (Table 32).

The lives of kehilla members converged in several places. The synagogue and prayer houses were principal in the community's social consciousness and integrity. Not only observant members of the community but practically all Jews assembled there. Those who went through the preliminaries of auto-emancipation from the bonds of tradition grouped around several institutions that acted on behalf of non-observant groups. Others, however, broke all ties with the kehilla. An example is Leopold Piekarski, owner of the Złotków estate within Kleczew municipal limits. Officially defined as an irreligionist and the father of a convert to Catholicism, Piekarski felt obliged to remit his contributions to the local Roman Catholic parish. Despite his irreligious status, the kehilla dunned him for 300 złoty in synagogue dues in 1925. Protested the charge, Piekarski stated, among others things, "[...] I have nothing in common with the Jewish religion and rituals [...]."[106] His appeal was turned down, evidently on the grounds that his status had

Table 31 Kleczew kehilla budget, 1919–33 (income)

Planned income	1919 Sum (mkp)	1919 %	1921 Sum (mkp)	1921 %	1929 Sum (zł)	1929 %	1930 Sum (zł)	1930 %	1931 Sum (zł)	1931 %	1932 Sum (zł)	1932 %	1933 Sum (zł)	1933 %
Dues	8,440	52.6	124,700	46.6	6,085	33.9	6,079	31.5	6,163	33.5	4,529	29.7	4,080	35.2
Dues and overdue fee	-	-	-	-	-	-	2,000	10.4	2,147.45	11.7	1,645	10.8	-	-
Synagogue & donations	-	-	5,500	2.1	4,270	23.8	2,400	12.4	403.03	2.2	100	0.7	35	0.3
Ritual slaughter	7,600	47.4	130,500	48.7	7,200	40.1	8,400	43.6	9,000	48.8	8,200	53.7	7,460	64.5
Cemeteries	-	-	4,500	1.7	-	-	-	-	-	-	560	3.7	-	-
Ritual pool	-	-	2,500	0.9	400	2.2	400	2.1	400	2.2	100	0.7	-	-
Rent	-	-	-	-	-	-	-	-	300	1.6	100	0.7	-	-
Total income	16,040	100.0	267,700	100.0	17,955	100.0	19,279	100.0	18,413.48	100.0	15,234	100.0	11,575	100.0

Source: APKonin, SPSłupca, classification nos. 212, 215, 232, 233; APKonin, SPKonin, classification no. 380.

Table 32 Kleczew kehilla budget, 1919–33 (expenses)

Planned expenses	1919 Sum (mkp)	1919 %	1921 Sum (mkp)	1921 %	1929 Sum (zł)	1929 %	1930 Sum (zł)	1930 %	1931 Sum (zł)	1931 %	1932 Sum (zł)	1932 %	1933 Sum (zł)	1933 %
Rabbi	3,500	21.8	52,000	19.4	4050	22.6	4,050	21.0	4,860	26.4	4,860	31.9	4,860	42.0
Secretary, synagogue and houses of prayer staff	-	-	-	-	-	-	-	-	-	-	300	2.0	300	2.6
Collector	-	-	-	-	500	2.8	624	3.2	625	3.4	720	4.7	-	-
Office expenses	-	-	4,000	1.5	100	0.6	100	0.5	250	1.4	260	1.7	300	2.6
Synagogues, houses of prayer	1,000	6.2	9,000	3.4	1,865	10.4	1,899	9.9	1,753	9.5	1,550	10.2	1,300	11.3
Ritual slaughterers	3,000	18.7	62,500	23.3	3,940	21.9	3,900	20.2	4,420	24.0	3,934	25.8	3,176	27.5
Cemetery and gravedigger	1,500	9.4	12,000	4.5	-	-	-	-	-	-	240	1.6	240	2.1
Mikve	1,500	9.4	42,000	15.7	400	2.2	400	2.1	400	2.2	100	0.6	50	0.4
Charity	4,300	26.8	57,000	21.3	400	2.2	600	3.1	450	2.4	1,700	11.2	750	6.5
Repairs	800	5.0	16,400	6.1	4,500	25.1	1,020	5.3	400	2.2	450	2.9	100	0.7
Taxes and insurance	200	1.2	2,600	1.0	700	3.9	4,636	24.0	2,490.60	13.3	500	3.3	150	1.3
Miscellaneous	240	1.5	10,200	3.8	1,500	8.3	2,050	10.7	2,800	15.2	620	4.1	349	3.0
Total expenses	16,040	100.0	267,700	100.0	17,955	100.0	19,279	100.0	18,413.48	100.0	15,234	100.0	11,575	100.0

Source: APKonin, SPSłupca, classification nos. 212, 215, 232, 233; APKonin, SPKonin, classification no. 380.

not been properly formalized. It took until the early 1930s to correct the deficiency; only then was his name removed from the list of contributors to the kehilla budget.[107] Aleksander Horensztejn held the same status, irreligious, from December 20, 1926, onward.[108]

Rabbis were highly respected in the community, especially among religious members. The post of rabbi was initially held by Szlam Hersz Kaufman,[109] who died in the second half of 1924.[110] After the community was served by a substitute rabbi for two years,[111] Hersz Zawłodawer was elected rabbi in 1926. Born in Kleczew on July 11, 1893, and trained in a rabbinic seminar, he settled on Konińska Street in Kleczew in 1926 with his wife Rojzla (b. January 21, 1899). The authorities considered Zawłodawer apolitical—which is possibly a simplified view of matters, given his active support of philanthropy and participation in many social and cultural events connected to the Orthodox world.[112] Perhaps they were convinced that he had the ability to differentiate between religious events/beliefs and political ones.

The following hired officials represented similar views: the circumcisers J. Sz. Przysucher and Henoch Brysz, the synagogue and prayer house caretaker I. Watman, the Talmud Torah teacher Gedalie Szejsznajder, and the elementary school instructors.[113] No data have been preserved to help us determine which Hasidic faction was most influential among the Jews of Kleczew. On the basis of information collected from Słupca and Konin counties, one may assume that the courts of Góra Kalwaria and Aleksandrów were the most powerful and those of Mszczonów and Warka were less so.[114] Disregarding the role of Jewish tradition among the older and middle generations in the 1920s and 1930s, a climate conducive to the jettisoning of Orthodox influences became entrenched in Kleczew and began to amass power. The catalyst of this state of affairs was mandatory elementary public education, which exposed Jewish children to the Polish language and culture. For this and other reasons, secular Jewish ideologies gained popularity and cultural changes set in motion a general revision of the value system.

The school system in Kleczew went only as far as the elementary level. When Poland regained its independence, the town had two people's (public) schools. In 1920, one of these institutions was transformed into a Seven-Grade Public Developmental School that was supposed to be attended by children of all faiths.[115] At first, however, most Jewish children attended the three-grade cheder located in Mojsze Brysz's house. After the fire of August 6, 1921, the cheder classrooms were taken over by the Kleczew Magistrate and allocated to victims of the fire. It took the cheder several years to get up and running again.[116]

In November 1921, an attempt was made to establish a religious school for all 150 Jewish children of school age. An application to this effect, submitted to the School Inspectorate in Słupca, emphasized the religious and cultural differences between these children and those attending the public school, as well as the fact that the kehilla members generated more than 50% of school tax revenue even though only 33% of children obligated by law to attend school were Jewish.[117] The request was denied; a separate and publicly financed public school for Jewish children was not established. Under these circumstances, some parents decided to give their children private religious educations, and several Jewish children attended non-public schools sponsored by the kehilla. A private Orthodox cheder run by a teacher named Watman was attended mostly by Hasidic children. A cheder for poor children, funded by the kehilla, and a Talmud Torah of similar character enrolled eight and nine boys, respectively.[118] Symche Złotogórski, Szmul Mojsie Fridenson, and Chaim Goldenberg were *melamedim* (teachers) in these institutions. They charged 3–4 złoty per month per child. Goldenberg taught eleven children for a monthly salary of 2.50 złoty per child.[119]

Photograph 20 shows the exterior view of the elementary school building in Kleczew as of March 1933.

In the 1938/39 school year, there were 605 registered schoolchildren in Kleczew, of whom eighty-four were Jewish (as opposed to 150 in 1921) and 103 others were otherwise not Catholic.[120] Photographs 22 and 23 show the student ID card and annual report card of a Jewish student in Kleczew's public elementary school.

Most members of the Jewish community were discomfited by this situation, especially after the authorities requisitioned the cheder's classrooms. Importantly, the cheder was what we would call today an Ultra-Orthodox institution and was for boys only. Ultra-Orthodox

20. Kleczew. Exterior view of elementary school building, March 1933.
(NAC, sign. 1-N-1581)

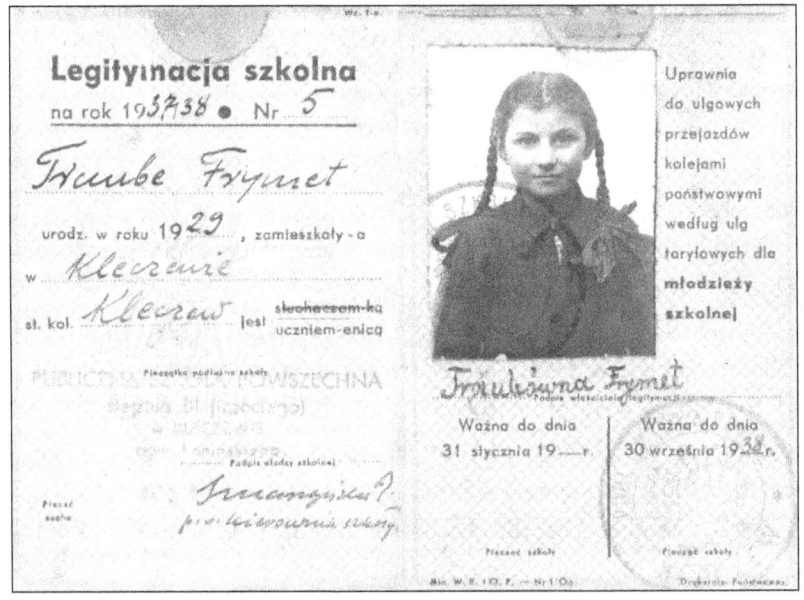

21. Frymet Traube's student ID card, Kleczew public school, 1937/1938
(Horev private collection)

22. Report card, Kleczew public elementary school, 1938
(Horev private collection)

girls attended public school and, from the 1930s, acquired supplemental traditional education at a Beis Yaakov Sunday school that had an enrollment of approximately thirty. Photograph 23, taken in 1938 or 1939, shows them and their teacher. It is believed that only one member of this group, Frymet Horev *née* Traube, survived the Holocaust.

23. Jewish girls with their teacher, Beit Yaakov school in interwar Kleczew
Third from left, second row: Frymet Traube; third from left, first row: her sister Hanna
(Horev private collection)

NOTES

1. *Dzieje Ziemi Słupeckiej,* collective work (Słupca-Poznań, 1960), 130.
2. In 1922 the town had ten streets: Słupecka, Rynek, Warszawska, Kościelna, Konińska, Wodna, Stodólna, Piaski Dolne, Piaski Górne, and Rutki. By the late 1930s, when the town limits were enlarged, their number grew to nineteen: Wjazdowa, Targowa, Jeziorna, Leśna, Piaski, Słupecka, Hejmana, Kościelna, Toruńska, Rynek, Nowa, Plac 11 Listopada, Chrzanowskiego, Ogrodowa, Żabia, Warszawska, Piłsudskiego, Serwitutowa, and Ślesińska.
3. APK, AmK, 447; APK, SPS, 217.
4. For more, see *Księga adresowa Polski (wraz z W. M. Gdańskiem) dla handlu, przemysłu rzemiosła i rolnictwa* (Warsaw, 1929), 854; J. Łojko, "Kleczew w okresie II Rzeczypospolitej," in *Dzieje Kleczewa*, 143-164.
5. Here is a brief example: Gittel Rachwalska (b. December 1845 in Kleczew) emigrated from Kleczew in 1866. Her second child, Harry, was born in 1867 in England; her third child, Tobias Asron, was born in 1869 in New York. Other members of the Rachwalski family who immigrated to the United States at that time were Rafael Rachwalski and his sister Trane Rachwalska (Thresa). The last mentioned (b. 1854 in Kleczew) departed with her husband Isaak Glucker (Ike Glasgow) from Hamburg to the U.S.A. on October 27, 1888. Three of Tobias Rachwalski's children—Abraham (Alfred) Moses Rachwalski (b. 1890 in Turek) and his brothers Majer Tobias

Rachwalski (b. 1895 in Kleczew) and Morton Rachwalski (b. 1908 in Kleczew) emigrated to the U.S. as well.
6   More about small town communities and demographic phenomena can be found in K. Urbański, *Gminy żydowskie małe w województwie kieleckim w okresie międzywojennym* (Kielce, 2006); T. Kawski, *Gminy żydowskie pogranicza Wielkopolski, Mazowsza i Pomorza w latach 1918-1942* (Toruń, 2008); and T. Kawski and M. Opioła, *Gminy żydowskie*.
7   Łojko, *Kleczew w okresie*, 145-146.
8   As illustrated by statistical data from January 1, 1936.
9   APK, SPK, 342. Municipalities: Brzeżno 11 (1.5% of the total municipal population), Ciążeń 2 (1.2%), Dąbroszyn 14 (0.01%), Gosławice 8 (0.07%), Golina 2 (0.033%), Grodziec 106 (1%), Kramsk 39 (0.9%), Lądek 32 (0.47%), Młodojewo 1 (0.0%), Oleśnica 17 (0.5%), Ostrowite 3 (0.0%), Stare Miasto 5 (0.06%), Skulska Wieś 179 (2.7%), Szymanowice 6 (0.02), Trąbczyn 7(0.01%), Tuliszków 9 (0.1%), Władysławów 216 (4.75%), Wilczogóra 146 (2.1%), and Wysokie 5 (0.13%).
10 In 1921, 101 Jews lived in villages in Koło County (0.1% of the population). The corresponding count in Turek County was 263 (0.3%) and in Kalisz County 76 (0.6%). Urban localities had larger Jewish populations: 2,930 (25.3%) in Koło County and 1,106 (12.9%) in Kalisz County. No Jews lived in Turek County. B. Wasiutyński, *Ludność*, Table IV, 70–71.
11 W. Grabski and the Office of Social Work, *Rocznik Statystyczny Królestwa Polskiego. Rok 1913* (Warsaw, 1914), Section I, Table III, 20, and Section I, Table IV, 33.
12 B. Wasiutyński, *Ludność żydowska w Polsce w wiekach XIX i XX. Studium statystyczne* (Warsaw, 1930), Table IV, 70-71.
13 APK, SPS, 217.
14 APK AmK, 450.
15 See the Kroner family story in Annex 2.
16 Źródło: APK, SPS, sign. 217.
17 Cf. T. Kawski, *Kujawsko-dobrzyńscy Żydzi w latach 1918-1950* (Toruń, 2006).
18 The Bagnos were a relatively large family in Kleczew. Chaim Laib Bagno owned both a bookshop and a photography shop/studio. He had at least two brothers: Tobiasz, a teacher, and Nachum Israel. Their father, Eliyahu Bagno, owned a grocery store, later a bakery, and then an oil factory. Moshe Bagno, Nachum's son, subsequently immigrated to Israel and became mayor of the town of Bnei Brak. His maternal grandfather, Abraham Makowski, was offered the position of rabbi of Kleczew but refused because he preferred to continue his occupation as a teacher and children's educator (source: Ms. Sarit Kav, daughter of Moshe Bagno).
19 YVA, O.3/3406, Testimony Eugenia Friedlender-Cyns, June 26, 1969, p. 21.
20 APK, AmK, 451.
21 APK, AmK, 451.
22 APK, AmK, 456. A document from mid-1919 confirms the economic and most probably the personal connections that existed. Entitled "List of people who were granted permits within Poland," it mentions Ludwik Dzieci, Rafael Jastrząb, Hejman Gembicki, Marceli Dzieci, Markus Kott, Jakub Krotowski, Salomon Krause, and Moryc Malarek.
23 APK AmK, 451.
24 APK, AmK, 251, 451.

25   APK, SPS, 252, 458.
26   APK, SPS, 253.
27   APK, AmK, 451.
28   APK, AmK, 459.
29   AP, SPS, 233; AmK 451, 458.
30   APK, SPS, 232.
31   APK, AmK, 456.
32   Archiwum Państwowe w Łodzi (State Archive in Łódź—hereafter: APŁ), Urząd Wojewódzki Łódzki 1918-1939 (Province Office in Łódź 1918-1939, hereafter: UWŁ), 541.
33   APK, SPS, 83,84; APK, SPK, 379.
34   APK, Komenda Powiatowa Policji Państwowej w Słupcy 1919-1932 (Słupca County Police Station 1919-1932—hereafter: KPPS), *Sprawozdanie Sytuacyjne Za Grudzień 1929 istyczeń 1930*.
35   APK, SPK, 379.
36   APK, AmK, 462.
37   A Zionist-religious youth movement affiliated with Mizrachi, established in Europe in 1929. During World War II, it merged with another Zionist-Religious youth organization, Bnei Akiva, which was also called the Torah ve-Avoda movement in several locations.
38   The name Hashomer Hatzair refers to a secular Socialist Zionist youth movement founded in 1913 in Galicia, then in Austria-Hungary. Its membership base was in Eastern Europe; by 1939, it had 70,000 members worldwide. With the beginning of World War II and the Holocaust, members of Hashomer Hatzair focused their attention on resisting the Nazis. Mordechai Anielewicz, leader of Hashomer Hatzair's Warsaw branch, became head of the Jewish Fighting Organization and one of the leaders of the Warsaw ghetto uprising.
39   Revisionist Zionism was a nationalist group within the Zionist movement. Its ideology was originally developed by Vladimir (Ze'ev) Jabotinsky, who advocated the "revision" of the "practical Zionism" of David Ben-Gurion and Chaim Weizmann, which focused on autonomous settlement in Eretz Israel. In 1935, after the Zionist Executive rejected Jabotinsky's political program and refused to declare the aim of Zionism "the establishment of a Jewish state," Jabotinsky resigned from the Zionist Organization and founded the New Zionist Organization (NZO) to conduct independent political activity in support of unrestricted immigration to Palestine and the establishment of a Jewish state there.
40   Poalei Tziyyon was a leftist Zionist movement established in Minsk in 1897. Its ideology was enunciated by Dov Ber Borochov in 1905. Key features of its ideology were acceptance of the Marxist view of history with the addition of the role of nationalism. At that time, the party's vision was that a Jewish proletariat would come into being in Palestine and then take part in class struggle.
41   APK, SPS, 199.
42   APK, KPPS, *Sprawozdanie sytuacyjne za grudzień* 1929 i styczeń 1930.
43   APŁ, UWŁ, 563; APK, AmK, 462.
44   APK, AmK, 461
45   APK, SPS, 84
46   APK, SPS, 214.

47 APK, SPS, 232.
48 APK, SPS, 83, 84.
49 The term "Rebbe" is often used by Hasidim to refer to the leader of a Hasidic movement.
50 Another variant was Agudas Shomrei Shabbos, Association of Sabbath Observers.
51 APK, SPS, 228.
52 APK, SPS, 86.
53 Tobiasz Rachwalski's son-in-law, husband of Fojgle Rachwalska (see Annex 2).
54 APŁ, UWŁ, mf L-12760, *Sprawozdania sytuacyjne z 1938*.
55 APK, SPS, 199; APK, AmK, 467.
56 APK, AmK, 462.
57 APK, AmK, 462.
58 APK, SPS, 199; APK, KPPS, *Sprawozdanie sytuacyjne za luty 1930 r.*
59 For examples of such attitudes, see T. Kawski, *Kujawsko-dobrzyńscy Żydzi*.
60 APK, SPS, 217, 225.
61 J. Łojko, *Kleczew w okresie II Rzeczypospolitej*, 144, 50; Z. Kaczmarek and K. Pawlak, "Endecja w Wielkopolsce Wschodniej w okresie międzywojennym," *Rocznik Wielkopolski Wschodniej* 4 (1976): vol. 4, table 6, p. 55.
62 APK, AmK, 449.
63 APK, AmK, 461; J. Łojko, *Kleczew w okresie II Rzeczypospolitej*, 153.
64 Archiwum Państwowe Miasta Stołecznego Warszawy (State Archive in Warsaw), Posterunek Policji Państwowej w Aleksandrowie Kujawskim 1918-1939 (Aleksandrów Kujawski Police Station 1918-1939), 680, *Raport Starosty Powiatowego Nieszawskiego dla Dowództwa Okręgu Korpusu w Łodzi za 26 październik—30 listopad 1921*. In Skulsk, the only event reported in source documents was the robbery of three Jewish merchants from Koło who were returning from the Skulsk fair on the night of November 14–15, 1921.
65 M. Gelbart, ed., *Kehilah Konin Befrihata uvehurbana* (Tel Aviv, 1968), 345-346, 365-366; T. Richmond, *Uporczywe echo. Sztetl Konin. Poszukiwanie* (Poznań, 2001), passim.
66 B. Szczepański, ed., *Dzieje Słupcy* (Poznań, 1996), 208-209.
67 APŁ, UWŁ, mf L-12770, card 62.
68 Z. Kaczmarek and K. Pawlak, *Endecja*, Table 6, p. 47.
69 Ibid., Table 6, p. 53.
70 APŁ, UWŁ, mf L-12769, card 450, *Sprawozdanie... za grudzień 1937*; Z. Kaczmarek and K. Pawlak, *Endecja*, Table 6, p. 47.
71 Z. Kaczmarek and K. Pawlak, *Endecja*, 47.
72 APŁ, UWŁ, mf L-12770.
73 APŁ, UWŁ, mf L-12769, card 450.
74 APŁ, UWŁ, mf L-12769, card 453.
75 M. Ringel, "Ustawodawstwo Polski Odrodzonej o gminach żydowskich," in *Żydzi w Polsce Odrodzonej. Działalność społeczna, gospodarcza, oświatowa i kulturalna*, ed. I. Schiper, A. Tartakower, and A. Haftka, vol. 2, 244-248; K. Krasowski, *Związki Wyznaniowe w II Rzeczypospolitej.Studium historyczno-prawne* (Warsaw-Poznań, 1988), 183-184; J. Tomaszewski, "Niepodległa Rzeczpospolita," in *Najnowsze dzieje Żydów w Polsce w zarysie (do 1950 roku)*, ed. J. Tomaszewski (Warsaw, 1993), 182-183, 187-189.

76   "Dziennik Urzędowy Rzeczypospolitej Polskiej" ("Official Journal of the Polish Republic"—hereafter: "Dz.U.RP") no. 52, item 500.

77   H. Świątkowski, *Wyznania religijne w Polsce ze szczególnym uwzględnieniem ich stanu prawnego*, Part 1. *Wyznania i związki religijne* (Warsaw, 1937), 113-115; F. Hefter, *Najnowsza ustawa kahalna* (Stanisławów, n.d.), passim. The Decree of the Chief of the State from February 7, 1919, was completed with regulations laid down by the Minister of Internal Affairs on March 28, 1919, concerning the organization of the Jewish Religious Society. The number of board members, with eight deputies, seems to have been introduced for some communities by MWRiOP under the regulation of December 23, 1927, which was subsequently repeated in Paragraph 2 of a law issued by MWRiOP on October 24, 1930, concerning regulations for elections of the organs of Jewish religious communities in the Republic of Poland, Silesia excluded.

78   *Rozporządzenie MWRiOP z dnia 24 października 1930 r. w sprawie regulaminu wyborczego do wyboru gmin wyznaniowych żydowskich na obszarze Rzeczypospolitej z wyjątkiem województwa śląskiego* (MWRiOP regulation of October 24, 1930, concerning voting rules for the election of organs of Jewish communities in Poland except Silesia Province), "Dz.U. RP," 1930, no. 75, item 592.

79   "DzURP" z 5 listopada 1930 r., no. 75, poz. 593 (from November 5, 1930, no 75, item 593).

80   Zarządzenie MWRiOP z dnia 28 grudnia 1936 r. o (MWRiOP Regulation of December 28, 1936, concerning salary and pension of rabbis and assistant rabbis and securing the fate of widows and orphaned children), *Urzędowy Ministerstwa Wyznań Religijnych i Oświecenia Publicznego* (Official Gazette of the Ministry of Religion and Public Education) no. 4 (1936): poz. 83 (no. 4, item 83).

81   Attachment to the edition: J. Grynsztejn and I. Kerner, *Przepisy o organizacja gmin wyznaniowych żydowskich. Nowe rozporządzenia, zarządzenia, przepisy.Rok 1931* (Warsaw, n.d.), 15-24.

82   This regulation was applied in practice. Given the growing poverty of community members in the 1930s, the dues imposed were usually the lowest irrespective of the size of the kehilla; most often it was 2-3 złoty.

83   Archiwum Żydowskiego Instytutu Historycznego w Warszawie (Archive of the Jewish Historical Institute in Warsaw—hereafter: AŻIH), Żydowska Gmina Wyznaniowa Włocławek (Włocławek Jewish Community—hereafter: ŻGWW), 113/11, *Regulamin Poboru Opłat i Składek gminnych w Żydowskiej Gminie Wyznaniowej w Lubrańcu z 1929 r.* (Regulation concerning the imposition of fees and contributions on the Lubraniec Jewish Community in 1929). It was assumed that all contributions for religious services (marriages, circumcisions, ritual baths, funerals) should be a function of the affluence of the community member (Paragraph 4). Dues were determined each year as Jewish families were counted and their wealth determined. Dues-payers were classified into four categories. The totality of community dues was divided into ten parts. The richest members (Category 1) paid 40%, Category 2 30%, Category 3 20%, and Category 4 10% (Paragraph 5). Similar solutions were also made use of in Kleczew.

84   AŻIH, ŻGWW. Cemetery fees amounted to 10-500 złoty in smaller communities and 10-1,000 złoty in large ones; for gravestones, the fee was 10-1,000 złoty and 10-10,000 złoty, respectively.

85 Kehillot were seated in the following locations: Konin County: Golina, Konin, Rychwal, Ślesin, Tuliszków, Władysławów; Słupca County: Kleczew, Pyzdry, Skulsk, Słupca, Wilczyn, Zagórów; Koło County: Babiak, Dąbie, Kłodawia, Koło, Izbica Kujawska, Sompolno; Kalisz County: Kalisz, Koźminek, Błaszki, Stawiszyn; Turek County: Turek, Dobra, Uniejow.
86 APK, SPK, 380, 381, 382, 383; SPS, 199, 228, 232, 233.
87 APK, SPS, 233.
88 APK, SPS, 233.
89 APK, SPS, 215; T. Kawski, "Inwentarze Gmin Żydowskich z Pomorza i Wielkopolski Wschodniej w latach 1918/20-1939," *Kwartalnik Historii Kultury Materialnej* 3-4 (2006): document 10, p. 83.
90 APK, SPS, 212, 214.
91 APK, SPS, 212, 217.
92 APK, SPS, 214.
93 APK, SPS, 216.
94 APK, SPS, 212.
95 APK, SPS, 217, 225.
96 APK, SPS, 199.
97 APK, SPS, 217.
98 APK, SPS, 199, 200.
99 APK, SPK, 380.
100 APK,SPK, 380, 385.
101 APK, SPK, 380.
102 APK, SPK, 383.
103 APK, SPK, 383. T. Kawski, "Społeczność żydowska na pograniczu kujawsko-wielkopolskim w XX wieku," in *Z dziejów pogranicza kujawsko-wielkopolskiego*. Collection of studies, ed. D. Karczewski (Strzelno, 2007), Table 5, 176.
104 APK, SPK 383.
105 APP, Urząd Wojewódzki Poznański 1919-1939 (Poznań Province Office—hereafter: UWP) 5708, *Sprawozdanie z życia mniejszości narodowych za kwiecień 1938 r.*
106 APK, SPS, 228.
107 APK, SPS, 232.
108 PK, SPK, 380.
109 APK, SPS, 214, 217; PK, AmK 448. He was born in 1860 or 1864. He lived on Konińska Street in Kleczew. His wife, Sara Kauffman, was 38 in 1924.
110 APK, SPS, 217
111 APK, SPS, 228.
112 APK, SPS, 199, 232.
113 APK, SPS, 214, 215; APK, AmK, 448
114 T. Kawski and M. Opioła, *Gminy*, passim.
115 J. Łojko, *Kleczew w okresie II Rzeczypospolitej*, 58-159.
116 APK, SPS, 213.
117 J. Łojko, *Kleczew w okresie II Rzeczypospolitej*, 159.
118 APK, SPS, 212, 215, 216, 232.
119 J. Łojko, *Kleczew w okresie II Rzeczypospolitej*, 159.
120 APP, Kuratorium Okręgu Szkolnego Poznańskiego (Poznań School District Department of Education), 55.

PART Two

"IN THE EYE OF THE STORM" JEWS IN OCCUPIED KLECZEW AND REICHSGAU WARTHELAND

4 The First Occupation Years: "Resettlement" and Deportation

1. THE SITUATION IN KLECZEW BEFORE SEPTEMBER 1939

In his speech to the Reichstag on January 30, 1939, Adolf Hitler proposed a horrifying solution to the "Jewish problem." (see document 7 in Annex 1)[1] The combination of his address and previous events in Germany, such as Kristallnacht (described below), could not have left Jews in neighboring countries unaffected. For the Jews of Kleczew, however, these preliminary events were somewhat distant.

The prewar situation for Jews in Kleczew and other towns in the area was to some extent a function of relations among Jews, Poles, and Germans at the time. Michel Prost describes relations between Poles and Jews in Kleczew as good. He reports having had many friends and observing no cases of violence. "There was 'separation without segregation' [among Poles, Jews and Germans]," he notes.[2] Things were quieter in Kleczew than in the major cities. Litigation took place, but physical violence was unknown, in contrast, for example, to the antisemitic attacks by groups of Poles in some Jewish quarters in Łódź.[3] Prewar testimonies in Kleczew report some 200 Jewish families among the approximately 700 families in the town. Jewish and Polish children grew up together, often attending the same Polish public schools and playing sports together—soccer was the favorite among boys. Children of all nationalities in Kleczew, mainly Poles and Jews, attended the same seven-grade public school. Jewish boys also attended religious schools in the afternoon.[4]

Blond, blue-eyed Bert Gembicki did not look Jewish and had many non-Jewish friends—a circumstance that would serve him well during the war.[5] In a video testimony, he relates that Kleczew did have some *narodowcy* (members or supporters of Polish nationalist organizations) who harassed girls. Bert Gembicki reports once having seen two *narodowcy* bullying girls in the street; he gave them a beating. The *narodowcy* promised revenge but he was undaunted, aware that few Poles belonged to this organization. Gembicki was also a member of the Zionist Hashomer Hatzair youth movement. At the meetings, outings, and summer camps of this organization, which were much like those of another Zionist youth movement, Hehaluts, Hashomer Hatzair taught members how to work toward emigrating to Palestine. Gembicki's parents, however, opposed his leaving Europe; life in Palestine was hard, they warned.[6] They were not alone in their opposition. For those who had resolved to resettle in Palestine anyway, Hashomer Hatzair had a branch and a training kibbutz (farming collective) in Wilczyn and a kibbutz in Ląd.[7]

The Jews of Kleczew knew about the persecution of Jews in Germany. In 1938, when many Polish Jews had been expelled from Germany and stranded in a provisional refugee camp in Zbąszyń (175 kilometers from Kleczew),[8] many Jewish communities in Poland had collected clothing and other necessities for them[9]. One of the deported Jewish families in Zbąszyń was the Grynszpans—husband, wife, and daughter. When their son in Paris learned what had happened to his family, he decided to take revenge. On November 9, 1938, he killed the Third Secretary of the German Embassy in Paris, Ernst vom Rath. The Nazi Party leaders in Germany reacted to the assassination by using it as a pretext to teach all the Jews of Germany a lesson. On the night of November 9/10, 1938, hundreds of synagogues in Germany were set afire and thousands of Jewish-owned shops and homes were plundered. Windows were shattered and buildings were defaced with Stars of David and antisemitic slogans. The pogrom acquired its name, Kristallnacht—the night of broken glass—from the glass of broken windows that littered the streets of Germany.

The events of Kristallnacht were not limited to German territory. Some Nazis evidently acted against Jews on the Polish side of their country's border. For example, they destroyed Jewish-owned shops and a synagogue in Wilczyn. A Jewish witness from Wilczyn recalls not having entertained fears of the Germans before Kristallnacht. That day, however (probably November 10, 1938), many young Germans wearing swastika armbands arrived in the town by truck and hurled stones at the synagogue. After breaking all the windows of the prayer house, they painted Stars of David on Jewish-owned shops and torched a building. No Poles came out to stop them. At that moment, the Jews of Wilczyn realized how intensely the Germans hated them. The perpetrators prepared the groundwork for Hitler's advent with masterful organization. Abram Landau recalls, "We knew something was cooking when they held organizing meetings. But after that night we understood. The Jews were afraid. The Jews didn't fight back. They were just afraid."[10] After Kristallnacht, Landau says, they repaired the damage and installed new books, but continued to be afraid.[11]

Continuing his testimony, Landau said,

> [...] It was a good life before the war in Wilczyn. I couldn't imagine losing it all. I liked the country. We lived well. We had fields, windmills, and a wine cellar. But I didn't like the government and the people. The teachers were antisemites. They resented [us]. I didn't feel comfortable with them.[12]

2. THE SEPTEMBER 1939 CAMPAIGN IN THE KLECZEW VICINITY

Poland declared a general mobilization immediately before the war broke out. Michel Prost of Kleczew, hearing the order, headed for his draft station at once. It was too late; he could not reach the center. Call-up order or not, he had no uniform and could not be considered a soldier even though as an army veteran he was prepared for war and had taken defense training (*przysposobienie obronne*) at school. He returned to Kleczew several days later.[13]

The weather in September 1939 was fantastic: no rain, sunshine all the time. Unfortunately, all this did was help the invading Wehrmacht to advance swiftly and the Luftwaffe to attack Polish towns and roads from the air. Kleczew was bombarded, though not heavily.[14]

A witness recalled that "The Germans entered [Grodziec, 50 kilometers from Kleczew] on September 5, 1939. From the beginning, they stole whatever property the Jews still had; shortly afterward, they began to arrest Jews and force them to wash cars."[15]

Another witness described how matters proceeded in Rychwał (43 kilometers from Kleczew):

> The Germans arrived on September 3, 1939. The first orders were that all Jews had to give up their weapons. The Jews were gathered in the marketplace with their hands up and an order to shoot anyone who moved was announced. A 74-year-old man could not stand. The SS approached him and beat him for a long time; [after that] the old man could not get out of bed. On September 12, 1939, they assembled all adult [Jewish men] in the street, shoved them to the ground, forced them to wear prayer-shawls and then cut them with knives. There were pogroms every day. Jews were beaten on the ground because someone thought they did not want to work. One time, Germans wanted to shoot all the Jews, but the rabbi collected gold for [the Jews'] survival. In spite of this, as punishment, they forced the Jews to walk ten miles every day to work without food.[16]

During the first days of September 1939, masses of Polish troops crossed towns in the Kleczew area. "We watched the Polish army, tanks and cavalry, pass through Wilczyn," one witness reported. The witness went on to state that after the Polish troops departed, the Germans came. German tanks rumbled into Wilczyn, 16 kilometers north of Kleczew and closer to the German border than Kleczew. The Jews in Wilczyn were frightened but had no idea of what awaited them. The Germans requisitioned a beautiful Jewish-owned home as their headquarters and announced that they were occupying the town.[17] Several additional towns in the vicinity,

24. Polish troops on the battlefield in defensive war, September 1939. Note abandoned equipment and weapons. (NAC, sign. 37-85-8)

which would soon become the Reichsgau Wartheland, often called the Warthegau, were occupied by German troops in mid-month after heavy fighting along the River Bzura on September 9–18, 1939, mainly around the town of Łowicz, impeded their invasion significantly.

When Kleczew's turn came, according to one witness, German soldiers entered the town and gathered in the marketplace. Intrigued children ran to them and handed out bread and candies; some brought soup. Some time later, SS and SA personnel in black and green uniforms arrived.[18] Several witnesses referred to the incoming Germans more generally, without identifying them with particular units or corps.

The Germans did not establish a ghetto in Kleczew; Jews continued to live in their houses. Soon, however, the new occupiers began to arrest Jews for forced labor. Having confiscated all privately held radios (a common German practice in Poland), the authorities presented their demands and other communications over loudspeakers or on broadsheets. Jews were assigned to various jobs, mainly road repair and stone work to be used for roads or as construction material. The Germans knew about the Jewish festivals and forced Jews to work specifically on these days. On Rosh Hashana, for example, Jews were taken straight from their synagogues to work.

The Germans destroyed sacramental Jewish objects, but generally left the buildings that housed them intact because they could be adapted to other purposes. In Kleczew, Torah scrolls were removed from synagogues and the buildings themselves were transformed into cinemas. Several months after their arrival, the German authorities also destroyed the Jewish cemetery. For this purpose, Polish residents were forced into forced labor. The ground was leveled; bones found were tossed into a nearby pit that had been excavated for the mining of peat. As they supervised the work, the Nazis, noticing that the corpse of a recently deceased haberdasher, one Pacanowski, was in good shape, decided to put on a show: the corpse, lying on a wooden board, was stood up so that it could "watch" the work. Gravestones in good condition were taken away for use in building sidewalks and curbs; those in poor condition were dropped into a nearby swamp. When the work was all over, as mentioned, a sports facility (*Sportplatz*) was built at the site.[19] The witness Leon Brener describes these events:

> In January 1940, all 2000 Jews from the area were deported to our town [Grodziec]. Every month, fifty Jews were taken from the town and were sent to Kleczew, Konin County, in order to destroy the Jewish cemetery and to create a sports ground, which was covered with asphalt, in its place.[20]

Similar testimony was given by a survivor from Rychwał:

> In September 1940, an order was given saying that all Jews should stand in the marketplace. Forty healthy Jews were chosen and sent to Kleczew near Konin. There was a cemetery there and the Jews had to turn over the cemetery grounds, dead bodies and all, and then pave the grounds with asphalt as is used for a parking lot. The dead were thrown into the river; their bodies floated to the surface.[21]

According to Gembicki, dozens of Jews were summoned to the *Kommandantur* (German headquarters) for labor. Some were put to work pulling weeds and pruning bushes.[22]

In Wilczyn, as in Kleczew, there was no ghetto and Jews lived in their own homes. However, Germans often ordered them out of their homes to perform sundry jobs for them, e.g., tailoring, repairing, cleaning, and mending leather jackets. Payment was made in food, never in coin. In the mornings, the Germans would deliver various items that had to be fixed or otherwise dealt with by the afternoon. It was a frightening time month and a half. A curfew was in effect from 8 p.m. onward; German soldiers looted houses.[23]

The German authorities dabbled in criminality from the beginning of the occupation. Some of their misdeeds are reflected in video testimonies given by Jews many years later. Abram Landau gave two examples. In one, the Germans arrested Prince Taczanowski (a local nobleman) together with his children, a priest, and seven nuns, and shot them to death in the woods. The murderers were probably members of an Einsatzgruppe (Einsatzgruppe der Sicherheitspolizei und des SD, mobile killing unit, pl. Einsatzgruppen) that operated on the basis of a list of wanted persons prepared before the war. Such lists contained the names of Polish patriots, intellectuals, patriotic clergy, and anti-German militants in Silesia and Greater Poland following World War I. According to Abram Landau, the assailants wished to instill fear in all hearts. Poles had to take the bodies and bury them. In the second example, Germans came in the middle of the night in quest of Jewish boys for labor. They rounded up some twenty boys and ordered them to go to a chapel where a sculpture of the Madonna had been placed in a wagon. They then announced the nature of the labor: the boys were to wheel the wagon around the square and hurl the Madonna sculpture through the window of the home of a wealthy Jew. After spending the rest of the night elsewhere, the Germans returned in the morning, alleged that the wealthy Jew was hiding someone important, and ordered the Jewish boys to bury the Madonna in the Jewish cemetery. It was all a game; few people were shot. Polish townspeople blamed the Jews for the desecration, although they were aware that the Jews had acted under duress.[24] (See also Document 8, Annex 1.)

Food was in short supply during the occupation of Kleczew. The Jewish townspeople were either unemployed or put to unpaid forced labor. A few enterprising Jews who had good relations with Poles managed to obtain food. Bert Gembicki's parents lost everything, making him the family provider. He had a bicycle and visited farmers to buy cattle, which he butchered, and then he sold the meat to others. He even went to Łódź by truck to do business.[25] He obtained chickens, flour, peas, and bread from the farmers in that area, who were not afraid because he was a member of the respected Gembicki family.[26] Bert Gembicki went about his cattle business so cleverly that he was able to "organize" (arrange clandestinely) food not only for his family but for others as well. Thanks to his friends in the cattle business, he obtained a special permit from the *Kommandantur* stating that he worked for the army as a meat supplier.[27]

Jews owned several large farms near Kleczew.[28] One of these landowners, named Piekarski, denied being Jewish when visited by the SS. The SS men led him away and asked the cooks and cleaners, "Where is your boss? Who is he?" All along, the man insisted that he was not Jewish. Then the SS men ordered the servants to procure a herring and wash it. Once the servants complied, an SS man seized the herring, hurled it in Piekarski's face, and then smacked him repeatedly with the fish. "You may wash it, but it's still herring." Then the SS men tied Piekarski's feet together and made a horse drag him around. Bert Gembicki witnessed this incident from his bicycle; Piekarski's neighbors' reports agree with what Gembicki heard.[29] Although the victim's first name is not mentioned in the testimony, he may have been related to Leopold Piekarski, the man who had severed all ties with the kehilla, held the official status of "irreligionist," and was the father of a convert to Catholicism (see Chapter 3).

Another witness, Hieronim Malarek, was away from Kleczew at the beginning of the war. He and his family attempted to escape from the war zone, but were unsuccessful because his father was mobilized. When some officers noticed that he was a Jew, they moved Malarek's father to another division. Later, when his unit was evacuated, Malarek's father remained at home instead of following the troops.[30] When the Germans approached, the father was very cautious. Wishing to flee to Russia—by this time, anybody who could flee was doing so—he appropriated a bicycle, loaded it with various possessions, and went with his entire family to Kleczew, where his parents lived. On the way, he bought a horse and wagon. As they traveled, however, the Polish army closed all the roads, forcing thousands of refugees to hide in the fields[31] and exposing them to strafing by German Messerschmidt aircraft. The Malareks survived the attack and continued to Kleczew.[32]

The Occupation of Kleczew

German troops marched into Kleczew on September 15, 1939, two weeks after the beginning of the war. After gathering all the Jews in the marketplace, they established a Judenrat (known there as the Ältestenrat, the council of elders) and installed Hersz Falc as the Judenälteste (elder of the Jews). Each day, a specified number of Jews had to be delivered for forced labor. All Jews, women and men, had to clean or repair streets, serve Wehrmacht soldiers, or perform other tasks. Men were tasked with rebuilding bridges, repairing roads, etc. Several days later, the Germans took hostages and released them only after the Judenälteste remitted a "contribution." This was repeated several times, the contribution set successively at 5,000 złoty, then 12,000, then 4,000, and finally at 20,000. By now, the Jews were totally dispossessed. Most of the persecution of Jews in Kleczew was perpetrated by police officers by the names of Fritz and Reich. Several weeks later, the Jews were ordered to wear a white armband with a blue Star of David as an identifying mark. They were forbidden to walk on sidewalks. They were stalked in the streets for beatings and shearing of beards.[33] Those doing forced labor were similarly abused. Before 1939 was out, the Jews were ordered to hand over a quantity of gold.[34] To ensure compliance, Jewish hostages were once again taken.[35]

The Germans destroyed all Jewish institutions. As noted, they seized the synagogue, desecrated it, and turned it into a cinema (or, according to another testimony, a dance hall).[36] The fate of the cemetery was described above.

Abuse of Jews in Kleczew

Survivors recall a number of instances of the abuse of Jews in Kleczew and separation imposed between them and their non-Jewish erstwhile friends. Before the deportation, there was an incident in which two Jews, a father and son, were shot dead by a German after curfew. The German coveted their house, to which the father and son had said the German had no right.[37] Soon after the occupation of the town, one of Michel Prost's German friends, Arthur Thenne, told him, "We aren't friends anymore; we cannot be friends. I am a German and you are a Jew."[38] Arthur Thenne was killed during the war.[39] Two other friends of Prost's received important postings—one as the municipal secretary and one with the police—but suddenly they weren't his friends anymore.[40] The Germans persecuted Poles as well as Jews, e.g., by proposing to shoot a Pole because he wore an old uniform with buttons that bore the likeness of an eagle, the Polish national emblem.

German authorities quickly renamed the town Lehmstädt. They installed a police force at once, relying on ethnic Germans (*Volksdeutsche*) who were willing to serve the Fatherland. The Volksdeutsche were well-organized and had been active before the war in the underground. The Jews knew that they would be victims but did not know how severely. From the first days of the occupation, Jews were put to forced labor in tasks such as widening and repairing roads. At first they thought their tasks made no sense. Later, however, they realized what it was for: to improve communication with the East.

The Ältestenrat was organized apace. It urged Jews to report for forced labor, as was its responsibility. A Polish Meister (overseer) supervised the works. At the beginning of the occupation, German troops on their way to the conquest of Warsaw stopped over to rule the town. Later, they were replaced by police.[41] German soldiers abused the local population, among other ways, by their buying habits. For example, they would tender ten Reichsmarks for an item worth much more, skirting the charge of shoplifting because, after all, they had paid something.[42] "Contributions" from Jews succeeded each other every few days, at about 2,000 Reichsmarks each time.[43]

Much the same happened in other towns in the area. Golina (about 100 kilometers from the German border, 22 kilometers from Kleczew) was heavily bombarded in September 1939. A *Sperre* (curfew) was imposed after the Germans came in. Jews were not permitted to walk on sidewalks, and Germans hacked the sidelocks of the Orthodox. The occupiers indulged in lawlessness.

However, if these problematic soldiers displayed hatred toward the Jews, the SS and Gestapo forces that came later were far worse.[44]

3. THE FIRST FEW MONTHS: CONSOLIDATING THE GERMAN INFRASTRUCTURE AND ADMINISTRATION

After securing Poland's defeat in September 1939, Nazi Germany annexed the central, western, and northern parts of the country. Military rule lasted until October 25, 1939; afterwards, some of these territories were incorporated into the Third Reich and the rest were ceded to the Generalgouvernement für die besetzten polnischen Gebiete (the General Government for Occupied Territories in Poland), renamed on July 8, 1940, the Generalgouvernement, to be described here as the General Government. The Poznań area was one of the areas incorporated into the Reich; it was called Reichsgau (Reich District) Posen and, from January 29, 1940, Reichsgau Wartheland or the Warthegau. The new district was divided into three governmental regions (Regierungsbezirke, singular: Regierungsbezirk): Poznań, Inowrocław, and Kalisz. The seat of Kalisz Regierungsbezirk was transferred to Łódź on April 1, 1940. Consequently, the region was renamed Łódź Regierungsbezirk. Reichsgau Posen included the prewar provinces of Posen, part of Pomerania, and (from September 4, 1939) Warsaw.[45] The territories of Eastern Greater Poland, a point of reference for our discussions above (Chapters 2 and 3), were incorporated into Inowrocław Regierungsbezirk along with Koło and Konin counties, and the Kalisz (later Łódź) Regierunsbezierk was aligned with Kalisz and Turek counties. Kleczew, like other towns in Konin County, became part of Inowrocław Regierunsbezirk.[46]

A "Model District"[47]

The lands incorporated into the Reich were predestined for rapid Germanization. To attain this goal, German civil law was applied at once, doing away with the Polish administration. The Reich Governor

ADMINISTRATIVE DIVISION OF THE REICHSGAU WARTHELAND
Łódź capital of the Regierungsbezirk
Kutno capital of the counties
---- boundary of the Wartheland
—— Regierungsbezirk boundaries (governmental region)
.... counties boundaries

(Reichsstatthalter) of the district, who wielded sovereign authority, intended the Warthegau to become a "model district" (*Mustergau*) and a testing ground (*Exerzierplatz*) for the attainment of planned goals with the utmost celerity. The idea was to use the experience gained for subsequent stages in the colonization of "the barbarian east of Europe."

On October 26, 1939, Gruppenführer Arthur Greiser became the Reichsstatthalter of the Warthegau. Since this position gave him enormous power over the future of the Jewish communities in the Warthegau, including that of Kleczew, it is worth presenting his personal characteristics and some milestones in the development of his career.

Arthur Greiser, Reich Governor (Reichsstatthalter) of the Warthegau[48]

Arthur Greiser was born on January 22, 1897, in Środa Wielkopolska. He attended high school in Inowrocław. When World War I began, he volunteered for the German Navy. In 1915 he made officer grade and in 1917 he became a naval aviation pilot. In 1918, he was wounded and placed in a military hospital in Gdańsk (Danzig). From then on, his fortunes would be linked to this city.

Greiser spent many years climbing the career ladder, attaining the governorship of the Warthegau after holding a variety of posts. He was not only the first but also the one and only governor of the region, where he had been born and raised. He joined the NSDAP (the Nazi Party) in 1929 but had been building personal relations with the party's top leaders since 1922–23 during his numerous stays in Munich. In those years, he centered his activities on the Free City of Gdańsk. In 1924, he founded the local cell of Steel Helm (*Stahlhelm*), an organization of German soldiers from World War I. A dispute with the Nazis in Gdańsk caused Greiser to eschew Party membership until 1929. Earlier that year, however, he had joined the SA. His enlistment in the Party, with the encouragement of Hermann Göring, marked the beginning of a brilliant career. In October 1930, when Hitler appointed Albert Forster to the post of *Gauleiter* (provincial governor) of Gdańsk, Greiser was named his deputy. On November 28, 1934, Greiser became president of the Senate of Gdańsk. He held this position until September 1, 1939. By then, he belonged not only to the SA but also to the SS. In recognition of his merits, he was promoted to high grades in the SS—Gruppenführer in 1939 and Obergruppenführer in 1942.

25. Arthur Greiser (1897-1946), Gauleiter and Governor of the Wartheland (YVA, sig. 228_183)

On October 21, 1939, Hitler appointed Greiser as *Gauleiter der NSDAP im Reichsgau Wartheland* (Party leader for the Warthegau); on October 26, 1939, he became the Reichsstatthalter of the district. The twin postings gave Greiser enormous—one might even say totalitarian—power in the territory that he ruled. The entire state administration and local government, as well as all organizations, police, and some of the military, were under his authority.

In addition to Hitler's support, Greiser was in very close contact with Göring and Heinrich Himmler. It is no coincidence that Himmler appointed Greiser to the post of the Reich Commissioner for the Promotion of German Nationhood in the Warthegau, a post usually held by the Higher Commander of SS and Police (HSSPF). As a loyal Nazi, he toed the party line in exercising his authority, filling senior administrative posts with party members. The result, in the Warthegau, was an imbalance between the state administration and the party, in favor of the latter. Either way, Greiser tried to control all major decisions in his fief. A faithful executor of orders from above, he energetically began to carry out a program of expulsion of Poles and Jews from the Warthegau in order to Germanize the area totally. To succeed in this mission, however, he—like others who held posts like his—would have to replace the Poles and Jews with ethnic Germans. This program met with difficulties and led to a moratorium on deportations. Therefore, Greiser and others began to look for additional solutions; Greiser striving all the time to make sure his district would be a model one.

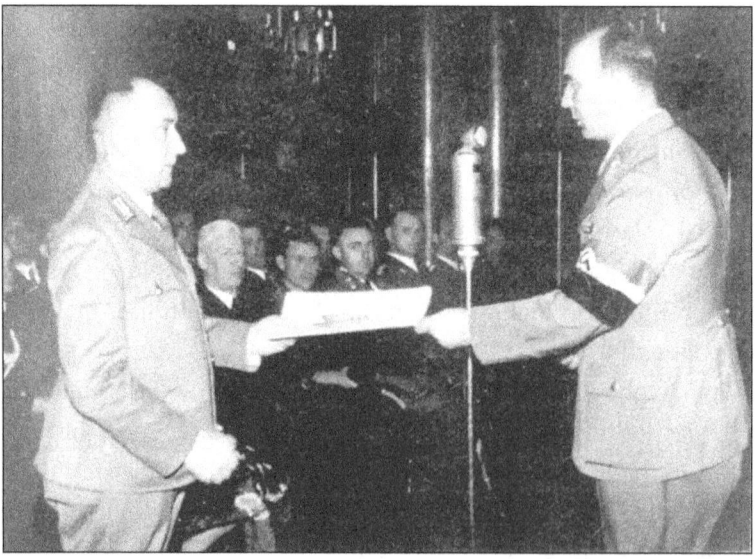

26. Arthur Greiser, Governor of the Wartheland (right) and Friedrich Übelhör (left) (YVA sig. 4949_9)

27. Arthur Greiser (second from right) and higher officials welcoming the millionth German settler in the Warthegau (YVA sig. 137BO7)

28. Poznań. German troops march with banners in front of Gauleiter Arthur Greiser (in car) on the occasion of second anniversary of the Wartheland, Oct. 1941. (NAC, sig. 2-3881)

Policy of Deportations from the Warthegau[49]

Expulsion of Jews and Poles

The conviction that it was necessary to expel the non-German population (Poles, Jews, Gypsies, and any others) and purportedly hostile and unnecessary groups (intellectuals, communists, homosexuals, tuberculosis patients, etc.) as soon as possible lay at the root of the Nazis' national policy in the Warthegau, as did its corollary, the replacement of the deportees with ethnic German settlers from various parts of Eastern Europe.

Jews were hated in the extreme; it was clear from the very onset of the Nazi occupation that their total elimination from social and economic life was a major objective. Polish residents were more tolerated, it being believed that they could be Germanized easily by being forced to sign the *Deutsche Volksliste* (DVL), a list of German nationals in occupied territories.[50] Exceptional treatment was prescribed for two kinds of Germans (*Reichsdeutsche* and *Volksdeutsche*) and those who, after special "racial" research, were deemed fit for Germanization. These people would be transported to the "Old Reich" (*Altreich*), i.e., Germany proper, for re-Germanization (*Wiedereindeutschung*). The Nazi authorities, basing their decision on "scientific" studies, believed that all individuals racially suitable for Germanization were of German origin (*Stammdeutsch*) although they might not even know it, having been Polonized. Hence the need for re-Germanization; only thus could the Nazi German Reich reclaim its lost blood.

After the annexation of Polish territories, the creation of the new district (the Reichsgau Wartheland), and the appointment of Arthur Greiser as Reich Governor, the purging of Jews and Germanization began. This policy was applied with much greater vigor in the Warthegau than in other annexed areas. It piqued the ambitions of Greiser, who sought to render his district *Judenrein* ("Jew-free") and "cleansed" of Poles as soon as possible. Those fit for Germanization under the racial criteria were to remain. This approach accorded with the official policy of the highest authorities in Berlin.

Reich Commissioner for the Consolidation of German Nationhood (RKFDV)

By decision of Hitler on October 7, 1939, Heinrich Himmler was appointed Reich Commissioner for the Consolidation of German Nationhood (*Reichskommissar für die Festigung deutschen Volkstums*—RKFDV). Hitler's decree, meant to reinforce German nationhood, created legal grounds for the displacement of the permanent population of the annexed Polish territories. It reads as follows:

According to my guidelines concerning the duty of *Reichsführer SS*, it includes:

1. Bring to the Reich those *Reichs-* and *Volksdeutsche* living abroad, which facilitated the final return to the country.
2. Eliminate the harmful effects of such foreign national groups which constitute a danger to the Reich and the German national community,
3. Create new German settlement areas through resettlement, and especially, the permanent settlement of *Reichs-*and *Volksdeutsche* returning to the country from abroad.[51]

The execution of this decree was tasked to Reichsführer SS Himmler, who delegated the job to plenipotentiaries (*Beauftragter Reichskommissars des für die deutschen Festigung Volkstums*), and more generally to Higher SS and Police Commanders (*Höhere SS und Polizeiführer*—HSSPF). On October 30, 1939, Himmler handed down his first order as the RKFDV. It was addressed to the Reich Security Main Office (Reichssicherheitshauptamt—RSHA) in Berlin and the Higher SS and Police Commanders—SS Gruppenführer Rediess in Königsberg, SS Gruppenführer von dem Bach-Zelewski in Wrocław, SS Gruppenführer Hildebrandt in Gdańsk, and SS Gruppenführer Koppe in Poznań—as Himmler's representatives in the areas where the Polish and Jewish populations were to be expelled.

Himmler also forwarded his order to SS Gruppenführer Friedrich-Wilhelm Krüger, Higher SS and Police Commander in the General Government, the area that was supposed to receive the displaced persons. The operation was to take place in November–December 1939 and January–February 1940. This marked the first wave of deportations. Of course, migrations of Poles and Jews from the Warthegau area had occurred earlier. Some civilians attempted to flee from the German troops even before the aggressors entered in 1939; others fled after the troops marched in. Some who had previously escaped returned to their homes, while others tried to move to other cities.

The November 8, 1939, Conference

On November 8, 1939, a conference was held in Kraków to discuss the deportation of Poles from the so-called Congress Poland (*Kongresspolen*) and Jews from the Old Reich (*Altreich*). The districts involved were Gdańsk, Poznań, Upper Silesia, and Eastern and Southeastern Prussia. Volksdeutsche from the Baltic countries, Volhynia, and elsewhere would settle in the vacated areas. The conference was attended by Krüger, presiding, and Hildebrandt, Koppe, von dem Bach-Zelewski, and Rediess, all as Plenipotentiaries for the Consolidation of German Nationhood. The conference was also attended by SS Brigadeführer Bruno Streckenbach, commander of the Security Police in the General Government, and Major General Becker, commander of the Order Police in the General Government.

At the conference, Krüger said, among other things:

> Wild resettlement should end as soon as possible. Countless Volksdeutsche are now returning in confusion through the Russian border. The most urgent task is to bring 25,000 Volksdeutsche from the Bug-Vistula region. By the spring, the General Government should adopt 1,000,000 Poles and Jews from the eastern and western areas of Poznań, the Gdańsk [region], Poland [probably Pomerania], and Upper Silesia. Bringing Volksdeutsche and the takeover of Poles and Jews (10,000 people every day) should take place as planned. Particularly urgent is the introduction of compulsory labor for Jews. The Jewish population should be removed as far as possible from Jewish-tenanted cities [*zażydzonych*] and employed at

road works. The question of lodging and meals for them is difficult and the problem has not yet been solved.⁵²

Streckenbach, tasked with the central planning of the displacement of the Polish population and the resettlement of Germans in the eastern territories, presented a proposal for the displacement. According to his scheme, all Jews and Poles in Congress Poland would be expelled by the end of February 1940. Poles often paid lengthy visits to the western areas for commercial purposes and sometimes for seasonal labor. Now the authorities decided to get rid of them. As for the other Poles, it was decided to conduct a study that would determine which of them were Volksdeutsche, i.e., "desirable" Poles. Only after this selection would the "unwelcome" Poles be resettled. This stage would take place in 1941.

The number of Poles and Jews to be deported by the end of February 1941 was estimated at approximately one million; the number of ethnic Germans who would enter the area as settlers was about 150,000. Thus, the displacement would also become an opportunity to carry out economic changes. With one new German settler replacing more than six displaced persons, the abandoned property—houses, apartments, etc.—would have to accommodate many fewer people, thereby improving the standard of living of those resettled. The property formerly owned by the more numerous deportees would be concentrated in the hands of the many fewer settlers. To compensate the settlers for the homes and homeland that they would leave behind, each farming household—for most of the settlers were farmers—would receive the land of several farms. Thus, as the German authorities wished, the agricultural holdings of small and large farms would be restructured. Of course, this restructuring of farmland by deportation was short-sighted and deceitful. From 1942 on, as more and more young men were inducted into the army, the Germans had to scour the General Government and the eastern territories for farm labor to replace the drafted men. Consequently, an opposite process, much different than that planned by Himmler, ensued: a growing multitude of people from the occupied areas flocked to Germany proper.

As the conference continued, the participants decided that the deported Poles and Jews would be allowed to take only a limited amount of belongings—hand luggage—and would not be permitted to bring foreign currency, precious metals, or works of art. The question of transport was worked out with the railway authorities. It was also decided that the Wehrmacht would cut off the General Government from the districts from which the population would be displaced, in order to thwart attempts by the displaced to return to their former places of residence. Notably, there was a border between the General Government and the annexed areas where travel documents were inspected and customs paid.

Adjourning their get-together in Kraków, the conferees set to attaining the goals of the Reich Commissioner for the Consolidation of German Nationhood beginning on October 30, 1939. Plenipotentiaries of the Higher SS and Police Commanders deported Poles and Jews and settled Germans in areas under their control. To do so, they issued the appropriate orders and created special offices and institutions, answering to Himmler as Reich Commissioner for the Consolidation of German Nationhood regarding all matters connected to the deportation.[53]

A few days after the conference—as early as November 12—the HSSPF in the Warthegau, Koppe, issued a secret circular concerning the resettlement of the Polish and Jewish population of this district to the General Government.[54] He wrote, *inter alia*, that by order of the Reichsführer SS and German Police Chief as Reich Commissioner for the Consolidation of German Nationhood, all Jews and all Poles who belonged to the intelligentsia or who, due to their national attitude, endangered the introduction and reinforcement of Germanism, were to be expelled from the former Polish territories and to be considered criminal elements. The purpose of the deportation, according to Koppe, was to cleanse and secure the new German territories and provide housing and income-earning opportunities for the arriving ethnic Germans. This would accelerate Germanization not only by purging the new German areas of Jews and Poles but also by increasing the German population of these areas via the introduction of Volksdeutsche. Underlined in the decree was the sentence, "Action must necessarily pursue these goals in principle, regardless of any other interests."[55] (See the full circular in Document 9, Annex 1, and another report about the resettlement in Document 10, Annex 1).

The deportation was worked out in conjunction with the Governor General, Dr. Hans Frank. Between November 15, 1939, and February 28, 1940, 200,000 Jews and 100,000 Poles were to be evicted and resettled in designated areas south of Warsaw and Lublin. The operation was intended to deport all Jews from the counties, not only the smallest districts—those with at least 2,000 Poles—but also from larger communities. In turn, the larger cities were obliged to deliver the following numbers of deportees: from Poznań: about 35,000 Poles and all Jews; from Łódź: about 30,000 Poles and approximately 30,000 Jews of Gniezno plus 2,300 Poles; and all Jews from Inowrocław.[56]

Koppe felt that preparations for the operation should begin at once. Thus, he issued his order on November 12, 1939—four days after the conference—and the operation was to begin on November 15. With so many more Poles and Jews designated for deportation than Volksdeutsche designated to be brought in from the Baltic countries, the General Government, and Volhynia, the police would have to protect property left behind, among their other duties. Koppe also said:

29. Poles being led to trains under German army escort as part of the Nazi German ethnic cleansing ("resettlement") of western Poland (the Wartheland), annexed to the Reich immediately after the 1939 invasion (Bundesarchiv R49 Bild-0131)

30. Expulsion of Poles from territories annexed to the Reich (1939–1943) (NAC, sign. 37-270-3)

31–32. Jewish property in the street after the deportation (YVA, sig. 3774_16; 3774_18)

Purification and securing of the territory will be achieved, with all the consequences, only when you remove the leading cultural stratum, all intellectuals, and all political and criminal elements. You shall also deport all individuals who willfully feel Polish. In the case of the intelligentsia, there is no need to establish evidence of political activity or hostility towards Germany. In addition, in

33. Deportation of Jews from Kutno. In the middle, in uniform: gendarmerie functionaries. On the right: German police (YVA, sig. 2do8)

every respect, it shall be done from the standpoint of creating residential opportunities and facilitating work for incoming Reichsdeutsche and Volksdeutsche. When determining if individuals or groups of people are politically dangerous, you shall consider all the attributed positions at stake—among other things, membership in Polish national groups. Political parties of all platforms, political associations of Catholic clergy and laity, etc., shall be purged.[57]

Since the purpose of the deportation was not only to free up housing but also to provide places of employment for ethnic Germans, a sufficient number of craft workshops and shops had to be liberated during the operation. One may assume that principles such as profession and wealth were applied, in addition to the political criteria and the elimination of criminal elements. Those who had larger and better housing, workshops, and shops appeared at the top of the list of deportees because their properties were more important to appropriate. Furthermore, "Blue-collar workers, petty officials, and employees who cannot be regarded as national-minded Poles or have not been punished for criminal offenses are excluded from the evacuation because they are needed as a labor force."[58]

Only six days remained (until November 18, 1939) to prepare a list of designated deportees for the *Ladräte* (county councilors), as per Koppe's order. That day, the Ladräte were to indicate the number of people suitable for deportation from their jurisdictions.

Building Capacity and Infrastructure for Successful Implementation of the Deportation Policy

The deportation from the Warthegau was led by Himmler as Reich Commissioner for the Consolidation of German Nationhood. Himmler did not appoint anyone in particular to do the work. As Reichsführer SS and German police chief, he relied on the proven worthiness of his secret security police apparatus, headed by a man who discharged various duties and had an ancillary structure with which to do so: Chief of Security Police and Security Service Reinhard Heydrich. The overall process of deportation and its preparations was directed by Department IV of the RSHA. Since the implementation was more complicated than had been expected, however, the department's normal modus operandi did not suffice. Therefore, after procedural meetings on December 19, 1939, it was found necessary to place someone in charge of "central proceeding of issues concerning security and police during the evacuation to the eastern territories." The people whom Heydrich appointed as his special aides for these matters were SS Hauptsturmführer Adolf Eichmann of Department IV and Eichmann's deputy, SS Hauptsturmführer Rolf Günther.[59]

A new *Referat* (specialist unit) was established at Kurfürstenstrasse 115/116 in Berlin. All correspondence concerning this department was to be sent not to this address but to RSHA Department IV (Amt IV) at Prinz Albrechtstrasse 8 in Berlin. Indeed, messages from this period were directed mainly to that address with the note "Attn. SS Hauptsturmführer Eichmann." Soon enough, Eichmann's Referat grew to office size and was designated RSHA IV D4. Following the reorganization of the office in 1941, it was redesignated IV B4.

By order of Heydrich on November 28, 1939, the deportation operation was to be carried out by the police apparatus, specifically the

Security Police and SD. Therefore, direct action and supervision of its course resided with Security Police Inspectors (IdS) who answered to the HSSPF. Special cells dedicated to the eviction action were set up at HSSPF headquarters in the districts. Initially, these cells were called "Special Affairs Staff for Deportation of Poles and Jews" (*Sonderstab Aussiedlung für die Juden und der Polen*). Subsequently they were renamed several times: first to "Office of Deportations of Poles and Jews" (*Amt für Polen und Aussiedlung von Juden*), then in late March 1940 to the "Resettlement Office" (*Umwanderungsstelle*), and then again to "Resettlement Central Office" (*Umwandererzentralstelle*)—under which title the office operated until it was liquidated.

A central office was established at HSSPF administrative headquarters, more specifically at the bureau of the inspector of Security Police and SD. This official later created outposts (*Aussenstelle*) in smaller centers. Each such outpost covered most of its jurisdiction (city or county) and prepared for resettlement activity there. German authorities believed that the largest number of people would be displaced from the Warthegau. In the other incorporated territories, especially Silesia and the so-called Western Prussia, most local people were fit for Germanization due to being "of German origin." This, however, did not apply to the Jews in these areas, all of whom would be expelled.

The technical preparations for the deportations included the issue of eviction notices, the keeping of records, and the construction of transit camps in conjunction with the railroad authorities.

As the deportation proceeded, efforts to improve its efficiency were made. At a conference at RSHA headquarters in Berlin on January 8, 1941, on the resettlement of Poles and Jews to the General Government from the lands annexed to the Reich, decisions were made to improve the coordination of transports to the General Government. According to the minutes of the conference, the organizers of the deportations

> promised to send transports according to a timetable on which the General Government authorities will be able to rely. The system of notification about the next transports, previously agreed upon with all details provided by the institutions of the Reich Security Main Office and the Eastern Railway (*Ostbahn*), will each time

advise the government of the General Government (Department of Home Affairs) of the arrival of another train in time, so that there will be enough time to make necessary preparations.[60]

In a memorandum prepared by Dr. E. Wetzel and G. Hecht of the NSDAP racial policy board in Berlin on the treatment of the occupied Polish population, dated November 25, 1939, the following clarification appears: "Jews—born or converted—shall be strictly and quickly deported from Poland irrespective of any of their claims."[61] Such a position was not new; it resulted from Nazi ideology. In the 1930s, the Nazis had sought to force German Jews to emigrate. This plan, however, had encountered considerable difficulties due to the refusal of many countries to accept refugees from Germany. The occupation of Poland changed the situation in this respect: now it was possible to expel Jews from Germany to "Polish territory," i.e., the General Government. According to the principles of Nazism, "[...] Only Germans have the right to Reich citizenship. All others are not entitled to Reich citizenship and, thus, have no political rights."[62]

Only Germans (Reichsdeutsche and Volksdeutsche) were to remain in the Warthegau. Those who, after a special "racial" investigation, would be considered suitable for Germanization woujld be spared from deportation from the Warthegau but would be taken to the Altreich for re-Germanization (*Wiedereindeutschung*). According to the Nazi authorities, all individuals who were racially suitable for Germanization—i.e., had German or Germanic features—were of German origin (*Stammdeutsch*) but might not be aware of it due to protracted Polonization. The Warthegau was ethnically diverse; given the high rate of ethnic intermarriage, national conscience or affiliation often traced to identification rather than biological characteristics. Such people, according to the Nazis, should be re-Germanized in order to restore lost blood to the German Reich.

The displacement of local Poles and Jews was apparently perpetrated on racial grounds alone, although demographic and economic factors were also important. From 1939 on, Himmler began a wide-ranging policy of transfer of German population, mainly from Soviet territories or other occupied areas. Volksdeutsche from the Baltic countries and Volhynia (Wołyń) were designated for resettlement in the Warthegau, where they

The First Occupation Years: "Resettlement" and Deportation | 159

34. Resettlement of Baltic Germans, column of trucks with displaced belongings, November 1939 (NAC, sign. 2-5731)

35. Plaszów, Kraków: resettlement of ethnic Germans (1939–1940). Reichsführer Heinrich Himmler (first on left) greets the displaced. One of the officers around him is Arthur Seyss-Inquart (second from left) (NAC, sign. 2-5750)

36. Resettlement of Volksdeutsche (ethnic Germans), 1940, column of carts of the displaced with their belongings on snowy road near Przemysl (NAC, sign. 2-5754)

37. Resettlement of Volksdeutsche (ethnic Germans), January 1940, displaced trucks loaded on railway wagons. Fig. Girwert (NAC, sign. 2-5757)

would be housed in properties once owned by deported Poles and Jews. Importantly, since deportees were allowed to take nothing but one small piece of hand luggage, not only population but also, and above all, property was exchanged in the operation, with Germans on the receiving end.

Organizing the Warthegau Administration[63]

The next orders were issued by Arthur Greiser, Reich Governor of the Wartheland, and by governors of smaller administrative units such as the Regierunsbezirk (president), the county (Landrat), selected towns (Oberbürgermeister), and village municipalities (commissioners). Greiser, in a speech titled "Judenpolitik" (Jewish policy) delivered in 1940, stated that the most important reason to concentrate Jews in the Łódź ghetto was to exploit them maximally by employing them in departments connected with the garment industry. His speech implies that those who did not work were to be exterminated, although he did not say this in so many words.[64] One quote that may reflect such an intent is: "[...] In the Łódź ghetto in the Warthegau, Jewish labor is exploited. Jews able to work live in the ghetto; they work in a three-shift system in the garment industry. I don't need to say what is going to happen with those Jews who do not work (that is, women, children, old people, the sick) [...]." Statements like these would be used by people such as Friedrich Übelhör, president of the Kalisz Regierungsbezirk, to make the final decision on the terms and method of purging Łódź of its Jews. Übelhör disclosed his decision in a secret circular of December 10, 1939: "[...] The final goal is to completely burn down the plague brotherhood...."[65]

The next level of regulations that sanctioned the extermination policy was created by the district central authorities and presidents and the governors of the Regierunsbezirke. In Inowrocław Regierunsbezirk, the following were governors: Hans Burckhardt (1939/1940–1944), William Pickel (1944), and Karl Wilhelm Albert (1944–1945); in Bydgoszcz Regierunsbezirk they were Günther Palten (1939–1940), Hans Kurt Schimmel (1940–1942), and Walter Kühn (1942–1945). They and their deputies, as well as the Landräte (plural of Landrat), Burgermeisters, Oberburgermeisters, and the elaborate German police, security, and army apparatuses in the area of the Regierunsbezirk, would be responsible for the extermination of Jews.[66]

Police Organization in the Warthegau[67]

The police and SS in the Warthegau played a special role in the persecution of the Jews from the very beginning of the German occupation of Poland—a particular function that invested their assignment with exceptional importance. Security police outposts were occupied by Einsatzgruppen (paramilitary units) that served in Poland from the first days of the occupation. Their task was to provide security at the rear of the fighting troops and to liquidate political opponents of the administration. After the Einsatzgruppen were dissolved, these tasks were assigned to the Security Police and SD outposts. In most cases, quondam officers in the Einsatzgruppen headed the newly created Sipo and SD institutions. Two Sipo and SD centers, those in Poznań and Łódź, were particularly important.

The internal structure of the state police (*Staatspolizei*, abbreviated as Stapo) was the same everywhere; its departmental structure mirrored that of the RSHA: I—Personnel Department, II—Administration and Law, III—Inland-*SD*, Department of Counterintelligence of the Security Service (*Sicherheistdienst*), IV—Secret State Police (*Geheime Staatspolizei*, the Gestapo), and V—Criminal Police (*Kriminalpolizei*, Kripo). There were also a Department VI—Foreign Intelligence—and a Department VII, the Ideological Department, which were not relevant at local levels of the RSHA. For the purposes of our discussion, one of the most important departments was IV, the Gestapo, within which Desk IV B4 (previously designated as II B4) dealt with Jews.

The police structure in the Warthegau stemmed partly from the transformation of Einsatzgruppe IV, which had operated in Poznań. SS Brigadeführer Lothar Beutel was Commander of EG IV. On November 23, 1939, SS Obersturmbannführer Josef Meisinger replaced him. EG IV, designed to function within the operational area of the Fourth Army, included two Einsatzkommandos (mobile squads): Einsatzkommando 1/IV, commanded by SS Obersturmbannführer Helmut Bischoff, and Einsatzkommando 2/IV, commanded by SS Sturmbannführer Regierungsrat Walter Hammer.

The Senior SS and Police Leader (HSSPF) in the Warthegau was SS Gruppenführer Wilhelm Koppe. The Security Police and Security Service Inspector (*Inspekteur der Sicherheitspolizei und des SD*—IdS) was Standartenführer Ernst Damzog. The commander of the Order Police in the Warthegau was SS Brigadeführer Oscar Knofe. A key personality at central police command in Poznań was SS Sturmbannführer Rolf Heinz Höppner, commander of the Security Service in Poznań (*der Führer des SD-Leitabschnitts Posen*), head of the District Office for National Affairs (*der für Gauamts Volkstumsfragen*), and head of the Migration Office (*Umwanderer Zentralstelle*, UWZ).

The Sipo and SD outpost in Łódź was established by the officers of the dissolved Einsatzgruppe III under the command of Hans Fischer and Einsatzkommando 2 commander Fritz Liphardt. Einsatzgruppe III, created on the eve of the invasion of Poland and headquartered in Wrocław (Breslau), was tasked with following the Eighth Army and acting within its operational area. After the dissolution of the operational groups, Einsatzkommando 1, part of Einsatzgruppe IV, which operated in the area of Poznań, also came to Łódź and established a Stapo outpost in Kalisz Regierungsbezirk.

In Łódź, the EK 1/III unit remained under Liphardt's command; it is from this unit that the Stapo of Łódź was created. The first head of the Stapo in Kalisz was the commander of EK 1/IV, Sturmbannführer Gerhard Flesch. In late 1939, Flesch was dismissed and replaced by Hauptsturmführer Dr. Robert Schefe. In 1942, Sturmbannführer Herbert Weygandt was temporarily appointed in his stead. After Weygandt's dismissal the same year, SS Sturmbannführer Dr. Otto Bradfisch became the head of Stapo in Łódź. Bradfisch had previously served in Mogilev, part of the German-occupied area in the east, where he had commanded Einsatzkommando 8 of Einsatzgruppe B. As commander of EK 8/B, he had been significantly involved in the murder of Jews. The unit he commanded from June to November 1941 had killed 28,219 people. Now, as commander of Stapo Łódź, Bradfisch was responsible for the Jews of Łódź. In addition to being chief of police in Łódź, he was also appointed representative mayor of Łódź in the autumn of 1943. Thus he possessed total police and civil power.

The Stapo outpost in Łódź, with more than 200 officials in early 1940, was divided into local outposts in Kalisz, Łęczyca, Sieradz, a border police commissariate in Wieluń, and a border police station in Łódź. In November 1940, its operational area was expanded to include Inowrocław.[68]

Nazi Legislation Concerning Jews in the Warthegau

Construction of the legal infrastructure began in late 1939 with the phased introduction of restrictions against Jews.[69] One of the first regulations in this process of gradual isolation was a ban on using sidewalks. The official who first introduced this rule was the Oberburgermeister of Włocławek, Hans Kramer, on September 29, 1939. Another new regulation specified the compulsory wearing of an identifying mark. In Włocławek, this regulation was issued on October 25, 1939. At first, Jews in Włocławek county had to sew yellow triangles on their backs at shoulder height and on their chests, with sides no shorter than 15 cm.[70] In 1940, the rule was changed; the Jews replaced the patches with a Star of David in a visible place.[71] In Nieszawa (Ciechocinek) county, a white Star of David patch with the inscription *Jude* was introduced.[72] Other methods appeared elsewhere, such as yellow stars on the chest and back, sometimes of considerable size (as in Aleksandrów Kujawski). In Włocławek, on November 11, 1939, the obligation to acknowledge all uniformed NSDAP members, soldiers, and police by removing caps or hats was imposed on Poles and Jews alike, on pain of a fine and, if the fine was unpaid, imprisonment.[73] Several residential restrictions were applied. By the late autumn of 1939, the right to change one's place of residence was limited, and essentially a Jew could not move to a new place of residence at all. Curfews were imposed, of hours that grew increasingly restrictive. At first they were from 8:00 p.m. to 5:00 a.m. for Jews and from 10:00 p.m. to 4:00 a.m. for Poles. Then in September, curfew for Jews was from 7:00 p.m. to 6:00 a.m.; in October from 6:00 p.m. to 6:00 a.m.; and in November and December from 5:00 p.m. to 6:00 a.m. For Poles, it was from 7:00 p.m. to 5:00 a.m.[74] Over time, Jews were banned from most public places (cinemas, parks, beaches, etc.) and the most elegant streets. Gradually, contact between Jewish and Polish citizens was restricted in administrative and non-administrative ways. By the time ghettos were established, all contact was forbidden.[75]

The purpose of this isolation was to exclude Jews from legal protection. Jews were classified as stateless and as such were subject to any repressive legislation. A decree on December 4, 1939, concerning penal procedure against Polish Jews in territories incorporated into the Third Reich imposed extremely severe penalties, including death, even for petty offences. Every penalty was to be immediately executed. In the months that followed, Jewish citizens were, for all intents and purposes, outlaws.[76] The court and penitentiary systems were completed with the establishment of labor camps for Jews.

4. EXPULSIONS OF JEWS AND POLES FROM REICHSGAU WARTHELAND

First Displacements, September 1939

In practice, the regulations concerning the solution of the "Jewish problem" in Inowrocław Regierungsbezirk and the Warthegau went into effect only when Wehrmacht forces arrived. Although the regulations were characterized by direct extermination actions, their scale was limited in comparison with the 1941–1942 standards. They were carried out in places where the number of Jewish inhabitants was quite small and their goal was to terrorize and induce emigration. Until November 1939, the German authorities did not impede voluntary changes of residence in counties that had large Jewish concentrations. They even considered such migrations desirable, and provoked Jews and forced them to leave their hometowns, e.g., in Ciechocinek or Radziejów (about 50 kilometers from Kleczew). "Wild" displacements (unauthorized and unorganized expulsions of Jews by low-ranking district officials with the intention of seizing their property) also took place.[77] Simultaneously, organized displacements were being prepared.

Evictions began in September 1939. Jews in Posen Regierungsbezirk and, to some extent, in Inowrocław Regierungsbezirk (Żnin, Szubin, and Mogilno counties) were concentrated on September 7, 1939, in Buk, Nowy Tomyśl County. A month later, they were transported to the Młyniewo transit camp near Grodzisk Poznański and thence to Szymanów in Sochaczew County in the General Government. Announcements ordering Jews to leave town were made in Pakość in October 1939 and in Inowrocław on October 20 and November 14, 1939. On October 20, 1939, women and children were transported from the latter location to Gniezno. Another transport, on November 14, 1939, delivered several people to Gniezno and Kruszwica. In late November and early December 1939, sixty-five Jews from Gniezno, forty-seven of whom had been brought to Gniezno from Inowrocław, and twenty Jews from Klecko, near Gniezno, were transported to Piotrków Trybunalski. The transport reached this destination on December 13, 1939, after almost two weeks en route. Ten people from Czerniejewo (Gniezno County) were sent to Łódź on November 10, 1939. In December 1939, a group of Jews from Szubin reached Gorzków. In February 1940, Jews from Gniezno and Gniezno County found themselves in Pruszków, near Warsaw.[78]

Displacements in Lublin

The counties in the western part of Inowrocław Regierungsbezirk (Gniezno, Inowrocław, Mogilno, Szubin, Wągrowiec, and Żnin) and Ostrów and Kępno counties in Kalisz Regierungsbezirk were "liberated" of Jews by December 1939. Operations for this purpose continued in some parts of the Posen Regierungsbezirk counties and in the central and eastern part of the Inowrocław Regierungsbezirk. To organize and carry out displacements in Nieszawa, Włocławek, Koło, Konin, Kutno, and Gostyń counties, more resources had to be engaged. Demography and socio-topography were decisive factors. Many towns had Jewish populations in the thousands (e.g., 13,000 in Włocławek, 6,800–6,900 in Kutno, 4,200 in Łęczyca, 9,400 in Zduńska Wola, 2,800 in Sieradz, and 4,500–4,600 in Koło).[79] Local authorities adjusted their policies to the central authorities' changing regulations. Initially there was no exact plan regarding what to do with the Jewish population. In September 1939, the intention was to deport all Jews from Polish areas incorporated into the Third Reich and from the Altreich to territory in southeastern

Poland; afterwards, they were to be expelled across the demarcation line into the Soviet Union. In reality, this proved impossible. The next plan was to enclose all Jews in an enclave in the southeastern part of the General Government, between the Vistula and Bug rivers. The Lublin vicinity was chosen as a preliminary location. Ultimately, a decision was made to concentrate the Jews in an enclave or transit camp in Nisko, situated in the District of Lublin. Implementation of this scheme began in November 1939 but was suspended in February 1940. By then, many people had been forced to leave their homes and had been shunted from place to place, subjected to hunger, and sentenced to a slow death.

The authorities in Inowrocław Regierungsbezirk implemented the plan in November 1939. Jewish communities were ordered to force Jewish landlords to draw up lists of their Jewish tenants. Non-Jewish landlords who had Jewish tenants were instructed to do the same. After the data were collected, a list of eviction designees was produced. The first to go were the poor. Ahead of the eviction, Jews were assembled at gathering points—mainly workshops, warehouses, schools, churches, and synagogues. A procedure laid down on November 24, 1939, determined that each transport of Jews had to be loaded in alphabetical order twenty-four hours before departure.[80] Transports often set out at night. The methods used in the displacement resulted in many casualties, as people were beaten, packed into unheated carriages for hours or even days, and denied food and water.[81]

The first mass displacements, from Włocławek, Konin, and Koło counties, ensued in December 1939. Two transports from Włocławek, with 500–550 people in each, were sent to Ożarów (December 1, 1939). In Konin, a group of 1,080–1,200 Jews was taken to the gathering points. On the night of November 30 to December 1, they were trucked to the railway station. On December 3, they reached Ostrowiec Świętokrzyski. Jews from Golina were also taken there. Some of those displaced from Konin found themselves in Turobin and Gorzków. Jews from Słupca and Skulsk were also taken to Gorzków. On December 10, 1939, 1,139 Jews from Koło were transported to Izbica Lubelska. Some of the newcomers were sent on to nearby towns and villages: 175 to Zamość and sixty-two to Krasnystaw, Turobin, Komarów, and Hrubieszów. On December 15, 1939, a transport from Włocławek and Włocławek County (Kowal and Lubień Kujawski) was directed to Zamość and Włoszczowa. Some people were sent to Wiskitki, Szczekociny, Tarnogród, Komarów, and Szczebrzeszyn. Jews from Ciechocinek County, mainly from Aleksandrów Kujawski, were displaced in December 1939. They found themselves in Sokołów Podlaski, Sokołów Małopolski, Grodzisk Mazowiecki, and Zamość. More displacements took place in February 1940. A transport from Włocławek and nearby towns was sent to Tarnów. Other groups from Nieszawa, Włocławek, and Koło counties were sent to locations in Masovia and Lesser Poland, in the General Government (Radom, Warszawa, and, in individual cases, Kraków). For example, Jews from Kowal and Lubień (Włocławek County) were sent to Żyrardów, Łyszkowice, Skierniewice, and Błonie. Jews from Włocławek were transported to Warsaw, Pruszków, Siedlce, Skierniewice, Piszczac (near Biała Podlaska), Grójec, Góra Kalwaria, Kozienice, and Limanowa. Jews from Aleksandrów Kujawski and Ciechocinek (Nieszawa County) found themselves in: Łyszkowice, Siedlce, and Grójec. It is interesting to note in passing that Jews in Gostyń and Kutno Counties were not displaced, even though the Jewish communities in the relevant towns were rather large.[82] Jews from Kalisz County (Łódz Regierungsbezirk), mainly from Kalisz, Koźminek, and Stawiszyn, were displaced.[83] Jews relocated from the territories of Reichsgau Danzig, Western Prussia, reached towns in Inowrocław Regierungsbezirk, mainly in Włocławek, Ciechocinek, and Kutno counties. In November and December 1939, Jews from Lipno, Dobrzyń on the Wisła, Lubicz, Kikół, and Toruń were banished to Włocławek and Aleksandrów Kujawski.[84]

On December 8, 1939, department heads at the office of the General Governor convened to discuss resettlement and Jewish policy. At the gathering, HSSPF SS Obergruppenführer Krüger, representing the German police in the General Government in Kraków, stated:

> From December 1, several trains carrying Poles and Jews from the areas recently annexed to the Reich will reach the General Government daily. These transfers will pour in until the middle of December. In Berlin, work on a central resettlement plan continues; on its basis the heads of districts will be

able to work to the longer term. This plan will determine how many Poles and Jews will have to be resettled in 1940. From mid-December, transports of Germans of Volhynia will come; they will be passing through the General Government area.[85]

The January 4, 1940, Conference

On January 4, 1940, Eichmann called a conference in Berlin to discuss further population displacements from the eastern areas. The discussants mulled a problem: more transports of displaced persons were reaching the General Government than had been planned. The General Government, beset with its own economic problems, was unprepared to receive them. The issue, however, went beyond the impossibility of deploying the displaced to different locations. Often lacking was elementary coordination between those responsible for deporting people and those responsible for receiving them. Sometimes the evictees spent eight days in sealed wagons. People froze in unheated trains, starved to death, or became ill due to exhaustion and unclean surroundings. Therefore, to improve the RSHA's performance in this matter, Eichmann decided to allocate Security and SD Inspectors—one assistant and one officer to each location—to carry out orders.

At first, the authorities allocated enough food for the transportees for two days. Given the organizational problems that prolonged travel and the food shortages in the General Government, however, the authorities later allowed, and still later even ordered, the displaced to take food with them. The destination, the General Government, was unable to provide the new arrivals with even minimal nourishment, especially in the first few days. In particular, local authorities in cities that received evacuation transports had no provisions for them. The General Government authorities threatened not to accept displaced people unless they were supplied with enough food for eight days and, subsequently, required that they have enough food for fourteen days; otherwise, they would send the transports back. These authorities repeatedly cited "the bad food situation in the General Government" and stated that it would not improve until the next harvest. Thus, the Reich would have to continue providing assistance. Reich Minister Seyss Inquart asked SS Gruppenführer Heydrich to support him on this. SS Brigadeführer Otto Wächter sought assurances regarding an adequate supply of food for evacuees arriving from areas where the food situation was generally better than it was in the General Government.[86]

The First Short-Term Plan (Der erste Nahplan): Discussion in January 1940

In his report on January 26, 1940, the Higher SS and Police Commander in the Warthegau wrote about the resettlement of Poles and Jews from the Warthegau to the General Government, thus summing up the first short-term plan.[87] According to the report, on November 28, 1939, an order requiring transportation to the General Government had been obtained for the period starting December 16, 1939, for 80,000 Poles and Jews. According to the author of the report,

The separation of quotas was based on studies of the population structure and the planned emigration of Germans from Baltic countries. In principle, at least one train of up to 1000 people was allocated for each rural county. For larger counties and cities or those that had a larger number of Jewish residents, a more appropriate assignment of trains was allocated.[88]

Within two days of the onset of the first short-term plan, eleven trains were made available for eight counties. Given the rapidly progressing operation and the transport difficulties, communication with Landräte and Oberbürgermeisters in the Warthegau, Higher SS and Police Commander, and, eventually, the Security Police and SD Commander and heads of districts or SS and police commanders in the General Government was made only by telephone and telegraph. Notably, the operation began only about six weeks after the end of military operations in Poland. Communication difficulties still prevailed and the Warthegau and the General Government were organized in diverse administrative units, further complicating matters. Thus, transports from the Warthegau set out and reached their destinations without proper coordination or notice of arrival. Although all offices involved in the deportation were constantly kept informed by daily reports to the RSHA, in practice there was much chaos.

Before beginning the ethnic cleansing of the Warthegau, Special Staff SS officers carried out inspections in many places to observe the state of preparations for deportation under the first short-term plan (*der erste Nahplan*). Although the preparations did not suffice for the start of displacements in November 1939, in some localities the authorities began to evict Poles from their homes and send them to transit camps (*Durchgangslager*) anyway.

The General Government principals convened again in Berlin on January 30, 1940, to discuss developments in the forced resettlement of the Polish and Jewish population from the Warthegau to the General Government. "The evacuations carried out up to now," their report stated, "have consisted of approximately 87,000 Poles and Jews from the Warthegau in order to make room for the Baltic Germans, who are to be settled there. In addition, there has been a spontaneous, so-called illegal, emigration."[89] Only in part was this illegal migration a willful flow to the General Government. In many cases, it constituted a forceful expulsion of Poles and Jews and was outside the official deportation statistics and plans. This confirms an observation made by Heydrich at the conference:

> SS Gruppenführer Heydrich noted that no objections in principle were raised against the evacuation in the direction of the General Government by the competent authorities of the General Government. The objections raised up to now had only been directed against the fact that in the earlier evacuations the figures originally set had been exceeded, and not kept.[90]

For a lengthy citation of remarks by Heydrich and General Government HSSPF Krüger at this conference, see Document 11 in Annex 1.

Difficulties and Challenges in Implementing the Deportation

Despite the overwhelming desire of Warthegau authorities to deport as many Poles and Jews as possible, the General Government authorities that were intended to receive the deportees encountered numerous difficulties and therefore sought to limit the influx. In the aforementioned conference, Obergruppenführer Krüger stated,

> [...] Fairly considerable training areas would have to be prepared in the Government-General for the Wehrmacht, Luftwaffe, and SS, which necessitate the relocation of about 100,000–120,000 people within the Government-General itself. It was therefore desirable to take this fact into account during the evacuations in the direction of the Government-General in order to avoid double resettlement.[91]

The problem was not only in transporting deportees to the General Government but also in dispersing them in densely populated areas that suffered from chronic scarcities of housing and food. To assist the reader in understanding the kinds of difficulties experienced in the field, part of a report from the *Kreishauptmann* of Krasnystaw about the establishment of Jewish quarters (ghettos) follows. First of all, much empty space was needed to receive so many deportees who had been so quickly evicted, and the Warthegau did not have it:

> The ordinance once published forbidding Jews to move freely should be used also against the Poles. The housing shortage in cities caused by transports of displaced Poles from the Warthegau has made itself felt in a very unpleasant way. Besides, there is also increase in demand from the German army and the German administration. A relevant Labor Office has already sent a report to the head of the Labor Department in Lublin District. I tried to avoid housing shortages by removing the Jews from the city center and creating a ghetto. However, Jewish homes are in such poor condition that large sums of money are needed for their minimal renovation. For Germans, these houses, naturally, are out of the question.[92]

The maintenance of the deportees could not rely on financial resources from the General Government budget; the deportees were to earn their livelihood from their own labor. This was obviously quite theoretical because such an outcome, based on ideological decisions, was altogether unrealistic. Five months into the war, the economic situation remained dire due to overcrowding caused by war-inflicted devastation, new administrative divisions, and the separation of the General Government from other areas by means that included the Reich customs border. The rupture of ties between manufacturing venues and export markets made things worse, as did widespread looting, rampant unemployment, and the masses of displaced persons who were exhausting the strained supplies. Under these circumstances, it was difficult to find suitable jobs for the deportees. The only reasonable solution seemed to be public works:

> Gruppenführer Heydrich observed in this connection that the building of the [defensive] ramparts and other plans in the East

would probably generate the concentration of several hundred thousand Jews in forced-labor camps. Their families would be dispersed among Jewish families already living in the General Government, which would solve the problem [...].⁹³

Housing and employment problems aside, nutrition posed multiple challenges. The conferees in Berlin on January 30, 1940, considered this as well:

> The poor food situation in the Government-General would not improve before the next harvest. This would make it necessary for the Reich to continue its subventions. Reich Minister Seyss Inquart requested SS Gruppenführer Heydrich to support him on this issue if it should become necessary to obtain further food subventions for the Government-General.[...] SS Brigadeführer Wächter requested that the evacuees, who came from areas where the food situation was considerably better than in the Government-General, should be provided with the appropriate foodstuffs."⁹⁴

Since the deportees would be coming from areas incorporated into the Reich, where the food situation was better, improving their food supplies would make things better only temporarily—there would still not be as much food available as there had been in their places of origin.

As for the resettlement of Poles,

> General Field Marshal [Göring] expressed the view that it is not far from a priority task, because the Poles are needed in rural areas as agricultural laborers, cultivating their land. If, for example, we would expel Poles from the Warthegau, who amount to only a small percentage of Germans [this presumably refers to the Volksdeutsche], who then would cultivate the land there? [...] As for the resettlement of Jews, General Field Marshal was of the opinion that this action should be carried out according to plan.⁹⁵

After the Germanization of the Warthegau, Western Prussia, Prussia, and Southeastern Upper Silesia, and the repatriation of Germans, long-term Germanization would be carried out in the General Government.⁹⁶

Mulling Madagascar, July 1940

In 1940, Jews in smaller ghettos were transferred to a central ghetto that had been established in Łódź for the ultimate purpose of shipping them to Madagascar. The possibility of resettling Jews in Madagascar was discussed extensively at a conference held on July 31, 1940, in Kraków, focusing on a common policy towards the Jewish and Polish population, attended by Arthur Greiser (Reich Governor of the Wartheland) and senior General Government and Warthegau officials.

Greiser found this possibility especially intriguing. During the conference, he said:

> Above all, the Jewish question should be considered. In this area, in the meantime, changes have occurred. There is now a different view on the question of the evacuation of the Jews. During a conversation with the Reichsführer SS the speaker, [I] learned of the intention to deport Jews to territories overseas. In this consultation, [I] said that [I am] forced to and wish to comply with this decision, but the Jewish problem—at least when it comes to Warthegau interests—must be resolved one way or another before the winter. It all depends, of course, on how long the war will continue. If it drags on, then one will need to find a temporary solution.⁹⁷

Despite the existence of the first short-term plan, which envisaged the deportation of hundreds of thousands of Poles and Jews from the Warthegau to the General Government, and despite the actual transportation of more than 87,000 people during the term of this plan, Greiser's dream of ridding the Warthegau of all Jews proved illusory. Although thousands of Jews had been deported from many counties, large concentrations remained, mainly in Łódź and the surrounding villages. Greiser mentioned this and expanded on it at the conference:

[...] A considerable number of Jews is concentrated in Łódź and its surroundings. In the city of Łódź, a ghetto for Jews has been set up. This operation is now virtually complete but is only temporary. There are about 250,000 Jews in the ghetto. These Jews, whose numbers could yet grow to 260,000, should leave the Warthegau in the future. [...] The plan was to transport them—based on some rational plans—to the General Government. Today's meeting was called, among other things, to establish rules for the reception of the Jews. In the meantime, the decision has been changed. Therefore, the speakers are very interested in the possibilities of the direction of their reception, as the Warthegau is in no way able to withstand these Jews, who have been crammed into the ghetto, even through this winter. This is because of both the food provisions policy and the danger of epidemic. If so, we must find a temporary solution that will allow these Jews to be taken elsewhere.[98]

The change of direction alluded to by Greiser was the plan to transport the Jews from the General Government to Madagascar. The purpose of this plan, like that concerning the forced emigration of Jews from Germany and Austria, was to render the Reich-occupied areas Judenrein. As Germany annexed more land, however, the population of Jews under German rule was growing. German Jewry, about 520,000 strong in 1933, had swelled by several hundred thousand after the annexation of Austria and the Sudetenland and the establishment of the Protectorate of Bohemia and Moravia; Jewish emigration from these areas did not reduce their numbers much. Furthermore, the conquest of Poland in 1939 increased the number of Jews in the German-occupied areas in a very significant way. For these reasons, solving the Jewish problem by emigration became impossible. Expulsion to the east was out of the question, because the Soviet authorities were disinclined to accept these Jews. In September and October 1939 the Germans attempted to exploit the chaotic situation in Poland to expel Jews from the Polish south to areas on the Soviet side of the demarcation line. Particularly active in this area was an Einsatzgruppe under the command of Udo von Woyrsch.[99] Several weeks after the end of the hostilities in Poland, however, the Soviet authorities sealed the border against the continued arrival of Jews from the German-occupied territories.

The "Jewish problem" was in fact a product of the racist Nazi ideology. Due to pressure from fanatical Nazis, including Himmler, it ballooned into one of the most urgent problems for Nazi Germany to solve. The displacement of hundreds of thousands of people without adequate preparation created a logistical quagmire that made the "Jewish problem" all the more acute. Extremist Nazi leaders such as Greiser, eager to show their zeal and achievements not only by promoting Germanization in their fiefdoms but also by "cleansing" them of Jews, further aggravated this predicament. Obviously the violent displacement of hundreds of thousands of people from their homes, businesses, and workshops could not but create an economic imbalance because it would transform the displaced into dependents. The fanatical leaders, however, craving for success at others' expense, did not consider the economic and social costs that would have to be borne. To deflect attention from such matters, they cynically used various arguments such as the threat of epidemics, food shortages, and a desire to extend Germanness to the areas that the Reich had annexed.

Gruppenführer Koppe, Higher SS and Police Commander in the Warthegau, said:

> [The] situation in the Warthegau regarding the Jewish question is deteriorating from day to day. The ghetto in Łódź was organized properly only on the condition that the shipping of Jews would begin by mid-year. Besides, the speaker [Greiser] emphasizes the renaming by the Führer of the former Łódź to Litzmannstadt, given that the city is conclusively, definitely, must, and will belong to the Warthegau.[100]

Koppe, still presenting a plan to settle Germans in the Warthegau, divulged the following information concerning settlement in Warthegau territory:

> The settlement plan for the Warthegau foresees an influx of sixty to seventy thousand Volksdeutsche. Besides them, 10,000

Germans from Bessarabia will arrive in the near future; they will also have to be accommodated. In the Warthegau at the moment, there are 588,000 Germans and 1.6 million Poles. Outside the General Government, there are still a total of eight million Poles.[101]

As it happened, scheming about Madagascar became increasingly unrealistic from August 1940 on for logistical and war-related reasons. By the end of that year, the plan was abandoned for good.

Challenges and Arguments Presented by Governor General Dr. Hans Frank

Plans to deport unnecessary Poles and Jews from the Warthegau met with understandable resistance from the chief of the General Government, Dr. Hans Frank. He seemed aware of the predicament that the situation posed as the General Government, being a vast concentration place of Jews and Poles, naturally became the destination of hundreds of thousands of deportees from the territories that the Reich had annexed. Appreciating the huge economic and social burden that the mass arrival of totally dispossessed deportees would foist on the local population and authorities,

> [Hans Frank] emphatically states that also due to the Jewish problem, the General Government is undoubtedly in a much more difficult situation than the Warthegau. The case of resettlement in the General Government becomes more complicated from day to day, among other things, in connection with plans of setting up new training areas for military exercises. To realize these plans, it will be necessary to resettle about 180,000 Poles.[102]

Frank's intention here was to inhibit Greiser's tendency to get rid of the superfluous population within a few months by sending it to the General Government. As the conference continued, Frank pressed his point:

Population density in the General Government is already 180 people per square kilometer. The average population density is much higher there than in Germany. Under these conditions, and with an increased influx of Poles to the General Government, the speaker does not guarantee that we can prevent epidemics or other disasters such as hunger. This is a very responsible task, which can be met only with the cooperation of all authorities concerned.[103]

SS Brigadeführer Bruno Streckenbach, commander of the Security Police in the General Government, also spoke at the conference:

[…] In addition to the Warthegau, East Prussia, West Prussia, and Silesia are also demanding to be rid of a great number of Poles. At this moment, the deportations of 120,000 Poles are being carried out from the Warthegau to provide empty space for Germans coming from Volhynia. Of this number, 58,000 people have been resettled in the General Government so far, leaving you with another 62,000 to accept. This action was to be properly completed by early July but dragged on due to transport difficulties.[104]

The General Government, however, had a serious food problem at the time of the conference, which coincided with the harvest season. The area was densely populated and not self-sufficient in food. As noted in the conference minutes, this state of affairs (which prevailed in the Reich as well) led Governor Greiser to conclude that the General Government lacked the wherewithal to accept these 250,000 Jews from the Łódź ghetto, even temporarily.[105]

Therefore, those who wished to keep the deportations going would have to explain how relations between the General Government and the Warthegau should proceed. Hans Frank and Arthur Greiser met to agree on such a clarification, but failed. Frank:

The situation in both territories is becoming desperate, so the problem must be solved in a fundamental way. The speaker feels obliged to admit that the Warthegau has absolute priority in the Germanization of this area. He is forced to give up the ambition of transforming the General Government into a German country. In any case, now is the time. However, the reception of such masses of displaced persons first requires a binding agreement on relevant conditions that will be acceptable to the General Government. If they are not met, it will be detrimental to national interests. The General Government has become a mass of Poles [and Jews] who have to be fed at the sole expense of the Third Reich. It has to be done if only because the General Government has important tasks to carry out in the interests of the German Reich.[106]

The problems attending upon the deportation of Poles and Jews from the Warthegau made it necessary to revise the plans. However, despite constant pressure from the likes of Greiser, the difficulties only grew, because the General Government was unable to accept deportees, especially during preparations for Operation Barbarossa. This led to a quest for solutions other and more extreme than deportation.

5. ATTITUDE TOWARD JEWS DURING THE DEPORTATION PERIOD

The Beginning of Nazi Policy toward the Jews in Poland

Within days of the conquest, the Nazis turned to the attainment of their goals. The mechanism for removing Jews from Reich-annexed lands went into action, but did so in inconsistent ways. Sometimes legislation was the deciding factor in promoting the extermination of Jews who lived in these areas. Legislation and other measures aimed to banish Jewish communities from public life. The process was implemented gradually, both at the legislative level among local governors of towns and Regierunsbezirke and in decisions from central authorities in Berlin. Local political and demographic conditions determined how matters evolved. In all locations, however, the process had several commonalities. The rules of conduct—if rules is the right word—were generally determined by the central authorities in Berlin. Instructions from Heydrich, chief of the RSHA, to commanders of the Einsatzgruppen by means of a cable (*Schnellbrief*) on September 21, 1939, informed recipients about the methods and stages of "solving the Jewish question" and serves as an exemplary document on the handling of the "Jewish problem" in the occupied Polish territories.[107]

In this classified cable, Heydrich referred to a conference held that very day, September 21, 1939, in Berlin. He mentioned "planned total measures" to achieve the final aim (*Endziel*), without explaining what they were. According to most researchers, this "final aim" should not, at this stage of the war and the occupation, be confounded with the "Final Solution of the Jewish Question" (*Endlösung der Judenfrage*) that came later. Without a doubt, however, it shows that the intention was to remove the entire Jewish population from German-occupied territories.[108] The methods to be used for this purpose would be determined later. As shown below, the German authorities' ideas on this topic varied according to developments in the war and the geopolitical situation. Importantly, Heydrich's instructions to the chiefs of the Einsatzgruppen specified the entity that would be responsible for dealing with the Jewish matters: the Security Police. It is also important to mention that the staff of the Einsatzgruppen in Poland became the permanent staff of the Security Police in various Polish cities and towns after the warfare in that country ended. In other words, essentially the same people would be dealing with Jewish matters in the coming years. In some cases, this continuity was maintained even as institutions came and went.

Although Heydrich mentioned the final aim without explaining it, his instructions concentrated on the preparatory stages. One of them was the concentration of Jews from the countryside in the larger cities. Here Heydrich distinguished between the zones of Gdańsk and West Prussia, Poznań, and Eastern Upper Silesia, and other occupied areas. By then, the Poznań vicinity and various other regions were already part of the Third Reich: they had been annexed, and were intended to remain so. This is a very important distinction, because annexation to the Reich meant a different policy toward the non-German population and, in particular, the Jews. Heydrich explained, "As far as possible, the [German-occupied] areas [...] are to be cleared of Jews; at least the aim should be to establish only a few cities of concentration."[109]

Despite the mention of cities as places of concentration, a different model of concentration was applied to the Jews in the Warthegau: concentration in small towns. However, two additional points deserve mention. First, Heydrich ordered the concentration of Jews only in localities that were rail junctions, in order to facilitate their subsequent removal to another and as-yet unknown destination. The second matter concerned the size of the Jewish communities involved: "On principle, Jewish communities of fewer than 500 people are to be dissolved and transferred to the nearest concentration center."[110]

Heydrich also instructed the Einsatzgruppen commanders on how to organize Jewish communities. By doing this, he demonstrated that he clearly intended to separate the Jewish and the Polish populations administratively, although this was not stated explicitly at this stage of the war, when the campaign against Poland had not yet ended but the country's fate was sealed. The German siege of Warsaw was continuing, most Polish troops had been destroyed, and the Soviet army was completing its occupation of the eastern part of Poland. Thus, Heydrich's directive was based on the knowledge that Poland would fall within days, after which the German authorities would carve up the country and commence a long-term occupation. Even at this early stage, the German authorities separated Poles and Jews by issuing separate instructions, laws, and decrees for each population.[111] The distinction between Poles and Jews also meant that the Jews would be excluded from the Polish or German administration and would be under the direct authority of the Security Police. Of course, in many matters—especially in cases of larger communities—there were contacts among Jews, Poles, and the German administration.

Heydrich's organizational vision for the Jewish communities included the establishment of a Jewish administration that would be accountable to the Germans. Thus, Germany intended to rule the Jewish population not directly but via the population's representatives. "In each Jewish community," Heydrich ruled, "a Council of Jewish Elders is to be set up which, as far as possible, shall be composed of the remaining authoritative personalities and rabbis. The Council is to be composed of up to twenty-four male Jews (depending on the size of the Jewish community)."[112] In smaller communities, councils were to be comprised of twelve members. Heydrich continued: "The Council is to be made fully responsible, in the literal sense of the word, for the exact and prompt implementation of directives already issued or to be issued in the future. [...] In case of sabotage of such instructions, the Councils are to be warned that the most severe measures will be taken."[113]

To bring the anti-Jewish policy to fruition, the German authorities needed information about the size of each Jewish community. Thus, one of the first tasks of the Jewish council, a.k.a. Judenrat or Ältestenrat, was to carry out an approximate census of the Jews. Next, "The Councils of Elders are to be informed of the date and time of the evacuation, the means available for evacuation, and, finally, the departure routes. They are then to be made personally responsible for the evacuation of the Jews from the countryside."[114] The councils would also be responsible for the appropriate housing of Jews arriving from the countryside and the suitable provisioning of Jews in transport.[115] More generally, Heydrich held the councils accountable for the exact and prompt implementation of German directives and for organizational issues relating to Jewish communities. Jews had little maneuvering room; noncompliance would be severely punished.

Even though Heydrich did not have to answer to anybody, he naturally proposed imaginary explanations for all his measures for the concentration of the Jews. "The reason to be given for the concentration of the Jews in the cities," he wrote, "is that the Jews have taken a decisive part in sniper attacks and plundering."[116] This was plainly ridiculous; very few Jews, if any, were allowed to possess arms and even fewer would dare shoot German soldiers. Even so, this fictitious claim of partisans or snipers was widely invoked during the September 1939 campaign in Poland, when there were no Polish or any other partisans. At a stretch, armed Polish soldiers from defeated units may have been in the field. Most Polish soldiers, however, had been briefed on, and complied with, the international conventions concerning warfare. Arguments regarding hidden partisans and snipers were extensively made as German soldiers and the Security Police operational units combed for excuses to justify their crimes.[117]

Even then, the German authorities had already made plans for the economic exploitation of the country. These plans are also reflected in Heydrich's instructions:

> In the execution [of this plan], it must be taken into consideration that economic requirements in the occupied areas do not suffer. Above all, the needs of the army must be taken into consideration. For instance, for the time being, it will scarcely be possible to avoid, here and there, leaving behind some skilled Jews who are absolutely essential for the provisioning of the troops, for lack of other options. But in such cases, the prompt Aryanization of these enterprises is to be planned and the move of the Jews to be completed in due course, in cooperation with the competent local German administrative authorities. For the preservation of German economic interests in the occupied territories, it is obvious that Jewish-owned war and other essential industries and also enterprises, industries, and factories important to the Four Year Plan[118] must be maintained for the time being. In these cases too, prompt Aryanization must be aimed for and the move of the Jews completed later.[119]

By "Aryanization," Heydrich meant the transfer of all Jewish-owned or -managed businesses to German hands. This policy was plainly a corollary of the Nazis' experience in Germany, where by the middle of the 1930s Jews were ousted from public-service positions and, eventually, all their businesses were Aryanized. It had taken several years to accomplish this feat in Germany; in occupied Poland, the goal was to get it done with all possible celerity. For the time being, deviations from the plan to remove Jews from the economy were dictated only by the need to secure German interests in the occupied territory. The sudden banishment of all Jews from the economy would disrupt production and distribution processes that had been badly affected by the war and its attendant migrations to begin with. This interim tolerance of Jews in the economy, however, was intended to be short.

The matter of the Polish economy in September 1939 was undoubtedly very important to the Germans. The impression of German economic strength in 1939 may be misleading. Despite the annexation of Austria in spring 1938 and of the Sudetenland the same year, as well as the creation of the Protectorate of Bohemia and Moravia in the spring of 1939—which brought in all the economic resources of these areas—the German economy was short on raw materials, machinery, labor, and other resources. In the German view, Poland should ideally be partly annexed to the Reich and treated as part of the Reich. In practice, however, the Warthegau and other annexed territories remained very different from the Reich in numerous ways, including the ethnic factor. The remaining Polish territories, by contrast, were intended to be a kind of German colony, and would be reduced to a subsistence level to provide the Reich with natural resources, raw materials, food, and labor.

The German authorities also wished to preserve food resources. Heydrich stated:

> [...] The food situation in the occupied territories must be taken into consideration. For instance, as far as possible, land owned by Jewish settlers is to be handed over to the care of neighboring German or even Polish farmers to work on commission in order to ensure the harvest of crops still standing in the field and replanting.[120]

The notion of removing Jews from agriculture and replacing them with German settlers was later implemented in the Warthegau, where Germans from the East and the Baltic countries were to be settled.

The guidelines in Heydrich's September 21 Schnellbrief had long-term implications. During the occupation, most of these ideas were realized sooner or later, even if the final objective had not been explained in any concrete manner. They included the establishment of Judenräte, the conducting of censuses of Jews, the concentration of Jews in selected places, deportations, Aryanization, and much more.

The guidelines also prescribed "regulations in these cities which will forbid [the Jews] entry to certain quarters completely and [rule] that—but with due regard for economic requirements—they may not, for instance, leave the ghetto, nor leave their homes after a certain hour in the evening, etc."[121]

The policy designed for the Jewish population of Warthegau was introduced gradually, as more and more drastic methods of direct and indirect extermination were put in place.[122] In practice, different means of repression were employed. First came physical, economic, legal, and moral terror; then were mass displacements to the General Government. The remaining population underwent isolation, ghettoization, or dispatch to Jews-only labor camps. The final stage was the elimination of the ghettos and camps, accompanied by technologized extermination in the first mass extermination camp established on Polish soil, at Chełmno on the Nerem (Kulmhof).

Before that, however, Jews in Inowrocław and Kalisz (Łódź) Regierungsbezirke became the objects of a genocidal experiment, the first on such a large scale on Reich-annexed soil. The governor's ambition to make his district "exemplary," coupled with his close connections with Hermann Göring and Heinrich Himmler, allowed the experience gained in this region to be used and gradually "refined" in the remaining Polish territory. The introduction of new measures directed at "solving the Jewish problem" in the Warthegau proceeded with different intensities at different times. How the methods were used depended on the decisions made by Adolf Hitler and other high-ranking state and Party officials, influenced by local factors and regional national policies at the Regierungsbezirk, county, or even town and municipal levels.

Persecution of Jews in Towns and Settlements of Inowrocław Regierungsbezirk

As noted above, Kleczew, like other towns in Konin County, became part of Inowrocław Regierunsbezirk, one of three Regierungsbezirke in the Warthegau (the other two being Poznań and Kalisz).

From the first days of the Nazi occupation, Jews in towns and settlements of the Regierungsbezirk were persecuted by Wehrmacht units, the SS Totenkopf Standarte Brandenburg, Einsatzgruppe IV, Einsatzkommando 16, and finally the *Selbschutz* (self-defense organization). These actions were widespread and brutal across the entire region. In the western and northern parts of Inowrocław Regierungsbezirk, they obliterated the Jewish population altogether. First, German authorities began to take hostages among local Jewish and Polish inhabitants—six in Koło, twelve in Nieszawa, and four (including the rabbi) in Konin. Similar events took place in Słupca, Ślesin, and other towns in the Regierungsbezirk. Several hostages were shot in public executions (Konin).[123]

During the period of military administration in the Warthegau, Einsatzgruppen and Waffen-SS killed some 10,000 people. At this time, Jews were not the main targets of the Einsatzgruppen; the principal objective of these killing units was the liquidation of the Polish intelligentsia, political opponents, and pro-independence activists. Even so, many Jews who belonged to the Polish intelligentsia were swept up in this wave of terror in the autumn of 1939.[124]

During the initial phase of the occupation, the Jewish inhabitants were not completely aware of the new situation. Some, especially the elderly, remembered the occupation that had taken place in World War I and expected something similar. A survivor who gave testimony captured this mindset:

> Then the war broke out. Mother remembered the Germans from the First World War, a cultured nation. She said it was impossible what the Germans were supposed to be doing to the Jews—she could not imagine it. She remembered that her father had been a trader in eggs and dealt with Germans all the time. They used to come to our house, and we had many German buyers living in Poland, and they were real friends of ours, and she judged the Germans by this. When I was in the war and saw so many horrible things, I thought of how naive she had been.[125]

It seems that not all German soldiers had been indoctrinated in hatred of Jews. A witness reports that some treated the Jews humanely and even tried to warn them:

The German soldiers [who occupied Konin in 1939] wanted to buy butter and cheese, and Mother was selling to them. They were very nice and glad that Mother spoke fluent German. One night one of them came to visit us—probably Mother used to speak to him during the day. He was not a young soldier, and they sat round the table and talked. I understood that he told Mother that bad times were coming, and there would be murder; he told her what Hitler had done in Germany—killing old people, the sick and handicapped, and he felt he must warn her because he had seen her a few times and saw she was a widow with children. He apologized because he would not be coming again to buy, but he advised Mother to do something, to disappear, to leave, because things would be very bad.[126] Mother called on one of the neighbors [...] and he simply wouldn't believe her. They thought she was fantasizing. We talked about it among ourselves all day. After a few days, the Germans took hostages, and two of them, a *goy* and a Jew, were executed in the big square [in Konin].[127]

In general, however, the persecutions began soon after Wehrmacht forces entered the country.[128] They were either individual in character, i.e., implemented pursuant to initiatives "from the ranks" by individual people or formations, or organized. In both cases, hatred of and disinclination toward Jews were brought into play. In Włocławek, Nieszawa (Ciechocinek), Koło, Konin, Kutno, and Gostynin counties, a specific scenario was used to justify mass persecution: there was repression of Jewish festivals and times of prayer under the pretext of the Jews forming illegal gatherings.

On September 22, 1939, in Włocławek, twenty-three men were arrested while praying in an apartment. Several others were killed during this action. A day later, large-scale searches of Jewish apartments on one of the city streets took place; 300 men were arrested. The next day, two synagogues and the *kloyzn* (smaller, less formal prayer houses; singular: *kloyz*) of the Ger Hasidim[129] were set afire. The Nazis blamed the destruction on the Jews and, while they were at it, accused "Jewish arsonists" of torching the adjacent houses. In retaliation for these alleged crimes as well as for their impudence toward the Nazis, the "arsonists" were arrested by SS police. Several hours later, 800–1,200 Jews were arrested as well, and were treated as hostages. As they were being escorted to prison, two people were shot, and one of them was severely wounded. Under similar circumstances, the synagogues in Lubień and in Przedecz and Radziejów were destroyed, the former on September 16, the latter on a later date. In the last-mentioned location, the accusation that Jewish arsonists had set two synagogues ablaze was based on the discovery of a box of matches on one of the detainees. By the end of 1939, synagogues and *batei midrash* (religious study halls) in most locations in the region had been burned, devastated, or torn down.

On September 15, 1939, thirty-two of the most affluent Jewish residents in Nieszawa were arrested, incarcerated for several hours, and then publicly flogged in the market square, each struck with a stick forty to seventy times. One of the victims, daring to protest, was subjected to three such beatings, kept in prison for two additional days, and finally murdered along with two Poles accused of theft.[130] The standard operating procedure in the first weeks of 1939 was intimidation and humiliation. Rapes also took place. Public spectacles, in which victims were tortured by partial or total hacking of beards, beatings, and so on, were organized. Parades of Orthodox Jews were often arranged that required them to wear religious garments, clutch Torah scrolls, and sing.[131] Another "game" was public destruction of the property of Jewish institutions. Most often, synagogues, study halls, *chadarim* (boys' elementary schools), and libraries were razed. Their paraphernalia were taken to the main square in town and burned. Then Jews were forced to sing and dance around the bonfire. In Przedecz, after the synagogue had been set afire, the rabbi was forced to haul heavy wooden logs around the market square. In Osięciny, the rabbi had to seat himself atop the pile of things to be burnt. He was spared by a large ransom.[132]

Similar events took place in practically all locations of Eastern Greater Poland. Kleczew was no exception. While the town was under military rule in 1939, all Jews were gathered in the market square, where the men had their beards ripped off. "The screams and weeping were incredible," recalls Józef Bartnicki of Kleczew, "My neighbor Heber (a trader in soap) was left with a ragged beard glued with blood. Although it was still warm outside, he always wore a scarf around his neck and beard. He never told anyone what had happened...." J. Kamiński remembered more:

> While the rabbi was placed in his liturgical robe on a special platform by the military police, the hair was torn out of his beard and blood spurted on and on. As the "game" continued, they kept spitting on him and hitting him. Such scenes were preserved in pictures showing Jews and their persecutors.

The military policeman Otto Katzberg conducted humiliating acts in the market square. Jews were forced to sing songs under soldiers' derisive gaze.[133]

Another witness recalled those days:

> Life could not be called life. You went to sleep in the evening not knowing what would happen the next morning. Jews were severely beaten. People were afraid to go out. We sat together, with neighbors, wondering what to do, where to go, how to prevent disaster. We thought they would beat us, take money, but no one could imagine the Shoah. Some Jews with money ran away and many families escaped to Russia. They found no paradise there but at least they stayed together as whole families. We couldn't move because we had no money and had no food.[134]

In the towns, it was a common to see uniformed Germans beating Jews in the street for trivial reasons or for no reason at all. "Games" involving Jews continued; in many cases Jews were compelled to stand many hours with their hands up or were shot in the head, stabbed with bayonets, or struck with rifle butts "for educational purposes." They might be thrown down stairs, forced to stand lightly dressed in freezing weather for hours on end or do squat-thrusts or roll in mud and puddles, and could be drowned in rivers and lakes—all "for fun."[135] The injunction against Jews' use of sidewalks allowed for staged car accidents that left some Jews dead or injured as they walked in the street (there is a specific record of this in Włocławek).[136] For some Jews, walking in the street risked not only their safety but possibly also, if not primarily, their honor. According to the testimony of a Jewish girl from Konin:

> They [the German authorities] said we had to wear a yellow patch and walk only in the road. For me it was terrible because Polish school-friends of mine walked on the pavement and were laughing at me. And I was the one who went on errands because it was dangerous for my brothers to go out. Having to walk in the street made me feel so ashamed I just wanted to hide. Many times, without telling Mother, I took off the yellow patch and walked along [on the sidewalk], my heart pounding. I wasn't afraid of the Germans because they didn't know who I was. I was afraid that the *goyim* would reveal that I was a Jew.[137]

The invaders destroyed not only buildings and objects of material value but also many cultural items, as well as Jewish holy books. A witness recalled:

> The Germans, after invading Ląd, looted the mansion of [Ajzyk Nelken and] destroyed the large Judaic library of Mordechai Teitelbaum. I remember his office full of shelves and shelves of books, bound in leather, with gold lettering. Behind the small orchard flowed a tributary of the Warta, partly covered with water plants. One part of the river was full of clean water, which we always used for bathing. In the other part of the river, when I went down some time after the German invasion, I noticed huge swollen volumes of Mordechai Teitelbaum's books floating by. The sight was shocking and to this day memorable. Today, I associate this view with an adage from a poem by Heinrich Heine:[138] "Where books are burned, they will burn people."[139]

The Eviction Method

To facilitate the deportations of Jews, a tactic of surprise was introduced. The population was given no notice of the impending deportation when it actually was to occur, so that the Jews would have no opportunity to hide movable property, especially valuables, or to escape and go into hiding. Therefore, evictions were carried out mostly at night or early morning.

> One day they said that no one was allowed to leave their home, and that the Germans would go from house to house and we would be sent away from Konin. In our house everyone packed a suitcase. Our aunt, Marysia, came to us and put her two little children on the floor to sleep. We were all together except for our grandparents, who were in the town, and we were sitting and waiting for the Germans to come and tell us to leave. Then, in the corridor outside, we heard one German say to the other. "Prost lives here. She stays." We heard this but still we knew it was not a good idea to go out and look. They took about 60 percent of the Jewish families and sent them away. At that time, we didn't know where they were going, but later we learned they were sent to Ostrowiec. We remained in Konin, and for some reason Grandfather and Grandmother also stayed.[140]

All individuals displaced from each locality were brought to a collection point from which they were transported to the General Government. At first, the trips were direct. Later, the deportees were transferred to temporary camps, from which they were transported to the General Government in special evacuation trains. Relocation camps were situated in Toruń, Potulice, Jabłonów, Tczew, Działdowo, Poznań, and Łódź, among other places, with a central resettlement camp in Łódź.

The camps were sited in existing buildings or in prefabricated barracks that had been erected for this purpose. Conditions were appalling—congestion and filth reigned and displaced people slept on straw and received minuscule food rations. Conditions were particularly severe in the winters of 1939–1940. Disease spread and poor sanitary conditions and lack of medical care and medications caused high mortality, especially among the elderly and children.

Kraków District Governor Otto Wachter, in his report for January 1940, wrote about the inhuman conditions of displaced Poles and Jews being moved from the Warthegau to Kraków District:

> It should be emphasized that the number of people unable to work was greatest among the evacuees from Poznań and the Warthegau. Further difficulties arose from unplanned dispatch of trains. And so, transports of Jews and the urban population were directed to rural counties, while other transports of the rural population reached urban areas. Shipments of women and children were sent in overloaded and unheated cattle cars without minimum food for those inside. The result was repeatedly confirmation of cases of death during transport as well as numerous incidents of bodily injury and frost.[141]

Jews displaced from Inowrocław Regierunsbezirk also experienced war trauma. The fate of some of them can be traced in the following examples. A group of forty women, elderly people, and children from Włocławek was sent to Zamość in late 1939 and lodged in the uninhabited apartments of Jewish families. About 150 men from the same transport were assigned to a "Jewish camp" located in the local synagogue and supervised by the SS. After a month, the camp was dissolved, and on January 15, 1940, its residents were transported to Szczebrzeszyn, 20 kilometers away. They could migrate further but were forbidden to settle in Zamość on pain of death. Having been separated from their families, they illegally sneaked into the town anyway to be reunited with them. Seventeen Jews were captured along the Szczebrzeszyn–Zamość road. Cold water was poured on them until they became "ice pillars" standing along the road as a warning for others. Another group of several dozen young Jews from Włocławek worked at a former agricultural school in Janowice, near Zamość. In the winter of 1940/1941, SS overseers forced them to disrobe and then poured water on them for several hours in temperatures below -10 degrees Celsius. Then, naked, the victims were locked into a shed, where they froze to death.

The displaced people who were sent to Warsaw fared no better. Henryk Bryskier (Władysław Janowski) describes what became of Jews from Włocławek, Kalisz, Poznań, and Łódź who were transferred to the Polish capital. They were lodged in a four-storey building at 9 Stawki Street. The elderly, the ill, and the children were given rooms on the top floor. Due to their state of health, they could not go down to the latrine, which was situated in the back yard, and had to relieve themselves in the stairwell. Within a few days, the building was full of excrement. Within three weeks, in January 1942, 228 of the 1,200 Jews who had been packed into the building died. Ultimately, most survivors of this treatment were murdered in extermination camps: those who found themselves in the Łódź ghetto perished at the camp in Chełmno on the Nerem, and those who were sent to the General Government were liquidated in Bełżec, Treblinka, or Sobibór. Some members of the latter group were sent to Auschwitz.[142]

The few who managed to survive extermination and return to their families told the living what the term "displacement to the east" concealed. One of them was the son of a displaced person from Włocławek named Wolsztein. Taken away in the first transport from Zamość to Bełżec on April 11, 1942, he managed to escape and returned to Zamość on April 13, 1942.[143] Szlojme Wiener (referred to as Jakob Grojnowski vel Grojanowski in the Ringelblum Archive)) from Izbica Kujawska was one of three surviving fugitives from Chełmno on the Nerem in January 1942 who made Jews aware of the role Chełmno on the Nerem played. He was also one of the first who informed others about goings-on in Bełżec.[144]

Dispossession was rife during the deportation process. Since one of the objectives of resettlement was to free housing for Volksdeutsche who had been displaced from the Soviet-occupied areas, deportees were not allowed to sell real estate or even small household items, carry large pieces of luggage or furniture, hide belongings, or place things in storage. They could take only small hand luggage. The authorities' purpose in making these rules was to leave as much as possible behind for newly resettled Volksdeutsche, so they could have a fully equipped apartment. Thus,

[…] The entire housing unit, such as furniture, bedding, even much of the clothing and underwear, had to be left in place. The same applied to tableware, cooking vessels, etc. The deported were not allowed to take tools of their trade such as medical instruments, dental equipment, crafts tools, etc. They were also not allowed to take works of art, jewelry, foreign currency, larger sums of money, or even savings passbooks. At first, Poles were theoretically entitled to take 200 złoty per person; Jews could take 50 złoty. In practice, it often happened that they could not raise these sums. Thereafter, the amount allowed was reduced to 80 złoty.[145]

In another form of legalized plunder, any assets, even ones the Jews were told they were permitted to keep, became de facto Reich property once acquired by the German authorities. Jews and Poles were totally dispossessed and uncompensated at the time of deportation. As some deportations were carried out at night or early morning in winter, people driven from their beds had no time to prepare for a calm journey by planning and packing the direst necessities. They were often treated brutally and at gunpoint. Moreover, those transported were searched at transition points, in resettlement camps, and at the General Government customs

38. Jewish property in the street after deportation (YVA, sig. 3774_19)

border. Thus, any remaining belongings in the deportees' possession were also looted.

Economic Exploitation of the Jews

The pilfering of Jewish property was a characteristic of the Nazi occupation policy.[146] It was not by chance that one of the Nazis' first anti-Jewish regulations required warehouse owners to report the addresses and contents of their businesses. The information collected enabled the Nazis, from the first days of the occupation, to systematically rob Jewish-owned shops, warehouses, and furnished apartments, and to steal valuables. Initially, only individuals (soldiers, military police, Volksdeutsche, SS, police, etc.) stole, but in time it appeared that the state was involved in the organized transfer of ownership of large units of property. Large businesses were sold to Germans from the Reich; smaller ones were leased to Volksdeutsche or handed over without charge to German settlers who had been displaced from the Reich. Former Jewish owners were personally forced to remove their wares and furniture from their shops or houses, most probably to accent their humiliation even more. Some new German proprietors retained former Jewish owners as unsalaried managers.[147] Less valuable property (everyday objects, home appliances, craft workshops, shops, etc.) was appropriated by Poles. Objects were bought at much reduced prices or were simply taken.[148] To expedite the looting of secreted property, deception was often used. The German mayor of Zagórów promised to liberate Jews displaced from Kleczew in exchange for their valuables. Those who wished to return to Kleczew for their hidden belongings were given special permits. Once they returned to Zagórów, not only were they not set free; they were forced to turn the valuables over to the Germans.[149]

"Contributions" and Head Tax

"Contributions" that the Germans required from municipalities in the first weeks of the occupation encouraged property exploitation.[150] Justified by alleged acts of arson perpetrated by Jews, they amounted to astronomical sums (e.g., in Przedecz—55,000 złoty;[151] in Włocławek—a first contribution of 100,000 złoty). When the regulations imposed were not obeyed, various measures were imposed. In Włocławek, there was a second contribution of 200,000 złoty demanded "for not following the rules of crossing the street," and a third, of 250,000 złoty, for "not obeying the regulation concerning yellow patches." Elsewhere, the reasons for the demanded contributions could be robberies (Ciechocinek) or provocative behavior (Lubraniec: 70,000 and 10,000 złoty). In Kleczew, penalties were imposed for "lost equipment"—for example, from September 22 to September 30 Jews had to remit 1,820 złoty for missing equipment worth 182 złoty.[152]

The final example of financial exploitation of Jews preceding the total cleansing of Jewish areas in the Warthegau in 1941 and 1942 was the poll tax.[153] Property left over after the displacement was sold, and local authorities transferred the money to the bank account of the German administration of the Łódź ghetto.[154]

Some Jewish community property was destroyed in a senseless way. A number of synagogues were demolished (Skulsk, Konin, and Turek), and their appurtenances completely ruined. Others were torched or torn down (Radziejów, Włocławek, and Uniejów). Yet others, however, were converted into warehouses, workshops, stables (Słupca, Osięciny, Konin, Izbica Kujawska, and Lubraniec), or movie theaters (Kleczew). Buildings in Jewish districts were pulled down (Chodecz, Lubień, Inowrocław, and Kleczew) for construction material or, in some cases, to find hidden valuables left by the displaced people. Books from Jewish synagogues, libraries, and houses of study were burned (Chodecz, Włocławek, Izbica Kujawska, Słupca, and Konin). Nearly all of the Jewish cemeteries in Inowrocław Regierungsbezirk were destroyed; the gravestones were used as construction material (e.g., in Kleczew). In Kleczew, Osięciny, and Radziejów, the cemetery hill was excavated and the soil was used to level streets. The few graveyards that survived the war, e.g., in Włocławek or Inowrocław, were devastated after the war.[155]

6. THE JEWISH COMMUNITY IN KLECZEW IN 1939–1940

The situation of Jews in Kleczew in 1939–1940 may be partially reconstructed from survivors' testimonies and the few documents that outlasted the war. The collections of the Jewish Historical Institute in Warsaw include several letters from representatives of the Jewish community in Kleczew to the "Joint" (the American [Jewish] Joint Distribution Committee) in Warsaw, whence the Jews of Kleczew could seek aid even after the Germans annexed the Warthegau. Later, when the Joint in Warsaw could not provide material assistance, the representatives asked the Reichsvereinigung der Juden in Deutschland [Reich Association of the Jews in Germany[for help. The letters describe the Jews' plight after their banishment from economic life and the German authorities' persecutions.

In the first months of the occupation, the wealthier members of the Jewish community appear to have had some reserve funds, which, however, soon ran out for two basic reasons: Jews had no way to generate income during the German occupation, and what remained of their capital was steadily consumed by taxes, repayment of loans, and so on. The result in Kleczew, as in nearby towns, was sudden impoverishment. In a letter to the Joint in Warsaw on March 26, 1940, the community representatives wrote:

> In our town, Kleczew, 90% of the population is impoverished. They lack the means to make ends meet, have no clothing and shoes, it is very cold, and there is great distress. All the goods the Relief Com.[mittee] has supplied until now to ease the distress have been exhausted. We cannot afford to support 150 Jewish families with even a piece of bread, and soon it will be Passover and we do not have the means to keep them alive. Therefore, we appeal to the honorable Joint Com.[mittee] to have pity on the 150 Jewish families and send us some help soon [...]. You must know if you don't take pity on us and send the necessary help our lives will be in danger.[156]

The second part of the letter explains in part why things had come to such a state: "We add the remark that there was a Savings Bank [Volksbank] and a Gm.[ilat] Chesed Bank [free loan fund], which were requisitioned by the county commissioner [Landrat] of Konin, and we had to pay back all our loans at once."[157] The letter was signed by H. Frenkel, H. Segał, and

Sz. Leszczyński as representatives of the Jewish Relief Committee in Lehmstädt (Kleczew). The Joint in Warsaw gave them a small amount of help (2000 złoty). The Joint's confirmation of the transfer of this aid, in a letter dated May 27, 1940, stresses that it was nonrecurrent and that the Joint did not undertake to provide continuous support.[158] The representatives of the committee in Lehmstädt acknowledged the receipt of the money on May 28, 1940, but asked for an alternative way to obtain assistance because "[…] the situation is getting worse every day. Relief is urgently needed. Of the Jewish population of 160 families, more than 130 families need relief."[159] (For additional correspondences see documents 12-21 in Annex 1.)

The Establishment of Ghettoes in the Warthegau

The isolation policy culminated with the establishment of ghettos in the Warthegau that would play an important role in the extermination process. The ghettoization order was handed down by Heydrich on September 21, 1939, in a phone message to the commanders of the Einsatzgruppen. The ghettos were to serve as places where Jews could be concentrated and more easily supervised. The Ältestenräte (plural of Ältestenrat, council of elders), established by German directive, were responsible for implementing German orders in a precise and timely manner. The ghettos were to be sealed; the introduction of a curfew was considered. Concentration would be justified on the grounds of alleged participation of Jews in partisan attacks and looting.[160] As a consequence, the first plans to establish ghettos in what would become Reichsgau Posen (Reichsgau Wartheland) were already formulated in the Kalisz and Inowrocław Regierungsbezirke in October 1939. From February 1940 on, ghettos were established in the Inowrocław and Kalisz (Łódź) Regierungsbezirke, but not in Posen Regierungsbezirk, which had already been emptied of Jews.[161]

In the transfer to these collective "village ghettos" (*Dorfghetto*), the Jews usually made the trip on foot and were allowed to bring nothing but the direst necessities, such as clothes and personal items. In general, the apartments they had left behind were earmarked for German settlers who would need them. Thus a witness described the transfer from Konin to the village ghetto in Królików, some 20 kilometers from Konin:

After a few months [in July 1940] it was announced that Konin must be *Judenrein* [free of Jews]. Wagons and horses were supplied. Everyone had to put their little bits and pieces on the wagons. A few old people were permitted to sit on the wagons. The rest of us had to walk. It was terrible to walk in the streets—the *goyim* were looking out the windows at us. The SS lashed out with whips and shouted. Dogs barked. People wept. It was terrible. Along the way, the Germans treated us very harshly. When their eye caught someone, they just beat him to death. We walked a long time. In every village some families were ordered to stay. We came to a village named Królików [about 20 kilometers from Konin].[162]

Deportation to Zagórów

In February 1940, many of the 250 Jewish families that had been counted in Zagórów (Konin County) in 1939 were transferred to Bochnia. After two days there, they were ordered to disperse to different towns in the area.[163] As of December 1940, there were 2,170 Jews in Zagórów, of whom 1,582 were deportees who had arrived that year from many towns in the area, including Kleczew, Słupca, Konin, Ślesin, and Golina, and were deported to the village ghetto in Zagórów.[164] A surviving witness, Josef Kazimierski of Golina, described the deportation to Zagórów as follows:

> One day, the German authorities announced that all Jews in town had to reach the marketplace in order to leave the township. They were allowed to take only such luggage as they could carry; bringing furniture or heavy objects was forbidden. The people prepared cloth sacks in order to pack as much as possible. After reaching the marketplace, they were ordered to place their sacks on several horse carts and march out of town. According to Kazimierski, the Poles did not even give them water to drink. They were evacuated on foot to Zagórów, about 30 kilometers from Golina.[165]

Another witness, Bert Gembicki of Kleczew, recalled that after the deportation was announced, the Jews took their personal things and went to Zagórów. He, too, noted that they could place some of their belongings in horse carts.

The Germans wished to make Golina (20 kilometers from Kleczew) and other towns in the area free of Jews (*Judenfrei*) by evicting Jews from their homes. Thus, many thousands of Jews from various towns, including all of those in Golina, were concentrated in Zagórów in 1940. In the ghetto, it was common practice to pack two to three families into one room. Charles Lepek's family spent its first two or three weeks in a stable. Unlike many other Jews, the Lepeks had managed to bring some fabric with them. In their new "home," they cut pieces of fabric every now and then and sold them to others in Zagórów and to Polish peasants in the area.[166]

According to Michel Prost, before the deportation from Kleczew, all the town's Jews were told to be ready at 5:00 a.m. on a certain day and to stand in front of their apartment doors along with their hand luggage. The doors had to be closed and the keys, bearing their names, were to be left in the lock. However, they were not deported. Several uneventful days later, the order was repeated. Prost considered this a Nazi ruse to disempower the Jews. This recurred for weeks, the *Judenälteste* preparing for evacuation each time.

One day, however, all the Polish peasants in the area arrived at 5:00 a.m. with their horse carts. They did not know where they would be sent; the Germans had told them only to take a one-day supply of food for their horses. At 5:00 p.m. that day, with the carts ready, the order was given: go to Zagórów, which Prost estimated as being 40 kilometers from Kleczew.[167] The operation was well organized. All the Jews were standing in front of their homes as the Poles pulled up with their carts, one of which carried the policemen who orchestrated the action.[168]

Zagórów was a mixed town—part Polish, part Jewish. Some of the Poles had already been evicted from town; now the Jews were moved to the municipal school and gymnasium.[169] Some witnesses reported that the ghetto in Zagórów resembled Kleczew but was much more populous because the Jews of Kleczew had been put together with those from Golina and Konin. It was an open ghetto, run by the police and the Jewish Council.[170] According to another witness, the distance to Zagórów was about 35 kilometers. The Jews had brought clothing and some necessities but little else. In Zagórów, fifty-six families went to the *shul* (synagogue) and others to a church (or a convent), since the nuns were not there. Hygienic conditions were bad; personal needs were met in outhouses.[171]

During the transfer to Zagórów from Kleczew in the summer of 1940, according to Tzvi Malron, the Jews had taken nothing but clothing, a few pots, and something to eat. They were forbidden to take furniture. In Zagórów, Malron's family rented a place that sufficed for the extended family. Afterwards, his father rented a room and the immediate family stayed there.[172]

According to Abram Landau, the deportation from Wilczyn to Zagórów on February 2, 1940, was much harsher than the deportations from other places in the area. Out of nowhere, the loudspeakers ordered all inhabitants of Wilczyn, without exception, to leave town within one hour. Horse carts were ready. Everyone was to lock their homes and hand the keys to Gestapo men equipped with dogs and weapons. The Jews—angry, frightened, and disoriented—did not know what to take. They packed what they could into small rucksacks but in many cases chose badly. In chilly weather, they walked to the carts. Abram Landau, seventeen years old at the time, reports that the family left his 95-year-old grandmother behind because she was blind and unable to walk. Consequently, the Germans shot her, as they did anyone who was not ambulatory. According to Landau, there was complete chaos during the deportation. The deportees could not grasp that they were to leave everything behind, head for the square, and depart from town.[173] Landau noted that the journey from Wilczyn to Zagórów was made by horse carts belonging to Polish farmers. Jews were placed aboard them and SS men followed each. (In all likelihood, these were not SS men but police.) The distance from Wilczyn to Zagórów was about forty-five kilometers, and nobody knew where the convoy was going.

Zagórów (Hinterberg) Ghetto, 1940–1941

Again, the eviction of the Jews of Kleczew to Zagórów, Konin County, took place in 1940. In the Zagórów ghetto, Jews from Golina, Konin, Słupca, Skulsk, Ślesin, and Wilczyn were also gathered.[174]

The Zagórów ghetto was an open one. There were private apartments but relations were sour. Bert Gembicki, who spent nine or ten months in Zagórów,[175] describes men who were hunted down and forced to perform different jobs. Newly-arrived Jews were placed by members of the Jewish community in various dwellings, mainly with local families but some living in communal buildings. Those who had relatives in Zagórów could count on living with them, despite the crowding. Josef Kazimierski reports that his parents were taken in by their relatives but, due to the lack of space in their apartment, he and his brothers had to remain in what used to be the public study hall.[176] The new arrivals received food at a public kitchen organized by the Zagórów kehilla.

39. Members of the Jedwab family in Zagórów ghetto, 1940 (YVA, sig. 3774_19)

Housing conditions in Zagórów were grim, with many people sleeping in each room. Men age eighteen and up were taken away for forced labor in road-building, road repair, and stone-hauling. This situation continued for nine months.[177] Afterward that time, men over age thirty were excused from labor.[178]

After their arrival in Zagórów, Jews were completely dependent on Judenrat assistance because they had not been able to bring much food or money. They were assigned to different types of work—cleaning, teaching, etc.—at sundry institutions. Hunger existed, but one witness described the food situation as relatively good.[179] Some Jews had a few second-hand things to sell in addition to occasional valuables that they had held back for the darkest hour.

Since the ghetto was an open one, some young men "organized" supplies on their own. Bert Gembicki returned to Kleczew and procured supplies. He was considered a "good organizer," and joined a friend for his initial visit to Kleczew. At the entrance to the town, he noticed signs warning inhabitants not to help Jews,[180] phrased roughly: "Do not admit Jews. If you see Jews, tell the *Kommandantur* [probably police or army officers—the witness frequently uses this word in reference to different things]. If you do not denounce the Jews, you will be hanged." Ignoring the signs, Gembicki entered town and approached his erstwhile Polish neighbors. Since his family had dealt in the cattle trade, Gembicki had many Polish acquaintances and enjoyed very friendly relations with them. Choosing farmers whom he knew well, Gembicki procured flour, bread, wheat, beans, meat, and other staples—everybody contributed something—and handed all the provisions to one of the farmers. Two days later, Gembicki paid this farmer to bring the harvest to Zagórów. Gembicki placed the entire inventory in the farmer's horse cart and covered it with boards. Then he and his friend seated themselves on the boards and were driven back to Zagórów.[181] Gembicki relates that he did this several times until he became too afraid to continue. After he had abandoned that venture, he continued to trade with local farmers and was able to bring food into the ghetto even though the farmers were afraid to help the Jews.[182] Gembicki said that one could go out during the daytime but not at night due to curfew.[183]

In another testimony, Abram Landau mentions occasions when he and others left the ghetto and went to a Polish farmer begging for food. Some farmers responded favorably; others were afraid and did not open the doors, he reported.[184]

Tzvi Malron's father and sisters gave private lessons in German and Polish to children in Zagórów. Once the ghetto was created, they were no longer able to practice this occupation, so Tzvi's father took whatever odd jobs he could find.[185] Men aged eighteen and up were taken to forced labor camps. At first, men who were sent to forced labor camps could come home on Shabbat; later, this was forbidden. Consequently, the Jewish population of Zagórów largely comprised children, women, and the elderly. Malron's father was an exception; he did physical jobs for the Judenrat. In some places, some but not all people were paid for their work. Food was scanty, but bread and potatoes were available.[186]

Zagórów had a synagogue—a small *shtibl*, to be exact—and Malron celebrated his bar mitzvah there when he turned thirteen, wearing a tallit and tefillin, after a religious Jew "from among the Ostjuden" had coached him for the event. The celebratory meal was very modest.[187]

One day, the Germans ordered the Judenrat to provide a list of persons for deportation to the East for farm labor. The Judenrat did as told, producing an alphabetized list of some 7,000 names. Subsequently, grand announcements regarding deportation *nach Osten* followed. People were permitted to prepare some luggage, not including furniture but including personal items such as clothes, pots, kettles, and shoes. Each day, a number of people were summoned to a gathering point on the basis of their addresses.[188] The whole process took about ten days.

The Malareks were scheduled for deportation on Friday. Shortly before their eviction, the Judenrat told them that they were going not to the East but to Sompolno. The family reported to the collection point, situated in a cattle market, and found Jews congregated there, many crying, with sacks of clothing and other belongings. The Germans ordered the assemblage to write their names (*genau namen abschrieben*) on their packages correctly in order not to lose anything.[189]

There were few escapes: fleeing from the ghetto in Zagórów was too frightening a thing to do. The Germans selected and removed people from the ghetto until Tisha be-Av, in mid-summer.¹⁹⁰ That day, Landau's father was away, his sisters were working in the square, and Landau himself was at home with his sick mother.¹⁹¹ Sirens sounded at 10:00 a.m. Loudspeakers barked: 200 boys were needed. Somebody came to the door; when Mrs. Malarek opened it, an SS man and a dog pushed their way in. The officer asked Landau how old he was and then said: *Jude aus!* [Jew, out!] Trucks were ready in the market square. Landau's mother, crying, came to the square—whereupon the SS man grabbed a machine gun and murdered her.¹⁹²

The deteriorating conditions, the atmosphere of dread, and the desperation among the remaining deportees in the Zagórów ghetto at this time may be adduced from Landau's testimony. According to this witness, the Germans had packed Jews from all over the county—as many as twenty-four smaller towns—into the ghetto. When Landau's family had arrived, they had received a room that they would have to share with twenty-three people. There were no indoor toilets; the facilities were outside. There was no food other than what they had brought with them. They ate it and then tried to carry on despite their hunger.¹⁹³ People contracted typhus and other diseases; they were hungry, cold, and beaten. Every day, 100–150 men and women were summoned to the marketplace, underwent a selection, and were taken away, ostensibly for labor. No one knew what became of them; they never returned.¹⁹⁴ Landau described the ghastly conditions in Zagórów: dwindling food supplies and frightened, tired, angry people. A few committed suicide, including one mentally ill man.¹⁹⁵

The Jewish Relief Committee from Lehmstädt (Kleczew) in Zagórów

On July 16, 1940, the entire Jewish community of Kleczew was deported to the ghetto in Zagórów, where other Jewish communities from surrounding towns had already been taken.¹⁹⁶ However, these communities did not fuse into a new community; they retained their organizational independence. After its transfer to Zagórów (Hinterberg), the Jewish Relief Committee in Lehmstädt became the Jewish Relief Committee from Lehmstädt in Hinterberg. Its members continued to plead to the Joint and other institutions on behalf of the Jews of Kleczew. A letter dated July 29, 1940, reports that 750 people, of whom "600 people lack any means of support," were moved from Kleczew to Zagórów. The rest of the letter confirms the receipt of RM (Reichsmarks) 1,000 in assistance from the Joint, of which only RM 400 was allocated to the needy, because the mayor of Kleczew appropriated the rest at the post office to cover head-tax obligations.[197] It should be emphasized that this was two days before the deportation. That very day, representatives of the Kleczew community wrote to J. Wolman of Kleczew, an employee of the Joint in Warsaw, asking him to intercede for the poor of Kleczew in Zagórów and help them to obtain additional aid.[198] Another letter to Wolman, sent on August 28, 1940, provides some details about the RM 600 that the mayor had appropriated, an act that left those deported to Zagórów even more impoverished. The Jews of Kleczew had been deprived of money at a time of distress, when they had not expected to be deported and had been allowed to take only hand luggage, leaving all their possessions behind. Thus the community wrote to Wolman:

> The total amount of the municipal tax amounted to RM 9000 and a greater sum was to be paid by the poor, as Heber Sz. N. RM 190, Fogiel Ch. RM 230, and Weinberg RM 70. Therefore sir, you can imagine that we were forced to collect RM 5000 to cover the tax that was to have been paid by the poor—and that was two days before the deportation.[199]

The letter went on to describe the wretched living conditions in the collective ghetto in Zagórów:

> Housing conditions in Zagórów are critical. Most people live 10–15 per room and many families still remain in the school and at the communal house. All of us are without jobs but we have a lot of time to enjoy the summer holidays (*sic*). We organized a kitchen at our expense, which serves 300 lunches a day. Half [of those using the facility] pay 5 pfennig and half [eat] for free. In general, our position can not be described clearly, as you can imagine, sir. We stress that if we do not receive external assistance, which must now be given, we cannot be responsible for the fate of all who are facing the worst for lack of bread.[200]

In their desperation, the Kleczew community representatives in Zagórów tried to approach people originally from Kleczew to receive some help:

> [...] And maybe, thanks to the forces of the Kleczewiaków [former residents of Kleczew] community who live in Warsaw, we can get help, because we have no other option.[201]

J. Wolman attempted to help the Kleczew Jews in Zagórów by sending a letter of recommendation to Mr. Borensztejn, director of the Joint in Warsaw.[202] We do not know who urged the members of the Kleczew Jewish Council in Zagórów to write to the Reichsvereinigung (Reich Association of Jews in Germany) for aid. We do know, from a letter dated November 24, 1940, that the Hinterberg (Zagórów) Ältestenrat had not received any money from the Reichsvereinigung even though the Joint in Warsaw had recommended that this be done:

> The distress of the refugees in our town grows with each passing day. Our welfare activities and public soup kitchen are feeding about 500 people, the allocation of apartments and medical and sanitary help will have to cease because all of our resources are exhausted. Now, facing the coming winter, our burden is getting even heavier and we are helpless.[203]

According to a letter of December 12, 1940, the Ältestenrat in Hinterberg received a RM 500 subsidy from the Reichsvereinigung.[204] The last letter, dated December 17, 1940, is a report of sorts on the activity of the Ältestenrat's relief committee. Evidently, this Ältestenrat considered itself a relief committee above all, as opposed to the typical Judenrat, which was responsible for a wide spectrum of activities. It goes without saying that the German authorities in Kreis Konin limited the Ältestenrat's remit to relief endeavors,[205] as follows:

1. Allotting housing; due to the severe housing shortage, several families had to be assigned to one large room.

2. Establishing a soup kitchen; this kitchen worked around the clock, delivering 400 lunches per day—a nutritious and well-prepared soup and 200 grams of bread per person.
3. Caring for the elderly and the ill; for this purpose, a special institution operating under medical supervision was set up.
4. Procuring of straw, tin ware, and kitchenware.
5. Caring for sanitary fixtures and medications.[206]

According to the December 1940 letter from Zagórów, there were 2,170 Jews in the ghetto, including 1,582 deportees. The public kitchen prepared 400 meals a day. The committee, however, was unable

[…] to supply the needy with heating, beds, wooden shoes, and the like; these [tasks] are impossible because our resources are completely exhausted. We were able to make an exception for the men who were drafted from here to the Jewish work camp in Konin and supplied some members of this group with wooden shoes.[207]

The letter concluded with one great cry for help: "It is no longer possible to obtain the necessary resources from the local Jewish population of Hinterberg, which itself is completely economically ruined. Hoping the praiseworthy Joint will continue supporting us in our great relief activity."[208]

Fragments of testimonies also give us some insight into religious life in Zagórów. Religious activity seems to have been much less intense at this time than it had been before the deportations from surrounding towns. The sudden and massive influx made it necessary to convert public buildings into lodgings: the study hall became sleeping quarters for many young men,[209] the synagogue courtyard became the public kitchen, etc., to the detriment of their original uses as places of prayer and study. Moreover, family discipline loosened somewhat. The abrupt change of roles had forced many young people to become their families' main breadwinners. During the deportation, their parents had lost not only property but also their prestige. Young men were less attracted to religion in these times of crisis. Older men, however, continued to pray regularly. Many *minyanim*[210] formed in private houses and held regular services.[211]

We have no detailed information about the final months of the ghetto in Zagórów. We may imagine, however, a steady deterioration until the fateful days of September or October 1941, when the final liquidation came.

Operation Barbarossa Disrupts the Deportation Process

In early 1941, preparations for Operation Barbarossa caused serious difficulties in implementing the deportation plan due to the high demand for transportation, especially railways. The General Government had to accommodate masses of troops—the majority of the German divisions, in fact—because it lay on the main route of the planned strikes. This meant some 1.5 million soldiers had to be housed and provisioned at a time when food was short in the General Government. Since the Barbarossa preparations were a priority, everything else slid into the background. Even so, on January 8, 1941, the RSHA hosted a conference on the resettlement of Poles and Jews from lands annexed to the Reich to the General Government. In the minutes of this conference, the participants explained what had to be done:

> During 1941, we will need to relocate a total of 831,000 people from the German Reich's eastern territories to the General Government, but resettlement for only about 180,000 has been provided for within the General Government, mainly in connection with the needs of the Wehrmacht.[212]

The number of people from the Warthegau to be resettled in the General Government was 148,000.[213]

As the conference proceeded, General Government officials argued that further deportations would become a burden on their territory. The displacements already carried out, they added, had caused population density in the General Government to surpass that of the Reich and had stunted the area's economic development badly. Furthermore,

[… The] area of the General Government has in fact been reduced significantly by about 12,000 square kilometers, of which 2,500 are due to the Wehrmacht objectives while the rest—the entire military protection zone along the rivers Narew, Vistula, and San—the General Government had to evacuate. This increased population density in the rest of the General Government by 170 people per square kilometer. Besides, the General Government lacks all natural conditions for the absorption of such a mass of people. The Reich is more powerful in this respect. If so, comparison of population densities inevitably leads to erroneous conclusions.[214]

The policymakers in Berlin were not convinced. The governors and mayors, they insisted, should be held responsible for accommodating displaced people who showed up in their areas. This task indeed seemed very difficult, due to the lack of available unoccupied space. However, "… as a representative of OKW said, [215] the number of troops stationed in the General Government is expected to increase. The accommodation of so many incoming people has to rely mainly on directing them to local housing occupied by families, notwithstanding the overcrowding that already exists."[216] Large-scale troop transports to the General Government had been proceeding systematically since early 1941, but the strongest flow of such transports began at the beginning of April 1941 and lasted until Operation Barbarossa commenced on June 22.

Since those being resettled in the General Government were deprived of any way of making a living, their employment had to be ensured—no small matter given the dire economic condition of the General Government. Public works appeared to be the only solution. As stated in the minutes:

> Able-bodied displaced people should be mobilized immediately. During the winter, this work should be limited mainly to clearing snow and doing some preliminary construction work […]. These public works, organized solely for the employment of displaced

people, often fail to yield great practical benefit and, basically, can be financed neither by the General Government nor by municipalities nor by associations of municipalities [*Gemeindeverbünde*]. It is therefore necessary to apply for a subsidy from the Reich.[217]

Secretary of State Dr. Joseph Bühler spoke in a similar vein. He considered the intended deployment of one million people in the General Government impossible. The resulting oppressive situation, he said, would be so dangerous in terms of security, policing, epidemics, and nutrition that unrest could not be avoided for long. He proposed to arrange organized work and to place evacuees in labor camps. The Governor General replied that these concerns were being tackled with the most severe measures. If you have difficulty with food, he counseled, the Reich must help.[218]

This opposition of General Government circles to the reception of deportees from the Reich-annexed areas led to an exaggerated view of the problem and placed those involved in the deportations of Jews, including Arthur Greiser and his retinue, under increased pressure. The effects described above were recognized and supported by high-ranking leaders such as Reichsführer SS Heinrich Himmler and Reinhard Heydrich. On the other hand, the Governor General, Dr. Hans Frank, knew that he could not resist the pro-deportation camp despite his high position in the Nazi hierarchy. Thus, despite loud expressions of resistance, he tried to find a way to agree to the deportation on the grounds of its being in the Reich's best interest. In this context we may read some of his remarks on the matter:

> As the General Government lives under the most extraordinary and difficult economic and transportation conditions, general policy and defense of the reception by the General Government of hundreds of thousands of people of foreign nationality and, in general, aliens, causes an additional and almost unendurable burden. These people were expropriated

in Germany. So they come here dispossessed, into a territory where they have no chance whatsoever of reconstructing their lives in any way. Considering this whole matter, however, we must be guided by considerations dictated only by *raison* of the Reich. [...] We should cease all criticisms of such moves that are based on debates and reflections about their advisability. Deportation must occur and the General Government must accept these people, this being one of the great tasks that the Führer has set before the General Government.[219]

Although Hans Frank's consent to the deportation of Jews and Poles to the General Government worked to his advantage, factors beyond his control eventually brought the deportation process to its knees. The aforementioned transport difficulties only worsened with the increasing involvement of German forces on the eastern front. These vicissitudes were followed by additional demands for labor in the Reich. This further demonstrated the disutility of deporting Poles to the General Government; after all, they were increasingly needed in the Reich, including the Warthegau. For Jews, the consequences were much graver because the impossibility of deporting them led the authorities to seek other solutions—ultimately resulting in the concept of physical extermination.

NOTES

1   For details about the speech, see Document 7, Annex 1.
2   Yad Vashem Archives (hereinafter: YVA), O.93/24710, video testimony Michel (Mendel) Prost, b. October 1, 1920, in Kleczew, VT-1.
3   YVA, O.93/24710, video testimony Michel (Mendel) Prost, b. October 1, 1920, in Kleczew, VT-1.
4   YVA, O.93/24854, video testimony Bert (Baruch) Gembicki, b. October 15, 1916, in Kleczew, VT-1.
5   YVA, O.93/24854, video testimony Bert (Baruch) Gembicki, b. October 15, 1916, in Kleczew, VT-1.
6   YVA, O.93/24854, video testimony Bert (Baruch) Gembicki, b. October 15, 1916, in Kleczew, VT-1, 10:00-12:00.
7   YVA, O.93/9257, video testimony Abram Landau, b. April 25, 1922, in Wilczyn, VT-2.

8   *Do zobaczenia za rok w Jerozolimie—deportacje polskich Żydów w 1938 roku z Niemiec do Zbąszynia* (See you next year in Jerusalem—Deportation of Polish Jews in 1938 from Germany to Zbąszyń), ed. I. Skórzyńska i W. Olejniczak, Fundacja TRES, Poznań 2012; Jerzy Tomaszewski, *Preludium Zagłady: wygnanie Żydów polskich z Niemiec w 1938 r.*, PWN, Warsaw, 1998.
9   YVA, O.93/24854, video testimony Bert (Baruch) Gembicki, b. October 15, 1916, in Kleczew, VT-1.
10 YVA, O.93/9257, video testimony Abram Landau, b. April 25, 1922, in Wilczyn, VT-2.
11 Ibid.
12 Ibid.
13 YVA, O.93/24710, video testimony Michel (Mendel) Prost, b. October 1, 1920, in Kleczew, VT-1.
14 YVA, O.93/24854, video testimony Bert (Baruch) Gembicki, b. October 15, 1916, in Kleczew, VT-1.
15 YVA, M.1.Q/138, testimony Leon Brener, 1-4.
16 YVA, M.1.Q/387, testimony Leybush Aaron from Rychwał.
17 YVA, O.93/9257, video testimony Abram Landau, b. April 25, 1922, in Wilczyn, VT-2.
18 Malron Malarek, VT-2.
19 YVA, O.93/24854, video testimony Bert (Baruch) Gembicki, b. October 15, 1916, in Kleczew, VT-1, YVA-M-1-Q/176, testimony Dawid Rygiel, February 26, 1948, in Ansbach, 2-4; M. Gelbart, ed., *Kehillat Konin bi-f'rihata u-ve-hurbana* (Konin Memorial Book), Memorial Committee of the Association of Konin Jews in Israel (Tel Aviv, 1968).
20 YVA, M.1.Q/138, testimony Leon Brener, 1-4.
21 YVA, M.1.Q/387, testimony Leybush Aaron.
22 YVA, O.93/24854, video testimony Bert (Baruch) Gembicki, b. October 15, 1916, in Kleczew, VT-1.
23 However, the Germans left the Landau family alone. YVA, O.93/9257, video testimony Abram Landau, b. April 25, 1922, in Wilczyn, VT-2.
24 Ibid.
25 YVA, O.93/24854, video testimony Bert (Baruch) Gembicki, b. October 15, 1916, in Kleczew, VT-1.
26 Ibid.
27 Ibid.
28 Ibid.
29 Ibid.
30 YVA, O.93/26326, video testimony Tzvi Malron (Hieronim Malarek), b. October 10, 1927, in Mogilno, VT-1.
31 Ibid.
32 Ibid. 10, 1927, in Mogilno, VT-1.
33 YVA-M-1-Q/176, testimony Dawid Rygiel, February 26, 1948, in Ansbach, 2-4.
34 YVA-M-1-Q/177, testimony Bert Gembicki, May 6, 1948, in Ansbach, 2-5.
35 YVA-M-1-Q/176, testimony Dawid Rygiel, February 26, 1948, in Ansbach, 2-4.
36 R. Grzonkowski, *Kleczew*, 236-242.
37 YVA-M-1-Q/176, testimony Dawid Rygiel, of February 26, 1948, in Ansbach, 2-4.

38 *Wir sind keine Freunde mehr, wir kennen keine Freunde mehr sein. Ich bin Deutsche und du bist Jude.* YVA, O.93/24710, video testimony Michel (Mendel) Prost, b. October 1, 1920, in Kleczew, VT-1.
39 Ibid.
40 YVA, O.93/24710, video testimony Michel (Mendel) Prost, b. October 1, 1920, in Kleczew, VT-2.
41 Ibid.
42 Ibid.
43 Ibid.
44 YVA, O.93/5585, video testimony Charles Lepek (Jechiel Chaim Łepek), b. August 28, 1923, in Golina, VT-1.
45 More in Cz. Łuczak, *Pod niemieckim jarzmem (Kraj Warty 1939-1945)* (Poznań, 1996).
46 The following counties also belonged to Inowrocław Regierungsbezirk: Ciechocinek (previously Nieszawa), Gniezno, Gostyń, Inowrocław, Koło, Kutno, Mogilno, Szubin, Wągrowiec, Włocławek, Żnin. For more, see W. Jastrzębski, "Kujawy w obrębie rejencji inowrocławskiej czasu wojny i okupacji (1939-1945)," in *Dwie części Kujaw. Związki i podziały w dziejach regionu*, ed. D. Karczewski, M. Krajewski, and S. Roszak, (Włocławek-Inowrocław, 2001), 113-127.
47 M. Alberti, *"Exerzierplatz des Nationalsozialismus": Der Reichsgau Wartheland 1939-1941*, in *Genesis des Genozids: Polen 1939-1941*, ed. K.M. Mallmann and B. Musial (Darmstadt, 2004), 111-126.
48 J.A. Młynarczyk, *Wpływ inicjatyw oddolnych Arthura Greisera i Odilona Globocnika na decyzję o wymordowaniu Żydów*, in *Zagłada Żydów na polskich terenach wcielonych do Rzeszy*, ed. A. Namysło (Warsaw, 2008), 15-17; Polski Instytut Wydawniczy, *Proces Artura Greisera przed Najwyższym Trybunałem Narodowym* (Warsaw, 1946); J. Sawicki, *Przemówienie końcowe prokuratora Jerzego Sawickiego przed Najwyższym Trybunałem Narodowym w sprawie przeciwko Arturowi Greiserowi* (Poznań, 1946); Cz. Łuczak, *Arthur Greiser: Hitlerowski władca w Wolnym Mieście Gdańsku i w Kraju Warty*, (Poznań, 1997).
49 "*Wysiedlanie ludności z ziem polskich wcielonych do Rzeszy*," Biuletyn Głównej Komisji Badania Zbrodni Hitlerowskich w Polsce [Bulletin of the Main Commission for Investigating Nazi Crimes in Poland—hereafter: BGKBZHP] 12, 23-31.
50 Such a policy was successfully implemented in Gdańsk Pomerania by Albert Forster, the Governor of Reichsgau Danzig-Western Prussia. For more, see W. Jastrzębski, *Polityka narodowościowa w Okręgu Rzeszy Gdańsk—Prusy Zachodnie (1939-1945)* (Bydgoszcz, 1977); idem, "Ludność niemiecka i rzekomo niemiecka na ziemiach polskich włączonych do rzeszy Niemieckiej (1939-1945)," in *Ludność niemiecka na ziemiach polskich w latach 1939-1945 i jej powojenne losy*, ed. W. Jastrzębski (Bydgoszcz, 1995).
51 "Dekret A. Hitlera o umocnieniu niemieckości polecający Himmlerowi przeprowadzenie masowych przesiedleń ludności polskiej, 1939, październik 7, Berlin," in *Okupacja i ruch oporu*, 112.
52 "Report W.F. Krüger on the state of German police in the General Government and resettlement politics, November 8, 1939, Kraków," in *Okupacja i ruch oporu*, 86.
53 *Wysiedlanie ludności z ziem polskich*, 25.
54 From a circular of the Higher SS and Police Commander in Warthegau, Koppe, on the resettlement of Jews and Poles from Warthegau to the General Government,

November 12, 1939, Poznań, in *Eksterminacja Żydów na ziemiach polskich w okresie okupacji hitlerowskiej: Zbiór dokumentów*, ed. T. Berenstein, A. Eisenbach, and A. Rutkowski (Warsaw, 1957), 32-33.
55 Ibid.
56 *Eksterminacja Żydów na ziemiach polskich w okresie*, 32-33.
57 From a circular of the Higher SS and Police Commander in Warthegau, Koppe, on the resettlement of Jews and Poles from Warthegau to the General Government, November 12, 1939, Poznań, in *Eksterminacja Żydów na ziemiach polskich w okresie*, 32-33.
58 Ibid.
59 *Wysiedlanie ludności z ziem polskich*, 26-27.
60 Report on conference concerning resettlement of Poles and Jews to the General Government from lands annexed to the Reich, held on January 8, 1941, at Reich Security Main Office in Berlin, January 13, 1941, Kraków, in *Okupacja i ruch oporu*, 319-320.
61 Excerpt from remarks by Dr. E. Wetzel and G. Hecht of the NSDAP Board for Racial Policy on the treatment of people in occupied Poland, November 25, 1939, Berlin, in *Okupacja i ruch oporu w dzienniku Hansa Franka 1939-1945*, vol. I, *1939-1942* (Warsaw, 1970), 134.
62 Ibid.
63 M. Alberti, "Exerzierplatz des Nationalsozialismus", 111-126; M. Alberti, *"Nikczemna perfidia"*, 71-72.
64 Quoted from A. Pakentreger, "Polityka władz niemieckich tzw. Kraju Warty wobec Żydów," *Biuletyn Żydowskiego Instytutu Historycznego w Warszawie*, no. 4 (1977): 35.
65 D. Michman, "Postawy i zachowania wobec Zagłady" in *Zagłada Żydów na polskich terenach wcielonych*, 163.
66 J. Sziling, "W latach okupacji hitlerowskiej (1939-1945)," in *Dzieje Inowrocławia*, vol. 2, ed. M. Biskup (Warsaw-Poznań-Toruń, 1982).
67 K.M. Mallmann, "'Rozwiązać przez jakikolwiek szybko działający środek': Policja Bezpieczeństwa w Kraju Warty," in *Zagłada Żydów na polskich terenach wcielonych*, 87-91.
68 K.M. Mallmann, *Rozwiązać przez jakikolwiek*, 89-90.
69 K.M. Pospieszalski, *Hitlerowskie "prawo" okupacyjne w Polsce: Wybór dokumentów*, Cześć I—*Ziemie "wcielone,"* "Doccumenta Occupationis" V (Poznań, 1952).
70 Instytut Pamięci Narodowej. Delegatura w Gdańsku.Oddział w Bydgoszczy (Institute of National Remembrance, Gdańsk Representation. Bydgoszcz Branch, hereinafter: IPN-B), Ds. 25/66, vol. 1.
71 This obligation was referred to again in the end of 1940: "Amtliche Bekantmachungen für den Kreis Leslau," 1940, no. 15, from November 15, p. 8.
72 T. Kawski, *Kujawsko-dobrzyńscy*, 251.
73 "Leslauer Bote. ABC dla Włocławka i Kujaw," no. 33, November 12, 1939.
74 "Amtliche Bekanntmachungen für den Kreis Leslau," no. 7, July 25, 1940.
75 "Amtliche Bekantmachungen für den Kreis Leslau," 1940, no. 7, July 25, p. 6, 1940, no. 9, August 29, p. 6; cf. T. Prekerowa, *Wojna i okupacja*, in *Najnowsze dzieje Żydów w Polsce w zarysie(do 1950 roku)*, ed. J. Tomaszewski (Warsaw, 1993), 278-279.
76 F. Friedman, *Zagłada Żydów polskich w latach 1939-1945*, BGKBZNP, vol. I, p. 173; A. Pakentreger, *Polityka władz*, 36-37.
77 AŻIH, Ring I, 796; AŻIH, 301/372, card 1.

78   AŻIH, American Joint Distribution Committee in Poland, (hereinafter: AJDC), 210/15; AŻIH, Ring I, 974; Fundacja "Pomorskie Archiwum Armii Krajowej" w Toruniu (Foundation "Pomerania Archive of the Home Army" in Toruń—hereafter: PAAK), Spuścizna W. Drzewieckiego (The Legacy of W. Drzewiecki), część 2. Relacje i wspomnienia. Relacja R. Brodeckiego (part 2. Reports and Recollections. Report of R. Brodecki), część 3.Inne materiały (part 3. Other Materials); Z. Klukowski, *Dziennik z lat okupacji Zamojszczyzny (1939-1944)* (Lublin, 1958), 85, 116; D. Dąbrowska, "Zagłada skupisk żydowskich w Kraju Warty w okresie okupacji hitlerowskiej," *Biuletyn Żydowskiego Instytutu Historycznego w Warszawie*, nos. 13-14 (1955): 166-173 tables 9-15, 128-130, and 181-184; T. Berenstein, "Martyrologia, opór i zagłada ludności żydowskiej w dystrykcie lubelskim," *Biuletyn Żydowskiego Instytutu Historycznego w Warszawie*, no. 21 (1957): 60-61 table 3, 70-72 table 7, 81 table 10, and 82-83 table 11; T. Kaliski, "Lata wojny i okupacji," in *Dzieje Pakości*, ed. W. Jastrzębski (Warsaw-Poznań, 1978), 198; T. Łaszkiewicz, *Żydzi w Inowrocławiu w okresie międzywojennym (1919-1939)* (Inowrocław, 1997), 68-72.
79   T. Kawski, *Gminy*, passim.
80   YVA, O.53/48, cards 617-618; YVA, JM/4207, document no. 40/19740.
81   AŻIH, 301/375, card 4.
82   YVA, JM/4207, 40/19740 and 053/48, card 632-636; AŻIH, AJDC, 210/15; AŻIH, Ring. I, 940, card 7; 871, cards 1, 3; 974; AŻIH, 301/375, card 4; Sz. Datner, J. Gumkowski, and K. Leszczyński, "Wysiedlenia ludności z ziem polskich wcielonych do Rzeszy," in *Biuletyn Głównej Komisji Badania Zbrodni Hitlerowskich w Polsce* (Warsaw, 1960), vol. XII, Document no. 18; T. Jaszowski, *Okupacyjna martyrologia włocławskich Żydów*, in *Z badań nad eksterminacją Żydów na Pomorzu i Kujawach*, ed. T. Jaszowski (Bydgoszcz, 1983), 26; T. Richmond, *Uporczywe echo*, 100-101; T.Berenstein, *Martyrologia*, 60-61 table 3, 70-72 table 7, 81 table 10, 82-83, table 11; D. Dąbrowska, *Zagłada*, 166-173 tables 9-15, 181-184; Z. Klukowski, *Dziennik*, 85, 116; T. Berenstein, *Martyrologia i zagłada*;T. Łaszkiewicz, *Żydzi*, 68-72.
83   More in A. Pakentreger, "Losy Żydów m. Kalisza i powiatu kaliskiego w okresie okupacji hitlerowskiej (od 1940 do 9 VII 1942 r.). Martyrologia i Zagłada," *Biuletyn Żydowskiego Instytutu Historycznego w Warszawie*, no. 2-3 (1980); M.A. Woźniak, "Getta i obozy pracy dla Żydów na terenie kaliskiego w okresie okupacji hitlerowskiej," *Zeszyty Kaliskiego Towarzystwa Przyjaciół Nauk*, no. 2 (1997).
84   T. Kawski, *Kujawsko-dobrzyńscy Żydz*, 241.
85   Minutes of conference of managers at the office of the General Governor on resettlement policy, Jewish policy, and the state of the German police in the General Government, December 8, 1939, Kraków, in *Okupacja i ruch oporu*, 93.
86   From speech of RSHA chief Heydrich and General Government HSSPF Krüger, delivered at a conference in Berlin about the forced resettlement of Polish and Jewish populations in the Warthegau to the General Government, Berlin, January 30, 1940, recorded in. T. Berenstein, A. Eisenbach, and A. Rutkowski, eds., *Eksterminacja Żydów na ziemiach polskich w okresie okupacji hitlerowskiej: Zbiór dokumentów* (Warsaw, 1957), 44-45.
87   From report of Higher SS and Police Commander in Warthegau about resettlement of Poles and Jews from Warthegau to the General Government, January 26, 1940, Poznań, recorded in *Eksterminacja Żydów na ziemiach polskich*, 40-41
88   Ibid.

89 Discussion of compulsory evacuation of Jewish Population of the Wartheland to the Government-General, January 30, 1940, in Yitzhak Arad, Yisrael Gutman, et al., *Documents on the Holocaust: Selected Sources on the Destruction of the Jews of Germany and Austria, Poland and the Soviet Union*, (Jerusalem, 1987) (hereinafter: *Documents on the Holocaust*), 183-185.
90 Ibid.
91 Ibid.
92 Report of the Krasnystaw county governor about creating Jewish quarters in connection with housing difficulties, September 10, 1940, Krasnystaw, recorded in *Eksterminacja Żydów na ziemiach polskich*, 91.
93 Discussion of compulsory evacuation of the Jewish population of the Wartheland to the Government-General, January 30, 1940, in *Documents on the Holocaust*, 183-185.
94 Ibid.
95 Minutes of conference of directors of departments in the Governor's General office with the participation of Hermann Göring, Johann L. Schwerin von Krosigk, Hans Frank, et al., on the General Government economy, February 15, 1940, Kraków, recorded in *Okupacja i ruch oporu*, 150.
96 *Okupacja i ruch oporu*, 150.
97 Conference with participation of Arthur Greiser and senior General Government and Warthegau officials on a common policy towards the Jewish and Polish population, July 31, 1940, Kraków, recorded in *Okupacja i ruch oporu*, 235.
98 Ibid.
99 A.B. Rossino, "Nazi Anti-Jewish Policy during the Polish Campaign: The Case of the Einsatzgruppe Woyrsch," *German Studies Review* 24 (2001): 35-54.
100 Conference with participation of Arthur Greiser and senior General Government and Warthegau officials on a common policy towards the Jewish and Polish population, July 31, 1940, Kraków, recorded in *Okupacja i ruch oporu*, 236.
101 Ibid., 236-237.
102 Ibid.
103 Ibid., 237.
104 Ibid.
105 Ibid.
106 Ibid., 237-238.
107 Instructions from Heydrich on policy and operations concerning Jews in the occupied territories, September, 21, 1939, recorded in *Documents on the Holocaust*, 173-178.
108 "Nazi Resettlement Policy and the Search for a Solution to the Jewish Question 1939-1941," in *The Path to Genocide*, 8-9.
109 Instructions from Heydrich on policy and operations concerning Jews in the occupied territories, September, 21, 1939, recorded in *Documents on the Holocaust*, 173-174.
110 Ibid., 174.
111 The position of Gypsies was less prominent; the German authorities often issued local instructions or made *ad hoc* decisions concerning them.
112 Instructions from Heydrich on policy and operations concerning Jews in the occupied territories, September, 21, 1939, recorded in *Documents on the Holocaust*, 174.

113 Ibid.
114 Ibid., 175, Part II, 4.
115 Ibid.
116 Ibid.
117 J. Böhler, *Zbrodnie Wehrmachtu w Polsce: Wrzesień 1939: Wojna totalna* (Kraków, 2009); K. Böhler (Hg), *"Größte Härte...." Verbrechen der Wehrmacht in Polen September—Oktober 1939* (Osnabrück, 2005); A.B. Rossino, "Nazi Anti-Jewish Policy during the Polish Campaign: The Case of the Einsatzgruppe Woyrsch," *German Studies Review*, no. 24 (2001): 35-54; idem, *Hitler Strikes Poland: Blitzkrieg, Ideology and Atrocity* (Lawrence, KS, 2003).
118 H. D. Petzina, *Autarkiepolitik im Dritten Reich. Der nationalsozialistische Vierjahresplan* (Stuttgart, 1968); A. Barkai, *Nazi Economics: Ideology, Theory and Policy* (New Haven, 1990); H.D.Petzina, *Der nationalsozialistische Vierjahresplan von 1936.* (Mannheim, 1965); Cz. Łuczak, *Przyczynki do gospodarki niemieckiej w latach 1939-1945* (Poznań, 1949); W. Jarzębowski, *Gospodarka niemiecka w Polsce 1939-1944* (Warsaw, 1946), 100-143.
119 Heydrich's instructions on policy and operations concerning Jews in the occupied territories, September, 21, 1939, recorded in *Documents on the Holocaust*, 176.
120 Ibid.
121 Ibid. 175.
122 M. Alberti, "Nikczemna perfidia, niska, bezmierna chciwość oraz zimne, wyrachowane okrucieństwo—ostateczne rozwiązanie kwestii żydowskiej w Kraju Warty," in *Zagłada Żydów na polskich terenach wcielonych do Rzeszy*, ed. Aleksandra Namysło (Warsaw, 2008), 69-71.
123 T. Berenstein and A. Rutkowski, "Prześladowania ludności żydowskiej w okresie administracji wojskowej w Polsce (1.IX.1939 r.—25.X.1939 r.)," *Biuletyn Żydowskiego Instytutu Historycznego w Warszawie*, no. 38 (1961): 8-16.; P. Rybczyński, "Zbrodnie Wehrmachtu w rejonie konińskim," in *Zbrodnie Wehrmachtu w Wielkopolsce w okresie Zarządu Wojskowego (1 września-25 października 1939)* (Kalisz, 1986), 85 and 100-101.
124 A. Galiński and M. Nudziarek, eds., *Eksterminacja inteligencji Łodzi i okręgu łódzkiego 1939-1940* (Łódź, 1992).
125 T. Richmond, *Konin: A Quest* (New York, 1995), 363.
126 Ibid.
127 Ibid.
128 J. Böhler, *Zbrodnie Wehrmachtu w Polsce: Wrzesień 1939: Wojna totalna* (Kraków, 2009), 27-60; Sz. Datner, *55 dni Wehrmachtu w Polsce: Zbrodnie dokonywane na polskiej ludności cywilnej w okresie 1.IX—25.X.1939 r.*, (Warsaw, 1967); A.B. Rossino, "Nazi Anti-Jewish Policy during the Polish Campaign: The Case of the Einsatzgruppe Woyrsch," in *German Studies Review*, no. 24 (2001): 35-54; idem, *Hitler Strikes Poland: Blitzkrieg, Ideology and Atrocity* (Lawrence, KS, 2003).
129 Followers of the Gerrer Rebbe (head of the Hasidic court in Góra Kalwaria).
130 T. Kawski, *Kujawsko-dobrzyńscy*, 249-252; M. Alberti, Nikczemna perfidia, niska, bezmierna chciwość oraz zimne, wyrachowane okrucieństwo—ostateczne rozwiązanie kwestii żydowskiej w Kraju Warty," in *Zagłada Żydów na polskich*, 80.
131 D. Sztokfisz, ed., *Kutno we ha Sewiwa* (Tel Aviv, 1968), 449; P. Rybczyński, *Zbrodnie Wehrmachtu*, 85 and 100-101.

132 ŻIH, Dział Dokumentacji (Department of Documents, hereinafter: DD), B. Chojnacka, *Dzieje Żydów w Osięcinach* (photocopied manuscript); J. Böhler, "Prześladowanie ludności żydowskiej w okupowanej Polsce podczas trwania zarządu wojskowego (od 1 września do 25 października 1939 r.)," in *Zagłada Żydów na polskich*, 46-58.
133 Quoted from R. Grzonkowski, *Kleczew*, 242.
134 T. Richmond, *Konin*, 364.
135 YVA, O.33/654; AŻIH, 301/375, c. 1-4; AŻIH, Podziemne Archiwum Getta Warszawskiego "Oneg Szabat"—Archiwum Ringelbluma I (The Oneg Szabat Underground Archive of the Warsaw Ghetto, a.k.a. Ringelblum's Archive I—hereinafter: Ring I), Ring I/936, cards 2-4; Ring I/940, cards 5, 13.
136 AŻIH, Ring. I/940, card 7.
137 T. Richmond, *Konin*, 363-364.
138 The quote is from Heine's play *Almansor* (1821): "*Das war ein Vorspiel nur, dort wo man Bücher verbrennt, verbrennt man auch am Ende Menschen.*" (That was but a prelude; where they burn books, they will ultimately burn also people.)
139 YVA-O.3/3406, testimony Eugenia Friedlender-Cyns, June 26, 1969, pp. 19-20.
140 T. Richmond, *Konin*, 364-365.
141 Report of Kraków District Governor Wächter for January 1940, about inhumane conditions of displaced Poles and Jews from the Warthegau to Kraków District, February 19, 1940, Kraków, recorded in *Eksterminacja Żydów na ziemiach polskich*, 46.
142 T. Richmond, *Sztetl*, 100-101; T. Kawski, *Kujawsko-dobrzyńscy*, 242-243.
143 YVA, 033/322
144 *Archiwum Ringelbluma*, 113, fn. 1; J. Gulczyński, *Obóz śmierci w Chełmnie nad Nerem* (Konin, 1991), p 39.
145 *Wysiedlanie ludności z ziem polskich*, 28.
146 M. Alberti, *Nikczemna perfidia, niska*, 72-73; K.M. Mallmann, *Rozwiązać przez jakikolwiek*, 85-99.
147 After the war (1945), some equipment that had been appropriated by Germans in this manner was "re-stolen" by the Soviets; other businesses were nationalized by the Polish State.
148 IPN-By.Ds. 25/66; AŻIH, Report 301/372, card 1-2; AŻIH, Ring. I, classification no. 940, cards 1-2, 7-8 and classification no. 871, card. 3; A. Pakentreger, *Polityka*, 36; Cz. Łuczak, "Demograficzne i ekonomiczne aspekty zagłady Żydów w okupowanej Polsce," *Przegląd Zachodni*, no. 56 (1989): 119.
149 R. Grzonkowski, *Kleczew*, 236-242.
150 Regulation Respecting the Laws and Customs of the War on Land, articles 36-56, recorded in D. Schindler and J. Toman, eds., *The Laws of Armed Conflicts: A Collection of Conventions, Resolutions and Other Documents* (Geneva, 1988), 87-92; Forced Labor Convention, 1930, articles 9-13.
151 Złoty refers to the Polish Zloty.
152 T. Kawski, *Kujawsko-dobrzyńcy*, 261; R. Grzonkowski, *Kleczew*, 242.
153 AŻIH, Ring I/381.
154 *Faschismus-Getto-Massenmord. Dokumentation über Ausrottung und Widerstand der Juden in Polen während des zweites weltkrieg* (Berlin, 1961), 399.

155 R. Grzonkowski, *Kleczew*, 242; B. Szczepański, ed., *Dzieje Słupcy* (Poznań, 1996), 225-226; J. Szymczak, ed., *Uniejów. Dzieje miasta* (Łódź-Uniejów, 1995), 278; T. Kawski, *Gminy*, passim; T. Kawski and M. Opioła, *Gminy*, passim.
156 AŻIH, 210/401, Kleczew, see Document 12 in Annex 1 (Letter 1).
157 Ibid.
158 Ibid.
159 Ibid.
160 *Eksterminacja Żydów*, 21-25.
161 W. Długoborski, "Żydzi z ziem polskich wcielonych do Rzeszy w KL Auschwitz-Birkenau," in *Zagłada Żydów*, 134. The author is mistaken in stating that ghettos were not established in Inowrocław Regierungsbezirk.
162 T. Richmond, *Konin*, 469.
163 YVA, M.1.E/338, testimony Melech Szafraniecki.
164 YVA-M-1-Q/176, testimony Dawid Rygiel, of February 26, 1948, in Ansbach, pp. 2-4.
165 YVA, O.93/29952, video testimony Josef (Joshu) Kazimierski, b. March 31, 1924, in Golina, VT-2, 9:50-15:00,
166 YVA, O.93/5585, video testimony Charles Lepek (Jechiel Chaim Łepek), b. August 28, 1923, in Golina, VT-1.
167 YVA, O.93/24710, video testimony Michel (Mendel) Prost, b. October 1, 1920, in Kleczew, VT-2.
168 Ibid.
169 Ibid.
170 Ibid.
171 YVA, O.93/24854, video testimony Bert (Baruch) Gembicki, b. October 15, 1916, in Kleczew, VT-1.
172 YVA, O.93/26326, video testimony Tzvi Malron (Hieronim Malarek), b. October 10, 1927, in Mogilno, VT-1, 26:00-29:00.
173 YVA, O.93/9257, video testimony Abram Landau, b. April 25, 1922, in Wilczyn, VT-2, 28:00-30:00.
174 YVA-M-1-Q/177, testimony Bert Gembicki, of May 6, 1948, in Ansbach, pp. 2-5.
175 Ibid.
176 YVA, O.93/29952, video testimony Josef (Joshu) Kazimierski, b. March 31, 1924, in Golina, VT-2, 12:00-15:00.
177 YVA-M-1-Q/176, testimony Dawid Rygiel, of February 26, 1948, in Ansbach, pp. 2-4.
178 Ibid.
179 YVA, O.93/5585, video testimony Charles Lepek (Jechiel Chaim Łepek), b. August 28, 1923, in Golina, VT-1.
180 Ibid., VT-1.
181 Ibid.
182 YVA, O.93/24854, video testimony Bert (Baruch) Gembicki, b. October 15, 1916, in Kleczew, VT-1, 25:00-27:00.
183 Ibid., VT-2.
184 YVA, O.93/9257, video testimony Abram Landau, b. April 25, 1922, in Wilczyn, VT-3.

185 YVA, O.93/26326, video testimony Tzvi Malron (Hieronim Malarek), b. October 10, 1927, in Mogilno, VT-2, 5:00-7:30.
186 Ibid.
187 Ibid.
188 Ibid., 8:30-11:00.
189 Ibid., 10:00-12:00.
190 The ninth day of the Jewish month of Av, when Jews mourn the destruction of the First and Second Temples in Jerusalem by fasting from sunset to the following night.
191 YVA, O.93/9257, video testimony ram Landau, b. April 25, 1922, in Wilczyn, VT-3, 10:00-12:00.
192 Ibid., 12:00-15:00.
193 Ibid., VT-3.
194 Ibid., VT-3, 5:00-7:00.
195 Ibid., VT-2, 22:50-25:00.
196 The deportation was reported in a letter dated July 29, 1940, to the Joint in Warsaw. AŻIH, 210/738, Zagórów; see Document 15, Annex 1 (Letter 4).
197 Ibid.
198 Ibid. see Document 16, Annex 1 (Letter 5).
199 Ibid. see Document 17, Annex 1 (Letter 6).
200 Ibid.
201 Ibid.
202 AŻIH, 210/738, Zagórów, see Document 18 in Annex 1 (Letter 7).
203 AŻIH, 210/738, Zagórów, see Document 19 in Annex 1 (Letter 8).
204 AŻIH, 210/738, Zagórów, see Document 20 in Annex 1 (Letter 9).
205 AŻIH, 210/738, Zagórów, see Document 21 in Annex 1 (Letter 10).
206 Ibid.
207 Ibid.
208 Ibid.
209 YVA, O.93/29952, video testimony Josef (Joshu) Kazimierski, b. March 31, 1924, in Golina, VT-2, 24:00-26:00.
210 A minyan (pl. *minyanim*) is a group of at least ten Jews that gathers for collective worship.
211 YVA, O.93/29952, video testimony Josef (Joshu) Kazimierski, b. March 31, 1924, in Golina, VT-2, 21:00-22:00.
212 Minutes of government meeting: report of conference on resettlement of Poles and Jews in the General Government from lands annexed to the Reich, January 8, 1941, at RSHA headquarters in Berlin, January 13, 1941, Kraków, recorded in *Okupacja i ruch oporu*, 317.
213 "Protokół posiedzenia rządu. Sprawozdanie z konferencji w sprawie przesiedlenia Polaków i Żydów do Generalnej Guberni z ziem włączonych do Rzeszy, odbytej 8 stycznia 1941 r. w Głównym Urzędzie Bezpieczeństwa Rzeszy w Berlinie, 1941 styczeń 13, Kraków," in *Okupacja i ruch oporu*, 318.
214 Minutes of government meeting: report of conference on resettlement of Poles and Jews in the General Government from lands annexed to the Reich, January 8, 1941, at RSHA headquarters in Berlin, January 13, 1941, Kraków, recorded in *Okupacja i ruch oporu*, 320.

215 OKW—*Oberkommando der Wehrmacht* (Wehrmacht High Command).
216 Minutes of government meeting: report of conference on resettlement of Poles and Jews in the General Government from lands annexed to the Reich, January 8, 1941, at RSHA headquarters in Berlin, January 13, 1941, Kraków, recorded in *Okupacja i ruch oporu*, p. 321.
217 Ibid.
218 Statements by Senior SS and Police Commander Krüger, State Secretary Bühler, and General Governor Frank at conference on January 8, 1941, at RSHA headquarters on the resettlement of Polish and Jewish population to the General Government, January 15, 1941, recorded in *Eksterminacja Żydów na ziemiach polskich*, 59-60.
219 Ibid., 61.

5 Forced Labor

1. JEWISH FORCED LABOR IN THE WARTHEGAU

From the first days of the Nazi occupation, Jews were put to grueling forced labor such as leveling ground, digging fire trenches, cleaning streets, collecting garbage, emptying cesspools, and burying the bodies of the murdered and the deceased.

Jewish forced labor was systematized after civil administrative authorities came into being. Once police-controlled Judenräte were empaneled, they were handed orders relating to the provision of forced labors. Only in 1940, however, due to the political and economic situation, did forced labor in the Warthegau begin to take on increasingly organized forms. During the autumn and winter of 1939, Jews were employed in sundry toils and in sweeping snow from streets and roads. After the German administration organized and went into action, its policies toward the Jews shifted from the somewhat unstructured form that was typical of the November 1939–early 1940 period into a more cohesive shape. This coincided with the first large wave of deportations of Poles and Jews from the Warthegau to the General Government, the German authorities hoping that the Warthegau would be emptied of Jews within a few months. The

Jews were under the similar impression that what awaited them in the near future was forced deportation to the east.

In late 1939 and early 1940, the authorities prepared economic plans for the Warthegau, including extensive infrastructure development. This effort was fundamentally connected with Germany's changing strategic situation. After the victories in Western Europe (especially in France, whence British forces had been evacuated to their home islands), a change of direction toward preparations for war with the USSR began. To prepare for Operation Barbarossa, infrastructure development accelerated, with particular reference to communication lines, railways, and roads, accompanied by the construction of new bridges and viaducts. The works were carried out mainly in the General Government and in the context of Operation Otto. Much of the rail and road link from Berlin to Warsaw, however, ran through the Warthegau; it, too, had to be developed.

Plans for the evacuation of Jews to Madagascar were drawn up but soon proved unworkable. As shortages of food, housing, and transport snarled the forced deportation of Jews to the General Government, the German authorities began to mull the possibility of exploiting Jewish forced labor from the Warthegau in the Old Reich (Altreich), in a departure from their actions thus far toward Jews in the territories that the Reich had annexed as a result of the war against Poland. On November 1, 1940, the injunction against sending Jewish forced labors to the Old Reich was lifted by decision of Gestapo chief SS-Obergruppenführer Heinrich Müller,[1] and in December 1940, a transport of Jewish workers was organized for the construction of a motorway from Frankfurt an der Oder to Poznań.

In the Warthegau, as opposed to the General Government, there were no clearly formulated rules regarding Jewish forced labor. Only Circular No. 557, of September 12, 1941, regulated the employment of Jews. By decision of Reich Governor Greiser, employment matters relating to Jews were transferred to the leadership of the National Labor Office (*Landesarbeitsamt*) in Poznań; only this office could grant permission for the employment of Jews in the Warthegau.[2] Greiser's directive forbade the transfer of workers from one job to another without permission. Appointed governors (*prezesi rejencji*) were responsible for implementing these regulations. These officials, in turn, supervised county governors (*Landräte*) and mayors (*Oberbürgermeister*).

Most employment of Jews in the Warthegau took place outside settled localities and ghettos. The sole exception was in the Łódź ghetto, where large-scale manufacturing activity took shape. Since the Łódź ghetto was almost hermetically sealed and a special ghetto scrip was used there instead of legal tender, all of its residents depended on external elements and may be considered forced laborers.

In other communities and, later, in collective ghettos, the situation was more fluid. After the first few months, in which deportations took place and the Jews' economic situation was grim, things stabilized in 1940. It was then that production in the Łódź ghetto developed on a massive scale. Elsewhere, however, economic conditions remained very difficult. The transfer of Jews to rural ghettos and the concentration of Jews in the Łódź ghetto did little to improve the situation. In late 1940 and early 1941, mobilization of the young and strong for work in forced labor camps began; these camps became the main venues for such labor. In some villages, forced labor of a local nature took place.

In discussing the problems of forced labor, it bears repeating that forced labor played a secondary role in ghettos and localities, with the sole exception of the Łódź ghetto, which also became a labor camp for all intents and purposes. In the Warthegau, unlike the General Government, labor details (*placówki*) of Jews who lived in ghettos and worked outside of them had very limited significance. In Poznań, for example, several labor camps were set up, one at the city stadium. In other ghettos, most forced laborers were housed separately from their families.

Labor camps had no unified organization. The Warthegau had no central supervisory organization for labor camps. As mentioned, the National Labor Office (*Landesarbeitsamt*) in Poznań was responsible for Jewish forced labor. At the level of local government, however, presidents, governors, and mayors were responsible for carrying out Greiser's directives. Infrastructure projects was entrusted to private firms. For these reasons, different kinds of labor camps went by different names, i.e., those exclusively for Jews, and those that had mixed populations (Jews and Poles), among other distinctions. Forced labor camps were

40. Jewish forced laborers deported from Sompolno and other localities to Blechhammer in 1941 (YVA, sig. 1088_2)

frequently called *Zwangsarbeitslager* (ZAL) or *Arbeitslager* (AL). There were also names like *Judenarbeitslager* (labor camps for Jews) or *Judenlager* (Julag—Jew-camps). Sometimes the name *Arbeitslager für Juden* (labor camps for Jews) was used. Labor camps set up along the highway under construction from Frankfurt to Poznań were called *Reichsautobahn-*

41. Jewish forced laborers on the way to work (YVA, sig. 1088_2)

lager (RAB, national highway camps). Labor camps set up to upgrade the rail line were called *Reichsbahnlager*—Reich railway camps. Camps where different companies employed Jewish workers were called *Gemeinschaftslager* (collective camps).

In May 1942, following a reorganization of the forced-labor system, control of labor camps changed hands. By decision of Fritz Sauckel, the supervision of labor camps was handed over to DAF (*Deutsche Arbeitsfront*, the German Labor Front), which introduced registration and standard numbering of the camps. From then on, DAF required the camps to submit monthly reports to its district offices, which forwarded them to DAF headquarters in Berlin.

Labor Camps

The establishment of this network of forced labor camps accelerated the decline of the Jewish population in Inowrocław Regierungsbezirk. Jews who reached these venues rarely returned to the places from which they had been taken. Moreover, the labor camp mechanism shattered relations within families and larger social groups. It weakened the potential of the "ghettoized" communities, which, deprived of its young and able-bodied members, strained to keep body and soul together. Only the elderly, children, women, the ill, and those unfit for work remained in ghettos. Along with their demographic contraction, the geographic confines of the ghettos were steadily being reduced to make them easier to supervise. Simultaneously, the Nazi authorities fine-tuned their regulations, most often impeding Jews from circulating outside Jewish districts and preventing non-Jews from entering them. The resulting state of affairs fostered residential, natural, and moral degradation.

In 1939–1940, referral to labor camps was limited in scale. On November 7, 1939, several dozen Jews from Lubień were sent to the labor camps in Buk and nearby locations in Nowy Tomyśl County. In a roundup in Kutno on September 19, 1939, captives were closed in a church and the Moderne Cinema, after which seventy of them were selected and sent to a camp for civilian prisoners of war in Łęczyca. Some 10,000 civilian prisoners, Polish and Jewish, found themselves interned in Sieradz, where they were persecuted and tortured, robbed, humiliated, and starved. Terms of detention lasted from several days (e.g., in Kutno) to several weeks or months. When the summer of 1940 turned to autumn, hundreds of Jews from different parts of Inowrocław Regierunsbezirk were directed in groups to the transit camp in Błonie in Inowrocław. Some of them, after interrogation, were transferred to other locations. In July 1940, forty Jews from Inowrocław Regierunsbezirk reached the Cieślin camp. A group of a hundred people from Nieszawa County (Radziejów, Piotrków Kujawski) was sent to Łojewo in the autumn of 1940. In December 1940, a selected group of men from Koło was sent to Poznań. This led to the establishment of several camps in Kalisz County.[3]

Displacements to camps increased considerably in the middle of 1941. Jews from Inowrocław Regierunsbezirk were usually taken to forced-labor camps within the Regierunsbezirk, in Mogilno, Inowrocław, Konin, and Żnin Counties. Many transports terminated in Posen Regierungsbezirk. Although the number of people directed to different camps cannot be determined, the available details suffice to describe the phenomenon.

One of the first transports, sent from Kłodawa on June 6, 1941, consisted of 150 men who initially reached the ghetto in Koło and subsequently (on June 20, 1941) were sent to a camp in Bolewice near Nowy Tomyśl. Another transport, sent to Poznań District on or around June 18, 1941, included Jews from Izbica Kujawska. Initially, this transport, too, was taken to Koło. When local Jews were added to the group, it numbered 500 people. On June 18 and 20, 1941, they reached the camp in Poznań; afterwards they moved on to camps in Krzyżowniki and on the Dąbie road. Another group of 225 people from Izbica Kujawska was taken to Poznań and Inowrocław on June 24, 1941. A transport from Włocławek and nearby towns with 651 people aboard (230 from Lubraniec, 159 from Włocławek, 126 from Brześć Kujawski, 51 from Kowal, 51 from Chodecz, 30 from Zduńska Wola, and four from other towns) reached Radziwiłł Fort in Poznań on June 26, 1941. A week later, 500 Jews were sent en bloc to Chodzież. The last transport of men from Włocławek and nearby towns took place on April 26, 1942. Transports from Żychlin, Sompolno, Kutno, Zagórów, and Krośniewice were initially sent to Poznań in July 1941. Also in 1941, groups of Jews from various regions in Poland, mainly Kalisz (Łódź) Regierunsbezirk, and local Jews from Kutno, Konin, and Koło Counties in Inowrocław Regierunsbezirk went to labor camps for Jews in the Inowrocław Regierunsbezirk. In autumn 1941, sixty-five people from Łódź, Pabianice, and Gostynin were taken to a camp in Papros. Those from Pabianice and nearby villages were sent on to Kruszwica. Jews from Warsaw, Kalisz, and Piotrków Kujawski were placed in Broniewo. Three hundred people from Gąbin, Gostynin, Koło, Łódź, and Służew were taken to Janikowo. In 1941–1943, Jews from Radziejów, Pabianice, and Łask County were placed in Radojewice. Jews from Poddebice, Gostynin, and Sanniki found themselves in a camp in Konin-Czarków on March 9, 1942. In the autumn of 1942, 200 people from the Łódź ghetto were placed in Orłowo.[4]

Mobilization for Service in Labor Camps

Workers for labor camps were drafted in accordance with orders pertaining to Jewish forced labor in different localities. People had an incentive to accept work in labor camps due to high unemployment and an inability to feed their families; they were promised a small sum for their toil in the camps. Only in the first few weeks, however. did people eagerly report to the labor camps. After that, very bad news about the treatment of Jewish workers in these camps began to arrive, speaking of beatings of Jewish laborers and poor nourishment that soon impaired their health. Once these messages reached home, young Jews began attempting to evade this kind of service. Therefore, to mobilize the requisite number of workers, the German authorities turned to other methods. In the Łódź ghetto, convicted criminals were sent to labor camps first. Opponents of Chaim Rumkowski's Ältestenrat regime in Łódź were also among the first to be sent. When these did not suffice, the authorities began to fill their quotas by coercion and arrests. Those who missed summonses to forced labor suffered sanctions such as the withholding of ration cards—a penalty that affected family members as well. Before being shipped to the camps, candidates underwent a medical examination in front of a commission that was supposed to exempt the unfit.

Deportation of Young Men to Labor Camps: The Case of Zagórów

Deportations from many Jewish communities in the area to Zagórów caused its Jewish population to balloon to several thousand. Some were employed, especially the young; older individuals were unlikely to be employed and began to scavenge for any job they could find. In some cases, they switched crafts. Either way, the possibilities of employment remained very limited in most cases. The biggest employers of Jews in Zagórów were the German authorities and the kehilla (i.e., the Judenrat). Jews not employed by either of these had to seek work at their own initiative or remain unemployed.

The German authorities posted young Jews to labor in different places in Zagórów and elsewhere. Some were recruited for cleaning jobs in Zagórów. Every day, young men were taken to a monastery that had been converted into a Wehrmacht base for this kind of labor. According to witnesses, the Wehrmacht treated the Jews well. After a day's work, the workers received a loaf of dark rectangular army-issue bread that they could take home to help feed their families.[5] Much in contrast was the *Arbeitsamt* (labor office) in Zagórów. It was run by a German named

Kessler, who drank around the clock. Every Jew who had to visit his office trembled with fear. Kessler habitually brandished and discharged his handgun, shouting and cursing as he implored the workers to put in an honest day's labor.[6]

Young people were systematically taken from the village ghetto in Zagórów to forced labor outside the ghetto, usually within a radius of 30 kilometers.

The assignment of people to forced labor followed rules. Testimonies report consistently that each family had to send two men to work each day. In families that had a preponderance of able-bodied sons, the young went first. According to the witness Josef Kazimierski, sometimes the laborers were sent to work in the woods. This had some advantages: workers there had to clear the woods of dry branches, which they were allowed to take home afterwards. Although they could not carry much of it on their backs, they came home each day with some firewood, with which they stoked their typical *tall chimneyed* brass stoves.[7]

As noted, Jews from the Zagórów ghetto were also assigned to labor out of town. In many cases, young men were taken to Konin (nearly 39 kilometers away). Josef Kazimierski reports having been sent to Konin in lieu of his older brother Jonathan. He and others were employed by the Germans in a project outside of Konin en route to Golina: the construction of a villa for a high-ranking German functionary in Konin. After completing the work, the laborers were posted to the construction of a road to Warsaw, most likely in preparation for Operation Barbarossa. After finishing this job, they were freed and sent back to Zagórów, unguarded and on foot.[8]

Wishing to Germanize Konin, the Germans had to modify and reorganize the town by destroying and rebuilding part of it. They did the same in other Polish towns and cities, especially Kraków. According to a witness from Kleczew, Jews who were selected for these labors in Konin were required to empty the synagogue of sundry objects in the course of the demolition work.[9] However distasteful this duty was, it was organized autonomously. There were no police. According to Michel Prost, the workers seized all Jewish libraries and holy books and gathered them in one place. Since many of the books were bound in leather, the workers had to tear them apart to retrieve this reusable material.[10]

On one occasion, the Germans loaded ten to twelve workers into large trucks and drove them to Konin. Their task was to unlock Jewish-owned houses, load their furniture and clothing into the trucks, and deliver the loot to the Gestapo office in the Zagórów ghetto for the use of Gestapo men's families.[11] The supervisors gave the Jewish workers nothing to eat all day. Lucky workers found something nutritious in the houses they were emptying. The witness Bert Gembicki tried to take something with him to sell while assigned to these tasks. Although the supervisors once caught him and beat him severely, he continued to do it in order to earn some money for himself and his family.[12] In the summer, a loudspeaker summoned all men to report to the Gestapo at 7:00 a.m. for daily assignments.[13]

Although the ghetto in Zagórów was open (not fenced), signs forbade the inmates to leave without a permit. Since nobody really guarded the ghetto, it could be exited and re-entered. Still, there was a curfew in the ghetto and one defied it at one's peril.

Some Jews, at their own initiative, began to do service jobs for peasants of the area. One of Josef Kazimierski's brothers, for example, a tailor who had his own portable sewing machine, performed sundry jobs for the peasants, mainly mending used clothes. Since new consumer goods, including clothes, were in very short supply during the war, most of the population had to mend used clothing constantly. Kazimierski's brother worked not for money but for food—bread, meat, lentils, flour, beans, etc. With rationing in effect, it was not possible to buy food in shops without ration cards.

In the second half of 1941 (most likely September), mobilizations of young men for forced labor increased considerably. Although evidence for this is lacking, the authorities may by then have set a time for the liquidation of the ghetto and wished to deport able-bodied young men first. If this was the case, it means that the pattern applied in Zagórów was different than that used in many other ghettos in the Warthegau and the General Government. In most places, pre-deportation selections removed most of the population and left able-bodied men, or in some cases women, behind. In Zagórów, the authorities may have wished to extract the men first in order to avoid unrest.

According to the witness Leon Jedwab, in the autumn of 1941 the authorities announced that they needed 450 young men for work in a labor camp.[14] Those who agreed to enlist were taken to the labor camp in Inowrocław but were not told that their destination would be far from the ghetto. Since they had packed few personal items and clothing, after a few weeks their clothes became dirty and threadbare. Therefore, two of their number, Chaim Sieradz and Yeshaya Brysz, asked the camp commander for permission to go to Zagórów and replenish their supplies. Permission was granted—this was before the deportation of the ghetto population—and each family that had somebody in the camp prepared a sack with clothing and personal items with their respective loved one's name on it. Leon Jedwab recalled that his mother packed not only clothes but also a golden chain and a gold watch—her engagement presents. These items helped him to survive the camp.[15]

Another witness recalled that his family had been asked one day, possibly in the summer or autumn of 1941, to send two men to work in an unspecified location. Two of four brothers—Josef and Shlomo—were taken by truck to the labor camp in Inowrocław, a journey several hours long.[16] Then some of those recruited were sent on to the Hohensalza forced-labor camp in Inowrocław to mine salt.[17] About six weeks later, all remaining Jews in Zagórów were led into a nearby forest and exterminated. By the end of 1941, Zagórów was judenfrei.[18]

Siting and Organization of the Camps

Most labor camps in the Warthegau were temporary and sited in public buildings such as schools, granaries, barns, pigsties, mansions, forester quarters, and mills. In a few cases, barracks built specifically for labor camps were used. Such facilities were erected in labor camps that the Organisation Todt[19] built during the construction of the highway and railway extension to the east. A specific example of the use of public buildings was a labor camp set up at the municipal stadium in Poznań. About 900 prisoners were concentrated there, some sleeping under the stands and the rest under the sky. Here existing buildings were used for obvious reasons: it saved money and it allowed the camp to pop into existence instantaneously. Besides, many camps were temporary and their workers were transferred to other places after the completion of specific jobs.

Importantly, these were labor camps in name only. They were actually places of lodging; the work took place elsewhere. In fact, there were no permanent labor camps near factories in the Warthegau, as was the case in the General Government from 1942 on.

Each camp was run by a camp leader (a *Lagerführer*—an SS officer). Other important functions were discharged by both Germans and Volksdeutsche. Germans served as *Wachmänner* (guards) and in other capacities. On the railway, the sentries were also railway guards (*Bahnschutz*). In agricultural estates and factories, watchmen doubled as foremen. In some camps, the wardens were Poles.[20] In the camps for Jews, older Jews did certain tasks, e.g., work as camp doctors, and occasionally there was a Jewish Order Service (internal police). Most tasks associated with the operation of the camp—cooking, working at the warehouse, providing technical services, etc.—were performed by the Jews themselves.

Living Conditions in the Camps

Living conditions in the camps were influenced mainly by such factors as food, labor, sanitary conditions, and medical care. Food rations for Jewish workers in camps in the Warthegau were regulated by Circular B/9 of July 9, 1941. This document, issued by the State Office for Supplies (*Landesernährungsamt*), set the weekly ration at 250 grams of horsemeat, 100 grams of fat, and 2250 grams of bread.[21] The cost of food was set at RM (Reichsmark) 1. With the approval of Ernst Kendzi, Reich trustee for labor in the Warthegau (*Reichstreuhändler bei der Arbeit Reichsstatthalter*), this amount could be exceeded. On June 25, 1942, by decree of the Department of Economics and Labour (*Arbeit und Wirtschaft*) of the Warthegau governorate, the daily budget for meals and lodging was reduced to less than this sum.[22]

Even though the official standards of nutrition were too low to allow the inmates to perform hard physical labor, the reality in the camps was even worse than it appeared because the standards were not respected. Due to endemic corruption, workers received reduced food rations and meals of poor quality, resulting in gastrointestinal diseases. The combination of hard labor and malnutrition sapped the workers' strength quickly, inducing high rates of disease, emaciation, and work accidents.

To improve the food situation, Jewish workers attempted to interact with the local population and often resorted to theft, for which, if caught red-handed, they could expect severe punishment. Those working in the countryside or on estates were somewhat better off, as opportunities for food supplementation were more common there.

The aforementioned woes were compounded by poor hygienic conditions. Since most camps were organized *ad hoc* and were not designed to accommodate large numbers of people, crowding and filth prevailed. Workers often had no place to wash, received minuscule allocations of soap and washing powder, had no change of clothes, and slept on makeshift bunks and straw. The camps quickly became infested with lice and bedbugs, causing illnesses to spread rapidly. The most common illness was typhus, which heavily beset those workers who were less resistant to disease. Physicians were available in larger camps but they lacked enough medicine to cope with the spread of disease and could not influence the root cause of the morbidity: the living conditions. Thus, their ministrations were mainly ineffective.

In addition to diseases, work-related injuries and wounds were grounds for medical intervention. Jewish workers whose labors were associated with moving heavy objects, such as the expansion of railway lines, or using sharp tools often succumbed to injuries. Other significant causes of injury were beatings by supervisors and guards. To make matters worse, employers bore the cost of retaining workers whether they worked or not; thus, they strove to rush the disabled back to work. Yet another threat was the selection and shooting of inmates who ceased to be able-bodied, a practice found in many camps.

As for wages and working conditions, in the early years of the labor camps Jewish workers' wages were set at RM 0.3 per hour, with tax deducted at source and deposited to a special account of the Łódź ghetto board. From this account, RM 13 assistance grants were paid to families of workers who remained in the ghetto. On June 26, 1942, however, a new regulation introduced the principle of paying Jewish workers nothing whatsoever and established a "Jew-loan" (*Judenleigebühr*) set at RM 0.7 RM per calendar day. Employers of Jews had to remit this fee to the account of the Łódź ghetto board or that of the mayor or commissioner of the workers' places of origin. Since most Jewish communities in the Warthegau were liquidated between the beginning of 1941 and 1942, the Łódź ghetto board became the legal heir of all Jews in the Warthegau and received remittances on account of all Jews employed in labor camps.[23]

Examples of Forced-Labor Camps in the Warthegau

Jews' working conditions in labor camps were largely a function of a system that not only crimped the camps' spending on the maintenance of Jewish labor but also encouraged the maximization of the workers' use due to their low cost. Another factor working against the Jews was the lack of supervision regarding treatment of labor and compliance with rules, encouraging abuse and impunity.

A witness recalled:

> [...] Jews were sent to various places for hard labor. On the way, they were beaten under the pretext that they had been working too slowly, and when they walked faster they were beaten for trying to escape [...]. Jews were forced to clean toilets with their bare hands, lick the floors with their tongues, carry heavy rocks to and fro, and dig pits and then fill them in—all under a hail of beatings. Jews worked all day without any food. Going home late at night, these exhausted Jews had to sing merry folk songs to the accompaniment of beatings with rubber truncheons by the Germans.[24]

Workers were chosen on the basis of their appearance, with the Nazis eagerly selecting the Orthodox.[25] Sometimes "moral" aims were taken into consideration. As residents of Koło were forced to repair a destroyed bridge, for example, they had to sing a song titled "Our Śmigły Rydz" repeatedly.[26] This ditty had several slightly different versions; in Kleczew, for example, on their way to work they had to sing, "*Śmigły-Rydz, hyc, hyc!* He taught us nothing. And our Hitler, the man of gold, taught us how to work."[27]

"Undisciplined" compulsory labor quickly succumbed to regulation. Jewish men aged fourteen to fifty were caught in the snare. Every day, Jewish community administrations (kehillot) and the Judenräte that oversaw them had to supply a predetermined number of workers on pain of severe penalties against both the Jews and the councils.

Forced Labor in Kleczew

Kleczew was one of the towns in which groups were housed in barracks. The sizes of these groups varied: 800–1,200 in Włocławek, 300 in Uniejów, and so on.[28] In Kleczew, the working group numbered forty to fifty, most aged 13–30 and hailing from Kleczew, Wilczyn, and Ślesin. Women were also included. The place of detention was a cluster of farm buildings belonging to Bronisław Żołnierkiewicz. Living conditions were ghastly. The inmates, supervised by local military police, were put to diverse clearing and building tasks, such as the construction of a military police station, building the Kleczew–Budzisław Kościelny road[29] (roadwork was very common), cleaning river banks, digging drainage ditches, and so on.[30] In many locations, German or Volksdeutsche farmers "hired" Jews for heavy field work and paid them a few pfennigs per day. Sometimes grueling make-work was assigned, such as carrying stones from one side of a field to the other. In the Wrocław ghetto, Jews compressed mud in the street with garden rollers.[31]

The Labor Camp in Inowrocław

In the summer of 1941, the authorities demanded two people from every family. Thus, Charles Łepek and one of his brothers stuffed some personal necessities into a small pack, reported for labor, and were registered. They were transported by truck to a location three or four hours away; unbeknownst to them, it was the labor camp in Inowrocław. There they did various jobs, mainly railroad construction. They were beaten with whips and treated worse than horses. Charles' brother sustained a bad cut and nearly lost his hand; it healed crooked for lack of proper treatment.[32]

Michel Prost of Kleczew testifies that 300–350 people aged 17–30 were rounded up by military police for labor in July 1941. The authorities selected the best professionals for work on the German railway and took them to the Hohensalza (Inowrocław) camp. Although they were not free, they were not strictly supervised even though there were guards. Firma Fischer of Frankfurt am Main moved tons of earth for a viaduct that would expand the existing linle by carrying a new track. The conditions and the labor were grim but generally survivable; according to Prost, only one prisoner died of tuberculosis. Prost and the others remained in the camp until late 1942 or early 1943. Then they were transferred to the next camp, there being many camps along the railway. When work on one section of the track was done, the workers were forwarded to another section and another camp.[33]

Given the insufficiency of official rations in the camp, the prisoners tried to augment their nutrition in any possible way. They could go out at night to obtain food from peasants, often through theft. They sometimes managed to get hold of marmalade and other staples and, after work in the evenings, could cook on a stove or oven in their barracks. Once, as Michel Prost had ten liters of soup made of potatoes, tomatoes, and other vegetables cooking on the stove, the Lagerkommandant barged in and demanded to know who was cooking and what was being cooked. It's soup, Prost replied, offering offered some to the commandant, who tasted the potatoes and complimented the chef. According to Prost, one could never know how the staff members would react.[34] Their attitudes depended on their ideology. Some were ideological Nazis, others were not. When the Lagerkommandant was a Nazi, life in the camp was much more difficult than it was with the Lagerkommandant of the soup anecdote, who was not.[35]

After working in Żegotki, Bert Gembicki (originally from Kleczew) was transferred in early 1942 to the camp in Inowrocław, where many young men from the Zagórów ghetto were interned in a males-only facility. Life there was a little better, Gembicki reports: the inmates were housed in barracks, and could even wash their underwear,[36] and they partook of better (but still insufficient) food. At night, prisoners left the camp through holes in the barbed wire to approach farmers for victuals.[37] The inmates leveled earth and loaded and unloaded rails under appalling conditions, especially when it was raining. Punishments were meted out within minutes of the onset of work.[38]

Abram Landau's testimony illuminates the practice of transferring laborers from one labor camp to another. In his case, after finishing a section of work, the Jewish laborers were transferred by foot to Rąbinek, a camp situated in a forest that had barracks large enough to accommodate fifty to sixty boys. The task in this camp was the construction of a railway station. It was hell, Landau reports. The guards killed people; prisoners had to "organize" food (potatoes) and even pilfered from dogs.[39] All the guards in Rąbinek were German civilians. The work was arduous and involved the moving of heavy objects. Prisoners harvested potatoes and carrots from a field. They slept on the floor, contracting worms, scabies, and miscellaneous diseases. After enduring this for four or five months, they went on to another camp.[40]

Michel Prost provides another example of labor mobilization among camps. In 1942, he was transferred from Hohensalza to a labor camp in Andrzejów. This place, he reports, had been a popular vacation site before the war. During summer holidays, children and women from Łódź came there for long stretches while men arrived for weekends only. In this camp, Jewish prisoners worked for the *Hoch und Tief Baugesellschaft Frankfurt an der Oder* Railway Company. According to Prost, the work was good. He worked there as a mechanic, looking after machinery, tending petrol pumps, and cleaning machines.[41] When the camp was liquidated, the prisoners were transported to the railway station, loaded into cattle cars by the Gestapo, and taken to Birkenau. This probably occurred in 1944.[42]

The Żegotki Labor Camp

Charles Łepek was also transferred from camp to camp along the railway. According to his testimony, after several months at the Inowrocław labor camp, about forty people, including him, were sent to the forced-labor camp in Żegotki.[43] The selectees were ordered to board trucks and were taken to the camp, eighty to ninety kilometers from Zagórów, leaving their families behind. Gembicki recalls spending the winter of 1941 in a house with broken windows and no heating. Instead of beds, he and the others had shelf-like bunks with no mattresses. To soften the hard surface, the inmates laid clothes on the planks. Rats from a nearby farm proliferated like stray cats. The house did have a stove on which the prisoners could cook a stew of unwashed potatoes, horsemeat, and bits of vegetables.[44]

Men worked in the fields under the supervision of one German and two Poles. The field was haphazardly demarcated and had to be re-measured, a grueling task entailing many consecutive days of shoveling. The laborers in the field received soup for dinner and drew water from a well, there being no plumbing. To wash, they filled a barrel with water outdoors in freezing cold and under Volksdeutsche guard. Their shirts were washed along with the worms that had stuck to them, due to the laborers' work of turning the soil, and hung on a rope to dry. The worms froze along with the wet clothes, which the men wore to work afterwards. Some inmates sat on their clothes to dry them.[45] Winter was grim: rats, worms, and lice abounded, but warm clothes were absent.[46]

Laborers worked twelve hours a day. In the winter, they shoveled snow and pushed trucks that got stuck in the muddy road. The guards hit them. Everything was wet. "I don't know how we survived. There was no food. Two people died there from rats that attacked them," relates Gembicki.

Two girls from another camp were sent there to cook. The German guards sexually assaulted them, impregnating one. When the owner of the farm heard about the incident, he called the police, who asked who was responsible. Somebody accused Bert Gembicki and another man. The police questioned them, subjected each to a beating, and then ordered them back to the fields to work. Several weeks later, when the girl's pregnancy became obvious, the commandant said that if the girl had the baby, she would have to kill it.[47]

Another pregnant Jewish girl was present and Bert Gembicki and another prisoner assisted during childbirth, although Gembicki did not really know how. After the birth, they swathed the baby in rags. A few days later, the girl was forced to kill the infant. She fed it vinegar, Gembicki reports, though he admitted that the cause of death may have been something else. Either way, the baby died.[48]

Charles Łepek and his brother went first to Żegotki and then to Wiesengrund, near Poznań, where a *Meister* commanded a group of Jewish workers who lived in a little house surrounded by a barbed-wire fence. When the detainees were sent to work, the guards opened a gate to let them out. They performed hard labor, such as draining fields in a *folwark* (large farm) where various crops (peas, potatoes, wheat, etc.) were grown. However, the field was muddy and workers had to dig channels for drainage pipes—first smaller ones, then larger ones. There was no medical aid in the camp. Łepek and others worked there between 1941 and 1943.[49]

Some Jews committed suicide in forced-labor camps. An individual named Podchlebnik is mentioned as having climbed to an attic in order to leap to the ground for this purpose. He was one of many. Hard labor in mud and cold water sapped inmates' health, inflicting many illnesses, including urinary tract problems. The prisoners suffered from hunger and were given no clothes. There were cases of harassment by other prisoners; in one known case, three brothers helped one another fend off bullies.[50] Those who died were buried near the camp.[51]

One day the Germans informed the detainees that they would be sent to a prison camp (*Straflager*). The day before they were supposed to make the move, a Sunday morning, a miracle happened: instead, SS men took all the prisoners to Inowrocław. About a week after that, the prisoners were taken to Buna. Although hungry, they were still alive, in a train, in the winter.[52] Of the approximately forty men who had begun the stint in Żegotki, twenty-three or so survived.[53]

2. THE FATE OF THE FORCED LABORERS

The forced-labor inmates often met a tragic fate. Persecution, labor beyond their abilities, lack of proper sanitary infrastructure, and scanty food rations killed them en masse. According to estimates, 600 men and 100 women died in camps scattered across Inowrocław County in 1939–1944.[54] Those who survived the liquidation of their first camps were transferred to other camps. Such transfers were preceded by selections, with the sick and those unfit for work removed from the camp and murdered under unknown circumstances. Sometimes, so-called "return transports" were created for them. Anna Ziółkowska presumes that most were taken to the death camps in Chełmno on the Nerem (Kulmhof) and Oświęcim-Brzezinka (Auschwitz-Birkenau).[55] Those detained in the Papros camp were taken to Edwinów in early 1943 and then, most probably, to Essen in August 1943. A group of thirty from the Broniewo camp was delivered to Radojewice on October 5, 1942. When this camp was dissolved in the summer of 1943, all the inmates were sent to a concentration camp. In early 1943, people from Inowrocław were taken to the camp in Andrzejów, near Łódź, where they were joined by 200 Jews from the camp in Cieślin in March 1943 and by others from Jaksice Borkowo in July 1944. Smaller groups vanished without a trace as the camps were liquidated. One may be fairly sure that they were murdered in secret locations. Jewish women from Orłów shared such a fate.[56] The following case study, concerning the forced-labor camp in Czarków, may serve as an example of the fate of many labor-camp inmates elsewhere.

The forced-labor Camp in Czarków and its Liquidation

The forced-labor camp in Czarków belonged to the chain of labor camps along the Berlin–Warsaw–Poznań railway. To excavate and level the ground for an extension of the track at the Konin station, a large number of Polish workers—approximately 200—was engaged by the Brietz firm. In the course of 1942, when this labor force proved insufficient, an Arbeitslager für Juden (labor camp for Jews) was established. Polish workers erected several wooden barracks on Bydgoska Road in Czarków, running from Konin to Niesłusz and Ślesin, and enclosed the facility with barbed wire. The first superintendent of the camp was Hausbrandt; he was succeeded by Wolf.[57]

The first group of workers was from a transport of Jews that had reached Konin station from various places such as Gostynin. In the freight cars were more than 1,000 people, including many boys just over thirteen years of age. The inmates, all of whom spoke Polish, formed a column for the march into Czarków.[58] In addition to this transport, other Jews were probably brought to the camp. Living conditions in the camp were difficult, because—again—the authorities delivered insufficient amounts of food for prisoners performing hard physical labor. Mortality in the camp was high on this account; additional prisoners died from beatings and shootings by the guards and from disease. Their corpses were hauled by horse cart to the Catholic cemetery on Kolska Street in Konin and buried there. These special transports were accompanied by a group of

Jewish workers under guard that tended to the haulage and the interment. According to the witness Józef Kantarowski, at least a hundred corpses were transported in this manner during the lifetime of the camp. Many of these people had succumbed to exhaustion; other bodies had smashed skulls, the result of baton blows, or evidence of wounds from guards' shotguns, rifles, and pistols.[59]

In his diary, Rabbi Yehoshua Moshe Aaronson of Sanniki describes the burial of Jews from Czarków labor camp at the Catholic cemetery:

> We buried the dead of the Konin camp as best we could, according to Jewish rites and traditions, but they would not permit us to bury them in the Jewish cemetery, only in the Christian graveyard. In every grave I tried to place a bottle in which there was a note giving the name of the dead, date of death, etc. In July 1942, some twenty men were taken from us for work in the Polish cemetery. Some Jews had been buried in special graves among those of the Poles, and the mayor of Konin ordered these bodies to be exhumed, and reburied in a communal grave at the southwest corner. There a pit was dug, about twenty meters long and two meters wide. Into this pit were placed all the dead and the killed who had previously been buried separately on a hill opposite. The work was hard as well as saddeningly painful, the more so as it was carried out under the supervision of an armed guard, who obliged the Jews to labor to the end of their strength. With his watch in hand, he allowed five minutes for the removal of each corpse to the new place. He would not allow a single minute to be spent on taking a look at the bodies of the martyrs. This was the method of removal: the bodies were lifted by garden forks poked into the eyeholes or the skull or body. Then lime was thrown onto each body before it was thrust into the pit. Those who carried out this work included relatives of the dead. They were forbidden to take the bottles containing details of each of the dead. I did manage to throw a few of these bottles into the pit without the guard noticing, but most of these bottles remained where I had first put them –though the dead, to whom they refer, do not lie there.[60]

After the war, the following inscription was placed at the location of the mass graves:

To the Jews abominably murdered by the Nazi oppressors in the camp in Czarków in 1942–43. Compatriots. Konin XI 1945.[61]

In addition, hundreds of enfeebled and ill Jews were trucked into the woods in the Kazimierz Biskupi area and shot.[62] Prisoners were also shot inside the labor camp by policemen from Konin. During one of these shootings twelve inmates were killed and their unburied bodies were left in the camp for several days.[63] This was probably done for show, in order to deter others from trying to escape or resist. Prisoners were also killed outside the camp, while working on excavations and railway construction.

The inmates in this camp were employed by two private German companies. Inspector Krein supervised all German companies that held contracts for the expansion of the railway junction at Konin. One of the companies, the aforementioned Brietz, was headquartered in Hannover. Its manager and foremen treated detainees humanely and, according the Regional Commission for the Investigation of Nazi Crimes in Poznań, refrained from abuse. The second company was Ostdeutsche Tiefbau Gesellschaft Jędrecki Stanislaus und Stoike Naumburg am Bober der Bob51er. Co-owned by Jędrecki and Stoike, it was established in a town in Zielona Góra district that bore the name Naumburg during the war and was renamed Nowogród Bobrzański afterwards. While Stoike behaved correctly toward the detainees, Jędrecki harassed them, thrashed them with a leather truncheon until they lost consciousness, and beat them as they lay on the ground. After work, the beaten prisoners were brought back to the camp by their peers. In addition to Jędrecki, two company supervisors mistreated prisoners: construction manager (*Bauführer*) Schönemann and Schachtmeister Eder. They were known to beat prisoners with knife handles and iron poles.[64]

According to witnesses, Jews who worked at expanding the railway line in Konin were less productive than Polish workers because they were poorly nourished and, for the most part, exhausted. Many were not used to hard physical labor. Thirteen-year-old boys worked among them. Unable to perform the arduous labor, they were beaten by overseers and guards.[65]

Primarily responsible for the policy of violence and abuse against prisoners at the labor camp for Jews in Czarków were the camp commandants, Hausbrandt and Wolf, and officers at the Gestapo base in Konin— especially Hugo Arendt, who visited the camp often. Executions there were carried out by members of a military police unit that was stationed in Konin in 1942–1943. Among the guards in the camp, Aleksander Grabowski and Seher were notorious for their exceptional cruelty; they carried out many killings during their army service. After the war, Grabowski was sentenced to death by a district court in Kalisz and executed.[66] One of Polish overseers, Stanisław Szczepaniak, was recognized by Jews who came to Konin after the war and informed on him to the Security Office (*UB—Urząd Bezpieczeństwa*) in Konin. The District Court in Kalisz, meeting in special session in Konin, sentenced Szczepaniak to ten years in prison.[67]

In late July 1943, the Gestapo in Konin conducted a selection of prisoners in the camp, separating those unfit for labor from the able-bodied in what amounted to a stay of execution for the latter. One cannot say whether this was related to Himmler's decision on August 9, 1943, to liquidate all forced-labor camps for Jews,[68] a decision that spelled the execution of all prisoners, able-bodied or not. Either way, prisoners in the camp swiftly mounted an uprising. The prisoner Rabbi Yehoshua Moshe Aaronson reported the run-up to this event in his diary:

> Yesterday the Gestapo men came and made a list. The signs are the same as they were last year for those taken to the valley of the shadow of death at Chełmno. We all have the impression that they will soon come to take us. Our question is whether we are finished and about to perish. But our own wills are as naught before the will of the Most High, the True Judge.[69]

On August 12, 1943, Jewish prisoners set fire to a barracks that housed a steam room, a coach house, and the morgue. Several inmates committed suicide by hanging themselves, among them a big and tall Jew named Philip. According to one witness, there were nine suicides.[70]

Several people accomplished this by injecting themselves with poison that had been prepared by the camp doctor,[71] who was afterwards killed by the Gestapo.[72] Others threw themselves into the flaming barracks. Many of those who did not die during the uprising were finished off by the gunshots of the Gestapo in Konin. According to Anna Ziółkowska's research and Rabbi Aaronson's memoirs,[73] the "elders of the Jews" in the camp—Fiszel Zielonka, Fajwisz Kamlarz, Abraham Zajft, Gecel Klejnot, Abraham Najdorf, Salomon Nusynowicz, Szlama Michalski, and Abraham Tabacznik—and the Jewish camp physician Hans Knopf all died during the uprising.[74]

The witness Shmulek Mottel says that preparations for the uprising that led to the resistance and suicide of many prisoners in Czarków began on August 7, 1943, several days before the event. His account follows:

> On August 7, 1943, the Gestapo returned and we understood immediately that there was to be another "selection." We knew well enough what this meant. It meant yet more torture, suffering, and death. We decided not to allow ourselves to be led like sheep to the slaughter, and that as the last choice open to us—if it were to become clear that the end was near and that we were to be martyred, as Jews-we would join together to destroy the camp by fire.
>
> On August 9, the uprising broke out. [This date is almost certainly a mistake: there is strong evidence that the uprising occurred on August 13.] Tabaczinski and Kleinot from Gostynin, and Kamlazh from Gąbin, set fire to the sheds and hanged themselves in the blaze. In the main barracks, Seif from Gostynin and Philip from Gąbin hanged themselves. The same fate befell Nusenowicz and Shlomo Michelski from Gostynin and Dr. Knopf, a Jew from Germany. The bloody nightmare of that event will stay with me all my life […].
>
> After firemen put out the blaze, we miraculously remained alive, surrounded by a strong guard. The Germans ordered us to drag out all the dead, the burnt, and the hanged, and asked me and an elderly Jew from Gąbin to deal with the corpses.

As it happened, the first body was that of a young friend of mine, Shlomo Michelski. My brother cut him from the rope, and kept the rope in order to hang himself—such was the suicidal psychology that swept over us that day. When we cut Shlomo down, he was still alive, and an SS man put a bullet through his eye. I went up to Shlomo, and despite all that had happened to him—the hanging and the shooting, and with it all he had always been a weak lad—he, to my great shock and distress, opened the other eye and recognized me. I could not stand the heartache. I approached the German and begged him to shoot me too. As usual, they refused a request […]. The bloody specter of those hard days in the Konin camp whirls around in my head like a demon, wherever I look or turn. The tragic occurrence made a powerful impression on the people of Konin. We, the fortunate survivors, stood with bowed heads before our heroes who would not allow the name Jew to be shamed.[75]

At the end of the uprising, about 200 detainees remained alive because they had been at work outside the camp. Several prisoners in this group managed to escape and survive. Soon after their return to the barracks, the remaining inmates were loaded into trucks and taken away in the direction of Niesłusz. Three hypotheses about their fate have been presented. One is that they were murdered in the forests near Kazimierz Biskupi.[76] Another is that they were loaded into cattle cars and deported to Germany.[77] However, according to a third opinion, all surviving prisoners were transported to the concentration camp in Auschwitz-Birkenau.[78]

After the uprising was suppressed, the camp was abandoned. The barracks remained uninhabited until the end of the war and were then dismantled.[79]

Himmler's decision of August 9, 1943, concerning the liquidation of all forced-labor camps for Jews set in motion a process in the Warthegau that ended in October 1943. Such prisoners as remained in the camps at that time were transported by train to Auschwitz-Birkenau.

3. ESTIMATES OF THE NUMBER OF POLES AND JEWS DEPORTED

The expulsion of the local population started in November 1939 and accelerated during the peak of German military successes in the west. At this time, intensive settlement of Germans in lieu of the deported Poles and Jews ensued.

In the buildup to Germany's attack on the Soviet Union (up to June 22, 1941), the deportations began to slow but continued nonetheless. One witness reports:

> Around March 1941, the Jews of Konin were deported to Józefów Biłgorajski. First, all Jews in Konin and its vicinity were deported to Grójec. Then some were deported to Józefów and others to Zagórów in Konin County. In Zagórów, after a short time, there was an "Aktion"—the Jews there were shot in the woods […] and buried in mass graves.[80]

This conduct was associated with an increase in demand for troop accommodations, food, and transport. After 1943, deportations in the Warthegau came to a virtual halt for several reasons, the foremost of which were failures on the eastern front and a shortage of German settlers who could populate areas abandoned by displaced Poles.

In the spring of 1942, the RSHA launched a massive extermination campaign against the Jews, known as the Final Solution of the Jewish Question. Tasked with the management of this action, which started as the "resettlement" of Jews from several West European countries to the "east," was RSHA Department IV, specifically the Department's *Referat* (specialist) office, directed by Adolf Eichmann. The Final Solution definitely abetted the waning of deportations because deportation was no longer a priority for Eichmann's office. An additional reason was the shortage of manpower in the Warthegau and the Reich. Many young men who had been inducted into the army during the war died and did not come home. Others sustained injuries that rendered them unfit for work. Therefore, their places were filled by Poles who knew German. In the early going, these Poles performed Germans' duties, e.g., guarding forced-labor camps for Jews.

Expulsions of Poles from the Zamość area were initiated in 1942, coinciding with the deportation of Jews to the death camps in *Aktion Reinhardt*. Nevertheless, the German authorities, Himmler above all, tried to force the implementation of their country's agricultural settlement program. To "liberate" the area, Poles were brutally expelled from their villages. The Germanization campaign in the Zamość area made it increasingly difficult to find German settlers who were ready to settle in both the Warthegau and the Zamość area.

As for the efforts to deport the local Polish population, in the spring of 1940, when the plans for mass displacement to the General Government failed and preparations to attack the Soviet Union were devised, this population became indispensable as an exploitable and cheap labor force that would keep the economy going. Polish workers, shipped forcibly to Germany, were supposed to be gradually replaced by Germans returning from different parts of conquered Europe. After the conquest of Eastern Europe, the remaining part of the able-bodied Polish population was to be relocated to the east and forced into the service of the Reich. Those unable to work, such as ethe ill, were to be exterminated. The German colonization of these territories could not have succeeded as well as it did without the sanctioned plundering of the displaced persons' property and the obliteration of all traces of local material culture and civil achievements. Regardless of ethnic or social affiliation and status, every group that the Nazis considered redundant or potentially dangerous was supposed to disappear from the Polish areas that were incorporated into the Third Reich.[81]

The estimated results of the mammoth deportation effort suggest the following: the process of concentrating and displacing Jews and Poles was initiated in spring 1940. The concept of "solving the Jewish problem" gradually matured in the following months. In the autumn of 1940, population transfers from the territories incorporated into the Reich were to be reconsidered. In Berlin, on January 8, 1941, the decision to transfer 831,000 Poles and Jews, including 60,000 Jews from Vienna, to the General Government was made. Some 90,000 Poles and Jews were designated for transfer from the Warthegau by April 1, 1941. Additionally, 19,000 people were to be removed in order to free land for firing grounds in Konin County, among other places. During this period, however, the scale of displacements was much smaller than originally planned. Slightly more than 19,000 people, 2,140 of them Jews, were evicted from the Warthegau. As part of the same operation on March 9 or 10, 1941, approximately 1,000 Jews were displaced from Grodziec County in Inowrocław Regierungsbezirk and were taken to Krasnystaw, Izbica, Lublin, and Józefów. In March 1941, Jews from Koło shared this fate; they were sent to Komar in the Zamość County and Żółkiewka in Krasnystaw County via Łódź. Jews from Ślesin, Konin County, were displaced on March 15, 1941. They found themselves in Łódź, whence they were transferred to Długi Kąt.[82]

According to official German data, however, 534,384 Poles were displaced from the Warthegau alone between December 1, 1939, and December 31, 1943.[83] This does not include "wild" expulsions, which were omitted from the statistics. In November 1939, such deportations included many thousands of people.

NOTES

1 A. Ziółkowska, "Obozy pracy przymusowej dla Żydów w Kraju Warty," in *Zagłada Żydów na polskich terenach wcielonych*, 101.
2 Ibid., 102.
3 T. Berenstein, A. Rutkowski, *Prześladowania ludności żydowskiej w okresie administracji wojskowej*, 68-71; J. Libiszewski, "Żydowskie obozy pracy przymusowej na terenie byłego powiatu inowrocławskiego," in *Z badań*, 45-52; J. Libiszewski, "Obóz na Błoniu w Inowrocławiu," in *Z badań*, 53-57; A. Ziółkowska, *Obozy pracy przymusowej dla Żydów w Wielkopolsce w latach okupacji hitlerowskiej (1941-1943)* (Poznań, 2005), 90; T. Stokfisz, J. Pawlak, "Eksterminacja ludności żydowskiej w Kutnie w XX wieku," *Kutnowskie Zeszyty Regionalne* 3 (1999): 41-52.
4 AŻIH, 301/375, p. 8, 11; 301/4070, c. 1; YVA, O.33/312, pp. 5-7; O.33/1343, pp. 9-11; D. Dąbrowska, *Zagłada*, 172 Table 14; *Kutno we ha Sewiva...*, 459-460; T. Bernstein, *Martyrologia*, no. 21, 60-61, Table 3, 70-72, Table 7, and 82-83, Table 11; D. Dąbrowska, *Zagłada*, 166-173 and 181-184, Tables 9-15; R. Sakowska, ed., *Archiwum Ringelbluma. Konspiracyjne Archiwum Getta Warszawskiego*, vol. 1, *Listy o Zagładzie* (Warsaw, 1997), 84, no. 40; Z. Czyńska and B. Kupić, "Obozy zagłady, obozy koncentracyjne obozy pracy na ziemiach w latach 1939-1945," *BGKBZNP*, 1 (1946): 14-25; T. Kawski, *Kujawsko-dobrzyńscy*, 244-245; A. Ziółkowska, *Obozy*, 85-96, 195.
5 YVA, O.93/29952, video testimony Josef (Joshu) Kazimierski, b. March 31, 1924, in Golina, VT-2, 12:00-15:00.

6   YVA, O.93/5585, video testimony Charles (Jechiel Chaim) Łepek, b. August 28, 1923, in Golina, VT-1.
7   YVA, O.93/29952, video testimony Josef (Joshu) Kazimierski, b. March 31, 1924, in Golina, VT-2, 12:00-15:00.
8   Ibid., VT-2, 26:00-29:00.
9   YVA, O.93/24710, video testimony Michel Prost (Mendel Prost), b. October 1, 1920, in Kleczew, VT-2.
10 Ibid., VT-2, 21:00-23:00.
11 YVA, O.93/24854, video testimony of Bert (Baruch) Gembicki, b. October 15, 1916, in Kleczew, VT-2.
12 Ibid., VT-2, 3:30-6:00.
13 Ibid., VT-2, 3:30-6:00.
14 YVA, O.93/4469, video testimony Leon Jedwab (Lipman-Jedwab), b. October 30, 1923, in Zagórów, VT-2, 14:00-17:00.
15 Ibid., VT-2, 19:50-23:00.
16 YVA, O.93/29952, video testimony Josef (Joshu) Kazimierski, b. March 31, 1924, in Golina, VT-3, 1:00- 9:00.
17 YVA-M-1-Q/177, testimony Bert Gembicki of May 6, 1948, in Ansbach, pp. 2-5.
18 Ibid.
19 Organisation Todt (OT)—formed in 1938 in Nazi Germany, an organization with the task of construction of military facilities, led initially by engineer Fritz Todt. It created both private construction companies and state enterprises. Organisation Todt employed Germans who were initially unfit for military service, as well as men awaiting induction who were required in the interim to work for some organization. During World War II, OT also employed forced laborers and engineers from occupied countries.
20 *Sprawozdanie OKBZH w Poznaniu*, YVA, TR.17/36, OKBZH w Poznaniu, OKP III. Ds 99/67, p. 39; Testimony of Stanisław Szczepaniak, YVA, TR.17/36, OKBZH w Poznaniu, OKP III. Ds 99/67, p. 14.
21 A. Ziółkowska, *Obozy pracy przymusowej dla Żydów w Kraju Warty*, in *Zagłada Zagłada Żydów na polskich terenach wcielonych*, 106.
22 Ibid.
23 Ibid., 111-112.
24 September 1939, Łowicz—anonymous author, "Repression against the Jews after the entry of German troops to Łowicz," in *Wybór źródeł do nauczania o zagładzie Żydów na okupowanych ziemiach polskich*, ed. A. Skibińska, R. Szuchta, W. Młynarczyk (Warsaw, 2010), 99-100.
25 AŻIH, Ring. I/796; T. Kawski, *Kujawsko-dobrzyńscy*, 244-245.
26 Cz. Łuczak, *Dzień po dniu w okupowanym Poznaniu 10 września 1939-23 lutego 1945*, (Poznań, 1989), 286; A. Pakentreger, *Polityka*, 39-41.
27 R. Grzonkowski, *Kleczew*, 236-242.
28 AŻIH, Ring. I/871, p. 1-2; 940, pp. 20, 26-27; *Uniejów*, 278.
29 R.Grzonkowski, *Kleczew*, 236-242.
30 AŻIH, 301/375, p. 2-3; AŻIH, Ring. I/936, pp. 4; 301/275, p. 2, 5, 7; K.F. Tchrusch and M. Korzen, eds., *Włocławek ve-ha-seviva, Sefer zikkaron* (n.p., 1967), 760-761.
31 T. Kawski, *Kujawsko-dobrzyńscy*, 260-262.

32 YVA, O.93/5585, video testimony Charles (Jechiel Chaim) Łepek, b. August 28, 1923, in Golina, VT-1.
33 YVA, O.93/24710, video testimony Michel Prost (Mendel Prost), b. October 1, 1920, in Kleczew, VT-3, Prost VT-2.
34 Ibid., VT-3.
35 Ibid., VT-2.
36 YVA, O.93/24854, video testimony Bert (Baruch) Gembicki, b. October 15, 1916, in Kleczew, VT-3.
37 Ibid., VT-3, 3:20-6:00.
38 Ibid.
39 YVA, O.93/9257, video testimony Abram Landau, b. April 25, 1922, in Wilczyn, VT-3.
40 Ibid., VT-3, 21:00-23:00.
41 YVA, O.93/24710, video testimony Michel Prost (Mendel Prost), b. October 1, 1920, in Kleczew, VT-3.
42 Ibid., VT-3, 8:45-11:00.
43 YVA, O.93/5585, video testimony Charles (Jechiel Chaim) Łepek, b. August 28, 1923, in Golina, VT-2.
44 YVA, O.93/24854, video testimony Bert (Baruch) Gembicki, b. October 15, 1916, in Kleczew, VT-2, 5:22-7:00.
45 Ibid., VT-2, 9:00-12:30.
46 Ibid., VT-3.
47 Ibid., VT-2, 12:30-17:00.
48 Ibid., VT-2, 17:00-19:00.
49 YVA, O.93/5585, video testimony Charles (Jechiel Chaim) Łepek, b. August 28, 1923, in Golina, VT-2.
50 Ibid., VT-2, 11:20-13:00.
51 Ibid., VT-2, 9:00-12:00.
52 Ibid., VT-2, 12:00-15:00.
53 Ibid.
54 J. Libiszewski, *Żydowskie obozy*, 45-46.
55 A. Ziółkowska, *Obozy*, 185-188.
56 J. Libiszewski, *Żydowskie obozy*, 51.
57 Report OKBZH in Poznań, YVA, TR.17/36, OKBZH w Poznaniu, OKP III. Ds 99/67, p. 36.
58 Testimony Józef Kantarowski, YVA, TR.17/36, OKBZH w Poznaniu, OKP III. Ds 99/67, p. 2.
59 Ibid.
60 T. Richmond, *Konin*, 453.
61 Ibid.
62 Estimate of the Regional Commission for the Investigation of Nazi Crimes in Poznań.
63 Testimony Józef Wiatrowski, YVA, TR.17/36, OKBZH w Poznaniu, OKP III. Ds 99/67, p. 14.
64 Report OKBZH in Poznań, ibid., 38.
65 Testimony Bernard Klimczak, ibid., 5.
66 *Sprawozdanie OKBZH w Poznaniu*, ibid., 39.
67 Testimony Stanisław Szczepaniak, ibid., 14.

68 A. Ziółkowska, "Obozy pracy przymusowej dla Żydów w Kraju Warty," in *Zagłada Żydów na polskich terenach*, 113.
69 T. Richmond, *Konin*, 338.
70 Testimony Józef Wiatrowski, YVA, TR.17/36, OKBZH w Poznaniu, OKP III. Ds 99/67, p. 14.
71 Ibid., 2.
72 Testimony Aniela Pecelrowicz, ibid., 8.
73 I. Brzeska, "Obóz pracy w Koninie-Czarkowie na podstawie pamiętnika rabina Jehoszua Aaronsona Alei Merort," in *Ośrodek zagłady w Chełmnie nad Nerem w świetle najnowszych badań* (Konin, 2004), 29-36; Aronson and Joshua, *'Alei Merorot* (Bnei Brak, 1996) [Hebrew].
74 A. Ziółkowska, *Obozy pracy przymusowej dla Żydów w Kraju Warty*, in *Zagłada Żydów na polskich terenach*, 114.
75 Quoted from T. Richmond, *Konin*, 338-339.
76 Testimony Aniela Pecelrowicz, YVA, TR.17/36, OKBZH w Poznaniu, OKP III. Ds 99/67, p. 8.
77 Testimony Bernard Klimczak, ibid., 5.
78 A. Ziółkowska, "Obozy pracy przymusowej dla Żydów w Kraju Warty," in *Zagłada Żydów na polskich terenach*, 114.
79 After the liberation, in 1947, two former prisoners, Majlich Szatan and Chaim Strykowski of Gąbin, reached Konin. Later, they emigrated.
80 YVA, M.1.E/1407, testimony Abraham Obarzanek.
81 More in Cz. Łuczak, *Polska i Polacy w drugiej wojnie światowej* (Poznań, 1993), 98-196.
82 D. Dąbrowska, *Zagłada*, passim.
83 *Wysiedlanie ludności z ziem polskich*, 30.

PART Three

FIRST TO BE DESTROYED: THE BEGINNING OF ORGANIZED MASS EXTERMINATION

6 | "Piloting" the Organized Mass Extermination of Jews

1. DECISION-MAKING IN THE EXTERMINATION OF JEWS IN THE WARTHEGAU

Inowrocław Regierungsbezirk

Activities involving the mass extermination of people in the Warthegau began in October 1939 and expanded in the autumn of 1941 into the "Final Solution of the Jewish Question" (*Endlösung der Judenfrage*) in the Łódź and Inowrocław Regierungsbezirken. Mass extermination started in late 1941, first in the woods near Konin and then at an extermination center in Chełmno on the Ner. During 1942, the systematic liquidation of all ghettos for Jews in the Warthegau, with the sole exception of the Łódź ghetto, occurred. By the end of that summer, the Jewish areas in this administrative district no longer existed, again with the exception of the Łódź ghetto, which served as a transit ghetto of sorts through which deportations were performed. In this transit process, the able-bodied were left in the ghetto while others, from local ghettos and the Łódź ghetto itself, were exterminated in Chełmno. The Łódź ghetto remained in existence until August 1944.[1]

This chapter describes the decision-making process and several milestones and key players on the road to the extermination of Jews in the Warthegau.

The Decision to Exterminate the Jews in the Warthegau

In 1941, Reich Governor Arthur Greiser wished to deport fewer Jews from his Gau (District) than the original plans had envisaged, and managed to convince Himmler and Heydrich to cut the number to 20,000 people in all, including some 5,000 Sinti and Roma. Since this was still a large number of people, Greiser submitted an additional proposal, requesting permission to liquidate the unproductive Jews of the Warthegau. The proposal was considered at length among the different levels of the civil and military administrations until September 19 or 20, 1941, when Hitler and Himmler accepted it.[2] Apparently Greiser used primarily economic arguments to further his plan. The liquidation of Jews unable to work would facilitate the elimination of the remaining rural ghettos in the Warthegau, which would reduce the cost of maintaining the Jews, allow the reduction of the police force that serve as ghetto guards, and free housing for ethnic German settlers—which was an urgent necessity. The creation of a central ghetto in Łódź to which able-bodied Jews would be transferred would increase production and profitability.[3]

Greiser and Himmler talked it over and the mass murder of Jews in Warthegau began shortly after. The process near Konin was initiated in late September 1941 by a unit called SS Sonderkommando Lange (see below). These murders, while massive in scale, amounted to a pilot operation. After their completion in October 1941, preparations to run a death camp in Chełmno on the Nerem got under way. The experience gained from the mass murder of Jews in Konin District (described in greater detail below) also influenced the shape and functioning of the center in Chełmno and the location of mass graves in the Rzuchowski forest. It would also serve as the starting point for the subsequent perfection of methods of mass murder in Chełmno and the Rzuchowski forest, as well as in the death camps in the General Government such as Bełżec, Sobibór, and Treblinka.

Sonderkommando Lange

As noted, mass extermination activities in the Warthegau had been proceeding since October 1939, with mentally ill Poles and Jews from Poznań as the victims. At that time, independent of T4 at Berlin headquarters[4] (which "euthanized" the mentally ill in Germany), an autonomous detail in Poznań went about such work: Sonderkommando Lange (Special Detail / a.k.a. Special Detachment Lange), named for its commander, SS-Obersturmführer Herbert Lange.[5] From October 1939 through the summer of 1941, Sonderkommando Lange murdered 5,726 patients from hospitals for the mentally ill in the Warthegau, and killed 1,808 people in eastern Prussia in the summer of 1940, in the town of Soltau among other locations.[6]

In the Warthegau, in contrast to Germany, the murder of the mentally ill went unprotested and could therefore take place without hindrance. In both regions the motive was to get rid of individuals who were burdensome to society, who failed to produce anything meaningful—"the destruction of life unworthy of life" (*Vernichtung lebensunwertem von Leben*) in the Nazi jargon. Consequently, the mentally ill and the genetically defective were murdered.

In this first period of activity, Sonderkommando Lange murdered the mentally ill in the cellars of Fort VII in Poznań and in a wagon that had been converted into a mobile gas chamber, its purpose masked by a sign that read "Kaisers Kaffe Geschäft" and a drawing of a steaming cup of coffee on the outside. The killing agent was carbon monoxide (CO) pumped from gas cylinders into the wagon, a method that was also used for murders at a clinic in Kościan.[7]

According to the Polish researcher Arthur Hojan, before the gassing of patients under T4 auspices, the use of this gas for this purpose had been piloted by Lange and his unit, part of Einsatzgruppe VI under the command of SS-Oberführer Erich Naumann, which had operated in the Poznań area in September 1939. Einsatzgruppe VI consisted of officers of the Security Service (SD) who arrived in Poznań on September 12, 1939. Einsatzgruppe VI took part in Operation Tannenberg (Unternehmen Tannenberg), in which Polish political and social leaders, political opponents of German rule including participants in the Wielkopolskie uprising, and other anti-German activists were liquidated. As part of this activity, Lange was ordered to establish a concentration camp in Poznań. To perform this task, he carried out reconnaissance of various locations to consider their usefulness and chose Fort VII, part of a Prussian system of fortifications built at the turn of the nineteenth and twentieth centuries and known as the Fortress of Poznań (Festung Posen). The fort, located on the outskirts of the city but relatively close to police and Gestapo headquarters, had facilities where prisoners could be detained.[8]

Herbert Lange was the first commandant of the camp; he held this position from October 7 to October 16, 1939. SS-Hauptsturmführer Hans Weibrecht replaced Lange when the latter was transferred after the dissolution of Einsatzgruppe VI. Wilhelm Koppe was the Higher SS and Police Commander (HSSPF) in Poznań SS-Gruppenführer. In this capacity, he was subordinate to both the Reichsstatthalter in the Warthegau, Arthur Greiser, and Reichsführer SS Heinrich Himmler.

SS Sonderkommando Lange probably reported directly not only to the HSSPF in the Warthegau but also to Greiser as the plenipotentiary of the RKFDV in this district. If so, Greiser had much sway over the detail's activities. Once Adolf Hitler signed the "euthanasia" order (as he did in early October; the order was pre-dated to September 1), Sonderkommando Lange began operations for the elimination— the murder—of people with mental illness or congenital genetic defects. They began at the Regional Psychiatric Hospital in Owińsk, near Poznań. After arranging with a German physician, Dr. Rudolf Bartussek, to take over the management of the hospital, they removed most of its Polish doctors and nurses. Then, of the roughly 1,100 patients, approximately 150 of German nationality were selected; they were transported to the Dziekanka psychiatric institution in Gniezno.

Sonderkommando Lange came to the center in Owińsk in late October 1939. The patients were then informed that they would be transported to a better place. Those who resisted were treated brutally and injected with sedatives. The patients were trucked under police escort to Poznań, each truck holding twenty-five to thirty people. The trucks reached Fort VII and the patients were led to Bunker 17 at the top of the fort, comprised of a room about seven meters long and two and a half meters wide, with a 2.5-meter semicircular vaulted ceiling. The cell had a metal door. Gassing took about eight minutes once the gas was discharged from its container. After that, the cell was opened and ventilated. Since it was at the top of the fort, servicemen and other prisoners were at no risk of being poisoned. From the closed bunker, the gas could disperse into the tunnels of the fort.[9]

Some fifty people could be accommodated in the gas chamber. To prevent fear and resistance, several ceiling lamps were lit before the ill were led in. Subsequently, the soothing deceit of turning on a light would be employed regularly in gas chambers and gas wagons.[10] After the cell was loaded, the door was closed and sealed with clay. The gas was kept in a container from which members of the Lange detail, stationed outside the room, discharged it into the chamber through an aperture of some kind. About eight minutes later, the soldiers opened the door, ventilated the room, and removed the corpses. Since the original cell door of Bunker 17 had no peephole, the victims' behavior inside the chamber could not be monitored. The corpses were taken to the Rożnowski forest near Obornik, not far from Poznań, and buried there.[11]

A great deal of information on the process of murder by gas comes from Polish prisoners who belonged to a Polish detail that was employed in "euthanizing" the mentally disabled. One member of this detail described it as follows:

> The SS men ordered us to bring patients out of the car and run to the bunker. SS men guarded, shouted, and pushed us. We also took iron gas containers, like oxygen, out of the car and we put them close to the bunker. After leading the sick into the bunker and closing the iron door, we were told by the SS to seal the door with clay. Then they sent us to a cell. After a short time we were led out into the courtyard again. We were told to remove the clay, pull open the door, and remove the corpses of the patients who had been poisoned by gas. [...] I took the corpses thrown out of the bunker into the car. That was a description of gassing the mentally ill and it was repeated several times, but I am not able to determine how often and how many people were

killed [...]. Later I learned that the bodies of the gassed patients were transported by cars from Fort VII to the woods in the area of Obornik and buried in mass graves.[12]

An estimated 250–300 patients from a hospital in Owińsk and elsewhere were murdered in Fort VII. Because it was possible to kill about fifty people each time, there must have been at least five or six gassings. Soon after these first instances of gassing, a portable gas chamber was built. This chamber was used to murder the mentally ill in institutions similar to Owińsk in the area, such as Dziekanka in Gniezno, of which the remaining patients were liquidated. This portable gas chamber was a modified wagon with a closed cabin, camouflaged in the manner described above.[13] Again, carbon monoxide (CO) was used, dispensed from containers supplied by T4 staff. The patients destined for death were loaded into the car in their hospital clothing. As in the previous case, aggressive individuals were injected with sedatives; some were treated brutally. After the wagon was loaded, the gas was released into the cabin and the passengers died in transport. Men from the detail then took the corpses to desolate woods, where they were unloaded and buried in mass graves that had usually been prepared in advance. In later transports, live patients were delivered in trucks, loaded into a wagon gas chamber on site, and murdered there. A special detail from Fort VII which remained apart from other prisoners did the unloading and the burying.

In November and December 1939, Sonderkommando Lange murdered the patients who had been in the institution in Owińsk, the psychiatric clinic of the University of Poznań, and the Dziekanka institution in Gniezno, which had held 1,044 people. All were murdered at the asylum in Kościan, located in Osieczna near Leszno, or in an institution in Lębork. The buildings of now-closed institutions for the mentally ill were taken over by the SS or designated as barracks for the Wehrmacht.[14]

After the murder of psychiatric patients in Poznań, Sonderkommando Lange moved on to Kochanówka, near Łódź. The psychiatric patients at an institution in this location were murdered on March 10–15, 1940. A group of blind and retarded children from Łódź was transported to an institution in Kochanówka and were murdered on March 27, 1940.

Four hundred ninety-nine more ill people, these from the sanatorium in Warta near Łódź, were murdered on April 2–4, 1940, and buried in the woods in Włyń-Rossoszyca.[15]

In mid-1941, the Lange detail perpetrated a second round of "euthanasia" among institutionalized adults in Dziekanka, Warta, Gostynin, Śrem, and Bojanowo. In this action, like in that of 1940, German doctors participated, filling out questionnaires that were later sent to T4 headquarters. One of the doctors, Dr. Ratke, inspector of the establishment in Dziekanka, drew up a list of patients destined to die. This second phase of "euthanasia" was held on the following dates: ninety patients in Dziekanka on June 3–4, seventy patients at the institution in Gostynin, and fifty-six at the institution in Śrem on June 10–12; eighty-two patients at the sanatorium in Warta on June 16; and sixty-eight women at a social care establishment in Poznań on July 3–5. All told, Sonderkommando Lange murdered 4,219 institutionalized patients in Poznań and about 2,000 in facilities around Łódź and other cities.[16] It is important to add that the use of exhaust gas to murder people began in 1941. This represented technological "progress" because it obviated the need to transport large numbers of gas cylinders.[17]

Due to the aforementioned protests in Germany, Hitler ordered the "euthanasia" to be stopped in August 1941. It is important to note, however, that only official "euthanasia" ceased; "wild euthanasia" continued in various locations until the end of the war. Different methods were used. One was murder by starvation; another was the injection of substances such as chloral hydrate, luminal, morphine, and scopolamine, among others.

In July 1941, after murdering mentally ill adults and children, people with congenital defects, the blind, and abusers of social services, Sonderkommando Lange prepared to embark on a new phase of its activity. This time, "unproductive" Jews in the Warthegau—at least 100,000 people— would be among the targets. The Sonderkommando received the order from its superordinate, the Stapo (State Police) in Poznań. After Greiser and Himmler finalized their decision on this matter, they passed the word on to Herbert Lange via Wilhelm Koppe, HSSPF, in the Warthegau, or, at some later time, to the head of the Poznań Stapo via Ernst Damzog and Sturmbannführer Helmut Bischoff.[18] Sonderkommando Lange was definitely the best unit to choose for this mission, given its experience in organizing mass murder for thousands of victims.

Many questions concerning the relationship of Sonderkommando Lange with T4 headquarters and administrative authorities and police in the Warthegau remain unanswered. As mentioned, the decision to murder at least 100,000 Jews in the region was made on September 19 or 20, 1941. However, the Sonderkommando apparently began this new phase of activity much earlier—as early as July 1941. It is not clear whether this was related to a letter from Rolf-Heinz Höppner, head of the SD in Poznań, to Eichmann on July 16, 1941 (discussed below), in which Höppner proposed to find an "effective measure" that would facilitate the liquidation of Jews.[19]

The document that provides information about launching a new phase of Sonderkommando Lange activity in the summer of 1941 served the Inspector of Security Police and SD in Poznań as justification for granting the II Class Cross of Military Merit to Walter Burmeister, Herbert Lange's personal driver, on July 16, 1943.[20] The decoration was awarded for Burmeister's participation in actions from July 1941 to April 5, 1943. Indeed, Sonderkommando Lange, which had already gained experience in mass murder in 1939–1940, could be used in the further extermination of Jews. Walter Burmeister testified as follows:

> One day in autumn 1941, I was summoned to the office of Hauptsturmführer Lange. He told me I would be assigned to a special unit whose task it would be to undertake a covert action in the interests of the Reich, of which I could not tell anybody [...]. In preparation for this, I learned from Lange that the task of this department would be the killing of people delivered there.[21]

This may indicate that both Lange and Burmeister began the action that, although it had not yet been named, appears—on the basis of information from other sources—to have been a murder campaign against the Jews of the Warthegau. In this action, a preparatory period may be discerned—from July to about December 5–8, 1941—during which experimental murders of Jews in the forests around Konin were carried out and the preparation and construction of the extermination center in Chełmno began. The second stage began with the activation of the Chełmno death camp and ended at the terminus of the camp's initial period of activity in April 1943.

It is odd and extremely difficult to comprehend the justification for awarding Burmeister with the Cross of Merit. In support of the decision, we read:

> Activity in [Sonderkommando Lange], consisting of direct combat and destroying enemies of the State, took place under constant threat of loss of life and required an unusually courageous and strong spiritual attitude [...]. This activity was of decisive importance for the solution of one of the most important national problems.[22]

Factual confirmation of experiments in murder is also provided in the post-war testimony of Wilhelm Koppe, Higher SS and Police Commander in the Wartheland:

> Dr. Brand [Himmler's personal assistant] told me that Dr. Brack [head of the T4 "euthanasia" program] experimented in Berlin with various gases; the experiments were to end soon and experiments with Brack's gases would take place in the Warthegau under his, Dr. Brack's, supervision. The carrying out of the gassing was commissioned to Lange's unit, of course.[23]

This demonstrates a close link between the Berlin headquarters of Operation T4 and Sonderkommando Lange. What the Sonderkommando did could not have been done without the consent of the HSSPF in the Warthegau, Wilhelm Koppe. Rolf-Heinz Höppner, head of the SD in Poznań and the author of the memorandum of July 16, 1941, who will be discussed later in this chapter, was not only aware of these connections—this is beyond doubt—but also, in all probability, involved in its context.

It also could not have been done without the knowledge of Arthur Greiser. This means that a well-functioning low and middle level apparatus designed the methods of mass extermination that would be brought against the Jews of the Warthegau. Greiser's role in this case was reduced to making high-level political decisions and obtaining the consent of Himmler and Hitler to kill "unnecessary" Jews in the Warthegau. If this was the decision-making process, we are speaking of a bottom-up regional initiative to annihilate Jews, one that met the expectations of the highest Reich authorities, gained their acceptance, and may have influenced the decision to apply the Final Solution of the Jewish Question in the territories occupied by the Germans and their allies.

Rolf-Heinz Höppner's Role and his Ideas on Extermination

In a letter to Eichmann on September 3, 1941, Höppner wrote:

> I could well imagine that large areas of the present Soviet Russia are being prepared to receive the undesired ethnic elements of the greater German settlement area [...]. To go into further details about the organization of the reception area would be fantasy, because, first of all, basic decisions must be made. It is essential in this regard, by the way, that total clarity prevails about what finally shall happen to those undesirable ethnic elements deported from the greater German settlement area. Is it the goal to ensure them a certain level of life in the long run, or shall they be totally eradicated?[24]

Höppner had no illusions when it came to the fate of the Jews. He seemed to realize, especially after the experiments in deporting Jews to the General Government in 1939–1941, that deportation, this time to Soviet-controlled areas of Poland, would be difficult if not impossible to realize. Thus, he sought to solve the "Jewish problem" at the local level, through their physical elimination.

The extermination of Jews in the Warthegau was certainly connected to the events taking place in the east during Operation Barbarossa. Since the war against the USSR had begun on June 22, 1941, crimes had been perpetrated on a massive scale. The main groups targeted by the extermination policy were political commissars, communist activists, prisoners of war, and Jews.

The crimes committed in Soviet-annexed territories—eastern Poland, the Baltic states, Bessarabia, and Bukovina—influenced the attitude held toward Jews elsewhere. In the Warthegau, however, the onset of mass murders of Jews was precipitated by grassroots initiatives. One of the key documents relating to these initiatives is a letter from Rolf-Heinz Höppner, head of the SD in Poznań, written on July 16, 1941.[25] This letter was the result of discussion and reflection about the Jewish problem in the Warthegau in the summer of 1941. At this time, as noted, the plan to deport Jews from the Warthegau to the General Government and thus to solve the Jewish problem and make the district Judenfrei had totally collapsed. The third short-term plan in March 1941 had led to the deportation of 19,226 people, including 2,140 Jews.[26] During this time, as the numbers make clear, primarily resettlement of rural Poles took place in order to free houses and farms for Germans who were being relocated from farming areas in Volhynia and Bessarabia that had been annexed to the USSR.

Thus, in the process of deportations from the Warthegau, Jews were relegated to a secondary priority; the evacuation of the roughly 250,000 Jews who inhabited the district was utterly unlikely. First, the intensive preparations for Operation Barbarossa in the spring of 1941 had committed all means of transport to the military. Second, a huge number of troops—around 2.5 million—was massing in the General Government in anticipation of Barbarossa, engulfing transport, board, and lodging in logistical difficulties. Such a concentration of troops seriously burdened the General Government economy, making the deportation of Jews to this area out of the question. Thus, the Warthegau remained alone with its unsolved Jewish problem. Unable to count on help from the outside, its authorities decided to seek solutions at home and use their own resources.

In the Warthegau, as in other areas, the initial looting that accompanied ghettoization had deprived the Jews of sources of livelihood, stocks of goods and food, and movable and immovable property. Thus the Jews had become a burden on the local economy, clashing with the Nazi idea that Jews should be self-sufficient. Under the German regime of central economic management, including food rationing on the basis of ration cards, Jews were denied cards and were thus threatened with starvation. People responsible for both economic affairs and Jewish affairs began to notice problems connected with the prolonged stay of Jews, particularly those unable to work, in the Warthegau. The German authorities saw these Jews as unproductive and immensely burdensome to the German economy. It became urgent to unburden the system of them with all possible celerity.

For this purpose, various proposals were raised. All, of course, led in one direction: get rid of the Jews. In fact, no positive solutions, e.g., organizing the large-scale employment of Jews in a ghetto outside of Łódź, were considered. The Jewish problem was taken up in numerous discussions but its causes, all of which were well known, were not discussed. After all, Jews had lived to a certain standard in interwar Poland, belonging to varied economic classes from manual labor to commerce or crafts to the liberal professions. Only after the Germans occupied Polish territory did the Jewish problem escalate into a mass crisis. As mentioned, the German administration had, through its laws and its predatory policy towards the Jews, pauperized the Jewish community very quickly, resulting in economic disequilibrium and deprivation in cash and kind. In the deportation to rural ghettos and the Łódź ghetto, Jews lost virtually all their possessions; from then on, their consumption (in cash or by bartering personal belongings) was negligible. Since the sale of belongings could assure survival only in part, deportees had to rely on self-labor or public assistance. The German authorities that could provide such assistance, however, had other interests in mind: dispossessing the Jews to the extent of eliminating them from economic life. Hence they began to talk about deportation to remote areas somewhere in Russia and, if this were to prove impossible, outright physical elimination as the only remaining option.

Another argument that led in this direction concerned health. According to people surrounding the German authorities, Jews were responsible for outbreaks of typhus and other epidemic diseases. On July 8, 1941, the Inowrocław regency president, Dr. Hans Burckhardt, wrote the following in a situation report:

There is an endless epidemic of typhus in the Jewish camp in Kutno. Therefore, again we point out that ghettos and camps for Jews are the worst kind of breeding ground for pestilence [...]. From a health point of view, we demand the immediate transfer of all Jews to a place completely separated from the rest of the public.[27]

In his letter to Eichmann, Rolf-Heinz Höppner mentions "various discussions [...] held locally in the office of the Reich Governor."[28] Similar discussions took place elsewhere, primarily at meetings between the Governor General, Dr. Hans Frank, and Arthur Greiser. They reached the same conclusion: "The situation in both territories is becoming desperate; therefore, the problem must be solved in a fundamental way."[29]

Greiser, interested mainly in the total deportation of Jews from the Warthegau, sought "fundamental" solutions by using various arguments, most commonly relating to the health situation. At one of the conferences, Greiser said:

The Warthegau can in no way retain these Jews, who are crammed into the ghetto, even through this winter, both because of food shortages and because of the danger of epidemics. We must, therefore, necessarily find a temporary solution that will allow those Jews to be transported to another area.[30]

He repeated this in another speech:

[...] Keeping these Jews crammed into the ghetto even through the winter would thrust the Warthegau into an unbearable situation for reasons related to food shortages and policy but also, and particularly, related to epidemics and policing. In any case, then, we must find a temporary solution that will create the possibility of deporting the Jews to other territories.[31]

Greiser's arguments supported those of his subordinate, HSSPF Koppe, who described the situation concerning the Jewish question in the Warthegau as deteriorating from day to day. The ghetto in Łódź had been organized on the assumption that the Jews would begin to be shipped out by mid-year.[32] In mid-1940, some hope was given to the idea of deporting Jews to Madagascar; as noted above, however, several weeks after the conquest of France, the idea appeared unfeasible. Resonance of this scheme is found in a statement that Greiser entered into the minutes:

> Based on conversations with Reichsführer SS [Himmler] he could tell that there is now the intention of deporting Jews to the overseas territories [...]. The Jewish problem—when it comes to his district [the Warthegau]—must be solved in some way before winter. This naturally depends on how long the war will take. If it lasts much longer, one will need to find a temporary solution.[33]

Thus, the quest for a solution regarding the Jews was discussed in Greiser's circles and at meetings with Governor General Hans Frank. Unsurprisingly, Höppner uses similar language in his correspondence: he, too, writes that a solution needs to be found before the winter. Höppner asked for a reaction to his proposals, which he judged as possibly seeming "in part fantastic but [...] thoroughly feasible."[34] In the first two paragraphs of his memorandum, Höppner proposes to create a camp for Jews from the Warthegau that could accommodate 300,000 people. In this camp, he proposes the construction of barracks enclosed by barbed wire. These barracks should be capable of accommodating workshops for tailors, shoemakers, and other producers of goods. In addition, ablebodied Jews could form working details that might be deployed outside the camp. The guarding of such a camp, Höppner proposed, would require a much smaller police presence than the guarding of the existing ghettos did. Moreover, such a camp would mitigate the epidemiological threat to local residents of Łódź and other cities that had ghettos.[35]

Apparently, however, Höppner did not believe in the very solution that he proposed, since in the fourth paragraph of his memorandum he writes that in the upcoming winter it would be impossible to feed most of the Jews; they would be threatened with starvation. Therefore, "One should honestly weigh whether the most humane solution might not be to finish off those of the Jews who are not employable by means of some quick-working device. At any rate, this would be more pleasant than letting them starve to death."[36] If the encampment of the Jews were to be chosen nevertheless, he continued, Höppner proposed to sterilize all Jewish women "so that the problem may actually be completely solved within this generation."[37]

The decisions about mass extermination of Jews in the Warthegau were made in subsequent weeks. We do not know, however, to what extent Höppner's memorandum contributed to the discussions that were held at the office of Reich Governor Greiser or at the different levels of state administration and police and security forces, which must have led to the determination.

One of the important factors in deciding on the mass murder of the Jews was the existence and functioning of Sonderkommando Lange in the Warthegau. The detail was able to carry out the liquidation mission on its own, with no need for outside reinforcements. Notably, during the summer and autumn of 1941, as the Wehrmacht swept into the east, demand for additional police forces to fill new positions in the occupied territories increased steadily. Therefore, a request for even a small number of reinforcements might encounter difficulties and be denied. The use of local forces independent of external elements would also make the scheme faster and less complicated to implement. Even if Höppner did not explicitly say as much in his memorandum, he was undoubtedly referring to Sonderkommando Lange, of whose activities he must have been very well informed as a senior SD officer in the Warthegau. Importantly, Höppner was not asking about the ways and means of murdering Jews who were considered unproductive; mainly, he simply sought permission to do the job.

It should also be emphasized that, given the disastrous economic situation in the ghettos brought on by economic policy and persecution, the Nazis had not tried to find opportunities to improve the Jewish population's living conditions. In their decision-making, they preferred to follow the path of radical solutions involving the removal of "unnecessary" Jews by physical elimination. Such action was certainly not dictated by economic necessity; the Nazis' economic policies toward the Jews were unidirectional, moving toward radicalization. Once the Jews' stolen goods could not be returned, the Jewish community was impoverished irreparably. If any actions designed to improve production efficiency were taken, they were not for the Jews' benefit but rather for German companies, administration, and police. Ghetto Litzmannstadt, the German name for the Łódź ghetto, may serve as an example: despite the elimination of "unproductive" Jews and improvements in industrial production, famine still claimed many Jewish lives there. Thus, the sole justification for seeking methods to eliminate "unproductive" Jews was racist ideology—the perception of Jews as unnecessary and worthy first of exploitation and then of physical elimination. The de-economization and ghettoization of Jews no longer satisfied the Nazi decision-makers due to the onerous burden that the masses of pauperized Jews in the ghettos imposed on the Nazi economy.

The quest for a "good" modus operandi was not rhetorical; it was a proposal to seek new methods of mass extermination of people. Höppner clearly knew of two tried-and-true methods: gunfire and gassing. However, although both methods had been used extensively in the Warthegau since September 1939, Höppner apparently was not convinced that they were appropriate for the liquidation of at least 100,000 Jews.[38] This number is based on the estimate of approximately 250,000 Jews in the Warthegau, the majority of whom, taking into account children, the elderly, and women unfit for hard labor, would not be considered able-bodied and would be eliminated. We do not know of further correspondence about methods of annihilation, but the issue was important enough that within months three different methods would be piloted (discussed below); after proving successful, they would undergo further technical improvements for greater efficiency. Thus, the Warthegau became a de facto testing ground for mass murder. The experience gained in this trial period would be employed in the construction of extermination camps in the General Government in the spring of 1942.

The decision to exterminate Jews in the Warthegau was apparently made at the beginning of the second week of September 1941 and was connected with Himmler's decision concerning the deportation of some 60,000 Jews from the Greater Reich and the Protectorate of Bohemia and

Moravia to the Łódź ghetto. A transfer of Jews on such a scale would have disrupted ghetto life and toppled the production process. Indeed, the local authorities protested and Arthur Greiser tried to prevail on Himmler to cut down the deportation. Greiser, who had also funneled money from the Łódź ghetto into the accounts of the Organization of Friends of the Warthegau—a body that he had established himself—was interested in maintaining the production process without interference.[39] Höppner was well aware of the business related to manufacturing in the Łódź ghetto and the conflict between the security apparatus and civil administration in the Warthegau. In the last section of his memorandum, he wrote:

> The Reich Governor [Greiser] has not yet expressed an opinion in this matter [creation of a great camp for Jews and seeking an appropriate method for the liquidation of non-productive Jews and the sterilization of women]. There is an impression that Government President Übelhör does not wish to see the ghetto in Łódź disappear, since he [his office] seems to profit quite well from it. As an example of how one can profit from the Jews, I was told that the Reich Labor Ministry pays six Reichsmarks (RM) from a special fund for each Jew employed, but that a Jew costs only 80 Pfennig.[40]

In addition to accepting this fee, Nazis could exploit Jewish labor by cutting expenditures on food set aside for them and pocketing profits from the Jews' manufacturing output.

As mentioned above, one of the alternative proposals was the sterilization of Jewish workers. Indeed, there was a detailed proposal for the sterilization or castration of two to three million able-bodied Jewish men and women.[41]

2. EXECUTIONS IN KAZIMIERZ BISKUPI

The process of mass murder in the area of Kazimierz Biskupi and the Długa Łąka woods may be reconstructed on the basis of several survivors' statements and the testimonies of witnesses who lived in the area.

According to these sources, the mass murder of Jews in the woods near Kazimierz Biskupi took place in the autumn of 1941. Since some of the Polish witnesses have difficulty establishing the exact times of the events, we quote several plausible versions. One witness sets the slaughter "in mid-November 1941, at about 4:00 a.m."[42] Another witness reports, "Transports of people to the forest in Krężel took place twice in September 1941. I cannot say exactly when."[43] A third witness recalls:

> I worked for several years during the war time as a forestry worker in the forests of Kazimierz. I remember in the fall, it might have been in September 1941, when Germany conducted a massive liquidation of Jews collected from different parts of the Konin – Zagórów district. Then Jews from Konin and Golina were brought by truck for a few weeks.[44]

Thus, the local population knew that Jews were being transported to the murder site, even if those able to observe the transports were unaware of what was going on. It is quite characteristic of the Germans to have allowed some forest workers to continue working even during the mass murders. One of these workers recalls:

> During the German occupation in 1941, I worked as a laborer in the forests cutting wood for a mine in Kazimierz forest not far from the narrow-gauge railway station in Kaizmierz Biskupi. It was near a lodge called "Wygoda." In September 1941, I had a feeling that I could not have had in 1940. Working along the highway that cut the Kazimierz forest in two parts and that links Kleczew and Golina, many times I saw German trucks that were used to carry people into the woods [...]. The trucks were covered with canvas, but sometimes the wind blew the cover open and then I saw a tight cluster of people. Children in the truck were standing among them. A four-wheeled trailer attachment loaded with suitcases, bundles belonging to the people transported by trucks, was at the rear. One day I noticed that Romania was written on one of the bundles. Where the people

were taken, I cannot say […]. After driving about 2–3 km, these cars turned into the forest.[45]

Transports to the Place of Execution

The victims were transported to their executions in trucks escorted by armed soldiers or policemen in cars. One of the witnesses to these events recalls:

> The convoy transporting the people for execution was usually composed of one truck with an attached trailer and one personnel car, in which uniformed police were probably sitting. These convoys sometimes went by several times a day.[46]

The deportees' personal items were transported in trailers attached to trucks. Since the German authorities in charge of the deportation tried to keep the Jews ignorant of both their destination and the fact that mass executions were being carried out, they usually told them that they would be deported to the east to live and work. Sometimes the authorities told victims that their destinations were labor camps for Jews and that they should therefore pack hand luggage, everyday items, valuables, and money. Accordingly, the deportee-designates tried to pack valuables and cash for the purchase of necessities in their new location. An important element in deceiving the doomed was convincing them that resettlement necessitated money and valuables. Since permissible luggage was limited to a few kilograms, they could take only the most valuable or essential items. This luggage was later searched for valuables, jewelry, and money at the scene of the crime.

As Jews were being murdered in the forest, the area of Sonderkommando activity was closed to outsiders and secured by armed guards. One witness states, "During this time, access to the forest in the area was closed. German authorities announced that crossing and remaining in the area would be forbidden for some time."[47] Another witness recalls: "Close to the road [leading into the heart of the forest] was a bulletin board with text in German and Polish, warning that entrance into the forest was strictly prohibited."[48]

Some people, however, inadvertently found themselves there regardless—several of them forest workers who were allowed to continue working despite the closure. Locals who had been able to observe the transports to the forest realized that those being transported were Jews and that their fate was to be murdered. One witness said this in so many words:

> One time I went in the direction of Kleczew by bike and heard from the depths of the forest a short series of machine gun shots, probably coming from a military firearm. I realized that the Germans had shuttled people to the forest and killed them there on the spot and buried them in mass graves.[49]

The Execution Site

After the war, representatives of the District Commission for the Investigation of Nazi Crimes in Poznań opened an investigation into these events and sought witnesses to gather evidence and conduct a site visit. Most accounts of the mass execution of Jews in the woods near Kazimierz Biskupi and Konin originate in the materials accumulated by this investigation. They are stored in the collections of the District Commission, which subsequently metamorphosed into the Institute of National Remembrance—Commission of Investigation of Crimes against the Polish Nation.

Here is how one witness describes the execution site in the Kazimierz Biskupi forests:

> I would like to supplement my testimony in this way: the transports of people to the "Krężel" forest took place on two occasions in September 1941. I cannot precisely indicate the time. The part of the forest that I described, where mass graves were located, exists to this day. The entire area of forests called "Kazimierskie" covered a total of 350 ha. "Krężel" is located within the confines of Kazimierz Biskupi. I could indicate the place even today.[50]

Another witness provides the following description: "Huge transports of people and cars were turning past the forester's house, 'Wygoda,' onto the road [*dukt*] in the depths of the forest."[51]

Mieczysław Sękiewicz, taken with a group of inmates from the prison in Konin to operate the place of execution, survived the war and gave testimony about the crimes perpetrated against Jews in Kazimierz Biskupi. Sękiewicz joined employees of the District Commission for the Investigation of Nazi Crimes in Poznań in an on-site visit to a forest in Kazimierz Biskupi. An excerpt of the minutes of the local version, which describes the witness's experiences and the place of execution, follows:

> Then the Gestapo officers got in and the car started moving towards the railroad station, turning on the road to Golina, then turning again by the mill and heading in the direction of Kazimierz Biskupi. It was light out, and seated with my face forward I was able to observe the road. Having passed Kazimierz Biskupi, the car turned left into the forest. Today I can recognize the path as a forest track, marked on Sketch I. The car passed one track running crosswise and reached the second track running crosswise to the right. Those tracks are marked on sketches with the numbers two and three. Next, the car with us inside turned around at the second crosswise track and headed back, stopping between the first and second tracks, a few meters away from the second track. I recognize the site very well. We were unshackled, led out of the car, and positioned with our backs to a clearing, where today the mass graves are marked on sketches I and II. We stood here for half an hour. Then we were led into the clearing, which I recognize perfectly today marked on the sketch with the letter "A." This clearing was not as overgrown as it is today.[52]

The German Detachment

Due to uncertainties in identifying the perpetrators of the mass executions in the woods near Kazimierz Biskupi, we present various witness accounts below. The killing squads were probably composed of members of different units that performed different duties. Undoubtedly, the groups heading the executions were officers of the State Security Service (SD) and the Security Police (Sipo), since they were responsible for Jewish affairs and were functionaries of the organization accountable for the liquidation of Jews in most areas of the General Government, the Warthegau, and the Soviet areas to their east. It is reasonable to assume that they played a leading role in exterminating the Jews. The main questions concern where they originated and to which unit they belonged in organizational terms. Such questions are not discussed in this study.

Either way, the leading role of the SD and Sipo does not preclude participation in deportations and liquidation operations by other agencies such as the civilian and military police, which could have played an executive or supporting role. Indeed, one witness recalled, "The tracks, the clearing, and the surrounding forest teemed with Gestapo officers."[53] The Gestapo, as part of the Security Police, certainly could have taken part in the action. An allegation to this effect, however, should be treated critically because civilians often had difficulties in telling apart different organizational apparatuses that included uniformed officers. Since the Gestapo was the organization responsible for persecuting the underground and the political opposition in the occupied and annexed territories, it had gained notoriety; witnesses often abused its name or confused it with other police agencies.

Another witness who was employed for a time at the office of the Konin Landrat described his knowledge of the liquidation of the Jews at the headquarters of the local administration:

> As an employee of the [police] department at the office of the Landrat of Konin, I met with German workers very often. I got the impression that any civilian employee of the police was thoroughly familiar with the liquidation of all Jews. During the quiet conversations in my presence, not once was it mentioned [...].
>
> My German friends refrained in conversations with me from describing scenes of the murder of Jews. These matters were kept in deep secrecy. In my time, random killings were carried out in Grodziec and Kazimierz Biskupi. This news was leaked to me from the mouths of Gestapo functionaries who participated in those murders.[54]

This information is vital because it attests that, in principle, Gestapo and police officers had been executing different people in the forests around Konin, especially those near Kazimierz Biskupi and Grodziec, since the beginning of the war. The forest in Kazimierz Biskupi is one of the largest northwest of Konin, a relatively short distance from the city. During the occupation, it became commonplace to murder prisoners and Jews in forests. There were very few witnesses in these cases, and therefore, news about them spread to a limited and local distance only. The victims remained anonymous. In addition, it was a relatively simple matter to bury the victims at the execution site. When executions took place in prisons, the removal of the corpses was much more difficult: it required the involvement of more people and entailed burial in cemeteries. Thus, in the vicinity of Konin the most convenient form of execution was the transport of victims into the forest, where they were murdered and interred on site.

Witness Ciurzyński continues: "There weren't any special units called Einsatzkommando to eliminate the Jews in Konin County until the end of my stay there, namely the end of February 1941."[55] Notably, the witness could not have known about the existence of a special squad in February 1941, since such a unit existed in Poznań and was sent to the Konin area only a few months later, in late August or in September 1941.

The Polish Detail

For reasons not completely known, the Germans decided to co-opt Poles in the extermination of the Jews. Thus, in addition to the German force that perpetrated the murders in the Konin area, a number of Poles were taken from the prison in Konin to the aforementioned location for various tasks during the execution. In a manner typical of executions in the woods, the Germans used hand-picked Jewish crews to perform all labors related to the digging, filling, and camouflaging of mass graves, as well as to sort clothes and search for valuables. After the *Aktion*, the members of these Jewish details were themselves murdered in pre-excavated graves and buried by members of the German squad. Jewish crews of this kind participated in mass executions in the course of Einsatzgruppen activity in the Soviet-annexed areas and in concentration and extermination camps. They also formed the Kommando 1005 unit that was set up at the end of the war to reopen communal graves and burn the corpses of victims of mass executions so as to destroy all evidence of the crimes committed.

It is most likely that the Germans did not use Jews in the units responsible for the actual murder-related tasks for several reasons. First, many young men in the Zagórów ghetto had been sent to work in Jewish labor camps; thus it seems possible that most men among those delivered to the murder site were unfit for efficient hard labor. The non-employment of Jews in such a depressing task may be understood as a lack of confidence in them because, as witnesses have stated, they could not cooperate with criminals and might interfere with their work, or hide valuables while searching clothes. Moreover, if the German detail wished to have efficient people at their disposal, whom they could trust to work the next day, Polish prisoners were a better choice. Notably, the mass executions in the woods near Kazimierz Biskupi were among the first of their type to be carried out on a large scale, unless one counts mass exterminations in these areas by Einsatzgruppen and the Selbstschutz during the September 1939 campaign and later that autumn. Selbstschutz was a name used by several paramilitary organizations created by ethnic Germans in Poland and other countries in Central and Eastern Europe. During the invasion of Poland of 1939, several such units operated in Poland, led by volunteers trained in Nazi Germany. In due course they were officially merged into one organization, the Ethnic German Self-Defense Force (Volksdeutsche Selbstschutz). These units took part in fighting as a fifth column, served the Gestapo, SS, and SD as auxiliary forces in the early stages of the occupation of Poland, and helped the civil administration in the Warthegau and other German occupation institutions as local controllers, informers, and members of execution squads, particularly in Operation Tannenberg (the eradication of the Polish intelligentsia) and other more local and vengeful atrocities. The killings of Polish and Jewish men, women, and children that can be traced specifically to the more-than-100,000-strong Volksdeutsche Selbstschutz are numbered at a minimum of 10,000. The force was disbanded in the winter of 1939/40; most its members joined the German SS or the Gestapo by the spring of the following year.

42. A Selbstschutz unit on parade (NAC, sign: 2-17112)

The crimes in 1939, however, were committed mainly by the SD and Sipo Einsatzgruppen, which specialized in mass murder. In 1941, the Einsatzgruppen operated in vast portions of the USSR, where they engaged in the homicide of hundreds of thousands of Jews and communists. As for the Warthegau, there was only a rather small local detail, which was not logistically prepared to execute thousands of Jews in improvised on-the-spot executions. It was, however, linked to the highest echelons of power in Nazi Germany—mainly to the central staff that ran Operation T4, the Nazi regime's program of systematic murder of the physically and mentally handicapped and psychiatric hospital patients, largely in 1939–1941. Initially the victims were shot by Einsatzgruppen and others, but gas chambers, as discussed above, were being used by the spring of 1940. Thus, the results of these experiments and improvisations led to the mass murder of Jews in the Chełmno extermination camp several months later and by the same detail.

Mieczysław Sękiewicz, whose testimony is one of the primary witness sources for the execution of Jews in the forests near Kazimierz Biskupi, described how he was taken to the murder site:

Gestapo officers came to the prison cell where I was locked up and told me to get ready to leave. They handcuffed me and led me to a passenger car, where two companions in misery from a prison in Konin were already sitting in the back seat shackled to each other at the arms and legs. Their names were Walenty Orchowski from Golina and Kazimierz Tylżanowski from the Rzgów commune. When I sat down next to them, the Germans shackled my legs.[56]

In addition to the three prisoners from Konin, other Polish prisoners from elsewhere were brought to the extermination site. "Apart from the three of us from Konin, about thirty Poles had already been brought to the site; I do not know where from."[57] Arriving at the place of execution, the prisoners were uncuffed so they could carry out their work freely. However, "The Gestapo officers warned us that they had the forest surrounded and under guard, and if we tried to escape, we would get a bullet in the head."[58]

Preparations for the Crime

Sękiewicz's testimony also reveals the identity of the victims who had been transported to the scene of the crime and how they looked:

> Groups of Jews were standing and sitting around the whole clearing, with the exception of the edge of the side where the tracks intersect, in the place marked with the letter "B" on the sketch. I cannot say how many of them there were, as they were standing among trees. The largest group was standing [here the witness shows the place] at the point marked "X" on the sketch. Among the crowds, there were women, men, and children; mothers with babies in their arms. I don't know whether these were Jews only from Poland. Later I was told that they came from the village of Zagórów. From among them, I recognized a tailor and a shopkeeper from Konin, but I cannot give their names.[59]

In addition to Sękiewicz's eyewitness report, the victims are described in other ways, usually by witnesses who saw them in the trucks during the transport to the forest. "Several times, due to wind, the tarpaulins that covered the cars blew open and then I saw the men, women, and children of Jewish nationality who were in the car."[60]

Preceding the executions in the forest near Kazimierz Biskupi, the victims were ordered to undress, after which they stood among the clothing and other items that they had brought, strewn in disarray. As mentioned earlier, a group of Polish prisoners had been enlisted to collect and sort these articles: "We were ordered to walk among the Jews standing next to the graves and to collect the scattered clothes and shoes."[61] Elsewhere in his testimony, Sękiewicz wrote, "All that time we had to collect and sort the scattered clothes, shoes, packs, food, eiderdowns, etc."[62] After the collection of clothes and other objects was completed, "[…] We were ordered to throw particular things into a truck—clothes separately, shoes separately, and other items."[63]

A witness reports that officers on site appropriated some of the victims' valuables, violating an express prohibition from Himmler in so doing. Himmler defined victims' belongings as state property that should be deposited. Misappropriation of valuables by members of the SS was disciplined in accordance with accepted rules and punishable by death. Common practice, however, was another matter, even though several senior SS officers were penalized for embezzlement. One such official was Odilo Globocnik, who was deposed as Gauleiter of Vienna on June 30, 1939. Another was Karl Lasch, Governor of Radom District in the General Government from 1940 to July 1941 and of Galicia District from August 1941 to January 1942. Lasch was told that before the end of his investigation he would have to commit suicide or be shot on Himmler's order.

Just the same, Sękiewicz reports the appropriation of large quantities of valuables by Gestapo officers:

> I witnessed scenes where Gestapo officers approached the places where we collected watches, rings and other pieces of jewelry in piles. The officers took fistfuls of these things and stuffed them into their pockets […]. Seeing this, some of us, including me, stopped putting the valuables in piles, and instead we threw the watches and rings carelessly into the forest.[64]

It is unlikely, however, that prisoners threw significant quantities of Jews' belongings into the woods, because such an act would have put them at the risk of murder by the officers. Certainly it was very risky; items flung away by workers could be found by the guards. However, this type of action—burying valuables or tossing them away to keep them out of criminals' hands, is known to have taken place in other camps, including death camps.

When Did the Executions in Kazimierz Biskupi Forest Take Place?

Exactly when the executions in the Kazimierz Biskupi forests took place is not known but may be estimated at late September, October, and possibly the first few days of November. It should be borne in mind that the liquidation of the Zagórów ghetto, with its several thousand inhabitants, took many days—about ten, according to Malron. This being the case, the German detail had to lead hundreds of Jews to the place of execution every day. Since the Kazimierz Biskupi forest was 25–30 kilometers from Zagórów, partly on dirt roads, a truck would need at least an hour to make the round trip. Allowing time to load and unload the trucks and accomplish any additional activity, each round trip took three to four hours, leaving time for three or four journeys per day. Various testimonies indicate that some Jews were brought to the murder site in covered trucks and others were delivered in gas vans. Since the gas vans were smaller and slower, it was irrational, from the perpetrator's point of view, to use them for long-distance transport. Because it was an experimental execution system, one supposes that various means of transport and methods of execution were used. Research has not yet fully answered these questions; one hopes that it will in the future.

A local researcher, Piotr Rybczyński, estimated the number of Jews in the Zagórów ghetto at the time of the liquidation at 2,500–3,000.[65] There were three collective village ghettos in Konin County—in Grodziec, Rzgów, and Zagórów—holding a combined total of about 6,000 Jews. In March 1941, about 1,000 Jews were deported from the ghettos in Grodziec and Rzgów to Izbica Lubelska, Janów Lubelski, and Krasnystaw, and some young men were transferred to a labor camp near Gdańsk. According to Rybczyński, the first to be liquidated were the ghettos in Rzgów and

Grodziec. The same pattern was used in each: after SS men reached the location, police forces and local Germans were organized. They informed the Jews that they were to be transported to the east for living and for agricultural forced labor. The Jews had to pay RM 4 for the transport, pass a medical examination to evaluate their able-bodiedness, and concentrate their luggage in one place in order to pass it on. The victims were then relocated to the Konin vicinity. On the basis of Rybczyński's research, it is assumed that the Jews from Rzgów and Grodziec were transported to the Niesłusz-Rudzica forest (Długa Łąka). The extermination there took place over several days during the last ten days of September and the first ten days of October 1941.[66]

According to Rybczyński, the Zagórów ghetto was liquidated later, between late October and early November 1941. The Jews of Zagórów were murdered in an area of the Kazimierz Biskupi forest called Krężel, near the Wygoda forester's house.[67]

Rybczyński's research evaluated the beginning of the action in Rzgów in the last ten days of September and the end of the action in Zagórów in the first ten days of November. There is, however, a problem with this timeline, since Sonderkommando Lange began the extermination in Chełmno on December 8, 1941. Assuming that the detail needed a few weeks to make the Chełmno facility operational, it is implausible that it was still involved in liquidating ghettos at the beginning of November.

Michael Alberti pinpoints the time of the murders in the woods near Konin and Kazimierz Biskupi at the end of September and the first days of October and no later; he estimates the number of Jews in the collective village ghettos in Konin County at around 3,500.[68] If this number of Jews designated for murder is accurate, it would take less time to do the job. According to Alberti, a diary composed of letters of the Landrat in Konin includes a note on a letter to the Regierungspräsidium in Hochensalza of September 20, 1941, concerning *Kennenzechnung für Juden*. On October 3, 1941, an answer was given along with the note *Kreis ist judenfrei* (County is free of Jews).[69] If this note is authentic, it would mean that all Jews in Konin County had been murdered by October 3, 1941. A second document quoted by Alberti is an internal document of Referat II E (Einsatz fremder Arbeitskräfte) (Desk II E [mobilization of foreign labor forces]).

It comprises lists of clothing and materials received by Stapoaußenstelle Konin (the Konin branch of the State Police) on October 11, 1941, with the notation *"aus abgeschlossenen Judenvorgängen"* (from completed Jewish operations). In the Nazi jargon, this denoted the belongings of murdered Jews.[70] This information confirms the previous theory—that by the beginning of October no Jews remained in the ghettos of Konin County. Thus, all remaining Jews in the collective village ghettos of Grodziec, Rzgów, and Zagórów had been murdered by the end of September 1941.

Method of Execution: Ready-Made Graves and Lime Pits

At the execution site in the forest near Kazimierz Biskupi, mass graves had been prepared before the Jews arrived. This was done to enhance the efficiency of the execution; if future victims had to wait at the execution site, the whole process would be delayed for hours, inconveniencing the members of the German squad and possibly causing additional panic among the victims and requiring increased efforts to keep the victims from running away. The witness Sękiewicz describes the size and location of the mass graves:

> Roughly parallel to the track marked as number one, only at a slight angle to the clearing, two large trenches had been dug. The first one, closer to the track, was about eight meters long, about six meters wide, and about two meters deep. At the far edge of the clearing along its entire width was a second trench roughly parallel to the first, with the same depth, about six meters wide and about fifteen meters long. Between the two trenches there was an empty space.

Here the witness, accompanied by the judge and others present, pointed out the place that he mentioned in his testimony, along with the precise location of the mass graves as marked on Sketches I and II.[71]

After the Jews were transported to the execution area and removed from the wagon, the preparations for their mass murder continued. At this point, it was clear to all that the Jews were not going to any forced-labor camp or place of resettlement but to the site of their murder.

Sękiewicz describes the dramatic scenes that immediately preceded the genocidal act.

> Then the Gestapo officers ordered the assembled Jews to undress, first those standing closest to the larger trench. Then they ordered the naked to move to the area between the two trenches and to jump into the larger pit. The screams and cries were indescribable. Some Jews—even most of them—jumped by themselves; others resisted and were beaten and pushed into the hole. Some of the mothers jumped holding their babies; others threw their children aside, while still others threw their children into the pit separately and jumped in themselves separately.[72]

The murder site in the forest near Kazimierz Biskupi became a kind of testing ground for the German squad. In the autumn of 1941, German authorities both in the Warthegau and the General Government mulled the possibility of expelling the Jews. However, since emigration or deportation to the east were not options, some high-ranking functionaries began to consider new methods: mass killing in various ways. The aforementioned experiments served as a basis for the development of the methods that would be employed in the annihilation of European Jewry. Although mass executions of both Polish and Jewish populations had been taking place by this time, there was no standard method for the elimination of thousands of Jews in one go. The numbers killed in shootings did not exceed several hundred at a time. The Einsatzgruppen used similar methods in operations in the areas annexed to the Soviet Union after September 17, 1939, and in the Baltic states and the Soviet territories that Germany occupied in the summer of 1941. In these operations, the Einsatzgruppen murdered thousands of Jews and communists en masse. Some Einsatzgruppen commanders, however, found that these techniques were hard for the murderers to implement over a lengthy period and on such a scale.[73] Attempts to involve the local population in pogroms and mass murder proved successful from the propaganda point of view but disastrous for the Germans in terms of the effective liquidation of masses of Jews and communists. Especially in areas occupied by Romanian troops, this technique ended in great failure because the local population, as well as Romanian soldiers and officers of the security forces, left thousands of corpses in the streets, roads, fields, and vineyards after the pogroms and murders that they had perpetrated. Therefore, the German officers in charge of Jewish affairs sought new methods of liquidation of Jews on a mammoth scale, as well as corpse removal. The mass murder in the forest near Kazimierz Biskupi appears to have become a paradigm for the piloting of these new methods. To describe this event, we will use selected parts of Mieczysław Sękiewicz's testimony. It should be borne in mind, however, that his testimony is reinforced by additional testimonies.

Sękiewicz testifies: "At the bottom of the larger trench I saw a layer of chunks of unslaked lime. I do not know how thick the layer was. There was no lime in the smaller grave."[74] There is no absolute certainty about the identity of the substance used by the German detail. We do not know if it was unslaked lime or lime mixed with other chemicals. Being familiar with the properties of unslaked lime, however, we know that this substance when combined with water may cause a rapid increase in temperature and become highly corrosive.

Sękiewicz continues:

> [...] Then a truck came from the direction of the road, and stopped at the track near the clearing. I noticed four vat-like things on the truck. Next, the Germans started to put a small engine in place, which probably was a pump. They connected it to one of the vats with a hose, and then two of the Gestapo officers pulled the hose from the motor to the large pit. They started the motor and these two Gestapo officers holding the hose began pouring something onto the Jews crowded in the large pit. I think it was water. That's what it looked like, but I am not sure. As the water was pumped, the hose was moved from one vat to another. Apparently, as a result of the slaking of the lime, those people started to be boiled alive, and an incredible scream emerged so that those of us seated near the clothing shredded the clothes and stuffed bits of cloth into our ears. The terrible screams of

those being boiled in the pit were joined by the screaming and wailing of the Jews still waiting to be executed. It went on for about two hours—maybe even longer.[75]

Despite the planning, it was probably difficult to predict how the whole operation would play out in terms of how long it would take to kill the victims and how many victims could be killed at once. The following account makes it clear that many more people were brought to the execution site than could be murdered in one go:

> At a certain point, the Gestapo officers ordered the Jews to stop undressing because the trench was already full. From above, the only thing visible was tightly crowded heads. Those Jews who had hurried and already undressed were thrown into the pit on top of the heads of those crammed inside.[76]

Murder by quicklime or lime turned out be very time-consuming and caused unbelievable suffering. All told, it proved to be a very cruel method, and, from the Germans' perspective, an inefficient one.

The use of the forest near Kazimierz Biskupi as a testing ground for methods of mass murder is reflected in witnesses' testimonies, according to which several different killing techniques were implemented there. In addition to the one described above using lime, quicklime, and perhaps other chemicals, the perpetrators used a truck that had an airtight cabin connected to its exhaust pipe. In this manner, the people in the cabin were murdered by means of the exhaust fumes:

> By the afternoon a large, dark gray ambulance-like wagon that opened in the rear drove into the clearing several times; after the doors were opened, human corpses of men, women, and children, all Jews, fell out from inside. I do not know whether the vehicle kept coming after I had been taken away from the clearing.
>
> The corpses pouring out of the truck were affixed to one another, as if in convulsive grasps, in contorted positions,

sometimes with chewed-up faces. I saw one with his teeth sunk into somebody else's jaw, while others had their noses or fingers chewed up. Many held hands in a violent grasp; they had obviously been family.[77]

The witness had no doubt that the victims had been killed by gas: "The corpses brought in the gray car had clearly been gassed. The inside of the car and clothes on the corpses gave off the smell of gas."[78]

We do not know where the victims unloaded near the mass graves in the Kazimierz Biskupi woods had come from, but the presumed timing of the operation suggests that the point of origin had not been far away. The presence of an unusually shaped vehicle was confirmed by other witnesses who lived in the area. From Sękiewicz's testimony, it appears that the gas wagon transported Jews from nearby villages to the place in the forest where they were murdered and buried.

The following account may indicate how the gas wagon was used in a stationary manner:

In the depths of the forest, a huge truck the size of a large bus, completely covered with [armored] plating, stood all day long. We supposed that Jews were being killed by gas in that vehicle. [...] The sound of gunfire was rare.[79]

This testimony may indicate that murder by shooting was relatively uncommon in Kazimierz Biskupi, supporting reports of attempts by the German detail to employ other methods of killing. Firearms were most likely used to finish off victims or to stop those who tried to flee.

Sękiewicz notes that murder by calcium quicklime was particularly cruel and caused the victims untold suffering by subjecting them not to immediate death but to prolonged agony: "The screams could still be heard. I heard them until I fell asleep. Because of weariness and tribulations, I was able to doze off relatively quickly."[80]

As the operation proceeded, some Jews in the forest begged the killers for mercy. "Some of them crawled at the Gestapo officers' feet, kissing their shoes, rifle butts, etc."[81] This got them nowhere, the decision to liquidate the Jews having already been made irreversibly. There was also no place for a selection among the Jews designated for death. The use of a working group of Polish prisoners in support tasks for this operation was probably meant to avoid the employment of any of these Jews. There may have been another important motive: preventing the possibility that Jews might escape and advise other Jews, back in the ghetto, of the fate of those recently deported—fomenting panic and hampering the murder process. Indeed, the Einsatzgruppen in the Soviet Union had tried to keep what awaited the victims a secret. The same modus operandi was used in deportations to death camps under Aktion Reinhard.

Eyewitnesses also reported cases of abuse of victims during the execution. Sękiewicz describes one such scene:

> I remember one more thing from the clearing during the killing of the Jews—how one of the Gestapo officers took a baby from her mother's arms and smashed the baby's little head against the edge of a car right in front of the mother's very eyes, and when the mother started screaming, he hurled the baby's head at her so violently that the brains filled her mouth. Then he took something, some lime or plaster from the car, and rubbed it on her mouth. Other women who screamed loudly were treated in the same manner. I saw how one Gestapo officer grabbed a young beautiful Jewish woman and, having torn off her dress and underwear, tied her arms behind her back, and hanged her naked by the arms from a tree. Then, using a utility knife, he cut her right breast in slices, and then cut her stomach open and rummaged around in her entrails. The Jewish woman died on the tree. I did not know any of the Gestapo officers who were there.[82]

Burial of Victims

Once the killing was done, the officers ordered Polish prisoners to cover up and conceal the mass graves. "We covered the grave carelessly; arms from some of the corpses were still sticking out when we were ordered to stop filling [it]."[83] The work was halted because new trucks, in which Jews had been killed by gas—probably exhaust fumes—had arrived. Such gas was used in the extermination camp at Chełmno, where later the German details also used trucks to asphyxiate people in this manner. Subsequently, hundreds of thousands of Jews were murdered in Bełżec, Sobibór, and Treblinka by means of stationary engines that had been lifted from Russian tanks and stationed next to the gas chambers. One cannot exclude the possibility that the experiments with gas wagons in killing people in the forest near Kazimierz Biskupi had become the basis for further technical improvements that were used on a massive scale in the death camps at Chełmno and in the General Government.

The corpses that arrived by gas wagons were difficult to unload for burial due to the Dantean scenes that had accompanied the process inside the van. Suffocating victims had trampled each other in their quest for survival; some were interlocked with others in ways that made them hard to separate:

> The Gestapo officers ordered us to tear the corpses apart, and if this did not work, then to chop them up, cutting off hands, legs, and other parts. Next, we had to place the corpses in a smaller trench in the clearing, positioning them tightly together with the heads alternating from one side to the other. We were ordered to stuff the chopped off parts between the bodies. While I was there, three such layers of people were arranged and one truck was still not unloaded.[84]

After each group was murdered, Polish prisoners were ordered to cover the victims' mass graves:

> The following day in the morning, the Gestapo officers ordered us to cover the large hole with dirt. The mass of people inside sort of collapsed and drifted downward towards the bottom of the pit. The bodies were so crowded together that they still remained in a somewhat standing position, only their heads were tilted to all sides […].[85]

The reason for this sloppy treatment and poor concealment is not clear. Probably it was a combination of indifference, carelessness, neglect, and lack of fear that news of the crime would spread. Presumably, the perpetrators realized that local people were aware of the executions and judged that it would not matter to them. It should be borne in mind that at this time, the autumn of 1941, the Germans were at the peak of their power and feared no one, least of all in the areas that they had incorporated into the Reich.

After the execution, local inhabitants were barred from the forest for a certain period of time. Even after the formal prohibition was lifted, locals were most likely afraid to enter the scene of the crime for some time. One witness recalls:

> About a one month after the facts described above, and once the ban of access to the forest was lifted, I went into the forest alone and found the following. At a distance of about three kilometers from the Wygoda forester's house, on the left side of the road leading to Kleczew, is a wooded area called Krężel. The graves were 400–500 meters away from the road in the woods, where there was a young forest, that is, a mixed forest several years old composed of pines, hornbeams, and birches.[86]

It was there that the witness discovered the mass graves:

> There were two huge and three smaller pits dug. The tops of the pits were covered with turf and planted with young spruces. A fetid white liquid was escaping from these graves. Two years later, it might have been in the winter or spring of 1943 or 1944, the German authorities again closed the forest where the young spruces had been planted.[87]

It is difficult to determine what the "fetid white liquid" oozing from the graves was. It may have been related to decomposition of the bodies due to the use of lime and, possibly, other corrosives and chemicals in the killing process and in an attept to "burn" the bodies in order to hide all evidence of the horrible crime.

Escape from Execution Sites

Only a few successful escapes of prisoners from places of execution are known to have occurred. In the case of Kazimierz Biskupi, no survivors are known; most of our detailed knowledge of the mass murder originates in Sękiewicz's testimony. Other information comes from local inhabitants who were able to observe the scenes of murder or evidence of it, such as seeing the transportation of the victims to the place of execution or the movement of wagons empty of passengers but full of clothes, hearing machine-gun fire, or otherwise being aware of the murders.

There was, however, one known case of escape of a prisoner from an execution site on another occasion. We do not know who he was, whether he was Jewish or not, or whether he managed to avoid arrest later. A local inhabitant describes an encounter with him as follows:

> I had such an event in the summer of 1943 that while riding a bicycle from Konin to my home, near the village of Grąblin, I stumbled on an unknown Pole hiding in the rye who asked for bread and water. He told me that he had fled from the Germans in the forest and had been hiding for two days in the fields and that he wanted to go to Zgierz. He told me briefly that he was one of the prisoners who had been employed in the forest to bury corpses brought by wagons by the Germans. I didn't have time to inquire about the prisoner's details because I saw that he was very scared and haggard and hungry. It was evident that he was afraid of me, and I also feared that someone would notice us. I gave him a piece of bread and rode home.[88]

Sękiewicz, supposedly the only prisoner who could testify about the murder in the forest near Kazimierz Biskupi, survived the war after enduring various prisons and concentration camps. He explains his survival in the following way:

[...] The Gestapo officers beat me with riding crops all over my face [at the execution site near Kazimierz Biskupi] and then took me to a prison in Konin together with my companions, all of us shackled just like when we were taken away. A few weeks later, we were transported to a camp in Inowrocław, then to Mauthausen and finally to Gusen. I remained in Gusen until my liberation on May 5, 1945. My companions could not last in the camp and they died there.[89]

Reports about the Mass Murder in the Kazimierz Biskupi Forests

Word about the mass murder spread relatively quickly. As early as April 1942, Hersh Wasser, then in the Warsaw ghetto, wrote about it to Aleksander Kamiński,[90] chief editor of *Biuletyn Informacyjny*, a Polish underground news bulletin published by the main Polish resistance organization. The main problem, however, was how much was known and how precise and detailed the available information about the mass murder in Kazimierz forest was. Wasser wrote:

> In the second half of November 1941, news spread through the cities of Koło District (*Kreis Wartbrücken*) that the entire Jewish population of these villages was to be resettled in Pińszczyzna or Eastern Galicia. The German authorities have imposed a poll tax of RM 4 on the entire Jewish population, and all men from age 14 to 60 and women under age 50 have undergone medical examinations to determine their ability to work. Concerned about these facts, the Jewish community endeavored to obtain any news about the deportation, but their efforts remained fruitless. The only thing that has been determined is that the Jewish population, counting three thousand people from Zagórów, Konin County, after similar preparations, was transported in cars to the Kazimierz forest near the town, where all traces of them have disappeared.[91]

All we can learn from this account is that thousands of Jews disappeared near Konin. Local inhabitants had much more precise information but were not connected to any underground organization and could not forward their knowledge to organizations that could disseminate it.

In his testimony, Bert Gembicki said that about six weeks after the arrest of several hundred young men for the labor camp in Inowrocław, all the Jews in Zagórów were taken to a nearby forest and exterminated. In 1941, Zagórów became judenfrei.[92] According to Michel Prost, in 1941 the Jews knew that Zagórów had been liquidated—Poles had told them—but did not know what to think about the information. That the Germans had been able to murder all the Jews in Zagórów was beyond their grasp.

> One couldn't imagine it. It was unbelievable until we finally realized that they [the Jews of Zagórów] no longer existed. We had no confirmation of the murder [apart from information that Poles living in the area related]. Some said that they had been moved to the Łódź ghetto. But there were some Jews from the Łódź ghetto whom we could ask to verify this report. We couldn't imagine they [the Jews of Zagórów] didn't exist. It was difficult to believe because in the labor camp in Inowrocław only one person had died.[93]

Abram Landau testified:

> They said that there were Raventrucks [a word probably derived from the German *Ravenwagen*]. A Pole who worked there said that the ghetto in Zagórów had been completely destroyed; nobody knew what had really happened. Some told about pits and lime; some said they were living; some said that they were electrocuted—that the Germans did it.[94]

Several attested to having thought about their families that had been interned in a ghetto or, possibly, in Chełmno. They had known what had happened, they said, but could not truly grasp it; they did note that some of the victims had been very young.

Some Jewish workers in labor camps had no contact with their families and, in fact, no communication with anyone on the outside.

Bert Gembicki testifies that an acquaintance from a village not far from Kleczew told him what had happened to his family. At that time (December 1941 or early 1942), Gembicki was an inmate at a forced-labor camp in Żegotki. One morning, he and his peers headed out for work on a large farm and had to go via the highway. On the way, Bert Gembicki saw a Pole named Josi [Józef] Kowalski, who recognized him and called out, "Gembisiu, Gembisiu." Kowalski, who lived about five kilometers from Kleczew, had been drafted for compulsory labor but received a home furlough once every two weeks. "I have to tell you something," he divulged to Gembicki. "They took all the Jews from Zagórów."[95]

Gembicki describes the rest of Kowalski's information:

> They took a trailer with Jews to the forest. One mile from there was a forest, a big forest. They took them to the forest, dug a big grave, put water into this big hole, and then threw lime inside. Lime together with water has a chemical reaction; it becomes very hot. It can burn hands....[96] They threw the Jews [into the hole], used an electric wire, and tied up the hands. This Pole told me this; he said that he had seen it. They killed 3,000–4,000 people there. Later they covered the pits but the earth started to move....[97] The earth started to shake. This man had a sister not far from Kazimierz [Biskupi] forest. It was a beautiful forest, between Kleczew, Kazimierz, and Konin.[98]

When Bert Gembicki heard this, he fainted. "I can't forget what [the Pole] said, but we had to ignore this news. We worked. It was a very tough winter in Żegotki, near Strzelno, not far from Inowrocław."[99]

There were cases in which Jewish forced laborers saw the trucks en route to the forest. Charles Lepek testifies that in the winter, due to the frozen ground, there was no work in agriculture but the Jews in the labor camps had to go to the highway to clear it of snow and make it passable. While doing this labor one day, Lepek reports having seen a "phony truck," about ten meters long and very tightly closed. He describes it as fake—like a tank, but a truck. Outside, there was a "Jewish guy" making sure the door was closed. He asked Lepek, "*Hey, wie geht es?*" [Hello, how are you?]. Later Lepek learned that there were graves in the woods. He could not call them graves at that time; they were more like holes into which people had been thrown, probably after having been gassed with exhaust fumes. "Many people with bad hearts went quickly. I don't know. They wouldn't let anybody out, of course."[100] From the moment Lepek left Zagórów, he did not know what had become of his parents. They may have been taken in this truck, he speculated. Modern cars would make the trip from Zagórów to the woods in the Kazimierz Biskupi area in about two hours. The operation may have proceeded around the clock. Since many Jewish communities had been concentrated in Zagórów, it was difficult to say how long the action continued. Lepek added: "They were packed like herring in a barrel. We speculated about how it had been done; they couldn't get out."[101]

According to the survivor Tzvi Malron, closed trucks resembling ambulances arrived during the deportation from the Zagórów ghetto. People were packed into these vehicles; their belongings were loaded into separate trailers that were attached to the trucks and held bundles of clothes:

> I remember—the whole family went. My grandfather entered such a car. I will not forget—cousins, everyone all together. It was two days before [our turn], when we had to go. My father said he was not going; he wanted to wait for the last day.[102]

One of the major factors that overshadowed the news about the mass murder of Jews from Zagórów ghetto in the Kazimierz Biskupi forest was a new wave of information about deportations from various towns in the Warthegau to Chełmno, where Jews were being murdered on a far greater scale than in Kazimierz Biskupi. Early in Chełmno's history, in January 1942, Rabbi Jacob Szulman wrote a dramatic letter to his relatives in the Warsaw ghetto about deportations to, and mass murder of Jews in, Chełmno.[103] His knowledge was based on information from escapees from Chełmno, one of whom, known as "Szlamek," gave a timely testimony about mass murder in Chełmno.[104] Once information about mass murder in Chełmno had begun to spread, the preceding murders in Kazimierz Biskupi paled in comparison. Thus, unfortunately, the fate of the Jewish community in the village ghetto in Zagórów remained insignificant for years in Holocaust historiography.

The Sole Surviving Family

The Malareks (subsequently the Malrons) were probably the only family that managed to escape from the Zagórów ghetto during the murder deportations to the Kazimierz Biskupi forest.

Tzvi Malron recounts how his family survived. His father, wishing to see where the Judenrat was going, put Tzvi's mother to bed and wrote "Typhus" on the door. In the meantime, the Germans went from house to house with a Polish policeman. When they came to Malron's home, his father went out and said, "*Meine Frau ist krank* ["My wife is ill"]; maybe we'll go after tomorrow." Hearing this and seeing the word "typhus" on the door, the Germans became afraid. That night, Zvi's father awakened the family and told them to get dressed and go. The Malrons crossed orchards, fields, and gardens:[105]

> Nearly every house in Poland had a garden. We went and went and went. We took hardly anything with us. My mother balanced a package on her head. Why on her head? Because we had to cross to the other side of the Warta River. My father knew how to swim. He knew where to cross. We followed him to the other side of the river. And we went through fields only at night. Not on the roads, only through fields. During the day, we lay among the bushes in the fields. My brother couldn't go on. We were wet for one or two days. We continued to go and Father said it wasn't far. Then we finally came to the place. A Pole whom my father knew saw us. They talked. The Pole was afraid. If somebody saw him, he could get a bullet in the head just because he'd spoken with Jews. Then [the Pole] said, "Come in. Quickly." He spoke to his wife and then moved a cupboard at an angle. We were not small. We understood. We were silent. We spent a few days there. At night we slept on the floor. During the day we were behind the cupboard. After that, [the Pole and his wife] took us in the

morning, before dawn, in a straw-filled wagon. We hid under the straw [...]. We went to Sompolno, where my aunt lived. It was in October–November 1941.[106]

Sompolno was very cold in autumn. We stayed there all winter. I don't know who prepared this, but we lived in a cellar. Father worked for a German butcher who had a sausage factory. Sompolno was an open ghetto. He worked every night and was able to get some sausages that he used to bring us. We cooked those sausages in a pot with water. It was good. My mother added something.

Then there was forced labor. They started taking people for work. I had to go as well. I was thirteen years old. I was registered. My father found somebody, a tailor named Fogel who was working for the Germans, and they took me to be like an apprentice. It was Father's friend from before the war; he worked only for the Germans. My father was registered at the butcher and I was registered there.

My uncle was taken to a forced-labor camp. One day after three or four months, he returned, maybe because of his eyes. He was sick.[107] We were registered and had documents. The Judenrat could arrange everything—all kinds of things. We worked officially. My father waited for the Judenrat from Zagórów, but they didn't come.[108]

Then the news arrived—that everyone [from Zagórów] had been taken to the woods near Kazimierz [Biskupi] and killed.[109] Nobody remained from Zagórów. Not even one family came. Nobody escaped. Only my father. He was an optimist. He was the only one. They finished off everybody there.[110]

In Sompolno, my father did not wait but thought about the future. We went to Radziejów, not far from there; about fifteen kilometers away. There was a *selekcja* [selection]. A number of men from there were taken to HASAG in Częstochowa. They took everybody from Sompolno and Radziejów.[111]

My father wanted to go to the Protektorat [in fact, the General Government], to Wiśnicz Nowy, near Bochnia. People were being sent to the Protektorat and my father wanted to go there. Even though he had no [travel] documents, he bought tickets. We wore the Star of David. They arrested us and checked us in every way. Then we were released. It was in Kłobuck. After our release, we went to Wiśnicz Nowy, via Częstochowa.[112]

It was 1942, before Passover. In Radziejów or Sompolno, my father had a $1,000 banknote and he managed to sell it. We had Father's watch and there was a fox fur. My parents sold all this. We came to Wiśnicz without anything—destitute. There was a Polish administration, Polish police, and Polish schools.[113]

3. EXECUTIONS IN DŁUGA ŁĄKA

The second mass execution site in the vicinity of Konin was Długa Łąka, several kilometers north of Konin. The Rudzica forest around Długa Łąka and that near Kazimierz Biskupi form a large complex of forests that stretches for many kilometers to the northwest from Konin to several kilometers from a border town. This made it a convenient place for the local Gestapo to murder masses of Jews and prisoners. Here, two modes of homicide—airtight gas trucks and shooting—were probably used. Kazimierz Szymczak testified: "In the forest, Germans carried out the murder of Jews for a long time, killed [them] in many ways, and then buried them in mass pits.... The whole area of the execution was overgrown with large trees, including birch, oak, and hornbeam."[114]

The exact location of these mass graves is noted in the minutes of the District Commission for the Investigation of Nazi Crimes in Poznań, which examined the crime in the woods of Długa Łąka:

> A witness led those present to inspect the current locality of the mass graves of murdered Jews. Two of these graves are located on the left side of the dirt road at a distance of approximately 100 meters apart. One of these burial places has a rise with a tapered tip, whose base has dimensions of 3.5x2.5 meters. The inspectors marked a mound over a big hole in which bodies of the murdered Jews were buried. The second grave is located a

bit farther towards the wide clearing cut out of the forest, now overgrown with grass and small bushes. Witness Szymczak indicates the current supposed location of the grave not marked in the field.[115]

It should be emphasized that although the crime in the Długa Łąka woods took place far from towns or settlements and the forest was closed to strangers at the time, several local residents were able to observe the activities. The District Commission minutes contain witnesses' testimonies, including that of Szymczak:

At the conclusion, the witness Szymczak shows the place where he worked as a forestry worker at the time of liquidation of the Jews. This place is just about 150–200 meters from the mass graves, except that the visibility in the forest was then much better, because now the slope is covered with tall trees.[116]

Szymczak explains how he was able to determine this:

I was about 100 meters from the place where I watched the whole operation and it took place over a period of several days. Because I was carrying out my work, the Germans did not interfere in my observation. I cannot tell from which city the Jews were brought to the place of execution.[117]

It is hard to determine, even roughly, when the executions of Jews in Długa Łąka occurred and how long they lasted on the basis of local witness reports. "The operation of killing the Jews lasted for several weeks," said Szymczak;[118] "It may have been the period from harvest to potato lifting."[119] Other witnesses cannot even report the year. The time of the year, however, is much easier to isolate: "It was the autumn of 1941 or 1942."[120] In the woods of Długa Łąka, as in the aforementioned case of execution in the forest near Kazimierz Biskupi, a restricted zone had been set up. "One morning, I do not remember the date, I noticed German troops surrounding a certain part of the forest."[121] Another witness recalled: "They surrounded the forest with checkpoints and didn't let anyone in."[122] Additional testimonies confirm the closure of the area:

> I recall that on September 26, 27, and 28, 1942—it seems to me that it could not have been in 1941—a larger group of Gestapo men, military police, and other auxiliary police came to the woods Długa Łąka [pow. Konin, gm. Gosławice], who closed forests in Długa Łąka for an indefinite period. The forest was surrounded by police checkpoints. I and my subordinates [foresters] had no access to the forest.[123]

Another witness said, "A large part of the deciduous and conifer forest opposite the forester's house in Długa Łąka by the flowing stream had been surrounded."[124] Yet another witness gave us some information about the size of the closed area:

> During the war I lived in a forester's house in Długa Łąka, about 1.5 km from Niesłusz.... I remember that once German police surrounded a part of the forest, the length and width of 1 km with checkpoints, and had banned everyone in the area from going into that part of the forest.[125]

According to one witness, the closure lasted two weeks.[126]

Another witness, a young boy at the time, was hired by officers at the checkpoints around the sequestered section of forest: "At a certain time in the morning, according to an officer's orders, I had to bring a chair for the German soldier at the checkpoint on the road. In the evening I had to take the chair back."[127]

Several testimonies refer to the crime and the perpetrators:

> From the stories of various people, I know that this whole action was led by the Gestapo from Konin. Several times I saw that the area of forest in the Długa Łąka, during the murder of Jews, was guarded by German soldiers from SS troops. I recognized their uniforms and the skull [the Totenkopf] on their caps.[128]

Others describe the kinds of functionaries and officers who comprised the German detail that carried out the executions in Długa Łąka:

> I knew almost all the military police in Konin, but I had no acquaintance with the other policemen among them, whom I saw as a convoy. Later, in a conversation with one of the Gestapo men, I learned that the Gestapo and the police came from Poznań.[129]

An additional witness gave details that established the kind of officers who were present: "The soldiers had uniforms with greenish bronze tabs at the collar and on the chest had a crescent-shaped plate."[130]

Methods of Execution

In the Długa Łąka woods, as opposed to the forest near Kazimierz Biskupi, a Jewish detail was employed to perform all work associated with the burial of the victims,[131] such as the digging of mass graves:

> These pits were dug by Jews who had been brought by cars to the forest. I do not remember the date or month in which the Germans began a massive liquidation and murder of Jews. I only remember that it was in the autumn. I can not specify the year.[132]

The size of the graves was "12–15 meters long, two meters wide, and as deep as the height of a man...."[133] Some [members of the Jewish commando] worked at digging pits and others unloaded corpses of Jews from cars and rolled them into mass graves."[134]

A witness from the local population had an opportunity to communicate with members of the Jewish details when two boys came with one of the German officers to his home:

> One day as I took water from the well, a German soldier with two Jewish boys aged 16–17 years, who had buckets, came into the courtyard and took water from the well. Having bread, I gave the boys half a loaf because one of them asked for bread. The soldier

did not notice. The officer came to the forester's house on several occasions, warmed up and ate.[135]

Kazimierz Szymczak's testimony indicates that the murders in the Długa Łąka woods were perpetrated by means of gas vans. Other reports speak of the burial of people who had been killed by special trucks. The witness Piotr Zalas recalls: "Again, the next day, several similar large trucks and one large car covered with a tarpaulin, similar in appearance to a furniture van, arrived. These cars, we thought, were bringing people to be liquidated."[136]

The perpetrators appear to have used different techniques for murder by means of exhaust fumes. One method was stationary, using an internal combustion engine connected by pipes to a car that was hermetically sealed on all sides. A description of the testimony of one witness gives more information on the method of killing:

> Then the witness, after passing about 40 meters through the forest that currently is 30 years old, shows the way—where the engine was—which in his opinion produced the exhaust gases that were fed into a large [hermetically] closed car; where each time a large group of Jews was closed inside. Corpses of those people poisoned by the gas were pulled out of the car and transferred to the three mass graves located a bit below—30–40 feet from here.[137]

Szymczak provides similar evidence:

> The killing of Jews was carried out in this way: at the place they had a very strong engine and a tube connected to the chassis of the car and the gas went into the car. Jews engaged in this operation pulled the dead from the car and rolled them into the graves.[138]

Two witnesses, Szymczak and Lucjan Zalas, concur that a special unit was used to prepare a forest clearing and that its members were the ones who connected the pipes to the hermetically sealed cars:

I got to the Marantowska Road [Aleja Marantowska]. A larger number of troops and trucks was standing there. At the Marantowska Road intersection, where I was walking, was a trailer that had four wheels and was completely covered. Next to it stood a unit [*agregat*] that had two wheels and was activated. Very close to Marantowska Road I noticed a group of naked people and another group of people dressed with stars indicating their Jewish nationality.[139]

According to witnesses, the Jews were murdered in a tightly closed trailer. If this is so, we have discovered yet another "invention" in the mass murder of Jews—the use of mobile gas chambers in the form of sealed trailers rather than vans, to which a special gas-producing unit was attached. This portable gas chamber could be used to murder Jews and others in different locations, obviating the need to build permanent gas chambers. One witness relates:

> One day I noticed how from the enclosed trailer human bodies were pulled out—naked. It was done by Jews with the stars. They were surrounded by armed German soldiers. Each time I was there, I saw a pile of clothes near the enclosed trailer. I also noticed, in the forest by the stream, two pits 15 meters in length. I also saw how the Jews were digging these pits. Among the Jews were adults, adolescents, and children holding the hands of women and men.[140]

It is also beyond doubt that many of the victims were shot to death. It is difficult to tell whether shooting was one of the basic methods of murder or just an auxiliary method. According to one witness, only Jews trying to escape were shot: "Some Jews who tried to flee were killed by shots from the guards' rifles."[141] According to another witness, mass executions of larger groups of Jews in the Długa Łąka forest may have taken place in this manner: "On the evening of the first day, that is, September 26, 1942, I heard several series of shots, issued by machine guns. These bursts lasted about an hour."[142] Another local resident said:

Once, when I ran away from a cow into the forest "by the stream" [*przy strudze*], I saw that there were a lot of men, women, and children in that place. It seems to me that there could have been about 300 people. The cars that brought these people usually came in either the afternoon or the evening [...]. In those days, when people were brought to be executed, I heard a series of machine gun shots during the day. At home, we talked among ourselves and concluded that the Germans had shot the people they brought there.[143]

As in other locations and the mass extermination crimes in the camps, the victims were ordered to strip naked and leave their clothes behind before being killed. According to witnesses' reports, in the Długa Łąka woods the dead Jews' clothes were also collected and taken away for reuse:

... After each transfer of the Jews to the clearing, clothes of Jews who were executed were collected and placed inside the cars. These cars left the forest uncovered, so that the clothes could be seen sitting in them. I recall that after the action, a group of Germans appeared who systematically cleaned up the clearing, and possibly also the adjacent area, so that the traces [of the activity] were obliterated.[144]

Other testimonies pertaining to the observation of transports that moved into the Długa Łąka woods prove that in many cases Jews were taken into the forest alive. Piotr Zalas reports:

I saw in one car, which was partly open, a great number of people who were being transported. On the third day a situation similar to that discerned on September 26 was repeated [...]. I noticed that the first day trucks arrived in the forest. Throughout the day there were about 20 trucks covered with canvas. At the head of the procession a green truck belonging to the Gestapo was being driven. I had not seen another convoy.

These cars arrived to the junction in the forest, located in the middle of the forest, and left their cargo there.[145]

The tarpaulin-covered trucks were much different from the tightly enclosed trucks used for gassing people. Therefore, they may have carried living people or almost-dead victims who had been shot during the liquidation of the ghetto or while trying to escape to the forest. It is unlikely that the executions took place in the cities or ghettos and that dead victims were then transported. This was not done on a large scale; the perpetrators did not wish to conduct mass executions in front of the local population. In addition, it was easier to transport live people to the place of execution and then kill them in the forest. It had an important psychological effect: victims brought to the forest were placed on unfamiliar terrain and felt lost, which weakened their desire to escape.

The witness Kazimierz Szymczak, confirms that living people were trucked to the forest. "To the place, they brought a larger group of Jews in trucks covered with tarpaulins."[146] In the minutes of September 1, 1968, he specified the location of mass graves where Jews had been taken for execution, as is noted in this description of his testimony:

> This place [of execution] is about 700 meters from the highway from Niesłusz to Maliniec. In the distance, about 400 meters from the highway on the fork of that branch of the road leading to Rudzica, he [the witness] pointed the way where the trucks during the extermination of Jews, which imported the Jews from a city unknown to him, had stopped.[147]

Other witnesses give more precise information about the Jews who were taken to the Długa Łąka forest:

> I noticed that for a long time Germans kept bringing in trucks with a larger number of people from Niesłusz.... I repeatedly saw these trucks covered with tarpaulins on the road from Niesłusz to Rudzica. Sometimes the people inside looked through the

cracks and therefore I knew the trucks were carrying people. The Germans unloaded the consignment on the corner of the road from Marantów leading to the road linking the "Solanki" with the chalet where my parents lived.[148]

Another witness provides similar information:

At the end of October 1942 [...] by the house where we lived, a few trucks rode by. They were covered with carpets or some other big pieces of material. The trucks came from Niesłusz through Marantów in the direction of the forest known as "Długa Łąka." Throughout the day, from early morning until dusk, 8–10 trucks could drive in the direction of Długa Łąka. Initially, we did not realize that the Germans were transporting Jews for liquidation. Once, I went for a walk and cycle trip and found that in one of the wagons there were a lot of people: women, youths, and children. On the back of the car was a German soldier, probably an SS man armed with a machine gun. The first action of transporting Jews to Długa Łąka lasted several days. Later there was quite a short break and then once again trucks began to circulate.[149]

Another witness states that after the first wave of liquidation of Jews there were some days when no traffic could be observed. This meant, however, that the action had been suspended, not completed:

After these three days the forest was still closed. It was likely that there was an action of liquidation [of people] in progress, because cars no longer passed through, and traffic on that section started up again on October 3 in the morning. Once again people to be liquidated were transported. The transportation of these people was repeated approximately every half-hour. We deduced that the Germans were transporting Jews from Konin and the surrounding area, meaning Rychwał, Zagórów, Golina, and other places, to be executed.[150]

Others witnesses assumed that the victims came mainly from the Zagórów ghetto. "They were probably people of Jewish nationality from Zagórów," said one.[151] Another commented:

> Based on my observations, I concluded that Jews were brought to the Długa Łąka forest not only from Konin but also from other towns in Konin County. I suppose they also were taken from the town of Zagórów, which then belonged to Konin District. Zagórów was a concentration area for Jews that [the German authorities] had decided to liquidate.[152]

When the truck returned from the forest, it did not contain any people, local residents noticed. "These cars, coming back, were not covered with tarpaulins and were used to carry clothes, items, bundles, etc. I surmised that a great number of people had been brought to the forest to be liquidated."[153]

The victims included women and children. One witness describes this:

> At this point [...], Jews of both sexes and of various ages, not excluding small children, still hand-in-hand, exited from the trucks. This is where the Germans threw turnips or carrots as food among the crowd of Jews and gave them a brief opportunity to rest. From this point, at the bend into the depths of the Długa Łąka forest, runs a dirt road about two feet wide, which [...] was at the time of the liquidation of the Jews a normal forest road [*leśny dukt*].[154]

An additional witness corroborates:

> A few trucks passed by, some of which went towards the forest in Rudzica and some to the forests of Gocław. As I recall, there were four or five wagons. All were covered with tarpaulins. I do not remember whether the trucks were escorted by cars. At one point one of those trucks passed by with its tarpaulin folded

back. Then I saw several women and children who were crying. According to their appearance they were Jews.[155]

Number of Victims

The exact number of victims of mass murder in the woods of Długa Łąka is not known. Kazimierz Szymczak offers a plausible estimate: "I cannot determine even approximately how many Jews were taken to the place of their liquidation, but it seems to me that there were very many. It appears to me that one can determine the total number executed to at least 2,000."[156] The website of the State Museum in Konin sets the number of victims murdered in the Długa Łąka woods at 1,600.[157]

One of the witnesses offers another approximation:

During the first day we heard several series of machine gun fire. Later, only occasionally shots were heard from the Długa Łąka. We established among ourselves, when talking with the members of our family, that in total 100 trucks loaded with Jews were transported to the Długa Łąka. In each truck there could have been 20–30 people. Thus, later we reached the conclusion that about 3,000 Jews were executed and buried in the Długa Łąka forest.[158]

Another witness, testifying after the war about the massacre in the Długa Łąka woods, used observations of mass graves (among other things) to estimate a number similar to the foregoing:

One day, after the completion of this mass murder at the end of 1940, I went walking in the woods of Długa Łąka and found three mass graves there. One was very large and measured approximately 12 meters in length and 4–5 meters in width. The other two grave pits were much smaller. Based on the appearance of the graves, I came to the conclusion that the total of Jews murdered and buried in them amounted to about 2,000–3,000.[159]

Mass Graves after the Execution

After the mass murder, some local residents went to the forest to see where it had happened. Their testimony to the District Commission for the Investigation of Nazi Crimes in Poznań suffices to verify the appearance and condition of these graves. One witness testified:

After some time, Germans notified that they had taken down the posts and access to the forest was open again. Then my father sent me as the first to establish what had changed in the closed part of the forest. I ran there with the cows, so as not to arouse suspicion, and found clear evidence of large pits. If I'm not mistaken, there were about four altogether. Superficially, it does not exclude the possibility that there were four. They were about 10–12 meters long and approximately 1.5 meters wide. They were covered with yellowing leaves. Trees growing out of these pits were not cleared and continued to grow. On the trunks of these trees I noticed traces of fresh yellow sand.[160]

The boy quoted above, accompanied into the forest by his uncle, also testified before the commission:

After some time we realized that the army had left the closed-off area of the forest at night. Finally, they left the forest area. Then I, with my uncle, went to see what the Germans had done in the guarded section of the forest. I led my uncle to Marantowska Road and then I found that there were three holes—not two—which I had seen in the beginning. These pits were concealed by turf and forest undergrowth. After some time, I also reached the conclusion that these pits were collapsing.[161]

Zdzisław Kazimierz Olejnik, who was at the crime scene with Piotr Zalas, describes his impressions of his visit:

In mid-November 1942, after the completion of the whole action, I went accompanied by Piotr Zalas—the forester—to the place where they had buried the corpses of the Jews. We both found that the place where Jews were unloaded from trucks had been cleared. On the grass of the clearing there were remnants of clothing and food. From this clearing Jews, already naked, were transported about 300 meters toward the village of Solanka. From there the car turned into the forest that was composed of old trees, where prepared graves had already been dug. I established then together with Zalas that there were two or three graves. Each of them was about 20 meters long and several meters wide. These graves were camouflaged well with leaves, and it was difficult to figure out how many bodies they could contain.[162]

A local resident described his visit to the scene of the mass murder as follows:

My house where I lived in Długa Łąka was about 400 meters from the place of execution. After October 3, 1942, I visited the place of execution, which was not guarded, and found that there were covered-up graves 12–15 meters long and two meters wide. From the mass graves, which had already settled, fetid pus was discharging. But I got the impression that it was not necessarily from human bodies. It was mixed with some chemicals. The graves were concealed by leaves. They planted some trees and shrubs were dug near the place of execution. From the following day, access to the forest was open to forestry workers and visitors.[163]

As the postwar years passed, it became difficult to identify the mass graves. By the 1960s, when an attempt was made to investigate the murders in the Długa Łąka forest, it had become especially complicated to determine the exact location of the mass graves, in part because sophisticated research techniques were not in use. In 1968, the District Commission for the Investigation of Nazi Crimes in Poznań explained:

Identifying the exact location of three mass graves in the current situation is impossible, and the witness says that at this point a tall forest grew, similar to that which extends to the other side of the ground path. None of these mass graves has a board or a sign as a reminder that this is a place of mass executions of innocent people by Nazi occupiers.[164]

Another witness also had difficulty in identifying the crime scene and determining the location of the mass graves:

By then, short trees had grown, mostly birch and various weeds. The witness cannot pinpoint the location of these three graves. The witnesses insist that the bodies of those murdered people had not been exhumed by the Germans because there was no need to do so.[165]

Masking the Mass Graves

The area of the mass graves was disguised to hinder the detection of their location. "The forest that then grew in that area was cut, and afterwards young trees were planted."[166] Referring to experiments that the German detail carried out in the mass-murder site in the Długa Łąka woods, we can conclude on the basis of witness testimonies that chemical agents were used to accelerate the decomposition of the bodies in the mass graves. Some witnesses identify the agent as carbide:

> According to a witness, the corpses were completely decomposed because of the effect of large amounts of carbide when they buried the bodies of the murdered. Then the graves were covered with earth and quite a large number of shrubs and trees were planted on top of them for better camouflage. The location where the mass graves are is in the area of the forest managed by the District Forest Administration in Sompolno.[167]

The witness Szymczak testifies:

> I declare that, in my opinion, the Germans did not remove the bodies of murdered Jews because the graves were filled with carbide, which resulted in the complete elimination of the bodies of victims. There was no need to unearth the dead because the carbide had caused the corpses to decompose. After the Soviet Army entered the area, I was interrogated by an officer of the Soviet Army, who carried out the investigation. I recall that the officer discovered the bones of small children in one of the graves and was full of compassion for their fate.[168]

In 1944, as discussed below at greater length, a special detail acted to destroy all traces of the mass murders that had taken place in the Kazimierz Biskupi and Długa Łąka forests. The unit was based on the Kommando 1005, a German unit composed of the Security Police (Sipo) and Security Service (SD). Günther Fuchs, the Gestapo Commissar from Łódź, commanded this unit in the Warthegau. Work in these places began in early February 1944; its purpose was to eliminate all traces of the mass graves by opening them and exhuming and cremating the corpses. The members of the detail stayed there for several months until they finished the job.

NOTES

1 For details on its demise and the downscaling of its population as a task for SS Hauptsturmführer Bothmann's Sonderkommando to perform, see Document 22 in Annex 1.
2 M. Alberti, *Nikczemna perfidia*, p. 81.
3 M. Alberti, *Die Verfolgung und Vernichtung der Juden im Reichsgau Wartheland 1939-1945* (Wiesbaden, 2006), 395-405.
4 P. Heberer, "Ciągłość eksterminacji: Sprawcy 'T4' i '"Akcja Reinhardt,'" in *Akcja Reinhardt: Zagłada Żydów w Generalnym Gubernatorstwie*, ed. Dariusz Libionka (Warsaw, 2004), 285-308.
5 J.A. Młynarczyk, "Wpływ inicjatyw oddolnych Arthura Greisera i Odilona Globocnika na decyzję o wymordowaniu Żydów," in *Zagłada Żydów na polskich terenach wcielonych*, 25, 27; K.M. Mallmann, *Rozwiązać przez jakikolwiek*, 94-95
6 M. Alberti, *Nikczemna perfidia...*, 80; H. Friedlander, *Der Weg zum Ns-Genozid: Von der Euthanasie zur Endlösung* (Berlin, 1997); V. Rieß, "Zentrale und dezentrale Radikalisierung: Die Tötungen "unwerten Lebens" in der annektierten west- und nordpolnischen Gebieten," in *Genesis des Genozids: Polen 1939-1941*, ed. K.M. Mallmann and B. Musial (Darmstadt, 2004), 127-144.
7 V. Rieß, *Die Anfänge der Vernichtung "lebensunwerten Lebens" in den Reichsgauen Danzig-Westpreußen und Wartheland 1939/1940* (Frankfurt a.M., 1995), 317-320, 330-332; E. Kogon et al., *Nationalsozialistische Massentötungen durch Giftgas: Eine Dokumentation*(Frankfurt a.M., 1983), 63-65.
8 In the early years, it was called Sicherheitspolizei Chef der Einsatzgruppe VI Konzentrazionslager Posen. It was later renamed Geheime Staatspolizei, Staatspolizeistelle Posen, Übergangslager—Fort VII. See A. Hojan, "Komora gazowa w forcie VII w Poznaniu (Początek nazistowskiego ludobójstwa)," in *Studia nad dziejami obozów koncentracyjnych w okupowanej Polsce* (Oswiecim, 2011), 170.
9 Ibid., 171-173.
10 Ibid., 173.
11 Ibid.
12 Testimony H. Mana, investigation of the case of the mentally ill, Archiwum OKBZH w Poznaniu, I Ds. 24/67, quoted from A. Hojan, *Komora gazowa*, 173.
13 M. Kaczmarek, "Eutanazja w tzw. Kraju Warty," in *Kronika Wielkopolski* (Warsaw, 1985), 75.
14 Ibid., 76.
15 Ibid., 75.
16 Ibid., 78-79.
17 Ibid., 78.
18 K.M. Mallmann, *Rozwiązać przez jakikolwiek*, 94.

19 Letter SS-Major Rolf-Heinz Höppner in German-occupied Poland to Adolf Eichmann, Reich Security Main Office, Berlin, in S. Lehrer, *Wannsee House and the Holocaust* (Jefferson, NC, 2000), 142-143. For additional details, see Document 23 in Annex 1.
20 Quoted from J.A. Młynarczyk, *Wpływ inicjatyw oddolnych Arthura Greisera*, 25, original quotation from P. Klein, "Die Rolle der Vernichtungslager Kulmhof (Chełmno nad Nerem), Belzec (Bełżec) und Auschwitz-Birkenau in den frühen Deportationsvorbereitungen," in *Lager, Zwangsarbeit, Vertreibung und Deportation: Dimensionen der Massverbrechen in der Sowjetunion und in Deutschland 1933 bis 1945*, ed. D. Dahlmann and G. Hirschfeld (Essen, 1999), 475.
21 Quoted from J.A. Młynarczyk, *Wpływ inicjatyw oddolnych Arthura Greisera*, 27; original quotation from *Nationalsozialistische*, 113-114.
22 Quoted from ibid., 25, original quotation from P. Klein, *Die Rolle der Vernichtungslager Kulmhof*, 475.
23 Przesłuchanie Koppego, quoted from J.A. Młynarczyk, *Wpływ inicjatyw oddolnych Arthura Greisera*, 2008, 25; original quotation from E. Kogon et al, *Nationalsozialistische Massentötungen durch Giftgas: Eine Dokumentation* (Frankfurt a.M., 1983), 112.
24 United States Holocaust Memorial Museum—hereafter USHMM), RG 15.007M, roll 8/file 103, pp. 45-62 (Höppner to Eichmann and Hans Ehlich, 3.9.41, with proposal of 2.9.41), quotation according to Ch. Browning, *Nazi Policy, Jewish Workers, German Killers* (Cambridge, 2000), 37.
25 Letter SS-Major Rolf-Heinz Höppner in German-occupied Poland to Adolf Eichmann, Reich Security Main Office, Berlin, in S. Lehrer, *Wannsee House*, 142-143.
26 UWZ itd, BGKBZHP, 21, 1970, p. 106.
27 Situation report of the president of the Inowrocław regency, July 8, 1941, quoted in M. Alberti, *Nikczemna perfidia*, 254.
28 Letter SS-Major Rolf-Heinz Höppner in German-occupied Poland to Adolf Eichmann, Reich Security Main Office, Berlin, in S. Lehrer, *Wannsee House*, 142-143.
29 Conference with the participation of Arthur Greiser and senior officials of the General Government and Warthegau on a common policy toward the Jewish and Polish population, July 31, 1940, Kraków, in *Okupacja i ruch oporu*, 237-238.
30 Ibid.,235.
31 July 31, 1940, Kraków, from statements of Gauleiter Arthur Greiser and General Governor Hans Frank on the resettlement of the Jews of Łódź to the General Government and a plan to deport Jews to Madagascar, in *Eksterminacja Żydów na ziemiach polskich*, 54-55.
32 Conference with the participation of Arthur Greiser and senior officials of the General Government and Warthegau on a common policy towards the Jewish and Polish population, July 31, 1940, Kraków, in *Okupacja i ruch oporu*, 236.
33 July 31, 1940, Kraków, from statements of Gauleiter Arthur Greiser and General Governor Hans Frank on the resettlement of the Jews of Łódź to the General Government and a plan to deport Jews to Madagascar, in *Eksterminacja Żydów na ziemiach polskich*, 54-55.
34 Letter SS-Major Rolf-Heinz Höppner in German-occupied Poland to Adolf Eichmann, Reich Security Main Office, Berlin, in S. Lehrer, *Wannsee House*, 142-143.
35 Ibid.

36 Ibid.
37 Ibid.
38 J.A. Młynarczyk, *Wpływ inicjatyw oddolnych Arthura Greisera*, 26.
39 "Konto specjalne Przyjaciół Kraju Warty," Młynarczyk, Jacek Andrzej, "Wpływ inicjatyw oddolnych Arthura Greisera i Odilona Globocnika na decyzję o wymordowaniu Żydów," in *Zagłada Żydów na polskich terenach wcielonych do Rzeszy*, ed. Aleksandra Namysło (Warsaw, 2008), 23.
40 Letter SS-Major Rolf-Heinz Höppner in German-occupied Poland to Adolf Eichmann, Reich Security Main Office, Berlin, in S. Lehrer, *Wannsee House*, 142-143.
41 See Document 24 in Annex 1.
42 Quoted from Ł. Pawlicka-Nowak, ed., *Chełmno Witnesses Speak*, (Konin-Łódź, 2004), 93-96. A copy of the Polish document is kept at YVA, O.4/222, pp. 1-6.
43 Testimony Stanisław Majewski, March 20, 1969, YVA-TR.17/7 (OKP.III.Ds.19/68), 9.
44 Testimony Szczepan Osińsk, ibid.,. 4.
45 Testimony Stanisław Majewski, ibid., 9.
46 Ibid.
47 Ibid.
48 Testimony Aleksander Konstanty Pecyna, January 18, 1978, ibid., 7.
49 Testimony Jan Zalas, February 3, 1969, YVA-TR.17/2 (OKP.III.Ds.21/68), 18-21.
50 Testimony Stanisław Majewski, March 20, 1969, ibid., 9.
51 Testimony Szczepan Osiński, March 20, 1969, ibid., 4.
52 Testimony Mieczysław Sękiewicz, Western Institute in Poznań. Doc. III-42, Konin County, quoted from Ł. Pawlicka-Nowak, *Chełmno Witnesses Speak*, 93-96. A copy of the Polish document is also kept in YVA O.4/222, pp. 1-6.
53 Testimony Mieczysław Sękiewicz, Western Institute in Poznań. Doc. III-42, Konin County, quoted from Ł. Pawlicka-Nowak, *Chełmno Witnesses Speak*, 93-96. A copy of the Polish document is kept at Yad Vashem Archives, O.4/222, pp. 1-6.
54 Testimony Jerzy Ciurzyński, November 10, 1945, YVA-TR.17/2 (OKP.III.Ds.21/68), 10-11.
55 Ibid.
56 Testimony Mieczysław Sękiewicz, Western Institute in Poznań. Doc. III-42, Konin County, quoted from Ł. Pawlicka-Nowak, *Chełmno Witnesses Speak*, 93-96. A copy of the Polish document is kept at Yad Vashem Archives, O.4/222, pp. 1-6.
57 Ibid.
58 Ibid.
59 Ibid.
60 Testimony Szczepan Osiński, March 20, 1969, YVA-TR.17/7 (OKP.III.Ds.19/68), 4.
61 Testimony Mieczysław Sękiewicz, Western Institute in Poznań. Doc. III-42, Konin County, quoted from Ł. Pawlicka-Nowak, *Chełmno Witnesses Speak*, 93-96. A copy of the Polish document is kept at YVA Archives, O.4/222, pp. 1-6.
62 Ibid.
63 Ibid.
64 Ibid. For the detailed testimony of Mieczysław Sękiewicz, see Document 25 in Annex 1.
65 P. Rybczyński, "Likwidacja skupisk ludności żydowskiej w powiecie konińskim," in *Ośrodek zagłady w Chełmnie nad Nerem i jego rola w hitlerowskiej polityce eksterminacyjnej: Materiały z sesji naukowej* (Konin, 1995), 111.

66 Ibid., 112.
67 Ibid.,
68 M. Alberti, *Die Verfolgung und Vernichtung*, 412.
69 *Landratsamt Konin, Tagebuch "geheim," 1939-44* (APP, LAK 2. Fol67f.). in M. Alberti, *Die Verfolgung und Vernichtung*, 412.
70 Stapostelle Hohensalza, Abt. II E, Aufstellung vom 13.10.1941 (AGK, zbiór mikrofilmów 864, fol. 43+Rs) in M. Alberti, *Die Verfolgung und Vernichtung der Juden im Reichsgau Wartheland 1939-1945* (Wiesbaden, 2006), 412.
71 Testimony Mieczysław Sękiewicz, Western Institute in Poznan. Doc. III-42, Konin County, quoted from Ł. Pawlicka-Nowak, *Chełmno Witnesses Speak*, 93-96. A copy of the Polish document is kept at Yad Vashem Archives, O.4/222, pp. 1-6.
72 Ibid.
73 *Documents on the Holocaust: Selected Sources*, 344-345.
74 Testimony Mieczysław Sękiewicz, Western Institute in Poznan. Doc. III-42, Konin County, quoted from Ł. Pawlicka-Nowak, *Chełmno Witnesses* Speak, 93-96. A copy of the Polish document is kept at Yad Vashem Archives, O.4/222, pp. 1-6.
75 Ibid.
76 Ibid.
77 Ibid.
78 Ibid.
79 Testimony Szczepan Osiński, March 20, 1969, YVA-TR.17/7 (OKP.III.Ds.19/68), 4.
80 Testimony Mieczysław Sękiewicz, Western Institute in Poznan. Doc. III-42, Konin County, quoted from Ł. Pawlicka-Nowak, *Chełmno Witnesses Speak*, 93-96. A copy of the Polish document is kept at Yad Vashem Archives, O.4/222, pp. 1-6.
81 Ibid.
82 Ibid.
83 Ibid.
84 Ibid.
85 Ibid.
86 Testimony Stanisław Majewski, March 20, 1969, YVA-TR.17/7 (OKP.III.Ds.19/68), 9.
87 Ibid.
88 Testimony Aleksander Konstanty Pecyna, January 18, 1978, ibid., 7.
89 Testimony Mieczysław Sękiewicz, Western Institute in Poznań. Doc. III-42, Konin County Quoted from Ł. Pawlicka-Nowak, *Chełmno Witnesses Speak*, 93-96. A copy of the Polish document is kept at Yad Vashem Archives, O.4/222, pp. 1-6.
90 Aleksander Kaminski (1903-1978)—the most important editor in chief of the underground ZWZ-AK *Biuletyn Informacyjny* (Information Bulletin), a member of the Headquarters and the clandestine scouts organization *Szare Szeregi*, and the author of the acclaimed book *Kamienie na szaniec* (Stones for the Rampart, 1945).
91 April 1942, Warsaw ghetto, report by Hersh Wasser, "Chełmno events" addressed to Aleksander Kamiński and published in "Bulletin Oneg Shabbat" [excerpts], in *Wybór źródeł do nauczania o zagładzie Żydów na okupowanych ziemiach polskich*, ed. A. Skibińska, R. Szuchta, and W. Młynarczyk, (Warsaw, 2010), 227-229. The report is quoted at greater length in Document 26, Annex 1.
92 YVA-M-1-Q/177, testimony Bert Gembicki, May 6, 1948, in Ansbach, 2-5.
93 Prost, VT-3.

94 YVA, O.93/9257, video testimony Abram Landau, b. April 25, 1922, in Wilczyn, VT-3, 25:30-27:30.
95 YVA, O.93/24854, video testimony Bert (Baruch Gembicki), b. October 15, 1916, in Kleczew, VT-2, 20:00-23:00.
96 Ibid., 22:17-24:00.
97 Ibid., 24:00-25:30.
98 Ibid., 25:30-27:00.
99 Ibid., 26:40-29:00.
100 YVA, O.93/5585, video testimony Charles Lepek (Jechiel Chaim Łepek), b. August 28, 1923, in Golina, VT-2.
101 Ibid.
102 YVA, O.93/26326, video testimony Tzvi Malron (Hieronim Malarek), b. October 10, 1927, in Mogilno, VT-2, 11:00-14:00.
103 January 21, 1942, Grabów-ghetto. Letter Rabbi Jacob Szulmana to relatives in Warsaw ghetto reporting about mass murder of Jews, in *Wybór źródeł do nauczania o zagładzie Żydów na okupowanych ziemiach polskich*, 226-227.
104 Testimony "Szlamek," January 1942 concerning death camp in Chełmno on the Ner, given in February 1942 in the Warsaw ghetto. "Szlamek," alias Jakub Grojnowski, was really Szlama Ber Winer of Izbica Kujawska, who managed to escape and reach the Warsaw ghetto.
105 YVA, O.93/26326, video testimony Tzvi Malron (Hieronim Malarek), b. October 10, 1927, in Mogilno, VT-2.
106 Ibid., VT-2, 13:30-17:00.
107 Ibid., VT-2, 17:00-20:00.
108 Ibid., VT-2.
109 Ibid.
110 Ibid., VT-2, 23:30-26:00.
111 Ibid., VT-2, 23:30-26:00.
112 Ibid., VT-2.
113 Ibid., VT-2, 27:30-29:00.
114 Testimony Kazimierz Szymczak, July 18, 1968, YVA-TR.17/2 (OKP.III.Ds.21/68), pp. 6-7.
115 Minutes of September 1, 1968, ibid.
116 Ibid.
117 Testimony Kazimierz Szymczak, July 18, 1968, ibid., 6-7.
118 Ibid.
119 Ibid.
120 Testimony Lucjan Zalas, April 7, 1970, ibid., 22-24.
121 Ibid.
122 Testimony Kazimierz Szymczak, July 18, 1968, ibid., 6-7.
123 Testimony Piotr Zalas, November 10, 1945, ibid., 12-13.
124 Testimony Lucjan Zalas, April 7, 1970, ibid., 22-24.
125 Testimony Jan Zalas, February 3, 1969, ibid., 1918-1921.
126 Testimony Lucjan Zalas, April 7, 1970, ibid., 22-24.
127 Ibid.
128 Testimony Kazimierz Janicki of May 23, 1974, ibid., 32-33.
129 Testimony Piotr Zalas, November 10, 1945, ibid., 12-13.

130 Testimony Lucjan Zalas, April 7, 1970, ibid., 22-24.
131 Testimony Kazimierz Szymczak, July 18, 1968, ibid., 6-7.
132 Ibid.
133 Ibid.
134 Ibid.
135 Testimony Lucjan Zalas, April 7, 1970, ibid., 22-24.
136 Testimony Piotr Zalas, November 10, 1945, ibid., 12-13.
137 Minutes of September 1, 1968, ibid., 6-7.
138 Testimony Kazimierz Szymczak, July 18, 1968, ibid., 6-7.
139 Testimony Lucjan Zalas, April 7, 1970, ibid., 22-24. For a transcript of Lucas Zala's testimony, see Document 27 in Annex 1.
140 Ibid.
141 Testimony Kazimierz Szymczak, July 18, 1968, ibid., 6-7.
142 Testimony Piotr Zalas, November 10, 1945, ibid., 12-13.
143 Testimony Jan Zalas, February 3, 1969, ibid., 18-21.
144 Testimony Zdzisław Kazimierz Olejnik, April 19, 1974, ibid., 26-28.
145 Testimony Piotr Zalas, November 10, 1945, ibid., 12-13.
146 Testimony Kazimierz Szymczak, July 18, 1968, ibid., 6-7.
147 Minutes of September 1, 1968, ibid., 6-7.
148 Testimony Jan Zalas, February 3, 1969, ibid., 18-21.
149 Testimony Zdzisław Kazimierz Olejnik, April 19, 1974, ibid., 26-28.
150 Testimony Piotr Zalas, November 10, 1945, ibid., 12-13.
151 Testimony Zdzisław Kazimierz Olejnik, April 19, 1974, ibid., 26-28.
152 Testimony Kazimierz Janicki, May 23, 1974, ibid., 32-33.
153 Testimony Piotr Zalas, November 10, 1945, ibid., 12-13.
154 Minutes of September 1, 1968, ibid., 6-7.
155 Testimony Zenobia Mikołajczyk of June 12, 1974, ibid., 37.
156 Testimony Kazimierz Szymczak, July 18, 1968, ibid., 6-7.
157 Pages of the District Museum in Konin, http://www.muzeum.com.pl/en/chelmno.htm; or in Polish http://www.muzeum.com.pl/content/view/137/243/.
158 Testimony Zdzisław Kazimierz Olejnik of April 19, 1974, YVA-TR.17/2 (OKP.III. Ds.21/68), 26-28.
159 Testimony Kazimierz Janicki, May 23, 1974, ibid., 32-33.
160 Testimony Jan Zalas, February 3, 1969, ibid., 18-21.
161 Testimony Lucjan Zalas, April 7, 1970, ibid., 22-24.
162 Testimony Zdzisław Kazimierz Olejnik, April 19, 1974, ibid., 26-28.
163 Testimony Piotr Zalas, November 10, 1945, ibid., 12-13.
164 Minutes of September 1, 1968, ibid., 6-7.
165 Ibid.
166 Testimony Kazimierz Szymczak, July 18, 1968, ibid., 6-7.
167 Minutes of September 1, 1968, ibid., 6-7.
168 Testimony Kazimierz Szymczak, July 18, 1968, ibid., 6-7.

7 Establishment and Operation of the First Extermination Camp

1. THE MASS EXTERMINATION CAMP IN CHEŁMNO ON THE NEREM

The mass extermination camp in Chełmno on the Nerem played a special role in eradicating the Jews from the Warthegau. It was the first camp of its type in Europe and its technological innovations were subsequently replicated in other extermination camps. They included mobile gas chambers (*Spezialwagen* or *Sonderwagen*) that used combustion gas and the administrative pretense of encouraging victims to shower before entering them. Construction of the Chełmno center began in November 1941 and the facility went into action on December 8, 1941. The first stage of its operation was completed on April 7, 1943. It was reactivated in the summer of 1944; its last prisoners were eliminated by the guards on the night of January 17–18, 1945.[1] During this period, statements about the purpose of the place—the extermination of Jews—were repeatedly transmitted to field officers by high-ranking officers from Germany. Reichsführer SS Heinrich Himmler's speech on October 4, 1943, to senior SS officers in Poznań, is a case in point. On this occasion, he was very specific in explaining his views and orders regarding the extermination of Jews.[2]

The Camp at Chełmno on the Nerem: General Characteristics

The extermination camp at Chełmno on the Nerem was the first permanent mass-murder facility established during the Holocaust. It was located in the village of Chełmno nad Nerem, about 14 kilometers from Koło and about 60 kilometers from Łódź, on the Łódź–Kutno–Poznań railway line. Chełmno was connected to Koło via a narrow-gauge track.

The Chełmno extermination center was set up in two different localities about four kilometers apart. The first was in the village itself, in an abandoned palace owned by the state that was unused at the beginning of the German occupation. A large park approximately 2.7 hectares in area surrounded the premises; when the death camp was established, it was encased in a board fence to make the camp difficult to view from the outside. The local Polish population was expelled from the village; except for a few forced laborers who were put to various ancillary tasks, Chełmno was inhabited by Germans during the war. In the park next to the palace, a brick building that had once housed a granary stood. Two additional

43. The church in Chełmno, near the palace building whence gas vans drove to the woods. In some cases, Jews awaiting murder were kept inside the church
(YVA, sig. 1427_367)

barracks were also built in the park. The second site was in the Rzuchów forest; the corpses were incinerated there.

Organization of the camp began in October or November 1941, after the mass murders perpetrated by Sonderkommando Lange in the Kazimierz Biskupi and Długa Łąka forests north of Konin. These crimes may be considered "pilots" for the next phase of the liquidation of Jews in the Warthegau, since immediately after them the Sonderkommando and its commander, SS Obersturmführer Herbert Lange, sought a convenient place to establish a permanent extermination center.

In December 1941, when the camp was ready for operation, 262,000 Jews still remained in the Warthegau, 31,440 of them in Inowrocław Regierungsbezirk.

The location of the camp was carefully chosen. Situated in Koło County (in the south of which was Inowrocław Regierungsbezirk) and bordering Łódź Regierungsbezirk, it allowed the rapid extermination of Jews from the neighboring ghettos in Koło and Turek counties. Again, witnesses who could report the Germans' crimes had been removed. It was relatively close to the Łódź ghetto, and thus solved the problem of getting rid of "unproductive" Jews there. When the latter ghetto was partly emptied, able-bodied Jews from the provincial ghettos, which had been gradually dissolved, were sent there to replace them.

44. Herbert Lange, commander of Sonderkommando Lange, responsible for the "euthanasia" program in the Warthegau and the murder of Jews in the Konin area, 1939-1941, and first commander of the Chełmno death center, December 1941–April 1942 (Bundesarchiv, sign.).

Notably, Chełmno was not what would become a typical camp like Bełżec, Sobibór, or Treblinka.³ The main difference is that the other camps were built several months after Chełmno and used Chełmno's experience to improve their mass-murder capabilities. Chełmno killed Jews on a massive scale but did so in a logistically cumbersome way. In its first stage of activity, victims were delivered from several transfer points using relatively difficult means of transportation, entailing extensive coordination and much administrative effort. Furthermore, as noted, two locations were used—the palace grounds in the town of Chełmno and the Rzuchów forest. Therefore, Chełmno is better described as an extermination center than as an extermination camp, although the latter name is in common use. Its capacity for murder and incineration did not exceed 1,000 per day; other camps under *Aktion Reinhardt* had six times that capacity, if not twelve. Auschwitz-Birkenau, at the peak of its activity in 1944, attained the unprecedented murder and cremation capacity of up to 20,000 people per day.

The essence of Chełmno lies in the fact that it was the first to develop a method of killing victims, mostly Jews, on a massive industrial scale and pace. It served as an experimental center from which others benefited—mostly the staffs of T4[4] and of Aktion Reinhard.

'Aktionen' and Transports

Aktionen involving Chełmno began unexpectedly—very often at night or in early morning. People were rushed out of their apartments, expelled into the street, and usually directed to one building, most often a church or synagogue. They were packed into the building, typically without food or water, and left there for up to several days. Those who tried to escape were killed. In Włocławek, a group that had received consecutive numbers beforehand spent several days waiting in the open air for their transport from the ghetto. Gradually, within a few days, successive groups were transported to Chełmno. While being loaded onto their means of transport, many people were hurt or killed.[5]

A witness describes the deportation from the ghetto in Koło:

> At the end of December 1941 (I do not remember exactly the date) the town of Koło was surrounded by units of the NSKK

[*Nationalsozialistisches Kraftfahrkorps*—National Socialist Motor Corps] (members of this organization were dressed in green "khaki" uniforms and black forage caps). Jews were taken from their apartments and transferred to the Jewish Committee building that was adjacent to the synagogue. Wagons arrived and the Jews left the building with their families, carrying their luggage. Before departing, the Germans set up a table where an SS officer sat. This officer had a list of all the Jews living in Koło; the person signed that list before getting into the van. Luggage was loaded into a trailer. The guards who watched the Jews and members of the Jewish Committee said that Jews were being transported "to work on the railways."

About forty people were loaded into the vehicle. Two trucks that were driven by Germans transported Jews from Koło. Every day about 1,000 people were deported.[6]

The witness was completely oblivious to the true purpose of the journey. He demonstrated this by saying, "I went to the truck that my father, mother, sister together with her five children, and father's brother with his wife and their three children took. I also helped to load the packages [into the trailer]. I even volunteered to go with my parents, but I was not allowed to do so."[7]

Before a community was eradicated, the members of its Judenrat were often killed (e.g., in Żychlin and Krośniewice).[8] After a ghetto was dissolved, a few Jews (fifty in Kutno–Konstancja, for example) would be left behind for cleanup duties. Alternatively, labor details were brought from the Łódź ghetto. Once the area was clean, after several days or weeks, the remaining people were executed or taken to Chełmno.[9]

Transports of Jews to Chełmno were made by rail. A special train of about twenty carriages was put together for this purpose. Roughly 1,000 Jews were placed in such a train. The train went as far as the Koło station. There, the passengers were transferred to a narrow-gauge train that went to Powiercie, where they were dispossessed of their luggage.

A witness described how this worked: "The luggage was transported in the last two cars. After arrival at the junction of the road with

45. Deportation of Jews to Chełmno by means of narrow-gauge railway
(YVA, sig. 3331_66)

the railway tracks, it was unloaded. On the same day, it was taken by cars to a big hut at Chełmno, where it was sorted."[10] The people in the transport were then marched to the village of Zawadki, where they were put up in a large building that housed a motorized mill. The next day, they were taken by trucks to Chełmno, about two kilometers away. Between 100 and 150 people were transported at one time; usually, about 1,000 people were hauled to Chełmno by 1:00 or 2:00 p.m. The Jews behaved calmly during the transport because their guards behaved correctly. A witness explains why they did so:

> Bothmann issued instructions according to which Jews were not allowed to be beaten and should be handled well. [The purpose] was to keep Jews uncertain about their fate. If they knew what awaited them, it would have hindered the work. For example, the total transport of Jews from Konin to Chełmno was accompanied by only six policemen. If they had known what awaited them, [the Jews] could have easily scattered.[11]

Reception at the Rzuchowski Forest Camp

Victim-filled cars from Chełmno arrived at a fenced-in area approximately 33 hectares large in the Rzuchowski forest, heavily secured by armed guards and patrolled all around. "[The] forest of Chełmno was guarded by about eighty SS men," a witness reported.[12] When cars containing gassed people reached the camp, the doors were opened and the cars were ventilated for about ten minutes. One witness recalled: "The first car from Chełmno arrived at about 8:00 a.m. When its door was opened, a thick whitish smoke belched out."[13] Despite having been exposed to the gas for several minutes, not all of the people were dead. A witness who unloaded gas wagons said, "The corpses were still warm. I did not notice any characteristic smell of gas. Some people were still alive and the SS men shot them in the head; most were shot in the back of the head."[14]

All subsequent operations were performed by a Jewish labor detail. First the members of this group unloaded the corpses from the car and inspected them thoroughly. Gold teeth were removed and any gold rings were taken off of fingers. All bodily orifices were inspected for hidden valuables. The policeman Bruno Israel testifies:

> Valuables were given to Richter and Gilf, who placed them in an iron box. Richter had the key of the strongbox. How the valuables were transported to Łódź, I don't know. Jewish workers in Chełmno searched clothes and luggage in a special barrack. Valuables were also given to Richter.[15]

In the initial period of the Chełmno center—the cold winter months—the corpses, after being searched, were buried in enormous mass graves. One of these places of interment was 270 meters long, eight to ten meters wide, and six meters deep. The graves had been dug by Jewish workers and others. Burying large numbers of victims in the frost of winter had no consequences; however, problems arose in the spring. According to one witness:

> When it got hot, the corpses buried in mass grave began to decompose. The earth moved. The air over a large area was poisoned. There were incidents of typhus. The Germans stopped receiving transports; two crematorium furnaces were hastily constructed (you could see the chimneys) and they started

burning the corpses. Mass graves were excavated and the Jews (especially the beefed-up *Waldkommando* [forest detail]) were ordered to incinerate the corpses in crematoria. I heard that the furnaces were fueled by wood. Following the burning of corpses (the pause lasted about two months), Jewish transports started to arrive again.[16]

It was not until the spring of 1942 that the construction of crematorium furnaces began. Local residents' testimonies indicate that they had two tall chimneys. After the construction of two furnaces that spring, corpses of victims who were murdered on an ongoing basis and those that had already been buried and were now exhumed were incinerated. Eyewitness accounts of escapees from Chełmno allow us to reconstruct the appearance of these furnaces:

> These ovens were built in the ground, not protruding above ground level. They had the shape of a rectangular stool turned downwards. The top of the stove had a surface of 6 x 10 meters; its depth was 4 meters. At the bottom of the furnace was an ash collector of 1.5 x 2 meters. The grates were made of railroad rails. A channel leading to the ash provided air but also served to remove the ashes and bones. The furnace walls were made of fire-clay bricks and fire-clay cement. In the furnace three layers of wood alternated with layers of corpses, assuring that the corpses would not come into contact with each other, to allow faster burning. The crematoria capacity amounted to 100 corpses. As the burning corpses fell downwards, new corpses were added from the top. Ashes removed from the crematoria and the rest of the bones, after they were ground using pestles, were initially poured into specially dug trenches, and later, in 1943, the bones and ashes were taken secretly at night in cars to Zawadki and there they were thrown from a bridge into the river.[17]

This was done by members of Sonderkommando Lange. Bruno Israel testifies:

Ashes and bones were carried away by Laaps, Runge, and Kretschmer. Loaded cars were waiting in Chełmno until 11 or 12 p.m., and at this hour, cars departed in the direction of the Koło.[18]

Later on, the Sonderkommando "borrowed […] a mill for crushing bones and also a traction engine from Powiercie."[19]

After the incineration, the ashes and the unburned remnants of bones were removed. Initially, the bones were manually pulverized by using pestles:[20] "The first time (1942–1943), hand pestles were used to crush the bones." Later, according to a witness:

> [There] was a machine for grinding bones at Chełmno. I saw it with my own eyes—the load, the entire truck, was filled with paper bags in which were ground bones. It was the spring of 1943, when the first camp at Chełmno was liquidated. To where the bones were taken, I do not know.[21]

Another witness testified:

> Ashes and bones were loaded into sacks made of sewn blankets brought by Jews from the transports. The bones had to be smashed into fine particles with clubs on a special slab of concrete so that no one could tell if they had been human bones or not. Filled bags were taken mostly at night.[22]

The Extermination Method

After the Jews were driven to the deserted palace and removed from the trucks, a member of the German detail told them that they were going to the east, where they would work and enjoy better living conditions. A witness recalled:

> In the morning at roughly around 8 o'clock, a car arrived at the palace. I heard a German speaking to those who had come. He said, among other things, "You will go to the east, there are large

areas to work; you just have to dress up in clean clothes, which will be given to you, and to take a bath." Applause rang out![23]

Even at this stage of the extermination, the perpetrators went out of their way to spread disinformation by asking the deportees to write letters to their families in the ghettos. One witness attests:

> [...] The Jews, before they were gassed, wrote letters to their families about their trip to Germany. In every shipment, 10–15 Jews who were held back from the transport wrote such letters. How they were killed, I do not know. This was to reassure the remaining Jews in the ghetto and to facilitate our future work. To mislead the Jews as to the nature of their intentions concerning them, in the barracks where the Jews undressed before gassing were appropriate signs: *Arzt, Baderaum* (physician, baths). I would like to emphasize that the Jews were so misled that after Bothmann's speech, they shouted in honor of Germany.[24]

The next stage, they were told, was disinfection. The deportees were led into a large, heated room in the palace, where they had to undress down to their underwear and then move down the corridor to the bath. This explains the wording of the signs "Physician" and "Baths." The undressed victims followed the "Baths" arrow down the hall to the exit door. Before reaching the door, they were told that they would be transported to the baths in a closed car. The exit door led directly to the closed vehicle, which stood on the road. Members of the German detail rushed the victims through the corridor and into the car so that they would not have time to figure things out and resist.

> Some time later we heard the shuffling of bare feet in the basement corridor—near the cellar, in which we were closed. We heard the Germans shout: "Move it, move it!" I realized that they were leading Jews through the corridor to the inner courtyard.[25]

Bruno Israel testifies:

> Jews were told that the car would go to the bath. They were given soap if they did not have their own. It was said that they would get bath towels on the spot. The Jews, even in the wagon, still behaved calmly. [The driver] Laaps closed the car door and started the motor. Before he turned on the engine, he went under the car and connected the exhaust pipe to a tube that reached the engine. I would like to stress that the exhaust pipe went through the floor to the center of the car, so that the combustion gas, after turning on the engine, went inside the car, thus poisoning the people inside. If someone poured chloroform, ether, or other components into the gasoline, I cannot say.[26]

After the Jews entered the car, the doors were immediately latched and the engine was switched on. Thus began the process of gassing people. A witness remembers: "After a while I heard the rumble of the car doors being locked. There was shouting and knocking on the walls of the car. Then I heard the noise of the motor being turned on. When 6–7 minutes passed, the cries quieted and the car left the yard."[27] After the engine was turned on, the truck did not move immediately but remained motionless for about five minutes. During this time, the victims inside tried to escape; this explains their pounding on the door and walls of the chamber. Had the car been driven at this time, the Jews' exertions might have caused it to wobble, making the trip difficult. Only after five minutes did the truck start moving toward the Rzuchowski forest, about four kilometers from Chełmno.

As the transport set out from Chełmno to the forest, the process of erasing the traces of the previous group of victims began. The floor was washed and clothes and shoes were removed. A witness recalls:

> We were called—that is, ten Jewish workers—to a large room on the upper floor in which women's clothing, coats, and shoes lay scattered on the floor. We were told to quickly take the clothes

and shoes to another room. In that room, there were a lot of other clothes and shoes. Shoes were put into a separate pile.[28]

Another witness states:

After the car—[called] "the hell"—drove away, the clothes were thrown through the windows into the courtyard. Then a group of Jews—workers—had to take them to the general pile of clothes that was in the garden. The pile was three to four meters tall and at least ten to fifteen meters wide. The police rushed us and mercilessly beat the Jews who were removing the clothing. Only after the area was cleared was a new batch of Jews brought to the palace.[29]

Thus the people in the next transport to Chełmno from Zawadki did not know what had happened to those in the previous transport. Surely they did not know that they had been murdered. There was no contact between one transport and another. Each step of the journey was a great unknown; the victims had no reason to believe that something amiss awaited them.[30]

Gas vans were first used in the Warthegau to murder the mentally ill and the disabled in the autumn of 1939, as was discussed earlier. They were also used for killing the mentally ill from Kochanówka Hospital near Łódź in March 1940.[31] We may assume that the gas-chamber vehicle used to murder patients from Kochanówka Hospital was a prototype; it was a van converted from a vehicle used by *Kaiser Kaffe Wien*.[32]

Gas wagons were also employed in the massacres in the Kazimierz Biskupi and Długa Łąka forests in late September 1941. After the establishment of the killing center in Chełmno, such vehicles were regularly used in both the first and the second period of this extermination center. There were three such cars, imported from Berlin. One could hold about 150 people; the others were smaller, with a capacity of 80–100.

The gas wagons used to kill the victims in Chełmno are known only by their descriptions. In 1944, after the liquidation of the mass-murder center, they were exported to Germany. Information about them comes from the mechanics who worked in the Kraft and Reichstrassenbauamt garages in Koło and from other witnesses.[33] During the investigation of the Chełmno center, eight Poles employed in the workshops were interviewed and gave details about the design of these cars. The largest vehicle was about six meters long and 2.5–3 meters wide. The smaller cars were 4.5–5 meters long and 2.3–2.5 meters wide. Their bodies were constructed of closely placed boards. The interior was enclosed and hermetically sealed with a laminate. The vehicles were painted dark gray. An exhaust pipe passed underneath the car and extended into the interior at half of its length. The outlet was secured by steel mesh to prevent jamming. A wooden grille was placed on the floor of the car. According to the mechanics, the engines of the vehicles had been produced by the Saurer firm. Near the cab was the inscription: *"Baujahr 1940—Berlin"* [year of construction 1940—Berlin]. The drivers wore gas masks.[34]

Bruno Israel testifies:

> There were two death cars in Chełmno. At the time I was in Chełmno, essentially only one car was used. A second, smaller car,

46. Gas van from Chełmno being examined by a member of the Polish Commission of Inquiry (YVA, sig. 1264_2)

47. Gas van from Chełmno—wooden construction of mobile gas chamber, originally covered with metal plates (YVA, sig. 1427_83)

with a capacity of about 80 people, stood in reserve in Chełmno. Both cars had been shipped from Berlin. They were driven by Laaps and Runge, who were absent during one week. Moreover, there was yet a third car, which was used to disinfect clothing. This car had its wheels removed. Did it serve for the gasification of people? I don't know. Into the car where the clothes were hung and the underwear was put on special benches someone placed a basin of burning sulfur and closed the door for the night.[35]

Sonderkommando Kulmhof

A special unit responsible for the murder of Jews at Chełmno was called Sonderkommando Kulmhof or SS-Sonderkommando Kulmhof, Kulmhof being the German name for Chełmno. This SS unit numbered around twenty people. The rest of the German detail comprised over one hundred people from various agencies, mostly the German military and civilian police. They performed auxiliary guard duty at the palace in Chełmno, watched over the camp in the Rzuchowski forest, and patrolled surrounding areas. This brought the strength of the whole detail to 150–180. One witness reports: "Besides the SS, the military police and

48. Canteen of the Sonderkommando and guards at the camp in Chełmno (YVA, sig. 1007_3)

criminal police collaborated with Sonderkommando Kulmhof. Initially, a total of 120–150 Germans served in Chełmno. Afterwards, their number increased to approximately 180. Originally the commander was Lange."[36]

SS-Obersturmführer Herbert Lange, the first commander of SS-Sonderkommando Kulmhof, was succeeded by SS-Haupsturmführer Hans Bothmann, whose deputies were Otto Platte and Willi Piller. Others discharged important duties as well: operations in the palace at Chełmno were supervised by SS-Untersturmführer Alois Heffele (Häfele); the detachment in the forest was supervised by Wachmeister Wilhelm Lenz; and the incineration of corpses was overseen by SS-Hauptscharführer Johann Runge and, later, by SS-Unterscharführer Erich Kretschmer. The gas wagons were driven by Lange, SS-Hauptscharführer Gustav Laaps, SS-Hauptscharführer Bursting, and Gilow.

As stated, ordinary policemen also served in Chełmno. One of them, Bruno Israel (a Volksdeutsche despite his last name), testified later about how they became part of Sonderkommando Kulmhof:

> Before the war, I worked as a dyer for the Leber and Lewandowski Company. I signed Volksliste in 1940. I began to work at Hilfspolizei in 1941. In 1943, I was drafted into the military police and received the rank of Wachtmeister. Later, when I was assigned to the Sonderkommando Kulmhof, I was promoted and became an Oberwachtmeister. I would like to mention that all the policemen who were assigned to Kulmhof were

49. Hans Bothmann, second commander of Chełmno death center (April 1942–April 1943 and May 1944–January 1945) (YVA)

at least at the rank of Oberwachtmeister. Only two military policemen had the rank of Wachtmeister.... In July or August 1944, when I served at the IV police station of the State Police, I was assigned to Sonderkommando Kulmhof. I would like to mention that from each police station one policeman was taken and assigned to the Sonderkommando. As I recall, then 22 policemen were assigned.[37]

The members of Sonderkommando Kulmhof were paid very well, much better than average officers performing comparable duties. In her memoirs, Rosalie Peham, the wife of a policeman who served in Chełmno, states: "When my husband worked at Chełmno, he received monthly salaries of RM 150 and RM 10–13 per day as *Schweiggeld* [hush money]. The latter sum, the *Schweiggeld*, was a special allowance for keeping secret what was happening in Chełmno."[38]

Members of Sonderkommando Kulmhof behaved cruelly toward Jewish prisoners who were employed in the Hauskommando and the Waldkommando. Israel characterizes this:

> The commander of Sonderkommando Kulmhof was Hauptsturmführer Johann Bootmann [Bothmann—author] (tall, redheaded, aged 36, slightly freckled). His deputy was Hauptscharführer Piller (it seems he was called Willi). He was a member of the SD and had a proper stripe on his sleeve. In addition to the stripe, "Prinz

Eugen" was written on his sleeve.[39] He was a burly blond man, aged about 36–40. In addition, the following served in Sonderkommando Kulmhof: Untersturrnführer Heffele (I do not know his first name) tall, aged about 50, very stout. He was the head of the Hauskommando. The head of the Waldkommando [one of two Jewish details in Chełmno] was Lenz. Hauptscharführer Johann Runge was the head of one of the crematoria. He was characterized by extreme cruelty. I saw how the Jews were beaten on their backs with a chain. I do not know where he came from. Unterscharführer [...] Kretschmer also worked at the crematoria. Hauptscharführer Gustav Laaps was a driver of the cars called Sonderwagen in which Jews were gassed. Laaps [...] was also cruel to the Jews.[40]

Officers and guards at Chełmno pilfered victims' valuables. Rosalie Peham testifies:

I received from my husband a gold watch, a gold bracelet, and a gold ring with a stone. These things came from Chełmno. He paid nothing for them. I received an outfit, but my husband said that he bought it from a colleague in Italy and had sent it from there. I received leather for shoes. Besides that, I bought a dress for one hen from a driver in Chełmno called Tonni.[41]

Despite receiving a special allowance for their silence, the officers and guards were not content with their salaries; they augmented them by bartering with the surrounding population. Rosalie Peham says, "Tonni often sold dresses and other items to the local people in exchange for food."[42]

The extermination center at Chełmno was visited by senior Nazi officials, including Gauleiter Arthur Greiser and Reichsführer SS Heinrich Himmler. According to witnesses, Greiser rated their efforts in the liquidation of Jews in the Warthegau very highly. A witness reports:

In early March 1943, Greiser was at Chełmno. He organized a party for members of the Sonderkommando, during which he gave each member of the Sonderkommando RM 500 and invited everyone for a four-week vacation on his property.[43] What was the name of his property? I don't know. I know that Himmler was in Chełmno in 1944. Further details of his whereabouts I do not know.[44]

Chełmno was also visited frequently by representatives of the police and administrative authorities of Łódź, including Dr. Otto Bradfisch and Hans Biebow.[45]

The Jewish Detail

Most heavy physical work was performed by the Jewish detail. Jews were employed in two squads—one, called the Hauskommando, at the Chełmno palace and the other, termed the Waldkommando, in the forest. Some members of the Waldkommando unloaded the corpses from the gas wagons and searched their bodies for valuables; others transported the corpses, after the search, to the crematorium. A special group was responsible for incinerating corpses and removing ashes. In total, the Jewish detail had about seventy people. The camp also recruited eight Polish prisoners from concentration camps. The Jews who worked in the palace (the Hauskommando) did cleaning labors and removed and sorted victims' clothing. In Chełmno, all workers lived in the granary—tailors and shoemakers on the upper floor and the Waldkommando and Hauskommando on the bottom floor.[46]

> The Jews lived in the palace storehouse in Chełmno. Forest workers were at the bottom, on the floor. Tailors and shoemakers worked for the Sonderkommando and various German dignitaries, such as Greiser, Biebow, and others. Bothmann himself had, for example, seventeen pairs of shoes made by Jewish shoemakers.[47]

In a later testimony (probably related to the second wave of exterminations at Chełmno), the witness Andrzej Miszczak said:

The Jews lived in the granary. Tailors and shoemaking facilities were housed there. Jewish tailors were kept in chains on the granary floor. A short time ago there were 47 Jews in Chełmno, and before that there were 80 to 90 Jews.[48]

Members of the forest detail, the Waldkommando, worked under terrible conditions, chained and starved. One witness reports cases of cannibalism:

> The forest department had Jewish workers. They walked in chains, handcuffed. Their legs were shackled with chains so that they could only take small steps. Chains that shackled their feet were attached to the waist. Jewish workers had to work in November without caps and half-naked. They were starved, so that they toasted corpses by the fire and ate human flesh. My husband told me about this.[49]

Members of the Jewish detail were often killed and replaced by new prisoners. This usually happened every few weeks. Prisoners working in the handling and disposal of crematorium ashes were replaced more frequently—every few days. A witness confirms this: "The work during the extraction of the ash was very difficult and risky. No one could stand there longer than 2–3 days. After that, he was already unfit for work and they killed him."[50] Another witness explains why this happened: "I underline that when bones were smashed, workers had to stand by the ashes, which were still very hot. They burned themselves in this way and had a lot of pain in their legs. Jewish workers who were according to officers unfit for work were shot."[51] One report describes such executions:

> Sometimes during the day Bothmann came and ordered the workers to gather. He chose a few laborers who had already, in his opinion, worked too long in the camp. Moniek Reich took off the chains from the people selected by Bothmann. Bothmann then ordered these people to lie face down on the ground by the

stove and shot them in the back of the head, killing them with his own hands.[52]

A survivor testifies about the working conditions of the Jewish ash removers:

> Work in the forest lasted from dawn to dusk. During the work there was only a ten-minute break when we were given coffee and bread. The whole time we worked with chains on our feet. All around the clearing, every ten meters, was a policeman with a machine gun. Workers were often killed for no reason. There was not a day they did not kill somebody.[53]

The murder of Jews in Chełmno was associated with their dispossession. Stealing took place at different stages of the eviction of Jews from the ghettos. Although the great majority of Jews had already been deprived of most of their property, frequently they had cached small, precious objects for the "blackest hour." Transport from the ghettos to "work in the east," in their estimation, would be just another step in their wanderings. They would have to leave their families, making it important to bring the most precious and necessary items. These things were often sewn into clothing, hidden in shoes, or concealed in other objects. When designated for murder at the Chełmno complex, the inmates were robbed of these last remaining possessions.

Looting occurred in several stages. The first was the appropriation of victims' suitcases while they still were at the mill in Zawadki. The victims were promised that their luggage would be transported in a separate car. Reaching the palace at Chełmno, they were ordered to undress before going to the showers and to leave their clothes and shoes behind. It was then that most remaining items were taken from them. If they managed to hide anything, it was in their underwear and on their fingers, in the form of rings. The last step was the search of the corpses after their deaths in the Rzuchowski forest. There, Jewish workers extracted the victims' gold teeth, removed rings, including wedding rings, and searched bodily orifices. A witness testifies:

By the time the camp was functioning, belongings of the victims were separated and divided in the palace in Chełmno. Every day three cars were sent. To where they were going—I do not know. Valuables were sent as well. I myself saw 6.5 kilograms of valuables sent in my presence. Gold from crowns of pulled teeth; there was a special team that had to pull out teeth and to remove rings.[54]

Leaving clothing and shoes behind before going to "bathe" made sense, because this way clothes could be sorted in sets and shoes arranged in pairs. The victims had to tie pairs of shoes together lest collection be impractical. Clothing was transported to the Łódź ghetto, where an inspection followed to remove labels (Stars of David) and prepare the items for cleaning, sorting, and packing. Clothing was re-used. Some was transferred to organizations such as the Winterhilfswerk des Deutschen Volkes (WHW). Other German charities received murdered victims' clothing as well. Forced laborers sometimes received them. Presumably the German charities knew where the clothing and shoes came from, since Stars of David were not always removed. In other cases, bloodstains might reveal the provenance of the clothing.[55] The inhabitants of the Łódź ghetto who sorted clothing also knew where it came from, of course. There were cases in which items belonging to the murdered were found in the clothing, or personal documents or records were chanced upon.

Clothing unsuitable for reuse was recycled into raw material. "Old clothes were processed by using a machine called a 'wolf' that had been specially imported for this purpose. I would like to stress that the Jews before their execution were stripped naked."[56] Other items that were deemed useless or unnecessary were thrown out and burned. A witness relates: "[…] Lumpy papers and photographs were burned in a pit at the end of the park, where there were three apple trees. I could point out this place. There was a fire there day and night."[57]

Information and Disinformation about the Deportation and Mass Murder

The Nazis took care in preparing to eradicate Jewish population centers. Their first tool was disinformation, i.e., the spreading of rumors about displacement. In the case of Konin County, the information disseminated was that the Jews were going to be sent away for labor. Men aged 14–60 and women aged 14–50 even underwent medical examinations to determine who was fit to work in Eastern Galicia. Many Jews fell for the deceit. One witness recalls:

> I witnessed how someone named Goldberg, owner of the flour mill, after the deportation of his son, applied to the German authorities to be named head of the camp for Jews from Koło in the east. His application was accepted and the Germans promised him that he would be the manager.[58]

Before that, each person had been asked to remit an RM 4 poll tax. Reassured about their fate, they were gradually taken, sixty people at a time, to the Kazimierz Biskupi forest near Zagórów and murdered. Similar "displacements" were carried out in Koło County. Again RM 4 was collected from everyone to cover the costs of travel and medical examinations were performed. A witness confirms this: "The Germans kept accurate records of those exterminated in Chełmno. Jewish communities were obliged to pay RM 4 for the transport of every Jew to Chełmno. In addition, each of the drivers had a list of the Jews whom he was to transport."[59]

The official version was that they were going to Chełmno, where a center for all Jews in the county was being established. Another version had it that after they assembled, they would be taken to work in Galicia or eastern Poland. To surprise their future victims, the Nazis never revealed an exact date for the "displacement." Before the Aktion, police and military units were called to surround the ghettos. Their task became easier and easier as time passed, because the ghetto perimeters were moved inward after each previous displacement and transport to camps.

Despite attempts to conceal the mass murders in Chełmno, news about deportations from the ghettos to the death camp reached the Warsaw ghetto by January 1942. It is important to quote a dramatic letter from Rabbi Jacob Szulman of Grabów, asking for prompt action to save the remaining Jews. The letter confirms that the Jews in the area not only knew about the mass murder, albeit only in general terms, but also understood perfectly the Nazis' intention to eradicate the Jews completely.

With divine help.

Grabów, Wednesday, January 21, 1942

To my beloved and dear relatives!
    It is very surprising that for a long time you have not written to us. How are you doing?
    What about the children of Milsztajn, Chanele Kenigsberg, and others?
    And now we pass you news of the terrible things that happened near our town, which for the last days were shrouded in mystery, namely: four weeks have elapsed since they took all the Jews, without exception, from Koło—men, women and children. Removed them all by cars, we do not know to where. Then the same happened in Dąbie, Kłodawa, Izbica [Kujawska], and other towns of the county. Despite strenuous efforts to learn something about their fate, we have received no news about them. Only this week fugitives who had fled from there have come to us. They told us everything—so that it will not happen to us—that there they [Germans] killed, poisoned by gas, and buried 50–60 in one grave. They constantly brought new victims. The threat has not yet passed.
    All this, of course, caused a terrible panic and indescribable horror among us. As of today, the third day of [the Jewish month of] Shevat, a fast was proclaimed and we are collecting money in the hope of saving lives. But you should know that what had happened until now was secret; you should announce it to all. You should sound the alarm. Look for some way out. Don't waste any time. Find a way to save the remaining Jews before—God forbid—the death sentence. Do not surrender. Do not be silent. Do everything to save the lives of thousands of brothers. Every

moment counts! You are, after all, to be so honored, one of the largest Jewish communities.

Ask the rabbis of Israel if relatives of the dead must observe seven days of mourning and what we should do. May God Almighty have mercy on the Jews and protect [them] from evil. May he send rescue in time, so that we might receive some good news! Please answer immediately.

And how are you? Here—apart from all this—nothing is new. Send our regards to all. I expect a speedy response.[60]

From January 1942 on, the mass murders in Chełmno were common knowledge in the Warsaw ghetto. In April 1942, Hersh Wasser wrote the following to Aleksander Kamiński, editor of *Biuletyn Informacyjny*, a leading underground bulletin in occupied Poland:

In mid-December 1941 the entire Jewish populations of Koło (2,000 people) and Dąbie on the Ner (1,000 people) were expelled. Deportation included all the Jews without exception. They were loaded on trucks—infants, children, elderly, and chronically ill. Along with their belongings, they were transported to the village of Chełmno, 12 kilometers from Koło on the road to Dąbie. Local ... peasants reported that no food was brought into the palace [in Chełmno] and that a gray truck arrives and departs several times a day, traveling to and from the direction of the Rzuchowski forest. ...Jews were brought in groups of 60, and later of 90 people. Luggage was dropped off at the local church buildings, which were seized by the Gestapo. Then the cars drove up to the palace, where the displaced got out.....

In addition to the Jews of Koło and Dąbie, from January 2 to 9, 1942—Gypsies brought from the Łódź ghetto; on January 10 and 12—Jews from Kłodawa; on January 13—Jews of Bugaj; on January 14 and 15—Jews from Izbica Kujawska; and from January 16 onwards and until the beginning of April—the Jews from the Łódź ghetto and in all probability also from Krośniewice, Żychlin and Kutno, were gassed at Chełmno.... These details are derived from the testimony of the local population in which, despite all precautions, word of the tragedy taking place in the "Chełmno Palace" echoed, originating above all in descriptions thrown from the windows of the car by the unfortunate gravediggers. As stated above, their authenticity is not subject to any doubt....[61]

The last clause of the letter stresses the importance of the entire missive: "Their authenticity is not subject to any doubt." Like other reports about mass murder in other German-occupied areas, however, this one was considered unreliable. Importantly, too, in addition to the Germans' attempts at spreading disinformation, any information about mass murders that did manage to reach Jews elsewhere was likely to be considered reportage about wartime atrocities rather than the premeditated, planned, and systematic murder of the Jewish people as such. As a case in point, by the summer of 1941 Jews were being systematically murdered in Ponary near Wilno. These murders reduced the size of the Jewish community but did not lead to its extermination. When couriers affiliated with Jewish youth movements brought news about the murders in Ponary to the Warsaw ghetto, many there reacted with disbelief. In other cases as well, Jews who reported systematic mass murder first had to convince the populace that they were telling the truth.

Local Polish residents also tried to spread the news about the extermination in Chełmno. This, however, was very difficult and dangerous for people who lacked connections with the Polish underground. One such case follows:

Initially, the SS used the phone in the community offices. Apparently, the community secretary, Stanisław Kaszyński, knew too much, since he was arrested and finally sentenced to death. Kaszyński had sent a letter to diplomatic representations describing the events which took place in Chełmno. This letter apparently fell into the hands of the Germans.[62]

Similar attempts to communicate by Jews who had escaped from places of execution were very desperate but not effective. When the messages actually reached the hands of the local population, the latter did not know what to do with such knowledge except to be frightened. In most cases, such despondent tidings were ineffective unless they were strong enough to stay in the memory of the local population. Most of the victims remained unknown and anonymous.

> Jewish prisoners awaiting execution sometimes threw letters. I remember this. Once I myself picked up a letter. The text started with the words: "We Jews from Lwów...." I threw this letter away. Jews tore up money and valuable papers and threw them into the road. Jews were kept in uncertainty to the last moment about what concerned their fate and what awaited them; therefore they behaved so passively. There was no reflex of rebellion.[63]

Who were the Victims of Chełmno?

The death center in Chełmno was built primarily for the Jews of the Warthegau. Only later did it receive Jews from elsewhere.

Mass murder in Chełmno began with the elimination of the inhabitants of the village ghetto in Kowale Pańskie. The Jews of Turek County (Łódź Regierungsbezirk), over 4,000 people all told, had all been concentrated there. Following a selection among them on December 6, 1941, 3,000 were imprisoned in the church in Dobra. Four days later, they were sent to Chełmno. Those left behind in Kowale Pańskie were killed in Chełmno on July 20, 1942. Selections of this nature recurred in all ghettos in every location.

The first group that reached Chełmno came from Inowrocław Regierungsbezirk and comprised approximately 3,900 Jews from Koło County (from Koło, December 7–11, 1941, about 2,300 people; from Babiak, Bugaj, and Nowiny Brdowskie, January 14, 1942, about 600 people; from Dąbie nad Nerem, Izbica Kujawska, January 14–15, 1942, about 1,000 people; from Kłodawa, January 9–12, 1942; and from Sompolno, February 2, 1942, an unspecified number). They were murdered between December 7, 1941, and February 2, 1942. One example of further mass killings was that of 10,700 people from Kutno County in March 1942 (Kutno, March–April 1942, an unspecified number; Krośniewice, March

2, 1942, 900 people; March 3, 1942, 3,200 people). The extermination of communities in the following counties began in April 1942: 4,400 from Gostynin County (for example, on April 17, people from Sanniki were directed to Chełmno), 1,580 from Ciechocinek County (Osięciny April 22, 1942, Radziejów April 10–11, 1942, Służewo before May 16, 1942), and 2,557 from Włocławek County (April 30–May 2, 1942, Włocławek).

Jews from the Łódź ghetto were included in the extermination transports from Inowrocław Regierungsbezirk. In January–May and September 1942, 70,687 of them were exterminated. The next group of 7,196 was murdered in June–July 1944. In March 1942, 972 Jews from Kalisz and Kalisz County met this fate, as did 2,423 from Łódź County in May 1942. In May–August 1942, 8,760 people from Łęczyca County were murdered; between June and August 1942, 15,859 from Łask County; in August 1942, 9,589 from Sieradz County; and 9,498 from Wieluń County. More than a thousand Jews (probably 2,000–3,000) were transferred from labor camps, and more than 10,000 were transferred from Western Europe (mainly from Germany, Czechoslovakia, and Austria). A witness reports:

> Jews from neighboring towns were brought to the camp at first; then they arrived from the Łódź ghetto. In addition to these transports, Jews were brought from various parts of Europe: Hungary, Yugoslavia, Czechoslovakia, France, and Greece. After the arrival of such transports, the military police had cigarettes from the country from which the transport had originated. Most Germans paid for food (like eggs) [with cigarettes]; this is how we knew where the transports had come from. Moreover, the police did not hide these facts. They would reminisce, "I remember that a transport with wealthy Jews from Vienna and 'rich Jews from Hamburg' came." The people transported from these places had more luggage and were better dressed.[64]

It is important to note that there were non-Jews among the victims of Chełmno. One example is a group of Gypsies from the Austrian-Hungarian border. Various sources report the murder of some 5,000 Gypsies in Chełmno. On November 5–9, 1941, five transports of Gypsies from five locations in Austria—Furstenfeld, Hartberg, Mattersburg, Oberwart, and Rotter Thurm—arrived at the Łódź ghetto. They were held under appalling conditions and enjoined against using the many valuables and musical instruments that they had brought.[65] Here is a short description of the Gypsy camp in the ghetto:

> A ghetto within a ghetto. About 5,000 people, strange strangers, behind the barbed-wire fences of the Gypsy camp that has been established within the ghetto: women, men, and children. Are we weeping because Gypsies are before us? We know nothing about their past. They look like they've come from some European country. Their skin is white and the expression in their dark eyes is sad. They came to us by surprise and were immediately placed in a fenced, well-guarded cage. None of us knows what is going on behind that spiked barbed-wire fence. Only in the evenings can one sometimes hear from the direction of the new camp terrified screaming and strange cries that make the blood in our veins run cold. A tragedy behind a curtain. Torture of people behind closed doors. The days of the Roman emperors are returning. This time, however, nothing is being done on playing fields or at the circus, but behind veils of total secrecy, beneath the enchanted hat from the fable of the Brothers Grimm: whoever puts it on disappears from the view of strangers. One day a few nurses and doctors are recruited from the ghetto hospital and given permission to enter the camp. The gate is locked tightly behind them and no one leaves or enters again. Only a few closed wagons enter the camp and leave every day. We, the veterans, have no difficulty guessing what is in these wagons, as we encounter them very frequently in the ghetto, too.
>
> A strange quiet now prevails in the camp. A few weeks pass. No one leaves [the camp] and only the closed wagons become more numerous with each passing day. Suddenly something new and disturbing happens. A stretcher bearing an unconscious woman who is ill with spotted typhus is brought to the hospital for infectious diseases. She is one of the nurses who

volunteered to work in the camp. Only from the stammering of the woman, who is burning with fever, is it finally possible to penetrate the terrible secret of the Gypsy camp. Life there is horrific, the hygienic conditions inhuman. The disease spreads by the hour and no one recovers. Those who fall ill get no treatment; food is lacking, and there are no medicines. [The ill] lie there next to one another in excrement as the vermin gnaw at their feverish bodies. Corpses among living bodies. The smells are ghastly. Appalling filth. Human language cannot describe the death agonies of those in the camp. Every day more volunteers who have fallen ill are brought in. The disease does not sleep and is not afraid of barbed wire or armed Germans. The vermin pass swiftly through the fences and seek new victims.

First cases of spotted typhus in the ghetto. At first a few, then more. The Gypsy camp is eliminated totally. The last inspection there is carried out by two Jewish physicians who enter the camp specially outfitted, wearing masks on their faces and rubber gloves on their hands and covered with a special powder that exterminates lice to safeguard their health. They step into puddles of excrement and blood, circulate among human bodies and rodents, and do not find a single living soul. Utterly depressed, the doctors emerge from the horrible world of ghosts, and then, at the last minute, their gaze catches a small, trembling hand that is raised up. Out of some sort of hidden drawer crawls the small body of a pale, mute girl. Without giving much thought to the danger of what they are doing, the doctors lift the trembling body and enter the ghetto carrying the last remnant of the "Gypsy camp." A passenger cart harnessed to a horse awaits them and returns them to the hospital. Germans stand at the entrance, waiting for a final report. But first they shoot the girl, the last mute witness of those forbidden things. The physicians undergo thorough disinfection and are allowed to rest a little after their work and to draw up a brief report. Two weeks later, one of them [a doctor] takes to his bed, sick, and does not get up again. The masks and the gloves did not help. The disease vanquished his body, which lacked sufficient strength of body and mind to fight its illness.[66]

Rozalia Peham's testimony (June 27, 1945) delivers rather scanty information about the killing of 5,000 people: "Gassman the driver told me that in Chełmno, apart from Jews, 5,000 Gypsies were killed."[67]

Small groups of Poles, Soviet POWs, and Czech children were also put to death in Chełmno.[68] Several testimonies confirm the murder of Soviet POWs:

> If Poles were murdered there, I don't know. My husband said nothing about it. He said, however, that one day—I do not remember when—two cars brought Russian officers. I remember my husband using the term, [saying] that "they were such elegant officers." I do not know whether they were taken directly to the forest or pushed into *Spezialwagen* and thus killed.[69]

The Czech children were from the village of Lidice;[70] they were brought to Chełmno as a consequence of the assassination of Reinhard Heydrich. Heydrich—head of the Nazi security police (Sipo), the Security Service (SD), and the Reich Security Main Office (RSHA)—was one of the leading figures in planning and carrying out the Final Solution of the Jewish Question in Europe. However, he had another important function: governor of the Protectorate of Bohemia and Moravia. On May 27, 1942, Heydrich was seriously wounded in an attack on the outskirts of Prague by the Czech paratroopers Joseph Gabčik, Jan Kubis, and Josef Valčík, as part of Operation Anthropoid. They had been trained by the Special Operations Executive (SOE) in England and Scotland and parachuted into Czech territory. Eight days later, on June 4, 1942, Heydrich died from blood poisoning. In retaliation for his death, the Nazis razed Lidice and another Czech village, Ležáky, and murdered their inhabitants or deported them to concentration camps. Originally, Hitler had sought a still harsher response, the murder of many thousands of Czech civilians; the first response actually made was smaller in scale, confined to the two villages. Even so, it was severe. Both villages, Lidice and

Ležáky, were completely destroyed, and 1,300 of their inhabitants were murdered. More than 13,000 villagers were arrested and deported—men mainly to concentration camps and women to the Ravensbrück concentration camp, where most were kept as prisoners. Many children were sent away for Germanization. Eighty-one children from Lidice, however, were sent to Chełmno and murdered in gas vans. After Heydrich's death, the operation of the extermination of the Jews of Poland was renamed Aktion Reinhardt.

First Liquidation of the Chełmno Death Camp

When the camp in Chełmno was liquidated, Arthur Greiser, Governor of the Warthegau, organized a farewell party for the entire Sonderkommando as an expression of gratitude for its success in murdering Jews in his *Gau*.[71] Greiser wrote about the members of the detail in the following way:

> ... I became acquainted with the attitude of members of the special unit, which I would like to report to Sir, the Reichsführer SS. People not only faithfully and bravely carried out all tasks imposed on them by you, Sir, to the letter, but additionally presented the best attitude of any soldier.... The soldiers also expressed a desire to continue to carry out their responsibilities under the command of their commander, Haupsturmführer Bothmann. I promised the soldiers that their request would be passed on to you, Sir, Reichsführer. Please, Sir, give me your permission to invite these soldiers, as part of their holidays, to be my guests in my estates, which should provide them with substantial assistance and an enjoyable holiday.[72]

It was typical of Nazi jargon to define the members of the detail, composed mainly of SS men, police functionaries, and policemen, as "soldiers" and their task of murdering innocent Jews and other civilians as a "military action."

In early spring, an order from Berlin came to close [the Chełmno extermination center] [and to] destroy and obliterate all traces. [The members of the detail] were ordered to use the crematoria in the future. As a result, graves had to be dug and the corpses to be reduced to ashes in specially constructed crematoria or in huge fires prepared in the forest. A special commission came from Berlin to examine the status of the work. There was a terrible stench. My husband laughed, that *die Herren aus Berlin* (Berlin gentlemen) cannot stay by the dug graves for more than five minutes before fainting.[73]

This state of affairs lasted until April 1943. Liquidation of the camp and obliterating traces [of it] began. The fence was dismantled; the equipment had been transported, etc. On April 7, 1943, the crematorium furnaces and the palace were blown up to cover up the traces of their crimes. In the woods, they planted grass on the [mass] graves.... The crematorium furnaces were dismantled and the bricks were moved somewhere. On April 11, 1943, SS Sonderkommando Kulmhof left. A small unit of military police who guarded the "place of execution" remained in the place. These were policemen from local police stations. A police officer from Sompolno was their commander. When the Sonderkommando Kulmhof left, they took with them Poles who were doing auxiliary work.[74]

The Second Wave of Extermination in Chełmno on the Nerem and Rzuchów Forest

The Chełmno extermination center resumed operations in 1944 at a new location. One reason for the reactivation was a project that envisaged the annihilation of Hungarian Jews there. That project, however, was abandoned because the camp at Auschwitz-Birkenau had been expanded and adapted to accommodate these victims.[75] Auschwitz-Birkenau was much more convenient for the killing of Hungarian Jews, mainly because it was much closer to Hungary, which significantly shortened and facilitated transport; the Chełmno vicinity lacked a good rail network. Auschwitz also had much better facilities for the safeguarding of victims' belongings.[76]

During the second wave of murders at the Chełmno center, the process took place differently than in 1941–1943, mainly in that it had been simplified. This time, victims were transported by narrow-gauge railway directly to Chełmno.

The transports that arrived in Chełmno were sent to the church, where they stayed only overnight. Heilwehle used to come to this church and say: "All you have got with you, you may eat. You are leaving to work tomorrow." He used to say [they were going] even to Munich. The next morning, two trucks drove up; they put 100 people in each truck—a total of 200 people. These wagons were driven into the forest. In the forest there were barracks with the words: *Badeanstalt, zum Arzt* (baths, to the doctor) on the door. People had to undress there. Everyone got a towel and soap to go to the bath. People went into the wagon and were gassed there.[77]

The victims spent the night in the church of Chełmno, near the palace. In the earlier period of Chełmno's murderous activity, this had served as the reception area for the deportees, who had been required to undress before going to "disinfection." From there, instead of going to the bath, they had been pushed into a gas wagon and transported to the Rzuchów forest. In 1944, victims detained in the church were transported from there to the Rzuchów forest. A witness testified: "In the morning, from the church in Chełmno, they began to bring groups of Jews to the forest. Already in the church Wacht.[meister] Heffele promised the Jews that a better fate awaited them; therefore, the Jews departed to the forest calmly."[78]

In the forest, two barracks stood in an enclosed area. One served as a dressing room where victims had to strip before going to the "bath." Naked, they were led into the wagon, which was also a gas chamber. This car was supposed to deliver the victims to the bath. After the victims were murdered, the cars drove to another clearing, where the corpses were immediately incinerated at special stations. A witness describes this process:

> The transport of those who were brought in three cars was unloaded in the Chełmno forest near the clearing in front of the barracks. Bothmann spoke to the Jews brought there and said that Jews would be going to work in Munich or Leipzig and that he would lead them there. He spoke of himself as someone who was stern but fair, saying that no one would suffer. He also said that the elders would have to perform indoor duties and younger people outdoor ones. Further, he announced that they would go

to the showers. The Jews had to undress in the barracks, men and women separately.[79]

Another witness reports:

Each undressed person had to lay his or her clothes and underwear on a bench; rings and other valuables had to be placed on a shelf above the clothes. Then men and women were sent together to an outdoor fenced area where a Sonderwagen waited. Jews were violently pushed into the wagon. We could hear cries and lamentations.[80]

As before, clothing was separated in an orderly manner to make it easier to put to further use. "Better clothes were sent to Łódź. Clothes in worse condition—rough and tattered clothes—were sent to [the ghetto in] Łódź to be processed in a specially imported machine."[81]

As in 1941–1943, great importance was attached to misinforming and confusing the victims to preclude resistance or escape attempts. The problem was not that the victims could truly escape; once they were on the extermination center grounds, escape was difficult if not impossible. Any resistance, however, would impede the smooth operation of the murder process; therefore, the perpetrators tried to keep the victims calm to the last moment and convinced them that nothing threatened them. A witness reported: "Jews generally stepped quietly into the car. I would like to mention that they were given a towel and a piece of soap, to affirm the belief that they were going to bathe. All naked, Jews were conducted into the car and the door was closed."[82]

The Second Liquidation of Chełmno: The Jewish Detail Rebels

The witness Andrzej Miszczak recounts the background of a remarkable event:

In autumn 1944, the camp at Chełmno, near Rzuchowski forest, was essentially liquidated. Crematorium furnaces were blown up. The barracks were dismantled in order to remove traces of the crime. To supervise the process of obliterating the evidence, a special commission was sent for this purpose from Berlin. Crematorium furnaces were demolished, bricks scattered in the woods. Mills [for grinding bones] returned to Powiercie.[83]

A German Sonderkommando and a group of forty-seven Jewish workers remained on location. On the night of January 17/18, 1945, the members of the Sonderkommando began lead the Jews outside in small groups and shoot them. After several such groups had been murdered, the Jewish prisoners in the barracks resisted, killing two Germans and setting the barracks afire. Amid the confusion, two Jewish prisoners, Mieczysław Żurawski and Szymon Srebrnik, managed to escape. Thanks to them, the events in the last hours of the camp are known.

Żurawski, a butcher from Włocławek, describes what happened that night:

> The final liquidation took place on the night of 17–18 January. At 1 a.m., [Germans] surrounded the camp, where we lay in chains (because we were shackled), and wanted to shoot us. There were still 40 workers alive. [The Germans] dragged five men away every time. They already had shot the first three groups of five. When they came for the fourth group, only two guards turned up. I remember their names: Lenz and Haase. We attacked them. I managed to get to the door. They fired at me. I was shot in the leg. It was dark and they had only flashlights. So I ran away and they fired at me. They thought I was already a corpse and they looked for me by the fence, but I escaped over the fence and tried to get to the forest, about 4 kilometers away. They chased me. I heard chasing behind me. I was even able to recognize the voices of some *Wachmänner*. I hid in the trenches until I got to the forest.[84]

A German participant in this incident describes it from his vantage point:

> After the escape of Żurawski, Lenz and policeman Haase went inside the storehouse to force the Jews to leave. But the Jews

50. Two-storey building near the no-longer-existent palace at Chełmno, where Jewish prisoners lived and worked. In the last days of the camp, Jewish prisoners rebelled and killed two German staff members; one prisoner escaped. In response, the Germans burned the building together with the prisoners (YVA, sig. 1427_363)

hanged Lenz and shot Haase. Then Bothmann ordered an attack on the storehouse using grenades. A fire broke out and the Jews were burned up. In Chełmno there were only 45 Jewish workers.[85]

Continuing, Żurawski describes the course of his escape from Chełmno.

> I lay all night in the forest, and when it began to dawn, I got to a barn near the forest. I was lying the whole day in that barn. I tore my shirt and bandaged the wounds. I had a wounded leg and my face was cut up by the barbed wire through which I had escaped.[86]

Żurawski was saved by a Polish family that helped and hid him until Red Army forces liberated the area several days later, on January 20, 1945. Afterwards, Żurawski returned to the extermination camp in the

Rzuchowski forest and described what he saw: "… When I learned that the Russians had occupied Chełmno, I went there. I found burnt corpses in the camp. Germans had poured gasoline on the building and hurled grenades…."

Number of Victims in Chełmno[87]

Among the few known escapes from places of execution, four occurred at the Chełmno extermination camp. Two inmates escaped from Bełżec. More prisoners from Treblinka and Sobibór survived due to uprisings. From other places of execution, only a few people managed to escape—in some cases, none at all got away.

> Twelve or thirteen vehicles came to the forest every day. In this way, I calculate that approximately 1,000 people were poisoned by gas every day.[88]
>
> Initially 1,000 people per day were brought to Chełmno. Among the policemen we used to say *Ein Tag Ein Tausend* [another day, another thousand].[89]
>
> I was employed in the Waldkommando at burning corpses for about three weeks. During this time, ten transports of Jews arrived—a thousand people each day.[90]

The main annihilation activities at Chełmno lasted from December 8, 1941, to April 7, 1943. From April 1943 until the final liquidation of the camp in January 1945, the activity was less intensive (a total of ten transports, i.e., about 10,000 people). Taking into account only the 480 days of the first period, a two-month moratorium on transports in the spring of 1942 and several interruptions associated with inevitable technical mishaps, which, according to research, did not exceed seventy days in total, should be deducted. The subtraction of 150 days from the total of 480 leaves 330 days in which the Chełmno camp operated. At 1,000 murders per day, the toll is 330,000 victims in all. Adding the 10,000 Jews who were murdered in 1944, the minimum number of murdered victims in Chełmno—men, women, and children, from infancy to old age—may be set at 340,000.[91]

Many recent studies question this figure, leading us to consider the possibility that it is an overestimate. Peter Klein writes about more than 150,000 victims but suggests no maximum.[92] He quotes a report prepared by Eduard Korherr for Heinrich Himmler, titled *Die Endlösung der europäischen Judenfrage*, which states that in addition to the 1,274,166 Jews murdered in the General Government by January 15, 1943, 145,301 were murdered in Chełmno.[93] Several thousand Jews from other locations should be added to this tally (e.g., 7,176 Jews from the Łódź ghetto between June 23 and July 14, 1941[94]) as well as several thousand Gypsies, Czech children, Polish civilians, and Soviet POWs. This would bring the estimated number of victims in Chełmno to approximately 170,000.

2. ACTIVITIES OF KOMMANDO 1005

As the Red Army advanced toward the extermination site, the SS embarked on efforts to obliterate all traces of the mass graves. This was a difficult task, since the graves were dispersed across vast areas in the east. During the activity of the Einsatzgruppen in Soviet territory, about a million and a half people had been murdered, in addition to approximately two million Soviet POWs who had been starved to death. Mass murder also took place in POW camps and other places. To deal with the task of eradicating the

51. Death camp in Chełmno on the Nerem: collection of tombstones from Turek (2009) (photo: T. Kawski)

52. Death camp in Chełmno on the Nerem. One of the monuments based on ruins of the crematorium (2009) (photo: T. Kawski)

evidence, a special detail was established to open mass graves and incinerate their contents.

The establishment of Kommando 1005—a German unit composed of the security police (Sipo) and the Security Service (SD)—is associated with two principal causes, one internal and the other external. Since the mass extermination center at Chełmno began its operation in December 1941, during a harsh winter, its victims were initially buried in frozen ground and did not decompose until the snow started melting in the spring of 1942. Then, the thousands of rotting corpses produced a strong stench that diffused throughout the countryside and threatened the area with contamination, spread of disease, and poisoning of groundwater. Therefore, the process of extermination was temporarily stopped in order to get rid of the corpses by incinerating them. This marked the beginning of Kommando 1005. Thus, the initial goal was not to obliterate traces of the crimes but to attain sanitation goals, although the former outcome flowed from the latter.

The second reason for the establishment of Kommando 1005 was the Allies' knowledge of the mass crimes. The heyday of the Wehrmacht had ended in 1941; by now, the Soviet counteroffensive near Moscow and the expulsion of German forces from some of the areas they had occupied had led to the discovery of mass graves. In addition, refugees from German-occupied territories reported criminal acts in the areas of Dnepropetrovsk, Odessa, Kamenetz Podolsky, and other cities. This information was published by Vyacheslav Molotov, the Soviet Minister of Foreign Affairs, on January 6, 1942. In early 1942, information about the mass graves of Jews in the Warthegau reached Martin Luther at the Reich Ministry of Foreign Affairs. Luther discussed the matter with Gestapo chief Heinrich Müller on February 6, 1942. Müller responded immediately, instructing Adolf Eichmann's office (IV B4) to deal with the situation.[95] However, the issue was too complex to settle in one go. It was a state secret; it would take time. The right man had to be found, someone who had previously performed similar tasks and who had the technical and organizational ability to do it again.

The man tasked with removing the traces of the crime was SS-Standartenführer Paul Blobel. Until January 13, 1942, Blobel had commanded Sonderkommando 4a—part of Einsatzgruppe C—in Ukraine and had mass-murdered Jews in so doing. His major crime was the genocide at Babi Yar near Kiev in the last days of September 1941, which annihilated some 33,000 Jews within a few days. On January 13, 1942, Blobel was sent home for medical treatment and was now residing in Düsseldorf. En route to Germany, Blobel had met in Warsaw with the head of the Main Office for Reich Security (Reichssherheitshauptamt—RSHA), Reinhard Heydrich, who had assigned Blobel to service in Department IV—the Gestapo. Completing his convalescence in June 1942, Blobel visited Eichmann's office to acquaint himself with his future duties. Later that month, he began his activities as the commander of Sonderkommando 1005.[96]

Paul Blobel's stint at the helm of Sonderkommando 1005 began and ended in the Warthegau. In June 1942, he travelled to Łódź, the closest major city to the Chełmno death camp, to organize the work and obtain help from local Sipo and SD personnel. His first urgent task was to dispose of the bodies of those murdered in Chełmno. Blobel, an architect and builder by profession who had served in the engineering corps during World War I, had a method for accomplishing this task: incineration using grills made of railroad rails to provide adequate ventilation. To set the fire, wood doused in gasoline was used. To destroy the last traces of the bodies, Blobel introduced a process of grinding bones. Since the activity of the Kommando 1005 was secret, Bothmann's Sonderkommando Kulmhof and the Litzmannstadt [Łódź] ghetto administration (Ghettoverwaltung) provided the necessary equipment and materials.[97]

In addition to its activity in three extermination camps (Bełżec, Sobibór, and Treblinka), in 1943 Kommando 1005 began operations in the east, where the Einsatzgruppen, which had mass-murdered Jews, Soviet political commissars, and prisoners of war, had been active in 1941–1942. We learn about the doings of Kommando 1005 in and around Lwów from the memoirs of Leon Weliczker, a member of the Jewish detail that was tasked with opening the mass graves and cremating the bodies. Weliczker describes the minutiae of the incineration process and the treatment of prisoners.[98] Notably, the members of Kommando 1005 did not perform any physical work; they only organized and supervised it. They also made arrangements for supplies of the materials necessary to burn the corpses and murdered unnecessary prisoners.

Due to the large number of mass-murder sites and the quantity of corpses that had to be removed, Kommando 1005 was divided into several smaller units, each operating in its own area. Blobel was responsible for coordinating the process and all operations related to it, known collectively as the exhumation action (*Enterdungsaktion*). Günther Fuchs, the Gestapo Commissar from Łódź, commanded the Kommando 1005 unit in the Warthegau. Dr. Otto Bradfisch, district commander of the State Police (Stapo), ordered him to lead the operation in this area. The unit comprised three SS men, thirty to forty German policemen, and twenty shackled prisoners from the Łódź ghetto. The work began in early February 1944 in the Konin vicinity, with mass graves in the environs of Kazimierz Biskupi and the Długa Łąka forests. The unit then proceeded to the Łódź region, where it worked in the Zgierz area and elsewhere. By July 1944, when it wound up its duties, it had operated in twenty localities.[99]

Little is known about the details of the corpse-burning process in the Kazimierz Biskupi and Długa Łąka forests. According to the minutes of the District Commission for the Investigation of Nazi Crimes in Poznań:

> ... The Germans, apparently fearing accountability, began in March 1944 to destroy evidence of the killings carried out in 1941 and 1942 in Konin County, in the woods of Kazimierz Biskupi, and in particular in the forest near Długa Łąka. A special team was organized, consisting of people from unidentified uniformed formations[100] and Jewish men, who proceeded to exhume not yet decomposed corpses of Jews still found in mass graves in the Długa Łąka forest and then to burn them on a pile of wood.... It lasted almost a whole month, when the entrance to the woods was closed by German checkpoints and, at that time, above the forest was the visible thick smoke of burnt bodies, which had a very unpleasant odor. The same thing happened especially with the remains of Jewish children buried in the woods at Kazimierz

Biskupi and corpses of the Jews brought by cars; unknown policemen from the police station in Kazimierz Biskupi took part in this.... Since the burning of corpses in this way was very difficult if not impossible, the Germans withdrew from conducting the action to the end and restricted themselves to an even better way to mask the scene of the crime—by planting trees and other greenery.... The quantities of burned Jewish corpses or those of any other person could not be established. In addition, it could not be conclusively established, with particular names, who took an active part in burning of the corpses in the woods just next to the Kazimierz Biskupi and next to the Długa Łąka.[101]

Local inhabitants remembered this operation well. One recalled: "Once, I noticed as I was passing by bicycle that a truck covered with a tarpaulin emerged from the forest. I did not see any people in this car. Generally, it was said that the Germans had liquidated mass graves of the Długa Łąka woods."[102] A second witness reports: "From the first to the thirtieth of March 1945 [1944—author], the Germans organized a team that carried out the exhumation and burning of corpses. It lasted a whole month."[103] A third witness says: "I recall that the elimination of the mass graves in the woods of Długa Łąka took place in March or April 1944 the action. The operations lasted several weeks."[104]

As in the mass murders in the woods in 1941, the removal of traces began with surrounding the forest with guards to prevent the ingress of accidental witnesses. As one witness said, "After some time, the German police again informed my father that the forest would be closed for the second time for a certain period ... in the spring."[105] Other witnesses corroborate this: "Some time later, I cannot remember when, German troops once again isolated the same stretch of forest."[106] The witness Lucjan Zalas, who lived in the forest around Długa Łąka, said, "Two years later, it might have been in the winter or the spring of 1943 or 1944, the German authorities closed the forest again, at the same site, and erased the traces of the crime."[107]

After the month-long Aktion, "The forest was again opened and then I had the opportunity to go and make an inspection."[108] One witness describes what he saw after the traces of the crimes had been removed:

> After the Germans completed this action and left, I went to this place. I saw that holes had been dug and were covered with earth but were not camouflaged. There were traces of large fires. I add that during the first action I saw as the army brought the Jews in military vehicles coming on the Marantowska Road, from the side of the road that ran from Konin to Gosławice. However, the German soldiers were coming in the morning along the road going from Niesłusz to the Rudzica. The Jews were unloaded from the car at the corner of Marantowska Road and the forest road running from the forester's house to Długa Łąka.[109]

Another witness describes what he saw after Kommando 1005 had done its work:

> After the German elimination of mass graves, one day I went for a walk in the woods. Traces of the graves had been carefully obliterated. I understood then that in a young scrub forest were remnants of the furnace, in which probably the corpses were burned. This place was about 40 meters away from the mass graves. From this point to the furnace, clear traces of a well-trodden path led from the furnace to the graves. It seems to me that if I went to this place now, I could recognize the traces of the liquidated graves.[110]

As mentioned, the Germans brought in a Jewish detail to remove evidence of the mass murder. Its members were in appalling physical condition. A witness described his encounter with them:

> After some time I rode back by bike going to work in Konin and I noticed a group of men numbering five to ten people, looking very poorly, covered with rags, who worked on the exit from the road into the Długa Łąka forest. All these people were shackled.

Their feet were chained and their hands were also tied with a string. They moved with great difficulty.[111]

Another witness described the members of the Jewish detail as strangers who spoke an unknown tongue:

> On several occasions during that time I rode a bike from Rudzica in the direction of Niesłusz and I saw a few trucks transporting the working group that was employed to burn the corpses that had been buried in mass graves. I noticed a group of workers with dark skin and black hair, and I thought they were probably Jews from southern Europe who spoke a language quite foreign to me. These people were probably also murdered in order to cover traces. None of my acquaintances saw these people transported back to Konin.[112]

Despite its secretive nature, the Aktion could not be hidden, because the horrid stench of the burning corpses wafted to great distances. "After

53. Death camp in Chełmno on the Nerem. One of the monuments overlooking the site where victims' mass graves are located (2009) (photo: T. Kawski)

a certain period of time, smoke with a very unpleasant odor of burned flesh hovered over the forester's house in Rudzica and Niesłusz,"[113] one witness says. Another witness recalls: "Everyone who lived in the area then smelled the stinking smoke drifting from the woods. It lasted about a few weeks."[114] Yet another one remembers: "During the day you could see the smoke over that section of the forest and when the wind blew toward the forester's house there was a terrible stench."[115] The witness Antoni Śliwiński recalls, "Smoke hovered for a long time over the Długa Łąka forest and the nasty odor of burned flesh drifted to Rudzica village...."[116]

Characteristically, even a boy who had been ordered to provide food for German officers during the first mass murder of Jews was given different orders, as he remembered later with some surprise: "This time we were told not to come with food and I did not see what happened there."[117]

Little is known about what went on during the exhumation of the mass graves. However, one witness comments: "It was quiet during the day; there were shootings in the evening."[118] It is likely that, as was the case with other units that participated in the removal and incineration of corpses, debilitated prisoners or prisoners in general were murdered after the work day, to be replaced by new ones.

The local population had very little contact with the prisoners in Kommando 1005. In one case, however, an inhabitant did have an opportunity to see a prisoner: "A young Jew came to my home, escorted by police, to take water. He would take two buckets of water every day. I do not know for what purpose."[119] In general, very few prisoners who served in the details that were responsible for the elimination of traces of mass murder survived. In the operation around Kazimierz Biskupi, there is information about at least one survivor. A witness recalls meeting a man who had managed to escape from the detail that performed the ghastly exhumation and incineration work:

> A few months after the liberation, I met a man about 55 years old, who at that place in the forest said that he had been in the group of prisoners who had been transported from the prison into the Krężel forest, and there they burned the corpses. I do

not know either the name of the man or where he came from. He told me that he had jumped from the car and fled into the forest and thus saved himself. His fellow prisoners had been executed by the Germans as witnesses to crimes carried out. When the man told the story in the woods, a few dozen people—Poles—were present. He was a stranger in our area.[120]

3. THE TALLY OF EXTERMINATION IN INOWROCŁAW REGIERUNGSBEZIRK

The exterminations in Inowrocław Regierungsbezirk and the Warthegau at large exacted a tragic toll. The Jewish population was almost completely obliterated. Only a few percent of the Jews who had inhabited that area before 1939 survived, and this only because they had fled to the Soviet Union.[121]

According to research performed by S. Waszak soon after the end of the war, 54,087 Jews had lived in Inowrocław Regierungsbezirk before the war.[122] Danuta Dąbrowska's detailed research on the population of certain towns and villages found 54,641.[123] These numbers should be increased slightly if one takes into account the pre-war statistical data from all the Jewish communities in the area that was later incorporated into the Regierunsbezirk. These data yield a total population of 55,700–55,800 Jews.[124] However the borders are drawn, Jews were the third-largest national group in the region, after Poles (1,157,000) and Germans (89,100). The various tallies of the Jewish population must be considered approximations due to inaccuracies in pre-war municipal administrations and the large migrations of Jews that preceded the war. It is hard to establish how many Jews inhabited the Regierungsbezirk in the first weeks of the Nazi occupation. Some civilians died in September 1939. Men eligible for service in the Polish army were mobilized. An indeterminate number of them were killed; others were taken prisoner by the Germans or Soviets.[125] Many civilians escaped to the far ends of Poland. After several weeks, some began to return to their hometowns, while others managed to reach the eastern boundaries of the Polish Republic, which were occupied by the Soviet army after September 17, 1939.[126] Concurrently, waves of Jewish refugees from western and central Greater Poland and Pomerania flowed into many locations of the Regierungsbezirk.

Of the 55,770–55,800 Jews who had inhabited Inowrocław Regierungsbezirk before the war began in 1939, only 39,713 remained there in October 1940 (3.43% of the total population at the time). This population shrank to 31,782 (2.8%) in April 1941, edged upward to 34,488 (2.98%) in July 1941, fell back to 31,440 in December 1941, and contracted to 22,506 (1.93%) in January 1942. The major extermination phase followed the establishment of the Chełmno camp. In October 1942, only three Jews were found in Inowrocław Regierungsbezirk, and by July 1943, only two.[127]

During that time, virtually all Jews in the counties of Łódź Regierungsbezirk were eliminated. The process was basically completed by September 1942, with the sole exception of the Łódź ghetto. In the second half of 1944, the gradual dissolution of this entity also began. The few Jews who served in labor details saw the coming of the Soviet army in January1945.[128]

When the Jewish population in part of a given county was obliterated, the presence of several dozen to 200 local Jews was tolerated for a few weeks afterward to tidy up the sites of former ghettos and Jewish districts. Most often, however, the workers were Jews brought in from the Łódź ghetto. In addition, Jewish doctors could be found in prisons. In Inowrocław, for example, there were three Jewish physicians as of October 15, 1942. Jews in seclusion or awaiting trial in prisons across Inowrocław Regierungsbezirk are not included in the statistics.

From mid-1942 to mid-1944, larger groups of Jews were found only in labor camps. In 1944, labor details comprising several to several dozen people made their appearance in Inowrocław Regierungsbezirk. Comprising men brought in from the Łódź ghetto, they dealt with the process of removing bodies from mass graves. After the men finished their job, they were executed.[129]

Kleczew, renamed Lehmanstädt by the Germans, spent this period in the eye of the storm and paid a very high toll from the first day (September 12, 1939) to the last (January 21, 1945). For Jews in this town, the Nazi occupation meant almost total extermination. In September 1939, the Jewish population of Kleczew numbered 746 (see Table 20).

According to municipal records dated November 14, 1945, 725 Jews from Kleczew were killed in 1939–1945. Several men survived concentration camps and extermination camps (Berek, Kuczynski, Kutnowski, Obarzanek, Pachciarki, and Prost).[130] Some Jews survived in the Soviet Union. Others blended in by using "Aryan" documents.

The Polish population of Kleczew also sustained losses, but on a smaller scale. Eighty-five people were killed in single or group executions, several hundred were taken to the Third Reich for forced labor, and another several hundred were displaced to the far ends of the General Government. German settlers arrived in the partly deserted town, e.g., 213 between October and December 1940.[131] According to other sources, 5,500 people were murdered in mass executions in the towns and villages of the Regierungsbezirk. Some 4,000 were sent to concentration camps, and approximately 300 of them died.[132] About 81,500 people were driven out and 55,000 were sent to the Third Reich for forced labor.[133]

4. WHAT ABOUT THE PERPETRATORS?

The Chełmno trials: After World War II, a series of war-crime trials of Chełmno extermination-camp personnel took place in Poland and Germany, spread out across almost twenty years. The first trial of former SS men—members of SS-Sonderkommando Kulmhof—was held in 1945 at the District Court in Łódź, Poland. The next four, held in Bonn, Germany, began in 1962 and concluded in 1965 in Cologne.

Several camp officials, gas-van operators, and SS guards were arraigned before the Łódź District Court on charges of committing war crimes and crimes against humanity in Chełmno between December 1941 and January 1945. The evidence against the accused, including testimonies by surviving witnesses, former prisoners, and mechanics attending to SS repair needs, was examined by Judge Władysław Bednarz. Three defendants were convicted and sentenced to death, including the deputy commandant of the camp, Oberscharführer Walter Piller; the gas-van operator Hauptscharführer Hermann Gielow, and Bruno Israel of the Order Police (Ordnungspolizei or Orpo). (The sentence of the last-mentioned was commuted to life in prison by Polish President Bolesław Bierut.) All three had been members of the SS Sonderkommando responsible for the extermination of Jews and non-Jews during the Holocaust in Poland.[134]

In 1962–1965, a dozen SS men from Kulmhof (Chełmno) were arraigned before a German court in Bonn and charged with the murder of 180,000 Jews in the camp. After three years of deliberations, the jury handed down sentences ranging from fifteen years' imprisonment (to Gustav Laaps, a gas-van operator, and Alois Häfele, leader of the SS Hauskommando in the camp) to thirteen months and two weeks. Six defendants were acquitted and released.

The first commandant of the Chełmno camp, SS Sturmbannführer Herbert Lange, was killed during the war on April 20, 1945 near Berlin. Hauptsturmführer Hans Bothmann, his successor, committed suicide in British custody in April 1946.[135]

Arthur Karl Greiser was arrested by the Americans in 1945. Extradited to Poland, he was tried for war crimes by the Polish government (before the Supreme National Tribunal), found guilty on all counts, and

54. Witnesses at the Chełmno trial in Bonn, Germany, in 1963. First on left, bottom row: Chełmno survivor Szymon Srebrnik (YVA, sig. 7452_12)

55. Arthur Greiser, Governor of the Wartheland (middle, with bandaged head), during his extradition to Poland (YVA, sig. 5318_212)

sentenced to death by hanging, civil death,[136] and confiscation of all property. In the early morning of July 21, 1946, he was transported from prison to the slope of Fort Winiary, where he was hanged[137] in the last public execution in Poland. The place of hanging may be symbolic, as it had been the German army's last point of resistance in the Battle of Poznań (1945).

Establishment and Operation of the First Extermination Camp | 371

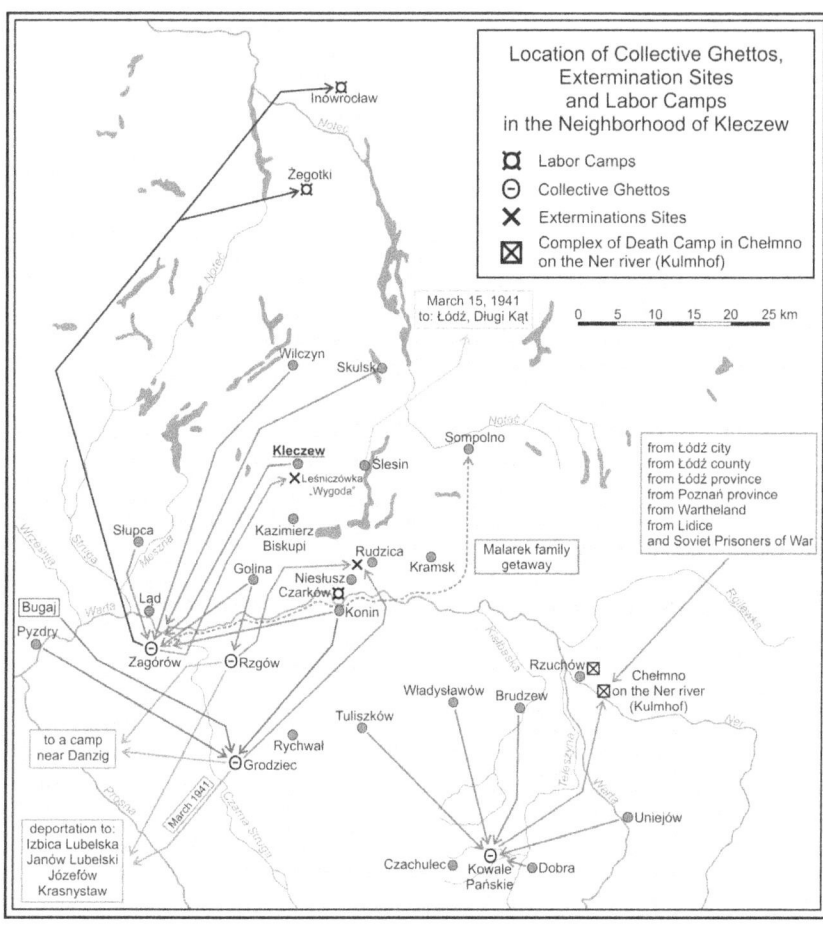

NOTES

1. J. Gulczyński, "Ośrodek zagłady w Chełmnie nad Nerem (przegląd i metodologia badań, aspekty muzealne)," in *Ośrodek zagłady*, 30.
2. See a paragraph of the speech in Document 28, Annex 1.
3. Y. Arad, *Bełżec, Sobibor, Treblinka: The Operation Reinhard Death Camps* (Bloomington, IN, 1987).
4. The term "T4" comes from the address Tiergartenstrasse 4 in Berlin, where the "euthanasia" program had its headquarters.
5. "Eksterminacja Żydów w latach 1941-1943 (Dokumenty Biura Propagandy i Informacji KG AK w zbiorach Biblioteki Uniwersytetu Warszawskiego)," *Biuletyn Żydowskiego Instytutu Historycznego w Warszawie* 2-3 (1992): 47 doc. 10 and 52 doc. 16.
6. Testimony Michał Podchlebnik, June 9, 1945, Koło, Nr akt III S. 13/45, in W. Bednarz, *Obóz straceń*, 1946, 39-40.

7   Ibid., 40.
8   *Eksterminacja Żydów w latach 1941-1943*, 51 doc. 15 and 55 doc. 18.
9   AŻIH, 301/314.
10 Testimony Bruno Israel, October 29, 1945, Łódź, in W. Bednarz, *Obóz straceń*, 69.
11 Ibid., 70.
12 Testimony Michał Podchlebnik, June 9, 1945, Koło, Nr akt III S. 13/45, in W. Bednarz, *Obóz straceń*, 44.
13 Ibid., 42.
14 Ibid.
15 Testimony Bruno Israel, October 29, 1945, Łódź, in W. Bednarz, *Obóz straceń*, 72. Bruno Israel was a gendarme who had been assigned to Sonderkommando Kulmhof. Despite his unusual name, materials collected by the judge Władysław Bednarz from the District Court in Łódź showed that he was of German origin and had signed the Volksliste. He belonged to the Evangelical Church.
16 Testimony Andrzej Miszczak, June 14, 1945, Chełmno, Nr akt III S. 13/45, ibid., 48-49.
17 W. Bednarz, "Chełmno," in *BGKBZNP* 1 (1946): 154-155.
18 Ibid.
19 Testimony Andrzej Miszczak, June 14, 1945, Chełmno, Nr akt III S. 13/45, in W. Bednarz, *Obóz straceń*, 52.
20 Ibid.
21 Testimony Rozalia Peham, June 27, 1945, Koło, in W. Bednarz, *Obóz straceń*, 58.
22 Ibid.
23 Testimony Bruno Israel, October 29, 1945, Łódź, ibid., 70.
24 Ibid., 74.
25 Testimony Michał Podchlebnik, June 9, 1945, Koło, Nr akt III S. 13/45, ibid., 41.
26 Testimony Bruno Israel, October 29, 1945, Łódź, in W. Bednarz, *Obóz straceń*, 70-71.
27 Testimony Michał Podchlebnik, June 9, 1945, Koło, Nr akt III S. 13/45, ibid., 41.
28 Ibid., 41-42.
29 Testimony Andrzej Miszczak, June 14, 1945, Chełmno, Nr akt III S. 13/45, ibid., 48.
30 For further description of the extermination process, see Jacob Grojanowski's detailed testimony in Document 29, Annex 1.
31 "Chełmno, in *BGKBZNP* 1 (1946): 153; Jerzy Lewiński, ed., *Proces Hansa Biebowa: Zagłada getta łódzkiego: Akta i stenogramy sądowe* (Warsaw, 1987), 228; "Zagłada chorych psychicznie," *BGKBZHP*. 3 (1947): 91-106.
32 *Proces Hansa Biebowa*, 228.
33 Ibid.
34 "Chełmno," 153.
35 Testimony Bruno Israel, October 29, 1945, Łódź, in W. Bednarz, *Obóz straceń*, 72.
36 Testimony Andrzej Miszczak, June 14, 1945, Chełmno, Nr akt III S. 13/45, ibid., 49.
37 Testimony Bruno Israel, October 29, 1945, Łódź, ibid., 68.
38 Testimony Rozalia Peham, June 27, 1945, Koło, ibid., 56.
39 Prinz Eugen—a division of the Waffen SS (SS combat troops).
40 Testimony Bruno Israel, October 29, 1945, Łódź, in W. Bednarz, *Obóz straceń*, 68.
41 Testimony Rozalia Peham, June 26, 1945, Koło, ibid., 55.
42 Ibid.
43 March 1943—letter Arthur Greiser to Himmler about retaining meritorious members of Special Kommando Lange at the death camp at Chełmno nad Nerem, in *Wybór źródeł do nauczania o zagładzie Żydów*, 236.

44 Testimony Rozalia Peham, June 27, 1945, Koło, in W. Bednarz, *Obóz straceń*, 58.
45 Testimony Bruno Israel, October 29, 1945, Łódź, ibid, 73.
46 Testimony Mordka vel Mieczysław Żurawski, July 31, 1945, Koło, ibid., 65.
47 Testimony Bruno Israel, October 29, 1945, Łódź, ibid., 73.
48 Testimony Andrzej Miszczak, June 14, 1945, Chełmno, Nr akt III S. 13/45, ibid., 52.
49 Testimony Rozalia Peham, June 27, 1945, Koło, ibid., 57.
50 Testimony Mordka vel Mieczysław Żurawski, July 31, 1945, Koło, ibid., 63.
51 Ibid.
52 Ibid., 64.
53 Ibid., 63.
54 *Proces Artura Greisera przed Najwyższym Trybunałem Narodowym* (Warsaw, 1946), 106.
55 "Chełmno," 160.
56 Testimony Bruno Israel, October 29, 1945, Łódź, in W. Bednarz, *Obóz straceń*, 72.
57 Ibid., 73.
58 Testimony Michał Podchlebnik, June 9, 1945, Koło, Nr akt III S. 13/45, ibid., 40.
59 Testimony Andrzej Miszczak, June 14, 1945, Chełmno, Nr akt III S. 13/45, ibid., 51.
60 January 21, 1942, Grabów ghetto. Letter Rabbi Jacob Szulmana to relatives in Warsaw ghetto about mass murder of Jews, in *Wybór źródeł do nauczania o zagładzie Żydów na okupowanych ziemiach polskich*, ed. A. Skibińska, R. Szuchta, and W. Młynarczyk (Warsaw, 2010), 226-227.
61 April 1942, Warsaw—the ghetto—Report of Hersh Wasser, Chełmno Events, addressed to Aleksander Kamiński and published in "Bulletin Oneg Shabbat" [excerpts], in *Wybór źródeł do nauczania o zagładzie,* 227-229.
62 Testimony Andrzej Miszczak, June 14, 1945, Chełmno, Nr akt III S. 13/45, in W. Bednarz, *Obóz straceń*, 50.
63 Ibid.
64 Ibid.
65 S. Krakowski, *Chełmno—A Small Village in Europe: The First Nazi Mass Extermination Camp* (Jerusalem, 2009), 51-57.
66 YVA, O.33/752, testimony Irena Libman, in S. Krakowski, *Chełmno: A Small Village in Europe*, 54-56.
67 "Gassman the driver told me that in Chełmno, apart from Jews, 5,000 Gypsies were killed." Testimony Rozalia Peham, June 27, 1945, Koło, in W. Bednarz, *Obóz straceń*, 57.
68 M. Budziarek, "Polacy, dzieci czeskie i jeńcy radzieccy zamordowani w Chełmnie nad Nerem," in *Ośrodek zagłady*, 69-72; A. Galiński, "Obóz dla Cyganów w Łodzi," *Biuletyn Okręgowej Komisji Badania Zbrodni Hitlerowskich w Łodzi—Instytut Pamięci Narodowej* 1 (1989): 47-57.
69 Testimony Rozalia Peham, June 27, 1945, Koło, in W. Bednarz, *Obóz straceń*, 57.
70 "Lidice," in *Encyclopedia of the Holocaust* (New York, 2006), 299-300; M. Budziarek, *Polacy, dzieci czeskie*, 69-72.
71 March 1943—letter Arthur Greiser to Himmler about retaining meritorious members of Special Kommando Lange at the death camp at Chełmno nad Nerem, in *Wybór źródeł do nauczania o zagładzie Żydów*, 236.
72 Ibid. For the full text of the letter, see Document 30, Annex 1.
73 Testimony Rozalia Peham, June 27, 1945, Koło, in W. Bednarz, *Obóz straceń*, 57.
74 Testimony Andrzej Miszczak, June 14, 1945, Chełmno, Nr akt III S. 13/45, in ibid., 49.

75 J.A. Młynarczyk, *Wpływ inicjatyw oddolnych Arthura Greisera*, 27; "Chełmno," 147-159.
76 Ibid., 161.
77 *Proces Artura Greisera*, 105.
78 Testimony Mordka vel Mieczysław Żurawski, July 31, 1945, Koło, in W. Bednarz, *Obóz straceń*, 61.
79 Testimony Bruno Israel, October 29, 1945, Łódź, in ibid., 70.
80 Ibid.
81 Testimony Andrzej Miszczak, June 14, 1945, Chełmno, Nr akt III S. 13/45, in ibid., 52.
82 Testimony Mordka vel Mieczysław Żurawski, July 31, 1945, Koło, in ibid., 62.
83 Testimony Andrzej Miszczak, June 14, 1945, Chełmno, Nr akt III S. 13/45, in ibid., 52.
84 *Proces Artura Greisera*, 105-106.
85 Testimony Bruno Israel, October 29, 1945, Łódź, in W. Bednarz, *Obóz straceń*, 74.
86 *Proces Artura Greisera*, 105-106.
87 *Chełmno*, 157.
88 Testimony Michał Podchlebnik, June 9, 1945, Koło, Nr akt III S. 13/45, in W. Bednarz, *Obóz straceń*, 42.
89 *Proces Artura Greisera*, 106.
90 Ibid.
91 "Chełmno," 156-157.
92 P. Klein, "Kulmhof/Chełmno," in *Der Ort des Terrors: Geschichte der nationalsozialistischen Konzentrantionslager*, Band 8, ed. Wolfgang Benz and Barbara Distel (Munich, 2008), 301.
93 Ibid., 310.
94 Ibid., 317.
95 S. Spector, "Aktion 1005: Effacing the Murder of Millions," in *Holocaust and Genocide Studies*, Vol. 5, No. 2, 158.
96 Ibid., 159.
97 Ibid. The detailed process of burning corpses is described in the chapter devoted to the Chełmno extermination center.
98 L. Weliczker, *Brygada śmierci (SK 1005): Pamiętnik* (Łódź, 1946).
99 S. Spector, "Aktion 1005," 170.
100 According to the testimony of the witness Lucjan Zalas (April 7, 1970), this unit was composed of soldiers.
101 The decision of suspending the proceedings of November 10, 1977, Okręgowa Komisja Badania Zbrodni Hitlerowskich w Poznaniu, YVA-TR.17/7 (OKP.III.Ds.19/68), 23-34.
102 Testimony Antoni Śliwiński, May 23, 1974, ibid., 29-31.
103 Testimony Piotr Zalas, November 10, 1945, ibid., 12-13.
104 Testimony Zdzisław Kazimierz Olejnik, April 19, 1974, ibid., 26-28.
105 Testimony Jan Zalas, February 3, 1969, ibid., 18-21.
106 Testimony Lucjan Zalas, April 7, 1970, ibid., 22-24.
107 Testimony Stanisław Majewski, March 20, 1969, ibid., 9.
108 Testimony Piotr Zalas, November 10, 1945, ibid., 12-13.
109 Testimony Lucjan Zalas, April 7, 1970, ibid., 22-24.
110 Testimony Antoni Śliwiński, May 23, 1974, ibid., 29-31.
111 Ibid.

112 Testimony Zdzisław Kazimierz Olejnik, April 19, 1974, YVA-TR.17/2 (OKP.III. Ds.21/68), 26-28.
113 Testimony Jan Zalas, February 3, 1969, ibid., 18-21.
114 Testimony Stanisław Majewski of March 20, 1969, ibid., 9.
115 Testimony Lucjan Zalas, April 7, 1970, ibid., 22-24.
116 Testimony Antoni Śliwiński, May 23, 1974, ibid., 29-31.
117 Testimony Lucjan Zalas, April 7, 1970, ibid., 22-24.
118 Ibid.
119 Testimony Piotr Zalas of November 10, 1945, YVA-TR.17/2 (OKP.III.Ds.21/68), 12-13.
120 Testimony Szczepan Osiński of March 20, 1969, ibid., 4.
121 Demographic balance for the northern part of the former Inowrocław Regierungsbezirk (Reichsgau Wartheland Province) and south-eastern part of the Bydgoszcz Regierunsbezirk (province of Reichsgau Danzig-West Prussia) presented by T. Kawski, "Żydzi z Kujaw, ziemi dobrzyńskiej oraz Bydgoszczy ocaleni z Shoah. Przyczynek do poznania struktury społeczno-zawodowej, zmian osadniczych oraz migracji ludności żydowskiej w Polsce po drugiej wojnie światowej," in *Wrzesień 1939 roku i jego konsekwencje dla ziem zachodnich i północnych Drugiej Rzeczypospolitej*, ed. R. Sudziński and W. Jastrzębski (Toruń-Bydgoszcz, 2001), 365-392.
122 S. Waszak, *Bilans*, 506.
123 D. Dąbrowska, *Zagłada*, 122. The calculations are based on reports of Jews who survived and information from national councils.
124 More in T. Kawski, *Gminy*, passim; T. Kawski, M. Opioła, *Gminy*, passim.
125 R. Grzonkowski, *Kleczew*, 195. Tadeusz Kroner, a Jewish doctor from Kleczew, was murdered by NKVD and died in Katyń.
126 For a detailed example, see the story of the Kroner family in Annex 2.
127 Instytut Pamięci Narodowej w Warszawie (Institute of National Remembrance in Warsaw, hereinafter: IPN-W), Reichsstatthalter im Wartegau 1939-1945, (hereinafter: RW), 120, cards 7-9, 39, 55.
128 More in L. Dobroszycki, ed., *The Chronicle of the Łódź Ghetto 1941-1945* (New Haven-London, 1984).
129 IPN-W, RW, 120, card 7-9, 75; AŻIH, 301/375, card 4; Cz. Łuczak, *Dzień po dniu w okupowanej Wielkopolsce i Ziemi Łódzkiej (Kraj Warty). Kalendarium wydarzeń 1939-1945* (Poznań, 1993), 116, 136-137; T. Kawski, *Kujawsko-dobrzyńscy*., 247.
130 R. Grzonkowski, "Kleczew w okresie drugiej wojny światowej," in *Dzieje Kleczewa*, ed. J. Stępien (Poznań-Konin, 1995), 236-242.
131 Ibid. Some 1,345 people were taken away and displaced during the war; about 600 people of them were taken to the Third Reich for forced labor. The first transport of this kind, on December 20, 1939, included 120 Poles; the next, on March 25, 1940, about 150, then another 100 were taken on April 3, 1941, and 570 in May and July.
132 S. Waszak, "Bilans walki narodowościowej rządów Greisera," *Przegląd Zachodni*, (1946): 490-491.
133 Z. Waszkiewicz, "Regencja inowrocławska podczas okupacji hitlerowskiej w historiografii polskiej," *Ziemia Kujawska* V (1978): 255-257, 268. The waves of displacement lasted from December 1939 to January 1941 and from January 1942 to November 1944. Their numbers: December 17, 1939—20,133; February 10—March

3, 1940—11,912; from March to January 1941—19,675; in January 1942—19,231; from January to November 1944—10,512.
134 P. Montague, *Chełmno and the Holocaust: The History of Hitler's First Death Camp* (Chapel Hill, NC, 2012). "The Gas Vans" (Appendix I), 206–209.
135 Ibid.
136 A term that refers to the loss of civil rights by a person due to a conviction or an act by a national government.
137 C. Epstein, *Model Nazi: Arthur Greiser and the Occupation of Western Poland*, 334-335.

PART Four

EPILOGUE: THE POSTWAR PERIOD

8 Kleczew after the War

Soviet forces seized Kleczew on January 21, 1945. Although the town had not been destroyed during the war, it was in a state of chaos and badly depopulated.

Few Jewish survivors returned to Kleczew after the war to witness the scale of the destruction. Most never came back; they rebuilt their homes in various countries, mainly Israel, France, the United States, and Canada.

The descendants of the Jews of Kleczew are spread in many countries today. They originate in two groups: those who left Kleczew before World War II and those who stayed when the war began but escaped later on. This chapter tells the stories of individuals who returned to Kleczew after the war. Two examples of families, one in each of the aforementioned categories, are discussed at length in Annex 2. The Rachwalski (Traube) family is an example of the first type, descendants of people who left Kleczew before the war, leaving their families behind. The Kroner family is an example of those who left Kleczew during the war and survived. One branch of the Rachwalski family (the Marks family) left for the United States; another branch (the Traubes) emigrated to British-ruled Palestine.

56. Thresa (TRANE) GLUCKER (*née* Rachwalski), daughter of Mordechai Rachwalski and Frymet Sztyler and sister of Tobiasz Rachwalski. She left Europe with her husband Isaak (Ike) Glucker (Glazgow) from Hamburg, Oct. 27, 1888, on the SS *Moravia*, and arrived in New York. She died on August 25, 1933 in Milwaukee, Wisconsin, U.S. (Marks private collection)

57. Three sons of Tobiasz Rachwalski from Kleczew, who emigrated to the U.S. in the early 20th century and changed their surname to Marks.
Standing (left to right): Morton, Alfred Mayer, and Alfred's wife, Helen
(Marks private collection)

Kleczew after the War | 381

58. Farewell party at Tobiasz Rachwalski's house for Tobiasz' daughter (Fojgel Traube), her husband, and their two daughters, who are about to leave for Palestine, July 1939
Seated in middle: Tobiasz Rachwalski.
Standing (right to left): Chaim (Tobiasz's son), Shlomo (Tobiasz's son), Fojgel Traube (née Rachwalski, Tobiasz' daughter), Rachel Pacanowski (Tobiasz's daughter), Frymet (Tobiasz's daughter)
Seated (right to left): Izaak Traube (Fojgle's husband), Pacanowski (Rachel's husband), Frymet and Hanna (daughters of Fojgel and Yzaak), Tobiasz Rachwalski, Hela Pacanowski (Rachel's daughter), Sarah (Tobiasz's wife), and an old lady adopted by Tobiasz and Sarah
(Horev private collection)

59. Left: Fojgel (Tzipora) Traube née Rachwalski with her daughters Fruma (Frymet) and Hannah, January 23, 1939, five months before they left to Palestine
(Horev private collection)

60. Right: Fruma and Hannah Traube with their uncle, Shlomo Rachwalski (Fojgel's brother), who perished in the Holocaust
(Horev private collection)

61. Two sisters: Fruma (Frymet) Horev née Traube (right) and Hannah Greenfeld (née Traube), 2013. Fruma was born in Kleczew and Hanna in Kalisz. They are daughters of Izaak Traube and Fojgle (née Rachwalski) and granddaughters of Tobiasz and Sara Rachwalski from Kleczew. Both Fruma and Hanna lived in Kleczew until July 1939. (Horev private collection) (2013, Israel)

Note: Presumably, Fruma is the last living Jewish person who was born in Kleczew before the war.

As mentioned, a few members the Kroner family managed to escape to the east during the war and survived.

Information about and descriptions of these families and several others are presented in Annex 2 as examples of people who emigrated several years before the war started, those who escaped during the war,

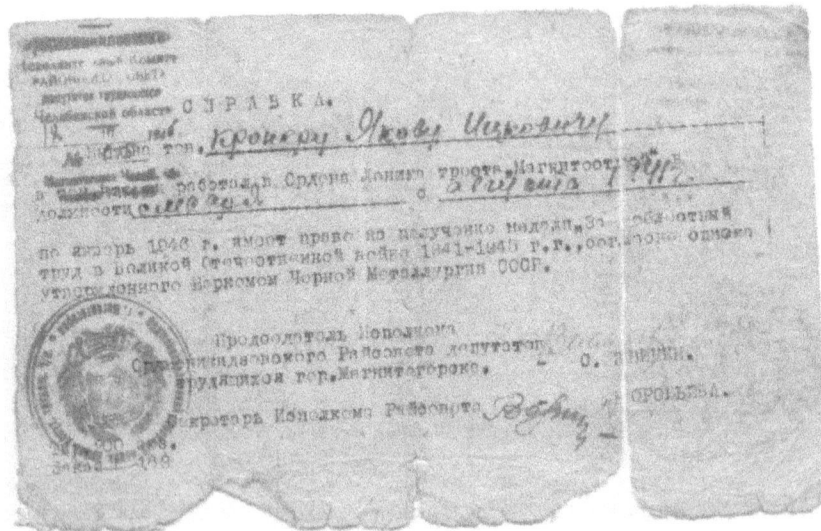

62. Jakub Itzkovich Kroner. Soviet certificate of award for good work during the "Great Fatherland War," 1941–1945 (Kroner private collection)

63. Jakub Kroner: membership card in the Professional Association of Miners, Wałbrzych branch, 1946. (Kroner private collection)

64. Jakub Kroner: membership card in Po'alei Tsiyyon-Ha-Shomer ha-Tza'ir in Poland (Kroner private collection)

and those who got out at the last minute. All left relatives behind in Kleczew; the latter were exterminated.

The Yad Vashem Archives in Jerusalem contain more than 300 names of former residents of Kleczew who could not escape the tragic end and perished in the Holocaust. Table M in Annex 3 presents this full list. Presumably many other victims were left out of the database due to lack of relatives and friends who could testify about them and fill in the requisite forms.

1. POSTWAR KLECZEW

After the war, de-capitalization of assets occurred and general confusion reigned, possibly aggravated by the presence of the Red Army. Kleczew underwent a major nationality change: once the Germans were displaced or escaped, it became nationally homogeneous. The infrastructure was rebuilt despite numerous obstacles. Construction of a housing estate on Stodólna Street, begun by the Germans, continued. A power plant was built. By 1951, the town had a dairy, an engine factory, a municipal cooperative called Samopomoc Chłopska (Farmers' Self-Help), a gardening enterprise, a bakery, six private shops, and a shoemakers' cooperative. Public buildings were adapted for use as a library, a school, and a Red Cross hospital that soon evolved into a medical center. The character of the town, however, remained agricultural. In 1951, there were ninety-six farms within the town limits.¹ This situation persisted until the 1970s. Objective factors inherited from previous centuries were inimical to local development.

Until 1975, Kleczew was located on the periphery of Poznań Province. There was no industry. Its population continued to decrease until the second half of the 1970s—from an estimated 2,430 in 1958 to 2,228 in 1965, 2,138 in 1970, and 2,097 in 1975. Minor gains were seen after that point, with 2,113 people residing there in 1978. Many residents found employment in nearby localities, mainly Konin. Consequently, the structure of employment changed. In 1970, 81.4% of occupationally active residents worked outside the agricultural sector and 18.6% made a living at farming. The industrialization of Konin County brought a new quality of life. Brown coal deposits in the region triggered industrial development in electrical power, mining, and metallurgical engineering. Coal extraction at the Jóźwin strip mine southeast of Kleczew began in 1971. The construction of this enterprise began in 1968; as the pits expanded, the town was so gravely endangered that its dissolution was considered at one point. Only in 1977, when the headquarters of the Konin Brown Coal Mine was transferred to Kleczew, was that idea abandoned. The location of a powerful company in a small town strongly influenced local life, gradually inducing urbanization and the development of infrastructure.

The employment structure began to change. Farming became less and less significant. Employment in the nationalized economic sector grew, mainly in manufacturing, transport, communication, trade, municipal economy, education, and administration. Employment in these sectors soared from 325 in 1973 to 1,787 in 1977. Concurrently, after considerable growth in the first half of the 1970s, the number of sales and service establishments diminished. In 1972, there were fifty-two such establishments—eight of them nationalized (state-owned or cooperative)—and by 1977 their number had decreased to nineteen, seven of them nationalized. In the 1980s, public institutions such as a primary school, a gymnasium, and a stadium were established. A residential high school, a new clinic, a cinema, and a cultural center were founded as well.² The old medical-center building was adapted to accommodate a kindergarten. The population grew. Kleczew had 3,234 residents in 1991, 3,470 in 1994, and 3,800 in 2004. The town's connections with Konin were sustained when it was administratively incorporated into Konin Province. Such was its status in 1975–1999. Beginning in 2000, Kleczew found itself again on the periphery of Greater Poland Province, within the boundaries of Konin County.

2. SURVIVORS AND DESCENDANTS OF KLECZEW'S JEWS

What traces remain of 300 years of Jewish history in Kleczew? Few Jews returned after the war, and if they did, it was only for a short time. The situation was similar in nearby localities.

According to several testimonies, only about twenty Jews who remained in Kleczew at the beginning of the war survived, all having gone through concentration camps.[3] One testimony—Bert Gembicki's early testimony—sets the figure at around fifteen, all having endured labor and concentration camps.[4] With one exception—Malron (Malarek)—all survivors from Kleczew who had been in Zagórów were removed from Zagórów before the mass murder in the forest of Kazimierz Biskupi. All of those who survived the forced-labor camp in Inowrocław, where they had been beaten and persecuted, were sent to different concentration camps in Germany. Although debilitated, several survived and were liberated at the end of the war in 1945.[5]

One of the survivors, Michel Prost, was in Buchenwald at the end of the war, working at an airplane factory in Magdeburg. Prost and others were first evacuated to the Elbe River and then to the north—to Rostock and Schwerin. It was a death march, guarded by *Volksturm*. There was a forest not far away. As they slept unguarded, they suddenly heard singing and saw a flag—a Soviet flag—and Russian soldiers. Poles, Jews, and Russians intermingled, asking each other, "Who are you? Where are you from?" Michel Prost continued: "Then we were free. We went to the village and searched for food. We took a sack of peas, but we couldn't cook them. Then, on May 8, 1945, a Russian officer told us that an armistice had been signed." In fact, it was Germany's capitulation.[6] Prost hoped that his brother had also survived and wanted to search for him. "If I survived, maybe he did, too," he thought. He and several other survivors approached the Soviets and told them they wished to go to Poland. For several days, they vacillated about what to do and where to go; they had no idea what had happened to the others. Then they headed toward the Oder River in the direction of Frankfurt am Oder. They proceeded to Frankfurt by foot or a horse cart that they had procured in one of the villages. At the Oder, Soviet soldiers appropriated their horses. After crossing the river on a pontoon bridge and entering Poland, the group of survivors continued by train. Some went to Poznań and other places. Michel Prost went alone to Kleczew. There he met one person who had been with him in a labor camp.[7]

Several additional Jews managed to return to Kleczew:

> After a few days, one Jew came and then three brothers arrived. The brothers were in three different camps and they met in Dachau. Then there were seven Jews from the camps. There were no survivors from Zagórów. Perhaps, all together, 15 Jews flocked to Kleczew.[8]

The situation in other towns was no different. After the war, only solitary survivors of once-flourishing communities returned. One of them recalled, "From our town [Grodziec] only three Jews survived; all of them had gone through concentration camps."[9] Rychwał was not much better: "Ten Jews [men] from the town survived: six who had been in concentration camps and four who were saved in other ways."[10]

There was no Jewish cemetery in Kleczew at this time. Everything had been planted over; the graveyard had become a football field. The synagogue had been turned into a cinema. The returning Jews spent a month or two there, though they felt that their lives could not be rebuilt in the town. Some of Prost's Polish friends who had been in the army turned up. Anyone who had had more than two years of elementary schooling had been liquidated by the Germans. The returnees had hoped to practice their occupations but found only agricultural villages around. There were no opportunities, no solutions. It was a poor country, a country in ruins.[11]

Eugenia Cyns, in the same area after the war, had the same impression of destruction and impoverishment:

There used to be many Jews in Pyzdry. Now, you can count the survivors on one hand. Before the war, it had been a vibrant city—there was a school. After the war, what had once been a Jewish town became a dead village. Currently, Polish provincial towns are not industrialized; there is no trade like there was before. There is no life in [the towns]. Numerically [demographically], the towns have not yet come back into balance.[12] ... When I was in those parts after the war, I could tell how impoverished these towns had become; they had completely lost their life and, in general, present a completely different face than I remember. All these [people] died.[13]

Some decided to go back to Germany and obtained *laissez passers* for this purpose. The best laissez passer, however, was cash or a half-liter of vodka. For the latter, Michel Prost noted, "A Russian soldier will open the gates of paradise for you."[14] He and his companions crossed the Soviet occupation zone and entered the American zone. American soldiers encountering them were astounded to find that they had come from Poland.

Most Jews who remained in Germany, Prost said, did not return to Poland. At a loss for what to do or where to go in western Germany, they went to the displaced person's (DP) camp in Feldafing, near Munich. Later, Prost went to Strasbourg and remained there for the rest of his life.[15]

Another survivor from Kleczew, Bert Gembicki, ended the war in a satellite camp of Buchenwald. He had been wounded; he had lost a finger and wore a bandage over the stump. Typhus had broken out. At the very end, the survivors had been given nothing to eat for three or four days. Gembicki had some bread that he tried to hide in a bag. He tied the bag to his leg with a piece of rope but found the bread gone the next morning.[16] In the last days, an attempt to kill all the Jews in the camp was made, but Gembicki survived. American soldiers liberated Buchenwald on April 11, 1945. After being emancipated, Gembicki returned to Buchenwald, met there his best friend from before the war, Szaye Pachciarski,[17] and went on to Weimar. When the Soviets reached Weimar, they told Gembicki to go home. "But where is my home? I have no home," he told himself. He then went to the American occupation zone, crossing the frontier, entered a little village, and proceeded to Ansbach.[18] He obtained an apartment from a German *Wohnungsamt* (housing office). Some time later, he emigrated to the United States.[19]

One of the factors that prompted Jews to return to their prewar habitats was an eagerness to reunite with someone from the past or to visit family members' graves. Eugenia Cyns and her brother returned to the area of Kleczew, Zagórów, and Ląd to find the grave of their father, who had died before the war. Here are their impressions of what was left:

> My brother went [to the Zagórów cemetery] after the war. At the cemetery in Zagórów was my father's gravestone. There was no trace of the cemetery. All that stood, near the cemetery gate, was Ajzyk Nelken's black marble gravestone . Apparently nobody tried to steal it. It was a big, beautiful headstone.[20] … The Jewish cemeteries of Zagórów, Kleczew, and Pyzdry were destroyed. Only the marble monument of Ajzyk Nelken was left in Zagórów after the war. Probably it was not noticed during the destruction of the cemetery, or someone deliberately left it. The cemetery in Pyzdry was [built] in sand. After the destruction of the cemetery, tombstones were removed, trees and shrubs cut, and the sandhills became mobile. When I arrived I saw the horrible sight. Human bones were scattered on the surface of the sands of which Jewish cemeteries had once been composed.

When she emigrated to Israel, Eugenia brought a bag of the sand with her.[21]

One way Kleczew's Jewish survivors could be traced was by scouring the National Archives in Konin for Jewish applications to the Kleczew Municipal Court. This was done to trace family members or their proxies who had asked the court for a legal statement declaring a person's death (e.g., during the war), on the basis of which a death certificate from the registry office could be requested.[22] This method was effective in settling many formal issues related to property (houses, shops, businesses, plots, etc.) left behind by people who had died or disappeared during the war.

In some cases, questions of pension or similar government or civilian arrangements had to be resolved.[23]

A unique story is that of Hannah Zakrzewska *née* Sokaszewska (b. 1910 in Kleczew, d. 1993). In December 1939, she married a non-Jewish Polish resident and, with the help of a German friend, obtained false documents. Hiding in a cellar for some time, she saw the deportation of Jews through a keyhole. Then, one of her husband's relatives denounced her. Fortunately, she managed to avoid prison and death, moved away from Kleczew, and returned with her husband after the war.[24] Theo Richmond tells her story in his book *Konin: A Quest*, published in 1995. The following excerpt describes his meeting with Hanna:

> A widow named Hannah was the sole Jewish inhabitant left in the little town of Kleczew, near Konin. Maybe the place was less torpid when the Jews lived here in considerable numbers. Mike Jacobs of Dallas had found Hannah on his last visit to the area and given me her address. We waited a long time before she appeared at the door, barefooted, a short, rotund woman with dark eyes and olive skin. She patted her dyed black hair into place while Izzy told her who we were. Hannah led us into her room, somber with dark furniture and a brown tiled stove. Seeing her unmade bed, I realized we had disturbed her afternoon nap. Above the bed were two religious pictures, one of Jesus bathed in a heavenly beam of light, the other of the Holy Virgin. Hannah put on her shoes and glasses and smoothed her dress. I gave her a color snapshot that Mike Jacobs's wife, Ginger, had asked me to give her. It was a photograph she had taken of Hannah standing next to her daughter's grave in Kleczew. Hannah looked at it silently for a while and then gave each of us an emotional kiss.
>
> Hannah was born into a Yiddish-speaking family in Kleczew in 1910. She had forgotten all her Yiddish, she said, and could speak only Polish. In December 1939 she married a local gentile, and soon after that a helpful German gave her false papers. She hid for a time in a cellar in Kleczew. One day, through a keyhole, she saw the Germans rounding up the Jews for deportation.

Later, one of her husband's relatives informed on her, but she managed to avoid arrest and left Kleczew.

She and her husband returned after the war. Parcels from her relatives in America helped them get by. The dress she was wearing today was made from material sent by an uncle in New York. She could have joined him in America but for one thing that prevented her ever leaving Kleczew: "How could I leave my daughter's grave behind?" She showed us a portrait of the young woman who had been her only child. From the clues offered, I guessed that she had died of cancer. Five weeks after her [daughter's] death, Hannah's husband hanged himself. Since then she had lived here on her own, coping with heart trouble but managing to look after herself. She was in touch with Teresa in Konin, whose mother, Nadzia, had been a friend.

In 1948, with the help of two non-Jews, one of them a stonemason, Hannah erected a few simple tombstones in the nearby forest at Kazimierz in memory of the Jews buried there in mass graves. It took more than thirty years before the local authorities got around to erecting an official memorial.

In 1954 she experienced "a period of hatred" when a group of local youngsters in their early twenties repeatedly scrawled "Dirty Jew" on her windows. They were caught and given heavy jail sentences, and since then she has been left in peace. The religious pictures above her bed were a present from a friend. Her daughter had been baptized and brought up in the Catholic faith. She seemed unwilling to discuss this or to describe her own feelings about being Jewish: "I am nearer death than life, so this is not the time for talking about such things and worrying about such things." I could pursue the subject no further.

We had tea in the dim, cool room, its thick walls protecting us from the sweltering heat outside. Later, Hannah took us on a brief tour to show us all that was left of Jewish Kleczew: the rabbi's house, the site of the synagogue (now a cinema), and a cement shack that was once the *mikve*. A drunk reaching out with one hand for a nonexistent wall was the only sign of human life as we made our way back to the car, where Feliks was fast asleep, hunched over the wheel. Hannah, reluctant to let us go, took a deep breath and released a drawn-out Jewish sigh: "*Oy vey!*" she said, speaking Yiddish for the first time. "*Dos lebn iz shver*"—Life is hard....²⁵

Hannah Zakrzewska (née Sokaszewska) died a year later [in 1993] in Kleczew and was buried near her daughter in the Catholic cemetery.²⁶

Several Jewish families or individual Jews, their number ranging from fewer than ten to several dozen according to different estimates, settled temporarily in nearby villages such as Tuliszków, Izbica Kujawska, and Sompolno.²⁷ In terms of organization, they were subject to the authority of district and local branches of the Central Committee of Jews in Poland (*Centralny Komitet Żydów Polskich*—CKŻP). Jews living in towns and settlements of Eastern Greater Poland were subordinated to the CKŻP district committees (*Komitet Okręgowy*—KO) in Włocławek and Kalisz. For some time, localities in Koło County were subject to the Włocławek KO; those in other counties were under the jurisdiction of the KO in Kalisz.²⁸ By the end of the 1940s, however, most Jews who had settled in these towns and settlements had left. They did so for various reasons—emotional or political factors, on economic grounds, or due to assaults and murders. Several groups that opposed the communist authorities operated in the counties of eastern Greater Poland and in Kuyavia. Other groups, under the mask of political activity, engaged in criminality. Often soldiers or militiamen committed criminal offenses against Polish and Jewish civilians. The latter seemed to be easy targets. For example, three Jews were murdered in Tuliszków and two in Osięciny, and many assaults were reported in Kutno, Koło, Konin, Inowrocław, and Nieszawa. Members of the offending groups were gradually arrested and severely punished; the death penalty was used in some cases.²⁹

In subsequent decades, the Jewish centers nearest to Kleczew were in Bydgoszcz, Łódź, and Włocławek. In 1961, their populations were seventy, 3,300, and 108, respectively.³⁰ In several cases, Jews who had settled in Poland made efforts to commemorate places of extermination and collect documentation on the extermination of the greatest part of their people. In 1948, with the aid of two Polish stonemasons, Hannah Zakrzewska erected a monument in the woods near Kazimierz Biskupi to commemorate the Jews who had been murdered there during the war. The inscription on the monument reads:[31]

> Here is the grave of innocent Jewish victims from Konin County, murdered by Nazi assassins in the years 1941–1944.

A photograph in the Yad Vashem Archives shows a group of survivors around a monument in the forest between Kleczew and Kazimierz Biskupi after the war—presumably one of those erected by Hannah Zakrzewska.

65. Old monument at one of the mass graves in the forest between Kleczew and Kazimierz Biskupi: "Grave of innocent Jewish victims from Konin District, murdered by Hitler's executioners in 1941–1944"

66. Kleczew, Poland, after the war: group photograph at the site where Jews were murdered. In the photograph are two children of victims who were murdered there (YVA, sig. 2071)

Members of the Jewish Historical Committee (*Żydowska Komisja Historyczna*), mainly from Włocławek and Łódź, acted to commemorate the mass extermination sites in Chełmno on the Nerem.[32] It took many years for the authorities to memorialize places of the extermination of Jews. In Kazimierz Biskupi, monuments were unveiled thirty years after the fact. Importantly, broken Jewish headstones have been found in the forest even in recent years, for unknown reasons.[33]

The case of Chełmno on the Nerem was similar. A monument was not unveiled there until 1964. Sometimes, however, the authorities took more conspicuous action. In Konin, they renovated the synagogue and the study hall adjacent to it and erected monuments in the Jewish cemetery and at the site of the forced labor camp for Jews. After the demise of communism, local authorities and other organizations started to show more concern about remembering the Jewish residents of their towns and villages. Attention began to be paid to ruined Jewish cemeteries, memorial plaques were installed, and cairns (memorial piles of stones) were erected. Of the Jewish cemetery of Kleczew, however, nothing remains. Long ago, as mentioned, it became a football pitch.

67-69. Krężel forest, near Kleczew: three Monuments commemorating the victims (2009) (photo: T. Kawski)

70-71. Jewish headstones, found in Krężel forest near Kleczew (2009) (photo: T. Kawski)

72. Site of the former Jewish cemetery in Kleczew, currently a football stadium: main entrance (2009) (photo: A. Głowacka)

73. Site of the former Jewish cemetery in Kleczew, currently a football stadium (2009) (photo: A. Głowacka)

Several physical traces of Jewish culture in Kleczew have survived. A commemorative plaque was installed in the façade of Kleczew town hall. During the war, the Germans opened municipal baths in a Jewish-owned building; they were used for over ten years. The town stable was also situated in a Jewish-owned building. The synagogue was transformed first into an auditorium, where traveling theater troupes performed, and then into the aforementioned cinema, which still exists. As the above quotation indicates, the rabbi's house survives, as does a concrete building that used to house a ritual bath. Many homes once owned by Kleczew Jews have been preserved. In 1948, the city market expanded into adjacent gardens that had belonged to two local Jews, Pacanowski and Grünfeld.[34]

The most recent symbolic event connected with the commemoration of the Jews of Kleczew took place in 2008: a special award was granted by the Prime Minister to students at the complex of secondary schools in Kleczew for participating in the seventh historical competition for secondary-school students, titled "History and Culture of Polish Jews," organized by the Shalom Foundation.[35]

74. Former synagogue in Kleczew (main entrance), currently a cinema (2009)
(photo: A. Głowacka)

3. A FINAL REMARK

Jewish life in Kleczew and neighboring towns that had smaller or larger Jewish communities no longer exists. Instead, the Polish population lives on and, in some cases, tries to discover its connections with the Jewish past, honor the memory of the former Jewish communities, and commemorate their extermination in the Holocaust. They have become the guardians of a memory, and we hope they will find followers so that the memory will be passed down and preserved. However, there are many descendants of the Kleczew Jewish community around the world who maintain their private or family memories. Ultimately, there are researchers, who dedicate their time and effort to the discovery and description of what happened during the Holocaust in Kleczew, Zagórów, Konin, Chełmno, the Warthegau, and elsewhere.

Ostensibly, this book has presented and analyzed developments and events through the prism of the Kleczew Jewish community from its inception, through its development into a vibrant community that was an essential part of the town of Kleczew, to its total destruction. In practice, the book has not limited its observation to the fate of a single community; instead, it has described and analyzed events that occurred during the war in this community and others in Inowrocław Regierungsbezirke and the Warthegau as a whole. The events in this area may be considered preliminary steps to what subsequently evolved into the planned industry of mass extermination in Poland and other countries in Europe. Nevertheless, we hope that this book will not only deepen what is known about what happened before and during the Holocaust in the Warthegau and in Inowrocław Regierungsbezirke, but will also safeguard the memory of the Jewish community that once lived in Kleczew.

NOTES

1   J. Stępień, "Od Polski Ludowej do III Rzeczypospolitej," in *Dzieje Kleczewa*, 274-275.
2   More in J. Stępień, *Od Polski Ludowej do III Rzeczypospolitej*, 261-321.
3   YVA-M-1-Q/176, testimony Dawid Rygiel, February 26, 1948, Ansbach, 2-4.
4   YVA-M-1-Q/177, testimony Bert Gembicki, May 6, 1948, Ansbach, 2-5.
5   Ibid.

6   YVA, O.93/24710, video testimony Michel (Mendel) Prost, b. October 1, 1920, in Kleczew, VT-3, 1:00-3:00.
7   Ibid., VT-3, 3:00-7:00.
8   Ibid., VT-3.
9   YVS, M.1.Q/138, testimony Leon Brener, 1-4.
10   YVS, M.1.Q/387, testimony Leybush Aaron.
11   YVA, O.93/24710, video testimony Michel (Mendel) Prost, b. October 1, 1920, in Kleczew, VT-3, 11:00-13:00.
12   YVA-O.3/3406, testimony Eugenia Friedlender-Cyns, June 26, 1969, 7.
13   Ibid., p. 21.
14   YVA, O.93/24710, video testimony Michel (Mendel) Prost, b. October 1, 1920, in Kleczew, VT-3.
15   Ibid., VT-3, 11:00-13:00.
16   YVA, O.93/24854, video testimony Bert (Baruch) Gembicki, b. October 15, 1916, in Kleczew, VT-5.
17   Ibid.
18   YVA-M-1-Q/177, testimony Bert Gembicki, May 6, 1948, Ansbach, 2-5.
19   YVA, O.93/24854, video testimony Bert (Baruch) Gembicki, b. October 15, 1916, in Kleczew, VT-5.
20   YVA-O.3/3406, testimony Eugenia Friedlender-Cyns, June 26, 1969, 22.
21   Ibid., 7.
22   As an example, a photocopy of such a decision by the Kleczew Municipal Court is presented in Document 31, Annex 1.
23   Data on cases submitted to the Kleczew Municipal Court, collected from Konin, are presented in Annex 2.
24   T. Richmond, *Uporczywe echo*, 473-475.
25   T. Richmond, *Konin: One Man's Quest for a Vanished Jewish Community* (New York, 1995), 471-473.xxx
26   Ibid., 473.
27   AŻIH, Central Committee of Jews in Poland, (hereinafter: CKŻP), Organization Department, classification no. 19, 106, 116; AŻIH, CKŻP, Department of Records and Statistics, classification no. 569, 571; T. Richmond, *Uporczywe*, 259. In Konin, for example, 46 Jews returned after the war, in Kolo 22; in Izbica-Kujawska 22–25; in Krośniewice 21; and in Sompolno 10.
28   Over 2,200 Jews settled in Kalisz after the war and approximately 800 did so in Włocławek. A. Pakentreger, "Statystyka Żydów m. Kalisza, ocalałych po II wojnie światowej," *Biuletyn Żydowskiego Instytutu Historycznego* (1974): 91; T. Kawski, "Mniejszość żydowska w województwie pomorskim (bydgoskim) w latach 1945-1956," in *Kujawy i Pomorze w latach 1945-1956. Od zakończenia okupacji niemieckiej do przełomu październikowego*, ed. W. Jastrzębski and M. Krajewski (Włocławek, 2001), 214 table 2.
29   State Archive in Płock, Kutno Branch, Kutno County Office 1945-1950, classification no. 24, *Sprawozdania sytuacyjne z lat 1945-1947*; APB, Pomerania Province Office in Bydgoszcz 1945-1950, classification no. 575, *Sprawozdanie sytuacyjne z powiatu włocławskiego za luty 1946*; T. Richmond, *Uporczywe*, p. 269; Z. Biegański, *Sądownictwo i skazani na śmierć z przyczyn politycznych w województwie pomorskim (bydgoskim) 1945-1956* (Bydgoszcz, 2003), passim.

30 A. Stankowski, "Nowe spojrzenie na statystyki dotyczące emigracji Żydów z Polski po 1944 roku," in G. Berent, A. Grabski, and A. Stankowski, *Studia z historii Żydów w Polsce po 1945 r.* (Warsaw, 2000), 134 table 14.
31 T. Richmond, *Uporczywe echo*, 473-475, 485-486.
32 AŻIH, CKŻP, Organization Department, classification no. 60. *Protokół posiedzenia OKŻ we Włocławku z 22 IV 1947.*
33 T. Richmond, *Uporczywe echo*, 473-475.
34 APKonin, Konin County in Konin 1945-1950, classification no. 271. *Lustracja Kleczewa z lipca 1946*; T. Richmond, *Uporczywe echo*, p. 473-475; J. Stępień, *Od Polski Ludowej*, 275.
35 http://www.kadysz.pl/articles.php?miId=259&lang=pl (accessed on July 10, 2009).

ANNEXES

Annex: 1
Documents, Letters, and Testimonies

List of documents, Letters, and Testimonies
1. Page of draft register from cities and towns of Greater Poland, Pyzdry, 1579
2. Excerpt from privilege granted to the Jews of Kleczew on June 21, 1776, by the owner of the town, Władysław Gurowski of Gurowo
3. Kleczew synagogue treasury register, 1851-1853, title page
4. Warsaw Guberniya Government Commission for Internal and Religious Affairs report on construction of Kleczew synagogue, June 24, 1853
5. Proposal from synagogue inspection in Kleczew to accept Kleczew synagogue construction project, filed with Warsaw Guberniya Government Commission for Internal and Religious Affairs, February 23, 1854
6. Kleczew synagogue plans, 1854 (Projections 1-4)
7. Excerpt of Hitler's speech, January 30, 1939
8. Attack on Jews of Włocławek after the onset of the German occupation
9. Excerpts of circular from Higher SS and Police Commander in Warthegau, Koppe, concerning plan for resettlement of Jews and

Poles from Warthegau to Generalgouvernement, Poznań, November 12, 1939
10. Excerpts of report from Higher SS and Police Commander in Warthegau on resettlement of Poles and Jews from Warthegau to Generalgouvernement, Poznań, January 26, 1940
11. Excerpts of speech by chief of Reich Security Head Office, Heydrich, and Higher SS and Police Commander in Generalgouvernement, Krüger, delivered at a conference in Berlin on forced resettlement of Polish and Jewish populations from Warthegau to Generalgouvernement, Berlin, January 30, 1940
12. Correspondence between Jewish representatives in Kleczew and Zagórów and JDC representatives in Warsaw—Letter 1
13. Correspondence between Jewish representatives in Kleczew and Zagórów and JDC representatives in Warsaw—Letter 2
14. Correspondence between Jewish representatives in Kleczew and Zagórów and JDC representatives in Warsaw—Letter 3
15. Correspondence between Jewish representatives in Kleczew and Zagórów and JDC representatives in Warsaw—Letter 4
16. Correspondence between Jewish representatives in Kleczew and Zagórów and JDC representatives in Warsaw—Letter 5
17. Correspondence between Jewish representatives in Kleczew and Zagórów and JDC representatives in Warsaw—Letter 6
18. Correspondence between Jewish representatives in Kleczew and Zagórów and JDC representatives in Warsaw—Letter 7
19. Correspondence between Jewish representatives in Kleczew and Zagórów and JDC representatives in Warsaw—Letter 8
20. Correspondence between Jewish representatives in Kleczew and Zagórów and JDC representatives in Warsaw—Letter 9
21. Correspondence between Jewish representatives in Kleczew and Zagórów and JDC representatives in Warsaw—Letter 10
22. Letter from Greiser, Gauleiter and Governor of the Wartheland, to Pohl, concerning the fate of the Łódź ghetto, February 14, 1944
23. Early documentary evidence of the Final Solution: letter from SS-Major Rolf-Heinz Höppner in German-occupied Poland to Adolf Eichmann, Reich Security Head Office, Berlin

24. Proposal for sterilization of 2–3 million Jewish workers, June 23, 1942
25. Testimony of Mieczysław Sękiewicz, Instytut Zachodni in Poznań
26. Excerpts of report from Hersh Wasser on "Chelmno events," addressed to Aleksander Kamiński and published in *Oneg Shabbat Bulletin,* Warsaw ghetto, April 1942
27. Testimony of Lucjan Zalas, April 7, 1970
28. Excerpts of Himmler's speech to senior SS officers in Poznań, October 4, 1943
29. Testimony of Jakob Grojanowski, a survivor from Chełmno.
30. Letter from Arthur Greiser to Himmler about retaining meritorious members of Special Kommando Lange at the death camp at Chełmno on the Nerem
31. Probate decision of Kleczew Municipal Court, December 28, 1949, concerning Chaskiel Kroner, d. May 10, 1942, in Wołkowysk

DOCUMENT 1

Page of draft register from cities and towns of Greater Poland, Pyzdry, 1579 (AGAD, ASK I, sign. 13, k. 756v)

DOCUMENT 2

Excerpt from privilege granted to the Jews of Kleczew on June 21, 1776, by the owner of the town, Władysław Gurowski of Gurowo[1]

... Be it known to all those concerned that under the continuous insistence of the Kleczew Synagogue and all common people in regard to their protection within the town and aiming at increasing the settlement and not decreasing it, I grant them the following permanent liberties:

First: The Synagogue and the whole congregation of the Kleczew Kehilla are allowed to practice any kind of trade that anybody may and can conduct.

Second: They will also be allowed to invite, even from abroad, other traders to their own homes and to dismiss those who mismanage trade.

Third: After paying a charge to the Court, producing and selling all kinds of liquors including vodka/hard liquor, beer, mead, wine, *wiśniak* [a dry alcoholic beverage made of cherries], *Malenniki*, and other beverages will be allowed.

Fourth: Traveling traders will not be allowed to bring and sell goods in the Town of Kleczew at any time other than during fairs, but then they will also need permission from the synagogue.

Fifth: Kleczew townspeople shall not interfere in Jewish trade apart from that in cattle, horses, hogs, and sheep.

Sixth: In case of the reconstruction (bricklaying) or construction of a synagogue, I pledge to provide the bricks they will need.

Seventh: Any disputes between a Jew and a Catholic or between a Catholic and a Jew shall be settled by the Town Mayor or by the Synagogue, respectively. They shall have the right to appeal to the Court if they feel aggrieved.

Eighth: Excepting Kurzyce cases, the entire kehilla and its successors shall remit to the Court treasury three thousand Polish zlotys from trade and distilling, apart from rent and taxes in the Republic of Poland established by Law, which I still wish to collect and declare to keep.

---
1 APP, KG, Konin, classification 118, cards 422-423.

DOCUMENT 3

Kleczew synagogue treasury register, 1851-1853, title page (AGAD, CWW, sign. 1546, k. 61).

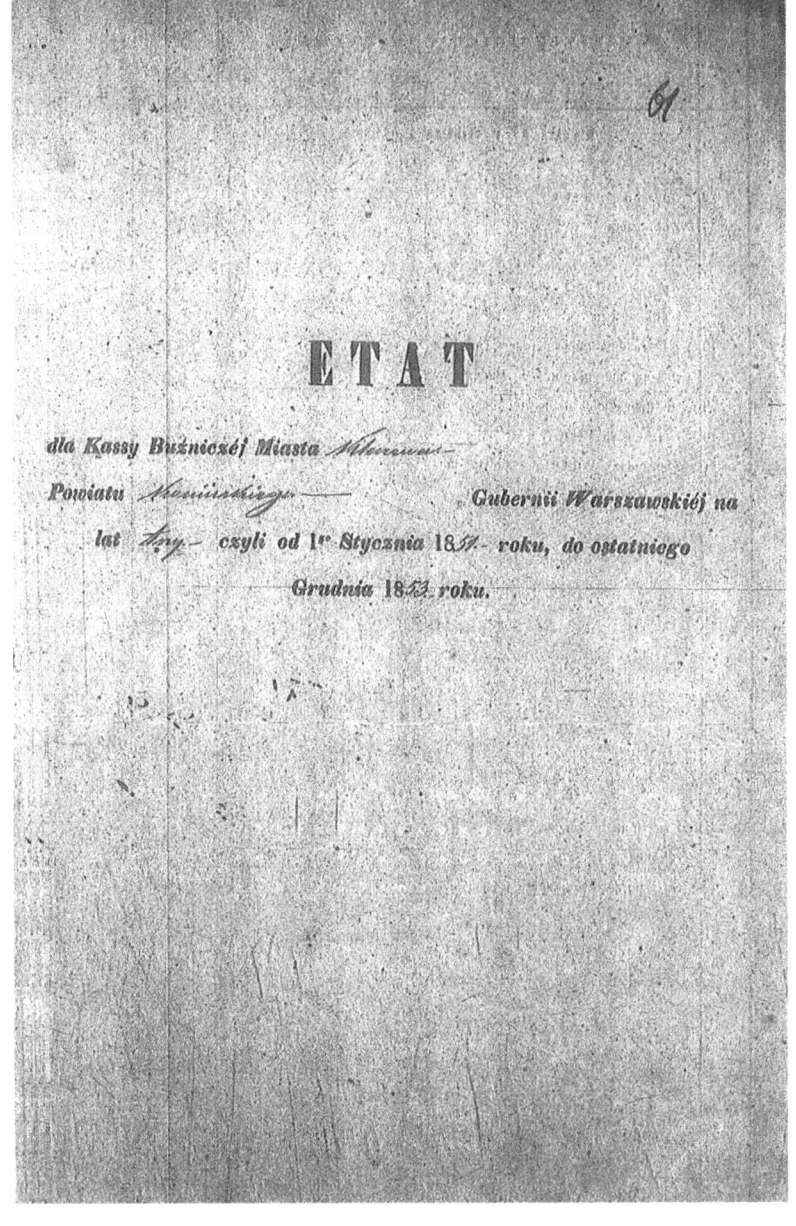

DOCUMENT 4

Warsaw Guberniya Government Commission for Internal and Religious Affairs report on construction of Kleczew synagogue, June 24, 1853

DOCUMENT 5

Proposal from synagogue inspection in Kleczew to accept Kleczew synagogue construction project, filed with Warsaw Guberniya Government Commission for Internal and Religious Affairs, February 23, 1854

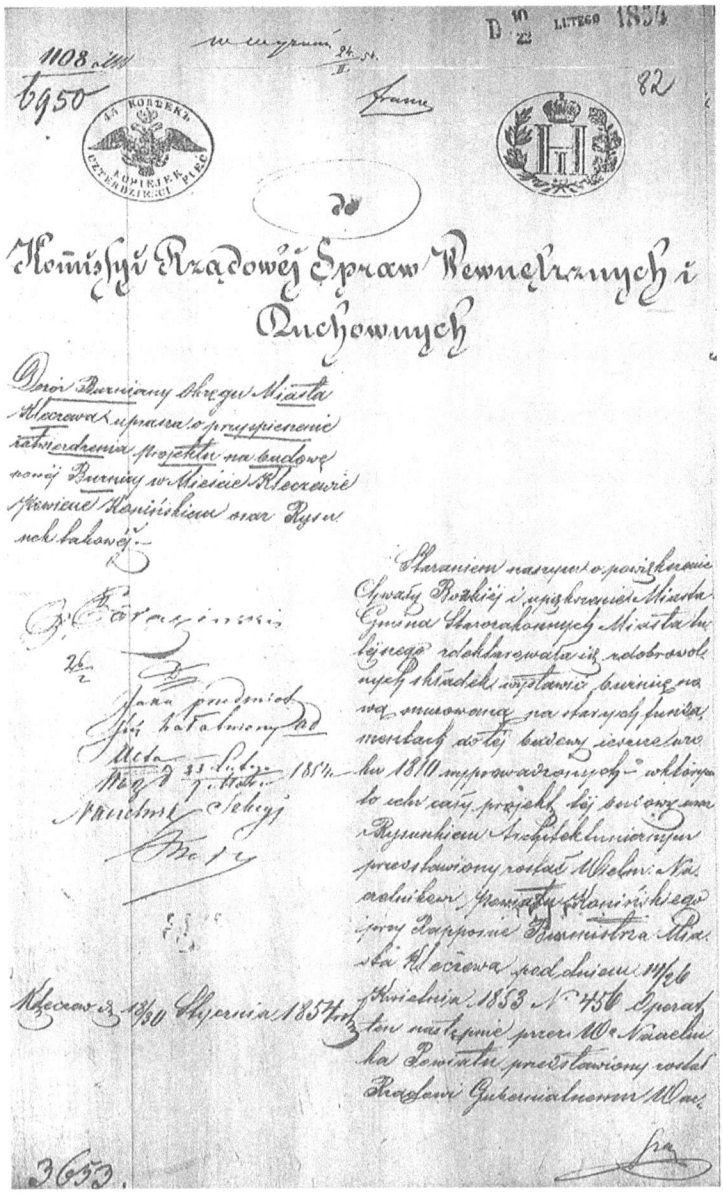

Annex: 1 | 411

DOCUMENT 6

Kleczew synagogue plans (Projections 1-4), 1854 (AGAD, Cartographic Collection, sign. 555-7)

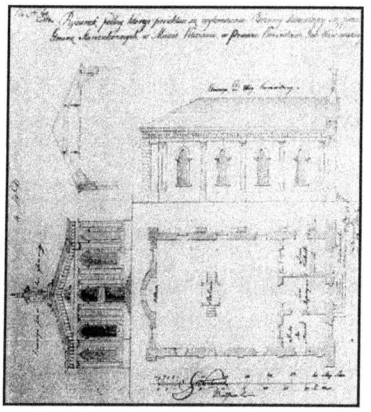
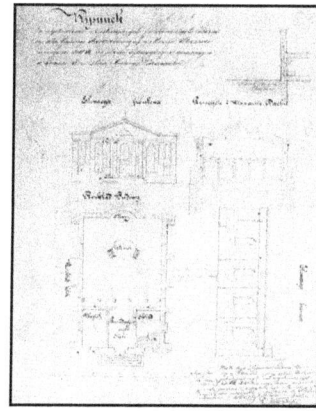
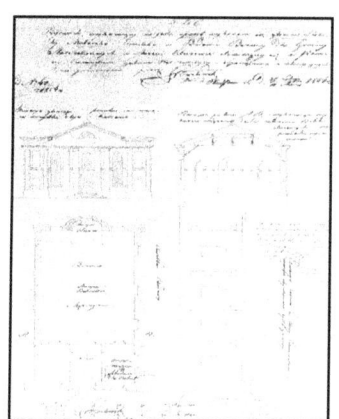

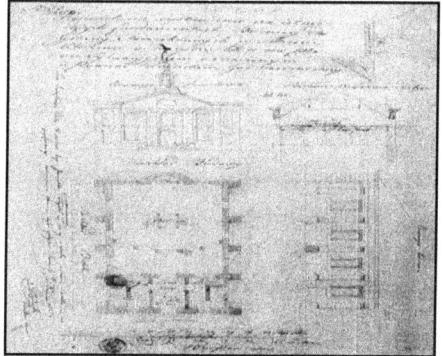

DOCUMENT 7

Excerpts of Hitler's speech, January 30, 1939[1]

... In connection with the Jewish question I have this to say: it is a shameful spectacle to see how the whole democratic world is oozing sympathy for the poor tormented Jewish people, but remains hard-hearted and obdurate when it comes to helping them—which is surely, in view of its attitude, an obvious duty. The arguments that are brought up as an excuse for not helping them actually speak for us Germans and Italians. For this is what they say:

1. "We," that is the democracies, "are not in a position to take in the Jews." Yet in these empires there are not even 10 people to the square kilometer. While Germany, with her 135 inhabitants to the square kilometer, is supposed to have room for them!
2. They assure us: We cannot take them unless Germany is prepared to allow them a certain amount of capital to bring with them as immigrants.

For hundreds of years Germany was good enough to receive these elements although they possessed nothing except infectious political and physical diseases. What they possess today, they have to a very large extent gained at the cost of the less astute German nation by the most reprehensible manipulations. Today we are merely paying this people what it deserves.

When the German nation was, thanks to the inflation instigated and carried through by Jews, deprived of the entire savings which it had accumulated in years of honest work, when the rest of the world took away the German nation's foreign investments, when we were divested of the whole of our colonial possessions, these philanthropic considerations evidently carried little noticeable weight with democratic statesmen. Today I can only assure these gentlemen that, thanks to the brutal education with which the democracies favoured us for years, we are completely hardened to all attacks of sentiment. After more than eight hundred thousand children of the nation had died of hunger and undernourishment at the close of the War, we witnessed almost one million head of milking cows being driven away from us in accordance with the cruel paragraphs of a dictate which the humane democratic apostles of the world forced upon us as a peace treaty. We witnessed over one million German prisoners of war being retained in confinement for no reason at all for a whole year after the war was ended. We witnessed over one and a half million Germans being torn away from all that they possessed in the territories lying on our frontiers, and being whipped out, practically with only what they wore on their backs. We had to endure having millions of our fellow countrymen torn from us without their consent, and without their being afforded the slightest possibility of existence. I could supplement these examples with dozens of the most cruel kind. For this reason we ask to be spared all sentimental talk. The German nation does not wish its interests to be determined and controlled by any foreign nation.

France to the French, England to the English, America to the Americans, and Germany to the Germans. We are resolved to prevent the settlement in our country of a strange people which was capable of snatching for itself all the leading positions in the land, and to oust it. For it is our will to educate our own nation for these leading positions. We have hundreds of thousands of very intelligent children of peasants and of the working classes. We shall have them educated—in fact we have already begun—and we wish that one day they, and not the representatives of an alien race, may hold the leading positions in the State together with our educated classes. Above all, German culture, as its name alone shows, is German and not Jewish, and therefore its management and care will be entrusted to members of our own nation. If the rest of the world cries out with a hypocritical mien against this barbaric expulsion from Germany of such an irreplaceable and culturally eminently valuable element, we can only be astonished at the conclusions they draw from this situation. For how thankful they must be that we are releasing these precious apostles of culture and placing them at the disposal of the rest of the world. In accordance with their own declarations, they cannot find a single reason to excuse themselves for refusing to receive this most valuable race in their own countries. Nor can I see a reason why the members of this race should be imposed upon the German nation, while in the States which are so enthusiastic about these "splendid people" their settlement should suddenly be refused with every imaginable excuse. I think that the sooner this problem is solved the better, for Europe cannot settle down until the Jewish question is cleared up. It may very well be possible that sooner or later an agreement on this problem may be reached in Europe, even between those nations which otherwise do not so easily come together.

The world has sufficient space for settlements, but we must once and for all get rid of the opinion that the Jewish race was only created by God for the purpose of being to a certain degree a parasite living on the body and the productive work of other nations. The Jewish race will have to adapt itself to sound constructive activity as other nations do, or sooner or later it will succumb to a crisis of inconceivable magnitude. One thing I should like to say on this day, which may be memorable for others as well as for us Germans: in the course of my life I have very often been a prophet, and have usually been ridiculed for it. During the time of my struggle for power it was in the first instance the Jewish race which only received my prophecies with laughter when I said that I would one day take over the leadership of the State, and with it that of the whole nation, and that I would then among many other things settle the Jewish problem. Their laughter was uproarious, but I think that for some time now they have been laughing on the other side of their face. Today I will once more be a prophet: if the international Jewish financiers in and outside of Europe should succeed in plunging the nations once more into a world war, then the result will not be the Bolshevization of the earth, and thus the victory of Jewry, but the annihilation of the Jewish race in Europe!

... The nations are no longer willing to die on the battlefield so that this unstable international race may profiteer from a war or satisfy its Old Testament vengeance. The Jewish watch-word "Workers of the world unite" will be conquered by a higher realization, namely, "Workers of all classes and of all nations, recognize your common enemy!"

DOCUMENT 8

Attack on Jews of Włocławek after the onset of the German occupation[2]

A few days after they entered Włocławek, [a group of] the Germans burst into a private house where Jews were standing in prayer on the eve of the Day of Atonement, and ordered those present to get out and run. Then they gave the order, "Stop," but some of the Jews did not hear this order being given and went on running; then the Germans opened fire and killed five or six of them. On the Day of Atonement itself the Germans burned down the two large synagogues. The fire also spread to several private homes. The Jews threw their possessions out [to save them] and there they were robbed by the Polish mob. These fires were set mostly by the men of the SS. The Jews tried to save the burning houses. The Germans then took all the Jewish men from one of the buildings, 26 persons, and forced them to sign a declaration that they themselves had set fire to the building. After the Germans had obtained this declaration they told the men who had been arrested that they would be punished for committing arson and could save themselves only if they paid a ransom of 250,000 złoty. The Jewish population of Włocławek collected the necessary sum amongst themselves and the men were released. Then [the Germans] began to launch hunting expeditions into the houses. They caught about 350 Jews and put some of them in barracks and some of them in the Mühsam factory. From there they were taken out to work every day, but given no food—only their families were permitted to bring them food. After many pleas those who had been arrested were permitted, after many checkings, to visit their homes from time to time in accordance with a special leave-of-absence permit, in order to wash, change their clothes, eat, and so on.

The regular work of the 350 who had been arrested did not by any means stop the abduction for work of Jews in the streets of the city. And apart from that there was the Jewish Council (Judenrat), which had been appointed in place of the former Community authorities; its activities were limited to nothing but carrying out the orders of the German authorities—it would supply a certain number of Jewish workers every day, in accordance with German demands. Those who had been taken away and those who were abducted for work were beaten and abused unmercifully. How they treated the Jews while they were working is shown by the fact that one of these Jews, Jacob Heiman, 52 years old and too weak for physical labor, was beaten and stabbed with a dagger while he was working, and a few days after he had returned home he died of his injuries.

In October, the Germans decreed that the Jews must attach a yellow badge to their clothes in back, and that they must not step on the sidewalks of the streets but walk in the middles of the streets. When they had collected the ransom of 250,000 złoty from the Jews for the imaginary arson, they imposed a new fine on the Jewish population after a short while, of 500,000 złoty, for the imaginary offense of not obeying the ban on using the sidewalk. The schools were closed. A few days after they moved into the city, the Germans closed and confiscated the factories and stores belonging to Jews. The Jews were required to register all their property, and a Jew was not permitted to keep more than 200 złoty in his home (in Warsaw, 2,000 złoty). There were many cases of Jews being beaten and tortured. They used to beat them not only during forced labor and not only when they had some complaint, but also for no reason at all: they would simply go up to Jews passing in the street, cry "Zhid" and stop to hit them.

DOCUMENT 9

Excerpts of circular from Higher SS and Police Commander in the Warthegau, Koppe, concerning plan for resettlement of Jews and Poles from the Warthegau to the General Government, Poznań, November 12, 1939[3]

Secret!

... Subject: Removal of Jews and Poles from the Wartheland region.

1. Reichsführer SS and chief of the German police as Reich Commissioner for the Consolidation of German Nationhood, ordered that the former Polish territories, now belonging to the Reich, will remove:
   a) all Jews and
   b) all those Poles who either belong to the intelligentsia or, by virtue of their national-Polish stance, may pose a danger to the introduction and strengthening of Germanism, to the same extent as criminal elements.

   The purpose of deportation is:
   a) cleansing and securing the new German land;
   b) providing housing and creating income-earning opportunities for arriving ethnic Germans.

   The evacuation action shall necessarily pursue these goals in principle, regardless of any other interests.

2. Based on conversations with the General Governor in Kraków, deportation from the Warthegau will take place between November 15, 1939, and February 28, 1940, and will actually concern 200,000 Poles and 100,000 Jews.

3. People deported will be settled in the designated areas south of Warsaw and Lublin.

4. During the first action, all Jews from counties shall be deported; moreover, from the smallest districts at least 2,000 Poles, and from bigger counties a proportionally larger number.

The following cities shall deliver the following for deportation:
Poznań: about 35,000 Poles and all Jews;
Łódź: approximately 30,000 Poles and about 30,000 Jews;
Gniezno: 2,300 Poles and Jews;
Inowrocław: 2,300 Poles and Jews.

Separate contingents will be provided for cities and counties of Jews and Poles for the deportation during the period specified in Section 2. Preparations should begin immediately. It should be borne in mind that the number of people leaving will be far greater than the number of ethnic Germans who will be resettled from the Baltic countries, the General Government, and Volhynia.

Cleansing and securing the territory, together with all its consequences, will be achieved only when the leading cultural stratum and the entire intelligentsia are removed, along with all political and criminal elements. All people who consciously feel Polish shall also be deported. In the case of the intelligentsia, proof of political activity or hostility towards Germany need not be established. In addition, the creation of residential and employment opportunities for arriving Reichsdeutsche and ethnic Germans should be upheld in every respect.

When determining if the person or groups of people are dangerous in terms of policy, stake attachment points must be taken into account. Accordingly, among other things, this includes belonging to Polish national groups, political parties of any view, belonging to Catholic political associations of both clergy and laity, etc.

5. Employing Volksdeutsche according to their professions is an urgent necessity in order to provide a sufficient number of craftsmen and shops. Laborers, lower officials, and employees who cannot be regarded as nationally conscious Poles or those who are not punished for criminal offenses shall be excluded from the evacuation because they are needed as a workforce.

6. County leaders (*Landrat*), taking into account the above principles, shall by November 18, 1939, provide the number of people who are to be deported from their subordinate areas.

DOCUMENT 10

Excerpts of report from Higher SS and Police Commander in the Warthegau on resettlement of Poles and Jews from the Warthegau to the General Government, Poznań, January 26, 1940[4]

I. Preparations

1) Planning for the resettlement of Poles and Jews in the General Government started on November 10, 1939, on the basis of the relevant agreement concluded on November 7–8, 1939, between SS-Obergruppenführer Krüger and SS-Gruppenführer Koppe. Taking as the basis, for the time being, the number of 300,000 people for deportation, this number has been allocated among the various cities and countries, according to their structure.

II. First short-term plan

1) On November 28, 1939, we received a decree ordering the deportation to the General Government, during the period of December 1–16, 1939, of 80,000 Poles and Jews.

   a) The allocation of quotas was based on studies on population structure and on the planned emigration of Baltic Germans. In principle, allocated to each rural county is at least one train for up to 1,000 people. If there is a greater number of Jewish residents in rural counties and cities, more trains will be assigned respectively....

   c) Eleven trains were made available to eight counties forty-eight hours after the announcement of the first short-term plan. Only brief communication about the terms was possible by telephone and telegraph between county leaders and town chiefs in the Warthegau and with higher SS and police commanders or with the Commander of the Security Police and SD, district heads, or SS and police commanders in the General Government.... In this way, all relevant authorities were constantly informed (daily reports to the Reich Security Head Office).

2) The first short-term plan was executed in the prescribed time. By December 12, 1939, eighty transports left, carrying a total of 87,883 displaced persons to the designated points of destination in the General Government.

III. Recognition and control of those selected for deportation

1) The first short-term plan flowed from the assumption that those individuals among the Poles who constitute a direct threat to Germanism must be deported first. Rich collections of material at the offices of the Security Service and the State Police were very helpful in determining the police's task.

   a) The first to be arrested were key members of Polish chauvinist parties and associations.[5] This circle of people was chosen first because of the people's intellect and professional status in the aforementioned establishments. Their positions shall be filled directly by Germans (especially from the Baltic areas and Volhynia). While the treatment of these individuals required extensive preliminary work, it was not complicated.
   b) Second, marking the antisocial (severely punished) elements among the Jews and Poles from Congress [Poland].

DOCUMENT 11

Excerpts of speech by chief of Reich Security Head Office, Heydrich, and Higher SS and Police Commander in the General Government, Krüger, delivered at a conference in Berlin on forced resettlement of Polish and Jewish populations from the Warthegau to the General Government, Berlin, January 30, 1940[6]

1. Gruppenführer SS Heydrich announces that today's meeting was convened by command of the Reichsführer SS to reach agreement with interested offices on a single line of resettlement tasks as instructed by the Führer. Evacuations carried out so far included approximately 87,000 Poles and Jews from the Warthegau to make room for resettled Baltic Germans there. Next to this was spontaneous, so-called illegal emigration.

   Based on the arguments of the Reich Minister, SS Gruppenführer Seyss-Inquart, and Obergruppenführer Krüger, Gruppenführer Heydrich states that important officials of the Governor-General have no major objections to the evacuation directed by the General Government. Previous complaints concerned only [the fact] that the evacuation did not comply with the original set of numbers, but exceeded them. With the creation of Referat IV D 4 to accomplish the tasks of central management, the objections fall away.

   It seems that it should be the primary purpose of the mission to make room for the Baltic Germans by deporting 40,000 Jews and Poles from the Warthegau to the General Government. Guidelines in choosing those to be deported are established in the order of Reichsführer SS, according to which Germans among others cannot be deported regardless of their past.

2. Gruppenführer SS Heydrich announces the following principal ordinance, issued by the Reichsführer SS:...

   On the general question of the recruitment of Polish farm workers, it had been ordered that there shall be no racial selections now. If a differentiated mass of good and bad Poles were to enter the Reich, this could cause confusion among the German population.

When employing Poles in the Reich, attention should be paid to the appropriate percentage ratio of male and female among them. According to recent statements, 800,000 to 1 million Poles, not including prisoners of war, are to be employed in the Reich. Selection shall be conducted by labor offices. Poles shall be partly taken from the eastern districts. In connection with the preparations, it was found that the local authorities in the eastern districts stated that these Poles are essential, as they are needed on site. For example, the Warthegau declared that it could withdraw only 20,000, while West Prussia-Gdańsk [district] wants to provide only 8,000. For this reason, it is absolutely necessary to gather all Poles in the eastern districts who may be considered farm workers. In the employment of farm workers, an exception may be made to the principal prohibition of racial selection, i.e., the Polish resettlement of farming families. Racially good elements may remain in Reich territory.

3. After both mass relocations:
   a) 40,000 Poles and Jews, in the interest of Baltic Germans, and
   b) 120,000 Poles, in the interest of Germans of Volhynia, should be the last resettlement, which shall include the deportation of all Jews from the new eastern districts and 30,000 Gypsies from the Reich to the General Government. Given the findings that the evacuation of 120,000 Poles will start more or less in March 1940, we must postpone the evacuation of Jews and Gypsies until the end of the previously mentioned actions. However, in any event, the General Government should send the allocation so that we can start planning. Obergruppenführer Krüger says that the General Government must prepare a fairly large range of training grounds for the Wehrmacht, the Luftwaffe, and the SS, entailing the resettlement within the General Government of some 100,000 to 120,000 people. It would be desirable—to avoid double displacement—to include them for resettlement to the General Government.

   Gruppenführer Heydrich mentions in this connection that the construction of the rampart [along the border with the USSR] and other projects in the East will presumably allow employment of hundreds of thousands of Jews in forced-labor camps. The families could then join them with other Jewish families already in the General Government, thus solving the problem. Obergruppenführer Krüger mentions that Volksdeutsche (mostly peasant elements) would be resettled in the General Government and then would come to the Reich. Therefore, Brigadeführer Greiser points out that Reichsführer SS set a later date to address this problem.

Gruppenführer Heydrich said that after these three aforementioned mass resettlements, racial selection will take place in the eastern districts, to be carried out in resettlement headquarters. Some of the Poles and their families would be scattered throughout the Reich. In mid-February 1940, the evacuation of 1,000 Jews from Stettin, where housing is urgently needed for military-economic reasons, should take place as they are to be deported to the General Government. Gruppenführer Seyss-Inquart reiterates the number of people whom the General Government should receive in the near future, namely:

40,000 Jews and Poles, 120,000 Poles, Jews, as well from all new eastern districts,

and 30,000 Gypsies from the Reich and the Eastern Marches [Austria].

He points to transport difficulties that the State Railways may encounter as a consequence and, finally, the bad food situation in the General Government, which will not improve before the next harvest. As a result, it is necessary that the Reich continue to provide assistance. Reich Minister Seyss-Inquart asked Gruppenführer Heydrich to support him on this if there was a need for further acquisition of food aid for the General Government. Brigadeführer Wächter asked evacuees arriving from areas where the food situation is generally better than that in the General Government to be provided with an adequate supply of food.

Gruppenführer Heydrich mentions, in connection with transport difficulties presented by Reich Minister Seyss-Inquart, to ensure that all movement of transports be prepared centrally at the Reich Ministry of Communications, thereby avoiding an unnecessary burden on the rolling stock.

DOCUMENT 12

Correspondence between Jewish representatives in Kleczew and Zagórów and JDC representatives in Warsaw—Letter 1[9]

Jewish Relief Committee Lehmstädt, March 26, 1940
in Lehmstädt

To the honourable Joint [Distribution] Com.[mittee]
in Warsaw

    With today's [letter] we approach you to ask the honourable Joint Com.[mittee] to fulfill our appeal, as 90% of the population in our town of Kleczew is impoverished. They lack the means that are necessary to make ends meet, no clothing, no shoes, and it is very cold, and there is great distress. All the goods the Relief Com.[mittee] has supplied until now to ease the distress have been exhausted. We lack the means to support 150 Jewish families with even a piece of bread, and soon it will be Passover and we lack the means to keep them alive. Therefore, we appeal to the honourable Joint Com.[mittee] to have pity on the 150 Jewish families and send us some help soon…. You must know if you do not take pity on us and send the necessary help, our lives will be in danger.

    But we sincerely hope that you, honourable gentlemen, will fulfill our urgent request very quickly, and thank you in advance.

    We add the remark that there was a savings bank (*Volksbank*) and a *Gm.*[*ilat*] *Chesed* bank [a free-loan fund] that were requisitioned by the county commissioner (*Landrat*) of Konin, forcing us to repay all our loans at once.

Respectfully,
H. Frenkel
H. Segał
Sz. Leszczyński

Photocopy of the first part of the letter from Jewish Relief Committee in Lehmstädt (Łódź) to Joint representatives in Warsaw, March 26, 1940

DOCUMENT 13

Correspondence between Jewish representatives in Kleczew and Zagórów and JDC representatives in Warsaw—Letter 2[10]

No. 0/627/40

American Joint Distribution Committee, Warsaw
Warsaw, May 27th 1940

To: Relief Committee for the Jewish Population in Lehmstädt

We politely notify you that on the 22nd of this month we transferred the sum of zł. 2,000. / two thousand złoty / to your address, for the relief action.

At the same time, we inform you that we cannot obligate ourselves to permanent subsidization for the future. Regarding this, we ask you to keep in contact. It is not necessary for your delegates to come to Warsaw.

Sincerely,
American Joint Distribution Committee

DOCUMENT 14

Correspondence between Jewish representatives in Kleczew and Zagórów and JDC representatives in Warsaw—Letter 3[11]

Jewish Relief Committee Lehmstädt, May 28, 1940
in Lehmstädt / Kleczew

To: American Joint Distribution Committee in Warsaw

We received your letter dated April 3, No. 0/124/40. Until now we could not give an answer on various issues, as it is in these times. Now we can answer that after long deliberations we have reached the decision that it is not possible for us to follow your request to officially acknowledge your three items.

We also politely ask you, G.H.C. [*Geehrtes Hilfskomitee*—Honourable Relief Committee], to give us alternative advice on how to receive support from you for our Jewish population, and your official acknowledgement.

At the same time, we ask that you please tell us about the extent of the subsidization to our town that your G.H.C. has granted, because the situation is getting worse every day. Relief is urgently needed—of the Jewish population of 160 families, more than 130 families need relief.

Hoping sincerely that you will answer soon,

Respectfully,
Hersz Segał
H. Frenkel

DOCUMENT 15

Correspondence between Jewish representatives in Kleczew and Zagórów and JDC representatives in Warsaw—Letter 4[12]

Jewish Relief Committee Hinterberg / Zagórów, July 29th 1940
von Lehmstädt in Hinterberg

To: Joint Committee, Warsaw

We the undersigned Jewish "Relief Committee" in Lehmstädt appeal with an alarming request to the aforementioned committee: we, all the Jews from Kleczew, counting 750 people, were expelled to Hinterberg-Zagórów, Konin County, on the 16th of this month [July], and 600 people are without any means of support. Since the situation is very serious, we ask for immediate weekly support.

Hoping that our call for help will be seriously considered.

Respectfully signed,
Jewish "Relief Committee" Lehmstädt, Hinterberg
Hersz Frenkel, Hersz Segał, B. Leszczyński

P.S. We confirm receipt of support in the sum of RM 1,000 [1,000 Reichsmarks], thank you heartily, and apologize for not answering and thanking you immediately. There was much annoyance because barely RM 400 went to the poor; the rest was taken by the mayor as a per capita tax [*Kopfsteuer*].

Please send a letter or money to these addresses:

Hersch Segał	Hinterberger Str.	18	for "Relief Committee"
F. Król	"	18	"
H. Frenkel	"	26	"
E. Goldenberg	"	10	"

DOCUMENT 16

Correspondence between Jewish representatives in Kleczew and Zagórów and JDC representatives in Warsaw—Letter 5[13]

Jewish Relief Committee   Hinterberg / Zagórów, July 29th 1940
von Lehmstädt
in Hinterberg

Dear Mr. Wolman!

Some time ago we wrote to you asking for your support for the poor Jews in Kleczew. We received RM 1,000 but the poor didn't get much of it because the mayor requisitioned the money already at the post office. The poor got RM 400; the rest he took as a per capita tax. Due to our chagrin, we were in no state of mind to answer immediately; now we thank you for your effort.

Now, *all the Jews* from Kleczew, 750 people, have been expelled to Zagórów / Hinterberg. Our situation is disastrous: 600 people are without any means of support, and the rest may be able to support themselves for 1–2 months.

Therefore, we appeal to you, a faithful compatriot from Kleczew, to use any means of the Joint or any other organization for immediate and weekly help. Hoping you will not forget us, we sign with most cordial greetings.

Hersz Segał
H. Frenkel
B. Leszczyński

Słupca, Konin, Skulsk, Ślesin, Rychwał, Peizen [Poniec] are within the villages from Zagórów to Grójec, Kleczew, Golina, Wilczyn are here. Today we also sent an appeal to the Joint.

Write to the mayor to return RM 600.

DOCUMENT 17

Correspondence between Jewish representatives in Kleczew and Zagórów and JDC representatives in Warsaw—Letter 6[14]

Zagórów (Hinterberg), August 28, 1940, and
recommendation from J. Wolman,
September 2, 1940.
Hinterberg, August 28, 1940

Dear Mr. Wolman,

We received your valuable postcard of August 4, 1940. We are thinking if it is worth intervening in regard to the RM 600 because this sum was taken by the Mayor for the *Bürgersteur* [municipal tax] for those who absolutely could not pay.

The total amount of the municipal civil [tax] amounted to RM 9000 and a greater sum was to be paid by the poor; for example, Heber Sz. N. RM 190, Fogiel Ch. RM 230, Weinberg RM 70, and therefore you can imagine, sir, that we were forced to collect RM 5000 to cover the tax that was owed by the poor—and this was two days before deportation.

Housing conditions in Zagórów are critical. Most people live 10–15 to a room and many families still remain in the school and at the communal house. All of us are without jobs and have much time to enjoy the summer holidays.

We arranged a kitchen at our expense, which serves 300 lunches a day. Half [of those who use it] pay 5 pfennig and half receive it for free. In general, our position cannot be clearly described, as you, sir, can imagine.

We stress that if we do not receive external assistance, which must now be given, we cannot be responsible for the fate of all who are prepared for the worst due to lack of bread. And maybe, thanks to the forces of the *Kleczewiaków* community [former Kleczew residents] who live in Warsaw, we can get help, because we have no other option.

Knowing that you, sir, feel compassion for us, surely you will not forget about us. The harvest took place with obstacles; however, we managed to complete the harvest without rain. Enclosed are cordial greetings from all of us to you, sir, your wife, and the rest of the family.

Yours,
H. Segal
[Unintelligible signature]

P.S. Leszczyński and Frenkel did not sign this letter because they left for the whole week.

P.P.S.
Money should be sent to the following addresses:
H. Segal, Hindenburgstr. 18
Paul Król, - „- 18
E. Goldenberg, - „- 10
Brisch L., Grosser [...] 7

DOCUMENT 18

Correspondence between Jewish representatives in Kleczew and Zagórów and JDC representatives in Warsaw—Letter 7[15]

Honorable Mr. Director Bornsztejn,
W.M.
Joint Distr.[ibution] Com.[mittee],
Jasna 11

Dear Mr. Director,
　I allow myself to send you, Mr. Director, a second letter we received from the Jews expelled from Kleczew, Ślesin, Wilczyn, Skulsk, Słupca, and Konin, and warmly recommend to send even small amounts to the addresses listed below.

Yours sincerely,
J. Wolman
Grochów, September 2, 1940

DOCUMENT 19

Correspondence between Jewish representatives in Kleczew and Zagórów and JDC representatives in Warsaw—Letter 8[16]

[Stamped] Hinterberg, November 24, 1940
Jewish Council of Elders
Hinterberg
Kreis Konin

American Joint Distribution Committee
Warsaw

Re: your letter of the 5th of this month, no. O/1307/40

We politely notify you that as of today we have not received any support from the Reichsvereinigung der Juden in Deutschland [Reich Association of the Jews in Germany]. The distress of the refugees in our towns is growing every day. Our welfare activities, a public soup kitchen feeding about 500 people, the allocation of apartments, medical and sanitary help, will have to cease because all our resources are exhausted. Now, facing the coming winter, our burden gets even heavier and we are helpless.

Therefore, we kindly ask you to immediately prompt the Reichsvereinigung der Juden in Deutschland to let us have the support as soon as possible.

Respectfully,
[Stamped]
Jewish Council of Elders
Hinterberg
Kreis Konin
[Two illegible signatures]

DOCUMENT 20

Correspondence between Jewish representatives in Kleczew and Zagórów and JDC representatives in Warsaw—Letter 9[17]

(Stamp:

[Stamped] Jewish Council of Elders
Hinterberg
Kreis Konin
Hinterberg, Dec. 12, 1940

To:
American Joint Distribution Committee
Warsaw

We politely inform you that today we received a subsidy in the sum of RM 500 from the Reichsvereinigung der Juden in Deutschland, as per your request.

With thanks for this support, we appeal to you for further help, because the vast majority of the refugees in our town are dependent on our support and our depleted resources are not sufficient to ease their distress.

Respectfully,
[Stamped]
Jewish Council of Elders
  Hinterberg
  Kreis Konin
  M. Dessauer [plus one illegible signature]

DOCUMENT 21

Correspondence between Jewish representatives in Kleczew and Zagórów and JDC representatives in Warsaw—Letter 10[18]

[Stamped] Jewish Council of Elders
Hinterberg
Kreis Konin
Hinterberg, Dec. 17, 1940

To:
American Joint Distribution Committee,
Warsaw

Re: your esteemed letter on Dec. 10th this year, No. O/1409/40 we inform you of the following:

On July 15, 1940, the whole Jewish population of the (Kreis) Konin County, from these towns: Lehmstädt (Kleczew), Golina, and Wolfsberg (Wilczyn), was deported to Hinterberg (Zagórów). Immediately upon arrival of the deportees, the local Jewish community started relief actions to support the deportees with housing, food, and medical aid. This relief action was organized by the local relief committee [*Hilfskomitee*], which was acknowledged as the "Jewish Council of Elders" [*Jüdischer Ältestenrat*] by the county chief of police [*Gendarmerie-Kreisführer*].

The Jewish Council of Elders conducts the following relief activities:

6. Housing allotment: due to severe housing shortage several families had to be assigned to one large room.
7. Establishment of a public soup kitchen that is working around the clock, delivering 400 lunches per day consisting of a nutritious and well prepared soup and 200 grams of bread per person.
8. Care for the elderly and the sick. For this purpose we established a special institution, which works under medical supervision.
9. Procurement of straw, tin ware, and kitchenware.
10. Sanitary facilities and medications.

With the beginning of winter, we face the impossible task of supplying the needy with heating, beds, wooden shoes, and the like, which is impossible because our resources are completely exhausted. We were able to make an exception for men who were drafted from here to the Jewish work camp in Konin and supplied some members of this group with wooden shoes.

Answering your questions, we notify you:
1. Number of Jews: 2170 people
2. Number of refugees / deportees: 1582
3. Number of people to take care of: 68
4. Number of emigrants: none
5. The soup kitchen is active every day.
6. The number of lunches is about 400 per day.
7. -----
8. There is no institution for children.
9. A home for the elderly and the ill exists.
10. Budget for social welfare for November 1940:

Budget for social welfare for November 1940

Public soup kitchen	RM	848,04
Support for heating		184,80
Support of the draftees in the Jewish work camp		
In Konin		34,75
Wooden shoes, 51 pairs		240,-
Sanitation, medications		25,-
Postage, stationery		5,25
		--
		1.340,84

11. The subsidies of 500 Reichsmarks from October 5 were used for the following purposes:

RM 250 to buy supplies of potatoes and vegetables for the soup kitchen,

RM 200 to buy beds for ill and elderly people
RM 50 for heating purposes.

The attached letter will show you how great our task is. It is no longer possible to procure the necessary means from the local Jewish population of Hinterberg, which itself is economically completely ruined. Hoping the honourable Joint will carry on supporting us in our great relief action.

We respectfully sign,
[Stamped]
Jewish Council of Elders
Hinterberg
Kreis Konin
M. Dessauer [plus one illegible signature]

DOCUMENT 22

Letter from Greiser, Gauleiter,[19] and Governor of the Warthegau, to Pohl, concerning the fate of the Łódź ghetto, February 14, 1944[20]

On the occasion of the visit of the RFSS [Reichsführer SS] in Poznan yesterday and the day before I had an opportunity to discuss and clarify two questions which concern the area of your work. The first question is as follows:

The ghetto in Łódź will not be converted into a concentration camp, as was emphasized at the discussion on February 5 held at my office, the Reich Governorate in Poznań, by SS Oberführer Baier and SS Hauptsturmführer Dr. Volk, who had been sent to my Gau (province) by your office. The Order of the RFSS of June 11, 1943, will therefore not be carried out. I have agreed the following with the RF:

1. The population of the ghetto is to be reduced to a minimum, and only those Jews who are absolutely required in the interests of the armaments industry are to remain.
2. The ghetto thus remains a Gau ghetto of the Reichsgau Wartheland.
3. The reduction of the population will be carried out by the Sonderkommando of SS Hauptsturmführer Bothmann, which had previously operated in the area. The RF will issue an order instructing SS Hauptsturmführer Bothmann and his *Sonderkommando* to leave their station in Croatia and be available for service in the Wartheland.
4. The disposal and use of the property of the ghetto will remain the responsibility of the Reichsgau Wartheland.
5. After the removal of all the Jews from the ghetto and its demolition, the entire area of the ghetto will become the property of the city of Łódź.

The RF will then give appropriate orders to the Central Trustee's Office for the East (Haupt-Treuhandstelle Ost).

Kindly convey your proposals on this subject to me.

Greiser

DOCUMENT 23

Early documentary evidence of the Final Solution: letter from SS-Major Rolf-Heinz Höppner in German-occupied Poland to Adolf Eichmann, Reich Security Head Office, Berlin[21]

L Hö/S
[Higher SS and Police Commander in the Warthegau]
SS-Major Rolf-Heinz Höppner

To
Reich Security Head Office
Office IV B 4
Attention SS-Lt. Col. Eichmann
Berlin
July 16, 1941

Dear Comrade Eichmann,
    Enclosed is a memorandum on the results of various discussions held locally at the office of the Reich Governor. I would be grateful to have your reactions sometime. These things sound in part fantastic, but in my view are thoroughly feasible.

1 enclosure
L Hö/S Poznan July 16, 1941 Memorandum

                Subject: Solution of the Jewish question

    During discussions in the office of the Reich Governor various groups broached the solution of the Jewish question in the Warthegau. The following solution is being proposed.

1. All the Jews of the Warthegau will be taken to a camp for 300,000 Jews which will be erected in barracks form as close as possible to the coal precincts and which will contain barracks-like installations for economic enterprises, tailor shops, shoe manufacturing plants, etc.

2. All Jews of the Warthegau will be brought into this camp. Jews capable of labor may be constituted into labor columns as needed and drawn from the camp.
3. In my view, a camp of this type may be guarded by SS-Brig. Gen. Albert with substantially fewer police forces than are required now. Furthermore, the danger of epidemics, which always exists in the Łódź and other ghettos for the surrounding population, will be minimized.
4. This winter there is a danger that not all of the Jews can be fed. One should weigh honestly whether the most humane solution might not be to finish off those of the Jews who are not employable by means of some quick-working device. At any rate, that would be more pleasant than to let them starve to death.
5. For the rest, the proposal was made that in this camp all the Jewish women from whom one could still expect children, should be sterilized so that the Jewish problem may actually be solved completely with this generation.
6. The Reich Governor has not yet expressed an opinion in this matter. There is an impression that Government President Übelhör does not wish to see the ghetto in Łódź disappear since he [his office] seems to profit quite well with it. As an example of how one can profit from the Jews, I was told that the Reich Labor Ministry pays 6 Reichsmark from a special fund for each employed Jew, but that the Jew costs only 80 Pfennige.

DOCUMENT 24

Proposal for sterilization of 2–3 million Jewish workers, June 23, 1942[22]

Reich Secret Document
Honorable Mr. Reichsführer,

On instructions from Reichsleiter Bouhler, I placed some of my men at the disposal of Brigadeführer Globocnik for his Special Task a considerable time ago. Following a further request from him, I have now made available more personnel. On this occasion Brigadeführer Globocnik expressed the view [p. 272] that the whole Aktion against the Jews should be carried out as quickly as possible, so that we will not be stuck in the middle should any difficulty arise someday making it necessary to stop the Aktion. You yourself, Mr. Reichsführer, expressed this view to me at an earlier time, stating that one must work as fast as possible if only for reasons of concealment.

Both reasons are more than justified according to my own experience and produce basically the same results. Nevertheless, I beg to be permitted to present the following consideration of my own in this connection:

According to my impression, there are at least 2–3 million men and women well fit for work among the approximately 10 million European Jews. In consideration of the exceptional difficulties posed for us by the question of labor, I am of the opinion that these 2–3 million should in any case be removed and kept alive. Of course, this can only be done if they are at the same time rendered incapable of reproduction. I reported to you about a year ago that people under my instruction have completed the necessary experiments for this purpose. I wish to bring up these facts again. The type of sterilization which is normally carried out on those with genetic diseases is out of the question in this case, as it takes too long and is too expensive. Castration by means of X-rays, however, is not only relatively cheap but it can be carried out on many thousands in a very short time. I believe that it has become unimportant at the present time. Rather, those affected will then in the course of a few weeks or months realize by the effects that they are castrated.

In the event, Mr. Reichsführer, that you decide to choose these means in the interest of maintaining labor-material, Reichsleiter Bouhler will be ready to provide the doctors and other personnel needed to carry out this task. He also instructed me to inform you that I should then order the required equipment as quickly as possible.

Viktor Brack

DOCUMENT 25

Testimony Mieczysław Sękiewicz, Instytut Zachodni in Poznań[23]

Doc. III-42, Konin County (copy)

Protocol

On October 27, 1945, the delegated Chief of the Municipal Court in Konin, District Judge Piotr Dulęba, pursuant to Article 254 of the Code of Penal Proceedings, visited the site of mass graves located in the national forests of Kazimierz Biskupi in Konin County, in Section 1, called "Wygoda," in order to present the graves and interrogate the witness, Citizen Mieczysław Sękiewicz, veterinarian. Present as individuals who know the terrain [were] Wójt of the Kazimierz Biskupi commune, Stanisław Radecki; [and] Citizen Aleksander Ciborski, dairy clerk of the Kazimierz Biskupi settlement. After reaching the site of the mass graves, it was confirmed that the state of the site was consistent with the one presented in the survey report of October 3, 1945, prepared by the head of the municipal court in Konin. Having recognized the place and been informed of criminal responsibility for false testimony, pursuant to Art. 107 of the Code of Civil Proceedings, Citizen Sękiewicz testified the following:

Mieczysław Sękiewicz, Konin, born on December 25, 1910, veterinarian, no criminal record, Polish, Catholic.

> In mid-November 1941, at about 4 a.m., Gestapo officers came to the prison cell where I was locked up and told me to get ready to leave. They handcuffed me and led me to a passenger car, where two companions in misery from a prison in Konin were already sitting in the back seat, shackled to each other at the arms and legs. Their names were Walenty Orchowski from Golina and Kazimierz Tylżanowski from the Rzgów commune. When I sat down next to them, the Germans shackled my legs. Then the Gestapo officers got in and the car started moving towards the railroad station, turning on the road to Golina, then turning again by the mill and heading in the direction of Kazimierz Biskupi. It was light out, and seated with my face forward I was

able to observe the road. Having passed Kazimierz Biskupi, the car turned left into the forest. Today I can recognize the path as a forest track, 25 on Sketch No. 1. The car passed one track running crosswise and reached the second track running crosswise to the right. Those tracks are marked on sketches 2 and 3. Next, the car with us inside turned around at the second crosswise track and headed back, stopping between the first and second track, a few meters away from the second track. I recognize the site very well. We were unshackled, led out of the car, and positioned with our backs to a clearing, where today the mass graves are marked on Sketches I and II. We stood there for half [an hour]. Then we were led into the clearing, which I perfectly recognize today marked on the sketch with the letter "A." This clearing was not as overgrown as it is today. Roughly parallel to the track marked as number one, only at a slight angle to the clearing, two large trenches had been dug. The first one, closer to the track, was about eight meters long, about six meters wide at the top, about two meters deep. At the far edge of the clearing along its entire width was a second trench roughly parallel to the first, with the same depth, and about six meters wide, about 15 meters long, and between the two trenches there was an empty space.

Here the witness, accompanied by the judge and those present, shows the place about which he is testifying, along with the precise place where the mass graves were located, marked on sketches I and II.

Groups of Jews were standing and sitting around the whole clearing, with the exception of the edge from the side where the tracks intersect, in the place marked with the letter "B" on the sketch. I cannot say how many of them there were, as they were standing between trees. The largest group was standing [here the witness shows the place] at the point marked "X" on the sketch. Among the crowds, there were women, men, and children, mothers with babies in their arms. I don't know whether these were only Jews from Poland. Later I was told that they came from the village of Zagórów. From among them, I recognized a tailor and a shopkeeper from Konin, but I cannot give their names. The tracks, the clearing, and the surrounding forest were teeming with Gestapo officers. Apart from the three of us from Konin, about 30 Poles had already been brought to the site. I do not know where they were brought from. At the bottom of the larger trench I saw a layer of chunks of unslaked lime. I do not know how thick the layer was. There was no lime in the smaller grave. The Gestapo officers warned us that they had the forest surrounded and under guard, and if we tried to escape, we would get a bullet in the head. Then the Gestapo officers ordered the gathered Jews to undress, first those standing closest to the larger trench. Then they ordered the naked to move to the area between the two trenches and jump into the larger pit. The screams and cries were indescribable. Some Jews—even most of them—jumped by themselves; others resisted and were beaten and pushed into the hole. Some of the mothers jumped holding their babies; others threw their children aside, while still others threw their children into the pit separately and jumped in themselves separately.

Some of them crawled at the Gestapo officers' feet, kissing their shoes, rifle butts, etc. We were ordered to walk among the Jews standing next to the graves and collect the scattered clothes and shoes. I witnessed scenes where Gestapo officers approached the places where we collected watches, rings, and other pieces of jewelry in piles, took fistfuls of these things, and stuffed them into their pockets. Seeing this, some of us, including me, stopped putting the valuables in piles, and instead threw the watches and rings carelessly into the forest. At a certain point, the Gestapo officers ordered the Jews to stop undressing because the trench was already full. From above, the only thing visible was tightly crowded heads. Those Jews who had hurried and already undressed, were thrown into the pit on the heads of those crammed inside. During this whole time we had to collect and sort the scattered clothes, shoes, packs, food, eiderdowns, etc. That lasted until midday, and then a truck came from the direction of the road, and stopped at the track near the clearing. I noticed four vat-like things on the truck. Next, the Germans started to put a small engine in place, which probably was a pump. They connected it to one of the vats with a hose, and then two of the Gestapo officers pulled the hose from the motor to the large pit. They started the motor and these two Gestapo officers holding the hose began pouring something onto the Jews crowded in the large pit. I think it was water, that's what it looked like, but I am not sure. As the water was pumped, the hose was moved from one vat to another. Apparently, as a result of the slaking of the lime, those people started to be boiled alive, and an incredible scream emerged so that those of us seated near the clothing shredded the clothes and stuffed bits of cloth into our ears. The terrible screams of those being boiled in the pit were joined by the screaming and wailing of the Jews still waiting to be executed. It went on for about two hours, maybe even longer. After it got dark, we were led from the clearing and along the forest track that lead to the road, towards the forest boundary to the very corner, and that's where we were stopped. This corresponds to the place marked as point "4" on the sketch [here the witness points out the place to the judge and others present]. They gave us some coffee to drink and a quarter of a kilogram of bread. There were six or seven tarpaulin-covered trucks parked along the forest border.

We were loaded in each of the trucks in such a way that one person lay down next to another person face down on the floor, unable to move, and that's how they ordered us to sleep. The screams could still be heard. I heard them until I fell asleep, which, due to weariness and tribulations, happened quite soon. The following day in the morning, the Gestapo officers ordered us to cover the large hole with dirt. The mass of people inside sort of collapsed and drifted downward towards the bottom of the pit. The bodies were so crowded together that they still remained somewhat in a standing position, only their heads were tilted to all sides. We covered the grave carelessly; arms from some of the corpses were still sticking out when we were ordered to stop filling [the grave] because trucks started arriving, and we were ordered to throw particular things into the truck—clothes separately, shoes separately, and other items. By the afternoon a large, dark gray ambulance-like wagon that opened in the rear drove into the clearing several times; after the doors were opened, human corpses of men, women, and children, all Jews, fell out from inside. I do not know whether the vehicle kept coming after I had been taken away from the clearing.

The corpses pouring out of the truck were affixed to one another, as if in convulsive grasps, in contorted positions, sometimes with chewed-up faces. I saw one with his teeth sunk into somebody else's jaw, while others had their noses or fingers chewed up. Many held hands in a violent grasp; they had obviously been family. The Gestapo officers ordered us to tear the corpses apart, and if this did not work, then to chop them up, cutting off hands, legs, and other parts. Next, we had to place the corpses in a smaller trench in the clearing, positioning them tightly together with the heads alternating from one side to the other. We were ordered to stuff the chopped-of parts between the bodies.

While I was there, three such layers of people were arranged and one truck was still not unloaded. That's when they took us to sleep in the cars like the night before, giving us a meal in the form of potato soup and bread. The following morning my prison companions and I were taken to the edge of the clearing border to be examined. A certain distance away, at a place marked with the number III on the sketch, we were arranged about a meter apart along the dug pit, which was more or less three by four meters in size. A Gestapo officer with a weapon stood facing each of us.

With my back turned, I was looking into the hole. A Gestapo officer ordered me to confess to all the activities, that is, reading illegal press, helping other Poles, etc. When I explained that the charges were false, he told me to turn around with my head down and warned me a few times that he would kill me if I did not plead guilty; if I did confess, then I would go home and be assigned to a good job.

When this did not bring any results, he shot at me from a few steps away. My nerves could not bear any more and I fell into the hole. In my consciousness I remember well that the thought crossed my mind that I was dead, yet I knew what was happening around me. Then I heard the Gestapo officers shout, "*Auf.*" I stood up rapidly and got out of the trench. All this lasted seconds. I was unwounded. I do not know whether the Gestapo officer missed or just shot to threaten me.

When I got out of the trench, the Gestapo officers beat me all over the face with riding crops and then took me to prison in Konin together with my companions, all of us shackled just like when we were taken away. A few weeks later, we were transported to a camp in Inowrocław, then to Mauthausen, and finally to Gusen. I remained in Gusen until liberation on May 5, 1945. My companions could not last in the camp and they died there. The corpses brought in the gray car had obviously been gassed. The inside of the car and the clothes on the corpses gave off the smell of gas. I remember one more thing from the clearing during the killing of the Jews—how one of the Gestapo officers took a baby from her mother's arms and smashed the baby's little head against the edge of a car right in front of the mother's very eyes, and when the mother started screaming, he hurled the baby's head at her so violently that the brains filled her mouth. Then he took something, some lime or plaster from the car and rubbed it on her mouth. Other women who screamed loudly were treated in the same manner. I saw how one Gestapo officer grabbed a young beautiful Jewish woman and, having torn off her dress and underwear, tied her arms behind her back, and hanged her naked by the arms from a tree. Then, using a utility knife, he cut her right breast in slices, and then cut her stomach open and rummaged around in her entrails. The Jewish woman died on the tree. I did not know any of the Gestapo officers who were there.

Here the protocol on-site visit was closed.

Chief of the Court
District Judge/ -/ Piotr Dulęba
/-/ Sękiewicz /-/ S. Radecki /-/ Ciborski
Recording Clerk: illegible signature

DOCUMENT 26

Excerpts of report from Hersh Wasser on "Chelmno events," addressed to Aleksander Kamiński[24] and published in Oneg Shabbat Bulletin, Warsaw ghetto, April 1942.[25]

Dear Sir,

We feel obliged to report authentic, beyond any doubt, events that took place in the western territories annexed to the Reich. News of these events has not yet arrived in the wide circles of Polish society. We believe that you, dear sir, will not keep them only for yourself.

In the second half of November 1941 a message spread through the cities of the Koło district (*Kreis Wartbrücken*) that the entire Jewish population of these villages was to be resettled in Pińszczyzna or Eastern Galicia. The German authorities imposed a poll tax of RM 4 on the entire Jewish population and all men from age 14 to 60 and women under the age of 50 underwent a medical examination to determine their ability to work. Concerned by these facts, the Jewish community made efforts to obtain any news about the deportation, but to no avail. The only thing that has been determined is that the Jewish population, including three thousand people from Zagórów, Konin County, was after preparations transported by cars to the Kazimierz forest, near the town, where all traces of them disappeared.

In mid-December 1941, the entire Jewish populations of Koło (2000 people) and Dąbie on the Ner (1000 people) were expelled. The deportation included all Jews without exception. They were loaded on trucks—infants, children, elderly, and the chronically ill. Along with their belongings, they were transported to the village of Chełmno, located 12 km away from Koło on the road to Dąbie. Local ... peasants reported that no food was brought to the palace [in Chełmno] and that a gray truck arrives and departs several times a day, going in the direction of Rzuchowski forest.... Jews were brought in batches of 60, and later on of 90, people. Luggage was dropped off at the local church buildings, which had been seized by the Gestapo. Then the cars drove up to the palace, where the displaced got out....

In addition to the Jews of Koło and Dąbie, [there were also killed] from January 2 to 9, 1942—Gypsies from the Łódź ghetto; on January 10 and 12—Jews from Kłodawa; on January 13—Jews of Bugaj; on January 14 and 15—Jews from Izbica Kujawska; and from January 16 onward and until the beginning of April—the Jews from the Łódź ghetto and in all probability from Krośniewice, Żychlin, and Kutno were gassed at Chełmno....

The details mentioned above are derived from the testimony of the local population which, despite all precautions, echoed the tragedy taking place in the "Chełmno Palace," mainly due to descriptions thrown from the windows of the car by the unfortunate gravediggers. As has already been said above, their authenticity is not subject to any doubt....

DOCUMENT 27

Testimony of Lucjan Zalas, April 7, 1970[26]

It was the autumn of 1941 or 1942. One day, I do not remember the date, I noticed in the morning German troops surrounding a certain part of the forest. The soldiers had uniforms with greenish bronze at the collars, and the pocket flaps on the chest had a crescent-shaped plate. This section of the deciduous and coniferous forest, composed of large trees, was opposite the Długa Łąka gamekeeper's cottage on the flowing stream. The guarding around the forest lasted at least two weeks. During this time, not long after the guards were positioned in the forest, the following event took place: to the gamekeeper's cottage an officer came with two or three soldiers being part of the guard [detail] and demanded eggs, butter, and fruit. They paid for this food. Given that the woman did not have sufficient quantities of products requested by a German officer, he commanded me, as the oldest of the children, to buy this food in the village of Możysław, which was adjacent to the forest, for him. I went to the village by bike and bought the food. I went back to the gamekeeper's cottage with the products, but the German officer was not there.

I was told to bring this food into the forest, to the surrounded section—the so-called Marantowska Avenue [road]. I went there. A soldier from the guard unit called me to him and told me to go straight to Marantowska Avenue. In front of Marantowska Avenue there was a duct [forest road] with a drainage ditch and from there I noticed a large group of German soldiers; and they also let me through. I got to Marantowska Avenue. There were a greater number of troops and standing trucks. Beyond the intersection of Marantowska Avenue with this forest road on which I walked stood a trailer which had four completely enclosed wheels. Next to it stood a machine on two wheels that was activated. Close to Marantowska Avenue I noticed a group of people, naked, and another group of people still dressedm with stars indicating their Jewish nationality. At one point the officer who had ordered the food came to me and took the food from the basket and he turned me away by the arm and said, "*Raus.*" Over the next few days I brought this officer more food.

One day I noticed how they were pulling out naked human bodies from the enclosed trailer. It was being done by Jews with stars [of David]. They were surrounded by armed German soldiers. Each time when I was there, I saw a pile of clothes near the enclosed trailer. I saw two dug pits, 15 meters in length, in the forest by the stream. I also saw how the Jews were digging these pits. Among the Jews were adult women and men, adolescents, and children. Each morning, I was ordered by an officer to bring a chair to the German soldier on duty at the post on the highway. In the evening, I had to take the chair back....

One day, when I was drawing water from the well, a German soldier with two Jewish boys about 16-17 years old, who had buckets, came into the courtyard and took water from the well. Having bread, I gave the boys half a loaf because one of them asked for bread. The soldier did not notice that. The officer came to the gamekeeper's cottage on several occasions, warmed up, and ate. After some time, we realized that the soldiers surrounding the area of the forest left during the night. Finally, they left the forest area. Then I, with my uncle, went to see what the Germans had done in the guarded section of the forest. I took my uncle to Marantowska Avenue and then we found that there were three holes, not the two that I had seen at the beginning. These pits were concealed by turf and forest undergrowth. After some time, we also discovered that these pits had collapsed.

Some time later, I cannot remember when, once again German troops surrounded the same section of the forest. During the day it was quiet and in the evening we heard shooting. During the day we could see smoke coming from that section of the forest and when the wind blew toward the gamekeeper's cottage there was a terrible stench. This time we were told not to come with food and I did not see what happened there.

After completing this action and after the departure of the Germans, we went to this place, I saw that holes were dug, covered with the earth, but were not masked. There were traces of large fires. I add that during the first action we saw how the army military vehicles were bringing the Jews along the road in the direction of Konin to Gosławice to Marantowska Avenue. However, the German soldiers who would come used the road going from Niesłusz to Rudzica. Jews were unloaded from the cars at the corner of Marantowska Avenue and the forest road from the Długa Łąka gamekeeper's cottage.

DOCUMENT 28

Excerpts of Himmler's speech to senior SS officers in Poznań, October 4, 1943[27]

... I am referring here to the evacuation of the Jews, the extermination of the Jewish people. This is one of the things that is easily said: "The Jewish people are going to be exterminated." That's what every Party member says: "Sure it's in our program, elimination of the Jews, extermination—it'll be done." And then they all come along, the 80 million worthy Germans, and each one has his one decent Jew. Of course, the others are swine, but this one, he is a first-rate Jew. Of all those who talk like that, not one has seen [mass murder] happen, not one has had to go through with it. Most of you men know what it is like to see 100 corpses side by side, or 500, or 1,000. To have stood fast through this and —except for cases of human weakness—to have stayed decent; that has made us hard. This is an unwritten, and never-to-be-written, page of glory in our history, for we know how difficult it would be for us if today, under bombing raids and the hardships and deprivations of war, we were still to have the Jews in every city as secret saboteurs, agitators, and inciters. If the Jews were still lodged in the body of the German nation, we would probably by now have reached the stage of 1916–17.

The wealth they possessed we took from them. I gave a strict order—which has been carried out by SS Obergruppenführer Pohl—that this wealth will of course be turned over to the Reich in its entirety. We have taken none of it for ourselves. Individuals who have erred will be punished in accordance with the order given by me at the start, threatening that anyone who takes as much as a single Mark of this money is a dead man. A number of SS men—they are not very many—committed this offense and they shall die. There will be no mercy. We had the moral right, we had the duty towards our people, to destroy this people who wanted to destroy us. But we do not have the right to enrich ourselves by so much as a fur, as a watch, by one Mark or a cigarette or anything else. We do not want, in the end, because we destroyed a bacillus, to be infected by this bacillus and to die. I will never stand by and watch while even a small rotten spot develops or takes hold. Wherever it may form we will together burn it away. All in all, however, we can say that we have carried out this most difficult of tasks in a spirit of love for our people. And we have suffered no harm to our inner being, our soul, our character....

DOCUMENT 29

Testimony of Jakob Grojanowski, a survivor from Chełmno[28]

Dear Sir,

We feel it our duty to inform you about a number of events, authentic beyond any doubt, which took place in the western territory annexed to the Reich and [news of] which, unfortunately, has not yet reached wide circles of the Polish public.

We hope that you, sir, will not keep this information only to yourself. In the second half of November 1941, news spread in the towns of Kolski district (now called Kreis Warthebrücken) that the entire Jewish population of these towns would be deported and resettled in Pińszczyzna or Eastern Małopolska. German authorities levied a poll tax of RM 4 on the Jewish population. In addition, all men aged 14 to 60, and women to 50, went through a medical examination to establish their ability to work. Alarmed by these facts, Jewish communities made efforts to obtain some details about the deportation, but in vain. The only fact they managed to establish was that the Jewish community of Zagórów, Konin District, numbering 3000 people, was after similar preparations deported by trucks to the town near the Kazimierz forest area, and nothing has been heard regarding them since.

In the middle of December, the entire Jewish population of Koło (about 2000 people) and of Dąbie on Ner (1000 people) was deported. The deportation included all Jews without exception. Babies, children, bed-ridden old men, all were loaded on trucks. All of them, together with their possessions, were taken to the village of Chełmno, situated 12 km away from Koło, on the way to Dąbie. Couriers sent by Jewish communities in Kłodawa, Izbica Kujawska, Bugaj, and Sempolina [Sempolno] to find out what had happened to the deported could only confirm that they had been placed in the Chełmno palace, from where they never exited. Local peasants report that no food supplies are being conveyed to the palace and that several times a day a gray truck drives to the palace and then leaves in the direction of the Luborodz forests. Only later did it become possible to establish more accurate details about what took place in the Chełmno palace.

Jews were brought in groups of 60 and later 90. Baggage was placed in the church, one of the buildings that had been requisitioned by the Gestapo. Then trucks drove to the palace, where the deported got off. The one-storey palace was destroyed during the previous war. The deported were brought to a large room, well-heated, with wooden slats laid out on the floor. Ladder-like stairs led from the room to a basement. In the basement there was a corridor exiting, with a ramp with stairs. From there a door led to a yard, and another door led to a different yard of the palace. An SS officer, together with a 60-year-old German, who with his very cordial behavior had already gained the sympathy of the deported while they were getting off the truck, now addressed the people, reassuring them that they would be resettled in the Łódź ghetto, where everyone would find work and the children would attend school. But before leaving for Łódź, they must go through disinfections and have a bath in the bathing room especially installed in the palace. In order to prepare for the disinfections, they were told to undress, men to their drawers, women to slips. Documents and valuables had to be tied in a handkerchief, and all the money sewn into the clothes had to be ripped out to prevent damage during the disinfections. After these preparations, the people were taken to the bathroom through the door leading to the stairs below; here the temperature suddenly dropped because the corridor was not heated at all. To the people's complaints the Germans answered politely that they should be patient until they would get to the bath.

The bath turned out to be a prepared ramp, to which these unfortunates were rushed with the help of whips, butts, and machine guns. They were then loaded into the execution van, which was standing on the opposite side of the ramp. The van into which the unfortunates were rushed was the size of a big gray truck, hermetically closed and furnished with tightly fastened doors bolted from the outside. The walls of the van were covered with tin; small ladders were laid out on the floor, covered with straw mats. Under the small ladders, on both sides of the van, two gas-pipe blowers, fixed with strainers, were placed. The two pipes led to the cab, where they were connected to a gas appliance that had a number of buttons. After the van had been loaded and the door hermetically closed, it drove to a forest, 7 km from Koło, where the slaughter took place. It was in a field surrounded by soldiers armed with machine guns, and mass graves prepared in advance ran in the middle of it. These were 5 meters deep, 1.5 meters wide at the bottom, and 5 meters wide at the top. The van stopped about 100 m from the grave. The driver/murderer pressed the buttons of the appliance in the cab and got out. The drivers were SS men in uniform, with skulls on their hats. Deadened cries and sounds of knocking on the walls came from inside the van. About a quarter of an hour later, the driver climbed a ladder and looked through a special eyehole into the van. After checking that all the victims were dead, he drove the van closer to the grave and five minutes later he gave an order to open the door of the van.

The burial was carried out by scores of Jewish forced-labor gravediggers. At the order of the commandant of the slaughter place—an SS-man—they started hurling the corpses, which smelled of gas and excrement and lay in great disorder, from the truck. The corpses were brutally pulled out by their hair, hands, and feet. The commandant shouted incessantly and struck the gravediggers. The corpses were piled up, and then two German civilians searched the still-warm bodies for valuables. The search was very scrupulous. Chains were torn from necks; gold teeth were extracted with pliers. They checked very closely to see if there were any valuables in female sex organs and in rectums. Only then were the corpses thrown into the grave, where two Jewish gravediggers arranged them with their faces to the ground, so that the feet of one were next to the head of another. Six to nine vans [worth of people] were buried a day. Each layer of corpses was covered with earth.

From January 17 on, they also added chloride. Eight gravediggers, who were dealing directly with the corpses, stayed in the grave all day long. Before the end of the day, one of the officers would order [some of] them to lie down facing the corpses and with a machine handgun put holes into their heads. The others covered the graves hastily and, at the order of the officers, went back to their special lodging in the palace. Apart from Jews from Koło and Dąbie, the following were murdered in Chełmno: from

January 2 to January 9, Gypsies were brought from the Łódź ghetto; on January 10 and January 12 Jews from Kłodowa; on January 13 Jews from Bugaj; on January 14 and 15 Jews from Izbica Kujawska; and from January 16 on—Jews from the Łódź ghetto.

There is no doubt that the action had been prepared in advance. Local police stations had accurate information about the fate that awaited the deportees. In spite of this, not only did they not inform the unfortunates about it but, on the contrary, they deceived them perfidiously, refusing to admit any knowledge of deportations. The Gestapo in charge of the executions in the palace acted according to a precisely worked-out plan. The main principle of its activity was total secrecy. Except for the groups of victims, absolutely no one was ever present in the area of the palace, and it never happened that two groups of "deportees" met anywhere. The aforementioned details come from accounts of the neighborhood population. In spite of all precautionary measures, echoes of the tragedy that was taking place in the Chełmno palace came to its attention—above all, from notes thrown out of the windows of the palace by the hapless gravediggers. As already mentioned, their authenticity is beyond doubt.

DOCUMENT 30

Letter from Arthur Greiser to Himmler about retaining meritorious members of Special Kommando Lange at the death camp at Chełmno on the Nerem,[29] March 1943

Reichsführer!

Several days ago, I visited the former Lange Special Unit, now under the command of the SS and Criminal Commissioner Hauptsturmführer Bothmann, as a special detail in Chełmno, Koło County, which is to be deactivated in mid-month. At this time, I became acquainted with the members of the Special Unit, whose attitude I would like to report to you, Herr Reichsführer SS. These men not only faithfully and bravely carried out all tasks imposed on them by you, sir, to the letter, but additionally presented the best attitude of any soldier.

Thus, during a very pleasant evening to which I had invited them, they handed me a contribution of RM 15,150 in cash, which they had spontaneously collected that day. I would like to contribute the money to the Fund for Aid to Children of Murdered Volksdeutsche, unless you, Reichsführer, see a more suitable purpose.

The soldiers also expressed a desire to continue to carrying out their responsibilities under their commander, Hauptsturmführer Bothmann. I promised the soldiers that their request would be passed on to you, Herr Reichsführer. Please, Sir, permit me to invite these soldiers, as part of their holidays, to be my guests in my estates, which should provide them with substantial assistance and an enjoyable holiday.

Heil Hitler
(-) Greiser

DOCUMENT 31

Probate decision of Kleczew Municipal Court, December 28, 1949, concerning Chaskiel Kroner, d. May 10, 1942, in Wołkowysk

NOTES

1. Yitzhak Arad, Yisrael Gutman, et al., eds., *Documents on the Holocaust: Selected Sources on the Destruction of the Jews of Germany and Austria, Poland and the Soviet Union* (Jerusalem, 1987), 132-135; N. H. Baynes, ed., *The Speeches of Adolf Hitler*, I (London, 1942),. 737-741.
2. *Documents on the Holocaust*, 185-187.
3. 12 listopada 1939 r., Poznań—Z okólnika wyższego dowódcy SS i policji w Warthegau, Koppe'go, dotyczącego planu przesiedlenia Żydów i Polaków z Warthegau do Generalnej Guberni, in *Eksterminacja*, 32-33
4. 26 stycznia 1940, Poznań, Ze sprawozdania Wyższego dowódcy SS i policji w Warthegau o przesiedleniu Polaków i Żydów z Warthegau do Generalnej Guberni, *Eksterminacja*, 40-41.
5. For a brief description, see Annex 2.
6. 30 stycznia 1940, Berlin. Z przemówienia szefa Głównego Urzędu Bezpieczeństwa Rzeszy, Heydricha i wyższego dowódcy SS i policji w Generalgouvernement Krügera, wygłoszonych na konferencji w Berlinie, u sprawie przymusowego przesiedlenia ludności polskiej i żydowskiej z Warthegau do Generalgouvernement., *Eksterminacja*, 44-45.
7. *Documents on the Holocaust*, 183-185.
8. NO-5322; *Documents on the Holocaust*, 183-185.
9. AŻIH, 210/401.
10. Ibid.
11. Ibid.
12. AŻIH, 210/738.
13. Ibid.
14. Ibid.
15. Ibid.
16. Ibid.
17. Ibid.
18. Ibid.
19. A Gauleiter was the Party leader of a regional branch of the NSDAP (=the Nazi Party) or the head of a Reichsgau (Reich District).
20. *Documents on the Holocaust*, 346-347.
21. Lehrer, Steven, *Wannsee House and the Holocaust*, (Jefferson, NC, 2000), 142-143; BGKBZHP 13 (1960): 69-70; AGK—Akta Sprawy Arthura Greisera, sign. 585/z/III, inw. 613, k. 567-568.
22. NO-205; *Documents on the Holocaust*, 272-273.
23. From Łucja Pawlicka-Nowak, ed., *Chełmno Witnesses Speak*, (Konin-Łódź, 2004), 93-96; a copy of the Polish document is kept in the Yad Vashem Archives, O.4/222, pp. 1-6.
24. Aleksander Kaminski (1903-1978), editor in chief of the most important magazine of the underground—ZWZ-AK, *Biuletyn Informacyjny* (Information Bulletin)— board member of the clandestine Scouts organization known as Szare Szeregi, and author of the acclaimed book *Kamienie na szaniec* (Stones for the Rampart), 1945.

25 A. Skibińska, R. Szuchta, and W. Młynarczyk, eds., *Wybór źródeł do nauczania o zagładzie Żydów na okupowanych ziemiach polskich* (Warsaw, 2010), 227-229.
26 Yad Vashem Archives, TR.17/2 (OKP.III.Ds.21/68), 22-24.
27 Himmler's speech to senior SS officers in Poznań, October 4, 1943, PS-1919; *Documents on the Holocaust*, 344-345.
28 Jewish Historical Institute in Warsaw (ŻIH), Ringelblum Archives, AR I/605; Joseph Kermish, ed., *To Live with Honor and Die with Honor: Selected Documents from the Warsaw Ghetto Underground Archives "O.S." (Oneg Shabbath)* (Jerusalem, 1986), 683-686.
29 A. Skibińska, R. Szuchta, and W. Młynarczyk, eds., *Wybór źródeł do nauczania o zagładzie Żydów na okupowanych ziemiach polskich* (Warsaw, 2010), 236.

Annex 2
Stories of Descendants and Survivors of the Jewish Community of Kleczew

A. RECONSTRUCTING SURVIVORS' WARTIME HISTORY: THE STORY OF THE KRONER FAMILY

Documents collected at the State Archives in Konin allow us to reconstruct the fate of entire families during the Holocaust. The case that follows concerns a group of applications for death certificates submitted by Jakub Kroner, involving several members of his family. Using documents stored at the State Archives in Konin and the Kroner family's private collections, it was possible to partly reconstruct the fate of some Kroner family members from Kleczew who perished during the Holocaust and one who, after surviving the war and the Holocaust in the depths of the Soviet Union, returned to Poland. Jakub Kroner returned not to Kleczew but to the "Recovered Territories"; in 1950 he emigrated, together with his family, to Israel.

Jakub Kroner applied to the Kleczew Municipal Court (*Sąd Grodzki w Kleczewie*) for death certificates for the following people: Lajb Kroner (b. 1909) [1] and his wife Chana Sura Kroner;[2] Lajb Kroner (b. 1861) [3] and his wife Laja Ruchla Kroner;[4] and Chaskiel Kroner[5], his wife Chana Kroner,[6] and their daughter Elżbieta Kroner.[7] Lajb Kroner, son of Icek Kroner and Adela Kroner *née* Skowron, was born on October 5, 1909. He was the brother of the applicant, Jakub.[8] Lajb Kroner was forcibly deported by the occupation authorities from Kleczew to Warsaw and subsequently was interned in the Warsaw ghetto along with his wife, Chana Sura *née* Szrajer.[9] Lajb Kroner, according to the testimony of the witness Henry Maliński, the son of Hersh and Itta-Rivka *née* Lewenberg, was shot in the Warsaw ghetto on July 23, 1942. After the deportation from Kleczew to Warsaw, Lajb Kroner lived, according to a witness's testimony, at 1 Smocza Street. In late October 1942, he was shot during a selection by German police. The case file, however, contains a contradiction, for another document—the application of judicial defender January Marciniak—states that Lajb Kroner was shot dead on July 23, 1942. Probably due to the confusion, as in similar cases involving the Kroner family, several other applications were filed. We do not know the outcome of this litigation.

Chana Sura Kroner *née* Szrajer is reported as having died of starvation in the Warsaw ghetto on June 5, 1942. She was born on February 13, 1912 in Słupca to Abram Benjamin Szrajer and Itta Szrajer *née* Latta. In this case, too, the witness Henryk Maliński furnished the foregoing details, but another witness testified to a different date of Chana Sura Kroner's death—October 5, 1942. The court dismissed this case, requesting the submission of additional documents. Again, we do not know the outcome of this litigation.

Jakub Kroner filed a request for the declaration of death of a different Lajb Kroner, this one the son of Elchana Kroner and Blima Kroner née Parzyński, born on July 15, 1861, in Kleczew. Lajb had also been deported to Warsaw, where he was killed on July 30, 1942.[10] In this case, the witness dated the death to early August 1942 and reported the cause of death as gunfire. With Lajb Kroner was his wife Ruchla Laja Kroner, daughter of Ajzyk Kroner and Rojza née Jagła, born in Kleczew in 1870.[11] The request for a declaration of death recorded the date of her demise as August 3, 1942, from a heart attack. In its decision, however, the court determined July 30, 1942, as the date of death.

Applications for declarations of death were filed for three other members of the Kroner family: Dr. Chaskiel Kroner, his wife Chana, and their daughter Elżbieta. Dr. Kroner, son of Chaskiel Lajb Kroner and Ruchla Laja Kroner née Jagła, was born on February 15, 1895, in Kleczew.[12] According to the witness Josek Mebler, Dr. Chaskiel Kroner was drafted into the Polish army in 1939 and was involved in the defense of Warsaw in September of that year. After the Germans occupied the capital, Dr. Kroner was released. It is unclear whether Dr. Kroner was imprisoned or managed to avoid that fate. Either way, he could not return to Kleczew and therefore headed east to Wołkowysk, which came under Soviet occupation on September 17, 1939. There he worked as a doctor. In late April 1942, during a selection and the exit of hundreds of Jews from Wołkowysk, he was shot dead in Kościuszko Square. The witness worked as a forced laborer in Wołkowysk and lived at 19 Mickiewicz Street, on the ground floor of the house where Dr. Kroner lived on the first floor. When the witness contracted typhus, Dr. Kroner treated him. He recalled that Dr. Kroner was shot at about 9:00 a.m. The witness, together with a group of other workers, received an order to bury shot Jews in the nearby woods. When the witness moved the corpses, he recognized Dr. Kroner. The Jews in Wołkowysk, he said, wore a metal plate with punched numbers sewn into their clothes; Dr. Kroner's number was 1422. About fifteen other Jews were shot at this time. The court decided to recognize the death of Dr. Chaskiel Kroner and determined the date of death as May 10, 1942, at 10:00 a.m., even though the date entered in the application was May 2, 1942.

Chana Kroner *née* Glazmann (b. January 14, 1906, in Łódź[13]), wife of Dr. Chaskiel Kroner and daughter of Chaskiel Glazmann and Kajla Chaja Glazmann *née* Hochberg, was forcibly deported by the Nazis to Warsaw in 1940 along with her daughter Elżbieta (b. April 25, 1938) . It was alleged that Chana Kroner died of starvation in the Warsaw ghetto on August 30, 1942. In this case, too, the witness was Henry Maliński. He stated in his testimony that Chana Kroner initially resided in Warsaw at 1 Smocza Street and died of exhaustion in late August 1941. Maliński claimed that he had been a caretaker at the house at 1 Smocza Street and clearly remembered what had happened there. He stated that he had seen the corpse of Chana Kroner and attended her funeral. The court determined the date of Chana Kroner's death as August 30, 1941. Her daughter, according to Henryk Maliński, died in late September 1941.[14] The court considered Elżbieta Kroner deceased and determined her date of death as September 30, 1941.

Jakub Kroner (1913–1970)

Jakub Kroner's life is a good example of the fate of those Jewish residents of Kleczew who, thanks to their escape to the east, found themselves in the Soviet Union. There Jakub Kroner survived the war and returned to Poland under the repatriation program thereafter, only to leave the country several years later and settle in Israel. Jakub Kroner was born on June 5, 1913, in Kleczew, to Icek Kroner and Adela Kroner *née* Skowron. From 1928 to 1930 he attended the Technical School of Wawelberg and Rotwand in Warsaw. In September 1939, he probably lived in Warsaw. In 1940, he was in Kowal and worked in a metal goods shop (as noted by a certificate of employment dated June 23, 1940). On January 8, 1941, in Magnitogorsk, Jakub Kroner married Zofia Wajsand (b. 1921 in Ostrowiec Świętokrzyski). During the war, Jakub Kroner was employed in Detachment No. 769 of the Working Battalion in Magnitogorsk. Jakub Itzkovich Kroner received the Soviet certificate award for good work in the Great Fatherland War of 1941–1945. He was a member of the Association of Polish Patriots in the Soviet Union. He also had a certificate issued by the Polish-Soviet Joint Commission for Evacuation Affairs (which handled matters relating to Polish citizens). Obtaining a certificate permitting him and his family to repatriate to Poland between April and June 1946, he reached Wałbrzych and joined the Walbrzych branch of the Professional Association of Miners in 1946. He also joined the Professional Association of Employees of Cooperatives and the Polish-Soviet Friendship Association in 1949. He maintained his Zionist and Jewish identity, as evidenced in his membership in the Po'alei Tsiyyon–ha-Shomer ha-Tza'ir Party in Poland and in the

Ha-Shomer ha-Tza'ir Jewish Labor Party (with membership card No. 3132).

Jakub Kroner was one of very few Jews from Kleczew who managed to receive his inheritance after the war. To proceed with the request for recognition of death before the Kleczew Municipal Court (*Sąd Grodzki w Kleczewie*), he hired a Polish lawyer to represent him while he lived in Silesia. At the meeting of the Municipal Court on December 28, 1949, Judge Edward Paszkowski, at the request of Yankev-Elkon [Jakub] Kroner, residing at 14 Roztafiński Street, Apartment 5, in Wrocław, and a permanent resident of Kleczew, Konin District, declared his rights to the estate of the deceased Chaskiel Kroner, son of Lajb Kroner and Ruchla Laja *née* Jagła, who was intestate in Wołkowysk on May 10, 1942.[15] Chaskiel Kroner had been born on February 15, 1895, in Kleczew and lived there. The Municipal Court judge ruled that the inheritance of the deceased, Chaskiel Kroner, was to be inherited in full by Yankev-Elkon [Jakub] Kroner, son of Ichak and Adel Kroner *née* Skowrońska, born on June 5, 1913, in Kleczew and cousin of the deceased. A copy of the request was issued to the applicant's attorney, defense court counsel January Marciniak, on February 3, 1950. On January 25, 1950, a valuation of real estate belonging to Chaskiel Kroner, son of Lajb and Ruchla Laja Kroner, who died on May 10, 1942, in Wołkowysk, was prepared. The property consisted of one single-storey brick building covered with tiles and a one-storey brick outbuilding roofed with asphalt and barewalled. The property and the buildings had been valuated at a minimum of 12.000 złoty before August 31, 1939, and 600.000 złoty at the time of the application. A certificate was issued by an expert witness, the Konin County architect Albert Gos.[16]

Another document in this case, a certificate from the Konin tax office dated January 30, 1950, demanded the payment of inheritance tax by Jakub a.k.a. Yankel Kroner Elkana [Yankev-Elkon Kroner], on the property of Chaskiel Kroner.[17] Following the decision of the Kleczew Municipal Court on December 28, 1949, concerning the transfer of the estate to the ownership of Jakub Kroner, he was obliged to pay an inheritance tax in the amount of 12,000 złoty. He made this remittance to the Konin tax office on February 3, 1950, thus allowing a deed of sale of the assets to be drafted or a record of ownership to be drawn up, possibly both in close succession. On June 19, 1950, the Kleczew Town Council Presidium issued another certificate,[18] declaring that Chaskiel Kroner had been the owner of the property at 16 Poznań Street for about ten years as of September 1, 1939.

A copy of a decision by the Kleczew Municipal Court on December 28, 1949, concerning Heir ("Spadek") after Chaskiel Kroner (d. May 10, 1942, in Wołkowysk) is presented in document 31, Annex 1.

On September 1, 1939, Chaskiel Kroner left his property, never to return. The property is bordered on the east by the property of Patałowski Abram. Another certificate, issued by the Kleczew Town Council Bureau on June 19, 1950, states that the property on 16 Poznańska Street (formerly Słupecka Street), which during the occupation had belonged to the deceased Chaskiel Kroner and then to the Town Council Presidium, underwent no repairs or investment. Jakub Kroner's motive for requesting the certificate was to present it to the Liquidation Office in Poznań. The document was signed by Bolesław Kachelski, Chairman of the Presidium.[19]

On June 28, 1950, Jakub Kroner and his wife and children (Tziva, b. 1941, and Yitzhak, b. 1946) left Poland via the border crossing in Zebrzydowice. On June 29, 1950, the three of them entered Austria at the border crossing in Hochenau. They left Austria on June 30, 1950. They went to Italy by train, crossing the border at Tarvisio. They boarded the *Galila* at Venice port on July 2, 1950, using Jakub Kroner's Polish identity card as a passport. They reached the port of Haifa, Israel, on June 6, 1950, as evidenced by the border control stamp in his Polish identity card. Jakub and his wife had two children, and Jakub died on April 18, 1970, in Hadassah Hospital, Jerusalem.

B. MORE THAN 100 YEARS OF DOCUMENTED RESIDENCY IN KLECZEW: THE RACHWALSKI GENEALOGY AS AN EXAMPLE

Background

The Rachwalski family tree reflects the lifespan of a typical Jewish family that lived in Kleczew. Members of this family probably reached Kleczew in 1829 or a few years earlier. They lived there in peace for more than 100 years, involved in the local economy and cultural life. As presented in previous chapters and tables, Tobiasz Rachwalski and his son Majer had a family-owned shoe store. Isaac Traube, Tobiasz's son-in-law, was among the first leaders of the Jewish Craftsmens Association in Kleczew. On a few occasions when times got tough, several members of the family left Kleczew for the United States and British-ruled Palestine. This happened in several waves. The first documented emigration (that of Gittel Rachwalski and her family) was in 1868; the last one was on April 24, 1939 (Pesse Rywa Rachwalski—Majer's wife, with their children). The last-mentioned members of the family left Poland only one week before Nazi Germany invaded Poland, joining Majer Rachwalski (Marks) and two of his brothers in the U.S.A. Only two months earlier, the Traube family (Tobiasz Rachwalski's daughter, her husband, and their two daughters) left Kleczew for British-ruled Palestine. Those who left at the last moment saved themselves and their descendants from the horrors of World War II in Poland. As shown in the Annex, most of the family chose to stay in Kleczew and perished in the Holocaust.

The following pages document the descendants of Mortke and Nechla Rachwalski and include, among others, families such as the Marks and Aarons families (residing in the U.S.A.) and the Traube, Greenfeld and Horev families (now in Israel).

> The annex is based on a research conducted by **Ms. Madeleine Okladek** of New York. The research was based mainly on JRI-Poland (Jewish Record Indexing) and the Polish State Archives project (PSA), in addition to direct information from descendants of the family. Some additional information is based on records in the Konin Archives (APKonin) records, collected by **T. Kawski** and **A. Głowacka-Penczyńska** (Poland). The names in the annex are spelled as they appear in the records.

The Rachwalski Family in Kleczew

Generation 1

1. **MORTKE[1] RACHWALSKI** was born c. 1773 and died before 1866. He married **NECHLA RACHWALSKA**. She died before 1866.[1]

The only record found regarding Mortke Rachwalski and Nechla Rachwalska's children relates to MOSIEK RACHWALSKI:

Generation 2

2. **MOSIEK[2] RACHWALSKI** (Mortke[1] Rachwalski) was born c. 1795. He died on April 4, 1866, in Kleczew. He married **RUCHEL KOZMINSKA** c. 1818. She was born in 1795 and died on February 9, 1880, in Kleczew.

Mosiek and Ruchel Rachwalski reached Kleczew with their children no later than 1829, and likely earlier.

Mosiek Rachwalski and Ruchel Kozminska had the following children:

   i.   ESTER[3] RACHWALSKA (daughter of Mosiek Rachwalski and Ruchel Kozminska) was born c. 1819. She died after 1867. She married (1) JOSEL RACZKA, born c. 1805, and after being widowed, (2) MAREK BAJNUS.

   ii. MORDECHAI[3] RACHWALSKI (son of Mosiek Rachwalski and Ruchel Kozminska) was born c. 1820. He married FRYMET SZTYLER on November 24, 1842, in Kleczew. She was born c. 1822 in Kazimierz.

   iii. SURA RYFKA[3] RYCHWALSKA (daughter of Mosiek Rachwalski and Ruchel Kozminska) was born c. 1826. She died after 1867. She married DAWID HERSZ FELTZER on January 15, 1852, in Kleczew. He was born in 1830 in Slesin and died in 1897 in Slesin PSA.

---

1   Superscripted numbers next to a name denote the generation number.

iv. ABRAM FUEL RACHWALSKI[3] (son of Mosiek Rachwalski and Ruchel Kozminska) was born in 1829 in Kleczew. He died before 1866.
v. MARJEM RACHWALSKA[3] (daughter of Mosiek Rachwalski and Ruchel Kozminska) was born c. 1833. She married LEIB BAUM ORZECHOWSKI in about 1850. He was born c. 1822.
vi. MINDEL RACHWALSKA[3] (daughter of Mosiek Rachwalski and Ruchel Kozminska) was born on December 16, 1836, in Kleczew.
vii. ZELDA[3] RACHWALSKA (daughter of Mosiek Rachwalski and Ruchel Kozminska) was born c. 1838. She married BORUCH STRZELINSKI in 1862. He was born in 1842 in Wilczyn.

> **Earliest date of arrival to Kleczew**
>
> According to vital records, **Abram Fuel Rachwalski** (son of Mosiek and Ruchel Rachwalski), was born in Kleczew in 1829, and his sister **Mindel Rachwalska** was born there on December 16, 1836. This means that **Mosiek Rachwalski** reached Kleczew before 1829. Notably, however, according to another source, Mindel reached Kleczew with her parents in 1837, when she was two years and nine months old (APKonin, AmKleczewa. File no. 220). One possible explanation is that the family may have left Kleczew for a short period in 1836 after Mindel's birth and returned in 1837. Their return is documented.

Generation 3

3. **ESTER**[3] **RACHWALSKA** (Mosiek[2] Rachwalski, Mortke[1] Rachwalski) was born c. 1819 and died after 1867. She married (1) **JOSEL RACZKA** (born c. 1805) and (2) **MAREK BAJNUS**.

Josel Raczka and Ester Rachwalska had the following children:

i. SURA[4] RACZKOWSKA (daughter of Josel Raczka and Ester Rachwalska) was born in 1838 in Kleczew. She married JOSEL FRIDENTHAL in 1858 in Kleczew. He was born 1838 in Kleczew.
ii. MENDEL[4] RACZKA (son of Josel Raczka and Ester Rachwalska), was born in 1843 in Kleczew. He married LIBA KOHN in 1866 in Kleczew. She was born c. 1841.
iii. MICHAL[4] RACZKA (son of Josel Raczka and Ester Rachwalska) was born in 1845 in Kleczew and died in 1847 in Kleczew.
iv. ELIASZ[4] RACZKA (son of Josel Raczka and Ester Rachwalska) was born in Kleczewa and died in 1848 in Kleczew.
v. MAJLECH[4] RACZKA (son of Josel Raczka and Ester Rachwalska) was born in 1852 in Kleczew.

Marek Bajnus and Ester Rachwalska had the following child:

i. GITEL[4] BAJNUS (daughter of Marek Bajnus and Ester Rachwalska) was born in 1867 in Kleczew.

4. **MORDECHAI**[3] **RACHWALSKI** (Mosiek[2] Rachwalski, Mortke[1] Rachwalski) was born c. 1820. He married FRYMET SZTYLER on November 24, 1842 in Kleczew. She was born c. 1822 in Kazimierz.

> Documentation in the Konin Archives shows that Frymet Rachwalska married and left Kleczew in 1843, at the age of 23 (APKonin, AmKleczewa. file no. 220). This, however, was probably a temporary move; as described below, all their children were born and registered in Kleczew.

Mordechai Rachwalski and Frymet Sztyler had the following children:

    i. HASKIEL[4] RACHWALSKI (son of Mordechai Rachwalski and Frymet Sztyler) was born on January 1, 1844, in Kleczew.

    ii. GITTEL[4] RACHWALSKA (daughter of Mordechai Rachwalski and Frymet Sztyler) was born on December 6, 1845, in Kleczew, and died in January 1935 in Milwaukee, Wisconsin, U.S.A. She married SZMUL SZMULOWICZ on December 7, 1864, in Kleczew. He was born April 1, 1842, in Kleczew.

    iii. ABRAM[4] RACHWALSKI (son of Mordechai Rachwalski and Frymet Sztyler) was born December 5, 1847, in Kleczew, and may have died in 1847 in Kleczew (PSA).

    iv. RAFAL[4] RACHWALSKI (son of Mordechai Rachwalski and Frymet Sztyler) was born December 12, 1849, in Kleczew, and died in Milwaukee, WI. He married TRANA LAJE SZULC in 1872 in Koło. She was born c. 1843.

    v. SZYMEK[4] RACHWALSKI (son of Mordechai Rachwalski and Frymet Sztyler) was born on December 12, 1849, in Kleczew, and died in 1850 in Kleczew.

    vi. FAYGELE[4] RACHWALSKA (daughter of Mordechai Rachwalski and Frymet Sztyler) was born. January 18, 1852, in Kleczew. She married FALEK SZULC in 1874 in Kleczew. He was born in 1848 in Koło.

    vii. TRANE[4] RACHWALSKA (daughter of Mordechai Rachwalski and Frymet Sztyler) was born January 29, 1854, in Kleczew, and died on August 25, 1933, in Milwaukee, WI. She married ISAAK GLUCKER in 1879 in Kleczew. He was born in May 1861 in Gostynin and died on February 23, 1942, in Milwaukee, WI.

    viii. ABRAM[4] RACHWALSKI (son of Mordechai Rachwalski and Frymet Sztyler) was born in 1856 in Kleczew (PSA).

Note for Abram Rachwalski: There is an Abram in the PSA records who died in 1863. This may be the same Abram.

ix. HERSZ[4] RACHWALSKI (son of Mordechai Rachwalski and Frymet Sztyler) was born in 1859 in Kleczew (PSA).
x. SURA[4] RACHWALSKA (daughter of Mordechai Rachwalski and Frymet Sztyler) was born in 1862 in Kleczew (PSA) and died in 1863 in Kleczew (PSA).
xi. ZELIG[4] RACHWALSKI (son of Mordechai Rachwalski and Frymet Sztyler) was born in 1862 in Kleczew (PSA).
xii. TOBIASZ[4] RACHWALSKI (son of Mordechai Rachwalski and Frymet Sztyler) was born in June 20, 1864, in Kleczew PSA. He died in the Holocaust. He married (1) HENDEL AUERBACH, who was born in 1870 and died in 1895, and (2) SARAH AUERBACH, who was born in 1880. The latter marriage took place between 1900 and 1902. Sarah too died in the Holocaust.

5. **SURA RYFKA**[3] **RYCHWALSKA** (Mosiek[2] Rachwalski, Mortke[1] Rachwalski) was born c. 1826 and died after 1867. She married DAWID HESZ FELTZER on January 15, 1852, in Kleczew. He was born in 1830 in Slesin and died in 1897 in Slesin (PSA) on Jan. 1897.

Dawid Hersz Feltzer and Sura Ryfka Rychwalska had the following children:

i. SYNE JOSKA[4] FELCER (son of Dawid Hersz Feltzer and Sura Ryfka Rychwalska) was born in 1858 in Slesin (PSA) and died in 1865 in Slesin.
ii. ABRAM[4] FELCER (son of Dawid Hersz Feltzer and Sura Ryfka Rychwalska) was born in 1853 in Slesin.
iii. FOJGEL[4] FELCER (daughter of Dawid Hersz Feltzer and Sura Ryfka Rychwalska) was born in 1854 in Slesin.
iv. BEJER[4] FELTZER (son of Dawid Hersz Feltzer and Sura Ryfka Rychwalska) was born on August 11, 1859, in Slesin. He died in 1862 in Slesin.

- v. PERLA ESTER[4] FELTZER (daughter of Dawid Hersz Feltzer and Sura Ryfka Rychwalska) was born in 1861 in Slesin, and died in 1862 in Slesin.
- vi. SYNA JOSKA[4] FELTZER (son of Dawid Hersz Feltzer and Sura Ryfka Rychwalska) was born in 1863 in Slesin.
- vii. ICYK[4] FELTZER (son of Dawid Hersz Feltzer and Sura Ryfka Rychwalska) was born in 1864 in Slesin.
- viii NACHA[4] FELTZER (daughter of Dawid Hersz Feltzer and Sura Ryfka Rychwalska) was born on August 9, 1867, in Slesin and died in October 1941 in the Zagórów ghetto. She married AJMAN.

6. **MARJEM[3] RACHWALSKA** (Mosiek[2] Rachwalski, Mortke[1] Rachwalski), was born c. 1833. She married LEIB BAUM ORZECHOWSKI c. 1850. He was born c. 1822.

Leib Baum Orzechowski and Marjem Rachwalska had the following children:

- i. FAJGELKA[4] ORZECHOWSKA (daughter of Leib Baum Orzechowski and Marjem Rachwalska) was born in 1851 in Kleczew. She married SZMUL LEIBUS LEWKOWICZ in 1875 in Kleczew. He was born c. 1851 in Sieradz.
- ii. SZMUL ABRAM[4] ORZECHOWSKI (son of Leib Baum Orzechowski and Marjem Rachwalska) was born in 1853 in Kleczew. He married TAUBA KINSTLER in 1878 in Koło. She was born c. 1858.
- iii. MINDLA[4] ORZECHOWSKA (daughter of Leib Baum Orzechowski and Marjem Rachwalska) was born c. 1855 and died 1866 in Kleczew.
- iv. RYFKA[4] ORZECHOWSKA (daughter of Leib Baum Orzechowski and Marjem Rachwalska) was born in 1858 in Kleczew.
- v. NECHE[4] ORZECHOWSKA (daughter of Leib Baum Orzechowski and Marjem Rachwalska) was born in 1867 in Kleczew.
- vi. MOSIEK[4] ORZECHOWSKI (son of Leib Baum Orzechowski and Marjem Rachwalska) was born in 1868 in Kleczew.

7. **ZELDA³ RACHWALSKA** (Mosiek² Rachwalski, Mortke¹ Rachwalski) was born c. 1838 and married BORUCH STRZELINSKI in 1862 in Kleczew PSA. He was born in 1842 in Wilczyn.

Boruch Strzelinski and Zelda Rachwalska had the following children:

i. ABRAHAM⁴ STRZELINSKI (son of Boruch Strzelinski and Zelda Rachwalska) was born c. 1863.
ii. HERSZ⁴ STRZELINSKI (son of Boruch Strzelinski and Zelda Rachwalska) was born in 1864 in Kleczew PSA.
iii. HAIE⁴ STRZELINSKA (daughter of Boruch Strzelinski and Zelda Rachwalska), was born in 1866 in Kleczew.
iv. ESTER⁴ STRZELINSKA (daughter of Boruch Strzelinski and Zelda Rachwalska) was born c. 1867 and died March 7, 1931, in London.
v. MOJSZE⁴ STRZELINSKI (son of Boruch Strzelinski and Zelda Rachwalska) was born in 1868 in Kleczew.
vi. FUL⁴ STRZELINSKI (son of Boruch Strzelinski and Zelda Rachwalska) was born 1870 in Kleczew and died c. 1965 in Berlin.
vii. SZAPSIE⁴ STRZELINSKI (son of Boruch Strzelinski and Zelda Rachwalska) was born in 1872 in Kleczew and married GITEL WILCZYNSKA in 1898 in Kleczew PSA.
viii. FAJGELE⁴ STRZELINSKA (daughter of Boruch Strzelinski and Zelda Rachwalska) was born in 1874 in Kleczew.
ix. SZYMON⁴ STRZELINSKI (son of Boruch Strzelinski and Zelda Rachwalska) was born in 1877 in Kleczew.
x. DWORA⁴ STRZELINSKA (daughter of Boruch Strzelinski and Zelda Rachwalska) was born in 1879 in Kleczew and died in 1879 in Kleczew.
xi. RUCHEL⁴ STRZELINSKA (daughter of Boruch Strzelinski and Zelda Rachwalska) was born in 1880 in Kleczew and married EFROIM GEMBICKI in 1897 in Kleczew (PSA).

Generation 4

8. **SURA**[4] **RACZKOWSKA** (Ester[3] Rachwalska, Mosiek[2] Rachwalski, Mortke[1] Rachwalski) was born in 1838 in Kleczew and married JOSEL FRIDENTHAL (b. 1838 in Kleczew) in 1858 in Kleczew.

Josel Fridenthal and Sura Raczkowska had the following children:

   i. TOBIE[5] FRIDENTHAL (son of Josel Fridenthal and Sura Raczkowska) was born c. 1864 and died in 1867 in Kleczew.
   ii. RUCHEL FRIDENTHAL (daughter of Josel Fridenthal and Sura Raczkowska) was born in 1870 in Kleczew and married MORDKE PRZEDECKI in 1897 in Kleczew (PSA).
   iii. FUEL FRIDENTHAL (son of Josel Fridenthal and Sura Raczkowska) was born in 1874 in Kleczew.
   iv. MOJZESZ FRIDENTHAL (son of Josel Fridenthal and Sura Raczkowska) was born in 1876 in Kleczew.
   v. BOAZ FRIDENTHAL (son of Josel Fridenthal and Sura Raczkowska) was born in 1879 in Kleczew.

9. **GITTEL**[4] **RACHWALSKA** (Mordechai[3] Rachwalski, Mosiek[2] Rachwalski, Mortke[1] Rachwalski) was born December 6, 1845, in Kleczew and died in January 1935 in Milwaukee, WI. She married SZMUL SZMULOWICZ on December 7, 1864 in Kleczew. He was born April 1, 1842, in Kleczew.

> *Gittel was known later (in the U.S.A.) as Gusta. She immigrated to the U.S.A. in 1868 and was buried in Spring Hill Cemetery in Milwaukee, Wisconsin. Szmul Szmulowicz was known later as Lehman Aarons.*

Szmul Szmulowicz and Gittel Rachwalska left Kleczew for the U.S.A. and changed their names. They had the following children:

   i. ESTER[5] AARONS (daughter of Szmul Szmulowicz and Gittel Rachwalska) was born in 1866 in Kleczew.

ii. HARRY[5] AARONS (son of Szmul Szmulowicz and Gittel Rachwalska) was born c. 1867 in England and died in January 1928.

iii. TOBIAS[5] AARONS (son of Szmul Szmulowicz and Gittel Rachwalska) was born on December 5, 1869, in New York and died on January 1, 1948, in Los Angeles. He married (1) FREDA HERSHER, who was born c. 1875 in Kentucky, and (2) SARA ROSENSTEIN, who was born c. 1902 in Wisconsin.

iv. CHARLES LEHMAN[5] AARONS (son of Szmul Szmulowicz and Gittel Rachwalska) was born in August 1872 in New York and died July 1952 in Milwaukee, WI. He married (1) ROSE SHEUERMAN, who was born c. 1878 in Iowa and died November 1945 in Milwaukee, WI, c. 1905, and (2) BECKY after 1946. She died in October 1971 in Milwaukee, WI.

v. SAMUEL[5] AARONS (son of Szmul Szmulowicz and Gittel Rachwalska) was born October 5, 1874, in Milwaukee, WI, and died December 10, 1943, in Los Angeles. He married BERTHA. She was born c. 1878 in Nebraska.

vi. BERTHA[5] AARONS (daughter of Szmul Szmulowicz and Gittel Rachwalska) was born 1877 in Milwaukee, WI.

vii. SYLVIA[5] AARONS (daughter of Szmul Szmulowicz and Gittel Rachwalska) was born c. 1880 in Wisconsin.

viii. JACOB L.[5] AARONS (son of Szmul Szmulowicz and Gittel Rachwalska), was born July 18, 1883, in Wisconsin and died February 19, 1935, in Olmsted, Minnesota. He married ELSIE. She was born c. 1887 in Minnesota.

10. **RAFAL[4] RACHWALSKI** (Mordechai[3], Mosiek[2], Mortke[1]) was born on December 12, 1849, in Kleczew, and died in Milwaukee, WI. He married TRANA LAJE SZULC (born c. 1843) in 1872 in Koło.

> *Rafal Rachwalski* came to the U.S.A. with his son Abram Mosiek (Albert) *Trana Laje* came to the U.S.A. with Chana and Ruchle. According to the 1900 census, she gave birth to six children, of whom several survived.

Rafal Rachwalski and Trana Laje Szulc had the following children:

i. ABRAM MOSIEK[5] RACHWALSKI (son of Rafal Rachwalski and Trana Laje Szulc) was born in 1872 in Koło.

> *Abram Mosiek Rachwalski* appears on the Hamburg Passenger List. According to this source, he resided in Koło and was 17 years old when he sailed April 26, 1890, from Hamburg to New York and and Baltimore on the SS Russia. Given the previous note regarding Rafal Rachwalski, April 26, 1890, may be considered the date of Rafal Rachwalski's arrival in the U.S.A. as well.

ii. CHANA[5] RACHWALSKA (daughter of Rafal Rachwalski and Trana Laje Szulc) was born in 1875 in Koło.

iii. CYWIE[5] RACHWALSKA (daughter of Rafal Rachwalski and Trana Laje Szulc) was born in 1878 in Koło and died in 1878 in Koło.

iv. EJDEL[5] RACHWALSKA (daughter of Rafal Rachwalski and Trana Laje Szulc) was born in 1879 in Koło.

v. RUCHLE[5] RACHWALSKA (daughter of Rafal Rachwalski and Trana Laje Szulc) was born in 1888 in Koło (PSA).

11. **FAYGELE[4] RACHWALSKA** (Mordechai[3] Rachwalski, Mosiek[2] Rachwalski, Mortke[1] Rachwalski) was born on January 18, 1852, in Kleczew. She married FALEK SZULC in 1874 in Kleczew. He was born 1848 in Koło.

Falek Szulc and Faygele Rachwalska had the following children:

i. EJDEL[5] SZULC (daughter of Falek Szulc and Faygele Rachwalska) was born in 1875 in Koło.

ii. CYWIE[5] SZULC (daughter of Falek Szulc and Faygele Rachwalska) was born in 1877 in Koło.

iii. SURA[5] SZULC (daughter of Falek Szulc and Faygele Rachwalska) was born in 1879 in Koło.

iv. MAJER^5 SZULC (son of Falek Szulc and Faygele Rachwalska) was born in 1881 in Koło.

12. **TRANE^4 RACHWALSKA** (Mordechai^3 Rachwalski, Mosiek^2 Rachwalski, Mortke^1 Rachwalski) was born on January 29, 1854, in Kleczew and died August 25, 1933, in Milwaukee, WI. She married ISAAK GLUCKER in 1879 in Kleczew. He was born in May 1861 in Gostynin and died February 23, 1942, in Milwaukee, WI.

Isaak Glucker and Trane Rachwalska had the following children:

i. RYFKA^5 GLUCKER (daughter of Isaak Glucker and Trane Rachwalska) was born in 1880 in Kleczew.
ii. SYLVIA^5 GLUCKER (daughter of Isaak Glucker and Trane Rachwalska) was born in June 1887 in Kleczew.
iii. LEON^5 GLASGOW (son of Isaak Glucker and Trane Rachwalska) was born on December 18, 1889, in Milwaukee, WI, and died September 1981 in Los Angeles. He married FRANCES KAUMHEIMER, who was born between 1892-1898.

> **Leon Glasgow** was noted in 1917–1918 to have a wife and three children. No further iformation about them is known.

iv. RUTH MIRIAM^5 GLASGOW (daughter of Isaak Glucker and Trane Rachwalska) was born on August 16, 1895, in Milwaukee, WI, and died on October 16, 1989, in Los Angeles. She married a person named POLK c. 1917.

> *Trane Rachwalska (Thresa)* left Hamburg on October 27, 1888, on the SS Moravia and arrived in New York. Volume 373-7I, VIII A 1 Band 062 C, page 1738. (Based on Hamburg Passenger Lists, Microfilm roll K_1738). According to the Wisconsin state census of June 1, 1905, she was the wife of Ike Glasgow and lived in Milwaukee, Wisconsin. Ike was 42, b. May 1861; he was a tailor. Theresa was 47, and had been born February 1857
>
> **Isaak Glucker is Ike Glasgow.** Ike's brother was Daniel Glasgow, who was born March 1882. He was a ladies' tailor. According to the 1900 census, Nathan Mape, age 21, was Ike's nephew. He was not living with them. His occupation was shoe cutter. He was naturalized on October 27, 1904, at the Milwaukee municipal court. 8434 V. 14 p. 148 Witnesses to his naturalization were A.K. Levy and Herm Grodzinsky.
>
> Thresa and Ike are buried in the cemetery "Second Home."

13. **TOBIASZ^4 RACHWALSKI** (Mordechai^3 Rachwalski, Mosiek^2 Rachwalksi, Mortke^1 Rachwalski) was born on June 20, 1864, in Kleczew (PSA), He probably died in 1942 in Chełmno. He married (1) **HENDEL AUERBACH**, who was born in 1870 and died in 1895, and (2) **SARAH AUERBACH**, who was born in 1880. The latter marriage took place between 1900 and 1904. Sarah too died in the Holocaust.

Tobiasz Rachwalski and Hendel Auerbach had the following children:

i. ABRAHAM MOSES^5 RACHWALSKI (son of Tobiasz Rachwalski and Hendel Auerbach) was born on April 14, 1890, in Turek and died on December 15, 1987, in Madison, WI. He married HELENE LEPEK, who was born in 1904.

ii. MAJER TOBIASZ^5 RACHWALSKI (son of Tobiasz Rachwalski and Hendel Auerbach) was born on September 10, 1892, and died January 31, 1979, in Milwaukee, WI. He married PESSE RYWA ZELKOWICZ. She was born on September 12, 1894, in Koło and died on December 14, 1979, in Milwaukee, WI.

iii. RACHEL^5 RACHWALSKA (daughter of Tobiasz Rachwalski and Hendel Auerbach) was born in 1894 and died in 1942 in the Holocaust. She married PACANOWSKI.

Tobiasz Rachwalski and Sarah Auerbach had the following children:[20]

iv. FOIGLE[5] RACHWALSKA (daughter of Tobiasz Rachwalski and Sarah Auerbach) was born c. 1903 in Turek. She married ITZHAK ABE TRAUBE in 1927 or 1928. He was born on April 1, 1903, in Kalisz. Both died in 1982 in Givatayim, Israel.

> *Itzhak Abe Traube* and *Foigle Tzipora* *(née Rachwalski) received the only family certificate (Palestine immigration visa) that was offered in Kleczew, winning it in a lottery-style drawing. They emigrated through Warsaw and Romania to British-ruled Palestine (pre-state Israel) in July 1939, two months before Nazi Germany invaded Poland.*

v. ISAAC[5] RACHWALSKI (son of Tobiasz Rachwalski and Sarah Auerbach) was born c. 1904, married and lived in Izbica, and died in the Holocaust.

vi. *MORTON[5] RACHWALSKI* (son of Tobiasz Rachwalski and Sarah Auerbach) was born in 1908 and died on August 15, 1967, in Milwaukee, WI. He married MINETTE between 1932 and 1936. She was born in 1912 and died August 29, 1997.

vii. CHAIM[5] RACHWALSKI (son of Tobiasz Rachwalski and Sarah Auerbach) was born c. 1914 and died in the Holocaust.

viii. SZLAME[5] RACHWALSKI (son of Tobiasz Rachwalski and Sarah Auerbach), was born c. 1916 and died in the Holocaust.

ix. FRYMET[5] RACHWALSKI (daughter of Tobiasz Rachwalski and Sarah Auerbach) died in the Holocaust.

14. **SZAPSIE[4] STRZELINSKI** (Zelda[3] Rachwalska, Mosiek[2] Rachwalski, Mortke[1] Rachwalski) was born in 1872 in Kleczew and married GITEL WILCZYNSKA in 1898 in Kleczew PSA.

Szapsie Strzelinski and Gitel Wilczynska had the following child:

i. TOSE[5] STRZELINSKI (daughter of Szapsie Strzelinski and Gitel Wilczynska) was born in 1899 in Kleczew (PSA).

Generation 5

15. **TOBIAS**[5] **AARONS** (Gittel[4] Rachwalska, Mordechai[3] Rachwalski, Mosiek[2] Rachwalski, Mortke[1] Rachwalski) was born on December 5, 1869, in New York and died on January 1, 1948, in Los Angeles. He married (1) **FREDA HERSHER**, who was born c. 1875 in Kentucky, and (2) **SARA ROSENSTEIN**, who was born c. 1902 in Wisconsin, the latter c. 1924.

> *Notes for Tobias Aarons: According to the 1910 census, Freda had no children. According to the 1930 census, Tobias was married to Sara and had a daughter.*

Tobias Aarons and Sara Rosenstein had the following child:
    i.   GOLDINA[6] AARONS (daughter of Tobias Aarons and Sara Rosenstein) was born c. 1925 in Milwaukee, WI.

16. **CHARLES LEHMAN**[5] **AARONS** (Gittel[4] Rachwalska, Mordechai[3] Rachwalski, Mosiek[2] Rachwalski, Mortke[1] Rachwalski) was born in August 1872 in New York and died in July 1952 in Milwaukee, WI. He married (1) **ROSE SHEUERMAN**, who was born c. 1878 in Iowa and died November 1945 in Milwaukee, WI, c. 1905, and (2) **BECKY**, after 1946. She died in October 1971 in Milwaukee, WI.

> *Charles Lehman Aarons was elected as a judge in the U.S.A., and served in that capacity from 1926 to 1950. He ran for re-election to the Circuit Court of the State of Wisconsin in 1931. He is buried in Spring Hill Cemetery along with other members of the Aarons family.*

Charles Lehman Aarons and Rose Sheuerman had the following children:

    i.   MATILDA[6] AARONS (daughter of Charles Lehman Aarons and Rose Sheuerman) was born c. 1908 in Milwaukee, WI.
    ii. LEHMAN CHARLES[6] AARONS (son of Charles Lehman Aarons and Rose Sheuerman) was born March 1, 1909, in Milwaukee,

WI, and died August 28, 1997, in Los Angeles. He married LOUISE, who was born March 16, 1911, in Pittsburgh, PA.

iii. LOUISE[6] AARONS (daughter of Charles Lehman Aarons and Rose Sheuerman) was born c. 1916 in Milwaukee, WI.

17. **SAMUEL**[5] **AARONS** (Gittel[4] Rachwalska, Mordechai[3] Rachwalski, Mosiek[2] Rachwalski, Mortke[1] Rachwalski) was born on October 5, 1874, in Milwaukee, WI, and died on December, 10, 1943 in Los Angeles. He married **BERTHA**, who was born c. 1878 in Nebraska.

Samuel Aarons and Bertha had the following children:

i. HARRIET[6] AARONS (daughter of Samuel Aarons and Bertha) was born c. 1906 in Milwaukee, WI.

ii. ROSLYN[6] AARONS (daughter of Samuel Aarons and Bertha) was born c. January 1910 in Milwaukee, WI.

18. **JACOB L.**[5] **AARONS** (Gittel[4] Rachwalska, Mordechai[3] Rachwalski, Mosiek[2] Rachwalski, Mortke[1] Rachwalski) was born on July 18, 1883 in Wisconsin and died on February 19, 1935, in Olmsted, Minnesota. He married **ELSIE**. She was born c. 1887 in Minnesota.

Jacob L. Aarons and Elsie had the following children:

i. ROBERT[6] AARONS (son of Jacob L. Aarons and Elsie) was born c. 1909 in Minnesota.

ii. DOROTHY[6] AARONS (daughter of Jacob L. Aarons and Elsie) was born c. 1912 in Minnesota.

19. **RUTH MIRIAM**[5] **GLASGOW** (Trane[4] Rachwalska, Mordechai[3] Rachwalski, Mosiek[2] Rachwalski, Mortke[1] Rachwalski) was born on August 16, 1895, in Milwaukee, WI, and died on October 16, 1989, in Los Angeles. She married a person with the last name POLK c. 1917. Polk and Ruth Miriam Glasgow had the following child:

i. JACK[6] POLK (son of Polk and Ruth Miriam Glasgow) was born c. 1919 in Milwaukee, WI.

20. **ABRAHAM MOSES**[5] **RACHWALSKI** (Tobiasz[4], Mordechai[3], Mosiek[2], Mortke[1]) was born on April 14, 1890, in Turek and died on December 15, 1987, in Madison, WI.[21] He married **HELENE LEPEK,** b. 1904.

> *Abraham Moses (a.k.a Alfred) Rachwalski immigrated to US in Sept 5, 1908 on the SS Pennsylvania. He left Hamburg Aug 21 1908 to New York After reaching the U.S.A., he changed his surname to Marks. Witnesses to his naturalization in Milwaukee, WI, were Milton Marks and Wm. H. Stein. A passport application dated April 15, 1924, states that he intended to sail aboard the SS Majestic on May 17, 1924, and return within six months. He intended to visit his parents in Poland, relatives in Germany, and the battlefield in France. His address at the time was 779 Parwell Avenue, Milwaukee, WI. He signed the application as Alfred Tobias Marks. Harry Louis, whose occupation was in the wholesale furniture trade, 579 Market Street in Milwaukee, vouched that he had known Alfred T. Marks for ten years.*

Abraham Moses (a.k.a. Alfred) Rachwalski and Helene Lepek had the following child:

i. MERTONE[6] MARKS (son of Abraham Moses Rachwalski and Helene Lepek) was born in 1932. He married (1) RUTH S. ECHER, who was born in 1933 in Vienna and died in 1965, (2) RADEE, who was born in 1931 in St. Paul, Minnesota, and died in 2006).

21. **MAJER TOBIASZ**[5] **RACHWALSKI** (Tobiasz[4], Mordechai[3], Mosiek[2], Mortke[1]) was born on September 10, 1892, and died on January 31, 1979, in Milwaukee, WI. He married **PESSE RYWA ZELKOWICZ** in Milwaukee, WI. She was born on September 12, 1894, in Koło and died on December 14, 1979, in Milwaukee, WI.

> *Majer Tobiasz Rachwalski* immigrated to US on November 22, 1922, on the SS Montclare from Liverpool to Detroit, MI crossing from Canada. U.S. naturalization records list his date of birth as August 22, 1892. Witnesses were Harry Boruszak and Chas Levy. The Social Security death index, however, has his date of birth as September 10, 1892. His SSN is 397-05-0567. The 1930 census gives his age as 38, meaning that he was born in 1892. According to the census, when he arrived, he lived with his aunt Theresa née Rachwalska Glasgow and her husband Isaac Glasgow (originally Glucker).
>
> **Pesse Rywa (nee ZELKOWICZ)'s** *passenger ticket was issued in Warsaw on August 14, 1939. She came on the SS Batory, which left from Gdynia, Poland, on August 24, 1939. According to the family history, she had earlier come to the U.S.A. with the rest of the family, but was sent back because she had trachoma.*
>
> *Majer and Pesse's place of residence in Kleczew was 33 Słupecka Street. This was documented for 1922, 1924, and 1927 in a list of people who held the right to vote in Kleczew (see Annex 3).* **Haja Sura Zelkowicz** *was Pesse's sister, nine years younger than Pesse. In 1927, she lived with them. (APKonin, AmKleczewa. files 448,449).*

Majer Tobiasz Rachwalski and Pesse Rywa Zelkowicz had the following children:

i. MORTKE LEZER[6] MARKS (son of Majer Tobiasz Rachwalski and Pesse RywaZelkowicz) was born on January 27, 1908, in Kleczew and died on September 23, 1989, in Milwaukee, WI. He married BECKY.

ii. HELEN[6] MARKS (daughter of Majer Tobiasz Rachwalski and Pesse Rywa Zelkowicz) was born in Kleczew. She never married and died c. 1972 in Tel Aviv, Israel.

iii. ZORACH LEZER[6] MARKS (son of Majer Tobiasz Rachwalski and Pesse Rywa Zelkowicz) was born in 1918 in Kleczew and died on July 2, 1981 in Milwaukee, WI. He married BEATRICE

RUTH SCHAEFFER. She was born in the U.S.A. and died August 13, 1965, in Milwaukee, WI.

22. **MORTON**[5] **RACHWALSKI** (Tobiasz[4], Mordechai[3], Mosiek[2], Mortke[1]) was born in 1908 and died in August 1967 in Milwaukee, WI. He married MINETTE between 1932 and 1936. She was born in 1912 and died August 29, 1997, in Milwaukee, WI.

> *Morton Rachwalski's date of arrival in the U.S.A. is unknown. In all probability he joined his brothers (**Alfred** and **Majer**) in the journey from Europe. Like his brothers and uncles, he changed his surname to Marks after reaching the U.S.*

Morton and Minette Rachwalski had the following children:

i. LOWELL[6] MARKS (son of Morton and Minette Rachwalski) was born c. 1937. He married MARGARET.

ii. JERRY[6] MARKS (son of Morton and Minette Rachwalski) was born in Milwaukee, WI.

23. **FOIGLE**[5] **RACHWALSKA** (Tobiasz[4] Rachwalski, Mordechai[3] Rachwalski, Mosiek[2] Rachwalski, Mortke[1] Rachwalski) was born c. 1903 in Turek or Kleczew. She married ISAAK ABE TRAUBE in 1927 or 1928 in Kleczew or Kalisz. He was born on April 1, 1903, in Kalisz. Both died in 1982 in Givatayim, Israel.

Isaak Abe Traube and Foigle Rachwalska had the following children:

i. FRYMET TRAUBE[6] (daughter of Itzhak Abe Traube and Foigle Rachwalska) was born on January 4, 1929, in Kleczew. She married ZEEV WOLF (CHORZEWSKI) HOREV, who was born on August 5, 1925, in Pajęczno, Poland.

ii. HANNA[6] TRAUBE (daughter of Itzhak Abe Traube and Foigle Rachwalska) was born in 1932 in Kalisz. She married YEHUDA GREENFELD (son of Ben Tzion Greenfeld) in Tel Aviv, Israel. He died in 2010 in Givatayim, Israel. Hannah died in January 25th, 2015.

Isaak Abe Traube and Foigle (Tzipora) née *Rachwalska left Kleczew for Israel with their daughters on July 7, 1939—two months before Germany invaded Poland in World War II.*

Tuvia HOREV (editor of this book) and his brother Menachem are the sons of Zeev HOREV (*né* CHORZEWSKI) and Frymet HOREV (*née* TRAUBE) and the grandsons of Isaak Aba TRAUBE and Foigle Tzipora (*née* RACHWALSKI)

Although intensive research and efforts were made in constructing the family tree, it may still include mistakes. We regret any such error that may have occurred. If you find one or if you can contribute additional information to this chapter, please send the information to the editor.

For reasons of irrelevancy and privacy, the continuation— three additional generations—is not presented. Requests for additional information regarding this genealogy should be forward to the editor.

C. RECONSTRUCTION VIA APPEALS TO KLECZEW MUNICIPAL COURT

One method used to trace Kleczew's Jewish survivors is by searching the National Archives in Konin for Jewish appeals to the Kleczew Municipal Court. As stated in the main text, family members of several people who were murdered or disappeared without a trace in the Holocaust attempted after the war to settle many formal issues related to property left behind. When applying for an inheritance of real estate, bank accounts, or other property, it was necessary to present relevant documents that would establish the entitlement. In the absence of death certificates—because they had not been issued by the population registry offices—it became necessary to obtain court orders. To procure them, applicants had to submit whatever documentation they possessed that would confirm the death; when these did not exist, they had to call witnesses who would file an affidavit. In their testimonies, the witnesses sometimes described the circumstances of the death and proved that they had resided at the locality of the deceased when the death took place or had participated in the victim's funeral. In other cases, witnesses attested to having learned of an individual's death through hearsay. In yet other testimonies, witnesses avowed to the last time they saw a particular person and the fact that that the person did not return. Of course, in some cases, there may have been errors or confirmations of a person's death when the person had actually been outside the country. That someone did not return after the war did not necessarily mean that he or she had died. However, given that over 96% of the prewar Jewish population in Poland had been exterminated, the margin of error was not large. In some cases, the court concluded that the testimonies of some witnesses were formulaic, recited, and inconsistent with basic facts known to the courts. Addressing issues of ownership was not only necessary for people who had died or were murdered during the war. In some cases, it was also required for people who had died before the war but had no legal heirs in view of evidence of the deaths of other family members. In cases of the succession of distant relatives, it was necessary not only to seek recognition of the death of wartime victims but also to restore the death certificates of people whose deaths had predated the war. Since the records of the Population Registry Office in Kleczew were destroyed, court decisions were necessary to restore the obliterated death certificates. This was performed when recognition of the deceased was required. An application to the court had to be submitted, including an indication of witnesses who testified under oath that the person had died before the war.

Importantly, some applications submitted after the war did not necessarily relate to people who had died during the war. The collections in the National Archives in Konin include records of court decisions concerning people who had died before the war. The case of Majer Kiwała, who died in Kleczew in March 1928, is an example.[22] Judge Józef Majewski of Kleczew Municipal Court decided on April 28, 1949, after scrutinizing the application of Adv. Stanisław Podlewski, representing Chaim-Zyjel Zylber of Koło, to restore Majer Kiwała's death certificate. The court decided to recognize the death of Majer Kiwała of Kleczew (b. 1867 in Kleczew), setting the date of his death at March 31, 1928, at midnight in Kleczew and instructing the Population Registry Office in Kleczew to issue a death certificate for him. The decision was based on the testimony of the applicant Chaim-Zyjel Zylber and the witness Lola Landau. Majer Kiwała was the son of Israel and Chana *née* Szajniak. The applicant stated that Kiwała's death certificate had been destroyed during the war, necessitating its restoration.

Similar to the above was a request to the Kleczew Municipal Court for a declaration of the death of Lajzer Śleszyński,[23] who had also died before the war. Here the applicant was Helena Drachman of Włocławek. On March 24, 1949, the court recognized the death of Lajzer Śleszyński, the son of Hersh and Golda *née* Papuszka, born on December 17, 1864, in Kleczew, setting the date of death at June 20, 1937, at midnight. The court then instructed the Population Registry to issue a death certificate for Śleszyński.

In several other cases, court decisions could reveal names and circumstances of people from Kleczew who had died during the war and identify their relatives, some of them survivors of the war. One example is the case of Moishe Jachimowicz of 9 Kiliński Street in Przedecz. Jachimowicz asked the Municipal Court to recognize the death of Hersh Frenkel, his cousin,[24] son of Ido Frenkiel and Gittel *née* Rozen Frenkiel, born January 30, 1899, in Skulsk. On July 20, 1924, Frenkel married Szajna-Hendel Elbaum and lived in Kleczew until 1940. That year he was deported, along with other Jews from Kleczew, probably to the ghetto in Zagórów, never to return. In another application submitted by Jachimowicz on July 24, 1948, we find that Hersh Frenkel was taken to Inowroclaw and in 1942 murdered there by the Gestapo on April 24, 1942.[25] Fishel Goldman of 9 Kiliński Street in Przedecz testified as a witness in this case. We do not know all the circumstances and actions taken by the court in Kleczew. The court decided, however, on June 30, 1949, to recognize Hersh Frenkiel as deceased and set the date of death at January 1, 1947, at midnight. The court placed a notice in the *Monitor Polski* (The Polish Monitor) instructing the person of interest to appear before the court or to send a message. After the passage of three months, with no news having arrived to indicate whether the person was alive or where he was, the court declared him dead. Such notice and the allowance of three months for a response was a common practice concerning missing persons under the law. The outcome could affect not only the recognition of the person as deceased but also matters relating to inheritance and other issues connected to real estate.

Tosia Buksztajn, daughter of Szepsi Buksztajn and Gitla née Wilczyńska, born on November 13, 1899, in Kleczew, was forcibly deported from the town in 1940.[26] She, her husband Michal Majer Buksztajn, and their daughter Rojza[27] were deported to the ghetto in Józefów Biłgorajski. After some time, they fled to Ostrowiec Świętokrzyski. Later, they were moved to the ghetto together with other Jews. On July 31, 1941, Tosia Buksztajn died during a typhus epidemic. Approximately six months later, on February 5, 1942, her daughter Rojza Buksztajn also died.

The Kleczew Municipal did not resolve all cases positively. Wherever conflicting evidence was submitted, it rejected requests. Such was the situation in an application for the recognition of the death of Szajna Hendel Frenkel,[28] wife of the aforementioned Hersh Frenkel. In this case, the problematic witness was Fishel Goldman. The court dismissed the application because Jachimowicz's application stated that Szajna Hendel Frenkel had been deported to Inowrocław in 1942 and murdered there on June 2, 1942. The witness, Fishel Goldman, stated that Szajna Hendel Frenkel was murdered in Inowrocław on June 2, 1942; however, in another case seeking recognition of the death of Gital

Frenkel *née* Rozen, Goldman said that she had died in Łódź on July 23, 1942. Kleczew Municipal Court found that Goldman could not have been simultaneously in Inowrocław and in the Łódź ghetto, present at the deaths of both women and giving the exact date of death. Therefore, the court found him not credible and rejected the petition. We do not know how these cases proceeded farther on. At times, however, the same witnesses appeared at several hearings and, if contradictions existed in their testimonies, the applications were rejected. Notably, it was possible to appeal to a higher court to reconsider the request by resubmitting the same documents but calling additional or new witnesses.

D. ADDITIONAL INFORMATION REGARDING DESCENDANTS AND RELATIVES OF JEWS FROM KLCZEW

> Most of the information in this section was obtained either via direct communication with families or through e-mail correspondence with relatives located following previous queries in a search for Kleczew families through the Jewish Gen Family Finder.

The Bagno Family

The Bagno family was a relatively large family in Kleczew. Eliyahu Bagno owned a grocery store, then a bakery, and finally an oil factory in the town. Chaim Laib Bagno, his son, owned both a bookshop and a photography shop and studio. He had at least two brothers: Tobiasz (a teacher) and Nachum Israel. Moshe Bagno, Nachum's son, was a Religious Zionist and was very active in establishing organizations such as Tzeirei Mizrachi and Hashomer Hadati in Kleczew. His maternal grandfather, Abraham Makowski, had once been offered the position of rabbi of Kleczew but had refused because he preferred to continue practicing his occupations as teacher and children's tutor. After extensive Zionist activity in Kleczew and the vicinity, Moshe Bagno emigrated to pre-state Israel in 1934. In his first years there, he lived in Hadera and served as a secretary of the Hapoel Hamizrachi Religious Zionist movement.[29] Later, he moved to the city of Bnei Brak with his family, where he was considered a leading figure graced with both vision and executive abilities. After heading the local branch of Hapoel Hamizrachi for several years, he became the second mayor of Bnei Brak, holding this position in 1954–1955 and 1957–1959. In July 1970, he was named Citizen of Honor of Bnei Brak.[30]

Leah (Lotka) Krzywanowski

Leah (Lotka) Krzywanowski was born in Kleczew in November 1913 to a family of twelve children. Her father, while neither Orthodox nor Hassidic, was religious and tried to maintain a bridge between Jewish tradition and the modern ideologies of the time, such as Zionism and

Communism. Lotka was a member of Hashomer Hatzair, a secular leftist Jewish youth movement. This drove a wedge between Lotka and her father, prompting her to emigrate to pre-state Israel without her father's blessing. She left Kleczew in July 1939 under Aliyah Bet[31] aboard the *Kołorado* and settled at first in Rehovot, where she and other youngsters prepared to establish a new settlement. In 1941 she and her group established Kibbutz Ramat Hashofet. While in Rehovot, she met and married Israel Hess. They had two children: Adam (who died in 1963 at age seventeen, from illness) and Edna. Israel Hess died in 1970. In 1972 Lotka married Mayer Holtzman (who, as it turned out, had also sailed to pre-state Israel on the *Kołorado*); they lived together in Kibbutz Ramat Hashofet for twenty-eight years.

Lotka was the only member of her family to survive the Holocaust.[32]

Meyer R. Mendelson

Meyer R. Mendelson was born on April 15, 1850, in Kleczew, emigrated to Chicago in 1890, and became a U.S. citizen in 1896. His birthplace, Kleczew, appears on a passport application that he made after he came to the U.S.A. He was married to Bertha Stifter (b. 1855 in Łódź). Bertha and their children joined Meyer in Chicago in 1891. Bertha's death certificate states that her father's name was Herman Stifter and that he was also born in Łódź. Her mother's name is unknown. Meyer died in Chicago in 1915; Bertha died in 1931. Their children—those about whom we know—were Max, Gertrude, Mannie, Morris, David, and Joseph. The family believes that all the children were born in Poland except Joseph.

The following information is based on the research of Abraham J. Harris of Goshen, New York, who compiled a genealogy of this family in 1968. Harris states: "At the beginning of the nineteenth century, Moses Raczkowski was a well-established and prosperous tanner in the town of Kleczew in the present province of Poznan. His prosperity is evidenced by the size of the dowries he gave his daughters, amounting to several thousand zlotys in each case. However, by the end of his life, the march of science and the resulting new technology made the old method of tanning obsolete. His sons struggled against the competition of the new plants for some years and finally had to give up."

Harris also says that the Sluzewskis of the Netherlands and the Lawtons of the U.K. are kin to the family members who came to the U.S.A. The details that he gives about this family are as follows:

MOSES RACZKOWSKI was born c. 1810 and died c.1882. He married **ESTHER** c. 1829. Their children were:

i. MENACHEM MENDEL, who was born c.1830 and died c. 1880. He married HANNE RIFKE SZKULNIK c.1851. Hanne died in 1904. This is the line of Shirley Ann Mendelson's husband; Meyer (Bertha) was their son.
ii. ITZEK HERSH, who was born in 1836 and died in 1923. He married RIFKE GLOCER c. 1854. Rifke died in 1898.
iii. ROSALIE, who died in 1901. She married ELKAN LEWANDOWSKI c. 1866. He died in 1928.
iv. SCHEINCHE.
v. GUSTA, who married UNKNOWN (probably named Schachtel) in 1869.

According to Harris, the children of Moses Raczkowski were probably all born in Kleczew.[33]

Marianna Juliana Salomea Koszerow

Marianna Juliana Salomea Koszerowa (also called, at various times, Sierpinska and Kleczkowski) was born in Kleczew in 1821, the daughter of Layzer Koszer (1770–1829), a day laborer in Kleczew, and his wife Rejza Kaufamnnova (1780–?). They were married in Kleczew on July 6, 1818. It is not known whether there were other children.

The family presumes that by 1844, Marianna was orphaned and went to Warsaw to take instruction in Roman Catholicism at the Wizytki Sisters convent. As the family understands, this was not uncommon; to encourage young Jews from rural communities to convert, the Church paid for their travel to and board in Warsaw. Unfortunately for her, Marianna was thrown out of the convent for blasphemous behavior and had to repay these subventions. She did, however, later marry as a convert and then began a long and quite well-documented life that took her to London and Paris until she died in 1903 in London. The family does not believe that she kept any connection with her home village, but she does appear to have adapted it as her surname in Paris in the 1870s and 1880s.[34]

Iciek Mosiek Zoberman

Isaac Soberman (b. 1848), the son of Layb Zauberman and Hinde Malarek, emigrated to England as a young man and worked as a tailor in the East End of London, where he married Elizabeth Samson and fathered nine children.[35]

The Wilcynski/Wilchinsky family

One branch of this family left Kleczew in the early twentieth century for London. Two first cousins, Rachel Leah of Kleczew and Jacob Wilchinsky of Sompolno, married in England. In 1927 or thereabouts, Rachel's brother was shot through a window and killed one Sabbath eve (Friday night) in Kleczew while making kiddush.[36] Rachel's father, known as Rebbi Selig, made a living by smuggling goods across the border. He too escaped to London, too. Sadly, none of the family members who remained in Kleczew survived the Holocaust.[37]

The Kalmanowitz family

Isaac Leib Kalmanowicz (b. 1846 in Kleczew, died c. 1927 in Kleczew) married Sara Lewinski of Pyzdry (b. March 10, 1847) on January 6, 1874. Both died before the Holocaust. They had five children (Lotta, Moses Nissen, Zigismund/Shimon, Herman/Hersz Zvi, and Betti). Most of them and their families perished in the Holocaust. Several descendants of this family emigrated to other countries; some now live in Israel.[38]

Josef Blitz (Joseph Cohen)

Josef Blitz (Joseph Cohen) left Kleczew for England sometime around 1880. According to the family, he had a ferocious temper (his nickname, "Black Joe," may have alluded to this or to his occupation—owner of a sweatshop). The expression "a real Kleczewer Cohen" survived in the family as an epithet for those who were quick to anger.[39]

The Kowalski family

Five brothers of this family emigrated to the U.S.A. in 1905-1906.[40]

Gerszon Eilenberg

His descendant, Jay Norwalk of the U.S.A., was not able to provide further details.

NOTES

Section A: Reconstructing survivors' wartime history: The story of the Kroner family

1. APK, Sąd Grodzki w Kleczewie, case 134.
2. Ibid., case 120.
3. Ibid., case 120.
4. Ibid., case 115.
5. Ibid., case 116.
6. Ibid., case 118.
7. Ibid., case 118.
8. Ibid., case 118.
9. Ibid., case 118.
10. Ibid., case 119.
11. Ibid., case 115.
12. Ibid., case 116.
13. Ibid., case 118.
14. Ibid., case 117.
15. Odpis postanowienia Sądu Grodzkiego w Kleczewie z dnia 28 grudnia 1949 roku, Nr. Akt Sp. 74/48 (private collection).
16. Szacunek wartości nieruchomości z dnia 25 stycznia 1950 (private collection).
17. Zaświadczenie Urzędu Skarbowego w Koninie z dnia 30 stycznia 1950 roku w sprawie opłaty podatku spadkowego przez Jakuba vel Jankiel Elkana Kronera w sprawie spadkowej nieruchomości po Chaskielu Kronerze.
18. Zaświadczenie Prezydium Miejskiej Rady Narodowej w Kleczewie z dnia 19 czerwca 1950 roku.
19. Zaświadczenie z dnia 19 czerwiec 1950 wystawione przez Prezydium Miejskiej Rady Narodowej w Kleczewie (private collection).

Section B: More than 100 years of documented residency in Kleczew: The Rachwalski genealogy as an example

20   According the Konin Archives and sources in the tables of Annex 3, their place of residence in Kleczew was 63/3 Rynek Street. This was documented for 1922, 1924, and 1927 (APKonin, AmKleczewa, file 447).

21   **Notes on Abraham Moses Rachwalski**: SSDI had a different date of birth (November 5, 1895) and of death (December 15, 1987), and reports his last residence as Madison, WI.

Section C: Reconstruction via appeals to Kleczew Municipal Court

22   APK, Sąd Grodzki w Kleczewie, case 140.
23   Ibid., case 97.
24   Ibid., case. 124.
25   Ibid., case 82.
26   Ibid., case 109.
27   Ibid., case 108.
28   Ibid., case 82.

Section D: Additional information regarding descendants and relatives of Jews from Kleczew

29   A religious Zionist political movement.
30   Based on e-mail correspondence with Ms. Sarit Kav, daughter of Moshe Bagno.
31   An organized effort by the Jewish leadership in Israel to increase Jewish immigration (both legal and illegal) to Eretz Israel in 1934–1939.
32   The information regarding this family is based on an English translation of relevant information from a paragraph written in Hebrew by Edna and Shaul Dan. Citation from the website of Ada Holtzman, daughter of Mayer Holtzman; Lotka was her step-mother. For more details, see: http://www.zchor.org/kleczew/kleczew.htm
33   Information regarding this family was received through e-mail correspondence with Shirley Ann Mendelson (Meyer R. Mendelson was her husband's great-grandfather).
34   Received through e-mail correspondence with Elizabeth Grainger, UK.
35   Received through e-mail correspondence with Annie Elizabeth Lindo, UK.
36   Jewish ceremonial blessing on wine.
37   Received through e-mail correspondence with Linda Geffon.
38   Received through e-mail correspondence with Jim Bennett, Israel.
39   Received through e-mail correspondence with David Conway (about his great-grandfather).
40   Received through e-mail correspondence with Kenneth L. Rattner, U.S. (Sept. 26, 2011).

Annex 3—Tables

A. House owners in Kleczew, March 27, 1810
B. Jews living in Kleczew on December 9–21, 1836
C. Contributions to Kleczew synagogue fund, 1844–1845
D. People who made contributions for repair of Kleczew synagogue in 1867
E. Number and percent of Jewish population in selected towns of Eastern Greater Poland, 1921–1939
F. Electors with active right to vote in Kleczew kehilla on May 27, 1924, by occupation, age, and address
G. Jewish voters to the Sejm of the Republic of Poland from Kleczew, 1935 (by occupation, place of residence, and date of birth)
H. Jews in Kleczew in 1919 who declared 10,000–30,000 mp in assets
I. Jewish inhabitants of Kleczew who paid local taxes and industrial and trade certificate taxes as of January 21, 1919
J. Payers of dues to Kleczew Jewish Community, 1919
K. People who remitted "supplemental dues" to the Kleczew Kehilla in 1921
L. Payers of dues to the Kleczew Jewish Community in 1933
M. Holocaust victims from Kleczew in the Yad Vashem database

Table A House owners in Kleczew as of March 27, 1810

No.	House no.	Owner's first name and surname	Number of houses with brick chimneys	Number of houses without brick chimneys
1.	2	Paweł Dyner	1	-
2.	5	Jakob Hern	1	-
3.	22	Stanisław Kopczynski		1
4.	24	Boruch Bengiamin		1
5.	25	Jan Gietrowski		1
6.	26	Walenty Malenczki		1
7.	29	Bartłomiej Kubuszewski		1
8.	38	Aron Wilczynski	1	
9.	56	Widow Sławoszewska	1	
10.	68	Po Benadzie	1	
11.	69	Dominik Jacquinot	1	
12.	71	Tuka Żydowska	1	
13.	75	Maciej Piotrowski	1	
14.	78	Kadmen Salamon	1	
15.	82	Boruch Majer	1	
16.	83	Pański Gościniec	1	
17.	87	Widow Kaczorkiewicz	1	
18.	93	Tomasz Madajewski	1	
19.	94	Piotrowa Iwemska		1
20.	95	Widow Olszakiewicz		1
21.	96	Krzysztof Kosiewicz		1
22.	97	Wojciech Iwemski	1	
23.	98	Szymon Orłowski	1	
24.	103	Alexander Zyske	1	
25.	104	Wigdor Haim		1
26.	105	Laib Psipsze	1	
27.	106	Hersz Golinski	1	
28.	107	Bartłomiej Zebrowski		1
29.	108	Kazimierz Iwemski	1	
30.	110	Widow Wojewodzina		1
31.	111	Franciszek Boruczki		1
32.	112	Poczmistrz Meister		1
33.	113	Stanisław Iwanski		1
34.	114	Frydrych Szczydynejk		1
35.	115	Trawinski		1
36.	116	Franciszek Kotłowski	1	
37.	117	Gościniec Piaski	2	
38.	118	Bernde Kazimierz	2	
39.	119	Tomaszowa Dąbrowska		1
40.	120	Kasper Drzynicki		1
41.	121	plant	1	

Table A, cont.

No.	House no.	Owner's first name and surname	Number of houses with brick chimneys	Number of houses without brick chimneys
42.	122	Painter Hubert		1
43.	123	Baker Konrat		1
44.	124	Widow Kubaszewska	1	
45.	126	Karnl Kin		1
46.	127	Widow Kowalska		1
47.	129	Widow Madajewska		1
48.	130	Wawrzyn Krop		1
49.	132	Józef Dzikowski		1
50.	133	Widow Kochen		1
51.	134	Rube Haim		1
52.	135	Laib Leszczynski		1
53.	139	Wdowa Baile	1	
54.	141	Hersz Rogozinski	1	
55.	142	Jcek Ber	1	
56.	144	Mosiek Epfraim	1	
57.	145	Szymon Szepsie	1	
58.	146	Maciej Lisek	1	
59.	147	Józef Pomierowski	1	
60.	150	Bartłomi Kewalek	1	
61.	NA	NA		1
62.	NA	NA	1	
63.	162	Bartłomi Wyrzutowicz	1	
64.	165	Stanisław Kopczynski		1
65.	166	Andrzej Liskiewicz		1
66.	167	Wyrwinska		1
67.	168	Franciszek Wałowski		1
68.	169	Andrzej Goinski		1
69.	170	Jakob Orłowski		1
70.	171	Wojciech Olkowicz		1
71.	172	Wojciech Dzikowicz		1
72.	173	Rachwał Olkowicz		1
73.	175	Szymon Lewandowski	1	
74.	178	Stanisław Piotrowski	1	
75.	185	Wojciech Liskiewicz	1	
Total number			39	38

Source: APK, AmK, classification no.148, classification no. 68-74

Note: Names are presented in their original order.

Table B Jews living in Kleczew on December 9–21, 1836

Full name	Age	Status	Occupation
Aronson Salomon	53	**Husband**	**Stall keeper**
Anna	22	Wife	Supported by husband
Naneta	2	Daughter	Supported by parents
Icek	3 months	Son	Supported by parents
Anszel Hersz Eliasz	63	**Husband**	**Speculator**
Łaje	53	Wife	Supported by husband
Rafał	21	Son	Supported by parents
Ryfka	19	Daughter	Supported by parents
Ester	11	Daughter	Supported by parents
Angart Izrael	21	**Single**	**Forwarder**
Aleksandrowa Ruchel	61	**Widow**	**Laborer**
Appel Herdke	44	**Widow**	**Laborer**
Frajdel	21	Daughter	Supported by mother
Hersz Leyb	16	Son	Supported by mother
Wolf	13	Son	Supported by mother
Łaje	9	Daughter	Supported by mother
Appel Frajde	13	**Single**	**Servant**
Appel Dawid	86	**Widower**	**Living on charity**
Appel Szmaje	71	**Widower**	**Supported by son-in-law**
Aronsowa Taube	36	**Widow**	**Laborer**
Maryem Łaje	10	Daughter	Supported by mother
Abram	7	Son	Supported by mother
Dawid	2	Son	Supported by mother
Ausbryan Szaje	36	**Married**	**Laborer**
Haje	39	Wife	Supported by husband
Ryfka	3	Daughter	Supported by parents
Appel Sure	18	**Single**	**Servant**
Appel Manasze	43	**Married**	**Dealer**
Gite	31	Wife	Supported by husband
Frojke	16	Daughter	Supported by parents
Haskel	12	Son	Supported by parents
Frayda	13	Daughter	Supported by parents
Rachel	10	Daughter	Supported by parents
Haje	9	Daughter	Supported by parents
Kalme	4	Son	Supported by parents
Bolk Ham	14	**Single**	**Supported by relatives**

Table B, cont.

Full name	Age	Status	Occupation
Bejer Herz	55	**Husband**	Tanner
Ryfke	43	Wife	Supported by husband
Łaje	21	Daughter	Supported by parents
Szmul	17	Son	Supported by parents
Małke	12	Daughter	Supported by parents
Rane	9	Daughter	Supported by parents
Taube	6	Daughter	Supported by parents
Hawe	1	Daughter	Supported by parents
Blitz Taube	48	**Widow**	Laborer
Sure	12	Daughter	Supported by parents
Majer	9	Son	Supported by parents
Beher Abram	46	**Husband**	Laborer
Sure	54	Wife	Supported by husband
Faygel	5	Daughter	Supported by parents
Baynus Abram	39	**Husband**	Dressmaker
Welke	26	Wife	Supported by husband
Chaje	10	Daughter	Supported by parents
Ester Bajle	6	Daughter	Supported by parents
Sure	5	Daughter	Supported by parents
Nache	2	Daughter	Supported by parents
Baruchowa Race	36	**Widow**	Laborer
Birnbaum Boruch	39	**Husband**	Dressmaker
Frajdel	29	Wife	Supported by husband
Layb	16	Son	Supported by parents
Chaim	9	Son	Supported by parents
Frymet	7	Daughter	Supported by parents
Abram	4	Son	Supported by parents
Baranek Zelik	34	**Husband**	Dressmaker
Ester	27	Wife	Supported by husband
Abram	6	Son	Supported by parents
Szlama	2	Son	Supported by parents
Bajnus Jakob	43	**Husband**	Dressmaker
Dwore	32	Wife	Supported by husband
Icyk	19	Son	Supported by parents
Hersz	17	Son	Supported by parents
Niehe	16	Daughter	Supported by parents
Peysa	14	Daughter	Supported by parents
Jakob	9	Son	Supported by parents
Bauman Lemel	30	Husband	Dressmaker
Ryfke	46	Wife	Dressmaker
Fraydel	21	Daughter	Supported by parents
Icyk Jakob	19	Son	Supported by parents
Ite	9	Daughter	Supported by parents
Baynus Chane	17	**Single**	Servant
Bauman Ruchel	19	**Single**	Servant

Table B, cont.

Full name	Age	Status	Occupation
Blitz Ryfka	18	Single	Servant
Baerwa Freide	43	Widow	Baker
Jakob	24	Married son	Salt seller
Rachel	20	Wife	Supported by husband
Dwore	7	Sister	Supported by parents
Baynusz Szymhe	54	Husband	Dressmaker
Rachel	31	Wife	Supported by husband
Mordka	14	Son	Supported by parents
Hinde	12	Daughter	Supported by parents
Dawid	10	Son	Supported by parents
Mendel	7	Son	Supported by parents
Sare	4	Daughter	Supported by parents
Bauman Morke	60	Husband	Laborer
Dwore	39	Wife	Supported by husband
Abram	20	Son	Supported by family, Dressmaker
Ryfke	16	Daughter	Supported by family, Dressmaker
Layb Jakob	13	Son	Supported by parents
Abram	12	Son	Supported by parents
Sare	10	Daughter	Supported by parents
Berliński Moszek	57	Husband	Laborer
Ryfke	36	Wife	Supported by husband
Draydel	11	Daughter	Supported by parents
Ester	7	Daughter	Supported by parents
Abram	2	Son	Supported by parents
Boruszak Layb	39	Husband	Dealer
Hane	46	Wife	Supported by husband
Boruch	13	Son	Supported by parents
Ryfke	4	Daughter	Supported by parents
Wolf	19	Son	Supported by parents
Joel	61	Widow	Supported by son
Bosak Dawid	50	Husband	Dressmaker
Rachel	50	Wife	Supported by husband
Beer	22	Son	Supported by parents
Jakob	19	Son	Supported by parents
Hane	16	Daughter	Supported by parents
Baum Abram	20	Single	Journeyman Dressmaker
Baum Icek	19	Single	Journeyman Dressmaker
Bendent Szmul	49	Husband	Stall keeper
Golde	33	Wife	Supported by husband
Bube Bayle	53	Widow	Laborer
Layb	31	Son	Supported by mother
Bauman Kadys	58	Widower	Laborer

Table B, cont.

Full name	Age	Status	Occupation
Boes Abram	42	**Husband**	**Dressmaker**
Sure	44	Wife	Supported by husband
Gerszon	18	Son	Supported by parents
Mosiek	19	Son	Supported by parents
Dwore	13	Daughter	Supported by parents
Hinde	9	Daughter	Supported by parents
Bayle	11	Daughter	Supported by parents
Boes	6	Son	Supported by parents
Blume	2	Daughter	Supported by parents
Beyer Szmul	41	**Husband**	**Dressmaker**
Branke	34	Wife	Supported by husband
Ester	19	Daughter	Supported by parents
Jenta	12	Daughter	Supported by parents
Tumerhe	10	Daughter	Supported by parents
Ulie	8	Son	Supported by parents
Ryfke	5	Daughter	Supported by parents
Icek	2	Son	Supported by parents
Mosze	1 month	Son	Supported by parents
Bokowa Ester	57	**Widow**	**Vodka seller**
Jakob	30	Son	Supported by mother / linen maker
Reka	29	Daughter	Supported by mother
Ryfka	16	Daughter	Supported by mother
Raychel	14	Daughter	Supported by mother
Bok Manche	53	**Mąż**	**Laborer**
Mendel	38	Wife	Supported by husband
Jentel	12	Daughter	Supported by parents
Guttel	13	Daughter	Supported by parents
Michle	8	Daughter	Supported by parents
Bok Szapsie	57	**Husband**	**Dealer**
Frayde	44	Wife	Supported by husband
Fiszel	22	Son	Supported by parents
Rachel	11	Daughter	Supported by parents
Chaje	10	Daughter	Supported by parents
Fajgle	4	Daughter	Supported by parents
Ester Hinde	1	Daughter	Supported by parents
Czernicki Boruch	79	**Widower**	**Speculator**
Sure	21	Daughter	Supported by father
Łaje	13	Daughter	Supported by father
Cyper Szmul	17	**Single**	**Apprentice, Dressmaker**
Cotek Ester	21	**Single**	**Servant**
Chaim Berek	28	**Married**	**Saddler**
Branke	25	Wife	Supported by husband

Table B, cont.

Full name	Age	Status	Occupation
Dawid Mayzelz Aron	37	**Husband**	**Dressmaker**
Ite	37	Wife	Supported by husband
Chaim	9	Son	Supported by parents
Rayzel	7	Daughter	Supported by parents
Hersz	4	Son	Supported by parents
Nysan	4	Son	Supported by parents
Anszel	1	Son	Supported by parents
Dawidowa Małke	36	**Widow**	**Laborer**
Aron Leyb	16	Son	Supported by mother
Henin	11	Son	Supported by mother
Szmul Abram	6	Son	Supported by mother
Dawidowa Rayzel	51	**Widow**	**Laborer**
Ryber	31	Son	Supported by mother, Dressmaker
Dawrys	25	Daughter	Supported by mother
Glaze Jude	14	Son	Supported by mother
Elkonier Boruch	43	**Husband**	**Trader**
Hane	35	Wife	Supported by husband
Szosze	14	Daughter	Supported by parents
Miryl	12	Daughter	Supported by parents
Aron Hersz	11	Son	Supported by parents
Szmul	8	Son	Supported by parents
Elka	4	Daughter	Supported by parents
Abram	1 month	Son	Supported by parents
Eliaszowa Myryl	16	**Single**	**Servant**
Feinkler Ester	58	**Widow**	**Supported by son-in-law**
Fajbus Jakob	51	Husband	Teacher
Bayle	31	Wife	Supported by husband
Nichem	19	Son	Supported by parents
Rayzel	13	Daughter	Supported by parents
Jude	4	Son	Supported by parents
Rayze	1	Daughter	Supported by parents
Frydental Hersz	28	**Husband**	**Salt seller**
Chace	26	Wife	Supported by husband
Abram	2	Son	Supported by parents
Dwore	7	Daughter	Supported by parents
Gostyński Jozef	15	**Single**	**Supported by a relative**
Grynfeld Haim	24	**Husband**	**Dealer**
Ruchel	24	Wife	Supported by husband
Icek	2	Son	Supported by parents
Kayle	2	Daughter	Supported by parents

Table B, cont.

Full name	Age	Status	Occupation
Gorzelany Abram	44	Husband	Dealer
Reyla	33	Wife	Supported by husband
Ryfke	15	Daughter	Supported by parents
Nieche	4	Daughter	Supported by parents
Maryem	2	Daughter	Supported by parents
Gębicka Freyda	16	Single	Servant
Goldman Jozef	49	Husband	Dealer
Rachel	36	Wife	Supported by husband
Hinde	16	Daughter	Supported by parents
Abram	2	Son	Supported by parents
Łaje	1	Daughter	Supported by parents
Tanner Szmul	79	Husband	Tanner
Raychel	41	Wife	Supported by husband
Aron	18	Son	Supported by parents
Hinde	17	Daughter	Supported by parents
Hendel	13	Daughter	Supported by parents
Ruchel	6	Daughter	Supported by parents
Hersz	4	Son	Supported by parents
Ester	1 month	Daughter	Supported by parents
Glazer Eliasz	54	Husband	Glazier
Libe	50	Wife	Supported by husband
Hudes	22	Daughter	Supported by parents
Grünfeld Aron	33	Husband	Dealer
Frayde	33	Wife	Supported by husband
Efraim Jozef	13	Son	Supported by parents
Hinde	11	Daughter	Supported by parents
Szymek	5	Son	Supported by parents
Salomon	3	Son	Supported by parents
Grünfeld Dawid	50	Husband	Dealer
Zysel	46	Wife	Supported by husband
Terche	16	Daughter	Supported by parents
Szmul	15	Son	Supported by parents
Sure	8	Daughter	Supported by parents
Gradycz Jozef	44	Husband	*Shochet* (ritual slaughterer)
Marye	41	Wife	Supported by husband
Haje	19	Daughter	Supported by parents
Skrajne Libe	14	Daughter	Supported by parents
Uszer	10	Son	Supported by parents
Dawid	8	Son	Supported by parents
Gryn Boruch	42	Husband	Tanner
Chaje	31	Wife	Supported by husband
Dobrys	13	Daughter	Supported by parents
Libe	10	Daughter	Supported by parents
Sure	9	Daughter	Supported by parents
Zelman	3	Son	Supported by parents

Table B, cont.

Full name	Age	Status	Occupation
Ryfka	3 months	Daughter	Supported by parents
Gębicka Małke	**21**	**Single**	**Servant**
Grabart Jakob	**68**	**Husband**	**Dressmaker**
Ester	54	Wife	Supported by husband
Layb	19	Son	Supported by parents
Dawid	13	Son	Supported by parents
Gryzda Aron	**25**	**Husband**	**Tanner**
Ite	21	Wife	Supported by husband
Hersz	2	Son	Supported by parents
Golińska Ester	**21**	**Single**	**Servant**
Grynfeld Szapsie	**30**	**Husband**	**Dealer**
Gitel	29	Wife	Supported by husband
Hinde Gołde	7	Daughter	Supported by parents
Szymek	5	Son	Supported by parents
Herzowa Hinde	**41**	**Widow**	**Laborer**
Hurwitz Gedalia	**42**	**Husband**	**Teacher**
Blume	51	Wife	Supported by husband
Chaje	21	Daughter	Supported by parents
Maryem Ruchel	2	Daughter	Supported by parents
Szmul	26	Son	Supported by parents
Hersz Layzer	**15**	**Single**	**Dressmaker's apprentice**
Hartate Łaje	**20**	**Single**	**Servant**
Holc Haje	**33**	**Widow**	**Laborer**
Sure	13	Daughter	Supported by mother
Salamon	11	Son	Supported by mother
Meyer	8	Son	Supported by mother
Haymowa Sure Rayze	**12**	**Single**	**Servant**
Jelenkiewicz Lemel Efraim	**14**	**Single**	**Living on capital**
Jelenkiewicz Icek Jakow	**61**	**Widower**	**Dealer**
Rayze	16	Daughter	Supported by father
Jelenkiewicz Rayze	**38**	**Widow**	**Trader's wife**
Gołde Łaje	17	Daughter	Supported by mother
Moszek	15	Son	Supported by mother
Sure	13	Daughter	Supported by mother
Ruchel	10	Daughter	Supported by mother
Abram	7	Son	Supported by mother
Bayla	2	Daughter	Supported by mother
Jelenkiewicz Dawid	**61**	**Husband**	**Innkeeper**
Mendel	51	Wife	Supported by husband
Judzki Jude	**24**	**Husband**	**Dressmaker**
Łaje	25	Wife	Supported by husband
Nudef	1	Daughter	Supported by parents

Table B, cont.

Full name	Age	Status	Occupation
Jajner Nyson	6	Single	Supported by relatives
Jozef Abram	21	Single	Journeyman, Dressmaker
Iwańczyk Szymche	34	Husband	Dealer
Hawe	31	Wife	Supported by husband
Zelik	9	Son	Supported by parents
Libe	11	Daughter	Supported by parents
Majer	3	Son	Supported by parents
Iwańczyk Layzer	72	Husband	Speculator
Tyfke	64	Wife	Supported by husband
Jelenkiewicz Lemel	34	Husband	Optician
Gerapie	32	Wife	Supported by husband
Moysze	6	Son	Supported by parents
Icek	4	Son	Supported by parents
Jarecki Hersz	32	Husband	Dealer
Hane	27	Wife	Supported by husband
Taube	2	Daughter	Supported by parents
Jabłoński Jakow	42	Husband	Fisherman
Aydel	25	Wife	Supported by husband
Sure	2	Daughter	Supported by parents
Jelenkiewicz Hersz	41	Husband	Tanner
Mendla	42	Wife	Supported by husband
Leyb	17	Son	Supported by parents
Ester	15	Daughter	Supported by parents
Rywele	11	Daughter	Supported by parents
Szymek	9	Son	Supported by parents
Jelenkiewicz Szmul	64	Husband	Speculator
Haye	39	Wife	Supported by husband
Bramache	20	Daughter	Supported by parents
Efraim	17	Son	Supported by parents
Izrael	13	Son	Supported by parents
Mordkie	7	Son	Supported by parents
Jelenkiewicz Lipman	67	Husband	Dealer
Nache	54	Wife	Supported by husband
Gitle	25	Daughter	Supported by parents
Lemel	22	Son	Supported by parents
Jakow	18	Son	Supported by parents
Parche	20	Daughter	Supported by parents
Łaje	16	Daughter	Supported by parents
Moryc	13	Son	Supported by parents
Efraim Zalmech	12	Son	Supported by parents
Kalmińska Schajche	79	Widow	**Supported by relatives**
Koźmińska Faygel	61	Widow	Widow

Table B, cont.

Full name	Age	Status	Occupation
Krerowa Faygelche	**54**	**Widow**	**Salt seller**
Izrael Ber	20	Son	Supported by mother
Brandel	18	Daughter	Supported by mother
Nusan	13	Son	Supported by mother
Kuczyński Faybus	**41**	**Husband**	**Hat maker**
Ester	29	Wife	Supported by husband
Chaje	16	Daughter	Supported by parents
Sure	14	Daughter	Supported by parents
Jude Layb	11	Son	Supported by parents
Ite	6	Daughter	Supported by parents
Ryfke	4	Daughter	Supported by parents
Benjamin	2	Son	Supported by parents
Szlama	4 months	Son	Supported by parents
Mayle Kuczyńska	68	Widow	Supported by son
Karcin Szlama	**20**	**Single**	**Servant**
Kaliski Szmul	**9**	**Single**	**Supported by relatives**
Koniński Lewek	**46**	**Husband**	**Butcher**
Frayde	44	Wife	Supported by husband
Ruchel	17	Daughter	Supported by parents
Szmul	16	Son	Supported by parents
Nyson	14	Son	Supported by parents
Eywe	13	Daughter	Supported by parents
Miryl	7	Daughter	Supported by parents
Hersz	4	Son	Supported by parents
Klepacz Moszek	**46**	**Husband**	**Dressmaker**
Ester	36	Wife	Supported by husband
Kępa Icek Jakob	44	Husband	Dealer
Udel	43	Wife	Supported by husband
Eliasz	16	Son	Supported by parents
Efraim	14	Son	Supported by parents
Łaje	7	Daughter	Supported by parents
Kaliska Gołde	**43**	**Widow**	**Laborer**
Manis	21	Son	Supported by mother
Majer	15	Son	Supported by mother
Koslawy Hemie	**36**	**Husband**	**Dressmaker**
Guberhie	35	Wife	Supported by husband
Hane	9	Daughter	Supported by parents
Maryem	4	Daughter	Supported by parents
Kaufman Koslawy	73	Widower	Supported by son
Krotoszyński Lewin	**36**	**Husband**	**Speculator**
Hawe	36	Wife	Supported by husband
aryem	15	Daughter	Supported by parents
Ayzyk	7	Son	Supported by parents
Hane Pese	4	Daughter	Supported by parents
Faymel	2	Son	Supported by parents

Table B, cont.

Full name	Age	Status	Occupation
Kohn Nathan	60	Husband	Teacher
Ester	41	Wife	Supported by husband
Cyrle	20	Daughter	Supported by parents
Moyżesz	10	Son	Supported by parents
Kalmiński Salomon	59	Husband	Dressmaker
Taube	46	Wife	Supported by husband
Perec	25	Son	Supported by parents
Aydel	23	Daughter	Supported by parents
Berek	21	Son	Supported by parents
Hinde	20	Daughter	Supported by parents
Jakob	17	Son	Supported by parents
Rachwał	14	Son	Supported by parents
Bine	13	Daughter	Supported by parents
Krzepski Eliasz	44	Husband	Teacher
Gitel	37	Wife	Supported by husband
Ryfke	19	Daughter	Supported by parents
Hinde	13	Daughter	Supported by parents
Tbe	10	Daughter	Supported by parents
Jukiew	8	Son	Supported by parents
Szlama	7	Son	Supported by parents
Halm Wolf	2	Son	Supported by parents
Krotowski Hersz	44	Husband	Laborer
Ides	31	Wife	Supported by husband
Raychel	14	Daughter	Supported by parents
Chane	12	Daughter	Supported by parents
Cyrol	10	Daughter	Supported by parents
Lota	5	Daughter	Supported by parents
Krotowski Michał	40	Husband	Speculator
Rachel	29	Wife	Supported by husband
Gitel	10	Daughter	Supported by parents
Ryfke	7	Daughter	Supported by parents
Dawid	2	Son	Supported by parents
Klepacz Jakob	58	Husband	Dressmaker
Hinde	36	Wife	Supported by husband
Wolf	20	Son	Supported by parents
Sure	12	Daughter	Supported by parents
Ite	4	Daughter	Supported by parents
Kohn Jude	32	Single	Dressmaker
Kleczkowska Szprynce	61	Widow	Laborer
Wolf	21	Son	Supported by mother, Dressmaker
Kleczkowski Wołek	46	Husband	Butcher
Bine	34	Wife	Supported by husband
Gintel	16	Daughter	Supported by parents
Haye	9	Daughter	Supported by parents

Table B, cont.

Full name	Age	Status	Occupation
Ruchel Gołde	3	Daughter	Supported by parents
Kalmanowicz Hersz	**26**	**Husband**	**Speculator**
Bayle	31	Wife	Supported by husband
Sure	2	Daughter	Supported by parents
Ryfke	3 months	Daughter	Supported by parents
Kalmanowicz Abram	**51**	**Husband**	**Tanner**
Hane	28	Wife	Supported by husband
Dobrys	12	Daughter	Supported by parents
Sure	7	Daughter	Supported by parents
Branke	5	Daughter	Supported by parents
Zelman	4	Son	Supported by parents
Mosiek	2	Son	Supported by parents
Korn Fszel	**49**	**Husband**	**Dressmaker**
Ester	35	Wife	Supported by husband
Abram	21	Son	Supported by parents
Ryfke	16	Daughter	Supported by parents
Jente	14	Daughter	Supported by parents
Hane	10	Daughter	Supported by parents
Icek	8	Son	Supported by parents
Łaje	3	Daughter	Supported by parents
Dwore	2 months	Daughter	Supported by parents
Kohn Efraim	**41**	**Husband**	**Collector**
Ester	36	Wife	Supported by husband
Jokew	13	Son	Supported by parents
Wołek	9	Son	Supported by parents
Layb	4	Son	Supported by parents
Taube	6	Daughter	Supported by parents
Szoel	1	Son	Supported by parents
Karo Zelig	**58**	**Husband**	**Dealer**
Gitle	42	Wife	Supported by husband
Ester	14	Daughter	Supported by parents
Hinde	22	Daughter	Supported by parents
Haye	9	Daughter	Supported by parents
Jakob	6	Son	Supported by parents
Zyze	4	Daughter	Supported by parents
Karo Hersz Lewin	66	Husband	Supported by son
Łaje	63	Wife	Supported by son
Krotoszyński Szmul	**52**	**Husband**	**Stall keeper**
Małke	42	Wife	Supported by husband
Frayde	19	Daughter	Supported by parents
Ester Peyse	17	Daughter	Supported by parents
Layb Haym	15	Son	Supported by parents
Icek Jozef	9	Son	Supported by parents

Table B, cont.

Full name	Age	Status	Occupation
Kotek Jakob	26	Husband	Collector
Zysel	24	Wife	Supported by husband
Marye	3	Daughter	Supported by parents
Lisner Jozef	59	Husband	Rabbi
Nysel	37	Wife	Supported by husband
Szlama	18	Son	Supported by parents
Dawid	15	Son	Supported by parents
Salomon	11	Son	Supported by parents
Maryem	13	Daughter	Supported by parents
Mayer	1	Son	Supported by parents
Lisner Łaje	70	Widow	**Supported by relatives**
Lewkowna Fraydel	31	Single	Servant
Łabiszyńska Bayle	18	Single	Servant
Leszczyński Lewin	61	Husband	Baker
Sure	51	Wife	Supported by husband
Rafał	20	Son	Supported by parents
Rayzel	22	Daughter	Supported by parents
Łabiszyńska Gittel	43	Widow	Laborer
Rywen	19	Son	Supported by mother, Dressmaker
Ryfke	18	Daughter	Supported by mother
Dobrys	14	Daughter	Supported by mother
Gittle	7	Daughter	Supported by mother
Udel	4	Daughter	Supported by mother
Leszczyński Salamon	36	Husband	**Dressmaker**
Perla	29	Wife	Supported by husband
Bayle	10	Daughter	Supported by parents
Szymek	8	Son	Supported by parents
Hane	3	Daughter	Supported by parents
Lewek Michał Layer	24	Single	Servant
Lisner Slama	37	Husband	**Stall keeper**
Cyryl Margen	21	Wife	Supported by husband
Abram	4	Son	Supported by parents
Cyryl Margem	5 months	Daughter	Supported by parents
Lipszyc Hersz	56	Husband	**Propinator/pub tenant**
Anna	42	Wife	Supported by husband
Ruchel	17	Daughter	Supported by parents
Bayle	8	Daughter	Supported by parents
Ite	4	Daughter	Supported by parents
Leszczyński Hersz	29	Husband	Shoemaker
Royze	30	Wife	Supported by husband
Moyszek Zalme	4	Son	Supported by parents
Mayer	2	Son	Supported by parents

Table B, cont.

Full name	Age	Status	Occupation
Lipski Tobiasz	39	Husband	Teacher
Ayde Blume	27	Wife	Supported by husband
Icek	7	Son	Supported by parents
Rayze	6	Daughter	Supported by parents
Jozef	5	Son	Supported by parents
Mendel	2	Son	Supported by parents
Jakob	1	Son	Supported by parents
Lubrańska Elżbieta	16	Single	Servant
Łabiszyńska Sure Haje	62	Widow	Laborer
Łabiszyńska Ester	73	Widow	Laborer
Abram	34	Son	Supported by mother
Izrael	27	Son	Supported by mother
Łabiszyński Eliasz	36	Husband	Dressmaker
Garche	26	Wife	Supported by husband
Leszczyńska Sure	61	Widow	Supported by son-in-law
Rychel Leszczyńska	26	Single	Supported by brother-in-law
Łata Layb	24	Single	Journeyman, Tanner
Łata Szymsie	20	Single	Supported by brother
Łachman Chaim	29	Husband	Dressmaker
Chaye	29	Wife	Supported by husband
Ryfke	2	Daughter	Supported by parents
Layzer Hersz	15	Son	Supported by parents
Malarek Ester	19	Single	Servant
Mazur Jakob	68	Husband	Dealer
Gitel	67	Wife	Supported by husband
Szmul	20	Son	Supported by parents
Dawid	18	Son	Supported by parents
Mise	12	Daughter	Supported by parents
Malarek Abram	34	Husband	Tanner
Golec	31	Wife	Supported by husband
Hersz Layb	6	Son	Supported by parents
Małke	4	Daughter	Supported by parents
Ruchel	4 months	Daughter	Supported by parents
Mydłek Hinne	40	Husband	Butcher
Szarne	30	Wife	Supported by husband
Jakob	21	Son	Supported by parents
Hane	20	Daughter	Supported by parents
Marge	17	Daughter	Supported by parents
Mazur Berendt	57	Husband	Dealer
Anna	23	Wife	Supported by husband
Manes Szayndel	19	Single	Servant

Table B, cont.

Full name	Age	Status	Occupation
Malarek Mosiek	58	Husband	Dealer
Ruchel	49	Wife	Supported by husband
Hersz	16	Son	Supported by parents
Gitel	14	Daughter	Supported by parents
Garche	10	Daughter	Supported by parents
Malarek Layb	24	Son	Supported by father, Baker
Reyla	23	Wife	Supported by husband
Ryce	2	Daughter	Supported by parents
Nanesan Sure	32	Widow	Laborer
Nayfeld Joef	23	Husband	Speculator
Hane	21	Wife	Supported by husband
Mejer	3 months	Son	Supported by parents
Najman Dawid	73	Husband	Baker
Gitle	40	Wife	Supported by husband
Terche	15	Daughter	Supported by parents
Bine	8	Daughter	Supported by parents
Jukew	5	Son	Supported by parents
Olejnik Aron	71	Husband	House owner
Frayde	72	Wife	Supported by husband
Proch Abram	21	Single	Servant
Pinkus Layzer	41	Husband	Dealer
Ruchel	31	Wife	Supported by husband
Pinkus	8	Son	Supported by parents
Icek	6	Son	Supported by parents
Poznański Jude	34	Husband	Dressmaker
Hane	29	Wife	Supported by husband
Abram	12	Son	Supported by parents
Jakob	8	Son	Supported by parents
Ester	2	Daughter	Supported by parents
Pietruszka Abram	32	Husband	Laborer
Aydel	31	Wife	Supported by husband
Icek	2	Son	Supported by parents
Gołde Pietruszka	66	Widow	Supported by son
Piotrowski Mendel	29	Husband	Tanner
Zyse	28	Wife	Supported by husband
Ruchel	2	Daughter	Supported by parents
Psipsie Frymel	44	Husband	Dressmaker
Haje	31	Son	Supported by husband
Layb	11	Son	Supported by parents
Szaje	3	Son	Supported by parents
Piekarski Izrael	41	Widower	Baker
Chaim	14	Son	Supported by father
Margen	13	Daughter	Supported by father
Taube	2	Daughter	Supported by father
Cyrel	8	Daughter	Supported by father

Table B, cont.

Full name	Age	Status	Occupation
Salamon	5	Son	Supported by father
Preger Dawid	**32**	**Husband**	**Goldsmith**
Rayzel	29	Wife	Supported by husband
Abram Jukew	4	Son	Supported by parents
Psipsie Abram	**43**	**Husband**	**Dressmaker**
Hane	33	Wife	Supported by husband
Jozef	16	Son	Supported by parents
Ryfke	15	Daughter	Supported by parents
Miryl	13	Daughter	Supported by parents
Peise	11	Daughter	Supported by parents
Gołde Szaynke	8	Daughter	Supported by parents
Hersz	2	Son	Supported by parents
Psipsie Nahman	**63**	**Husband, widower**	**Haberdasher**
Jude	19	Son	Supported by father
Piotrkowski Majer	**31**	**Husband**	**Soap Trader**
Bayle	29	Wife	Supported by husband
Dwore	4	Daughter	Supported by parents
Mosiek Jakob	4 months	Son	Supported by parents
Pakuczowa Aydel	**53**	**Widow**	**Laborer**
Dawid Hersz	16	Son	Supported by mother
Parzyński Haskel	**36**	**Husband**	**Shulklapper**
Ryfke	29	Wife	Supported by husband
Blume	7	Daughter	Supported by parents
Frayde	5	Daughter	Supported by parents
Icek	2	Son	Supported by parents
Layb	1	Son	Supported by parents
Psipsie Haim	**42**	**Husband**	**Stall keeper**
Machle	30	Wife	Supported by husband
Reyse	10	Daughter	Supported by parents
Abram	4	Son	Supported by parents
Chane Sure	1	Daughter	Supported by parents
Icyk Jakob Psipsie	11	Single	Supported by brother
Piotrkowski Szapsie	**62**	**Husband**	**Laborer**
Chaje	50	Wife	Supported by husband
Szmul	22	Son	Supported by parents
Gitel	11	Daughter	Supported by parents
Szymek	6	Son	Supported by parents
Przedecki Icek	**39**	**Husband**	**Laborer**
Chane	33	Wife	Supported by husband
Salaman	15	Son	Supported by parents
Małke	13	Daughter	Supported by parents
Sławe	5	Daughter	Supported by parents
Brane	2	Daughter	Supported by parents
Rachwalska Gitel	**20**	**Single**	**Servant**

Table B, cont.

Full name	Age	Status	Occupation
Rączkowski Mosiek	42	Husband	Tanner
Ester	35	Wife	Supported by husband
Mendel	7	Son	Supported by parents
Hersz	2	Son	Supported by parents
Rachwalska Marye	11	Single	Servant
Rachwalski Mosiek	43	Husband	Cap maker
Rachel	35	Wife	Supported by husband
Mordke	17	Son	Supported by parents
Ester	15	Daughter	Supported by parents
Margel	13	Daughter	Supported by parents
Sure Ryfke	8	Daughter	Supported by parents
Abram	8	Son	Supported by parents
Nache	6	Daughter	Supported by parents
Rączkowska Małke	59	Widow	House owner
Josel	33	Son	Supported by mother, Butcher
Rączka Mendel	23	Husband	Shoemaker
Michle	23	Wife	Supported by husband
Abram	3 months	Son	Supported by parents
Rogoziński Abram	21	Single	Servant
Rogoziński Lewek	76	Husband	Living on charity
Cyryl	56	Wife	Supported by husband
Rakowski Jude	34	Husband	Baker
Hane	45	Wife	Supported by husband
Gorie Bauman	14	Son	Supported by stepfather
Ester Bauman	9	Daughter	Supported by stepfather
Zelig Rakowski	6	Son	Supported by father
Gorie Rakowski	2	Son	Supported by father
Rachwalska Chaje	16	Single	Servant
Szmulewicz Wolf	21	Single	Teacher
Teacher Sure	53	Widow	Dealer
Mendel	21	Son	Supported by mother
Jakob	19	Son	Supported by mother
Marye Dwore	16	Daughter	Supported by mother
Hinde	12	Daughter	Supported by mother
Mosie Szmul	14	Son	Supported by mother
Teacher Szlama	54	Husband	Dealer
Tauba	45	Wife	Supported by husband
Mosiek	15	Son	Supported by parents
Dwore Hinde	12	Daughter	Supported by parents
Abram Ayzyk	8	Son	Supported by parents
Michał	13	Son	Supported by parents
Glazierowa Łaje	13	Single	Servant

Table B, cont.

Full name	Age	Status	Occupation
Sompoliński Jozef	59	Husband	Dressmaker
Dwore	48	Wife	Supported by husband
Icek	25	Son	Supported by parents
Szmul	19	Son	Supported by parents
Benjamin	6	Son	Supported by parents
Sure Gitel	3	Daughter	Supported by parents
Szklarka Sure	45	Widow	Laborer
Aron	15	Son	Supported by mother
Layb	6	Son	Supported by mother
Szwarc Mendel	10	Single	**Supported by relatives**
Szmul Icek	51	Husband	Laborer
Łaje	34	Wife	Supported by husband
Nansen Jakus	6	Son	Supported by parents
Glazier Layb	25	Husband	Glazier
Małke	22	Wife	Supported by husband
Layb	2	Son	Supported by parents
Michel Glazier	19	Single	Supported by brother
Majer Glazier	15	Single	Supported by brother
Chamie Glazier	15	Sister	Supported by brother
Minde Łaje	9	Sister	Supported by brother
Stemberg Icek	50	Husband	Glazier
Rayzel	44	Wife	Supported by husband
Gitel	14	Daughter	Supported by parents
Szwarek Blume	16	Single	Servant
Teacher Wolf	43	Husband	Laborer
Małke	51	Wife	Supported by husband
Morye	19	Daughter	Supported by parents
Abram Szmaje	12	Son	Supported by parents
Sendel Wołek	45	Husband	Laborer
Ite	35	Wife	Supported by husband
Bayle	16	Daughter	Supported by parents
Mosiek	14	Son	Supported by parents
Tylche	9	Daughter	Supported by parents
Morke	2	Son	Supported by parents
Teacher Marek	69	Husband	Laborer
Minda	62	Wife	Supported by husband
Ruchel	22	Daughter	Supported by parents
Teacher Sure	46	Widow	Laborer
Mosiek	7	Son	Supported by mother
Liebe	6	Daughter	Supported by mother
Teacher Zelig	31	Husband	Laborer
Ślesiński Hemie	39	Husband	Dressmaker
Hinde	34	Wife	Supported by husband
Efraim Hersz	10	Son	Supported by parents

Table B, cont.

Full name	Age	Status	Occupation
Rayzel	20	Daughter	Supported by parents
Jucek Lipman	**53**	**Husband**	**Dealer**
Judes	36	Wife	Supported by husband
Hane Ryfke	9	Daughter	Supported by parents
Udel Sure	**19**	**Single**	**Servant**
Wilczyńska Mindel	**20**	**Single**	**Servant**
Wilczyński Moszek	**42**	**Husband**	**Propinator / pub tenant**
Szajna	50	Wife	Supported by husband
Lewin	16	Son	Supported by parents
Jozef	13	Son	Supported by parents
Sare	10	Daughter	Supported by parents
Wilczyński Josef	**49**	**Husband**	**Dressmaker**
Hane	49	Wife	Supported by husband
Icek	19	Son	Supported by parents
Dawid	16	Son	Supported by parents
Zelig	14	Son	Supported by parents
Mindel	11	Daughter	Supported by parents
Marye	7	Daughter	Supported by parents
Witkowska Frayde	**44**	**Widow**	**Laborer**
Eliasz	24	Son	Dressmaker
Gitel	9	Daughter	Supported by mother
Benjamin	5	Son	Supported by mother
Wigdor Haim	**44**	**Husband**	**Laborer**
Icek	22	Son	Supported by father
Nemahe	11	Son	Supported by father
Layzer Hersz	7	Son	Supported by father
Witkowski Michał	**35**	**Husband**	**Laborer**
Ruchel	31	Wife	Supported by husband
Ryfke	7	Daughter	Supported by parents
Miehel	5	Son	Supported by parents
Maynus	4	Son	Supported by parents
Mirel	2	Daughter	Supported by parents
Blume	20	Single	Supported by relatives
Wrocławska Rayce	**25**	**Single**	**Servant**
Witkowski Szloma	**36**	**Husband**	**Dealer**
Frayde	24	Wife	Supported by husband
Rayze	1	Daughter	Supported by parents
Wilczyński Mosiek	**39**	**Husband**	**Dressmaker**
Chaje	39	Wife	Supported by husband
Łaje	15	Daughter	Supported by parents
Haim	7	Son	Supported by parents
Jayb	5	Son	Supported by parents
Frymet	3	Daughter	Supported by parents

Table B, cont.

Full name	Age	Status	Occupation
Warembrum Jakob	**36**	**Husband**	**Barber**
Ryfke	24	Wife	Supported by husband
Ester	5	Daughter	Supported by parents
Moysie	2	Son	Supported by parents
Witkowski Boruch	**73**	**Husband**	**Dealer**
Michle	59	Wife	Supported by husband
Mordke	36	Son	Supported by parents
Szmul	26	Son	Supported by parents
Wilczyńska Dwora	**54**	**Widow**	**Laborer**
Lewek	17	Son	Supported by mother
Ryfke	13	Daughter	Supported by mother
Manes	10	Son	Supported by mother
Witkowski Icek	**46**	**Husband**	**bingerbread maker**
Blume	41	Wife	Supported by husband
Hane	21	Daughter	Supported by parents
Layb	16	Son	Supported by parents
Royze	3	Daughter	Supported by parents
Benjamin	15	Son	Supported by parents
Wilczyński Hersz	**26**	**Single**	**Fisherman**
Wróblewski Mosiek	**53**	**Husband**	**Laborer**
Słodkie	43	Wife	Supported by husband
Morye	14	Daughter	Supported by parents
Abram	1	Son	Supported by parents
Hersz	2	Son	Supported by parents
Zoberman Layb	**33**	**Husband**	**Dressmaker**
Hinde	29	Wife	Supported by husband
Ester	5	Daughter	Supported by parents
Zyske Hersz	**35**	**Husband**	**Dressmaker**
Temerche	31	Wife	Supported by husband
Zelman	6	Son	Supported by parents
Ester	4	Daughter	Supported by parents
Zyze Hersz	**33**	**Husband**	**Dressmaker**
Aydel	23	Wife	Supported by husband
Zelmanowicz Szmul	**25**	**Husband**	**Singer**
Brane	20	Wife	Supported by husband
Fraydel	2	Daughter	Supported by parents
Symche Zelmanowicz	19	Single	Supported by brother
Zauberman Mahe	**80**	**Husband**	**Haberdasher**
Cyrel	60	Wife	Supported by husband
Chaim	41	Son	Supported by parents
Zelman Symhe	**14**	**Single**	**Servant**

Source: APK, AMK, classification number 220

Note: the order of records and bold type is presented identically to the original.

Table C Contributions to Kleczew Synagogue Fund in 1844–1845

No.	Full name 1844	Size of contribution (rubles, kopeks)	No.	Full name 1845	Size of contribution (rubles, kopeks)
				Inventory from bill for the year 1845	12.66
1	Abram Bujnis	0.15	1	Abram Bajnicz	0.1
2	Abram Jozef Glocer	0.75	2	Abram Jozef Glocer	0.6
3	Abram Kalmanowicz	2	3	Abram Kalmcunowicz	1.9
4	Abram Labiszynski	0.3	4	Abram Łabiszyński	0.3
5	Abram Nyzen	0.45	5	Abram Mysen	0.45
6	Abram Psipsie	0.6	6	Abram Pipcie	0.3
7	Abram Psipsie Plewinski	0.3	7	Abram Slesiński	0.3
8	Abram Wolnsztajn	0.6	8	Abram Wolsztein	0.75
9	Aron Boes	1.8	9	Aron Boes	1.8
10	Aron Grynfeld	8.25	10	Aron Grynfild	8.25
11	Aron Zyskin	13. 31 ½	11	Aron Liskind Szmulowicz	0.75
12	Aron Zyskind	0.75			
13	Aron Zyskind lease	7.94	12	Aron Lyskniel from a lease	26.62
14	Behr Kalniewski	0.45	13	Behr Kalmiński	0.45
15	Ber Heim Saddler	3	14	Beki Scielarz	3.15
16	Bernd Mazur	8.25	15	Berend Mazur	8.25
17	Boruch Elkunis	4.4	16	Bern Elkonis ?	13.11
			17	Borzich Boruszas/k	0.3
18	Chajm Grynfeld	7.5	18	Chajm Grynfild	7.5
19	Chajm Psipsie	1	19	Chajm Psipcze	0.3
20	Dawid Bezak	1.5	20	Dawid Bosak	1.15
21	Dawid Gnad	0.45	21	Dawid Gnat	0.45
22	Dawid Grynfeld	2	22	Dawid Grynfild	1.5
23	Dawid Mazur	4.5	23	Dawid Mazur	4.5
24	Dawid Przeger	2.25	24	Dawid Przgor /Pregor	2.25
			25	Dawid Toporski	0.15
25	Efrajm Kohn	0.75	26	Efrajm Kohu	1.5

Table C, cont.

No.	Full name 1844	Size of contribution (rubles, kopeks)	No.	Full name 1845	Size of contribution (rubles, kopeks)
26	Eliasz Glazer	0.45	27	Eliasz Glazer	0.15
			28	Eliasz Gleizer	0.15
27	Eliasz Łabiszyński	1.5	29	Eliaz Lubiczyński	1.5
28	Eliasz Shkolnik	0.15			
29	Eliasz Witkoski	0.3	30	Eliaz Wilkocki	0.15
30	From a lease	13.28	31	From a lease	26.62 ½
31	Geszron Baranek	0.9	32	Gerczon Baranek	0.75
32	Gierszon Klużkoski	0.3			
33	Hejm Izrael Piekarski	1.5	33	Hajm Picharski /Pickarzki	2
34	Hersz Frydenthal	1.2	34	Hersz Frydentka	1.2
35	Hersz Parecki!/ Jarecki	3.3	35	Hersz Garecki	3.3
36	Hersz Kalmanoms	1.8	36	Hersz Kahnananow	1
37	Hersz Kleczewski	0.15	37	Hersz Kalmińcki	0.15
			38	Hersz Kleczeski	0.15
38	Hersz Leszczyński	0.75	39	Hersz Leszczyński	0.5
39	Hersz Lipszyc	9	40	Hersz Lipszyc	7
40	Hersz Malarek	2	41	Hersz Malarek	2
41	Hersz Wilczyński	0.45	42	Hersz Wilczyński	0.6
			43	Izrael Barbaum	0.15
42	Izrael Kamlotek	0.6	44	Izrael Kamlotek	0.6
43	Izrael Krygier	0.3	45	Izrael Krygier	0.3
44	Izrael Piekarski	2.25	46	Izrael Piekarski	2.25
45	Jaiek Kohn	0.15			
46	Jakub Boes	4.5	47	Jakub /Boes/	6
47	Jakub Buzak	4.5	48	Jakuz Brzako /Brzosko	4.5
48	Jakub Grezibert	0.3	49	Jakub Grabor	0.3
49	Jakub Marek Shkolnik	1.5	50	Jakub Mosek Shkolnik	1.6

Table C, cont.

No.	Full name 1844	Size of contribution (rubles, kopeks)	No.	Full name 1845	Size of contribution (rubles, kopeks)
50	Jakub Sure Shkolnik	4.5	51	Jakub Sure Szkulnis	5
51	Jakub Mazur	10.3	52	Jakub Mazur	6.3
52	Jakub Nipen	0.75	53	Layb Jakub Nipen	0.75
			54	Jeyk Glazier	0.15
53	Jeiek Bornsztein	1.2	55	Jeyk Bernsztyn	1
54	Jozef Goldman	7.5	56	Jozef Goldman	7.5
55	Jozef Golihajmer	8.25	57	Jozef Gardhanin	8.25
56	Jozel Rączka	2	58	Jeszel Rączka	3
57	Jozef Kusnierczyk	0.6	59	Josef Kusmierczyk	0.6
58	Jozef Nayfeld	3.3	60	Jozef Majfelz	3.15
			61	Jayk Malarek	1.5
			62	Jeyk ?Kaher?	0.15
59	Jude Judzki	0.3	63	Jude Judzki	0.15
60	Jude Poznanski	0.6	64	Jude Poznanicki	0.6
61	Jude Rakoski	0.6	65	Jude Rakowski	0.6
62	Jude Zajdel	1.8	66	Jude Kaydell	2.3
			67	Jurzil? Kohu /Kahu/	0.15
			68	Jicek Baum Orzechowski	0.3
63	Lajb Baranek/ Baraszuk	1.8	69	Laib Boruszas/k	1.8
64	Lajb Jelenkiewicz	0.45	70	Laib Jelenkiewicz	0.45
65	Lajzer Bauman's house	0.75			
66	Leib Łata	0.45	71	Lajb Łata	0.45
			72	Lajb Danzygier	1
67	Lejbus Krotoszyński	1.2	73	Lajb Krotoszyński	1.1
68	Lewin Chajm Krotoszynski	0.6	74	Lajbus Krotoszyncki	0.3
69	Liser Radzijeski	0.3	75	Lajzer Radzijerski?	0.3
70	Lewek Pelenkiewicz	0.45	76	Leiwel Jelenkiewicz	0.45

Table C, cont.

No.	Full name 1844	Size of contribution (rubles, kopeks)
71	Lewek Przedborz	2.7
72	Lipman Majer Shkolnik	0.3
73	Lewek Wilczynski	3
74	Lewek Wilczynski	0.3
75	Lipman Glazier	0.45
76	Majer Pietrkowski	2.75
77	Manasze Appel	4.5
78	Mendel Sure Shkolnik	0.75
79	Merdke Witkowski	0.15
80	Michał Gębicki	0.25
81	Majer Glazier	0.3
82	Michał Pregler	0.45
83	Michał Shkolnik	0.3
84	Michał Witkowski	0.3
85	Mordke Rachwalski	0.45
86	Mosesz Aron Dawid	0.6
87	Mosiek Golinski	0.3
88	Mosiek Hertzberg	1.2
89	Mosiek Klepacz	0.45
90	Mosiek Shkolnik	1
91	Moszek Rączkowski	4.5
92	Moszik Rahwalski	0.6
93	Perec Salamon Ihalmiarz (?)	0.15

No.	Full name 1845	Size of contribution (rubles, kopeks)
77	Lejmen/Lipmen/Majer Shkolnik	0.45
78	Lewek Wilczynski	3
79	Liwek Knedborz	2.2
80	Sipman Glazier	0.45
81	Majer Harness Maker	2.7
82	Majer Pitrkowski	2
83	Menasze Appell	1
84	Mendel Sure Shkolnik	0.3
85	Merdle Witkowski	1
86	Michał Gękeiki?	0.45
87	Michał Glazier	0.15
88	Michał Prigler (Pregler)	0.3
89	Michał Shkolnik	0.15
90	Michał Wizkoski	0.45
91	Mordke Rahwalski	0.4
92	Mosie Aron Dawid	0.3
93	Moszek Goliński	1.2
94	Mosiek Herizberg	0.45
95	Mosiek Klepacz	1
96	Moziek Shkolnik	4.5
97	Mosiek Rączkoski	0.45
98	Mosiek Rahwalski	0.75
99	Moszek Herczynski	1
100	Moszek Jelenkiewicz	1
101	Pejcach Krygier	0.6

Table C, cont.

No.	Full name 1844	Size of contribution (rubles, kopeks)	No.	Full name 1845	Size of contribution (rubles, kopeks)
			102	Pejcacz Kryger	0.3
			103	Ppesczen Kluczkocki	0.75
94	Rafał Leszczyński	0.45	104	Rafał Leszczyński	0.6
95	Salamon Aroshorn	0.9	105	Salamen Aronsiher	0.15
			106	Salamon Blutz	0.6
96	Salamon Tanner	0.6	107	Salamon Tanner	0.45
97	Seszel Kohm	0.15			
98	Symke Jurańczyk	8	108	Smyrel Piotrkowski	11
99	Szapsie Grynfeld	11	109	Szajnce Grynfild	5.5
100	Szlama Lisner	4	110	Szlama Lisner	4.5
101	Szlama Witkowski	4.5	111	Szlama Witkocki	1.8
102	Szmul Bendend	1.8	112	Szmul Bendurz	1.8
103	Szmul Krotoszyn	1.8	113	Szmul Krotoszyński	0.55
104	Szmul Sompolinski	0.45	114	Szmul Sapolinski	0.4
105	Szmul Tanner	0.45	115	Szmul Tanner	8
			116	Szymche Iwanczyk	0.35
106	Widow Boes	0.3	117	Widow Boes	4.5
107	Widow Jelnikiewicz/Jelenkiewicz/Pelnikiewicz	3	118	Widow Jelenkiewicz	0.15
108	Widow Neyman	0.15	119	Widow Neyman	1.8
109	Widow Sure Shkolnik	1.8	120	Widow Sare Shkolnik	7.5
110	Widow Wilczynska	7.5	121	Widow Wilczyńska	2
111	Wolf Glocer	1.5	122	Wufe Glocer	1.5
112	Wulf Szlama Shkolnik	1	123	Wulf Szkulnik	1.8
113	Zelig Karo	1.8	124	Zelig Karo	0.75
114	Zelig Szkulnik	0.75	125	Zelig Shkolnik	0.75
Total annual contribution		**254.03**	**Total annual contribution**		**236.42**

Source: APK, Am K, classification number 19

Table D Donors for repair of Kleczew synagogue in 1867

Full name	Occupation	Amount (rubles)
Baranek Abram Moszek	Cap maker	0.20
Baum Icek Jakub	Dressmaker	0.50
Baum Icek Jukew	Dressmaker	0.50
Baum Perec	Glazier	0.50
Bauman Szmul Hersz	Dealer	0.30
Blachart Trocel	Dealer	0.50
Blitz Majer	Dressmaker	1.20
Blitz Szlama	Dressmaker	2.50
Boes Aron	Dressmaker	2
Boes Szmul	Dealer	4.50
Boes Wowa Frajlech	Dealer	0.75
Bok Fiszel	Cap maker	0.50
Bosak Jakub	Trader	33
Bosak Lejb Beer	Trader	17
Braun Jakub	Dealer	1.20
Dancygier Lejb	Trader	27
Dyndol Icek	Dealer	0.50
Ebert Abram	Dealer	4.50
Eliaszyk Majer	Dressmaker	1.20
Elkanus Samuel	Trader	6.50
Engel Dawid	Dealer	1.25
Fridental Abram	Dealer	0.50
Fridental Hersz	Dealer	3.50
Friedental Josef	Dealer	1
Gębicki Michał	Dressmaker	1.20
Glocer Abram Josef	Dealer	8
Glocer Efraim Lemel	Dealer	2.50
Glocer Wołek	Dealer	8
Goldbaum Bernard	Dealer	4.50
Grünfeld Abram	Dealer	3
Grünfeld Aron	Dealer	7
Grünfeld Chaim	Trader	30
Grünfeld Efraim Josef	Tobacconist	0.50
Grünfeld Salomon	Dealer	7
Grünfeld Szapsia	Trader	45
Grünfeld Szymon	Dealer	8
Hajman Jakub	Dealer	3.50
Heliczkowski Dawid	Dealer	1.25
Ilczyński Josef	Trader	15
Iwańczyk Majer	Tanner	11

Table D, cont.

Full name	Occupation	Amount (rubles)
Iwańczyk Zelig	Trader	18
Janecki Hersz	Dealer	8
Jelenkiewicz Lejb	Dealer	1.20
Jelenkiewicz Lemel	Dealer	0.50
Jelonkiewicz Efraim	Stall keeper	9
Kałmanowicz Abram	Dealer	4.50
Kałmanowicz Hersz	Dealer	3.50
Kałmanowicz Jakub	Dealer	1.25
Kałmanowicz Moszek Szlama	Dealer	1.25
Kałmiński Beer	Dressmaker	1.20
Kałmiński Rafał	Dealer	2
Kamiński Hersz	Butcher	0.30
Kärp Majer	Glazier	0.75
Kohn Jakub	Dealer	2
Kohn Manes	Dealer	2
Kohn Wowa	Dealer	0.50
Koniński Nusen	Butcher	1.50
Korn Boruch	Dressmaker	1.20
Koszer Mordka	Dressmaker	0.50
Krawczyk Chaim	Dressmaker	1.20
Krawczyk Hersz	Dressmaker	1.20
Krawczyk Moszek Aron	Dressmaker	2.50
Kroner Elka	Tinsmith	2
Krotoszyński Icek Josef	Dealer	3
Krotoszyński Lejb Chaim	Dealer	3.40
Krotowski Dawid	Dealer	2
Kryger Izrael Beer	Dressmaker	2.50
Kuczyński Juda Lejb	Cotton candy maker	3.50
Lememberg Szlama Hersz	Dealer	1.50
Leszczyński Rafał	Dressmaker	0.30
Lipszyc Hersz	Tavern keeper	17
Lisner Szlama	Dealer	8.50
Łabiszyński Rafał	Dealer	1.50
Łata Izrael	Dealer	2
Łata Szmul Hersz	Dressmaker	0.50
Malarek Hersz	Trader	9.40
Nasielski Izrael	Dealer	4.50
Nysenbaum Abram	Dressmaker	0.30
Orzechowski Lejb	Dressmaker	0.50
Piekarski Chaim	Trader	17
Piekarski Wowa Izrael	Dealer	3
Piotrkowski Majer	Dealer	0.75
Piotrkowski Nuta	Dealer	1
Poznański Wowa	Baker	0.55

Table D, cont.

Full name	Occupation	Amount (rubles)
Pregler Michał	Horse cart driver	2
Przedborz Lejb	Dealer	2.50
Przedecki Salomon	Fisherman	1.20
Psipsia Anszel	Dealer	2
Psipsia Lejb	Dealer	2
Psipsie Szalo	Dressmaker	0.50
Psipsie Wigdor	Dressmaker	0.50
Rachwalski Mordka	Cap maker	1.50
Rakowski Perec	Dressmaker	1.20
Rączkowski Icek Hersz	Tanner	3.50
Rączkowski Josek	*Shochet*	2
Rączkowski Manel	Tanner	6.50
Rączkowski Moszek	Tanner	11
Roterdam Benjamin	Tanner	1.20
Rozenkrantz Jakub Moszek	Dealer	0.50
Rozenkrantz Moszek	Tanner	1.20
Saddler Chaim	Tanner	8
Sompoliński Josef	Dressmaker	0.60
Sompoliński Szmul	Dealer	0.50
Sompoliński Wowa	Dressmaker	2
Szczeciński Hersz	Propinator / pub tenant	13
Glazier Abram	Glazier	0.50
Glazier Boruch	Glazier	0.75
Glazier Chaim Michał	Baker	2.50
Teacher Jakub	Trader	10
Szmerławski Josef	Dealer	2.50
Warmbrum Dawid	Medical assistant (feldsher)	2
Wilczyński Lejb	Dealer	8
Wilczyński Lejb	Dressmaker	1.20
Wilczyński Lejb	Dressmaker	0.50
Wilczyński Wowa Szamsie	Dealer	3.50
Witkowski Benjamin	Dealer	1.50
Witkowski Binem	Dressmaker	0.60
Witkowski Josef	Dealer	7
Witkowski Szlama	Dealer	13
Wołkowicz Moszek	Tobacconist	0.60
Wróblewski Eljasz	Trader	17
Zajdel Juda Majlech	Dressmaker	2.50
Zajf Moszek	Baker	1
Zyskind Ezryel	Dealer	0.75
Zyskind Szmul	Tanner	1.20
Total		**555.3**

Source: APK, AmK, classification number 22

Table E Number and percent of Jewish population in selected towns of Eastern Greater Poland, 1921–1939

Town	1921		1931		1936		1939	
	No.	Percent	No.	Percent	No.	Percent	No.	Percent
Babiak, Koło County	237	29.2	240*	-	240*	-	240-250*	-
Błaszki, Kalisz County	2,186	56.1	2,237	44.8	1,990	39.9	NA	-
Dąbie, Koło County	1,400	30.4	1,100	28.8	1,100*		1,100*	-
Dobra, Turek County	1,207	39.5	1,750*		1,850*		2,000*	-
Golina, Konin County	695	28.7	643	25.3	721	24	720-750*	-
Izbica Kujawska, Koło County	1,378	46.2	NA	-	1,525	42	1,550*	-
Kalisz, Kalisz County	15,566	34.9	19,248	35	26,070	34.1	NA	-
Kleczew, Konin County	894	32.6	NA	-	740	21	750*	20
Kłodawa, Koło County	1,148	29.4	NA	-	NA	-	1,350*	25-26
Koło, Koło County	5,159	45	5,000*	40	NA	-	4,560*	35
Konin, Konin County	2,902	28.9	3,600	34.6	2,235	20.8	2,500*	-
Koźminek, Kalisz County	729	32.1	NA	-	NA	-	800*	29
Pyzdry, Konin County	406	8.8	240*	5.5	229	4.7	230*	4
Rychwał, Konin County	244	21.8	250-270*	-	241	11	230-240*	
Skulsk, Konin County	228	25.9	160*	15	NA	-	140-160*	15
Słupca, Konin County	1,426	25.8	1,140	18.3	1,073	15.8	1,050*	15
Sompolno, Koło County	1,149	30.7	1,125	24.7	NA	-	1,100*	22
Stawiszyn, Kalisz County	672	26.2	650-700	-	600*	-	550-600*	-
Ślesin, Konin County	304	14.6	260*	10-11	265	9.9	250	9
Tuliszków, Konin County	260	11	198	-	202	8	200	9
Turek, Turek County	2,678	26.9	NA	-	2,762	29.4	2,395	24
Uniejów, Turek County	1,100	30.1	NA	-	NA	-	890	30.4
Wilczyn, Konin County	174	26.4	170*	22	162**	20	174	20*
Władysławów, Konin County	293	30.5	250	-	250*	-	280	-
Zagórów, Konin County	807	21.7	NA	-	722	16.7	628	15

Source: APK, SPK, classification number 342; D. Dąbrowska, "Zagłada skupisk żydowskich w Kraju Warty w okresie okupacji hitlerowskiej," *Biuletyn Żydowskiego Instytutu Historycznego* 13-14 (1955): 159, table 3; A. Pakentreger, *Żydzi w Kaliszu*, 9-10; H. Marcinkowska, *Miasteczko*, 41-42; T. Kawski, *Społeczność żydowska*, 162-163, table 1; T. Kawski, M. Opioła, *Gminy żydowskie*, passim.

*= Ca.

** Data from 1935.

Table F Electors with active right to vote in Kleczew Jewish kehilla on May 27, 1924, by occupation, age, and address

Family name and name	Age	Occupation	Address
Albert Michał Hersz	52	Huckster	Kleczew, ul. Chrzanowo
Bagno Chaim L.	42	Photographer	Kleczew, ul. Słupecka
Bagno Nuchem	45	Merchant	Kleczew, ul. Rynek
Bainus Wigdor	30	Huckster	Kleczew, ul. Kościelna
Bajmiś Gerszon	61	Huckster	Kleczew, ul. Kościelna
Bajmiś Michał	80	—	Kleczew, ul. Warszawska
Bamber Abram	32	Tailor	Kleczew, ul. Konińska
Bamber Mojsze	30	Saddler	Kleczew, ul. Słupecka
Berendt Berek	25	Huckster	Kleczew, ul. Słupecka
Berendt Hersz	44	Huckster	Kleczew, ul. Słupecka
Błaszkowski Josef	35	Huckster	Kleczew, ul. Rynek
Boas Josek	60	Hatter	Kleczew, ul. Rynek
Bock Szmul	75	Huckster	Kleczew, ul. Rynek
Brysz Godeł	28	Merchant	Kleczew, ul. Słupecka
Brysz Luzer	35	Merchant	Kleczew, ul. Rynek
Brysz Mojsze		Merchant	Kleczew, ul. Rynek
Czerwonka Izrael	42	Huckster	Kleczew, ul. Kościelna
Dawidowicz Chaskeł	36	Huckster	Kleczew, ul. Słupecka
Dobrzyński Kałme	48	Huckster	Kleczew, ul. Kościelna
Dyndol Izaak	49	Huckster	Kleczew, ul. Słupecka
Dzieci Idel	56	Huckster	Kleczew, ul. Słupecka
Dzieci Lejb	26	Huckster	Kleczew, ul. Słupecka
Ettinger Abram Icek	65	Citizen	Kleczew, ul. Słupecka
Fogiel Chaim	50	Merchant	Kleczew, ul. Słupecka
Fogiel Icek	34	Farmer	Kleczew, ul. Górne Piaski
Fogiel Szmaje	37	Farmer	Kleczew, u. Górne Piaski
Friedensohn Mojsze Sz.	50	Huckster	Kleczew, ul. Warszawska
Gembicki Abram Josek	72	Tailor	Kleczew, ul. Słupecka
Gembicki Chaim	36	Tailor	Kleczew, ul. Słupecka
Gembicki Efroim	65	Tailor	Kleczew, ul. Słupecka
Gembicki Zelig	34	Tailor	Kleczew, ul. Słupecka
Gostyński Hersz	44	Huckster	Kleczew, ul. Rynek
Grünbath Eljasz	65	—	Kleczew, ul. Rynek
Grünblath Icek	42	Huckster	Kleczew, ul. Słupecka
Grünfeld Dawid	61	Huckster	Kleczew, ul. Rynek
Haba Josef Eljasz	39	Baker	Kleczew, ul. Słupecka
Hamburg Symche	90	Fisherman	Kleczew, ul. Słupecka
Heber Szaja	39	Huckster	Kleczew, ul. Kościelna
Huberman Azrjel	60	Fisherman	Kleczew, ul. Słupecka

Table F, cont.

Family name and name	Age	Occupation	Address
Huberman Nachme	27	Fisherman	Kleczew, ul. Słupecka
Iławski Szaje	44	Huckster	Kleczew, ul. Kościelna
Jaffe Szyje	40	-	Kleczew, ul. Słupecka
Jakubowicz Hersz Lejb	26	Tailor	Kleczew, ul. Rynek
Joachimkiewicz Majer	33	Huckster	Kleczew, ul. Słupecka
Jutrzyński Wolf	80	Fisherman	Kleczew, ul. Słupecka
Kaufman Szlama Hersz	60	Rabbi	Kleczew, ul. Konińska
Kaźmierski Efroim	33	Butcher	Kleczew, ul. Słupecka
Kiwała Iszuel	30	Tailor	Kleczew, ul. Warszawska
Kiwała Lejb	27	Tailor	Kleczew, ul. Warszawska
Klamrowski Beer	49	Tailor	Kleczew, ul. Rynek
Klamrowski Hersz	45	Merchant	Kleczew, ul. Słupecka
Kleczewski Pinches	47	Merchant	Kleczew, ul. Warszawska
Klepacz Icek	28	Butcher	Kleczew, ul. Słupecka
Klepacz Jukew	58	Butcher	Kleczew, ul. Słupecka
Koner Abram	33	Huckster	Kleczew, ul. Słupecka
Koner Icek	52	Tinsmith	Kleczew, ul. Słupecka
Koner Icek Lejzor	63	Huckster	Kleczew, ul. Słupecka
Koner Lejb	62	Tinsmith	Kleczew, ul. Słupecka
Korn Fałek	44	Merchant	Kleczew, ul. Rynek
Korn Szmul	36	Merchant	Kleczew, ul. Słupecka
Koszarek Lejb	43	Tailor	Kleczew, ul. Słupecka
Koszcz Jakub	27	Tinsmith	Kleczew, ul. Konińska
Koszer Mojsze	58	Tinsmith	Kleczew, ul. Konińska
Koza Symche	40	Merchant	Kleczew, ul. Słupecka
Krotowski Fałek	38	—	Kleczew, ul. Słupecka
Krotowski Izrael	33	Merchant	Kleczew, ul. Konińska
Krzyżanowski Mojsze	57	Baker	Kleczew, ul. Konińska
Kuczyński Abram	32	Merchant	Kleczew, ul. Rynek
Kutnowski Luzer	40	Merchant	Kleczew, ul. Rynek
Leszczyński Lewek	61	Tailor	Kleczew, ul. Słupecka
Leszczyński Załme	32	Tailor	Kleczew, ul. Słupecka
Lewkowicz Icek	30	Huckster	Kleczew, ul. Warszawska
Lewkowicz Mojsze	36	Baker	Kleczew, ul. Słupecka
Lipman Chaim	48	Tailor	Kleczew, u. Słupecka
Łabuszyński Michał	26	Huckster	Kleczew, ul. Słupecka
Łatta Salomon	76	Tailor	Kleczew, ul. Słupecka
Łatta Szmul Jakub	52	Huckster	Kleczew, ul. Konińska
Marek Hersz Wolf	30	Tailor	Kleczew, ul. Słupecka
Markowski Chaim	30	Tailor	Kleczew, ul. Słupecka
Nalazek Icek Lejzor	72	—	Kleczew, ul. Słupecka
Neiman Mojsze	54	—	Kleczew, ul. Warszawska
Noss Dawid	38	Tailor	Kleczew, ul. Konińska
Obwarzanek Mordche	47	Tailor	Kleczew, ul. Słupecka

Table F, cont.

Family name and name	Age	Occupation	Address
Pacanowski Henoch	52	Huckster	Kleczew, ul. Piaski Górne
Pacanowski Icek	30	Huckster	Kleczew, ul. Piaski Górne
Pacanowski Luzer	31	Huckster	Kleczew, ul. Warszawska
Pachciarski Nuchem	60	Huckster	Kleczew, ul. Warszawska
Patałowski Abram	27	Hatter	Kleczew, ul. Słupecka
Pregler Ziskind	65	Citizen	Kleczew, ul. Słupecka
Presberg Jakub	50	—	Kleczew, ul. Warszawska
Prost Ichiel	59	Huckster	Kleczew, ul. Rynek
Prost Jakub	28	Huckster	Kleczew, ul. Warszawska
Prost Lemel	31	Huckster	Kleczew, ul. Słupecka
Prost Salomon	33	Huckster	Kleczew, ul. Piaski Górne
Przedecki Jozef	56	Merchant	Kleczew, ul. Słupecka
Przedecki Mordcha	28	Huckster	Kleczew, ul. Słupecka
Przysucher	69	Butcher	Kleczew, ul. Konińska
Psipsze Anszel	80	Merchant	Kleczew, ul. Słupecka
Rachwalski Tobjasz	60	Huckster	Kleczew, ul. Rynek
Rakowski Ichel	38	Merchant	Kleczew, ul. Słupecka
Reichenbach Mojsze	48	Merchant	Kleczew, ul. Rynek
Reichmann Mojsze	40	Merchant	Kleczew, ul. Słupecka
Rogoziński Izrael	60	Tailor	Kleczew, ul. Warszawska
Rogoziński Juda	32	Tailor	Kleczew, ul. Warszawska
Russ Gerszon	33	Merchant	Kleczew, ul. Słupecka
Rygiel Majer	60	Tailor	Kleczew, ul. Kościelna
Rygiel Salomon	46	Merchant	Kleczew, ul. Słupecka
Rygiel Wigdor	27	Tailor	Kleczew, ul. Słupecka
Samson Juda Lejb	40	Huckster	Kleczew, ul. Warszawska
Segał Dawid	57	Huckster	Kleczew, ul. Słupecka
Segał Hersz	25	Huckster	Kleczew, ul. Słupecka
Sender Rubin	40	Huckster	Kleczew, ul. Rynek
Szmelcyngier Nuchem	50	Huckster	Kleczew, ul. Warszawska
Szöhnsznader Gedalje	47	Teacher/Teacher	Kleczew, ul. Rynek
Sztachelberg Jakub Lejzor	32	Huckster	Kleczew, ul. Słupecka
Ślesiński Lejzor	58	Huckster	Kleczew, ul. Konińska
Śliwiński Icek	62	Huckster	Kleczew, ul. Konińska
Światowicz Kaufman	25	Huckster	Kleczew, ul. Słupecka
Urbach Icek Jojne	32	Huckster	Kleczew, ul. Słupecka
Urbach Jozef	56	Huckster	Kleczew, ul. Słupecka
Urbach Wolf Hersz	2	Huckster	Kleczew, ul. Słupecka
Wajsman Abram		Huckster	Kleczew, ul. Rynek
Warbrum Dawid	32	—	Kleczew, ul. Rynek
Wassermann Perec	37	Huckster	Kleczew, ul. Słupecka
Weingart Ichiel Majer	36	Huckster	Kleczew, ul. Słupecka
Weingart Sucher M.	64	Huckster	Kleczew, ul. Słupecka
Widawski Abram	48	Teacher	Kleczew, ul. Chrzanowo

Table F, cont.

Family name and name	Age	Occupation	Address
Widawski Szyje	64	—	Kleczew, ul. Słupecka
Witkowski Abram	32	Tailor	Kleczew, ul. Warszawska
Witkowski Fajwiś	38	Tailor	Kleczew, ul. Warszawska
Witkowski Henoch	40	Fisherman	Kleczew, ul. Słupecka
Witkowski Jojne	52	Tailor	Kleczew, ul. Słupecka
Witkowski Załkin	69	Fisherman	Kleczew, ul. Słupecka
Witkowski Zyszel	26	Fisherman	Kleczew, ul. Słupecka
Wolf Mendel	36	Huckster	Kleczew, ul. Rynek
Wolstein Abram	47	Huckster	Kleczew, ul. Rynek
Złotogórski Symche	54	Huckster	Kleczew, ul. Rynek
Żółty Abram W.	50	Huckster	Kleczew, ul. Warszawska

Source: Źródło: APK, SPS, case 217.

Table G Jewish voters for the Sejm of the Republic of Poland from Kleczew, 1935 (by occupation, place of residence, and date of birth)

Full name	Date of birth	Occupation	Place of residence (street)	Living in district since
Abramczyk Dawid	21.8.1910	Laborer	Chrzanowskiego	Birth
Brener Chaja Sura	25.9.1868	Laborer	Chrzanowskiego	Birth
Brener Bajla	26.12.1905	Supported by mother	Chrzanowskiego	Birth
Brener Chune	26.6.1911	Supported by mother	Chrzanowskiego	Birth
Dyndol Izaak	27.7.1896	Trader	Chrzanowskiego	Birth
Dyndol Jette	1.8.1896	Supported by husband	Chrzanowskiego	Birth
Dyndol Jankew	30.9.1908	Supported by parents	Chrzanowskiego	Birth
Dyndol Ajdel	30.1.1911	Supported by parents	Chrzanowskiego	Birth
Gembicki Abram Jankew	18.2.1852	Supported by son	Chrzanowskiego	Birth
Gembicki Zelig Chaim	1.5.1890	Dressmaker	Chrzanowskiego	Birth
Gembicka Rojza	15.12.1910	Supported by husband	Chrzanowskiego	1931
Huberman Nachem	14.6.1897	Fisherman	Chrzanowskiego	Birth
Huberman Rywka	14.2.1899	Supported by husband	Chrzanowskiego	1923
Huberman Azrjel	27.4.1868	Fisherman	Chrzanowskiego	1894
Huberman Gołda Łaja	1874	Supported by husband	Chrzanowskiego	Birth
Kiwała Zelig Hersz	31.10.1899	Trader	Chrzanowskiego	Birth
Kiwała Marjem	31.12.1900	Supported by husband	Chrzanowskiego	1933
Kiwała Giszuel	24.11.1894	Trader	Chrzanowskiego	Birth
Kiwała Jachet	25.12.1895	Supported by husband	Chrzanowskiego	1924
Lewkowicz Mosie	29.8.1888	Baker	Chrzanowskiego	1910
Lewkowicz Gitel	27.4.1888	Supported by husband	Chrzanowskiego	Birth
Pieterkowska Frajda	16.6.187	Laborer	Chrzanowskiego	1932
Patałowski Hersz	7.2.1904	Trader	Chrzanowskiego	Birth
Patałowska Bajla	26 years old	Supported by husband	Chrzanowskiego	Birth
Śliwicki Hersz	16.5.1901	Dressmaker	Chrzanowskiego	1930
Śliwicka Gołda	13.4.1902	Supported by husband	Chrzanowskiego	1930
Wilczyńska Mindel	22.1.1871	House owner	Chrzanowskiego	1900
Wilczyńska Udel	31.5.1902	Supported by mother	Chrzanowskiego	Birth
Wilczyńska Estera	29.1.1905	Supported by mother	Chrzanowskiego	Birth
Wołkowicz Abram	7.9.1904	Trader	Chrzanowskiego	1928
Wołkowicz Fajgla	21.9.1908	Supported by husband	Chrzanowskiego	Birth

Table G, cont.

Full name	Date of birth	Occupation	Place of residence (street)	Living in district since
Witkowska Libe	5.9.1900	Supported by husband	Chrzanowskiego	1934
Bruksztejn Michel Majer	23.2.1903	Dressmaker	Edwarda Hejmana-Jareckiego	1928
Bruksztejn Tosie	13.11.1899	Supported by husband	Edwarda Hejmana-Jareckiego	1928
Berent Majer Dawid	9.8.1897	Dressmaker	Edwarda Hejmana-Jareckiego	1911
Berent Gołda	20.6.1898	Supported by husband	Edwarda Hejmana-Jareckiego	1927
Bagno Chaim Lajb	15.10.1882	Bookstore owner	Edwarda Hejmana-Jareckiego	1915
Bagno Nacha	16.9.1882	Supported by husband	Edwarda Hejmana-Jareckiego	1915
Bagno Estera Chaja	21.4.1911	Supported by parents	Edwarda Hejmana-Jareckiego	1933
Berendt Hersz	28.2.1880	Trader	Edwarda Hejmana-Jareckiego	Birth
Berendt Sura	5.9.1881	Supported by husband	Edwarda Hejmana-Jareckiego	1903
Berendt Rojza	15.12.1906	Supported by parents	Edwarda Hejmana-Jareckiego	Birth
Berendt Frajdel	29.12.1909	Supported by parents	Edwarda Hejmana-Jareckiego	Birth
Bamber Mojsiej Chaim	12.12.1894	Saddler	Edwarda Hejmana-Jareckiego	Birth
Bamber Marjem	14.9.1901	Supported by husband	Edwarda Hejmana-Jareckiego	Birth
Chaba Josek Eljasz	11.8.1885	Baker	Edwarda Hejmana-Jareckiego	1913
Chaba Frajda	1.4.1895	Supported by husband	Edwarda Hejmana-Jareckiego	Birth
Chojnacki Chune	13.1.1891	Dressmaker	Edwarda Hejmana-Jareckiego	1926
Chojnacka Marjem	14.1.1892	Supported by husband	Edwarda Hejmana-Jareckiego	Birth
Dzieci Icek Lejb	30.1.1898	Trader	Edwarda Hejmana-Jareckiego	1906
Dzieci Itta	4.11.1895	Supported by husband	Edwarda Hejmana-Jareckiego	1922
Dzieci Idel	26.1.1867	Trader	Edwarda Hejmana-Jareckiego	1906
Dziei Estera	29.1.1872	Supported by son	Edwarda Hejmana-Jareckiego	1906
Ettinger Abram Icek	15.8.1856	House owner	Edwarda Hejmana-Jareckiego	1859
Ettinger Małka	20.9.1859	Supported by husband	Edwarda Hejmana-Jareckiego	Birth
Frenkiel Hersz	30.1.1899	Trader	Edwarda Hejmana-Jareckiego	1932
Frenkiel Szajem Guendel	35 years old	Supported by husband	Edwarda Hejmana-Jareckiego	1934
Gembicki Mojsie Aron	9.1.1887	Trader	Edwarda Hejmana-Jareckiego	1932
Gembicki Efrojm	1859	Dressmaker	Edwarda Hejmana-Jareckiego	Birth
Gembicka Ruchla	21.8.1880	Supported by husband	Edwarda Hejmana-Jareckiego	Birth
Gembicka Jentel	20.1.1905	Supported by parents	Edwarda Hejmana-Jareckiego	Birth

Table G, cont.

Full name	Date of birth	Occupation	Place of residence (street)	Living in district since
Huberman Szaje	3.5.1903	Laborer	Edwarda Hejmana-Jareckiego	birth
Huberman Ajdel	28 years old	Supported by husband	Edwarda Hejmana-Jareckiego	birth
Kroner Icek	6.7.1872	Tinsmith	Edwarda Hejmana-Jareckiego	birth
Kroner Zajdel	6.1.1885	Supported by husband	Edwarda Hejmana-Jareckiego	birth
Kroner Lejb	5.10.1909	Supported by parents	Edwarda Hejmana-Jareckiego	birth
Lewi Cyrla Itta	1870	House owner	Edwarda Hejmana-Jareckiego	1918
Litman Bine	12.12.1879	Trader's wife	Edwarda Hejmana-Jareckiego	1905
Litman Salka	28.2.1907	Supported by mother	Edwarda Hejmana-Jareckiego	birth
Litman Marjem Estera	20.3.1908	Dressmaker	Edwarda Hejmana-Jareckiego	birth
Łabiszyńska Dwojra	17.12.1875	House owner	Edwarda Hejmana-Jareckiego	1900
Łabiszyńska Rywka	14.4.1903	Supported by mother	Edwarda Hejmana-Jareckiego	birth
Łabuszyński Fuel	29.1.1909	Supported by mother	Edwarda Hejmana-Jareckiego	birth
Markowski Chaim	30.7.1894	Trader	Edwarda Hejmana-Jareckiego	1921
Markowka Chana Pessa	13.6.1897	Supported by husband	Edwarda Hejmana-Jareckiego	birth
Nelkan Hers Lejb	13.2.1857	Supported by son-in-law	Edwarda Hejmana-Jareckiego	1880
Obarzanek Mordka	31.8.1877	House owner	Edwarda Hejmana-Jareckiego	1919
Obarzanek Gitel	1.11.1879	Supported by husband	Edwarda Hejmana-Jareckiego	1919
Obarzanek Hersz	30.6.1909	Supported by parents	Edwarda Hejmana-Jareckiego	1919
Prost Lemel	20.8.1893	Trader	Edwarda Hejmana-Jareckiego	1905
Prost Liwsia Henka	13.5.1895	Supported by husband	Edwarda Hejmana-Jareckiego	1908
Prost Chana	25.5.1899	Supported by parents	Edwarda Hejmana-Jareckiego	1910
Pikus Jakub	27.12.1877	Dressmaker	Edwarda Hejmana-Jareckiego	birth
Pikus Ruchla	6.10.1885	Supported by husband	Edwarda Hejmana-Jareckiego	birth
Patałowska Cywia	16.2.1867	House owner	Edwarda Hejmana-Jareckiego	birth
Patałowski Majer	15.3.1907	Supported by mother	Edwarda Hejmana-Jareckiego	birth
Patałowska Gitla	16.8.1908	Supported by mother	Edwarda Hejmana-Jareckiego	birth
Patałowski Abram	16.2.1896	Supported by mother	Edwarda Hejmana-Jareckiego	birth
Patałowska Łaja	14.9.1900	Supported by husband	Edwarda Hejmana-Jareckiego	1924
Psipsie Ruchel	20.9.1858	House owner	Edwarda Hejmana-Jareckiego	1890
Przedecki Mordka	4.12.1896	Locksmith	Edwarda Hejmana-Jareckiego	birth
Przedecka Uchla	5.12.1905	Supported by husband	Edwarda Hejmana-Jareckiego	1910

Table G, cont.

Full name	Date of birth	Occupation	Place of residence (street)	Living in district since
Przedecki Josek	8.10.1866	House owner	Edwarda Hejmana-Jareckiego	1890
Rajchert Zysman	1909	Watchmaker	Edwarda Hejmana-Jareckiego	1930
Rajchman Mojsiej	15.1.1884	Trader	Edwarda Hejmana-Jareckiego	1914
Rajman Itta	7.3.1889	Supported by husband	Edwarda Hejmana-Jareckiego	1914
Rajchman Hersz Dawid	5.8.1910	Supported by parents	Edwarda Hejmana-Jareckiego	1914
Rygiel Jakub Salomon	22.4.1877	Trader	Edwarda Hejmana-Jareckiego	1900
Rygiel Małka Łaja	22.11.1869	Supported by husband	Edwarda Hejmana-Jareckiego	1900
Rozenblum Wolf	18.2.1904	Laborer	Edwarda Hejmana-Jareckiego	1932
Rozenblum Blima	15.8.1894	Supported by husband	Edwarda Hejmana-Jareckiego	Birth
Rozenberg Jochet	32 years old	housewife	Edwarda Hejmana-Jareckiego	1927
Strzelińka Gitla	4.2.1875	Supported by son	Edwarda Hejmana-Jareckiego	Birth
Strzeliński Rafał	31.7.1901	Trader	Edwarda Hejmana-Jareckiego	Birth
Strzelińska Rywka	27 years old	Supported by husband	Edwarda Hejmana-Jareckiego	27.5.1935
Strzelińska Ruchel	15.11.1903	Supported by brother	Edwarda Hejmana-Jareckiego	Birth
Strzelińska Estera	15.9.1909	Supported by brother	Edwarda Hejmana-Jareckiego	Birth
Segał Hersz	20.4.1899	industrialist	Edwarda Hejmana-Jareckiego	1924
Segał Mindel	25.5.1900	Supported by husband	Edwarda Hejmana-Jareckiego	Birth
Segał Dawid	14.5.1866	Trader	Edwarda Hejmana-Jareckiego	1927
Segał Chaja	1870	Supported by husband	Edwarda Hejmana-Jareckiego	1927
Segał Szajba	15.7.1910	Supported by parents	Edwarda Hejmana-Jareckiego	Birth
Swiatowicz Kaufman	16.9.1898	taxi-cab owner	Edwarda Hejmana-Jareckiego	1923
Swatowicz Michla	15.2.1901	Supported by husband	Edwarda Hejmana-Jareckiego	Birth
Sochaczewska Łaja	28.2.1890	Supported by son	Edwarda Hejmana-Jareckiego	Birth
Sochaczewska Rojza	4.5.1911	Supported by brother	Edwarda Hejmana-Jareckiego	Birth
Urbach Menachem Icek	28.5.1904	Trader	Edwarda Hejmana-Jareckiego	1914
Urbach Hana	15.9.1901	Supported by husband	Edwarda Hejmana-Jareckiego	Birth
Urbach Icek Jojne	13.9.1892	Dealer	Edwarda Hejmana-Jareckiego	1912
Urbach Gitla	14.11.1886	Supported by husband	Edwarda Hejmana-Jareckiego	1919
Witkowski Zułkin	24.3.1856	Fisherman	Edwarda Hejmana-Jareckiego	1880
Witkowska Bina	10.4.1860	Supported by husband	Edwarda Hejmana-Jareckiego	1883
Witkowski Enoch	1.6.1883	Fisherman	Edwarda Hejmana-Jareckiego	1883
Witkowski Rychier	22.9.1897	Fisherman	Edwarda Hejmana-Jareckiego	Birth
Witkowska Mila	30 years old	Fisherman	Edwarda Hejmana-Jareckiego	1925

Table G, cont.

Full name	Date of birth	Occupation	Place of residence (street)	Living in district since
Wassermann Chaim Perec	23.5.1884	Trader	Edwarda Hejmana-Jareckiego	1908
Wassermann Blima	27.6.1887	Supported by husband	Edwarda Hejmana-Jareckiego	1908
Wasserman Tobjasz	5.5.1911	Supported by parents	Edwarda Hejmana-Jareckiego	Birth
Abramowicz Alta	10.1.1873	Supported by son-in-law	Konińska	1926
Bamber Szajche	22.3.1866	Supported by son	Konińska	Birth
Bamber Abram	25.4.1892	Dressmaker	Konińska	Birth
Cygelsztroch Ajzyk Lejb	3.4.1902	Butcher	Konińska	1924
Cygelsztroch Randla	1901	Supported by husband	Konińska	1924
Koszer Jankew	13.9.1897	Tinsmith	Konińska	Birth
Koszer Parchje	2.1.1893	Supported by husband	Konińska	Birth
Krzyżanowski Mosiek	24.10.1870	Baker	Konińska	1907
Krzyżanowska Hana	13.12.1880	Supported by husband	Konińska	1907
Krzyżanowski Szlama	.12.1903	Supported by parents	Konińska	1907
Krzyżanowski Izrael Alter	9.5.1906	Supported by parents	Konińska	Birth
Krzyżanowska Bajla	28.10.1907	Supported by parents	Konińska	Birth
Krzyżanowska Marjem	8.7.1909	Supported by parents	Konińska	Birth
Łata Jakób Szmul	22.8.1872	Trader	Konińska	Birth
Łata Chaja Estera	12.12.1869	Supported by husband	Konińska	Birth
Łata Sładke	24.12.1897	Supported by parents	Konińska	Birth
Łata Fogel	17.7.1902	Supported by parents	Konińska	Birth
Łata Bajla	15.11.1906	Supported by parents	Konińska	Birth
Łata Szyme	5.10.1908	Dressmaker	Konińska	Birth
Roszkowicz Lejb	16.5.1908	Dressmaker	Konińska	1933
Moszkowicz Ruchla	25.5.1889	Supported by husband	Konińska	Birth
Nos Dawid	5.5.1885	Dressmaker	Konińska	1913
Nos Rachela	1888	Supported by husband	Konińska	Birth
Przedecka Rywka Fajgele	29.12.1863	House owner	Konińska	1895
Przedecka Pesa	4.1.1904	Dressmaker	Konińska	Birth
Rogoziński Izrael	13.5.1891	Dressmaker	Konińska	Birth
Rogozińska Parchie	2.1.1893	Supported by husband	Konińska	Birth
Rogoziński Izrael	70 years old	Supported by son	Konińska	1883

Table G, cont.

Full name	Date of birth	Occupation	Place of residence (street)	Living in district since
Ślesiński Lejzor	17.12.1864	Trader	Konińska	Birth
Ślesińska Tauba	24.3.1866	Supported by husband	Konińska	1894
Witkowski Icek Lejb	8.7.1864	Dressmaker	Konińska	1920
Witkowska Rojzla	1858	Supported by husband	Konińska	1920
Watman Jakub	29.3.1882	Watchmaker	Konińska	1913
Watman Chana	13.5.1884	Supported by husband	Konińska	1913
Wejnberg Icek	11.8.1851	Supported by kehilla	Konińska	1900
Wejnberg Icek	47 years old	Laborer	Konińska	1899
Wejnberg Chana	28 years old	Supported by husband	Konińska	1930
Zawłodawer Hersz	11.7.1893	Rabbi	Konińska	1926
Zawłodawer Rojzla	21.1.1899	Supported by husband	Konińska	1926
Bajduś Gerson	2.8.1861	Dressmaker	Kościelna	Birth
Bajduś Tauba	13.12.1860	Supported by husband	Kościelna	Birth
Dobrzyński Kałma	19.9.1875	Dealer	Kościelna	1902
Dobrzyńska Dwojra	4.3.1884	Supported by husband	Kościelna	Birth
Podchlebnik Załme	35 years old	Dealer	Kościelna	1934
Podchlebnik Małka	13.12.1896	Supported by husband	Kościelna	1934
Rygiel Jochel Majer	19.2.1864	House owner	Kościelna	1887
Rygiel Frajdel	28.12.1866	Supported by husband	Kościelna	Birth
Rygiel Liebe	14.6.1904	Supported by parents	Kościelna	Birth
Rygiel Machła	1904	Supported by parents	Kościelna	Birth
Rygiel Szelo	31.12.1910	Supported by parents	Kościelna	Birth
Rygiel Lajbuś	14.11.1906	Dressmaker	Kościelna	Birth
Szulc Jakub	5.11.1902	Dealer	Kościelna	1923
Szulc Hinde Bajle	25.4.1900	Supported by husband	Kościelna	1923
Samson Marjem Gołda	14.5.1906	Supported by husband	Kościelna	1934
Samson Szmul	9.6.1908	Trader	Kościelna	Birth
Traube Izaak Abe	8.9.1903	Dealer	Kościelna	1932
Traube Fojgel	22.10.1903	Supported by husband	Kościelna	1932
Roer Abram	23.1.1900	Butcher	Ogrodowa	1926
Roer Ides	1902	Supported by husband	Ogrodowa	1926
Boczko Lajter Towje	5.2.1905	Tinsmith	Piaski	1921

Table G, cont.

Full name	Date of birth	Occupation	Place of residence (street)	Living in district since
Boczko Rywka	14.9.1901	Supported by husband	Piaski	Birth
Rakowski Ichiel	4.3.1886	Watchmaker	Piaski	Birth
Rakowska Taube	5.10.1887	Supported by husband	Piaski	1929
Urbach Josek	18.12.1867	Trader	Piaski	1905
Urbach Rywka	1866	Supported by husband	Piaski	1905
Urbach Szyje	3.3.1894	Supported by parents	Piaski	1905
Urbach Fajbuś	15.1.1903	Supported by parents	Piaski	1905
Urbach Dwora	16.9.1899	Supported by husband	Piaski	1905
Berendt Regina	12.5.1876	Trader's wife	Plac 11 Listopada	1900
Berendt Hersz	7.6.1907	Supported by mother	Plac 11 Listopada	Birth
Berendt Jenta	19.10.1910	Supported by mother	Plac 11 Listopada	Birth
Bamber Izaak	20.12.1899	Dressmaker	Plac 11 Listopada	Birth
Bamber Rywka	27.8.1901	Supported by husband	Plac 11 Listopada	Birth
Bigos Lejb	9.7.1908	Dressmaker	Plac 11 Listopada	Birth
Bigos Bajla	18.5.1910	Supported by husband	Plac 11 Listopada	Birth
Fogel Chaim	13.1.1876	Trader	Plac 11 Listopada	1903
Fogel Bajla	17.5.1877	Supported by husband	Plac 11 Listopada	Birth
Fogel Abram	20.1.1906	Supported by parents	Plac 11 Listopada	Birth
Fogel Uren Majer	20.1.1911	Supported by parents	Plac 11 Listopada	Birth
Fogel Szifre	20.1.1911	Supported by parents	Plac 11 Listopada	Birth
Klepacz Szima	30.9.1904	Butcher	Plac 11 Listopada	Birth
Klepacz Hersz	8.11.1908	Butcher	Plac 11 Listopada	Birth
Leszczyński Załme	26.2.1892	Dressmaker	Plac 11 Listopada	Birth
Leszczyńska Zise	16.8.1898	Supported by husband	Plac 11 Listopada	1926
Leszczyński Lewek	7.7.1856	Supported by son	Plac 11 Listopada	Birth
Leszczyńska Frajdel	14.3.1904	Dressmaker	Plac 11 Listopada	Birth
Witkowski Jojne	31.1.1870	Dressmaker	Plac 11 Listopada	Birth
Witkowska Fojgel	6.11.1875	Supported by husband	Plac 11 Listopada	1900
Witkowski Mordka Hersz	15.11.1902	Supported by parents	Plac 11 Listopada	1900
Witkowski Jankew	21.12.1902	Supported by parents	Plac 11 Listopada	1900

Table G, cont.

Full name	Date of birth	Occupation	Place of residence (street)	Living in district since
Witkowska Łaja	16.1.1907	Supported by parents	Plac 11 Listopada	Birth
Witkowska Taube	23.5.1911	Supported by parents	Plac 11 Listopada	Birth
Brysz Mojsze	18.2.1882	Trader	Rynek	1904
Brysz Estera	31.7.1886	Supported by husband	Rynek	Birth
Brysz Rywke Nyche	10.11.1909	Supported by parents	Rynek	Birth
Bagno Nuchem Izrael	21.2.1879	Trader	Rynek	1903
Bagno Marta	13.11.1879	Supported by husband	Rynek	Birth
Bagno Abram	20.5.1908	Supported by parents	Rynek	Birth
Ber Mosiek Fajbiś	5.7.1900	hairdresser	Rynek	1924
Ber Łaja	1903	Supported by husband	Rynek	1924
Boes Sara	1861	Laborer	Rynek	1887
Boes Sala	28.7.1891	Laborer	Rynek	Birth
Brysz Luzer	22.10.1889	Trader	Rynek	1916
Brysz Sura	18.1.1891	Supported by husband	Rynek	1916
Grünfeld Dawid Lipman	20.7.1857	Trader	Rynek	Birth
Grünfeld Ajdel	28.6.1860	Supported by husband	Rynek	1885
Grünfeld Rywka	8.3.1896	Supported by parents	Rynek	Birth
Grünfeld Sure	13.5.1899	Supported by parents	Rynek	Birth
Goldenberg Emanuel	40 years old	Dentist	Rynek	1934
Goldenberg Eugenja	41 years old	Dentist	Rynek	1934
Goldenberg Ruwin	69 years old	Supported by son	Rynek	1934
Goldenberg Róża	62 years old	Supported by son	Rynek	1934
Herszkowicz Fajbuś	15.7.1901	Trader	Rynek	1933
Herszkowicz Rojza	27.4.1906	Supported by husband	Rynek	Birth
Jakubowicz Hersz Lejb	12.4.1898	Dressmaker	Rynek	Birth
Jakubowicz Taube	8.8.1896	Supported by husband	Rynek	Birth
Jakubowicz Rywka	16.5.1895	Trader's wife	Rynek	Birth
Klamrowski Berek	20.11.1873	Dressmaker	Rynek	1908
Kamrowska Marjem Estera	27.1.1878	Supported by husband	Rynek	Birth
Kleczewski Pinkus	11.6.1877	Dealer	Rynek	1912
Kleczewska Estera	1870	Supported by husband	Rynek	1912
Kleczewski Arja	31.1.1909	Dealer	Rynek	1912
Kiwała Lajbuś	5.5.1897	Dressmaker	Rynek	Birth

Table G, cont.

Full name	Date of birth	Occupation	Place of residence (by streets)	Living in district since
Kiwała Fojgiel	15.5.1899	Supported by husband	Rynek	1926
Korn Fiszel Icek	15.1.1883	Trader	Rynek	1908
Korn Salka	15.3.1880	Supported by husband	Rynek	Birth
Korn Berta	18.6.1909	Supported by parents	Rynek	Birth
Korn Tauba	1863	Supported by son	Rynek	1916
Klepacz Icek	27.4.1896	Trader	Rynek	Birth
Klepacz Ella	12.5.1908	Supported by husband	Rynek	1926
Łepek Sucher	70 years old	House owner	Rynek	1906
Łepek Tauba	63 years old	Supported by husband	Rynek	1906
Łepek Zelig	1907	Dealer	Rynek	Birth
Łepek Estera	8.3.1905	Supported by husband	Rynek	1934
Łepek Dobryś	14.4.1911	Supported by parents	Rynek	Birth
Łepek Majer	11.2.1901	Trader	Rynek	1906
Łepek Sura	25.12.1899	Supported by husband	Rynek	Birth
Nejman Mojsie Aron	24.3.1868	House owner	Rynek	1896
Nejman Rajzel	30.3.1870	Supported by husband	Rynek	1896
Pacanowski Luzer Ber	1893	Trader	Rynek	1916
Pacanowska Ruchel	25.3.1895	Supported by husband	Rynek	1916
Psipsie Symche	8.12.1902	Dressmaker	Rynek	Birth
Psipsie Machła	35 years old	Supported by husband	Rynek	1932
Prost Estera Hana	25.6.1868	Trader's wife	Rynek	1912
Prost Abram	26.12.1903	Trader	Rynek	1912
Prost Rajzer	2.8.1906	Supported by mother	Rynek	1912
Prost Aron	14.10.1910	Supported by mother	Rynek	1912
Rachwalski Tobjasz	7.7.1874	Trader	Rynek	Birth
Rachwalska Sura	10.10.1877	Supported by husband	Rynek	1899
Rodal Abram Izaak	2.5.1910	Laborer	Rynek	1933
Reich Moryc	11.6.1896	Trader	Rynek	1934
Rygiel Wigdor	8.5.1897	Dressmaker	Rynek	Birth
Rygiel Estera	25.12.1898	Supported by husband	Rynek	Birth
Szyke Icek	1.1.1904	Dressmaker	Rynek	Birth
Warmbrum Wigdor	13.1.1894	hairdresser	Rynek	Birth

Table G, cont.

Full name	Date of birth	Occupation	Place of residence (by streets)	Living in district since
Warmbrum Sura	14.12.1901	Supported by husband	Rynek	Birth
Wilczyńska Hinda	30.10.1897	Laborer	Rynek	1920
Wolsztejn Abram	21.12.1875	Trader	Rynek	Birth
Wolsztejn Łaja	19.1.1884	Supported by husband	Rynek	1905
Wolsztejn Jankew Lejb	28.10.1910	Supported by parents	Rynek	Birth
Witkowski Moszek	6.10.1897	Dressmaker	Rynek	1923
Witkowska Sura	8.7.1892	Supported by husband	Rynek	1923
Wózek Mojsie	19.9.903	Dealer	Rynek	1928
Wózek Łaja	15.7.1898	Supported by husband	Rynek	Birth
Wolf Mendel	14.11.1888	Trader	Rynek	1913
Wolf Estera Rojza	28.2.1894	Supported by husband	Rynek	Birth
Złotogórski Symche	17.7.1870	Teacher	Rynek	1894
Złotogórska Sura	16.1.1865	Supported by husband	Rynek	Birth
Złotogórska Gitel	15.1.1910	Supported by parents	Rynek	Birth
Gostyńska Sala	50 years old	House owner	Rynek	Birth
Frydenson Moszek Szmul	60 years old	Teacher	Generała Pierackiego	1917
Frydenson Sura Gitla	58 years old	Supported by husband	Generała Pierackiego	1917
Frydenson Perla	23.7.1908	Supported by parents	Generała Pierackiego	1932
Frydenson Złota	1910	Supported by parents	Generała Pierackiego	1917
Heber Szaja Nuchem	65 years old	Trader	Generała Pierackiego	1911
Heber Gitle	7.9.1886	Supported by husband	Generała Pierackiego	1911
Jastrząb Berek	5.2.1868	Fisherman	Generała Pierackiego	1920
Jastrząb Mindla Eiwala	2.6.1868	Supported by husband	Generała Pierackiego	1920
Kutnowska Chana Sura	1894	Laborer	Generała Pierackiego	1903
Kiwała Ruchel	1867	House owner	Generała Pierackiego	Birth
Kiwała Abram	23.1.1901	Dressmaker	Generała Pierackiego	Birth
Kiwała Henoch	14.6.1903	Dressmaker	Generała Pierackiego	Birth
Krotowski Izrael	8.3.1889	Dealer	Generała Pierackiego	Birth
Krotowska Machła	24.3.1904	Supported by husband	Generała Pierackiego	1927
Lewkowicz Icek	1897	Trader	Generała Pierackiego	Birth
Lewkowicz Sładka	1888	Supported by husband	Generała Pierackiego	1917
Marek Hersz Wolf	37 years old	Dressmaker	Generała Pierackiego	1920

Table G, cont.

Full name	Date of birth	Occupation	Place of residence (street)	Living in district since
Marek Chana Sura	30 years old	Supported by husband	Generała Pierackiego	Birth
Nüssenbaum Hinde Cywie	25.10.1861	House owner	Generała Pierackiego	Birth
Nüssenbaum Chana	19.11.1893	Supported by mother	Generała Pierackiego	Birth
Nüssenbaum Frymet	1.2.1901	Supported by mother	Generała Pierackiego	Birth
Nüssenbaum Blime	6.10.1895	Supported by mother	Generała Pierackiego	Birth
Pachciarki Nuchem	69 years old	Trader	Generała Pierackiego	1914
Pachciarska Hinda	62 years old	Supported by husband	Generała Pierackiego	1900
Prezberg Jakub	1.1.1873	Dealer	Generała Pierackiego	1892
Prezberg Gitla	54 years old	Supported by husband	Generała Pierackiego	Birth
Rajchenbach Mosiek Aron	24.12.1876	House owner	Generała Pierackiego	1916
Rajchenbach Mindla Ruchla	12.7.1876	Supported by husband	Generała Pierackiego	1916
Rajchenbach Chana Marjem	12.3.1908	Supported by parents	Generała Pierackiego	Birth
Rajchenbach Bajla Chana	128.1910	Supported by parents	Generała Pierackiego	Birth
Szapsiewicz Hinda	6.9.1890	House owner	Generała Pierackiego	Birth
Szyke Haskiel Chaim	13.1.1905	Cap maker	Generała Pierackiego	28.2.1935
Szmelcyngier Nuchem	1873	Trader	Generała Pierackiego	1914
Szmelcyngier Rasza	1879	Supported by husband	Generała Pierackiego	1914
Samson Juda Lejb	52 years old	Trader	Generała Pierackiego	1914
Samson Małka	45 years old	Supported by husband	Generała Pierackiego	1914
Samson Jakub	7.12.1910	Supported by parents	Generała Pierackiego	1914
Urbach Chaim	26.9.1906	Dealer	Generała Pierackiego	1914
Urbach Małka	1909	Supported by husband	Generała Pierackiego	1914
Widawski Szyje	1860	Trader	Generała Pierackiego	1917
Widawska Chaja	1866	Supported by husband	Generała Pierackiego	1917
Witkowski Abram	16.10.1892	Dressmaker	Generała Pierackiego	1915
Witkowska Dwojra Estera	34 years old	Supported by husband	Generała Pierackiego	1926
Wilczyńska Blima	35 years old	Laborer	Generała Pierackiego	Birth
Zyzek Lejb	28.1.1888	Butcher	Generała Pierackiego	1930
Zyzek Szajne	1882	Supported by husband	Generała Pierackiego	1930
Malarek Mojsie Chaim	28.2.1867	Farmer	Rutki	Birth
Malarek Amalia	14.7.1871	Supported by husband	Rutki	1892

Table G, cont.

Full name	Date of birth	Occupation	Place of residence (street)	Living in district since
Iłowski Szaja	24.3.1878	Dealer	Stodólna	1918
Iłowska Szenca	56 years old	Supported by husband	Stodólna	1918
Dzieci Menachem	24.8.1899	Trader	Słupecka	1905
Dzieci Chaja Sura	1902	Supported by husband	Słupecka	1905
Krotowska Hudes	27.12.1869	House owner	Słupecka	Birth
Krotowska Rywka	4.8.1905	Supported by mother	Słupecka	Birth
Krotowska Rachela	12.6.1907	Supported by mother	Słupecka	Birth
Krotowska Fajgel	12.6.1907	Supported by mother	Słupecka	Birth
Prost Aron	21.1.1895	industrialist	Słupecka	1931
Prost Małka	1899	Supported by husband	Słupecka	1931
Fogel Szarna	14.7.1883	Trader's wife	Toruńska	1916
Fogel Ruchel	1.8.1859	Supported by daughter-in-law	Toruńska	1918
Gembicka Ruchel Łaja	31.12.1896	Trader's wife	Toruńska	Birth
Kuczyński Abram	14.5.1892	Trader	Toruńska	1916
Kuczyńska Sine	29.3.1896	Supported by husband	Toruńska	1916
Lubraniecki Abram	14.5.1902	Trader	Toruńska	26.3.1935
Lubraniecka Pessa Sura	25.4.1904	Supported by husband	Toruńska	26.3.1935
Leszczyński Szaje	1894	Trader	Toruńska	1927
Leszczyńska Bajla	26.7.1907	Supported by husband	Toruńska	Birth
Koszer Ruchla Łaja	45 years old	Laborer	Wodna	1903
Koszer Frajdel	24.3.1903	Supported by mother	Wodna	Birth
Śliwicki Icek	15.3.1867	Dealer	Wodna	1902
Śliwicka Ruchel	14.1.1904	Supported by father	Wodna	Birth
Śliwicka Sura	1906	Supported by father	Wodna	Birth

Source: APK, AmK, classification number 450

Notes:

– Based on Kleczew as Voting District No. 55, Electoral Constituency No. 19 (1935)

– Presented in original order

Table H Jews living in Kleczew in 1919 who declared 10,000–30,000 mp* in assets

First name and surname	Type and value of property (mp)	Industrial or trade company and its value (mp)	Cash owned (mp)	Total value of all assets (mp)
Adler Eljasz		7,000		7,000
Bok Samuel	House, 9,000	2,000	3,000	14,000
Błaszkowska Małka	¼ of a house, 15,000			
Brysz Mojsze	¼ of a house, 40,000	14,000	1,000	550,000
Berendt Hersz	¼ of a house, 10,000	6,000		16,000
Dzieci Idel	House, 10,000	1,000		11,000
Chaim Fogel	20 Ks (?)., 15,000	2,000		17,000
Grynfeld Dawid	House, 10,000	8,000		18,000
Jastrząb Berek		30,000		30,000
Knopf Icek Szmul	2 houses, 13,000 and 6,000	2,000	1,500	3,500, debts 13,180
Łabuszyński Josef	10,000	5,000	3,000	18,000
Neumann Mojsze		1,500		1,500
Widawski Szyje	14,000	3,500		17,500
Wajngart Chiel Majer		15,000	2,000	17,000
Others who declared but no data exist regarding the value of their assets				
Baum Szmul Hersz	Pietrowski Jakub	Witkowski Abram	Koza Samson	
Brysz Lejzer	Pietruszka Zyskind	Warmbrum Szymon	Lewkowicz Mojsze	
Łatta Szmul Jukew	Raczkowski Icek Hersz	Witkowski Zołkind	Leszczyńsk Lewek	
Łatta – sons	Rachwalski Tobjasz	Urbach Josek	Wolf Mendel	
Eliasz Grynblat	Rygel Salomon	Kroner Lejb	Wajsman Abram	
Chale Grynfeld	Segał Dawid	Klepacz Jukew		
Psipsie Chaim Zelek	Samson Lejb Jude	Klamrowski Hersz		
Psipsi Anszel	Szmelczyngiel Nuchem	Kiwała Majer		
Prost Ichiel	Wilczyski Zelek	Kroner Icek		
Rajchert Mojsze	Wilczyński Abram Zelig	Klamrowski B.		

Source: APK, AmK, classification no. 451.

* mp = the marka, currency of the Kingdom of Poland and the Republic of Poland between 1917 and 1924.

Table I Jewish inhabitants of Kleczew who paid local taxes and industrial and trade certificate taxes as of January 21, 1919

Full name	Type of business	Price of industrial and trade certificate (in Polish marka*)	Amount of local tax (in Polish marka)	Total taxes paid (in Polish marka)
Albert Hersz	Junk sale	35	21	56
Alter Eljasz	Seed sale	35	21	56
Bagno Chaim	Accessories sale	35	21	56
Bagno Chaim	Miscellaneous products sale	35	21	56
Bagno Nuchem	Goods measured by elbow sale	35	21	56
Berendt Gedalje	Food products sale	35	21	56
Berendt Hersz	Timber trade	240	144	384
Berendt Hersz	Hardware trade	35	21	56
Berendt Rywe	Food products sale	35	21	56
Berendt Rywka	Tobacco trade	35	21	56
Biederka Izrael	Butchery	35	21	56
Błaszkowska Chawa	Tobacco trade	35	21	56
Błaszkowska Małka	Food products sale	35	21	56
Boas Jozef	Cap maker	35	21	56
Bok Samuel	Food products sale	35	21	56
Brysz Hersz	Food products sale	35	21	56
Brysz Lejzor	Accessories sale	35	21	56
Brysz Mojsie	Accessories sale	35	21	56
Brzuszek Wolf	Butcher	240	144	384
Chaba Jozef	Bakery	35	21	56
Cochner Icek	Groceries	35	21	56
Dawidowicz Chil	Groceries	35	21	56
Dawidowicz Chil	Trade	240	144	384
Dobrzyński Kalman	Groceries	35	21	56
Dzieci Idel	Groceries	35	21	56
Dzieci Idel	Tobacco trade	35	21	56
Fogiel Chajem	Goods measured by elbow sale	35	21	56
Fogiel Szmaje	Dairy	240	144	384
Gembicki Abram	Dressmaker	35	21	56
Gembicki Efraim	Soap trade	10	6	16
Grünblatt Icek	Butter and eggs sale	240	144	384
Grunfeld Dawid	Glass trade	35	21	56
Grynblatt Eljasz	Baker	35	21	56
Heber Szaja	Groceries	35	21	56
Heber Szlama	Tobacco trade	35	21	56
Hirszberg Izaak	Accessories sale	35	21	56
Inke Łaja	Accessories sale	35	21	56
Jakubowicz Kalma	Dressmaker	35	21	56

* The marka was the currency of the Kingdom of Poland and the Republic of Poland between 1917 and 1924.

Table I, cont.

Full name	Type of business	Price of industrial and trade certificate (in Polish marka)	Amount of local tax (in Polish marka)	Total taxes paid (in Polish marka)
Jaworski Kalman	Tobacco trade	35	21	56
Kaźmierski Hersz	Butchery	35	21	56
Kędzierski Mosze	Butcher	35	21	56
Kiwała Majer	Dressmaking	35	21	56
Klamrowski Binem	Dressmaking	35	21	56
Klamrowski Szmul	Butter trade	240	144	384
Kleczewski Pinkus	Accessories sale	35	21	56
Klepacz Jakub	Butcher	35	21	56
Knopf Icek	Groceries	35	21	56
Knopf Icek	Tobacco trade	35	21	56
Konet Icek	Accessories sale	35	21	56
Kott Helena	Hardware trade	240	144	384
Kott Markus	Trade	240	144	384
Kott Markus	Coal trade	240	144	384
Kott Markus	Groceries	35	21	56
Koza Simche	Ready-made clothes sale	35	21	56
Kroner Lejb	Groceries	35	21	56
Kroner Lejb	Tobacco trade	35	21	56
Krotowski Abram	Seed sale	35	21	56
Krzywanowski Rywen	Baker	35	21	56
Lejb Juda	Groceries	35	21	56
Lejb Juda	Accessories sale	35	21	56
Leszczyński Fuel	Groceries	35	21	56
Leszczyński Lejb	Dressmaking	35	21	56
Lewi Abram	Groceries	35	21	56
Lewi Itte	Goods measured by elbow sale	35	21	56
Lewi Itte	Goods measured by elbow sale	35	21	56
Lewin Abram	Accessories sale	35	21	56
Lewkowicz M.	Bakery	35	21	56
Lipszyc Salomon	Groceries	35	21	56
Lipszyc Salomon	Ready-made clothes sale	35	21	56
Lipszyc Salomon	Dressed timber trade	240	144	384
Litman Chaim	Hand-made articles sale	35	21	56
Łabuszyński Jozef	Groceries	35	21	56
Łabuszyński Jozef	Groceries	35	21	56
Łatte Jakub	Groceries	35	21	56
Łatte Jakub	Groceries	35	21	56

Table I, cont.

Full name	Type of business	Price of industrial and trade certificate (in Polish marka)	Amount of local tax (in Polish marka)	Total taxes paid (in Polish marka)
Nejman Mojsze	Accessories sale	240	144	384
Nisenbaum	Accessories sale	35	21	56
Noes Dawid	Dressmaking	35	21	56
Pachciarski Natan	Butter trade	35	21	56
Patałowski Izaak	Baker	35	21	56
Pregler Zyskind	Porcelain trade	10	6	16
Pregler Zyskind	Groceries	35	21	56
Presberg Jakub	Footwear trade	35	21	56
Prost Ichiel	Groceries	35	21	56
Prosta Lemel	Groceries	35	21	56
Psipsie Anszel	Tobacco trade	35	21	56
Psipsie Anszel	Groceries	35	21	56
Psipsie Rywen	Dressmaking	35	21	56
Rachwalski Abram	Footwear trade	35	21	56
Rajch Dorota	Hand-made articles sale	35	21	56
Rakowska Etta	Watchmaking and groceries	35	21	56
Rakowski Mojsze	Groceries	35	21	56
Reich Moryc	Accessories and hand-made articles sale	35	21	56
Reichman	Groceries	35	21	56
Russ Gerszon	Leather sale	35	21	56
Rygiel Salomon	Accessories sale	35	21	56
Rygiel Salomon	Groceries	35	21	56
Samson Juda Lejb	Groceries	35	21	56
Segał Chil	Trade	240	144	384
Segał Chil	Trade	240	144	384
Segał Dawid	Tobacco trade	240	144	384
Sender Rubin	Hand-made articles sale	35	21	56
Stab Chawa	Soda water trade	35	21	56
Szapszewicz Abram	Cap maker	35	21	56
Szklarek Mincia	Groceries	35	21	56
Szmeleinger Nuta	Butter and eggs sale	240	144	384
Sztachelberg	Women's clothing sale	35	21	56
Ślesińsk Lejzor	Tobacco trade	35	21	56
Ślesiński Lejzor	Tobacco trade	35	21	56
Ślesiński Lejzor	Groceries	35	21	56
Trobe Chawa	Accessories sale	10	6	16
Wajngart	Groceries	35	21	56

Table I, cont.

Full name	Type of business	Price of industrial and trade certificate (in Polish marka)	Amount of local tax (in Polish marka)	Total taxes paid (in Polish marka)
Wajngart	Accessories sale	35	21	56
Wajngart Markus	Oil mill	200	120	320
Waksman	Leather sale	35	21	56
Wartska Roza	Accessories sale	35	21	56
Wartska Roza	Ready-made clothes sale	10	6	16
Waserman	Goods measured by elbow sale	240	144	384
Widawski Abram	Accessories sale	10	6	16
Widawski Szyje	Restaurant	240	144	384
Wilczyński	Butcher	35	21	56
Wilczyński Zelek	Tobacco trade	35	21	56
Wilczyński Zelek	Groceries	35	21	56
Wilkowski Abram	Dressmaker	35	21	56
Wolf Mendel	Groceries	35	21	56
Wolf Mendel	Groceries	35	21	56
Wolman Hersz	Women's and men's clothing sale	240	144	384
Wolsztain	Haberdashery	35	21	56

Source: APK, AmK, classification number 451.

Table J Payers of dues to Kleczew Jewish Community, 1919

First name and surname	Sum (mp*)	Class of payer	First name and surname	Sum (mp*)	Class of payer
Adler Alje	50	II	Lewi Itte	80	II
Aurbach Josef	50	II	Lewin Abram J.	30	III
Bagno Ch. L.	25	III	Lewkowicz Dobrysz	20	III
Bagno Nuchem	60	II	Lewkowicz Mojsze	60	II
Beinusz Gerszon	40	III	Lipszyc Salomon	60	II
Benkel Icek	100	I	Lipszyc Sender	200	I
Berendt Gedalie	15	III	Littman Chaim	10	III
Berendt Hirsz	40	III	Łaboszyński Josef	120	I
Berendt Szosze	20	III	Łatta Szmul Jakub	20	III
Berendt – sons	50	II	Łatte Salomon	20	III
Błaszkowska Małka	15	III	Łepek Sucher	80	II
Boas Josef	20	III	Malarek Lejzor J.	200	I
Bock Szmul	15	III	Malarek M. Ch.	60	II
Brisz Luzer	15	III	Nejman Mojsze	60	II
Brisz Mojsze	50	II	Noss Dawid	40	III
Chaba	20	III	Pachciarski Nuchem	30	III
Chojnacka Estera	20	III	Patałowski Chaim	10	III
Czerwonka Hirsz	50	II	Piekarski Leopold	300	I
Dobrzyński Kalman	10	III	Piekarscy - synowie	200	I
Dzieci Idel	150	I	Pietruszka Zyskind	10	III
Engel Dawid	200	I	Pikus	10	III
Ettinger – married couple	600	I	Piotrkowski Luzer	10	III
Fogiel Chaim	30	III	Pregler Zyskind	60	II
Fogiel Icek	40	III	Prost Ichiel	60	II
Fogiel Szmaje	60	II	Prost Lemel	20	III
Gembicki Abram J.	120	I	Przedecki Josef	30	III
Grünblatt Eliasz	60	II	Psipsze Anszel	30	III
Grünblatt Icek	30	III	Psipsie Chaim Z.	25	III
Grünfeld Dawid	40	III	Rachwalski Tobiasz	40	III
Grünfeld – sons	30	III	Rakowski Izydor	15	III
Heber Szaje Nuchem	15	III	Rakowski Majer	80	II
Hirszberg Szyja	20	III	Reich – sons	400	I
Huberman Ezrjel	20	III	Reichert Lajbusz	80	II
Iwańczyk Eli	800	I	Reichman Mojsze	20	III
Jakubowicz Kasriel	40	III	Russ Gerszon	40	III
Jastrzem Ber	50	II	Rygiel Salomon	80	II
Kazimierski	10	III	Samson Lajbusz	40	III
Kazimierski Chemie	15	III	Segał Chiel	20	III
Kiwała Majer	120	I	Segal Dawid	80	II
Klamrowski Ber	60	II	Sender Rywen	300	I

Table J, cont.

First name and surname	Sum (mp*)	Class of payer	First name and surname	Sum (mp*)	Class of payer
Klamrowski Kirsz	80	II	Szapszowicz Abram	15	III
Klepacz Jakub	60	II	Szlesiński Lejzor	150	I
Knopf Icek Sz.	30	III	Sztachelberg Jakub L.	50	II
Koner Icek L.	25	III	Waksman Abram	150	I
Korn Fiszel	25	III	Warmbrun Szymon	50	II
Koszarek Lajbusz	25	III	Wasserman Perec	120	I
Kott Helena	80	II	Weingart Ichiel M.	20	III
Kott Samuel	60	II	Weingart Mordka	40	III
Korn Szmul	15	III	Weingart Sucher M.	60	II
Kott Markus	40	III	Widawski Szyja	20	III
Kroner Icek	40	III	Wilczyński Abram Z.	80	II
Kroner Lejb	80	II	Wilczyński Zelig	10	III
Krotowscy – sons	200	I	Witkowska Hana	80	II
Krzywanowski Mojsze	60	II	Witkowski Abram	25	III
Kuczyński Abram	40	III	Witkowski Jojne	30	III
Kutnowski Luzer	40	III	Witkowski Załkind	20	III
Leimer Abram	60	II	Wolf Mendel	80	II
Leszczyński Lenwie	60	II	Wollmann Hirsz	250	I
Leszczyński Rafael J.	15	III	Wolstein Abram	50	II
			Wróblowska Flora	60	II

Source: APPoKon, SPSłupca, classification number 212

* mp= the marka, currency of the Kingdom of Poland and the Republic of Poland between 1917 and 1924.

Table K People who remitted "supplemental dues" to the Kleczew Kehilla in 1921

First name and surname	Sum (mp*)	First name and surname	Sum (mp)
Albert M. Hirsz	200	Łabuszyński Jozef	1,000
Bagno Ch. Lejb	100	Łatte Jakub	200
Bagno Nuchem	300	Łatte Załme	200
Bainusz Gerszon	100	Łepek Sucher	400
Bamber – (successors)	100	Malarek L. Icek	600
Berendt - (successors)	300	Malarek Moryc	400
Berendt Hirsz	200	Najman Mojsze	200
Berendt Sz.	100	Noss Dawid	100
Blaszkowski Jozef	200	Obarzanek Mordka	100
Boar J.	100	Ofszinski E.	100
Bock Szmul	100	Pachciarski Nuchem	200
Brysz Mojsze	300	Piekarski Leopold	1,500
Brysz L.	150	Pikus Jakub	100
Chaba Alja	100	Pregler Zyskind	600
Czerwonki	800	Prost Ch.	200
Dzieci Idel	1,000	Prost Leon	100
Ettinger A. Icek	1,500	Przedecki Jozef	100
Fogel Chaim	200	Pszypsze (Psipsie) Anszel	100
Fogel Icek	600	Pszypsze (Psipsie) Zelig	200
Fogel Szmaje	600	Rachwalski Tobjasz	300
Gembicki A. Jakub	600	Raich - sukcesorzy	2,500
Gembicki Moryc	500	Rakowski Izaak	500
Grinblatt Icek	100	Rakowski Majer	1,500
Grinfeld Dawid	300	Reichmann Mojsze	100
Halperówna	100	Russ Gerszon	100
Iwańczyk Adam	3,000	Rygel Załme	600
Jakubowicz–(successors)	500	Samson Lejbusz	100
Jastrząb Beer	300	Seder Rywen	2,000
Kaźmierski Chemje	100	Segał Dawid	200
Kiwała – (successors)	600	Skurnik Mojsze	400
Klamrowski Beer	200	Szmelcynger	100
Klepacz Jakub	200	Sztachelberg J. Lejzor	600
Korn Fiszel	200	Urbach J. Jojne	300
Korn Szmul	200	Urbach Jozef	300
Koszarek	150	Waingart Mordcha	1,000
Kott Helena	500	Waingart S. Mendel	200
Krauze Lejb	200	Wajsman Abram	600
Krauze S.	200	Warmbrum–(successors)	100
Kroner Icek	200	Wassermann Perec	1,500
Kroner Lejb	200	Wemgort Ch. Majer	100
Krotowski- (successors)	600	Widawski Szyje	100
Krzyżanowski Mojsze	200	Wilczyński A. Zelig	500

Table K, cont.

First name and surname	Sum (mp)	First name and surname	Sum (mp)
Kuczyński Abram	600	Wilczyński Zelig	100
Lamer Abram	500	Wilkowski Abram	150
Leszczyński L.	600	Witkowska Hania	200
Lewi – (successors)	1,000	Witkowski Jojne	200
Lewin A. Jakub	200	Witkowski S. Lejb	100
Lewkowicz D.	400	Witkowski Zułkind	100
Lewkowicz Icek	100	Wolf Mendel	500
Lewkowicz Mojsze	300	Wollman Hirsz	1,500
Lipszyc Sender	400	Wolsztein Abram	500
Lipszyc Szlama	300		
Sub-total:	**20,600**	**Sub-total:**	**23,450**
Grand total:		44,050	

Source: APK, SPS, classification no. 213.

* mp= the marka, currency of the Kingdom of Poland and the Republic of Poland between 1917 and 1924.

Table L Payers of dues to the Kleczew Jewish Community in 1933

First name and surname	Occupation	Dues per year (złoty)	First name and surname	Occupation	Dues per year (złoty)
Bagno Abram	Tailor	15	Lewkowicz Icek	Trader	10
Bagno Chaim	Shopkeeper	20	Lewkowicz Mojsie	Baker	20
Bagno Nuchem	Shopkeeper	50	Łatte Szmul Jakub	Trader	15
Bamber Abram	Tailor	35	Łatte Załme	Real estate owner	10
Bamber Icek	Tailor	12	Łepek Majer	Grocer's shopkeeper	12
Bamber Mojsie	Harness-maker	10	Łepek Sucher	Real estate owner	25
Ber Mojsie	Barber	20	Malarek Moryc	Farmer	50
Berendt Hersz	Shopkeeper	40	Marek Hersz	Tailor	10
Berendt Majer Dawid	Tailor	12	Markowsi Chaim	Tailor	40
Berendt Rywka	Shopkeeper	35	Nejman Mojsie	Real-estate owner	65
Brukstein Jakub	Tailor	12	Noss Dawid	Tailor	10
Brysz Luzer	Shopkeeper	20	Obarzanek Mordke	Trader	12
Brysz Mojsie	Shopkeeper	18	Pacanowski Ber	Merchant	50
Chabe Josek	Baker	17	Pachciarki Nuchem	Real estate owner	10
Chojnacki Chune	Tailor	50	Patałowska Chaja	Real estate owner	8
Dobrzyński Kałme	Trader	14	Patałowski Abram	Cap-maker	20
Dyndol Icek	Trader	8	Pinkus Jakub	Tailor	35
Dzieci Idel	Shopkeeper	60	Presberg Jakub	Merchant	10
Dzieci Łaje	Grain merchant	45	Prost – synowie[sons](?)	Grocer's shopkeeper	35
Dzieci Menachem	Grain merchant	45	Prost Aron	Roof maker	12
Ettinger Abram	Real-estate owner	40	Prost Jakub	Shopkeeper	15
Ettinger Lejzer	Trader	12	Prost Lemel	Merchant	30
Feiwel Josef	hat-maker	10	Przedecki Mojsie Aron	Trader	10
Fiszer Mojsie	Trader	10	Przedecki Mordke	Laborer	8
Fogel Chaim	Shopkeeper	12	Psipsie Ruchla	Dress-maker	12
Fogel Mania	Real-estate owner	40	Pzedecka Fajgel	Real estate owner	10
Fogel Szmaja	Merchant	50	Rachwalska Pessa	Dress-maker	12
Frenkiel – bracia [brothers](?)	Leather-stitchers	15	Rachwalski Tobjasz	Trader	55
Gembicki Chaim	Horse Merchant	20	Rakowski Ichiel	Trader	15
Gembicki Zelig	Tailor	80	Reich Dora	Trader	70

Table L, cont.

First name and surname	Occupation	Dues per year (złoty)	First name and surname	Occupation	Dues per year (złoty)
Grünfeld Dawid	Shopkeeper	30	Reichenbach Mojsie	Trader	35
Heber Szaje	Trader	8	Reichmann Mojsie	Trader	8
Hornstein Aleksander	Dentist	125	Russ Gerson	Leather-stitcher	15
Huberman Azrjel	Fisherman	10	Rygiel Majer	Tailor	8
Huberman Nachme	Trader	8	Rygiel Majer Lejb	Tailor	12
Iwańczyk Adam	Land owner	900	Rygiel Salomon	Trader	20
Jakubowicz Hersz	Tailor	50	Rygiel Wigor	Tailor	10
Jakubowicz Majer	Furrier	30	Samson Lejb Juda	Shopkeeper	12
Jastrząb Berek	Fisherman	40	Segał Dawid	Shopkeeper	35
Joachimkiewicz Majer	Trader	12	Segał Hersz	Shopkeeper	35
Kiwała–spadkobiercy[heirs]	Tailors	60	Sender Sura	Real-estate owner	80
Kiwała Izrael	Tailor	15	Strzelińska Gitel	Real-estate owner	40
Kiwała Lejb	Tailor	40	Szmelcyngier Nuchem	Trader	12
Klamrowski Ber	Tailor	15	Szulc Jakub	Merchant	88
Klamrowski Hersz	Tailor	45	Ślesiński Lejzor	Shopkeeper	30
Klepacz Icek	Trader	15	Śliwicki Icek	Trader	10
Kołtyn Menachem Abram	Trader	12	Światowicz Kaufman	Car business owner	20
Korn Fiszel	Ironware	60	Urbach Jojne	Horse trader	60
Korn Jakub	Real-estate owner	50	Warbrum Dawid	Barber	18
Korn Szmul	Confectioner	25	Warbrum Wigdor	Barber	12
Koszarek Lejb	Tailor	18	Wasserman Perec	Grocer's shopkeeper	25
Kroner Chaskiel	Doctor	75	Widawski Szyje	Shopkeeper	20
Kroner Icek	Tinsmith	25	Wilczyńska Mindel	Real-estate owner	10
Kroner Lejb	Shopkeeper	75	Wilczyński Lemel	Tailor	15
Krotowski Fałek	Trader	12	Witkowski Abram	Tailor	12
Krzywanowski Mojsie	Baker	20	Witkowski Jojne	Tailor	20
Kuczyński Abram	Merchant	35	Witkowski Mojsie	Tailor	12
Kutnowski Lejzor	Trader	20	Wolf Mendel	Grocer's shopkeeper	25
Leszczyński Szyje	Merchant	50	Wollman Jakub	Land owner	300
Leszczyński Załme	Tailor	60	Wolstein Abram	Merchant	45
Lewi Itte	Real-estate owner	55	Wołkowicz Abram	Merchant	10
Lewi Lejb	Tailor	12	Wózek Mojsie	Trader	10
Lewkowicz Dobrysz	Grocer's shopkeeper	15			

Source: APK, SPS, classification no. 233

Table M Holocaust victims from Kleczew in the Yad Vashem database

No.	Surname	First name	No.	Surname	First name
1	Abkiewicz	Helena	32	Bielawski	Hena
2	Bagno	Abraham	33	Bielawski	Leibel
3	Bagno	Chaim Lajb	34	Bielawski	Mendel
4	Bagno	Chajcha [Chajcia]	35	Bigus	Kajle
5	Bagno	Estera	36	Bigus	Lajb
6	Bagno	Fishel	37	Blaszkowski	Abraham
7	Bagno	Mata	38	Bocko	Rywka
8	Bagno	Nachum	39	Cadik	Lola
9	Bagno	Shmuel	40	Dzieci	Mordchai
10	Bagno	Shulamit	41	Egal	Pesia
11	Bagno	Nache	42	Engel	Salomea
12	Bamber	Icchak	43	Fogel	Abraham
13	Bamber	Mania	44	Fogel	Aron
14	Bamber	Ruta	45	Fogel	Berta
15	Barysz	Chava	46	Fogel	Chaim
16	Barysz	Lea	47	Fogel	Chaja
17	Bejrysz	Mosze	48	Fogel	Dawid
18	Berendt	Beila	49	Fogel	Hersz
19	Berendt	Berek	50	Fogel	Lajb
20	Berendt	Dora	51	Fogel	Pesa
21	Berendt	Hers	52	Fridenzon (Friedensohn)	Mosze
22	Berendt	Hinda	53	Gelbfisch	Mordchai
23	Berendt	Jenta	54	Glocer	Abraham
24	Berendt	Jicek	55	Glocer	Eliasz
25	Berendt	Lea	56	Glocer	Henryk
26	Berendt	Mojsze Hersz	57	Gold	Josef
27	Berendt	Rywka	58	Goldman	Rachel
28	Berendt	Sara	59	Goliński	Baruch
29	Berendt	Sara	60	Goliński	Binyamin
30	Berent	Icek	61	Goliński	Ela
31	Bielawski	Breina	62	Goliński	Mendel

Table M, cont.

No.	Surname	First name	No.	Surname	First name
63	Goliński	Sarah	95	Kolton	Rachel Leja
64	Granek	Gedalia	96	Koniński	Majer
65	Granek	Shashona	97	Koren	Abram
66	Granek	Shlomo	98	Korn	Abraham, Ber
67	Grinfeld (Grünfeld)	Dawid	99	Korn	Berta
68	Grinfeld (Grünfeld)	Dawid Lejzer Leopold	100	Korn	Bronia
69	Grinfeld (Grünfeld)	Leopold	101	Korn	Fiszel
70	Gutner	Chana	102	Korn	Gerszon
71	Heiman	Sara	103	Korn	Jacob
72	Herman	Frieda	104	Korn	Moshe
73	Herman	Genia	105	Korn	Sala
74	Herszkowicz	Rosa	106	Korn	Sala
75	Herszkowicz	Shraga	107	Korn	Yakov
76	Herszkowicz	Tova	108	Korn	Dawid
77	Herszlikowicz	NA	109	Korytnicki	Etka
78	Jakobowicz	Moishe	110	Koscher	Ester
79	Jakubowicz	Boles	111	Koscher	Frida
80	Jastrząb	Berysz	112	Koscher	Iakow
81	Jastrząb	Mindel	113	Koscher	Mordchai
82	Kaczyk	Asias	114	Koscher	Rachel
83	Kaiser	Ada, Sara	115	Król	Fajwl
84	Kalmanowicz	Herman	116	Król	Hanyush, Zvi
85	Kalmanowicz	Yakob	117	Król	Pawel
86	Kaplan	Frejda	118	Kroner	Adek
87	Karl	Berta	119	Kroner	Anka, Anna
88	Kassa	Wolf	120	Kroner	Chana
89	Kleczewski	Menachem	121	Kroner	Eliezer
90	Kleczewski	Mendel	122	Kroner	Elza
91	Klein	Laja	123	Kroner	Elzunia
92	Klepacz	Hari	124	Kroner	Fisel
93	Klepacz	Iechak [Itzhak]	125	Kroner	Genia
94	Knochel	Mendel	126	Kroner	Henrick

Table M, cont.

No.	Surname	First name	No.	Surname	First name
127	Kroner	Heskel	159	Kwiatkowska	Ester
128	Kroner	Jhuda	160	Kwiatkowska	Shoshana, Roza
129	Kroner	Leib	161	Kwiatkowski	Brendel
130	Kroner	Richard	162	Kwiatkowski	Joseph
131	Kroner	Rozalja	163	Kwiatkowski	Yakov
132	Kroner	Rysio	164	Kzywanowski	Hana, Chana
133	Kroner	Yehezkel, Henrik	165	Lefkowits	Laib
134	Krooener (Kroner)	Hella	166	Leszczyńska	NA
135	Krooener (Kroner)	Maniah	167	Lewi	Irena, Yehuda
136	Krooener (Kroner)	Meer	168	Lipszyc	Salomon
137	Krooner (Kroner)	Adeck	169	Lissak	Jakow
138	Krooner (Kroner)	Ben	170	Lissak	Malka
139	Krooner (Kroner)	Ludwig	171	List	Jenta
140	Krooner (Kroner)	NA	172	Litman	Abram
141	Krzywanowska	Lotka	173	Litman	Bine
142	Krzywanowska	NA	174	Litman	Jadzia
143	Krzywanowski	Berta	175	Litman	Maria
144	Krzywanowski	Chaim Szlomo	176	Malarek	Amalia
145	Krzywanowski	Frania	177	Malarek	Amalia
146	Krzywanowski	Hanna	178	Malarek	Fela
147	Krzywanowski	Hersz	179	Malarek	Halina
148	Krzywanowski	Israel	180	Malarek	Maks
149	Krzywanowski	Jakow	181	Malarek	Maks
150	Krzywanowski	Mania	182	Malarek	Moryc
151	Krzywanowski	Michael	183	Malarek	Rutka
152	Krzywanowski	Michal	184	Malarek	Ryska
153	Krzywanowski	Moshe	185	Malaryk	Makel
154	Krzywanowski	Roza, Ruszka, Ruzka	186	Moskowicz	Mailech
155	Krzywanowski	Salek	187	Mozovisiky	Parl
156	Krzywanowski	Towa	188	Nelken	Hersz
157	Krzywanowski	Tzvi	189	Nissenbaum	Mordka

Table M, cont.

No.	Surname	First name	No.	Surname	First name
190	Noimark	Yoel	222	Rakoska	Leonja
191	Obarzanek	Hersz	223	Rakoski	Maks
192	Obarzanek	Jozef	224	Rakoski	Yakob
193	Obazanek	Gitel	225	Reichman	Cwi
194	Obazanek	Icchak	226	Reichman	Czarny
195	Obazanek	Mordchai	227	Reichman	Fishel, Fisher
196	Obazanek	Reuben, Reuvein	228	Reichman	Helen
197	Obaznak	Mordechai	229	Reichman	Hersz
198	Ogrodowski	Chana	230	Reichman	Icek
199	Pacanowski	Ber	231	Reichman	Jette
200	Pacanowski	Dawid	232	Reichman	Moishe, Moshe
201	Pacanowski	Henech	233	Reichman	Sala
202	Pacanowski	NA	234	Reichman	Yette
203	Pacanowski	Ruchel	235	Reichman	Zvi
204	Pendzel	Pejsach	236	Rejzin	Nisan
205	Pinkus	Anna	237	Rogozinski	Ester
206	Prost	Dudek	238	Rogoziński	Hanna
207	Prost	Lemel	239	Rosenblum	Anna
208	Prost	Liwcia	240	Rosenblum	Wolf
209	Prost	Rose	241	Rosenthal	Sara
210	Prost	Schlomi	242	Rozental	Wolf
211	Przedecki	Aron	243	Rozental	Balbina
212	Przedecki	Leon	244	Rozental	Moryc
213	Przedecki	Moniek	245	Rozental	Regina
214	Pszedecki	Mosze	246	Ruzevicz	Abraham
215	Rachwalski	Chaim	247	Rygiel	Ester
216	Rachwalski	Frymet	248	Rygiel	Fradel
217	Rachwalski	Sara	249	Rygiel	Leon
218	Rachwalski	Shlomo	250	Rygiel	Maier
219	Rachwalski	Tobiasz	251	Rygiel	Saul
220	Rajchman	Mojsze	252	Rygiel	Victor
221	Rajchman	Yeta	253	Samson	Malka

Table M, cont.

No.	Surname	First name	No.	Surname	First name
254	Samson	Samuel	282	Watman	Schmuel
255	Samson	Yuta	283	Watman	Tova, Towa
256	Schonschneider	Benzion	284	Weingort	Abraham
257	Schonschneider	Iechiel	285	Widawski	Abraham
258	Schonschneider	Zipora	286	Widawski	Towa
259	Segal	Ester	287	Wieselberg	Nachum, Nathan
260	Segal	Hirsz	288	Wilczynski	Bluma
261	Segal	Mirjam	289	Wiltszynka	Mindel
262	Segal	Yechiel	290	Witkowska	Fajga
263	Sochaczewski	Lea	291	Witkowska	Luba
264	Sojka	Alje Zalman	292	Witkowska	Rozka
265	Sudberg	Samuel	293	Witkowska	Tobcia
266	Szeimann, Szeynman	Basia	294	Witkowska	Tova
267	Szmidt	Mojzesz	295	Witkowski	Avraham
268	Sznaper	Rachmi	296	Witkowski	Benjamin
269	Sztarkman	Szewa	297	Witkowski	Hersh
270	Sztiller	Sala	298	Witkowski	Jakob
271	Vogel	Mania	299	Witkowski	Rivka
272	Vogel	Szyfra	300	Witkowski	Shlomo
273	Waingort	Toube	301	Witkowski	Yona
274	Wajnberger	Esther	302	Witkowski	Yzchak
275	Watman	Hannah	303	Witkowski	Zygmunt
276	Watman	Jacob, Yakov	304	Wolfstein	Lea
277	Watman	Koppel	305	Wolfstein	Luba
278	Watman	Miriam	306	Wolfstein	Szlomo, Salomon
279	Watman	Rachel	307	Wolfstein	Yakov
280	Watman	Roselle	308	Wolfstein	Yakov, Yehuda
281	Watman	Saul	309	Zumer	NA

Source: Central Database of Shoah Victims' Names, Yad Vashem Archives

Annex 3 | 561

List of Abbreviations

AGAD	–	Central Archives of Historical Records in Warsaw
AmK	–	Records of the town of Kleczew
APB	–	State Archive in Bydgoszcz
APŁ	–	State Archive in Łódź
APP	–	State Archive in Poznań
ASK	–	Archive of the Royal Treasury
AŻIH	–	Archive of the Jewish Historical Institute
CKŻP	–	Central Committee of Jews in Poland
CWW	–	Central Religious Denominations Authority in the Kingdom of Poland
DD	–	Department of Documents
IPN-B	–	Institute of National Remembrance. Gdańsk Office. Bydgoszcz Branch
IPN-W	–	Institute of National Remembrance in Warsaw
KG, Kalisz	–	Court Ledger, Kalisz
KG, Konin	–	Court Ledger, Konin
KPPS	–	County Police Station in Słupca
KZK	–	Kaiserliche Zivilververwaltung Konin
ŁGWŻ	–	Jewish Community in Łódź

OKBZH-B	–	District Commission for the Evaluation of Nazi Crimes in Poland. Bydgoszcz Branch
PAAK	–	Pomerania Archive of the National Army
Ring I	–	Ringelblum Archive
RW	–	Reichsstathalter im Wartegau
SPK	–	County Office in Konin
SPS	–	County Office in Słupca
UWP	–	Province Office in Poznań
YV	–	Yad Vashem
YVA	–	Yad Vashem Archive
ŻGWW	–	Jewish Community in Włocławek

Archival Sources

1. **Central Archives of Historical Records in Warsaw**
   a. Archive of the Royal Treasury I
   b. Archive of the Royal Treasury, royal bills
   c. Central Religious Denominations Authority in the Kingdom of Poland
2. **State Archive in Warsaw:**
   a. State Police Station in Aleksandrów Kujawski 1918-1939.
3. **State Archive in Bydgoszcz:**
   a. District Commission for the Evaluation of Nazi Crimes in Poland. Bydgoszcz Branch
   b. Pomerania Province Office in Bydgoszcz 1945-1950
4. **State Archive in Łódź:**
   a. The Jewish Kehilla in Łódź
   b. Province Office in Łódź 1918-1939
5. **State Archive in Płock: (Kutno Branch)**
   a. County Office in Kutno 1945-1950
6. **State Archive in Poznań:**
   a. Records of the town of Kleczew
   b. Records of the town of Konarzewo

c. Guilds of the town of Poniec
   d. Court Ledger, Kalisz
   e. Court Ledger, Konin
   f. Department of Education of the Poznań School District
   g. Province Office in Poznań 1919-1939.
7. **State Archive in Poznań: (Branch in Konin)**
   a. Registry Office Records, Synagogue District in Kleczew
   b. Records of the town of Kleczew
   c. Kaiserliche Zivilverwaltung Konin 1915-1918
   d. County Police Station in Słupca 1919-1932.
   e. County Office in Konin 1918-1939.
   f. County Office in Konin 1945-1950.
   g. County Office in Słupca 1918-1932.
8. **Archive of the Jewish Historical Institute in Warsaw. Research Institute:**
   a. American Joint Distribution Committee in Poland.
   b. Underground Archive of the Warsaw Ghetto (Ringelblum's Archive) part 1.
   c. Reports.
      1. Jewish Kehilla in Włocławek
      2. Central Committee of Jews in Poland, Organization Department
      3. Central Committee of Jews in Poland, Registration and Statistics Department Library in Kórnk
   d. manuscripts
9. **Institute of National Remembrance in Warsaw:**
   a. Reichsstathalter im Wartegau 1939 – 1945.
10. **Institute of National Remembrance. Gdańsk Office. Bydgoszcz Branch:**
    a. Collection Ok. By. Ds. 25/66
11. **Foundation "Pomerania Archive of the National Army" in Toruń:**
    a. The legacy of W. Drzewiecki, part 2. Reports and memoirs, part 3. Other materials.
12. **Yad Vashem. The Holocaust Martyrs and Heroes Remembrance Authority Archives in Jerusalem**

13. Archives of the Institute of National Remembrance (IPN)
14. Federal Archives in Germany (Bundesarchiv)
15. National Digital Archives in Poland (NAC)
16. Spielberg Foundation Video Testimonies Collection
17. The Martyrs' Museum in Żabikowo

Bibliography

Primary sources

Amtliche Bekantmachungen für den Kreis Leslau. 1940.

Arad, Yitzhak, Shmuel Krakowski, and Shmuel Spector, eds. *The Einsatzgruppen Reports: Selection from Dispatches of the Nazi Death Squads' Campaign against the Jews, July 1941-January 1943.* New York: Holocaust Library, 1989.

Arad, Yitzhak, and Yisrael Gutman, et al., eds. *Documents on the Holocaust: Selected Sources on the Destruction of the Jews of Germany and Austria, Poland and the Soviet Union.* Jerusalem: Yad Vashem, 1987

Baynes, Norman Hepburn, ed. *The Speeches of Adolf Hitler,* vol. I. London: Oxford University Press, 1942. 737-741.

Berenstein, Tatiana, Artur Eisenbach, and Adam Rutkowski, eds. *Eksterminacja Żydów na ziemiach polskich, Zbiór dokumentów.* Warsaw, 1957.

Berenstein, Tatiana, Artur Eisenbach, Bernard Mark, and Adam Rutkowski, eds. *Faschismus-Getto-Massenmord: Dokumentation über Ausrottung und Widerstand der Juden in Polen während des zweiten Weltkrieges.* Berlin: Rütten & Loenig, 1960.

Breitinger, Hilarius. *Als Deutschenseelsorger in Posen und im Warthegau 1934-1945: Erinnerungen.* Mainz, 1984.
Codex diplomaticum Maioris Poloniae. Poznań, 1840.
Cyprian, Tadeusz, and Jerzy Sawicki, eds. *Siedem procesów Najwyższego Trybunału Narodowego.* Poznań: Instytut Zachodni, 1962.
Das Deutschtum in Bessarabien: Insbesondere der im Warthegau anzusiedelnde Teil, Zusammengstellt von Fr. Fiechtner, SS-Ansiedlungsstaebe Warthe-Ost und Warthe-West. Ca 1940.
Datner, Sz., J. Gumkowski, and K. Leszczyński. "Wysiedlenia ludności z ziem polskich wcielonych do Rzeszy." *BGKBZHP* 12 (1960).
Dobroszycki, Lucjan. *The Cronicle of the Łódź' Getto 1941-1945.* New Haven: Yale University Press, 1984.
Dziennik Urzędowy Ministerstwa Wyznań Religijnych i Oświecenia Publicznego nr. 4 (1936): 83.
Dziennik Urzędowy Rzeczypospolitej Polskiej. 1928, nr 52, poz. 500; 1930 r., nr 75, poz. 592.
Einsatzgruppen (wyrok i uzasadnienie), opracowanie i tłumaczenie Sz. Datner, J. Gumowski, K. Leszczyński, Biuletyn GKBZHwP, vol. XIV, 1963.
Eisenbach, Artur, ed. *Dokumenty i materiały do dziejów okupacji niemieckiej w Polsce*, t. 3. *Getto łódzkie.* Warsaw, 1946.
"Eksterminacja Żydów w latach 1941-1943 (Dokumenty Biura Propagandy i Informacji KG AK w zbiorach Biblioteki Uniwersytetu Warszawskiego)." *BŻIH* 2-3 (1992).
Friedman, Tuvia, ed. *Der Höhere SS- und Polizeiführer beim Reichsstatthalter in Posen im Wehrkreis XXI Wilhelm Koppe.* Haifa: Institute of Documentation in Israel for the Investigation of Nazi War Crimes, 1997.
____. *Die NS-Prozesse in Deutschland: gegen die SS-Verbrecher, die in den 6 Vernichtungslager: Auschwitz, Belzec, Chelmno, Majdanek, Sobibor, Treblinka: Millionen Juden ermordet haben.* Haifa: Institute of Documentation in Israel for the investigation of Nazi war crimes, 2003.
Gebiet Wartheland der Hitler-Jugand, ed. *Führerdienst Gebiet Wartheland.* Posen: Bearbeitung u. Zusammenstellung Friedrich Hilgendorf, n.d.

Geisler, Walter. *Deutscher! Der Osten ruft Dich!*: Die wirtschaftlichen Entwicklungsmöglichkeiten in den eingegliederten Ostgebieten des Deutschen Reiches. Berlin: Volk und Reich, 1941.

Göldner, Paul. *Der Feldzug in Polen 1939: Dokumente, Bilder, Berichte mit Erlauterrugen*. Berlin: Frundsberg-Verl., 1939.

Greiser, Artur. *Proces Artura Greisera przed Najwyższym Trybunałem Narodowym*. Warsaw: PIW, 1946.

Grynsztehn, Jakub, and Ignacy Kerner, eds. *Dodatek do wydawnictwa Przepisy o organizacji gmin wyznaniowych żydowskich. Nowe rozporządzenia, zarządzenia, przepisy. Rok 1931*. Warsaw: Gmina Wyznaniowa Żydowska, 1931.

Guldon, Zenon, ed. *Lustracja województw wielkopolskich i kujawskich 1628—1632*. cz. 3. Bydgoszcz, 1967.

Günther-Swart, Imma von. *Grundlagen der Landwirtschaft im Reichsgau Wartheland und im Reichsgau Danzig-Westpreussen*. Leipzig: Hirzel, 1941.

Historische Gesellschaft fur Posen. *Deutsche Wissenschafliche Zeitschrift in Wartheland: neue Folge des Zeitschriften der historischen Gesellschaft fur die Provinz Posen und des naturwissenschaftlichen Vereins zu Posen sowie der deutschen wissenschaftlichen Zeitschrift für Polen, Herausgegeben von Alfred Lattermann*. Posen: Historische Gesellschaft für Posen, 1940.

Jevrejska Enciklopedija, vol-14. Petersburg, 1910-1913.

Kawski, Tomasz. "Inwentarze gmin żydowskich z Pomorza i Wielkopolski Wschodniej w latach 1918/20-1939." *Kwartalnik Historii Kultury Materialnej*, 2006, nr 3-4.

Kermish, Joseph, ed. *To Live with Honor and Die with Honor: Selected Documents from the Warsaw Ghetto Underground Archives "O.S." (Oneg Shabbath)*. Jerusalem: Yad Vashem, 1986.

Killinger, Manfred v. *Kampf um Oberschlesien 1921: bisher unveröffentlichte Aufzeichnungen des Führers der "Abteilung v. Killinger" genannt "Sturmkompagnie Koppe."* Leipzig: R.F. Koehler, 1934.

Kiock, E. *Der Kreis Eichenbrück: 800 Jahre deutsche Kulturleistung im Wartheland*. Posen, 1944.

Kleczyński, Józef, and Franciszek Kluczycki, eds. *Liczba głów żydowskich w Koronie z taryf roku 1765.*, Kraków, 1898.
Klukowski, Zygmunt. *Dziennik z lat okupacji Zamojszczyzny (1939-1944).* Lublin: Lublin Cooperative Publishing, 1958.
Krakowski, Shmuel (Stefan), and Łucja Pawlicka Nowak, eds. *Mówią świadkowie Chełmna*, Rada Ochrony Pamięci Walk i Męczeństwa. Konin: Muzeum Okręgowe w Koninie, 1996.
Księga adresowa Polski (wraz z W. M. Gdańskiem) dla handlu, przemysłu, rzemiosł i rolnictwa. Warsaw: Towarzystwo Reklamy Międzynarodowej, 1926/[19]27-1930.
Lange, Friedrich. *Ostland kehrt heim.* Berlin: Nibelungen, 1941.
Laubert, Manfred. *Studien zur Geschichte der Provinz Posen in der ersten Hälfte des 19. Jahrhunderts.* Posen: Historische Gesellschaft für den Reichsgau Wartheland, 1943.
Leslauer Bote. ABC dla Włocławka i Kujaw. 1939.
Lewiński, Jerzy, ed. *Proces Hansa Biebowa: Zagłada getta łódzkiego: Akta i stenogramy sądowe.* Warsaw: GKBZHP-IPN, 1987.
Mazura, Zbigniewa, Aleksandry Pietrowicz, and Marii Rutowskiej, eds. *Raporty z ziem wcielonych do III Rzeszy (1942-1944).* Poznań: Instytut Zachodni, 2004.
Miron, Guy, ed. *The Yad Vashem Encyclopedia of the Ghettos during the Holocaust.* Jerusalem: Yad Vashem, 2009.
NSDAP. *Gau Wartheland, Gebietliche Gliederung.* Posen: Gauorganisationsamt, 1940.
NSDAP. *Gau Wartheland, Verordnungsblatt (Gau Wartheland. Nationalsozialistische Deutsche Arbeiterpartei), Wartheland Poznan.* Poznań, 1940.
NSDAP. Gau Wartheland, Wartheland. Posen, 1942.
Ohryzko-Włodarska, Czesława, ed. *Lustracja województw wielkopolskich i kujawskich 1659-1665.* cz. I. Wrocław: Zakład Narodowy im. Ossolińskich, 1978.
Okupacja i ruch oporu w dzienniku Hansa Franka 1939-1945, vol. I, 1939-1942. Warsaw, 1970.
Ortsverzeichnis des Reichsgaues Wartheland. Posen: NS-Gauverlag [, 1941].

Parczewski, Alfons J., ed. *Rejestry poborowy województwa kaliskiego z lat 1618-1620*. Warsaw: Gebethner i Wolff, 1879.

Pawlicka-Nowak, Łucja, ed. *Mówią świadkowie Chełmna*. Konin: Muzeum Okręgowe, 2004.

Pospieszalski, Karol Marian, ed. *Polska pod niemieckim prawem, 1939-1945 (Ziemie Zachodnie)*. Poznań: Instytut Zachodni, 1946.

___. *Niemiecka lista narodowa w "Kraju Warty": Wybór dokumentów z objaśnieniami w języku polskim i francuskim*. Poznań: Instytut Zachodni, 1949.

___. "Hitlerowskie 'prawo' okupacyjne w Polsce: Wybor dokumentów, Cześć I—Ziemie 'wcielone." In *Doccumenta Occupationis V*. Poznań: Instytut Zachodni, 1952.

Proces Artura Greisera przed Najwyższym Trybunałem Narodowym. Warsaw: PIW, 1946.

Publicationsstelle Berlin-Dahlem. *Die Ostgebiete des Deutschen Reiches und das Generalgouvernement der besetzten polnischen Gebiete in statistischen Angaben*. Berlin: Ausgearbeitet und herausgegeben von der Publikationsstelle Berlin-Dahlem, Selbstverlag der Publikationsstelle, 1940.

"Regulation Respecting the Laws and Customs of the War on Land, art. 36-56." In *The Laws of Armed Conflicts: A Collection of Conventions, Resolutions and Other Documents*, ed. Dietrich Schindler and Jiri Toman. Geneva: Brill, 1988.

Rejestr miejsc i faktów zbrodni popełnionych przez okupanta hitlerowskiego na ziemiach polskich w latach 1939-1945: Województwo konińskie. Warsaw: GKBZHP, 1981.

Rejestr miejsc i faktów zbrodni popełnionych przez okupanta hitlerowskiego na ziemiach polskich w latach 1939-1945. Warsaw: GKBZHP-IPN, 1985.

Rocznik Statystyczny Królestwa Polskiego. Rok 1913. Warsaw: Biuro Pracy Społecznej pod kierunkiem W. Grabskiego, 1914.

Rohlfing, Theodor, and Rudolf Schraut, et al, eds. and compilers. *Die Neuordnung des Rechts in den Ostgebieten: Sammlung der Reichsgesetze, der Verordnungen der Militarbefehlshaber, der Reichsstatthalter Danzig-Westpreussen und Wartheland, des Generalgouveneurs für das*

Gouvernement Polen mit kurzen Anmerkungen. Berlin: de Gruyter, 1940.

Rosenkranz, Otto. *Siedlung und Landwirtschaft im Reichsagu Wartheland*. Berlin: Deutsche Landbuchhandlung, 1941.

"Rozporządzenie MWRiOP z dnia 5 kwietnia 1928 w sprawie ogłoszenia jednolitego tekstu rozporządzenia Prezydenta Rzeczypospolitej z 14 października 1927 r. o uporządkowaniu stanu prawnego w organizacji gmin wyznaniowych żydowskich na terenie Rzeczypospolitej Polskiej z wyjątkiem województwa śląskiego." *Dziennik Urzędowy Rzeczypospolitej Polskiej*, nr 52 (1928).

"Rozporządzenie MWRiOP z dnia 24 października 1930 r. w sprawie regulaminu wyborczego dla wyboru organów gmin wyznaniowych żydowskich na obszarze Rzeczypospolitej z wyjątkiem województwa śląskiego." *Dziennik Urzędowy Rzeczypospolitej Polskiej*, nr 75 (1928).

Sakowska, Ruta, ed. *Archiwum Ringelbluma: Konspiracyjne archiwum getta warszawskiego*, vol. 1. Warsaw: PWN, 1997.

Sauer, Willi. *Das Deutschtum im Buchenland, insbesondere der im Warthegau anzusiedelnde Teil, SS-Ansiedlungsstab Warthe-Ost und Warthe-West Planungsabteilung*. Informationsstelle [, ca. 1939].

Sauer, Willi, and Eginhard Hehn, eds. *Das Deutschtum im Buchenland, insbesondere der im Warthegau anzusiedelnde Teil*, SS-Ansiedlungsstab Warthe-Ost und Warthe-West Planungsabteilung, Informationsstelle. Ca. 1939.

Schauff, Rudolf. *Der polnische Feldzug: England! Dein Werk!* Berlin: Die Wehrmacht, 1939.

Schiller, Oskar. *Haulaenderein im Wartheland*. Posen: Hirt-Reger, 1943.

Schultz, Robert, ed. *Das Antlitz des Deutschen im Wartheland: Ein Bildband*, vom Gauhauptmann im Reichsgau Wartheland für den Heimatbund Wartheland, Schriften des Heimatbundes Wartheland. Posen: Hirt-Reger und V. Schroedel Siemau, 1942.

Schütze, Hermann. *Der Reichsgau Wartheland: eine Heimatkunde*. Breslau: F. Hirt, 1941.

Skibińska, Alina, Robert Szuchta, Wiesława Młynarczyk, et al., eds. *Wybór źródeł do nauczania o zagładzie Żydów na okupowanych ziemiach polskich*. Warsaw: Stowarzyszenie Centrum Badań nad Zagładą Żydów, 2010.

Słownik Geograficzny Królestwa Polskiego i innych krajów słowiańskich, t. 4. Warsaw, 1883.

Spatz, Otto H. *Wiedergewonnenes deutsches Land in Danzig-Westpreussen, Ostpreussen, Wartheland, Oberschlesien, Elsass, Lothringen, Luxemburg, Eupen-Malmedy*. Munich: J.F. Lehmann, 1941.

Spector, Shmuel. *The Encyclopedia of Jewish Life Before and During the Holocaust*, vol. II. New York University Press: Yad Vashem, New York.

Tomczak, Andrzej, ed. *Lustracja województw wielkopolskich i kujawskich 1564-65*. cz. II Bydgoszcz, 1963.

Verordnungsblatt für die besetzten Gebiete in Polen. Berlin, 1939.

Verordnungsblatt. Poznań: NSDAP, Gau Wartheland, Wartheland Poznań, 1940.

Von Srbik, et al. *Das grössere Reich: Grossdeutschland am Anfang des IX. Jahres nationalsozialistischer Staatsführung*. Berlin: Vlg. Für Sozialpolitik, 1943.

Weliczker, Leon. *Brygada śmierci (SK 1005), pamiętnik*. Łódź: Centralna Żydowska Komisja Historyczna, 1946.

"Zarządzenie MWR i OP z dnia 28 grudnia 1936 r. o pensji i emeryturze rabinów i podrabinów oraz o zabezpieczeniu pozostałych po nim wdów i sierot." *Dziennik Urzędowy Ministerstwa Wyznań Religijnych i Oświecenia Publicznego* no. 4 (1936): 83.

Źródła dziejowe, vol. XII, *Polska XVI wieku pod względem geograficzno—statystycznym opisana przez Adolfa Pawińskiego*, vol. 1, *Wielkopolska*. Warsaw, 1883.

Secondary Literature

Abramowicz, Sławomir. "Odpowiedzialność za zbrodnie popełnione na Żydach w łodzkiem." In *Getto w Łodzi 1940-1944: Materiały z sesji naukowej—9 VIII 1984*, 129-139. Łódź: OKBZHw Łodzi-IPN, 1988.

___. "Ofiary i sprawcy, świadkowie i dokumenty zbrodni w ośrodku zagłady w Chełmnie nad Nerem." In *Fenomen getta łódzkiego 1940-1944*, ed. Paweł Samuś and Wiesław Puś, 347-361. Łódź: Wydawnictwo Uniwersytetu Łódzkiegi, 2006.

___. "Zagłada ludności getta łódzkiego w ośrodku w Chełmnie nad Nerem." In *Dzieje Żydów w Łodzi 1820-1944: Wybrane problemy*, ed. Wiesłw Puś and Stanisław Liszewski, 338-351. Łódź: Wydawnictwo Uniwersytetu Łódzkiego, 1991.

Adamska, Jolanta. "Grabież mienia mieszkańców getta przez funkcjonariuszy hitlerowskich." In *Getto w Łodzi 1940-1944: Materiały z sesji naukowej—9 VIII 1984*, 81-97. Łódź: OKBZHw Łodzi-IPN, 1988.

Adelson, Józef. "W Polsce zwanej ludową." In *Najnowsze dzieje Żydów w Polsce w zarysie (do 1950 roku)*, ed. Jerzy Tomaszewskiego, 387-477. Warsaw: PWN, 1993.

Alberti, Michael. "'Exerzierplatz des Nationalsozialismus': Der Reisgau Wartheland 1939-1941." In *Genesis des Genozids: Polen 1939-1941*, ed. Klaus-Michael Mallmann and Bogdan Musial, 111-126. Darmstadt: Wissenschaftliche Buchgesellschaft, 2004.

___. *Die Verfolgung und Vernichtung der Juden im Reichsgau Wartheland 1939-1945*. Wiesbaden: Harrassowitz, 2006.

___. "'Nikczemna perfidia, niska, bezmierna chciwość oraz zimne, wyrachowane okrucieństwo'—ostateczne rozwiązanie kwestii żydowskiej w Kraju Warty." In *Zagłada Żydów na polskich terenach wcielonych do Rzeszy*, ed. Aleksandra Namysło, 69-84. Warsaw: IPN, 2008.

Arad, Yitzhak. *Belzec, Sobibor, Treblinka: The Operation Reinhard Death Camps*. Bloomington, IN: Indiana University Press, 1987.

Arani, Miriam Y. *Fotografische Selbst- und Fremdbilder von Deutschen und Polen im Reichsgau Wartheland, 1939-45, Vol. 1-2: Unter besonderer Berücksichtigung der Region Wielkopolska*. Hamburg: Kovac, 2008.

Arndt, Nikolaus, and Alexander Arndt. *Ein Wolhynier erzahlt: aus dem Leben von Alexander Arndt im zaristischen Ostwolhynien, im polnischen Westwolhynien, im "Warthegau" und in Unterfranken*. Wiesentheid: Schwabach, 1982.

Banasiewicz, Maria. *Polityka naukowa i oświatowa hitlerowskich Niemiec na ziemiach polskich "wcielonych" do Trzeciej Rzeszy w okresie okupacji (1939-1945)*. Poznań: Wyd. Naukowe UAM, 1980

Baranowski, Daniel. *Simon Srebnik kehrt nach Chełmno zurück: zur Lektüre der Shoah*. Würzburg: Königshausen & Neumann, 2009.

Baranowski, Julian. "Powstanie i organizacja getta [w Łodzi]," In *Getto w Łodzi 1940-1944: Materiały z sesji naukowej—9 VIII 1984*, 11-26., Łódź: OKBZHw Łodzi-IPN, 1988.

___. "Zagłada Żydów z Kraju Warty i z Europy Zachodniej w Chełmnie nad Nerem." In *Ośrodek zagłady w Chełmnie nad Nerem i jego rola w hitlerowskiej polityce eksterminacyjnej*, 19-25. Łódź-Konin: Muzeum Okręgowe, 1995.

___. "Utworzenie i organizacja getta w Łodzi." In *Fenomen getta łódzkiego 1940-1944*, ed. Paweł Samuś and Wiesław Puś, 127-128. Łódź: Wydawnictwo Uniwersytetu Łódzkiego, 2006.

Bednarz, Władysław. *Obóz straceń w Chełmnie nad Nerem*. Warsaw: PIW, 1946.

___. *Das Vernichtungslager zu Chelmno am Ner*. Warsaw: Staatliches Verlagsinstitut, 1949.

Berenstein, Tatiana. "Martyrologia, opór i zagłada ludności żydowskiej w dystrykcie lubelskim." *BŻIH* 21 (1957).

___. "Obozy pracy przymusowej dla Żydów w dystrykcie lubelskim." *BŻIH* 24 (1957): 3-20.

___ and Adam Rutkowski. "Prześladowania ludności żydowskiej w okresie hitlerowskiej administracji wojskowej na okupowanych ziemiach polskich (1 IX 1939 r.—25 X 1939 r.), cz. I- III." *BŻIH* 38 (1961): 3-38.

___. "Prześladowania ludności żydowskiej w okresie hitlerowskiej administracji wojskowej na okupowanych ziemiach polskich (1 IX 1939 r.—25 X 1939 r.), cz. IV-V." *BŻIH* 39 (1961): 63-87.

Bergman, Eleonora, and Jan Jagielski. *Zachowane synagogi i domy modlitw w Polsce. Katalog*. Warsaw: Żydowski Instytut Historyczny INB, 1996.

Bergman, Eleonora. *Nurt mauretański w architekturze synagog Europy Środkowo—Wschodniej w XIX i na początku XX wieku*. Warsaw: Neriton, 2004.

Biegański, Zdzisław. *Sądownictwo i skazani na śmierć z przyczyn politycznych w województwie pomorskim (bydgoskim) 1945-1956*. Bydgoszcz: Akademii Bydgoskiej im. Kazimierza Wielkigo, 2003.

Biskupa, Mariana, ed. *Dzieje Chełmna: zarys monograficzny*. Warsaw: PWN, 1987.

Bitner–Nowak, Anna, Zofia Wojciechowska, and Grzegorz Wojciechowski. *Dzieje Ponieca*. Poniec: Urząd Miejski w Poniecu, 2000.

Bogucka, Maria, and Henryk Samsonowicz. *Dzieje miast i mieszczaństwa w Polsce przedrozbiorowej*. Wrocław: Zakład Narodowy imienia Ossolińskich, 1986.

Böhler, Jochen, ed. *"Größte Härte...": Verbrechen der Wehrmacht in Polen, September-Oktober 1939*, Ausstellungskatalog. Osnabrück: Fibre, 2005.

Böhler, Jochen. *Auftakt zum Vernichtungskrieg. Die Wehrmacht in Polen 1939*. Frankfurt a.M., Fischer, 2006.

___. "Prześladowanie ludności żydowskiej w okupowanej Polsce podczas trwania zarządu wojskowego (od 1 września do 25 października 1939 r.)." In *Zagłada Żydów na polskich terenach wcielonych do Rzeszy*, ed. A. Namysło, 46-58. Warsaw: IPN, 2008.

___. *Zbrodnie Wehrmachtu w Polsce: Wrzesień 1939: Wojna totalna*. Kraków: Znak, 2009.

Bömelburg, H. J., and B. Musial. "Die deutsche Besatzungspolitik in Polen 1939-1945." In *Deutsch-Polnische Beziehungen 1939-1945-1949: Eine Einführung*, ed. Włodzimierz Borodziej and Klaus Ziemer. Osnabrück: Fibre, 2000.

Brones, Mieczysław. "Niektóre problemy grabieży ekonomicznej w Polsce dokonywanej przez Wehrmacht w okresie 1.9—25.10.1939 r." *BGKBZHP* XVIII (1968).

Broszat, Martin. *Nationalsozialistische Polenpolitik. 1939–1945*. Schriftenreihe der Vierteljahrshefte für Zeitgeschichte 2. Stuttgart: Deutsche Verlags-Anstalt, 1961.

Browning, Christopher. *Nazi Policy, Jewish Workers, German Killers.* Cambridge: Cambridge University Press, 2000.
Budziarek, M. "Polacy, dzieci czeskie i jeńcy radzieccy zamordowani w Chełmnie nad Nerem." In *Ośrodek zagłady w Chełmnie nad Nerem i jego rola w hitlerowskiej polityce eksterminacyjnej*, 69-72. Łódź-Konin: Muzeum Okregowe, 1995.
"Chełmno." *BGKBZNP* 1 (1946): 153.
Chojnacka, Beata. *Dzieje Żydów w Osięcinach*, (maszynopis powielony).
Cüppers, Martin. *Wegbereiter der Shoah: Die Waffen-SS, der Komandostab Reichsführer SS und die Judenvernichtung 1939-1945.* Darmstadt: Wissenschaftliche Buchgesellschaft, 2005.
Czubiński, Antoni, and Zenon Szymankiewicz. *Konspiracja Wielkopolska 1939-1945: Zarys dziejów.* Poznań: KAW, 1988.
Czyńska, Zofia, and Bogumił Kupść. "Obozy zagłady, obozy koncentracyjne i obozy pracy na ziemiach polskich w latach 1939-1945." *BGKBZNP* 1 (1946): 11-62.
Datner, Szymon. *Wilhelm Koppe: nieukarany zbrodniarz hitlerowski.* Warsaw: Zachodnia Agencja Prasowa, 1963.
___. *55 dni Wehrmachtu w Polsce: Zbrodnie dokonywane na polskiej ludności cywilnej w okresie 1.IX—25.X.1939 r.* Warsaw: MON, 1967.
___. "Sonderkommando 1005 i jego działalność ze szczególnym uwzględnieniem okręgu białostockiego." *BŻIH* (1976): 63-78.
Dąbrowska, Danuta. "Zagłada skupisk żydowskich w Kraju Warty w okresie okupacji hitlerowskiej." *BŻIH*, no. 13-14 (1955): 122-184.
Danielewicza, Jerzego, eg. *Dzieje Klecka.* Poznań: Koło Związku Bojowników o Wolność i Demokrację w Klecku, 1983.
Deportacje Polaków z północno-zachodnich ziem II Rzeczypospolitej 1940-1941. Źródła do historii Polski. Warsaw: Oficyna Wydawnicza Rytm, 2001.
Deresiewicz, Janusz. *Okupacja niemiecka na ziemiach polskich włączonych do Rzeszy (1939-1945).* Poznań: Instytut Zachodni, 1950.
Długoborski, Wacław. "Żydzi z ziem polskich wcielonych do Rzeszy w KL Auschwitz-Birkenau." In *Zagłada Żydów na polskich terenach wcielonych do Rzeszy*, ed. Aleksandra Namysło, 129-147. Warsaw: IPN, 2008.

Dyliński, Ryszard, Marian Flejsierowicz, and Stanisław Kubiak. *Wysiedlenie i poniewierka. Wspomnienia Polaków wysiedlonych przez okupanta hitlerowskiego z ziem polskich „wcielonych" do Rzeszy 1939-1945*. Poznań: Wyd. Poznańskie, 1985.

Eisenbach, Artur. *Hitlerowska polityka zagłady Żydów*. Warsaw: Książka i Wiedza, 1961.

___. *Z dziejów ludności żydowskiej w Polsce w XVIII i XIX w.* Warsaw: Państwowy Instytut Wydawniczy, 1983.

Galiński, Antoni, and Marek Budziarek, eds. *Eksterminacja inteligencji Łodzi i okręgu łódzkiego 1939-1940*. Łódź: Instytut Panieci Narodowej, 1992.

Epstein, Catherine. *Model Nazi: Arthur Greiser and the Occupation of Western Poland*. Oxford: Oxford University Press, 2010.

Esch, Michael G. *"Gesunde Verhältnisse": Deutsche und polnische Bevölkerungspolitik in Ostmitteleuropa, 1939-1950*. Marburg: Herder Institut, 1998.

Ettinger, Shmuel. "Sejm Czterech Ziem." In *Żydzi w dawnej Rzeczypospolitej*, 34-43. Wrocław: Ossolineum, 1991.

Farbstein, Esther. "Diaries and Memoirs as a Historical Source: The Diary and Memoir of a Rabbi at the 'Konin House of Bondage.'" *Yad Vashem Studies* 26 (1998): 87-128.

Fijałek, Jan. "Formy eksterminacji pośredniej mieszkańców getta w Łodzi." In *Getto w Łodzi 1940-1944: Materiały z sesji naukowej*, ed. Puś Wiesław and Liszewski Stanisław, 51-64. Łódź: Wyd. Uniwersytetu Łódzkiego, 1988.

Fijałkowski, Zenon. *Kościół katolicki na ziemiach polskich w latach okupacji hitlerowskiej*. Warsaw: Książka i Wiedza, 1983.

Förster, Jürgen. "The German Army and the Ideological War against the Soviet Union." In *The Policies of Genocide: Jews and Soviet Prisoners of War in Nazi Germany*, ed. Gerhard Hirschfeld, 15-29. London: The German Historical Institute, 1986.

Friedlander, Henry. *Der Weg zum Ns-Genozid: Von der Euthanasie zur Endlösung*. Berlin: Berlin-Verlag, 1997.

Friedman, Filip. "Zagłada Żydów polskich w latach 1939-1945." *BGKBZNP* 1 (1946).

Galiski, Antoni. "Policja w getcie." In *Getto w Łodzi 1940-1944: Materiały z sesji naukowej—9 VIII 1984*, 27-49. Łódź: OKBZHw Łodzi-IPN, 1988.

___. "Obóz dla Cyganów w Łodzi." In *BOKBZHŁ-IPN*, vol. 1, 47-57. Lodz, 1989.

Gelbert, Mendle, *Kehilat Konin befrikhata uvehurbana* [Memorial Book of Konin]. Tel Aviv: Association of Konin Jews in Israel-Memorial Committee, 1968.

Georg, Enno. *Die Wirtschaftlichen Unternehmungen der SS*, Deutsche Verlag-Anstalt, Stuttgart, 1963

Golczewski, Frank, *Ghettos im Reichsgau Wartheland incl. Des Ghettos Łódź/Litzmannstadt, unpublished*, Hamburg, 2006.

Gotz, Aly. *Endlösung: Völkerverschiebung und der Mord an den europäischen Juden*. Frankfurt a.M.: Fischer, 1995.

Grodecki, Roman, and Jerzy Wyrozumski. "Dzieje Żydów w Polsce do końca XIV w." In *Polska piastowska*. Warsaw: PWN, 1969.

Grot, Zdzisław, and Wincenty Ostrowski, eds. *Wspomnienia młodzieży wielkopolskiej z lat okupacji niemieckiej, 1939-1945*. Poznań: Instytut Zachodni, 1946.

Gruner, Wolf. *Jewish Forced Labor under the Nazis: Economic Needs and Racial Aims, 1938-1945*. Cambridge: Cambridge University Press, 2006.

Grynberg, M., *Żydzi w rejencji ciechanowskiej 1939 - 1942*, Warsaw, 1984.

Grynsztejn, Jakub, ed. *Przepisy o organizacji gmin wyznaniowych żydowskich. Nowe rozporządzenia, zarządzenia, przepisy. Rok 1931.* Warsaw: I. Kerner, 1931.). 15-24.

Grzeszczak, Maciej. "Społeczność żydowska Kleczewa w latach 1815-1863 w świetle Akt miasta Kleczewa." *Kwartalnik Historii Żydów* 3, 235 (2010): 345-354.

Grzonkowski, R. "Kleczew w okresie drugiej wojny światowej." In *Dzieje Kleczewa*, ed. Jerzy Stępnia, 165-260. Poznań-Konin, 1995.

Gulczyński, Janusz. *Obóz śmierci w Chełmnie nad Nerem*. Konin: Wojewódzki Ośrodek Kultury, 1991.

___. "Ośrodek zagłady w Chełmnie nad Nerem (przegląd i metodologia badań, aspekty muzealne)." In *Ośrodek zagłady w Chełmnie nad*

Nerem i jego rola w hitlerowskiej polityce eksterminacyjnej, 29-42. Łódź-Konin: Museum Okręgowe, 1995.

Guldon, Zenon, ed. *Lustracja województw wielkopolskich i kujawskich 1628-1632*, part III. Bydgoszcz: Zakład Narodowy im Ossolińskich, 1967.

Guldon, Zenon. "Skupiska żydowskie w miastach polskich w XV-XVI wieku." In *Żydzi i judaizm we współczesnych badaniach*, vol. II, ed. Krzysztof Pilarczyk and Stefan Gasiorowski. Kraków: Księg. Akademicka, 2000.

Guldon, Zenon, and Jacek Wijaczka. "Osadnictwo żydowskie w województwach poznańskim i kaliskim w XVI-XVII wieku." *BŻIH* 2-3 (1992).

———. "Ludność żydowska w Wielkopolsce w drugiej połowie XVII wieku." In *Żydzi w Wielkopolsce na przestrzeni dziejów*, ed. JerzyTopolski and Krzysztof Modelski. Poznań: Wydawn, 1999.

Gumkowski, Janusz. *Zbrodniarze hitlerowscy przed Najwyższym Trybunałem Narodowym*. Wyd. Prawnicze, 1967.

Gürtler, Paul. *Nationalsozialismus und Evangelische Kirchen im Warthegau: Trennung von Staat und Kirche im nationalsozialistischen Weltanschauungsstaat*. Göttingen: Vandenhoeck & Ruprecht, 1958.

Gutschow, Niels. "Stadtplanung im Warthegau 1939-1944." In *Der "Generalplan Ost": Hauptlinien der nationalsozialistischen Planungs—und Vernichtungspolitik*, ed. Mechtild Rössler and Sabine Schleiermarcher, 232-58. Berlin: Akademie Verlag, 1993.

Hahn, Issy. *A Life Sentence of Memories: Konin, Auschwitz, London*. London: Vallentine Mitchell, 2001.

Hansen, Georg. *Ethnische Schulpolitik im besetzten Polen: Der Mustergau Wartheland*. Münster: Brandenburgische Landeszentrale für politische Bildung, Waxmann, 1995.

Harvey, Elizabeth. *Women and the Nazi East: Agents and Witnesses of Germanization*. New Haven: Yale University Press, 2003.

Heberer, Patricia. "Ciągłaść eksterminacji: Sprawcy 'T4' i 'Akcja Reinhardt.'" In *Akcja Reinhardt: Zagłada Żydów w Generalnym Gubernatorstwie*, ed. Dariusz Libionka. Warsaw: IPN, 2004.

Hefter, Filip. *Najnowsza ustawa kahalna: Rozporz. z dnia 24 października 1930*. Stanisławów: A. Bodek, 1931.

Hilberg, Raul. *The Destruction of the European Jews.* New Haven: Yale University Press, 2003.

Hohenstein, Alexander. *Warthelӓndisches Tagebuch aus den Jahren 1941/42.* Stuttgart: Deutsche Verlags-Anstalt, 1961.

Hojan, Artur. "Komora gazowa w forcie VII w Poznaniu (Początek nazistowskiego ludobójstwa)." In *Studia nad dziejami obozów koncentracyjnych w okupowanej Polsce*, ed. Jadwiga Pinderska-Lech, 167-177. Państwowe Muzeum Auschwitz-Birkenau, 2011.

Horn, Maurycy. "Najstarszy rejestr osiedli żydowskich w Polsce z 1507 r." *BŻIH* 3 (1974).

___. "Chronologia i zasięg terytorialny żydowskich cechów rzemieślniczych w dawnej Polsce (1613-1795)." In *Żydzi w dawnej Rzeczypospolitej*, ed. Andrzej Link-Lenczowski and Tomasz Polansky, 201-213. Warsaw: Ossolineum, 1991.

Hundert, Gershon D. *Żydzi w Rzeczypospolitej Obojga Narodów w XVIII wieku. Genealogia nowoczesności.* Warsaw: Cyklady, 2007.

Jamroziak, Wojciech, ed. *Pamiętniki ocalonych: wspomnienia więźniów hitlerowskich miejsc kaźni w Wielkopolsce.* Poznań: Wyd. Poznańskie, 1983.

Janicka, Joanna. *Żydzi Zamojszczyzny 1864-1915.* Lublin: Norbertinum, 2007.

Janowicz, Zbigniew. *Ustrój administracyjny ziem polskich wcielonych do Rzeszy Niemieckiej, 1939-1945, tzw: Okręgi Kraju Warty i Gdańska—Prus Zachodnich.* Poznań: Instytut Zachodni, 1951.

Jasiewicz, Zbigniew. *Dzieje Ziemi Słupeckiej: Praca Zbiorowa.* Słupca-Poznań: Wyd. Poznańskie, 1960.

Jastrzębski, Włodzimierz. *Polityka narodowościowa w Okręgu Rzeszy Gdańsk—Prusy Zachodnie (1939—1945).* Bydgoszcz, 1977.

___. "Ludność niemiecka i rzekomo niemiecka na ziemiach polskich włączonych do Rzeszy Niemieckiej (1939-1945)." In *Ludność niemiecka na ziemiach polskich w latach 1939-1945 i jej powojenne losy.* Bydgoszcz: Wydawnictwo Uczelniane WSP, 1995.

___. "Kujawy w obrębie rejencji inowrocławskiej czasu wojny i okupacji (1939-1945)." In *Dwie części Kujaw. Związki i podziały w dziejach regionu*, ed. Dariusz Karczewskiego, Mirosław Krajewskiego, and Stanisław Roszaka. Włocławek-Inowrocław: Wyższa Szkoła Humanistyczno-Ekonomiczna we Włocławku, 2001.

Jaszowski, Tadeusz. "Okupacyjna martyrologia włocławskich Żydów." In *Z badań nad eksterminacją Żydów na Pomorzu i Kujawach*, 22-30. Bydgoszcz: Pomorze, 1983.

Jurek, T. "Mikrokosmos prowincjonalny. Nad najstarszą księgą Ponieca z przełomu XVI i XVI wieku." In *Aetas media aetas moderna. Studia ofiarowane profesorowi Henrykowi Samsonowiczowi w siedemdziesiątą rocznicę urodzin*, ed. Halina Manikowska, Agnieszka Bartoszewicz, and Wojciech Fałkowski. Warsaw: Instytut Historyczny Uniwersytetu Warszawskiego, 2000.

Kaczmarek, Marian. "Eutanazja w tzw. Kraju Warty." *Kronika Wielkopolski* (1985): 69-81.

Kaczmarek, Ryszard "Sytuacja ludności żydowskiej na obszarach zachodnich i południowych Europy wcielonych do Rzeszy Niemieckiej a polityka antyżydowska na polskich terenach wcielonych—próba porównania." In *Zagłada Żydów na polskich terenach wcielonych do Rzeszy*, ed. Aleksandra Namysło, 34-45. Warsaw: IPN, 2008.

Kaczmarek, Z., and K. Pawlak, "Endecja w Wielkopolsce Wschodniej w okresie międzywojennym." *Rocznik Wielkopolski Wschodniej* 4 (1976).

Kaliski, T. "Lata wojny i okupacji." In *Dzieje Pakości*, ed. Włodzimierz Jastrzębskiego. Warsaw-Poznań, 1978.

Kargel, Adolf. *Deutschtum im Aufbruch: Vom Volkstumskampf der Deutschen im östlichen Wartheland*. Leipzig: S. Hirzel, 1942.

Kawski, Tomasz. "Mniejszość żydowska w województwie pomorskim (bydgoskim) w latach 1945-1956." In *Kujawy i Pomorze w latach 1945-1956. Od zakończenia okupacji niemieckiej do przełomu październikowego*, ed. Włodzimierz Jastrzębskiego and Mirosław Krajewskiego. Włocławek: Wyższa Szkoła Humanistyczno-Ekonomiczna we Włocławku, 2001.

———. "Żydzi z Kujaw, ziemi dobrzyńskiej oraz Bydgoszczy ocaleni z Shoah. Przyczynek do poznania struktury społeczno-zawodowej, zmian osadniczych oraz migracji ludności żydowskiej w Polsce po drugiej wojnie światowej." In *Wrzesień 1939 roku i jego konsekwencje dla ziem zachodnich i północnych Drugiej Rzeczypospolitej*, ed. Ryszard Sudzińskiego and Włodzimierz Jastrzębskiego. Toruń-Bydgoszcz: Uniwersytetu Mikołaja Kopernika, 2001.

———. "Mniejszości narodowe i wyznaniowe w Radziejowie i okolicach." In *Radziejów poprzez stulecia*, ed. Dariusz Karczewskiego. Włocławek-Radziejów: Lega-Oficyna Wydawn, 2002.

———. "Inwentarze gmin żydowskich z Pomorza i Wielkopolski Wschodniej w latach 1918/20-1939." *Kwartalnik Historii Kultury Materialnej* 1 (2006): 73-96.

———. *Kujawsko-dobrzyńscy Żydzi w latach 1918-1950*. Toruń: Wydawnictwo Adam Marszałek, 2006.

———. *Gminy żydowskie pogranicza Wielkopolski, Mazowsza i Pomorza w latach 1918- 1942*. Toruń: Wydawn Nauk Grado, 2007.

———. "Społeczność żydowska na pograniczu kujawsko-wielkopolskim w XX wieku." In *Z dziejów pogranicza kujawsko-wielkopolskiego*, ed. Dariusz Karczewski, 161-187. Strzelno: Polskie Towarzystwo Historyczne, Oddział Inowrocław, 2007.

———. "Funkcjonowanie struktur biurokratycznych gmin żydowskich centralnej i zachodniej Polski w latach 1918-1939." In *Dzieje biurokracji na ziemiach polskich*, vol. 1, ed. Artura Góraka, Ireneusza Łucia, and Dariusza Magiera. Lublin-Siedlce: Instytut Historii Akademii Podlaskiej/Instytut Historii Uniwersytetu Marii Curie-Sklodowskiej, 2008.

———, and Monika Opioła. *Gminy żydowskie pogranicza Wielkopolski, Mazowsza, Małopolski i Śląska w latach 1918-1942*. Toruń: Wdawnictwo Adam Marszałek, 2008.

Kay, Alex J. "Germany's Staatssekretäre, Mass Starvation and the Meeting of 2 May 1941." *Journal of Contemporary History* 41, no. 4 (2006): 685–700.

Kershaw, Ian. "Improvised Genocide? The Emergence of the 'Final Solution' in the 'Warthegau.'" *Transactions of the Royal Historical Society* 2 [6th series] (1992): 51-78.

Kiełboń, Janina. "Deportacje Żydów do dystrykty lubelskiego (1939-1943)." In *Akcja Reinhardt: Zagłada Żydów w Generalnym Gubernatorstwie*, ed. Dariusz Libionka, 161-181. Warsaw: IPN, 2004.

Kiełboń, Janina. "Deportacje Żydów do dystryktu lubelskiego (1939-1943)." *Zeszyty Majdanka* 14 (1992): 61-92.

Klein, Peter. "Die Rolle der Vernichtungslager Kulmhof (Chełmno nad Nerem), Belzec (Bełżec) und Auschwitz-Birkenau in den frühen Deportationsvorbereitungen." In *Lager, Zwangsarbeit, Vertreibung und Deportation: Dimensionen der Massenverbrechen in der Sowjetunion und in Deutschland 1933 bis 1945*, ed. Dittmar Dahlmann and Gerhard Hirschfeld. Essen: Klartext Verlag, 1999.

___. "Kulmhof/Chełmno." *Der Ort des Terrors* VIII (2008): 301-328.

Kleinschmidt, Kurt. *Die Preisvorschriften in den eingegliederten Ostgebieten: Stand von Anfang März 1943*. Posen: Hirt, 1943.

Kogon, Eugen, et al., eds. *Nationalsozialistische Massentötungen durch Giftgas: Eine Dokumentation*. Frankfurt a.M.: Fischer, 1983.

Kołodziejczyk, Ryszard. "Miasta i mieszczaństwo w Królestwie Polskim w 1965 r. w świetle statystyki." In his *Dzieje burżuazji w Polsce. Studia i materiały*, vol. 2. Wrocław: Zakład Narodowy im. Ossolińskich, 1980.

Korn, Israel. *Ma survie: 17 Eloul 5699 - 24 Iyar 5705; Meine Mamme*. Jerusalem: I. Korn, 2001.

Körner, Hellmut. *Zwischen Warthegau und UDSSR*. Berlin: Reichsnährstand Verlags-Ges., 1941.

Krakowski, Shmuel. "Organizacje młodzieżowe w getcie łódzkim." In *Fenomen getta łódzkiego, 1940-1944*, ed. Paweł Samuś and Wiesława Pusia, 281-286. Łódź: Wydawnictwo Uniwersytetu Łodzkiego, 2006.

Krakowski, Shmuel. "Policy of the Third Reich in Conquered Poland." *Yad Vashem Studies* 9 (1973): 225-245.

Krakowski, Shmuel. "Relations between Jews and Poles during the Holocaust: New and Old Approaches in Polish Historiography." *Yad Vashem Studies* 19 (1988): 317-340.

Krakowski, Shmuel. "The Fate of Jewish Prisoners of War in the September 1939 Campaign." *Yad Vashem Studies* 12 (1977): 297-334.

Krakowski, Shmuel. "The Fate of the Jewish POWs of the Soviet and Polish Armies." In *The Shoah and the War*, ed. Asher Cohen, Yehoyakim Cochavi, and Yoav Gelber, 217-231. Berlin: Peter Lang, 1992.

Krakowski, Shmuel. "The Testament of the Last Prisoners of the Chelmno Death Camp." *Yad Vashem Studies* 21 (1991): 105-123.

Krakowski, Shmuel. *Chełmno—A Small Village in Europe: The First Nazi Mass Extermination Camp*. Jerusalem: Yad Vashem, 2009.

Krakowski, Shmuel. *Das Todeslager Chełmno/Kulmhof: der Beginn der "Endlösung."* Göttingen: Wallstein, 2007.

Kramer, Edith. "Meine Erfahrungen in Posen, Antoniek und Theresienstadt bis zur Rettung in der Schweiz." *Emuna/Israel Forum* 4 (1976): 28-36 and 5/6 (1976): 69-74.

Krasowski, Krzysztof. *Związki wyznaniowe w II Rzeczypospolitej. Studium historyczno-prawne*. Warsaw-Poznań: Państwowe Wydawn. Naukowe, 1988.

Krausnick, Helmut, et al. *Anatomy of the SS State*. London: Collins, 1968.

Krausnick, Helmut. *Hitlers Einsatzgruppen: Die Truppe des Weltanschauungskrieges 1938-1942*. Frankfurt a. M.: Fischer Taschenbuch-Verlag, 1985.

Kutrzeba, Stanisław. "Przywileje Kazimierza Wielkiego dla Żydów." *Sprawozdania PAU* 27, no. 10 (1922).

Kuwałek, Robert. "Getta tranzytowe w dystrykcie lubelskim." In *Akcja Reinhardt: Zagłada Żydów w Generalnym Gubernatorstwie*, ed. Dariusz Libionka, 138-160. Warsaw: IPN, 2004.

Lehnstaedt, Stephan. *Jüdische Arbeit in den kleinen Ghettos des Warthegaus*. Munich: Unpublished, 2009.

___. "Jewish Labor in the Smaller Ghettos in the Warthegau Region." In *Yad Vashem Studies* 38, no. 2 (2010): 47-84.

Lehrer, Steven. *Wannsee House and the Holocaust*. Jefferson, NC: McFarland, 2000. 142-143.

Leszczyński, Julian. "Od formuły obozu zagłady - Höppner - Chełmno n/Nerem - do Endlösung." *BŻIH* 101 (1977): 41-61.

Libickiego, Marcina, and Ryszarda Wryka, eds. *Zbrodnie niemieckie w Wielkopolsce w latach 1939-1945*. Poznań: Wyd. Poznańskie, 2004.

Libiszewski, Jerzy. "Getta w powiecie włocławskim." In *Materiały na sesję naukową „W 45 rocznicę zagłady skupisk żydowskich w Kraju Warty."* Zduńska Wola, 23 X 1987.

Libiszewski, Jerzy. "Obóz na Błoniu w Inowrocławiu." In *Z badań nad eksterminacją Żydów na Pomorzu i Kujawach,* ed. Tadeusz Jaszowski, 53-57. Bydgoszcz: Pomorze, 1983.

Libiszewski, Jersey. "Żydowskie obozy pracy przymusowej na terenie byłego powiatu inowrocławskiego." In *Z badań nad eksterminacją Żydów na Pomorzu i Kujawach*, ed. Tadeusz Jaszowski, 45-52. Bydgoszcz: Pomorze, 1983.

Jaszowski, Tadeusz. „Okupacyjna martylorogia Żydów włocławskich." In *Z badań nad eksterminacją Żydów na Pomorzu i Kujawach*, ed. Tadeusz Jaszowski, 22-30. Bydgoszcz: Pomorze, 1983.

Longerich, Peter. *Politik der Vernichtung: Eine Gesamtdarstellung der nationalsozialistischen Judenverfolgung*. Munich-Zürich: Piper, 1998.

Loose, Ingo. "Wartheland." In *Das "Grossdeutsche Reich" und die Juden*, ed. Wolf Gruner, 229-258. Frankfurt, a.M.: Campus Verlag GmbH, 2010.

Łaszkiewicz, Tomasz. *Żydzi w Inowrocławiu w okresie międzywojennym (1919-1939)*. Inowrocław: Oficyna Wydawnicza Muzeum im. Jana Kasprowicza, 1997.

Łojko, Jerzy. "Kleczew w okresie II Rzeczypospolitej." In *Dzieje Kleczewa:Praca zbiorowa*, ed. Jerzego Stępnia, 143-164. Poznań-Konin: Urząd Wojewódzki. [Wydział Spraw Społecznych], 1995.

___. "Kleczew w XVI-XVIII stuleciu." In *Dzieje Kleczewa: Praca zbiorowa*, ed. Jerzego Stępnia, 19-110. Poznań-Konin: Urząd Wojewódzki. [Wydział Spraw Społecznych], 1995.

___. "Miasto w latach 1793-1870." In *Dzieje Kleczewa: Praca zbiorowa*, ed. Jerzego Stępnia, 111-122. Poznań-Konin: Urząd Wojewódzki. [Wydział Spraw Społecznych], 1995.

Łuczak, Agnieszka. *Ze strachem pod rękę i śmiercią u boku...: Wielkopolanki w konspiracji, 1939-1945*. Poznań: Wojewódzka Biblioteka Publiczna, 2006.

Łuczak, Czesław. *Przyczynki do gospodarki niemieckiej w latach 1939-1945*. Poznań: Instytut Zachodni, 1949.

___. *Grabież polskiego mienia na ziemiach zachodnich Rzeczypospolitej "Wcielonych" do Rzeszy, 1939-1945*. Poznań: UAM, 1969.

___. *Wysiedlenia ludności polskiej na tzw. ziemiach wcielonych do Rzeszy, 1939-1945*. Poznań: Instytut Zachodni, 1969.

___. *Kraj Warty" 1939-1945: Studium historyczno-gospodarcze okupacji hitlerowskiej*. Poznań: Wyd. Poznańskie, 1972.

___. "Eksterminacja ludności powiatu tureckiego w okresie okupacji hitlerowskiej." *Rocznik Wielkopolski Wschodniej* 4 (1976): 76-82
___. *Polityka ludnościowa i ekonomiczna hitlerowskich Niemiec w okupowanej Polsce.* Poznań: Wyd. Poznańskie, 1979.
___. *Polityka ekonomiczna Trzeciej Rzeszy w latach drugiej wojny światowej.* Poznań: Wyd. Poznańskie, 1982.
___. *Położenie ludności polskiej w Kraju Warty 1939-1945.* Poznań: Wyd. Poznańskie, 1987.
___. "Demograficzne i ekonomiczne aspekty zagłady Żydów w okupowanej Polsce." *Przegląd Zachodni* 56 (1989).
___. *Dzień po dniu w okupowanym Poznaniu 10 września 1939-23 lutego 1945.* Poznań: Wydawn. Poznańskie, 1989.
___. *Dzień po dniu w okupowanej Wielkopolsce i Ziemi Łódzkiej (Kraj Warty). Kalendarium wydarzeń 1939-1945.* Poznań: Wydawn. Lektor, 1993.
___. *Polska i Polacy w drugiej wojnie światowej.* Poznań: Wyd. Naukowe UAM, 1993.
___. "Polityka Greisera w stosunku do Żydów." In *Żydzi w Wielkopolsce na przestrzeni dziejów*, ed. Jerzego Topolskiego and Krzysztofa Modelskiego, 212-219. Poznań: Wyd. Poznańskie, 1995.
___. *Pod niemieckim jarzmem (Kraj Warty 1939-1945).* Poznań: PSO, 1996.
___. *Arthur Greiser: Hitlerowski władca w Wolnym Mieście Gdańsku i w Kraju Warty.* Poznań: PSO, 1997.
___, ed. *Wysiedlenia ludności polskiej na tzw. ziemiach wcielonych do Rzeszy 1939-1945*, Documenta Occupationis T. VIII. Poznań: Instytut Zachodni, 1975.
Maas, Walther Gerhard Eduard. *Von der provinz Südpreussen zum Reichsgau Wartheland.* Poznań: S. Hirzel, 1942.
Macyra, Roman. *Prasa konspiracyjna w Kraju Warty w latach 1939-1945.* Poznań: Wyd. Poznańskie, 2006.
Madajczyk, Czesław. *Generalna Gubernia w planach hitlerowskich. Studia.* Warsaw: PWN, 1961.
Madajczyk, Czesław. *Generalplan Ost.* Poznań: Instytut Zachodni, 1962.

Madajczyk, Czesław. *Polityka III Rzeszy w okupowanej Polsce.* Warsaw: Państwowe Wydawnictwo Naukowe, 1970.
Madajczyk, Czesław. *Faszyzm i okupacje 1938-1945: Wykonywanie okupacji przez państwa Osi w Europie*, Vol. I: *Ukształtowanie się zarządów okupacyjnych.* Poznań: Wyd. Naukowe Semper, 1983.
Madajczyk, Czesław. *Faszyzm i okupacje 1938-1945: Wykonywanie okupacji przez państwa Osi w Europie*, vol. II, *Mechanizmy realizowania okupacji.* Poznań: Wyd. Poznańskie, 1984.
Madajczyk, Czesław. *Generalny Plan Wschodni: Zbiór dokumentów.* Warsaw: GKBZHP, 1990.
Madajczyk, Czesław, ed. *Generalny Plan Wschodni: zbiór dokumentów.* Warsaw: Główna Komisja Badania Zbrodni Hitlerowskich w Polsce, 1990.
Mallmann, Klaus-Michael. "'Rozwiązać przez jakikolwiek szybko działający środek': Policja Bezpieczeństwa w Kraju Warty." In *Zagłada Żydów na polskich terenach wcielonych do Rzeszy*, ed. Aleksandra Namysło, 85-99. Warsaw: IPN, 2008.
Marcinkowska, Halina. *Miasteczko w kolorze niebieskim. Żydzi z Błaszek.* Błaszki, 2001.
Marczewski, Jerzy. "The Nazi Nationality Policy in the Warthegau 1939-1945 (an outline)." *Polish Western Affairs* 30, no. 1 (1989): 31-50.
Marczewski, Jerzy. *Hitlerowska koncepcja polityki kolonizacyjno-wysiedlenczej i jej realizacja w "Okręgu Warty."* Poznań: Instytut Zachodni, 1979.
Materiały na sesję naukową „W 45 rocznicę zagłady skupisk żydowskich w Kraju Warty." Zduńska Wola: IPN, 1987.
Meissner, Blanka. *Ewakuacja niemieckich władz administracyjnych i niemieckiej ludności z okupacyjnych ziem polskich w latach 1944-1945.* Warsaw: GKBZHP-IPN, 1987.
Michałowska, Anna. *Między demokracją a oligarchią. Władze gmin żydowskich w Poznaniu i Swarzędzu (od połowy XVII do końca XVIII wieku).* Warsaw: Wyd. Akademickie Dialog, 2000.
Michman, Dan. "Judenraty, getto, ostateczne rozwiązanie kwestii żydowskiej. Trzy niezależne czy też powiązane ze sobą komponenty polityki antyżydowskiej? Kilka ogólnych spostrzeżeń i ich odniesienie do przypadku Łodzi (Litzmannstadt)." In *Zagłada Żydów na polskich*

terenach wcielonych do Rzeszy, ed. A. Namysło, 163-168. Warsaw: IPN, 2008.

Młynarczyk, Jacek Andrzej. "Wpływ inicjatyw oddolnych Arthura Greisera i Odilona Globocnika na decyzję o wymordowaniu Żydów." In *Zagłada Żydów na polskich terenach wcielonych do Rzeszy*, ed. Aleksandra Namysło, 14-33. Warsaw: IPN, 2008.

Mnichowski, Przemysław. "Hitlerowskie obozy pracy przymusowej dla Żydów z getta łódzkiego na środkowym Nadodrzu w latach 1940-1944." In *Getto w Łodzi 1940-1944: Materiały z sesji naukowej—9 VIII 1984*, ed. Jan Fijałek and Antoni Galiński, 105-116. Łódź: OKBZHw Łodzi-IPN, 1988.

Musial, Bogdan. *Deutsche Zivilverwaltung und Judenverfolgung im Generalgouvernement: Eine Fallstudie zum Distrikt Lublin 1939-1945*. Wiesbaden: Harassowitz, 1999.

———. "Niemiecka polityka narodowościowa w okupowanej Polsce w latach 1939-1945." *Pamięć i Sprawiedliwość* 6 (2004): 13-35.

Namysło, Aleksandra, ed. *Zagłada Żydów na polskich terenach wcielonych do Rzeszy*. Warsaw: IPN, 2008.

Nawrocki, Stanisław. *Policja hitlerowska w tzw. Kraju Warty w latach 1939-1945*. Poznań: Instytut Zachodni, 1970.

———. *Terror policyjny w "Kraju Warty," 1939-1945*. Poznań: Wyd. Poznańskie,1973.

Nowicki, Przemysław. "Ludność żydowska w Izbicy Kujawskiej w okresie międzywojennym (1918-1939)." *Debiuty Naukowe WSHE* 5 (2004): 129-150.

———. "Zanim 'przybył z zaświatów,' nazywł się Winer. Krąg rodzinny i konspiracyjny Szlamka, uciekiniera z ośrodka zagłady w Chełmnie nad Nerem." *Zagłada Żydów. Studia i materiały* no. 5 (2009): 163-192.

Ohryzko-Włodarska, Czesława, ed. *Lustracja województw wielkopolskich i kujawskich 1659-1665*, part I. Wrocław: Zakład Narodowy im Ossolińskich, 1978.

Ośrodek zagłady w Chełmnie nad Nerem i jego rola w hitlerowskiej polityce eksterminacyjnej. Łódź-Konin: Muzeum Okręgowe, 1995.

Pakentreger, Aleksander. "Statystyka Żydów m. Kalisza, ocalałych po II wojnie światowej." *BŻIH* 96 (1974): 81-92.

___. "Polityka władz niemieckich tzw. Kraju Warty wobec Żydów." *BŻIH*, no. 4 (1977): 33-48.

___. "Losy Żydów m. Kalisza i powiatu kaliskiego w okresie okupacji hitlerowskiej (od 1940 do 9 VII 1942 r.). Martyrologia i Zagłada." *BŻIH* no. 2-3 (1980): 3-21.

___. *Żydzi w Kaliszu w latach 1918-1939. Problemy polityczne i społeczne.* Warsaw: Państwowe Wydawn. Nauk, 1988.

Pawlak, Janusz. "Eksterminacja ludności żydowskiej w Kutnie w XX wieku." *Kutnowskie Zeszyty Regionalne* 3 (1999): 41-52.

Pawlicka-Nowak, Łucja, ed. *Chełmno Witness Speak*. Konin-Łódź: The Council for the Protection of Memory of Combat and Martyrdom in Warsaw, 2004.

___. *The Extermination Center for Jews in Chełmno-on-Ner in the Light of the Latest Research: Symposium Proceedings, September 6-7, 2004.* Konin: District Museum in Konin, 2004.

___. *Ośrodek zagłady Żydów w Chełmnie nad Nerem w świetle najnowszych badań: materiały z sesji naukowej.* Łódź: Oficyna Bibliofilów, 2004.

Petzina, Dieter. *Autarkiepolitik im Dritten Reich: Der nationallsozialistische Vierjahresplan.* Stuttgart: Deutsche Verlags-Anstalt, 1968.

Piechota, Zbigniew, and Janusz Wróbel. "Formy eksterminacji bezpośredniej mieszkańców getta w Łodzi." In *Getto w Łodzi 1940-1944: Materialy z sesji naukowej*, ed. Puś Wiesław and Liszewski Stanisław, 65-79. Łódź: Wyd. Uniwersytetu Łódzkiego, 1988.

Piechota, Zbigniew. "Likwidacja skupisk żydowskich w byłych powiatach tureckim i kolskim." In *Materiały na sesję naukową "W 45 rocznicę zagłady skupisk żydowskich w Kraju Warty,"* 5-16. Zduńska Wola 23 X (1987).

Pietrzak, Jan. *Hans Biebow—portret oprawcy, in Fenomen getta łódzkiego 1940-1944*, ed. Paweł Samuś and Wiesław Puś. Łódź: Wydawnictwo Uniwersytetu Łódzkiego, 2006. 185-203.

Pilarczyk, Krzysztof, and Gąsiorowski, Stefan, eds. *Żydzi i judaizm we współczesnych badaniach*, vol. 2. Kraków: Księg. Akademicka, 2000.

Pinkas ha-Kehillot. Encyclopaedia of Jewish Communities, vol. 1. Jerusalem: Yad Vashem, 1976.

Pinkas ha-Kehillot. Encyclopaedia of Jewish Communities, vol. 4, Jerusalem: Yad Vashem, 1989.

Porzycki, Wiesław. *Posłuszni aż do śmierci: niemieccy urzędnicy w Kraju Warty, 1939-1945*. Poznań: PSO, 1997.

Prekerowa, Teresa. "Wojna i okupacja." In *Najnowsze dzieje Żydów w Polsce w zarysie (do 1950 roku)*, ed. Jerzy Tomaszewski, 273-384. Warsaw: Wydawnictwo Naukowe PWN, 1993.

Redemacher, Michael. *Handbuch der NSDAP-Gaue, 1928-1945: Die Amtsträger der NSDAP und ihrer Organisationen auf Gau- und Kreisebene in Deutschland und Österreich sowie in den Reichsgauen Danzig-Westpreussen, Sudetenland und Wartheland*. Hamburg: Selbstverlag des Verfassers, 2000.

Richmond, Theo. *Uporczywe echo. Sztetl Konin. Poszukiwanie*. Poznań: Media Rodzina, 2001.

Richmond, Theo, *Konin: A Quest*. London: Vintage, 1996.

Riedel, Joachim. "Postępowanie karne w Niemczech w procesach o eksterminację Żydów na polskich ziemiach wcielonych do Rzeszy: Zarys problemu." In *Zagłada Żydów na polskich terenach wcielonych do Rzeszy*, ed. Aleksandra Namysło, 228-252. Warsaw: IPN, 2008.

Riess, Volker. *Die Anfänge der Vernichtung lebensunwerten Lebens in den Reichsgauen Danzig-Westpreussen und Wartheland 1939/40*. Frankfurt a.M.: Lang, 1995.

___. "Zentrale und dezentrale Radikalisierung: Die Tötungen 'unwerten Lebens' in der annektierten west- und nordpolnischen Gebieten.'" In *Genesis des Genozids: Polen 1939-1941*, ed. Klaus-Michael Mallmann and Bogdan Musial, 127-144. Darmstadt: Wiss. Buchges, 2004.

Ringel, Michał. "Ustawodawstwo Polski Odrodzonej o gminach żydowskich." In *Żydzi w Polsce Odrodzonej. Działalność społeczna, gospodarcza, oświatowa i kulturalna*, ed. Ignacy Schiper, Alexander Hafftka, and Arieh Tartakower, vol. 2, 244-248. Warsaw: Nakł. Wydawn., 1936.

Rogall, Joachim. *Die Räumung des "Reichsgaus Wartheland" vom 16. bis 26. Januar 1945 im Spiegel amtlicher Berichte*. Sigmaringen: J. Thorbecke, 1993.

Rosenkranz, Otto. *Siedlung und Landwirtschaft im Reichsgau Wartheland*. Berlin: Deutsche Landbuchhandlung, 1941.
Rossino, Alexander B. "Destructive Impulses: German Soldiers and the Conquest of Poland." *Holocaust and Genocide Studies* 7 (1997): 351-365.
Rossino, Alexander B. "Nazi Anti-Jewish Policy during the Polish Campaign: The Case of the Einsatzgruppe Woyrsch." *German Studies Review* 24 (2001): 35-54.
Rossino, Alexander B. *Hitler Strikes Poland: Blitzkrieg, Ideology and Atrocity*. Lawrence, KS: Kansas University Press, 2003.
Rückerl, Adalbert, ed. *Nationalsozialistische Vernichtungslager im Spiegel deutscher Strafprozesse: Belzec, Sobibor, Treblinka, Chelmno*. Munich: Deutscher Taschenbuch Verlag, 1979.
Rusiński, Władysław ed. *Dzieje Kalisza*. Poznań: Wydawnictwo Poznańskie, 1977.
Rutowska, Maria. *Straty osobowe i materialne kultury w Wielkopolsce w latach II wojny światowej*. Warsaw: PWN, 1984.
___. *Wysiedlenia ludności polskiej z Kraju Warty do Generalnego Gubernatorstwa 1939-1941*. Poznań: Instytut Zachodni, 2003.
___. *Lager Główna: niemiecki obóz przesiedleńczy na Głównej w Poznaniu dla ludności polskiej (1939-1940)*. Poznań: Instytut Zachodni, 2008.
Rybczyński, Piotr. "Zbrodnie Wehrmachtu w rejonie konińskim." In *Zbrodnie Wehrmachtu w Wielkopolsce w okresie Zarządu Wojskowego (1 września-25 października 1939)*, 69-102. Kalisz: Delegatura w Kaliszu Okręgowej Komisji Badania Zbrodni Hitlerowskich w Łodzi, Instytut Pamięci Narodowej, 1986.
___. "Likwidacja skupisk ludności żydowskiej w powiecie konińskim." In *Ośrodek zagłady w Chełmnie nad Nerem i jego rola w hitlerowskiej polityce eksterminacyjnej*, 109-115. Łódź-Konin: Muzeum Okręgowe, 1995.
Sawicki, Jerzy. *Przemówienie końcowe prokuratora Jerzego Sawickiego przed Najwyższym Trybunałem Narodowym w sprawie przeciwko Arturowi Greiserowi*. Poznań, 1946.
Seidler, Franz W. *Die Organisation Todt: Bauen für Staat und Wehrmacht, 1938-1945*. Koblenz: Bernard & Gräfe, 1987.

Serwański, Edward. *Obóz zagłady w Chełmnie nad Nerem, 1941-1945.* Poznań: Wyd. Poznańskie, 1964.

Sesja naukowa "W 45 rocznicę zagłady skupisk żydowskich w Kraju Warty: referaty i komunikaty. Zduńska Wola: IPN, 1987.

Sienkiewicz, Witold, and Grzegorz Hryciuk. *Wysiedlenia, wypędzenia i ucieczki 1939-1945. Atlas ziem Polski.* Warsaw: Demart, 2008.

Siepracka, Dorota. "Postawy Polaków wobec ludności żydowskiej Kraju Warty." In *Zagłada Żydów na polskich terenach wcielonych do Rzeszy*, ed. Aleksandra Namysło, 195-210. Warsaw: IPN, 2008.

Sierpowski, Stanisłav, ed. *Dzieje ziemi gostyńskiej.* Poznań: UAM, 1979.

Skórzyńska, Izabela, and Wojciech Olejniczak, eds. *Do zobaczenia za rok w Jerozolimie—deportacje polskich Żydów w 1938 roku z Niemiec do Zbąszynia / See You Next Year in Jerusalem—Deportation of Polish Jews in 1938 from Germany to Zbąszyń.* Poznań: Fundacja TRES, 2012.

Snyder, Timothy. *Bloodlands: Europe between Hitler and Stalin.* London: The Bodley Head, 2010. 162-188;

Spector, Shmuel. "Aktion 1005: Effacing the Murder of Millions." In *Holocaust and Genocide Studies* 5, no. 2 (1990): 158.

Stachiewicz, Piotr. *Akcja Koppe: krakowska akcja "Parasola."* Warsaw: MON, 1982.

Stankowski, Albert. "Nowe spojrzenie na statystyki dotyczące emigracji Żydów z Polski po 1944 roku." In *Studia z historii Żydów w Polsce po 1945 r.*, ed. Grzegorz Berendt, August Grabski, and Albert Stankowski. Warsaw: Żydowski Instytut Historyczny, 2000.

Stefański, Kazimierz. *Mieszczaństwo kaliskie w XVI wieku.* Kalisz, 1933.

Stępnia, Jerzy, ed. *Dzieje Kleczewa.* Poznań-Konin, 1995.

Stępnia, Jerzy. "Od Polski Ludowej do III Rzeczypospolitej." In his *Dzieje Kleczewa*, 261-326. Poznań-Konin, 1995

Streit, Christian. "The German Army and the Policies of Genocide." In *The Policies of Genocide: Jews and Soviet Prisoners of War in Nazi Germany*, ed. Gerhard Hirschfeld, 1-14. London: The German Historical Institute, 1986.

Struck, Manfred. *Chelmno Kulmhof: Ein vergessener Ort des Holocaust?* Bonn: Gegen Vergessen-Für Demokratie, 2001.

Świątkowski, Henryk. *Wyznania religijne w Polsce ze szczególnym uwzględnieniem ich stanu prawnego*, cz. 1. *Wyznania i związki religijne*.Warsaw: Pyz, 1937.

Sudziński, Ryszard, and Jastrzębski, Włodzimierz, eds. *Wrzesień 1939 roku i jego konsekwencje dla ziem zachodnich i północnych Drugiej Rzeczypospolitej*. Toruń-Bydgoszcz: Wyd. Uniwersytetu Mikołaja Kopernika, 2001.

Szczepańskiego, Bolesława, ed. *Dzieje Słupcy*. Poznań, 1996.

Sziling, Jan. "W latach okupacji hitlerowskiej (1939-1945)." In *Dzieje Inowrocławia*, ed. Marian Biskupa, vol. 2. Warsaw-Poznań-Toruń: Państ. Wydaw. Naukowe, 1982.

Sziling, Jan. *Polityka okupanta hitlerowskiego wobec kościoła katolickiego, 1939-1945: Tzw. okręgi Rzeszy: Gdańsk-Prusy Zachodnie, Kraj Warty i Regencja Katowicka*. Poznań: Instytut Zachodni, 1970.

Sztokfish, D. *Kutno ve ha-Seviva*. Tel Aviv: Former Residents of Kutno and Surroundings in Israel and the Diaspora, 1968.

Tchrusch, K. F., and Korzen, M., eds. *Wloclawek ve ha-Sviva. Sefer Zikkaron*. (N.p.,) 1967.

Terles, Mikołaj. *Ethnic cleansing of Poles in Volhynia and Eastern Galicia, 1942-1946*. Toronto: Alliance of the Polish Eastern Provinces, Toronto Branch, 1993.

Schindler, Dietrich, and Jiri Toman, eds. *The Laws of Armed Conflicts: A Collection of Conventions, Resolutions and Other Documents*. Dordrecht: Martinus Nijhoff, 1988.

Tomaszewski, Jerzy. "Niepodległa Rzeczpospolita." In his *Najnowsze dzieje Żydów w Polsce w zarysie (do 1950 roku)*, 143-269.Warsaw: PWN, 1993.

___. *Preludium Zagłady: wygnanie Żydów polskich z Niemiec w 1938 r.* Warsaw: PWN, 1998.

Tomczak, Andrzej, ed. *Lustracja województw wielkopolskich i kujawskich 1564-65*, part II. Bydgoszcz: Zakład Narodowy im Ossolińskich, 1963.

Topolski, Jerzy, ed. *Dzieje Wielkopolski*, vol. 1 *do roku 1793*. Poznań, 1969.

Trunk, Isaiah. *Judenrat: The Jewish Councils in Eastern Europe under Nazi Occupation*. Lincoln: University of Nebraska Press, 1996.

Tych, Feliks. "Typologia gett utworzonych przez okupantów niemieckich w Polsce (1939-1944)." In *Fenomen getta łódzkiego 1940-1944*, ed. Paweł Samuś and Wiesław Puś, 77-89. Łódź: Wydawnictwo Uniwersytetu Łódzkiego, 2006.

Tycner, Henryk. *Die Freiheit kam im Januar '45: Tatsachen und Erinnerungen an die Tage der faschistischen Okkupation in Poznan und an die Kämpfe zur Befreiung meiner Heimatstadt*. Berlin: Dietz, 1985.

Unger, Michal. *Reassessment of the Image of Mordechai Chaim Rumkowski*. Jerusalem: Yad Vashem, 2004.

___. "Jewish Forced Labor in the Lodz Ghetto and Its Influence on German Policy." In *Fenomen getta łódzkiego 1940-1944*, ed. Paweł Samuś and Wiesław Puś, 169-182. Łódź: Wydawnictwo Uniwersytetu Łódzkiego, 2006.

Szymczaka, Jana, ed. *Uniejów. Dzieje miasta*. Łódź-Uniejów: Towarzystwo Przyjaciół Uniejowa, 1995.

Urbański, Krzysztof. *Gminy żydowskie małe w województwie kieleckim w okresie międzywojennym*. Kielce: Muzeum Narodowe w Kielcach, 2006.

W 45 rocznicę zagłady skupisk żydowskich w Kraju Warty: referaty i komunikaty. Zduńska Wola: IPN, 1987.

Walendowska-Garczarczyk, Anna. *Eksterminacja Polaków w zakładach karnych Rawicza i Wronek w okresie okupacji hitlerowskiej, 1939-1945*. Poznań: Wyd. Naukowe UAM, 1981.

Wasiutyński, Bohdan. *Ludność żydowska w Polsce w wiekach XIX i XX. Studium statystyczne*. Warsaw: Kasy im. Mianowskiego, 1930.

Wasser, Bruno. *Himmlers Raumplanung im Osten: Der Generalplan Ost in Polen 1940-1944*. Basel: Birkhäuser, 1993.

Waszak, Stanisław. "Bilans walki narodowościowej rządów Greisera." *Przegląd Zachodni* 1 (1946).

Waszczyński, Jan. "Rola Hansa Biebowa w eksterminacji mieszkańców getta w Łodzi." In *Getto w Łodzi 1940-1944: Materiały z sesji naukowej—9 VIII 1984*, ed. Jan Fijałek and Antoni Galiński, 117-125. Łódź: OKBZHw Łodzi-IPN, 1988.

Waszkiewicz, Zofia. "Regencja inowrocławska podczas okupacji hitlerowskiej w historiografii polskiej." In *Ziemia Kujawska*, vol. 5. Poznań: Naukowe, Oddzial w Poznaniu, 1978.

Wąsicki Jan. *Opis miast polskich*, vol. 1. Poznań: Uniw. im. A. Mickiewicza, 1962.

Wegener, Karl-A. *Historisches Ortschaftsverzeichnis Wartheland*. Frankfurt a.M.: Verlag des Bundesamtes für Kartographie u. Geodaesie, 1998.

Weinberg, Gerhard L. *A World at Arms: A Global History of World War II*. Cambridge: Cambridge University Press, 2005

Weitz, Yechiam. "Himmler in Poznan: Evil Rationalized." In *Forum on the Jewish People, Zionism and Israel* 46/47 (1982): 97-103.

Wietrzykowski, Albin. *Powrót Arthura Greisera*. Poznań: Pomoc, 1946.

Witkowski, Antoni. *Mordercy z Selbstschutzu*. Warsaw: MON, 1986.

___. *Nieukarana zbrodnia*. Warsaw: Bellona, 1995.

Witte, Peter. "Two Decisions Concerning the 'Final Solution to the Jewish Question': Deportations to Lodz and Mass Murder in Chełmno." *Holocaust and Genocide Studies* 9, no. 3 (1995): 318-345.

Wozniak, Marian, ed. *Encyklopedia konspiracji wielkopolskiej, 1939-1945*. Poznań: Instytut Zachodni, 1998.

Woźniak, Mieczysław A. "Getta i obozy pracy dla Żydów na terenie kaliskiego w okresie okupacji hitlerowskiej." *Zeszyty Kaliskiego Towarzystwa Przyjaciół Nauk*, no. 2 (1997).

Wróbel, Janusz. "Specyfika polityki niemieckiej w Łodzi w latach 1939-1945." In *Fenomen getta łódzkiego 1940-1944*, ed. Paweł Samuś and Wiesław Puś, 63-76. Łódź: Wydawnictwo Uniwersytetu Łódzkiego, 2006.

Wyrozumski, Jerzy. "Żydzi w Polsce średniowiecznej." In *Żydzi w dawnej Rzeczypospolitej*, 129-135. Wrocław-Warsaw-Kraków: Ossolineum, 1991.

"Wysiedlanie ludności polskiej w tzw. Kraju Warty i na Zamojszczyźnie oraz popełnione przy tym zbrodnie, opracowanie, wybór dokumentów hitlerowskich i ich tłumaczenie na język polski mgra Wacława Szulca." *BGKBZHP* 11 (1970): 7-307.

"Wysiedlanie ludności z ziem polskich wcielonych do Rzeszy." *BGKBZHP* 12, (1960): 25

"Wysiedlanie ludności z ziem polskich wcielonych do Rzeszy. Wybór dokumentów. Oprac. Szymon Datner, Janusz Gumkowski, Kazimierz Leszczyński." *BGKBZHP* 12 (1960): 23-180.

Yahil, Leni. *The Holocaust: The Fate of European Jewry, 1932-1945*. New York: Oxford University Press, 1990.

"Zagłada chorych psychicznie." *BGKBZHP* 3 (1947): 91-106.

Zaremska, Hanna. "Przywileje Kazimierza Wielkiego dla Żydów i ich średniowieczne konfirmacje." In *Małżeństwo z rozsądku? Żydzi w społeczeństwie dawnej Rzeczypospolitej,* ed. Marcina Wodzińskiego and Anny Michałowskiej-Mycielskiej. Wrocław: Wydawn. Uniwersytetu Wrocławskiego, 2007.

Zbrodnie Wehrmachtu w Wielkopolsce w okresie zarządu wojskowego (1 września - 25 października). Kalisz: OKBZHP, 1986.

Zineman, Jacob, ed. *Almanach gmin żydowskich w Polsce*, t. 1. Warsaw, 1939.

Ziółkowska, Anna. *Obozy pracy przymusowej dla Żydów w Wielkopolsce w latach okupacji hitlerowskiej (1941-1943)*. Poznań: Wydawnictwo Poznańskie, 2005.

___. "Obozy pracy przymusowej dla Żydów w Kraju Warty." In *Zagłada Żydów na polskich terenach wcielonych do Rzeszy*, ed. Aleksandra Namysło, 110-115. Warsaw: IPN, 2008.

Żydzi w dawnej Rzeczypospolitej. Wrocław-Warsaw-Kraków: Ossolineum, 1991.

"Żydzi." In *Polacy-Żydzi 1939-1945*, ed. Andrzej Kunert. Warsaw: Rada Ochrony Pamięci Walk i Męczeństwa, 2001.

On-line sources

http://www.kadysz.pl/articles.php?miId=259&lang=pl (stan na 10.07.2009).
http://www.muzeum.com.pl/content/view/28/81/ (14.11.2011)
http://www.zchor.org/kleczew/kleczew.htm

Index

INDEX OF SUBJECTS

A

Administration, 2, 12, 22, 38, 42, 51–56, 58–60, 63, 65–66, 77, 106, 110, 153–164, 173, 182, 187, 197, 224, 238, 258, 268, 271–273, 278, 280, 301, 314, 360, 366, 384
Agriculture, 41, 185, 297
Agudas Isroel (Agudat Israel), 114–116
Agudas Shomrej Umachzikej Shabbos (Association of Sabbath Observers and Guardians), 100
Air and Anti-Gas Defense League (Liga Obrony Powietrznej I Przciwgazowej LOPP), 102
Aliyah Bet, 493
Ambulance, 289, 298, 447
American soldiers, 387
American zone, 387
Antisemitism, 78
Artisan, 41
Association of Jewish Craftsmen, 101, 468
Association of Polish Patriots in the Soviet Union (ZPP), 465
Associations, 65, 74, 94, 155, 212, 418, 420
Auditorium, 396
Authorities, 2, 30–32, 46, 51–52, 57–58, 60, 66–67, 69, 76–77, 92, 99, 103, 105, 107, 110–111, 114, 120–121, 137–139, 142, 148, 151–152, 157–158, 161, 165–167, 170–172, 176–185, 187, 191, 194–195, 197–198, 200, 208, 213, 224–225, 229, 231, 233–234, 238, 243, 250, 264, 266, 267–268, 273, 275, 287, 293, 295, 310, 338, 342, 362, 390–391, 393, 415, 419, 422, 449, 454, 463

B

Bailiff, 77
Baker, 23–25, 27, 35n48, 45, 49, 51, 54, 76, 81–82, 89, 112, 503, 512, 514, 516, 526, 527, 529–530, 533–534, 537, 546–548, 554–555
Baltic Germans, 159, 171, 419, 421–422
Bank, 60, 76, 78, 197–198, 238, 424, 488
Barber, 22, 24, 26, 30, 81–82, 519, 554–555
Baths, 13, 52–53, 58, 77, 106, 128n83, 330, 353, 396
Beit Yaakov, 124
Blacksmith, 23–25, 27, 35n48, 40, 46, 51, 76
Bnei Akiva, 126n37
Board, 53, 59, 63, 80, 94, 101–102, 105–106, 110–113, 115–116, 129n77, 138, 158, 204, 236–237, 240, 267, 313, 322, 333, 494

Bookshop, 77, 82, 84, 89, 492
Brewery, 26, 88
Brown Coal Mine, 384
Budget, 52–54, 77, 105–107, 118–120, 173, 235, 436
Bund, 114–116
Burial, 65, 244, 279, 291–294, 301, 304–305, 456
Business, 40, 45–47, 67, 74, 76, 81–85, 89, 110, 140, 177, 184, 196, 273, 388, 546–549
Butcher, 23–24, 26–27, 34n47, 35n48, 39, 49, 51, 76, 81, 89, 300, 355, 509–510, 513, 516, 526, 530–531, 537–539, 543, 547, 549

C

Cantor, 30, 58, 107
Carpenter, 23, 25, 27, 35n48, 47, 51, 76, 89
Catholic, 22, 26, 30–32, 42, 66, 69, 77, 121, 390–391, 407, 418, 443
Catholic cemetery, 243–244, 391
Central Committee of Jews in Poland (CKŻP), 391
Certificate, 52, 81, 88, 106, 388, 462, 465–467, 488–489, 493, 546–549
Charity, 53, 106–107, 119
Cheder, 52, 64, 109, 121
Cinema, 138, 141, 164, 229, 384, 386, 390, 396
Circumcision, 53, 57
City hall, 40
CKŻP, 391
Clinic, 259, 262, 384
Clockmaker, 89
Cobbler, 45, 47, 50, 90
Commandant, 239, 241, 246, 260, 368–369, 456
Commemorative plaque, 396
Communication, 110, 137, 142, 171, 225, 296, 384, 419, 423
Communist authorities, 391
Concentration camp, 243, 248, 260, 294, 338, 350–351, 368, 385–386, 438
Convert, 69, 117, 140, 158, 197, 209, 231, 259, 332, 438, 494
Cooper, 23, 25, 27, 35n48, 47
Cooperative, 76, 101, 383–384, 465
Cooperative Fund of Jewish Merchants, 101
Council of Elders, 53, 141, 182–183, 199, 202, 433–435, 437

Council, 29, 39, 42, 80, 102, 105–106, 110, 113, 114, 183, 208, 238
Councilor, 102, 156
Coup d'etat, 75
Court, 12, 14, 25–26, 28, 30–31, 46, 63, 66–67, 77, 100, 106, 110, 120, 164, 246, 368–369, 388, 407, 443, 459, 462–467, 488–491
Crafts, 24, 31, 35n48, 39, 41–42, 45–50, 76, 81, 89, 231, 268
Craftsmen, 10, 12, 14, 23–26, 28, 46, 49–50, 76, 81, 84, 88–89, 99, 101, 115–116, 418
Criminality, 139, 391
Cultural Center, 384

D

Dairy, 76, 81, 89, 383, 443
Day of Atonement, 415
Demography, 78–85, 166. *See also* Population
Dentist, 76, 82–83, 90
Deportation, 41, 142, 146, 148–164, 171–175, 179–197, 200–202, 205, 207, 209–213, 224–226, 231–234, 249–251, 257, 266–269, 272–273, 275, 278, 287, 291, 295, 298–299, 324, 326, 341–346, 389, 417–420, 422, 430, 449, 454, 457, 463
Displaced Person, 151, 169, 173, 180, 194, 250, 387, 420
Displaced Persons Camp, 387
District Committee, 391
Doctor, 27, 77, 83, 235, 247, 260, 263, 348–349, 353, 367, 442, 464
DP, 151, 169, 173, 180, 194, 250, 387, 420

E

Economy, 25–26, 42, 48, 76, 85–92, 184–185, 250, 267–268, 272, 384, 468
Education, 74, 99, 106–107, 120–121, 123, 384, 412
Einsatzgruppen, 4, 139, 161, 181–182, 187, 199, 279–281, 287, 291, 358, 360
Einsatzkommando, 162–163, 187, 279
Elections, 55, 77, 80, 102, 105–106, 110–115, 118, 129n77
Enlistment, 69, 145

Euthanasia, 260, 263, 265, 323
Executions, 149, 184, 246, 273–277, 279–282, 284, 286–291, 293–295, 301–302, 304–313, 341, 345–346, 352, 357, 370, 455
Extermination, 3, 161, 164, 180, 186, 194, 199, 213, 249, 257–315, 366–369, 391, 397, 453
Extermination Camp, 3, 186, 194, 321–360, 393

F

Factory, 39, 41, 47, 50, 76, 300, 383, 385, 415, 492
Fair, 26, 103–104
False documents, 389
Farmer, 82, 204–205
Farmer's Self-Help, 383
Fee, 25, 65, 104, 107, 120, 237, 273
Final Solution, 4, 181, 249, 257, 266, 350, 404, 439
Fire, 12, 16, 39–40, 43–44, 76–77, 79, 115, 121, 224, 246–247, 294, 311, 339, 341, 356, 360, 415
Fisherman, 39, 82
Folkist Party (Folkspartei), 115–117
Folkspartei, 115–117
Forced Labor, 137–138, 140–142, 174, 204–205, 224–251, 285–286, 297, 300, 368, 385, 393, 416, 422, 456
Frontier, 45, 388
Fund, 53, 99, 101, 106, 198, 273, 424, 440, 458, 498
Funeral Fraternity, 65

G

Gemilus Chesed, 99
General Zionists, 94, 114
Gentile, 389
Gentry, 41
Glazier, 35n60, 506, 517, 525–526
Goldsmith, 26, 35n60, 49, 515
Grave, 16, 65, 244, 288, 291, 297, 301–302, 311, 327, 343, 388–390, 392, 445–446, 456
Gravestone, 107, 388
Graveyard, 244, 386
Great Depression, 75, 103, 112
Great Fatherland War, 382, 465

Grocery, 125n18, 492
Guild, 25, 28, 31, 35n48, 65–66
Gymnasium, 201, 384
Gypsies, 148, 218n111, 344, 347–348, 350, 358, 422–423, 450, 457

H

Haberdashery, 26, 81, 83, 88–89, 549
Hapoel Hamizrachi, 492
Hashomer Hadati, 94–98, 492
Ha-Shomer ha-Tza'ir Jewish Labor Party, 465
Hashomer Hatzair, 94, 99–100, 127n38, 134, 493
Hasidic movement, 54
Haskala, 55
Hatred, 4, 143, 187–188, 390
Hatter, 529, 531
Hebrew, 29, 57–58, 106, 497n32
Hospital, 40, 64–65, 145, 260, 262, 281, 332, 348–349, 383, 467
Hotel, 77
House of Prayer, 40, 94, 109, 110–111
House of Study, 53

I

Industry, 42, 46–48, 78, 84, 99, 107, 160, 384, 397, 438
Infrastructure, 40, 42, 58–59, 64, 143–164, 225–226, 242, 383–384
Inheritance, 465–466, 488, 490
Inspectorate, 121

J

JDC, 2, 198, 217n78, 404, 424, 426–430, 432–435
Jewish Association of the Social Library and Reading Room, 99
Jewish cemetery, 138–139, 244, 386, 393, 395
Jewish community, 1, 3–4, 15, 19, 28–32, 43, 51–70, 77–78, 80, 105–125, 182–183, 197–213, 238, 268, 272, 295, 299, 345, 397, 435, 449, 454, 498, 550, 554
Jewish council, 183, 202, 208, 415, 433–435
Jewish Free Loan Fund, 101
Jewish Historical Committee, 393
Jewish Record Indexing, 468
Jewish Scouts, 99, 102
Jewish Small Business Association, 101

Joint (JDC), 2, 198, 217n78, 404, 424, 426–430, 432–435
Judenrat, 141, 183, 204–205, 208, 231, 299–300, 325, 415

K

Kehilla, 19, 28–32, 47, 51–55, 58, 60, 63–65, 77, 80–81, 84, 89–91, 94, 99, 102, 105–113, 115–116, 118–122, 140, 203, 231, 407, 498, 529, 552
Kindergarten, 385
KO (District Committee), 391
Komitet Okręgowy(District Committee), 391
Kommando 1005, 280, 314, 358–366
Kommando Lange, 4, 405, 458

L

Labor camp, 226, 228–248, 284, 286, 296–297, 300, 385–386, 393
Laissez passer, 387
Landlords, 41, 167
Landowner, 55, 82
Landrat, 160–161, 198, 278, 285, 418, 424
Lawyer, 466
Lignite, 1, 89
Liquor, 26–27, 407
Loan, 76, 99, 101, 198, 237, 424
Locksmith, 32, 39, 82
Luftwaffe, 136, 172, 422

M

Magistrate, 39–40, 60, 64, 66, 77, 121
Manufacturing, 28, 173, 226, 273, 384, 439
Marriage, 30, 473, 480
Mass extermination, 3, 186, 257–315, 321–359, 393, 397
Mass graves, 245, 249, 258, 262, 276–277, 279, 286, 290–293, 301–302, 304–305, 308, 311–315, 327–328, 352, 358–365, 367, 390, 443–444, 456
Mass murder, 4, 258, 264, 271–274, 281, 286–289, 294–299, 306, 311–314, 322, 324, 332, 341–346, 358, 361, 363, 365, 385, 453
Mayor, 30–31, 60, 63–66, 77, 163, 196, 207, 237, 244, 407, 428–430, 492

Melamed, 29–30, 53
Memorial, 2, 390
Memorial Plaque, 393
Midwife, 77
Mikve, 29, 58, 64, 106, 109, 119, 390
Militia, 143, 145, 161, 171, 178, 187, 189–190, 196, 211, 238, 246, 249, 258, 264, 267, 276, 278, 280, 303–304, 334–336, 342, 347, 351–352, 363, 423, 452
Mill, 40–42, 47, 76, 88, 135, 234, 277, 326, 329, 340, 342, 443
Mizrachi, 92–94, 102, 111–112, 114–117, 127n37, 492
Mohel, 58, 82
Monitor Polski, 490
Municipal Court, 46, 388, 405, 443, 459, 462, 466–467, 488–491
Murder, 4, 31–32, 163, 188–189, 194, 206, 224, 242–243, 245, 248, 258–265, 267, 271–276, 278–281, 284–292, 294, 296, 298–299, 301, 303–306, 311, 313–314, 323–324, 328, 332, 334, 340–342, 345–347, 350–355, 357–358, 391–392, 456, 488, 490
MWRiOP, 105–107, 129n77

N

National Party, 103–104
National Union Camp (Obóz Zjednoczenia Narodowego - OZON), 104
New Zionist Organization (NZO), 126n39
NKVD, 375n125
Notary, 77
Numerus clauses, 74
Numerus nullus, 74

O

Oil Refinery, 76
Orthodox, 55, 90, 92, 99–100, 110–114, 116, 120–121, 143, 189, 237, 492

P

Peasants, 201, 233, 239, 344, 413, 449, 454
People's Cooperative Bank Ltd., 76, 101
Photographer, 81–82, 89, 529
Po'alei Tsiyyon, 111
Po'alei Tsiyyon–ha-Shomer ha-Tza'ir Party, 383, 465

Pogrom, 16, 77–78, 104, 134, 136, 287–288
Polish Army, 101, 136, 141, 366, 464
Polish Military Organization (Polska Organizacja Wojskowa – POW), 104
Polish State Archives, 2, 462, 468
Polish-Soviet Friendship Association, 465
Polish-Soviet Joint Commission for Evacuation Affairs (Repatriation), 465
Population Registry Office, 488–489
Population, 9–10, 12–16, 19, 22, 24–26, 38, 40, 42–45, 48–50, 52, 54, 63, 76, 78, 103, 142, 148–152, 158, 160, 166, 169, 171, 175–176, 178–179, 181–182, 186–187, 192–193, 198–199, 205, 209–211, 217n86, 218n89, 223n218, 226, 228, 231, 233–234, 236, 249–250, 271, 274, 287–288, 295, 304, 308, 322, 337, 341, 344–346, 365–368, 384–385, 391, 397, 404, 415–416, 419, 421, 424, 426–427, 435, 437–438, 440, 449–450, 454, 457, 488, 498, 528
Power station, 76
Presbytery, 40
Prisoners of war, 229, 267, 360, 413, 422
Professional Association of Employees of Cooperatives, 465
Professional Association of Miners, 383, 465
Property, 12–13, 15–16, 22, 24, 39, 58–59, 84–85, 107, 109, 136, 151, 153–154, 160, 165, 189, 192, 195–197, 209, 250, 267, 283, 338, 340, 370, 388, 416, 438, 466–467, 488, 545
Protestant, 42, 77

R

Rabbi, 14, 29–30, 53–58, 60, 63–64, 66, 82, 83, 102, 105–107, 110, 113, 117, 119–120, 129n80, 136, 183, 187, 189–190, 244, 246–247, 298, 342, 344, 390, 396, 492, 512, 530, 538
Real estate, 14, 28, 48, 82, 86, 107, 194, 466, 488, 490, 554–555
Recovered Territories (Ziemie Odzyskane), 462
Red Army, 356, 358, 383
Red Cross, 383
Regierungsbezirk, 143, 161–162, 164–168, 186–191, 197, 199, 228–229, 251, 257–258, 323, 346–347, 366–368, 375n121, 397
Reichsdeutsche, 148, 155, 158, 418
Religious Zionists, 93, 94, 114, 492, 497n29
Republic, 26, 38–39, 74, 76, 85, 99, 105, 107, 366, 407, 533
Revisionist Zionists, 94, 114
Ritual bath, 29, 52–53, 58, 106, 128n83, 396
Ritual slaughterhouse, 52–53
Russian soldiers, 385

S

Saddler, 23, 27, 49, 61, 504, 520, 527, 529, 534
Sales, 22, 29, 384
Samopomoc Chłopska, 383
Sanation, 75
School, 30, 39–40, 42, 52, 54, 58–59, 64, 66, 74, 77–78, 106–107, 109, 121–125, 134–135, 144, 167, 189, 191, 193, 201, 207, 234, 301, 383–384, 386–387, 396, 416, 430, 455, 465
School Inspectorate, 121
Sejm, 80, 498, 533
Senate, 80, 145
Service, 13, 22, 48, 59–60, 63–66, 76, 84, 128n83, 210, 230–231, 233, 235, 246, 250, 263, 360, 366, 384, 438
Sexton, 15, 29, 57, 107
Shammes, 29–30, 57–58
Shkolnik, 15, 29–30, 57–58, 521–524
Shul-klapper, 53, 58
Shyster, 67–68
Smugglers, 45
Soldiers, 11–12, 137, 139, 141–143, 145, 163, 183, 187–188, 190, 196, 210, 261, 275, 288, 303–304, 306, 351, 363, 385–387, 391, 451–452, 456, 458
Soviet occupation zone, 387, 464
SS, 140, 202, 242, 261, 285, 327, 351, 361, 368–369, 453, 456
Stadium, 226, 234, 384, 395
Starosta, 103
Surgeon, 22, 24, 26–27, 30, 77, 90
Synagogue, 2, 14–15, 19, 21–22, 29–32, 40, 42, 52–66, 106–107, 110–111, 117–120,

134–135, 138, 141, 167, 188–189, 193, 197, 202, 205, 209, 232, 324–325, 386, 390, 393, 396, 403, 407–411, 415, 498, 520, 525
Szlojmej Emunej Isroel, 115

T

T4, 259, 262–265, 281, 324, 371
Tailor, 23–28, 35n48, 35n60, 39, 45, 47, 49–51, 62–63, 69, 81–82, 89, 112, 139, 233, 270, 282, 300, 338–339, 439, 445, 495, 529–532, 554–555
Talmud Torah, 109, 120–121
Tanner, 27, 47, 49, 493, 502, 506–508, 511, 513–514, 516, 524–525, 527
Tannery, 40–41, 47, 51, 89
Tax, 12, 15–19, 22–25, 28–30, 46, 53–54, 81, 85–86, 88–89, 107, 121, 196–198, 207, 236, 295, 342, 407, 428–430, 449, 454, 466, 498, 546–549
Teacher, 26, 30, 39, 53, 59, 61, 64, 81, 82, 106, 120–121, 123–124, 125n18, 135, 492, 505, 507, 510, 513, 516–517, 527, 531, 542
Technical School of Wawelberg and Rotwand, 465
Textile, 23, 28, 46–47
Theater, 197, 396
Tinsmith, 49, 81–82, 89, 112, 526, 530, 535, 537–538, 555
Tobacco, 78, 81, 83, 88–89, 546–549
Tombstone, 358, 388, 390
Torah ve-Avoda, 94, 126n37
Town Council Presidium, 466–467
Trade, 1, 14, 22–23, 25–28, 30, 35n48, 45–46, 48, 50, 63, 67–68, 76, 81, 83–84, 88–90, 99, 104, 107, 195, 204, 384, 387, 407
Traditionalist, 93, 113
Training commune (kibbutz), 95
Truck, 135, 140, 159–160, 206, 233–234, 238, 240–241, 245, 248, 260, 262, 274–275, 282–284, 288–292, 296–298, 301, 305–312, 325–326, 329, 331, 344, 353, 362, 364, 445–447, 449, 451, 454–456
tzadikim, 63
Tze'irei Mizrachi, 93
Tzeirei Mizrachi, 492

U

Urbanization, 10, 41, 46, 384

V

Valuables, 192, 196–197, 204, 275, 279–280, 283–284, 327, 337–338, 341, 348, 354, 445, 455–456
Vodka, 387, 407
Voivode, 105
Volksdeutsche, 142,1 48–153, 155, 158, 160, 174, 177, 194, 196, 235, 238, 241, 280, 335, 418, 423, 458
Volksliste, 148, 335, 372n15
Volkssturm, 385
Voter, 80, 498, 533

W

Waffen SS, 187
Weaver, 35n48, 47, 82
Wedding, 53, 57, 100, 106–107, 340
Wehrmacht, 136, 141, 152, 164, 172, 186, 188, 210–211, 231, 262, 271, 359, 422
Wheelwright, 23, 27, 35n48, 39, 47, 76
Windmill, 39, 76, 135
Wohnungsamt, 388
Workers, 41, 47–48, 51, 62, 88, 92,99, 155, 225, 228, 230–233, 235–239, 241–245, 250, 273–274, 276, 278, 284, 296, 313, 327, 331–332, 338–340, 355–356, 364, 367, 405, 414–415, 421–422, 441, 464
Working Palestine Support League, 114
Workshops, 41, 46–47, 50–51, 76, 89, 155, 167, 177, 196–197, 270, 333

Y

Yiddish, 57–58, 69, 98, 389, 391
Yom Kippur, 53
Youth movement, 93–94, 126n37–38, 134, 345, 493

Z

Zionism, 55, 92, 94, 102, 114–116, 126n39, 492
Zionist Organization, 94, 117, 126n39

INDEX OF NAMES[1]

A

Aaronson, Yehoshua Moshe (Rabbi), 244, 246–247
Abram (the butcher), 23, 35n60
Adler, Alje, 92, 550
Adler, Eliasz, 89, 545
Albert, Karl Wilhelm, 161
Alberti, Michael, 215n47, 216n63, 219n122, 220n146, 285, 315n2–3, 318n68
Aleksandrowicz, Aron, 27
Aleksandrowicz, Boruch, 22
Aleksandrowicz, Chersz, 22
Aleksandrowicz, Jakub, 30
Alexanderka, 23
Amsterdam, Cwi Hirsz (rabbi in Konin), 57
Aranowicz, Marek, 20, 23
Arendt, Hugo, 246
Auerbach, Fałek (rabbi of the Kleczew synagogue district), 57
Auerbach, Shlomo, 57

B

Bach-Zelewski, Erich von dem, 150
Bagno, Abraham (Abram), 540, 554, 556
Bagno, Chaim, 84, 89, 92, 546, 554
Bagno, Chaim L., 81, 492, 529, 550, 552
Bagno, Efrayim, 84
Bagno, Ester, 534, 556
Bagno, Frymet, 84
Bagno, Mate (née Grinblat), 84, 556
Bagno, Moshe, 93, 95–97, 492
Bagno, Nachum Israel, 84–86, 92–93, 102, 112,492 529, 540, 552, 554, 556
Bagno, Nachum Israel Ha'Levi
Bagno, Nuchem, 85, 92, 101, 111, 546, 550
Bagno, Ptachya, 84
Bagno, Rivka, 84
Bagno, Shmuel Yosef, 84, 556
Bakalarz, 23
Bakalarz, Jakub, 23
Bałecki, Aleksander, 23
Bamberg, Lejb, 58
Bartel, Samuel, 46
Bartnicki, Józef, 190

---

[1] The names in the index are limited to those appearing in the text and excluding the names in the tables and annexes.

Bartussek, Rudolf, 260
Bauman, Abraham, 55, 63
Bauman, Layzer, 48
Baunvater, Mikolaj, 13
Becker (commander of the Order Police), 150
Bednarz, Władysław, 368
Bednarz, Wojciech, 25
Bennett, Jim (Israel), 495
Ber, Hajm, 60–61
Berendt, 556
Berendt, C., 55–56
Berendt, Hersz, 88–89, 92, 529, 534, 539, 545–546, 554
Berendt, Lea, 96
Berendt, Mendel, 89
Berendt (Berendtowa), Rywka, 85, 89, 91, 546
Berger, August, 47
Berk, Jastrząb, 112
Bernd, Hersz, 102
Beutel, Lothar, 162
Biebow, Hans, 338
Bierut, Bolesław, 368
Bile, Jakub, 47
Birnbaum, Hajm, 64
Bischoff, Helmut, 162, 264
Blobel, Paul, 359–361
Boas, Josef, 102, 111, 546, 550
Boas, Szuml, 46
Boes, Jakub, 67, 521
Bogucka, Maria, 11
Boile, Jozef, 48
Boile, Salomon, 48
Bok, 23
Bolesław the Pious, 13–14
Bończa-Tomaszewski, Nikodem, xxi
Borensztejn (director of the Joint in Warsaw), 208
Boruch (the barber-surgeon), 21–22, 30, 35n60
Borzewicki, 13
Bossak, Maks, 55–56
Bothmann, Hans, 326, 330, 335, 338–339, 356, 360, 369, 438, 458
Bradfisch, Otto, 338, 361
Braun, Gotfryd, 47
Brener, Leon, 138
Brisch, M., 55

Bruksztajn, Majer M., 113
Bryskier, Henryk (Władysław Janowski), 194
Brysz, Henoch, 87, 120
Brysz, Luzer, 89, 101, 111–112, 529, 540, 554
Brysz, Mojsze (Mojsie), 112, 121, 529–540, 552, 554
Brysz, Yeshaya, 234
Bühler, Joseph, 212
Burckhardt, Hans, 161, 268
Burmeister, Walter, 264–265
Bursting (SS-Man), 335
Byk, Hemic, 66
Byk, Sara, 66

C

Casimir III the Great, 13–14
Casimir IV Jagiellon, 13–14
Cerulik, Boruch, 23, 50
Cerulik, Jakub, 23, 31
Cerulik, Marek, 23
Chaba (Haba), Josek, 90
Chaba Icek, 112
Chaba Josef Eliasz, 113–114, 534
Chersz (a furrier), 23
Chmielnicki, Bohdan, 10
Chojnacki, Chaim (Chune), 112, 534, 554
Cieśla, Piotr, 15
Cieśla, Regina, 15
Ciurzyński, 279
Conway, David, xxi, 497
Cukier, Efraim, 69
Cyns, Eugenia, 386, 388
Cyrulik, Masiek, 21, 30
Czarniecki, Jan, 16
Czernicki, Boruch, 50

D

Dąbrowska, Danuta, 366
Damzog, Ernst, 162, 263
Dan, Edna, 100, 493
Dawidziak, Usier, 23
Derengowski, Marceli, 58
Diane Plotkin, xx
Dobosiewicz, Walenty, 22, 31
Druenfeld, Dawid, 89
Dybała, Anna, xxi
Dyndol, Icek, 79, 89, 113, 525, 554

Dyner, Szymon, 79
Dzieci, Idel, 86, 90–91, 112, 529, 534, 545–546, 550, 552, 554
Dzikowski, Jakub, 31

E
Effaimowicz, Jek, 31
Eichmann, Adolf, 156, 169–170, 249, 264, 266, 269, 359–360, 404, 439
Eliasz, Anszel Hersz, 50, 501
Ettinger, Abram, 89, 91, 554
Ettinger Abram Icek, 111, 529, 534, 552
Etyngiel (Ettinger), Lejzer (Lejzor), 92, 111, 554

F
Fajeńczyski Mojsie, 113
Falc Hersz, 141
Fibich, Arnold Gustaw, 69
Figiel, Icek, 83
Figiel, Szmaja, 83
Fischer, Hans, 162
Flesch, Gerhard, 163
Fogel, Chaim, 86, 113, 539, 545, 552, 554, 556
Fogel, J., 101
Fogel, Szmaja, 86, 89, 554
Fogiel, Hanno, 47
Fogiel, M.H., 88
Fraiemowicz, Mosiek, 23
Frank, Hans, 153, 178–180, 212–213, 269–270
Frenkel, H., 198, 424, 427–429, 489-490
Fridenson, Szmul Mojsie, 121
Friedenson, Mojsie, 83
Friedlender-Cyns, Eugenia, 125n19, 220n139, 398n12
Fuchs, Günther, 314, 361
Fuga, Maciej, 31

G
Gabčik, Joseph, 350
Garbarz, Szmul, 47–48, 55–56, 60–61, 66
Gębicki, Abram, 85–86
Gębicki, Abram Jakub, 89
Gębicki, Chaim, 89
Gębicki, Mojsie, 89

Geffon, Linda, xxi, 497n37
Gembicki, Bert, 134, 139–140, 201, 203–204, 233, 239–241, 296–297, 385, 387
Gembicki, Jakub, 48
Gembicki, Zelig, 102, 529
Gembrocki, Majer Aron, 113
Gerszen, F., 88
Gerszon, Lejb, 102
Gielow, Hermann, 368
Gierszberg, Izaak, 55–56, 58
Gierszczen, Wolf, 32
Gilf (SS-Man), 327
Gilow (SS-Man), 335
Glauba, Lejbuś, 79
Gleiman, Michał, 46
Głowacka-Penczyńska, Anetta, xix, 468
Gluba, Nuchem, 79
Glucker, (Glazgow) Isaak (Ike), 124n5, 380, 472, 479–480
Glucker, (née Rachwalski) Thresa (Trane), 380, 472, 479
Golan, Nechama, xx
Goldbaum, B., 55–56, 525
Goldberg (owner of the flour mill), 342
Goldenberg, Chaim, 121
Goldenberg, Emanuel, 83, 428, 431, 540
Goldenberg, Eugenia, 83, 540
Goldman, Josef (Jozef), 506, 522
Golemowski, Lukasz, 25
Göring Hermann, 145, 186
Gośliński, Abraham, 23
Gośliński, Jachym, 23
Grabowski, Aleksander, 246
Grainger, Elizabeth, xxi, 497n34
Graydyc, Szainya Liba, 65
Graydycz, Józef, 65
Graydycz, Margie, 65
Greenfeld, Hannah, 382, 468, 486
Greenfeld, Yehuda, 486
Greenwood, Naftali, xx
Greinfeld, Szlama, 47
Greiser, Arthur, 144–148, 160, 175–180, 212, 218n97, 225–226, 258, 260, 263, 266, 269–271, 273, 316n32-33, 337–338, 351, 369–370, 404–405, 423, 438, 458
Grembart, Eiki, 69
Grembart, Szmul, 69
Grienfield, (née Traube) Hanna, 382

Grimm (Brothers – Jacob and Wilhelm), 348
Grinfeld, Hajman, 60
Gruchalski, Walenty, 31
Gruenfeld, Efraim Josef, 60
Grünblatt, Eliasz, 79, 90, 550
Grynfeld, Dawid Lipman, 65
Grynfeld, Hajm, 55–56
Grynszpans, 134
Guldon, Zenon, 1
Günther, Rolf, 156
Gurowski, Melchior, 13
Gurowska, Anna (of the Radomicki family), 39
Gurowski, Mikołaj, 39
Gurowski, Władysław, 26, 31, 403, 407

H

Haase (SS-man), 355–356
Habe, Josek, 102
Häfele (Heffele), Alois (SS-Man), 335, 369
Hammer, Walter, 162
Hartung, Karol, 46
Hausbrandt (functionary in Czerków), 243, 246
Haym, Kacper, 32
Heber, Mojsze, 113
Heber, Szaja, 88–89, 529,546, 555
Hecht, G., 158
Heine, Heinrich, 191
Herman, Leopold, 79
Hern, Jakob, 499
Hersz, M., 55–56
Heydrich, Reinhard, 156, 170, 172–174, 181–185, 199, 212, 218n109, 218n112, 258, 350, 360, 404, 421–423
Hildebrandt, 149–150
Himmler, Heinrich, 146, 149, 151–152, 156, 158–159, 177, 186, 212, 250, 258, 260, 263, 266, 270, 273, 283, 337–338, 358, 372n43, 373n71, 405, 458
Hirszberg, Izaak, 85–86, 91, 546
Hitler, Adolf, 133, 145, 149, 186, 188, 237, 258, 260, 263, 266, 350, 458
Hojan, Arthur, 259
Holibaba, 23
Holtzman (Holzman, née Krzywanowski) Lotka (Lea), 100
Holtzman, Ada, xx, 100

Holzmann, Lea (Lotka) (née Krzywanoska), xx
Höppner, Rolf-Heinz, 162, 264–273, 316n19, 316n28, 316n34, 317n40, 404, 439
Horensztajn, Rywen, 83
Horensztejn, Aleksander, 90, 120
Horev (née Traube), Fruma (Frymet), 123–124, 382, 487
Horev, Boaz, xxv, 476
Horev, Ehud, xxv
Horev, Einav, xxv
Horev, Mazal, xxv
Horev, Tuvia, xix–xx, 487
Horev, Ze'ev, xxv, 486–487
Horowitz, Gedalie, 58
Huberman, Azriel, 90
Huberman, Nachman, 113, 530, 533, 555

I

Israel, Bruno, 327–328, 331, 333, 335, 368, 372n15
Iwańczyk, Adam, 83, 90, 109, 552, 555
Iwańczyk, Eli, 109, 550
Iwańczyk, Layzer, 50, 508

J

Jachman of Kleczew (merchant), 32
Jacobs, Ginger, 389
Jacobs, Mike, 389
Jakubowicz, Hersz, 90, 555
Jakubowicz, Hersz Lejb, 112, 530, 540
Jakubowicz, Jankel lter, 112
Jakubowicz, Majer, 112, 555
Jakubowski, Majer, 89
Jan of Kleczew, 13
Jankowska, Renata, xxi
Jarecki, 66, 521
Jarecki, Hersz, 46, 60–61, 508
Jarocki, Elkowi, 64
Jastrząb, Berek, 87, 112, 126n22, 542, 545, 555
Jędrecki, Stanislaus, 245
Jedwab, Leon, 234
Jelenkiewicz (the widow), 48, 524
Jelenkiewicz, Fraiem, 23
Jelenkiewicz, Jakub, 20, 28, 30, 32
Jelenkiewicz, Lewek, 23, 47, 67–68
Jelenkiewicz, Mosiek, 48, 523

Jelenkiewicz, Szmul, 50, 508
Jelenkowicz, Maciej, 47
Jelonkiewicz, Abram, 55–56
Jelonkiewicz, Icyk Jakub, 48, 55–56
Jelonkiewicz, Lipman, 47, 55–56, 508
Jelonkowicz, Abram Jakub, 47
Jelonkowicz, Efraim Szlama, 47
Jeżowa, 23
Jick, 15
Joachimkiewicz, Majer, 89, 112, 530, 555
Jojne, Fajwisz, 113
Jóźwiak (a tailor), 23, 35n60

K

Kalina, Abram, 47
Kalmanowicz, Hersz, 50, 61, 511
Kałme (the butcher), 23
Kamiński, Aleksander, 295, 318n90, 344, 405, 460n24
Kamiński, J., 190
Kamlarz, Fajwisz, 247
Kamlazh (prisoner in Czarków), 247
Kantarowski, Józef, 244
Katzberg, Otto, 190
Kaufman, Rabbi Szlam Hersz, 83, 110, 120, 530
Kaufmann, Rabbi P., 55-56
Kav, Sarah (Sarit), xx, xxii
Kawski, Tomasz, xix, 358, 364, 394
Kazimierski, Chemje, 90
Kazimierski, Josef (Joshua), 200, 203, 232
Kaźmierczak, Efraim, 83
Kempel, Bogumił, 47
Kendzi, Ernst, 235
Kenigsberg, Chanele, 343
Kessler (chef of the Labor Office in Zagórów), 232
Kiwała, Lejb, 112, 530, 555
Kiwała, Majer, 86, 89, 91, 489, 545, 547, 550
Klamrowski, Ber (Baer, Beer), 86, 89, 530, 545, 550, 552, 555
Klamrowski, Hersz, 87, 89, 530, 545, 555
Kleczewski, Pinkus, 112, 540, 547
Klein, Peter, 316n20, 358
Kleinot (prisoner in Czarków), 247
Klejnot, Gecel, 247
Klepacz, Icek, 101, 112, 530, 541, 555
Klepacz, Jukew, 89, 530, 545

Kluczewski, Abram, 47
Kluczkowski, Lewek, 47
Klug, Jan, 39
Knofe, Oscar, 162
Knopf, Hans, 247
Kołacz, Grzegorz, xx, xxii
Koniarek, Lajbuś, 89
Konrad, Karol, 46
Kopczyński, Michał, 31
Koppe, Wilhelm, 149–150, 152–153, 162, 177, 260, 263, 265, 269, 403, 417, 419
Korherr, Eduard, 358
Korn, Fiszel (Fiszer/Fszel), 88, 89, 511, 551–552, 555
Korzew, Icek, 113
Koszerowa, Maryanna, 69, 494
Koszyczek, Lukasz, 25
Kotek, Jakub (Jakob), 60, 66, 512
Kotlarz, Izrael, 20, 23
Kowalski, Josi (Józef), 297
Koza, Simche (Simce/Symche/Symcha), 88, 89, 113, 530, 547
Kozłowski, S., 59
Koźmiński, Marek, 23
Kramarz, Mateusz, 26
Kramer, Hans, 163
Krawiec, Eliasz, 21, 23
Kretowski, Franciszek, 13
Kretschmer, Erich, 329, 335, 337
Kroner, Chaskiel, 83, 90, 99, 102, 111, 405, 459, 464, 555
Kroner, H. Dr., 90
Kroner, Icek, 86, 89, 91, 112, 463, 535, 545, 551–552, 555
Kroner, Jakob, xxii, 382, 383, 462–463, 465–467
Kroner, Lejb (Lajb), 87, 89, 112, 463, 535, 547, 551–552
Kroner, Yitzhak, xx, xxii
Krotoszyński, Lewek Chaim, 47, 522
Krotoszyński, Lewek Jozef, 47
Krotoszyński, Lewin, 47, 50, 55–56, 509
Krotoszyński, Szmul, 47, 61, 511, 524
Krotowski, Abram, 89, 547
Krotowski, Fałek, 89, 530, 555
Krotowski, Michał, 50, 510
Krüger, Friedrich-Wilhelm, 149–150, 168, 172, 217n86, 404, 419, 421–423

Kryger, Jakób (Jakub), 63, 64
Krygier, Peisach (Pejsach/Pejcacz), 47, 524
Krzywanowski (*née* Herszlik), Hana, 100
Krzywanowski, Berta, 100
Krzywanowski, Franja, 100
Krzywanowski, Jakob, 100
Krzywanowski, Machel, 100
Krzywanowski, Mojsie, 85, 89, 91, 555
Krzywanowski, Rosa (Ruzka), 100
Krzyżanowski, 110
Krzyżanowski, M., 530, 537, 552
Kubis, Jan, 350
Kuczyński, Abram, 86, 92, 101–102, 112, 530, 544, 551, 553, 555
Kuczynski, Berek, 368
Kühn, Walter, 161
Kupferman, Szlama Hersz, 83
Kuśnierka (a widow), 23
Kuśnierz, Salma, 23
Kutnowski, 368
Kutnowski, LejzoR (Luzer), 79, 87, 112, 530, 551, 555

L

Laaps, Gustav, 335, 337
Łabuszyński, Josek (Josef/Jozef), 86, 89, 91, 545, 547
Lachman, Hersz, 48
Lachman, Salomon, 20, 23
Lachmańczyk, Jachym, 23
Łachmanowicz, Lachman, 30
Łącki, Władysław, 13
Lamprecht, Gotlib, 60
Landau, Abram, 135, 139, 202, 205–206, 240, 296
Lange (SS-Man), 258–266, 271, 285, 323, 328, 335, 405, 458
Lange, Herbert, 259–260, 263, 323, 335, 369
Lasch, Karl, 283
Łatta (Łatte), Jakub Szmul (Szmul Jakub/Jukew), 112, 530, 550
Layzerowicz, Chersz, 23, 30
Layzerowicz, Michał, 21, 23, 30
Łazarek, 16
Leber, 335
Lebovitcz, Sarah, 96
Leibovitcz, Pnina, 96

Lenz, Wilhelm (SS-Man), 335, 337, 355–356
Lepek (Łepek), Charles, 238, 240–242, 297–298
Łepek, Majer, 101, 541, 554
Leśkiewicz, Rafał, xx, 524, 526
Leszczyńska, Maskowa, 23
Leszczynski, Chersz Salomon
Leszczyński, Icek, 89
Leszczyński, Litman, 23, 28
Leszczyński, Mosiek, 20, 23
Leszczyński, Salomon, 23, 30, 32
Leszczyński Sz., 199, 424
Leszczyński, Szyje (Szaje), 102, 544, 555
Leszczyński, Załme, 101, 112, 530, 539, 555
Lewandowski, 18, 335
Lewek, Efram, 27
Lewi, Itta (Itte), 87, 90, 547, 550, 555
Lewi, Lejb, 99, 555
Lewkowicz, Efraim, 27
Lewkowicz, Icek, 113, 530, 542, 553–554
Lewkowicz, Mojsze, 89, 112, 530, 545, 550, 553–554
Leymusiak, Lewek, 23
Leymusiewicz, Lewek, 28, 36n69
Lindo, Annie Elizabeth, xxi
Liphardt, Fritz, 162
Lipski, Tobiasz, 60, 513
Lipszyc, Hersz, 60, 66, 512, 521, 526
Lipszyc, Józef, 102
Lipszyc, S., 55–56
Lipszyc, Sender, 85–86, 91, 550, 553
Lipszyc, Szlama (Szlama Josek), 88–89, 91, 110, 553
Lisner, Jozef, 48, 512,
Liszkowski, Mateusz, 30-31
Litmann, Yehudit, 96
Litner Jozef (Józef), 60
Livushinska, Shoshanna, 96
Lubiszewski (of Giewartów) Tadeusz, 36n86
Lukas, Paweł, 16
Luther, Martin, 359

M

Malarek, Hieronim, 140
Malarek, Icek, 21, 23

Malarek, Icek Lejzor, 111, 552
Malarek, Izydor, 85–86, 91
Malarek, Maurycy, 58
Malarek, Moryc, 83, 85, 125n22, 552, 554
Malarek, Mosiek, 55, 60, 63, 514
Malarkowski, 23
Malron (Malarek), Tzvi, 202, 298–299, 385
Mansard, Salomon, 48
Markiewicz, Mosiek, 23
Markowski, Chaim, 101–102, 111–112, 530, 535
Marks (Rachwalski), Tobiasz, xx, 468
Marks family, 379–380, 468, 485–486
Marks, Richard, xx
Martynbaum, Szalma, 83
Masiek, Abram, 48
Maśkowicz (Jewish barber-surgeon), 22
Mazur, Berend (Bernd/Berendt), 55–56, 61, 67, 513, 520
Mazur, Stary, 23
Mazur, Wowa, 66
Mędykowski, Witold, xix
Meisinger, Josef, 162
Menclin, 13
Mendelsohn, Ezra, xx–xxi
Mendelson, Shirley Ann, xxi
Metlewski, Michal, 32
Michalski, Szlama, 247
Michelski, Shlomo, 247–248
Mikołaj (of Kleczew), 13
Milsztajn, 343
Minc, Mosze Ben Izaak, 14
Minicki, Pawel, 32
Miszczak, Andrzej, 338, 354
Molendski, Grzegorz, 22
Molotov, Vyacheslav, 359
Morton, Alfred Mayer, 380
Morton, Helen, 380
Mosiek,Izrael, 48
Mottel, Shmulek, 247
Müller, Heinrich, 225, 359

N

Najdorf, Abraham, 247
Napoleon, 38
Naumann, Erich, 259
Nayfeld, Joel, 50, 514
Nejman, Mojsie (Mojsze), 89, 541, 550, 554

Nejman, Ryfka, 64
Nelken, Ajzyk, 88, 191, 388
Nelkien, Szmul, 56
Neuman, Julian, 88
Neumann (doctor), 42
Norwalk, Jay, xxi, 496
Noss, Dawid, 89, 530, 550, 552, 554
Nusenowicz (prisoner in Czarków), 247
Nusynowicz, Salomon, 247

O

Obarzanek, 368
Okladek, Madeleine, xxi, 468
Olejnik, Zdzisław Kazimierz, 312
Oleynik, Iung, 23
Opioła, Monika, 1, 5n5, 71n33, 108, 528
Orchowski, Walenty, 282, 443
Otto, Wächter, 170, 193
Oyrzyński, Andrzej, 31

P

Pacanocski, (née Rachwalski) Rachel, 381
Pacanovski (Pacanowski), Hela, 381
Pacanowski, 138, 381, 396, 554, 559
Pacanowski, Ber, 112
Pachciarki, 368
Palten, Günther, 161
Parzyński, Haskiel (Haskel), 58, 515
Patałowska, Chaja, 89
Patałowski, Abram, 113, 467, 531, 535, 554
Peham, Rosalie, 336–337
Perlmuter, Abraham Tzvi, 57
Pessa, Rachwalski, 101, 554
Philip (prisoner in Czarków labor camp), 246–247
Pickel, William, 161
Piekarski (landowners), 140
Piekarski, Leopold, 90, 117, 140, 550, 552
Pietrkowski, Majer, 56, 523
Piller, Walter, 368
Piller, Willi, 335–336
Piłsudski, Józef, 75
Pinkus, Jakub, 87, 113, 554
Piotrowski, Jakub, 86, 89, 91
Piszczyk, 23
Platte, Otto, 335
Pomianowski, Bartłomiej, 22

Poradziński, Balcer, 31
Pregler, Zyskind, 85, 86, 89, 91, 531, 548, 550, 552
Prost, Chil (Ch. J./Ichel), 55–56, 86, 102, 110
Prost, Lemel, 87, 111–113
Prost, Michel, 133, 135, 201, 232, 238–240
Przedecki, Mordka, 113, 447, 535, 554
Przyjemski, Krzysztof, 13
Przysucher, J. Sz., 120
Psipsie, Chaim, 89, 91, 550
Psipsie, Ruchla, 89, 554
Psipsie, Symche J., 113, 541
Psiupsin, 23
Pupiek, Jakub (a.k.a. Chaskiel), 31

R

Rachwalczyk, Salamon, 32
Rachwalski, xix–xxi, xxv, 79, 86, 125n5, 379, 468–487
Rachwalski, Abraham Moses (Alfred), 480, 484
Rachwalski, Chaim, 93, 381, 481, 559
Rachwalski, Fojgel, 101, 381–382
Rachwalski, Frymet, 93, 96, 381, 481, 559
Rachwalski, Majer, 90-91, 480
Rachwalski, Rafał, 69
Rachwalski, Sarah (Sara), 381–382, 559
Rachwalski, Shlomo, 98, 381, 559
Rachwalski, Sura, 91
Rachwalski, Tuvia (Tobiasz / Tobjasz), xxiv, 79, 86, 90–92, 112, 381, 481, 484–485, 531, 541, 545, 550, 552, 554, 559
Rączkowski, Moszek, 55–56, 61, 523, 527
Radziejewski, Szmul, 64
Rakowski, Izydor, 88, 91, 550
Rakowski, Jechel, 102, 111
Rakowski, Majer, 86, 89, 91, 102, 550, 552
Rath, Ernst vom, 134
Ratke (Dr.), 263
Rattner, Kenneth L., xxi
Rediess (Redieß), Friedrich Wilhelm Otto, 149–150
Reich, Dora, 90, 554
Reich, Moniek, 339
Reich, Moryc, 102, 541, 548
Reichman, Sarah, 96
Ribbentrop, Joachim von, 74

Richmond, Theo, 389
Richter (SS-Man), 327
Rogozińska, Majer Szlama, 48
Rogoziński, Izrael, 86, 89, 91, 531, 537
Rubin, Sender, 85, 86, 92, 111, 531, 548
Runge, Johann, 329, 334–335, 337
Rusocka, Jadwiga, 13
Rusocki, 13
Russ, Gerszon, 87, 101–102, 111
Rybczyński, Piotr, 284–385
Ryczywolski, Mosiek, 47
Rygiel, Majer, 89, 91, 531, 538, 555, 559
Rygiel, Salomon, 89, 91, 112, 531, 536, 548, 550, 555

S

Sakashawska, Tova, 96
Salmanowicz, Abram, 47
Salomonowicz, Efraim, 47
Salomonowicz, Layzer, 28
Samson, Lajb Jude, 111, 531, 543, 545, 548, 555
Samsonowicz, H., 11
Sauckel, Fritz, 228
Schefe, Robert, 163
Schimmel, Hans Kurt, 161
Schönemann, 245
Schumper, Józef, 59
Ściński, Kazimierz, 31, 36n69
Segał, Dawid, 55–56, 87, 90, 101, 112–113, 531, 536, 545, 548, 552, 555
Segał, Hersz, 102–103, 198, 424, 427–429, 531, 536, 555
Segał, Ichiel, 87, 89
Seher (guard in Czarków), 246
Seif (prisoner in Czarków), 247
Sękiewicz, Mieczysław, 277, 281–283, 286–288, 290–291, 294, 317–318, 443
Sender, Sura, 90, 555
Seyss-Inquart, Arthur, 159, 421, 423
Shilo, Naama, xxi
Sieradz, Chaim, 234
Silberklang, David, xx
Skowron, Szraga, 88
Śliwiński, Antoni, 365
Smaklerz, Mosiek, 20, 22
Śmigły-Rydz, Edward, 237
Smulewicz, David, 64

Sochaczewska, Łaja, 87, 89, 536
Sokołowski, Julian, 46
Spale, Jakub, 113
Spławski, 13
Srebrnik, Szymon, 355, 369
Stankowski, Albert, xx, xxii
Stoike, 245
Streckenbach, Bruno, 150–151, 179
Strzeliński, Rafał, 102, 112, 536
Suproniuk, Jarosław, xx
Światowa (merchant's wife), 23
Światowicz, Kaufman, 84, 90, 531, 536, 555
Szaehsznajder, Gedalie, 83
Szafarz, Szymon, 48
Szaye, Pachciarski, 387
Szczepaniak, Stanisław, 246
Szejsznajder, Gedalie, 120
Szkolnik (a tailor), 23
Szkolnik, Jakub Sure, 66–68
Szkolnik, Mejer Szlama, 55–56
Szkolnik, Moszek, 67–68
Szkolnik, Wolf (Wołek) Szlama, 47, 55, 63, 66, 67, 68
Szkolny, Fryderyk, 46
Szlamek (prisoner in Chelmno), 298
Szmuchlerz, Musiek, 23
Sztachelberg, Jakub, 94
Sztyler, Frymet, 380, 469, 471–473
Szulman, Jacob (Rabbi of Grabów), 298, 342
Szyke, Chaskiel, 101
Szymczak, Kazimierz, 301–302, 305, 308, 311, 314

T
Tabaczinski, 247
Tabacznik, Abraham, 247
Taczanowski (nobleman and landowner), 139
Taraszuwski, W., 62
Teitelbaum, Mordechai, 191
Thenne, Arthur, 142
Traube (née Rachwalski), Fojgel (Tzipora), 381
Traube (née Rachwalski), Fojgle, 381–382, 538
Traube, Fruma (Frymet), 123–125, 381–382

Traube, Hanna (Hannah), 381, 486
Traube, Izaak, 102, 381–382, 468, 486
Tylżanowski, Kazimierz, 282, 443

U
Übelhör, Friedrich, 146, 161, 273, 440
Ulatowski, 31
Urbach, 87–89, 113–114, 53, 536, 539, 543, 552, 555
Urbach, Icek Jojne, 113, 531, 536
Urbach, Jojne, 89, 555

V
Valčík, Josef, 350

W
Waingot, (Weingot) Sucher Mendel, 110
Wajngart, Majer Ichel, 89, 545
Wajngart, Mordka, 89
Wajngot, Sucher, 85
Warbrum, Szymon, 91
Warmbrum, Wigdor, 101, 541
Waserman, Perec, 87, 89, 102, 531, 551–552, 555
Wasser, Hersh, 295, 344, 405, 449
Wasserman, D., 85
Waszak, S., 366
Watman (née Krzywanowski) Towa, 100, 560
Watman, I., 120
Watman, Schmuel, 560
Weibrecht, Hans, 260
Weingart, S. M., 55–56, 551
Weingarten, Moszek, 89
Weingot, Sucher Mendel, 110
Weisweller, Sucher, 88
Weliczker, Leon, 360
Wetzel, Dr. E., 158
Weygandt, Herbert, 163
Widawski, Abram, 83, 531, 549
Widawski, Szyja (Szyje), 83, 86, 90, 91, 532, 543, 545, 549, 551–552, 555
Wiener, Szlojme (Jakob Grojnowski vel Grojanowski), 194
Wijaczka, Jacek, 1, 17
Wilczyński, Abram, 86, 89, 91, 543, 545, 551, 555

Witkowski, Boruch, 55–56, 519
Witkowski, Icek Lejb, 89, 538
Witkowski, Jojne, 89, 111, 532, 539, 551, 553, 555
Witkowski, Zołkind (Załkin), 90, 532, 545
Włydelski, Hemie, 67
Włydelski, Sarne, 67
Woian, Michał, 46
Wojner, Samuel, 46
Wolf (functionary in Czarków), 246
Wołkowicz Moszkowa, Ryfka, 64
Wollmann-Goranin, H., 55–56
Wolman, 207, 429
Wolman, Hersz, 93, 103, 110, 549
Wolman, Jakub, 83, 90, 102, 111, 207–208, 430, 432
Wolstein, Abram, 112, 532, 551, 555
Woltmann, H., 55–56
Woyrsch, Udo von, 176
Woźnicki, Antoni, 31
Wrenson, Wolf, 55–56

Y
Yakobowitz, Yehudit, 97

Z
Zabelik, 16
Zajączek, Józef (General), 52
Zajft, Abraham, 247
Zakrzewska (*née* Sokaszewska), Hannah, 389, 391–392
Zalas, Lucjan, 305, 362, 451
Zalas, Piotr, 305, 307, 312–313
Zawłodawer, Hersz, 102, 114, 120, 538
Zawłodawer, Rojzla, 121, 538
Zielenkiewicz, Chersz, 23
Zielenkiewicz, Jakub, 23
Zielenkiewicz, Maciej, 32
Zielonka, Fiszel, 247
Ziółkowska, Anna, xxi, 242, 247
Złotogórski, Symche, 121, 532, 542
Żołnierkiewicz, Bronisław, 238
Żurawski, Mieczysław, 355–356

INDEX OF PLACES

11 Listopada Square (Plac), Kleczew, 81

A
Aleja Marantowska (Marantowska Avenue), 306
Andrzejów, 240, 243
Ansbach, 388
Auschwitz, 194, 352
Auschwitz-Birkenau, 242, 248, 324, 352
Austria, 176, 185, 347–348, 423, 467

B
Babi Yar, 360
Babiak, 108, 346, 528A
Baltic countries, 150, 153, 158, 171, 185, 418
Bartów, 96
Bełżec, 194, 258, 292, 324, 357, 360
Berlin, 148–149, 156–158, 168–169, 171, 174, 180–181, 211, 225, 228, 243, 250, 259, 265, 332–334, 351–352, 355, 369, 421, 439
Bessarabia, 178, 267
Birkenau, 240, 242, 248, 324, 352
Blachownia Śląska (Blechhammer), 227
Blechhammer (Blachownia Śląska), 227
Błaszki, 2, 528
Błonie (in Inowrocław), 168, 229
Bober, 245
Bochnia, 200, 300
Bohemia, 176, 185, 272, 350
Bojanowo, 263
Bolewice, 230
Bonn, 368–369
Borek, 17, 24
Bór Świnogacki (Świnogacki Forest), 32
Bracław, 63
Brdów, 24, 346
Breslau (Wrocław), 162
Breslav (Bracław), 63
Broniewo, 230, 243
Brudzew, 11–12
Brześć, 14, 230
Brześć Kujawski, 230
Buchenwald, 385, 387
Budzisław Kościelny, 238
Bugaj, 344, 346, 450, 454, 457
Buk, 165, 229
Buna, 242
Bydgoska, road (in Czarków, Konin), 243
Bydgoszcz, 161, 391
Bzura, River, 137

C

Canada, 379
Chełmno nad Nerem (Kulmhof), 186, 242
Chicago, 493
Chodecz, 197, 230
Chodzież, 17, 230
Chrzanowo, 80, 529, 531
Chrzanowskiego Street, Kleczew, 81
Ciążeń, 51, 80, 88
Ciechocinek, 163, 165, 168, 188, 197, 347
Cieślin, 229, 243
Cologne (Köln), 368
Czarków (Konin), 230, 243–248
Czechoslovakia, 74, 347
Częstochowa, 300–301

D

Dachau, 386
Danzig (Gdańsk), 145
Dąbie, 230, 343–344, 346, 449–450
Długa Łąka, 273, 285, 301–315, 323, 332, 361–363, 365, 451–452
Długi Kąt, 251
Dłusk, 80
Dnepropetrovsk, 359
Dobra, 346
Dobrocałowo, 52
Dunajec, 27
Düsseldorf, 360
Działdowo, 192
Dziekanka, 260, 262–263

E

East End (London), 495
East Prussia, 179
Eastern Europe, 4, 148, 250, 280
Eastern Galicia, 295, 342
Eastern Małopolska, 454
Eastern Marches (Ostmark), 423
Eastern Upper Silesia, 181
Edwarda Heimana Street, Kleczew, 99
Edwinów, 242
Elbe, River, 384
England, 350, 413, 495
Essen, 243

F

Feldafing, 387
Fort VII (Poznań), 259–260, 262,
France, 225, 270, 347, 379, 413
Frankfurt, 227, 239, 386
Frankfurt an der Oder (Frankfurt/Oder), 225, 240, 386

G

Galicia, 74, 283, 295, 342, 449
Gąbin, 230, 247,
Gdańsk (Danzig), 145, 149, 181, 284, 422
Gdynia, 485
Germany, 3–4, 42, 73–74, 133–135, 143, 148, 151, 154, 158, 176–177, 179, 182, 184, 188, 198, 208, 213–214, 225, 247–250, 259, 263, 274, 280–281, 287, 321, 330, 332, 347, 360, 368–369, 385, 387
Glasgow, 480
Gniezno, 14, 16, 25, 45, 88, 153, 165, 260, 262, 418
Golina, 4, 11, 51, 69, 98, 104, 113, 142, 167, 200–203, 274, 277, 282, 309
Goranin, 55–56, 90, 109
Gosławice, 303, 363
Gostynin, 188, 230, 243, 247, 263, 347
Góra Kalwaria, 63, 99–100, 120, 168
Górańska Street, Kleczew, 109
Górne Piaski, 80
Grabów, 342–343
Grąblin, 294
Greater Poland, 1–3, 10–12, 14–16, 19, 22–23, 25, 27–29, 42, 46, 73, 78–80, 103, 107, 108, 117, 139, 143, 189, 367, 385, 391
Greece, 347
Grodziec, 80, 136, 138, 251, 278–279, 284–286, 386
Grodzisk Wielkopolski, 16
Grójec, 168, 249
Grzywc, 65
Gur (Góra Kalwaria), 99
Gurowo, 403
Gusen, 295, 448

H

Hadera, 492
Haifa, 467

Hamburg, 347, 380
Hannover, 245
Hejmana-Jareckiego Street, Kleczew, 80
Hinterberg (Zagórów), 203–206
Hochenau, 467
Hochensalza (Inowrocław), 285
Hungary, 347, 352

I

Inowrocław (Hochensalza), 14–15, 78, 143–144, 153, 161, 163–168, 186–187, 193, 197, 199, 228–230, 234, 238–240, 242–243, 251, 257–258, 268, 295–297, 323, 346–347, 366–368, 385, 391, 397, 418, 448, 490–491
Israel (Palestine – British Mandate of Palestine), 14, 84, 100, 327–328, 331, 333, 335–336, 344, 368, 379, 382, 388, 462, 465, 467–468
Italy, 337, 467
Izbica, 2, 108, 167, 194, 197, 230, 251, 284, 343–344, 346, 391, 450, 454, 457
Izbica Kujawska, 2, 108, 194, 197, 230, 344, 346, 391, 450, 454, 457
Izbica Lubelska, 167, 284
Izdebno, 52

J

Jabłonów, 192
Jaksice Borkowo, 243
Janikowo, 230
Janowice, 193
Janów Lubelski, 284
Jarocin, 17
Jerusalem, 3, 383, 467
Józefów, 249, 251, 490
Józefów Biłgorajski, 249, 490
Jóźwin, 384
Jutrosin, 17

K

Kalisz, 2, 12–17, 19, 39–40, 47, 64–65 69, 76, 79, 95, 108, 113, 143, 161–163, 165, 168, 186, 194, 199, 229–230, 246, 347, 391
Kamenetz Podolsky (Kamieniec Podolski), 359

Kazimierz, 14, 17, 24, 31, 52, 274, 282, 297, 301, 305, 308, 311–312, 390, 443
Kazimierz Biskupi, 25, 52, 80, 109, 245, 248, 273–302, 304, 314, 323, 332, 361–362, 365, 385, 392–393, 443–444
Kazimierz Biskupi, Forest, 4, 274, 284–286, 295–299, 449, 454
Kcynia, 16–17
Kiev, 360
Kiszkowo, 17
Kłobuck, 301
Kłodawa, 11–12, 25, 108, 230, 343–344, 346, 450
Kobylin, 171
Kochanówka, 262, 332
Kolska Street, Konin, 243
Koło, 11–12, 17, 19, 24–25, 76, 78, 108, 113, 143, 166–168, 187–188, 229–230, 237, 251, 295, 322–325, 333, 342–344, 346, 391, 449–450, 454, 456, 458
Konińska Street, Kleczew, 59, 80–81, 120
Kopaszewo, 14
Koponin, 88
Koszewo, 52
Kościan, 14, 259, 262
Kościelna Street, Kleczew, 80–81
Kowal, 168, 230, 465
Kowale Pańskie, 346
Koźmin, 17
Koźminek, 17, 108, 168
Kórnik, 17
Krajenka, 17
Kraków, 14, 150, 152, 168, 175, 193, 232
Kramsk, 80
Krasnystaw, 167, 173, 251, 284
Krężel, 274, 276, 285, 293
Krężel, Forest, 276, 365, 394
Krośniewice, 230, 325, 344, 346
Krotoszyn, 16–17, 19, 47, 50, 55–56, 61
Królików, 199–200
Kruszwica, 165, 230
Krzyżowniki, 230
Kujawy (Kuyavia), 14, 42, 78, 391
Kulmhof (Chełmno nad Nerem), 186, 242, 334–338, 352, 360, 368–369
Kurzyce, 407
Kutno, 78, 155–156, 166, 168, 188, 229–230, 269, 322, 325, 344, 346, 391, 450

Kuyavia (Kujawy), 14, 42, 78, 391
Kwiatkowo, 12

L

Ląd, 12, 51, 85, 88, 134, 191, 248, 388
Lądek, 24, 51
Lehmstädt (Kleczew), 142, 188, 206–210, 424–429, 435
Leipzig, 353
Lesser Poland, 10, 14, 168
Leszno, 19, 65, 262
Ležáky, 350–351
Lębork, 262
Licheń, 12
Lidice, 350–351
Lithuania, 9, 25, 29, 74
Litzmannstadt (Łódź), 177, 272, 360
London, 495
Los Angeles, 477, 479, 482–483
Lubień, 168, 189, 197
Lublin, 9, 153, 165–169, 173, 251
Luborodz, Forest, 454
Lubraniec, 197, 230
Lwów, 346, 360
Łabiszyn, 16–17, 63
Łask, 230, 347
Łęczyca, 14–15, 88, 163, 166, 229, 347
Łękno, 17
Łobżenica, 16–17
Łojewo, 229
Łukom, 88

M

Madagascar, 175–178, 225, 270, 316n31
Madison, WI, 480, 484, 497
Magdeburg, 11, 385
Magnitogorsk, 465
Malbork (Marienburg), 11–12
Maliniec, 308
Małopolska Wschodnia
Marantowska, Road or Avenue, 306, 312, 363, 451–452
Marantów, 309
Margonin, 17
Marienburg (Malbork), 11–12
Masovia (Mazowsze), 14, 42, 79, 168
Mattersburg, 348

Mauthausen, 295, 448
Mazowsze, 14, 42, 79, 168
Mickiewicz Street, Wołkowysk, 464
Milwaukee (Wisconsin, USA), 380, 472, 476–477, 479–486
Miłosław, 17
Minsk (Soviet Union), 126n40
Młodojewo, 80, 125n9
Mogilno, 165, 215n46, 229
Moravia, 176, 185, 273, 350
Moscow, 359
Mostki, 52
Możysław, 451
Munich (München), 145, 353, 387

N

Nakło, 16–17
Narew, River, 211
Naumburg am Bober (Nowogród Bobrzański), 245
Nebraska, 477, 483
Netherlands, 494
New York, 124n5, 380, 390, 468, 477–478, 480, 482, 493
Niepodległości Square, Kleczew, 40
Niesłusz-Rudzica, Forest, 285, 301, 308, 310, 363–365, 452
Nieszawa, 163, 166, 168, 187–189, 229, 391
Nowa Street, Kleczew, 124n2
Nowe Miasto, 17
Nowiny Brdowskie, 346
Nowogród Bobrzański (Naumburg am Bober), 245
Nowy Tomyśl, 165, 229–230
Nowy Wiśnicz (Wiśnicz Nowy), 300–301

O

Oberwart, 348
Oder, River, 386
Odessa, 359
Ogrodowa Street, Kleczew, 81
Oleśnica, 80, 125n9
Orłowo, 230
Orłów, 243
Osieczna, 262
Osięciny, 189, 197, 347, 391

Ostrowiec Świętokrzyski, 167, 465, 490
Owińsk, 260, 262

P

Pabianice, 230
Pakość, 165
Palestine, British Mandate of (Israel), 468, 481
Papros, 230, 242
Paris, 134, 495
Peizen (Poniec), 24, 35n48, 429
Piaski Dolne Street, Kleczew, 124n2
Piaski Górne Street, Kleczew, 124n2
Piaski Street, Kleczew, 80–81, 124n2
Pińszczyzna (area of Pińsk), 295, 449, 454
Piotrków Kujawski, 229–230
Pobiedziska, 17
Poddębice, 230
Poland, 1–4, 9–16, 19, 22–23, 25, 27–29, 37–69, 73–81, 92, 103–105, 107-108, 117, 120, 134–135, 137, 139, 143, 150–151, 153, 158, 161–162, 167–168, 171, 176, 180–187, 189, 225, 230, 266–268, 280, 282, 299, 342, 344, 351, 366–370, 383, 385–387, 391, 397, 439, 444, 462, 465, 467–468, 482–488, 493, 528, 533
Pomerania, 143, 150, 367
Ponary, 345
Poniec, 24, 429
Posen (Poznań), 73, 143, 165, 199, 229, 260
Potulice, 192
Powidz, 45, 88
Powiercie, 325, 329, 355
Poznań (Posen), 2, 4, 9, 14, 16, 19, 25–26, 76, 113–114, 143, 147, 149–150, 153, 161–162, 181, 186, 192–194, 225–227, 229–230, 234, 241, 245, 259–265, 267, 276–277, 279, 301, 304, 312–313, 321, 361, 370, 384, 386, 466–467, 493
Poznańska Street, Kleczew, 40, 467
Protectorate of Bohemia and Moravia, 176, 185, 350
Prussia, 3, 22, 38–39, 42, 65, 150, 157, 168, 175, 179, 181, 259, 422
Przedecz, 12, 189, 196, 489–490
Pyzdry, 14–17, 25, 76, 80, 103, 108, 115–116, 129n85, 387–388, 403, 406, 528

R

Racięcice, 52
Radojewice, 230, 243
Radom, 168, 283
Radziejów, 165, 189, 197, 229–230, 300–301, 347
Radziwiłł Fort (Poznań), 230
Ramat Hashofet, 493
Raszków, 17
Ravensbrück, 351
Rawicz, 16
Rąbinek, 240
Red Ruthenia (Ruś Czerwona), 10
Reich, 143, 148–149, 150, 157–158, 168, 170, 173–174, 176–180, 185–186, 195–196, 210–213, 216n60, 225, 228, 249–250, 264, 272, 293, 417, 421–423, 449, 453–454
Romania, 274
Rostock, 385
Rotter Thurm, 348
Roztoka, 27
Rudzica, 285, 301, 308, 310, 363–365, 452
Russia, 3, 25, 29, 38, 140, 190, 266, 268
Rutki Street, Kleczew, 81, 124n2
Rychwał, 11–12, 24, 52, 115, 136, 138, 309, 386, 429, 528
Rynek (Market Square), Kleczew, 40, 80, 92, 124n2
Rzgów, 51, 282, 284–286, 443
Rzuchowski, Forest, 258, 326–329, 331, 334, 340, 344, 354, 357, 449

S

San, River, 211
Sandomierz, 14
Sanniki, 230, 244, 347
Schwerin, 385
Scotland, 350
Sępólno Krajeńskie, 17
Sieradz, 14, 163, 166, 229, 234, 347
Siernicze, 90, 109
Skoki, 17
Skulsk, 51–52, 79–80, 103, 108, 115–117, 127n64, 129n85, 167, 197, 203, 429, 432, 489, 528
Skulska Wieś, 80, 125n9

Sławoszew, 52
Sławoszewek, 109
Sławoszewo, 27
Śludzkie Budy, 52
Słupca, 2, 4, 11–12, 25, 51–52, 55, 76, 78–80, 85, 88, 103, 108, 109–110, 113, 115–117, 120–121, 129n85, 167, 187, 197, 200, 203, 429, 432, 463, 528
Słupecka Street, Kleczew, 80–81, 94, 467
Służew, 230
Służewo, 347
Smocza Street, Warsaw, 463–464
Sobibór, 194, 258, 292, 324, 357, 360
Sochaczew, 63, 165
Solanka, 312
Soltau, 259
Sompolno, 104, 108, 129n85, 205, 227, 230, 300–301, 314, 346, 352, 391, 528
Soviet Union, 74, 167, 249–250, 287, 291, 366, 368, 462, 465
Spławie, 52
Stadium (Poznań), 226, 234, 384
Stawiszyn, 108, 129n85, 168, 528
Stettin (Szczecin), 423
Stodólna Street, Kleczew, 81, 124n2, 383
Strasbourg, 387
Strzałków, 45
Strzelno, 297
Sudetenland (Sudety), 176, 185
Sudety (Sudetenland), 176, 185
Swarzędz, 19, 27
Sweden, 38
Szczebrzeszyn, 168, 193
Szymanowice, 80, 125n9
Ślesin, 12, 25, 51–52, 104, 108, 115, 129n85, 187, 200, 203, 238, 243, 251, 429, 432, 528
Śrem, 263
Środa Wielkopolska, 144
Świnogacki Forest (Bór Świnogacki), 32

T

Targowa, Street, Kleczew, 124n2
Tarvisio, 467
Tczew, 192
Toruń, 168, 192
Toruńska Street, Kleczew, 81
Trąbczyn, 80, 125n9

Treblinka, 194, 258, 292, 324, 357, 360
Trzemeszno, 25
Tuliszków, 12, 24, 52, 79, 108, 125n9, 129n85, 391, 528
Turek, 11–12, 76, 108, 113, 125n10, 143, 197, 323, 346, 528
Turkey, 38

U

Ukraine, 10, 360
Uniejów, 12, 108, 197, 238, 528
United States (of America), 124n5, 379, 388, 468

V

Venice, 467
Versailles, 73, 77
Vienna, 250, 283, 347, 484
Vilnius (Wilno), 345
Vistula, River (Wisła), 167, 211
Volhynia (Wołyń), 150, 153, 158, 169, 179, 267, 418, 420, 422

W

Wałbrzych, 383, 465
Warsaw (Warszawa), 2–3, 14, 25, 31, 41, 64–65, 88, 142–143, 153, 165, 168, 182, 194, 198–199, 207–208, 225, 230, 232, 243, 295, 298, 342, 344–345, 360, 416–417, 425, 463, 465, 494
Warszawa (Warsaw), 168
Warszawska Street, Kleczew, 80
Warta, 191, 263
Warta, River, 299
Wartbrücken (Koło), 295, 449
Warthegau (Wartheland, Kraj Warty), 3, 137, 143–158, 160–164, 170–180, 182, 185–187, 193, 197–200, 210, 213, 217n86, 224–242, 248–251, 257–273, 278, 280–281, 287, 298, 314, 321, 323, 332, 337, 346, 351, 359–361, 366, 397, 403–404, 417, 419, 421–422, 438–440
Weimar, 387
West Prussia, 179, 181, 422
Western Europe, 55, 225, 347
Wielkopolska (Greater Poland), 1

Wieluń, 163, 347
Wiesengrund, 241
Więcbork, 17
Wilcza Góra, 80
Wilczyn, 528
Wilno (Vilnius), 345
Winiary Fort, Poznań, 370
Wiśnicz Nowy (Nowy Wiśnicz), 300–301
Wjazdowa Street, Kleczew, 124n2
Władysławów, 79, 104, 108, 115, 125n9, 129n85, 528
Włocławek, 128n83, 163, 166–168, 188, 191, 193–194, 196–197, 215n46, 230, 238, 324, 347, 355, 391, 393, 398n28, 403, 415–416, 489
Włyń-Rossoszyca, 263
Winiary, fort (Poznań), 370
Wodna Street, Kleczew, 81
Wołkowysk, 405, 459, 464, 466–467
Wrocław (Breslau), 162
Września, 16–17, 45–46, 78
Wygoda, 274
Wygoda, Forest, 276, 285, 293, 443

Y
Yugoslavia, 347

Z
Zagórów (Hinterberg), 203–206, 208–209
Zamość, 167–168, 193–194, 250–251
Zawadki, 326, 328, 332, 340
Zbąszyń, 134
Zduny, 24
Zduńska Wola, 48, 166, 230
Zebrzydowice, 467
Zgierz, 294, 361
Zielona Góra, 245
Złotów, 16-17, 19
Żabia Street, Kleczew, 124n2
Żabikowo, 3
Żegotki, 239–242, 297
Żerków, 17
Żerniki, 17
Żnin, 165, 229
Żółkiewka, 251
Żychlin, 230, 325, 344, 450

www.ingramcontent.com/pod-product-compliance
Lightning Source LLC
Chambersburg PA
CBHW061339300426
44116CB00011B/1918